The Biblical "One Flesh" Theology of Marriage as Constituted in Genesis 2:24

The Biblical "One Flesh" Theology of
Marriage
as Constituted in Genesis 2:24

An Exegetical Study of this Human-Divine Covenant Pattern, Its New Testament Echoes, and Its Reception History throughout Scripture Focusing on the Spiritual Impact of Sexuality

René Gehring

WIPF & STOCK · Eugene, Oregon

THE BIBLICAL "ONE FLESH" THEOLOGY OF MARRIAGE AS CONSTITUTED IN GENESIS 2:24
An Exegetical Study of this Human-Divine Covenant Pattern, Its New Testament Echoes,
and Its Reception History throughout Scripture Focusing on the Spiritual Impact of Sexuality

Copyright © 2013 René Gehring. All rights reserved. Except for brief quotations in critical publications or reviews, no part of this book may be reproduced in any manner without prior written permission from the publisher. Write: Permissions, Wipf and Stock Publishers, 199 W. 8th Ave., Suite 3, Eugene, OR 97401.

Wipf&Stock
An Imprint of Wipf and Stock Publishers
199 W. 8th Ave., Suite 3
Eugene, OR 97401

www.wipfandstock.com

ISBN 13: 978-1-62032-849-1

Manufactured in the U.S.A.

For Catherina, Alicia, Finn, and Sem

For this reason a man shall leave
his father and his mother,
and be joined to his wife;
and they shall become one flesh.
(Genesis 2:24)

For love is as strong as death,
Jealousy is as severe as Sheol;
Its flashes are flashes of fire,
The very flame of Jahweh.
(Song of Solomon 8:6–7)

Contents

Foreword by Steven Thompson | xi

Introduction | xiii

Abbreviations | xv

I **The Old Testament Foundation** | 1
    I.1 The Original "One Flesh" Ideal | 2
        I.1.1 The Edenic Constitution of Marriage (Gen 1:26–27; 2:18–25) | 2
            I.1.1.1 Historical Context | 2
            I.1.1.2 Text and Translation | 3
                I.1.1.2.1 The Hebrew Text | 3
                I.1.1.2.2 Translation | 5
            I.1.1.3 Textual Analysis | 6
                I.1.1.3.1 Unity or Discontinuity in Genesis 1–2 | 6
                I.1.1.3.2 Genesis 1:26–27 | 7
                I.1.1.3.3 Genesis 2:18–25 | 10
            I.1.1.4 Wider Biblical Context | 32
                I.1.1.4.1 Gen 2:4–25 Foreshadowing the Fall | 33
                I.1.1.4.2 Covenantal Aspects | 41
            I.1.1.5 Summary and Final Considerations | 48
        I.1.2 Everlastingness and Monogamy (Deut 24:1–4 et al) | 55
            I.1.2.1 Divorce as Unintended Deviation | 55
            I.1.2.2 Polygamy as Cultural Digression | 66
            I.1.2.3 Summary and Final Considerations | 73
        I.1.3 Ritual Purity of Licit Sexuality (Lev 15:18) | 76
            I.1.3.1 Ancient Jewish Sources | 77
                I.1.3.1.1 Philo | 77
                I.1.3.1.2 Josephus | 78
                I.1.3.1.3 Rabbinic Notes | 80
                I.1.3.1.4 Conclusions | 81
            I.1.3.2 Current Interpretations and a Non-Defiling Alternative | 83
            I.1.3.3 Further Evidence? | 96

    I.1.3.3.1 Exod 19:14–15 | 96
    I.1.3.3.2 1 Sam 21:4–5 | 99
    I.1.3.3.3 "Humble Your Souls" or a Missing Precept? | 100
    I.1.3.3.4 A New Testament Hint? | 101
   I.1.3.4 Summary and Final Considerations | 102
 I.2 Approaching the Spiritual Sphere | 106
  I.2.1 Interaction Between the Two Levels | 106
   I.2.1.1 The "Sons of God" Going Astray (Gen 6:1–4) | 107
    I.2.1.1.1 Objections against the Human Character | 109
    I.2.1.1.2 Arguments in Favor of the Human Interpretation | 113
    I.2.1.1.3 Conclusions | 120
   I.2.1.2 Israel's Apostasy at Shittim (Num 25) | 121
   I.2.1.3 The Golden Calf (Exod 32) | 131
   I.2.1.4 Summary and Final Considerations | 137
  I.2.2 Marriage as Model of the Divine Covenant | 142
   I.2.2.1 Marriage and Prostitution Images | 143
   I.2.2.2 The "Covenant of Peace" | 148
    I.2.2.2.1 Human-Divine "Marriage" | 148
    I.2.2.2.2 The Marriage Covenant in Malachi | 154
    I.2.2.2.3 Divorce in the Prophets | 159
  I.2.2.3 Summary and Final Considerations | 160

II The New Testament Echoes of the Edenic Ideal | 164
 II.1 The Edenic Ideal in Prominent Ancient Jewish Literature | 164
  II.1.1 Philo | 165
  II.1.2 Josephus | 171
  II.1.3 Post-Canonical Jewish Literature | 173
  II.1.4 The Qumran Scrolls | 179
  II.1.5 Rabbinic Perceptions | 180
 II.2 Concrete NT References to the Edenic Ideal | 187
  II.2.1 Jesus about Divorce (Matt 5:32; 19:3–9; Mark 10:2–12; Luke 16:18) | 187
   II.2.1.1 Historical Context | 188
    II.2.1.1.1 The LXX as Basis of the Debate | 189
    II.2.1.1.2 Josephus and Philo about Divorce | 192
    II.2.1.1.3 Rabbinic Teachings on Divorce | 194
   II.2.1.2 Text and Translation | 203
    II.2.1.2.1 The Greek Text | 203
    II.2.1.2.2 Translation | 211
   II.2.1.3 Textual Analysis | 215
   II.2.1.4 Summary and Final Considerations | 225
  II.2.2 Paul's Spiritual Application (Eph 5:21–33; 1 Cor 6:12–20) | 235
   II.2.2.1 Historical Context | 236

            II.2.2.1.1 Ephesians | 236
            II.2.2.1.2 Corinth | 237
        II.2.2.2 Text and Translation | 239
            II.2.2.2.1 The Greek Text of 1 Cor 6:12–20 | 239
            II.2.2.2.2 Translation | 241
            II.2.2.2.3 The Greek Text of Eph 5:21–33 | 242
            II.2.2.2.4 Translation | 244
        II.2.2.3 Textual Analysis | 245
            II.2.2.3.1 Ephesians 5:21–33 | 245
            II.2.2.3.2 1 Corinthians 6:12–20 | 260
        II.2.2.4 Summary and Final Considerations | 274
    II.3 Further Allusions | 279
        II.3.1 Paul's Practical Application (1 Cor 7) | 280
            II.3.1.1 Notes on Lawful Sexuality | 281
            II.3.1.2 Paul on Marital Separation/Celibacy | 285
            II.3.1.3 Mixed Marriages and Singleness | 294
            II.3.1.4 Summary and Final Considerations | 299
        II.3.2 Nuptial Imagery | 300

III Results: Permanent Commitment to the Edenic Ideal | 310
    III.1 The Spiritual Level (Christ–Church): Toward a Successful Representation | 310
        III.1.1 Edenic Basis and Soteriological Oneness | 311
        III.1.2 Marriage as Image for the Plan of Redemption | 314
    III.2 The Literal Level (Husband–Wife): Toward a Sound Foundation | 318
        III.2.1 Significance and Responsibility of Sexuality | 319
            III.2.1.1 Consummation of Marriage | 320
            III.2.1.2 Social Security and Protection | 325
            III.2.1.3 Summary and Final Considerations | 328
        III.2.2 Further Legitimate Reasons for Divorce | 330
    III.3 Eternal Ideal or Final Abolishment? | 338
        III.3.1 Alterable or Permanent Pattern? | 340
        III.3.2 Text, Translation, and First Hints | 343
        III.3.3 Marriage Between Sin and Redemption | 345
        III.3.4 Summary and Final Considerations | 348

Epilogue | 351

Appendix | 355

Bibliography | 367

Foreword

THE CORE OF THIS study is a thoroughgoing exegesis of a single verse in the book of Genesis, followed by a patient tracking of its impact on the rest of the biblical canon. Working at a level of detail not achieved in previous studies of Genesis 2:24, author Dr René Gehring unpackages previously-overlooked nuances of the message of this paradigmatic verse. He then traces its reception through the Hebrew Bible and into the New Testament.

The result of Gehring's labor is a deeper awareness of the ways in which this Genesis creation motif, the uniting of man and woman in marriage, has re-emerged repeatedly across the biblical canon, enriching its expressions, not only of the nature of marriage, but also of Hebrew and early Christian expressions of YHWH's relationship to humanity.

Gehring's findings provide insights which should provoke re-evaluations of the biblical basis for a range of doctrinal and practical positions on marriage and family, on personal assurance of one's relationship to God, and on the relationship across denominational and religious boundaries which currently divide believing communities. His study provides fresh insights on a range of relational matters, such as: is there a "core" biblical perspective on marriage? Do Jesus' logia on marriage and divorce annul, or build upon, the Hebrew Bible position? Is the justification of divorce and remarriage by some faith communities still supported by the relevant biblical passages? Is there a "correct" biblical perspective on polygamy? Is there any fresh biblical insight impacting the issue of same-sex marriage?

It has been a privilege to be involved in a small way with the author in his development of this study. I happily anticipate its impact on the thinking and the life of communities which rely on Scripture for guidance in some crucial relational questions of our day.

Steven Thompson
(Supervisor of Higher Degrees by Research,
Avondale College of Higher Education, Cooranbong, Australia)

Introduction

> The Garden of Eden has turned out to be as alluring for biblical scholars as it was for Adam and Eve. Problems flourish amid the beauty of the verses describing life there, and scholars, as ever, are as much attracted by the problems as the beauty.[1]

ONE OF THE "PROBLEMS" of Eden continuously fascinating scholars is the Edenic marriage "ideal" in Gen 2:24. Although the literature about marriage and sexuality is very extensive, detailed exegesis within that literature is very limited—often reduced to a few brief exegetical observations. Profound exegesis of this verse is conspicuously absent in most of the literature dealing with the prominent topic of biblical marriage and sexuality.

> Although much has been written on sexuality and marriage from the perspective of the Old and New Testaments, little attention has been given to what is perhaps the most engaging and elusive expression relating to the whole topic, namely, the 'one flesh' expression which occurs in the poetic climax of the Genesis 2 account of creation and recurs as a technical expression in the New Testament writing.[2]

While a few scholars realize the significance of Gen 2:24 (including the immediate context: Gen 1:26–27; 2:18–25) for any research about biblical marriage, its meaning as divine covenant pattern has attracted only very little attention; the same can be noted concerning the NT texts, which are examined primarily in context of divorce (Matt 19:3–9; Mark 10:2–12) and sometimes concerning ecclesiology or gender roles (1 Cor 6:12–20; Eph 5:21–33). This study, however, will focus on what I suggest may be called the "Edenic ideal" of Gen 2:24, that is, the "one flesh" union and its various facets. The aim is to attempt to discover the main themes of Gen 2:24 and to trace their echo, development, and application throughout Scripture. This approach to marriage and sexual ethics was encouraged by Jesus pointing back to paradise in Matt 19:4–6 (cf. Mark 10:6–9) as his only foundation to settle queries in this realm. A comprehensive

1. Lawton, "Gen. 2:24," 97.
2. Stuhlmiller, "One Flesh," 3.

study, consequently, applying this perspective to the different biblical passages dealing with intimate relationships is missing in current research. The present study intends to fill this missing part of the puzzle.

The biblical theology of this "Edenic ideal" will be scrutinized concerning its practical, contextual meaning (questions about origin and purpose of marriage, sexuality, intimacy, divorce, gender roles etc.), but especially regarding its spiritual significance as a model for the divine-human relationship between God and Israel, and in regard to the NT church. The focus, then, is to explore and present evidence for a fundamental, harmonious teaching on marriage throughout Scripture, and suggesting that Gen 2:24, may at least subliminally present in the different marriage texts of Scripture.

The main emphasis in this study is the New Testament and its understanding and application of Gen 2:24. It is, however, impossible to obtain trustworthy results of the NT texts without at first closely researching the OT basis. The first part of this study, therefore, deals with "The Old Testament Foundation" concerning several significant aspects contributing to a right understanding of the "Edenic ideal" as given in Gen 2:24. The attitudes toward divorce and polygamy, as well as the ritual purity of the one flesh union, represent an important prerequisite for interpreting the New Testament texts. The subjects of divorce and polygamy interrelate directly with the discussions given in the New Testament and are significantly meaningful for an understanding of the deeper meaning of the exclusiveness and everlastingness of the Edenic ideal. The section on the Old Testament marriage metaphors and the three significant accounts of sexual sins and God's intervention is used as an instrument to approach the spiritual (divine-human) sphere as the basic pattern that is taken over by Paul in the New Testament. As will be developed and argued in more detail in that chapter, the model of Gen 2:24 comprises all the crucial steps necessary to represent the divine covenant of salvation; the three main "pillars" of building a covenant as given in Gen 2:24 are the same even at the spiritual level: (1) leaving (other Gods), (2) cleaving (to Yahweh), (3) becoming one (intimate union by יָדַע).

The second part of this study investigates "The New Testament Echoes of the Edenic Ideal" as given in the discussion about divorce in the gospels, and its figurative, spiritual application by Paul. It is introduced by a survey of the different perceptions about the Edenic ideal in ancient Jewish literature, and rounded off by further NT allusions concerning Paul's practical exposition of marriage, sexuality, and divorce (1 Cor 7). The New Testament nuptial imagery and its implications will also be considered.

The third part draws further conclusions from the previous investigations as a special contribution to the "one flesh" concept on the spiritual, as well as the literal, sphere. It completes the several foregoing "summaries and final considerations" given at the end of each chapter and finally reemphasizes the most important findings, concluding with a biblical statement about the possible future state of marriage in the world to come.

Abbreviations

Biblical Books

1 Chr	1 Chronicles	Acts	Acts	Isa	Isaiah	Nah	Nahum
1 Cor	1 Corinthians	Amos	Amos	Jas	James	Neh	Nehemiah
1 John	1 John	Col	Colossians	Jer	Jeremiah	Num	Numbers
1 Kgs	1 Kings	Dan	Daniel	Job	Job	Obad	Obadiah
1 Pet	1 Peter	Deut	Deuteronomy	Joel	Joel	Phlm	Philemon
1 Sam	1 Samuel	Eccl	Ecclesiastes	John	John	Phil	Philippians
1 Thess	1 Thessalonians	Eph	Ephesians	Jonah	Jonah	Prov	Proverbs
1 Tim	1 Timothy	Esth	Esther	Josh	Joshua	Ps	Psalms
2 Chr	2 Chronicles	Exod	Exodus	Jude	Jude	Rev	Revelation
2 Cor	2 Corinthians	Ezek	Ezekiel	Judg	Judges	Rom	Romans
2 John	2 John	Ezra	Ezra	Lam	Lamentations	Ruth	Ruth
2 Kgs	2 Kings	Gal	Galatians	Lev	Leviticus	Song	Song of Songs
2 Pet	2 Peter	Gen	Genesis	Luke	Luke	Titus	Titus
2 Sam	2 Samuel	Hab	Habakkuk	Mal	Malachi	Zech	Zechariah
2 Thess	2 Thessalonians	Hag	Haggai	Mark	Mark	Zeph	Zephaniah
2 Tim	2 Timothy	Heb	Hebrews	Matt	Matthew		
3 John	3 John	Hos	Hosea	Mic	Micah		

Post-Canonical Jewish and Christian Literature

1 Clem.	1 Clement	*Jdt.*	Judtih
1 Esd	1 Esdras	*Jub.*	Jubilees
2 En.	2 Enoch	*L.A.B.*	Liber antiquitatum biblicarum (Pseudo-Philo)
3 Macc.	3 Maccabees	*Liv. Pro.*	Lives of the Prophets
Apoc. Mos.	Apocalypse of Moses	*Sib. Or.*	Sibylline Oracles
Bar.	Baruch	Sir.	Sirach
Barn.	Epistle of Barnabas	Tob.	Tobit
Gos. Phil./Thom.	Gospel of Philip/Thomas	*T. Naph./Reu./Sim.*	Testament of Naphtali/Reuben/Simeon

Rabbinic Literature

'Abot R. Nat.	Abot de Rabbi Natan	*Nid.*	Niddah
b.	Babylonian Talmud	*Pesiq.*	Pesiqta
Ber.	Berakoth	*Pesaḥ.*	Pesaḥim
'Ed.	'Eduyyot	*Qidd.*	Qiddušin
'Erub.	'Erubin	*Rab.*	Rabbah
Giṭ.	Giṭṭin	*s.*	Sifra
Ḥag.	Ḥagigah	*Sanh.*	Sanhedrin
Ketub.	Ketubbot	*Šabb.*	Šabbat
Mak.	Makkot	*t.*	Tosefta
Mo'ed Qaṭ.	Mo'ed Qaṭan	*Ter.*	Terumot
m.	Mishnah	*y.*	Jerusalem (Palestinian) Talmud
midr.	Midrash	*Yad.*	Yadayim
Ned.	Nedarim	*Yebam.*	Yebamot

Flavius Josephus

A.J.	Antiquitates Iudaicae	*C.Ap.*	Contra Apionem
B.J.	Bellum Iudaicum	*Vita*	De sua Vita

Philo of Alexandria

Abr.	De Abrahamo	*Leg.*	Legum Allegoriarum
Agr.	De Agricultura	*Legat.*	Legatio ad Gaium
Cher.	De Cherubim	*Migr.*	De Migratione Abrahami
Conf.	De Confusione Linguarum	*Mos.*	De vita Mosis
Congr.	De Congressu Eruditionis Gratia	*Mut.*	De Mutatione Nominum
Contempl.	De Vita Contemplativa	*Opif.*	De Opificio Mundi
Decal.	De Decalogo	*Praem.*	De Praemiis et Poenis
Det.	Quod Deterius Potiori Insidiari Soleat	*QG*	Quaestiones et Solutiones in Genesim
Fug.	De Fuga et Inventione	*Sacr.*	De Sacrificiis Abelis et Caini
Gig.	De Gigantibus	*Somn.*	De Somniis
Her.	Quis Rerum Divinarum Heres Sit	*Spec.*	De Specialibus Legibus
Hypoth.	Hypothetica sive Apologia pro Judaeis	*Virt.*	De Virtutibus
Ios.	De Josepho		

Bible Versions

BHS	Biblia Hebraica Stuttgartensia	NASB	New American Standard Bible
LXX	The Septuagint	NET	The Net Bible
NA^{27}	Novum Testamentum Graece (Nestle-Aland, 27th ed.)	RSV	Revised Standard Version

Lexicons[1]

BDB	Brown/Robinson/Driver/Briggs/Gesenius, *A Hebrew and English Lexicon of the Old Testament*	LEH	Lust/Eynikel/Hauspie, *A Greek-English Lexicon of the Septuagint*
BDAG	Danker/Bauer/Arndt, *A Greek-English Lexicon of the New Testament and other Early Christian Literature*	LSJ	Liddell/Scott/Jones/McKenzie, *A Greek-English Lexicon*
CAL	Hebrew Union College, *Comprehensive Aramaic Lexicon*	TDOT	Botterweck/Ringgren/Fabry, *Theological Dictionary of the Old Testament*
FRI	Friberg/Miller, *Analytical Lexicon to the Greek New Testament*	THA	Thayer, *Thayer's Greek-English Lexicon of the New Testament*
HALOT	Köhler/Baumgartner/Richardson/Stamm, *The Hebrew and Aramaic Lexicon of the Old Testament*	TWOT	Harris/Archer/Waltke, *The Theological Wordbook of the Old Testament*

Other

ANE	Ancient Near East(ern)	p(p).	page(s)
fn.	Footnote	par.	parallel text(s)
lit.	Literally	Tg.	Targum
MT	Masoretic Text	trans.	translation
NT	New Testament	v(v).	verse(s)
OT	Old Testament	§(§)	paragraph(s)

---

1. See the general bibliography for more detailed information.

I

The Old Testament Foundation

FOR A THOROUGH AND trustworthy investigation of the New Testament "echoes" (or "developments") of Gen 2:23–24, the Old Testament foundation must be considered first.[1] This section consists of two main parts. The first part is directly related to the important texts establishing the ideal of marriage at creation and further facets thereof within the Pentateuch. Deviations in practice and perception are oftentimes held as some kind of a "legal/licit" distortion of the Edenic pattern (divorce and polygamy) and will be scrutinized and criticized for the purpose of "refining" the outcomes.

The second part approaches the spiritual sphere by exploring certain OT instances referring to significant experiences of the people both before the deluge and in the history of ancient Israel. These are important accounts of spiritual decline in close connection with a deviation from Edenic principles in marital (sexual) matters. The Old Testament marriage metaphors will further contribute to the covenantal aspects of the "marriage" relation symbolized in the relationship between Yahweh and his people.

---

1. The main Bible version generally used in this study is the NASB version (New American Standard Bible, 1995). When others are used and quoted they will be mentioned separately. The Hebrew Text and critical apparatus according to the BHS: Rudolph, Wilhelm, and Karl Elliger, eds., *Biblia Hebraica Stuttgartensia*, 5th ed. Stuttgart: Deutsche Bibelgesellschaft, 1997; the Septuagint from Rahlfs, Alfred, and Robert Hanhart, *Septuaginta*, 2nd ed. Stuttgart: Deutsche Bibelgesellschaft, 2006. The Mishnah is cited according to the English translation of Neusner, Jacob, *The Mishnah. A New Translation*. New Haven: Yale University Press, 1988. The Talmud is rarely quoted, but where a part of the text is given verbatim, I will add the concrete reference literature that provides an adequate translation. The English texts of Philo and Josephus are taken from the Loeb Classical Library (Philo) and the new translation of Mason (Josephus): Colson, F. H., Whitaker, G. H., and Ralph Marcus, eds., *Philo*, 10 vols., The Loeb Classical Library. Greek Authors. London/Cambridge: William Heinemann Ltd./Harvard University Press, 1929–1953; Mason, Steve et al., eds., *Flavius Josephus. Translation and Commentary*. Leiden/Boston: Brill, 2000–present.

The Biblical "One Flesh" Theology of Marriage as Constituted in Genesis 2:24

I.1 The Original "One Flesh" Ideal

I.1.1 The Edenic Constitution of Marriage (Gen 1:26–27; 2:18–25)

This section is an exegetical investigation of the pivotal verses of Gen 1:26–27 and Gen 2:18–25. After addressing some brief considerations about the historical background of Gen 1–3, the text of the given passages will be examined, drawing conclusions by investigating the obvious content, linguistic, literal, and other stylistic features, as well as the wider literary context.

I.1.1.1 Historical Context

Basically, it is unadvisable to search for some historical context of the events of the creation account, inasmuch as it deals with a prehistoric (even pre-worldly) period and its specific framework. Concerning the time and circumstances of the process of writing down these accounts, however, it is not necessary for this study to attempt to construct the historical setting of the composition of Genesis, or to trace its literary development. Instead, in order to investigate adequately the Old Testament from a New Testament perspective, as is requisite in this study, it is helpful to adopt the view of Jesus, the apostles, and the ancient Jewish as well as early Christian traditions; that means to assign the creation story and the remainder of the Pentateuch to Moses' pen, accepting as historical the events depicted in these books:[2]

> Moses received the Law on Sinai and delivered it to Joshua; Joshua in turn handed it down to the Elders; from the Elders it descended to the prophets, and each of them delivered it to his successors until it reached the men of the Great Assembly.[3]

> Moses also, a faithful servant in all his [i.e., God's] house, noted down in the sacred books all the injunctions which were given him, and when the other prophets also followed him, bearing witness with one consent to the ordinances which he had appointed.[4]

This is apparently the perspective which parallels the interpretation of the Pentateuch as viewed by the New Testament writers, the ancient Jewish scholars, and the members of the early Christian church.[5] Since this study aims to perceive the NT understanding

---

2. See for NT evidence: Matt 8:4; 19:7–8; 22:24; (23:2); Mark 1:44; 7:10; 10:3–5; 12:26; Luke 2:22; 16:29, 31; 20:37; 24:27, 44; John 1:17, 45; 3:14; 5:46; 7:19, 22–23; 8:5; 9:29; Acts 3:22; 6:14; 13:38; 15:1, 5; 21:21; 26:22; 28:23; Rom 10:5, 19; 1 Cor 9:9; 2 Cor 3:15; Heb 9:19; 10:28.

3. *M. Abot* 1:1. For further Jewish statements see Josh 1:7–8; 1 Kgs 2:3; 2 Kgs 23:21, 25; 2 Chr 8:13; 34:14; 35:12; Ezra 3:2; 6:18; Neh 8:1; 13:1; *b. Abot* 1; *Giṭ.* 60a.

4. *1 Clem.* 43:1; cf. also *Barn.* 10:1, 11.

5. The remainder of the OT was also viewed as authentic material truly narrating Israel's history. See all the numerous OT references in the NT that frequently hint at the ancient times which are perceived as authentic, historical reports of Israel's history.

of Gen 2:24 and its echoes, adopting this view is a presupposition that will consistently be carried out throughout the following investigations in the hope of discovering a fundamental, harmonious teaching of marriage throughout Scripture. It is furthermore suggested that Gen 2:24, as a conceptual foundation, is at least subliminally present in the different marriage texts of Scripture.

I.1.1.2 Text and Translation

I.1.1.2.1 THE HEBREW TEXT

A first step, not only to a close reading, but even more to a thorough investigation of the central text on the Edenic ideal, is the textual criticism and analysis. The necessary delimitation of the passages to be investigated is easily explained by taking a closer look at the concrete content. The beginning and the end of the focus on the man-woman story in Gen 2 is contained within vv. 18–25, while vv. 19–20 are a kind of pedagogic insertion (leading man to feel his need of a human counterpart),[6] not immediately belonging to God's primary working and creating for the sake of the man's "helper" (עֵזֶר; Gen 2:18). While vv. 16–17 may also be relevant for the interpretation of vv. 18–25, they do not necessarily pertain to the most salient verses concerning the woman's creation and marriage, but will be regarded when considering the immediate context. In chap. 1, vv. 26–28 briefly reflect humankind's story of Gen 2:18–25 with their own emphasis, while only vv. 26a and 27 are actually dealing with the relevant aspects to be examined exegetically.

At first it is necessary to scrutinize the Hebrew text of the above-mentioned verses in order to appraise possible textual lacks and variants. Differences between the Hebrew version and the Greek translation of the Septuagint will be mentioned in particular, since this Greek OT text was likely the basis of the Greek-writing New Testament authors. However, the possible intentions behind the Greek variants will not be discussed at this early stage of research, but will follow later within the exegesis of the particular verses. Also, grammatical and lexical hints as given by ambiguous or unusual grammatical elements, strange verbal tenses (aspects), or special meanings of keywords must be mentioned. Further literary features will be analyzed, preparing for the investigation of the literary context in the subsequent chapter, which emphasizes the various literary links within the entire creation account as well as in the wider biblical context.

To begin with, the Hebrew text of Gen 1:26–27 and 2:18–25, omitting Gen 1:26b and 2:19–20, reads as follows:

---

6. Similarly Anderson, "Reflections," 128; Ortlund, *Whoredom*, 18.

The Biblical "One Flesh" Theology of Marriage as Constituted in Genesis 2:24

(1:26a) וַיֹּאמֶר אֱלֹהִים נַעֲשֶׂה אָדָם בְּצַלְמֵנוּ כִּדְמוּתֵנוּ

(1:27) אֱלֹהִים אֶת־הָאָדָם בְּצַלְמוֹ בְּצֶלֶם אֱלֹהִים בָּרָא אֹתוֹ זָכָר וּנְקֵבָה בָּרָא אֹתָם וַיִּבְרָא

(2:18) וַיֹּאמֶר יְהוָה אֱלֹהִים לֹא־טוֹב הֱיוֹת הָאָדָם לְבַדּוֹ אֶעֱשֶׂהּ־לּוֹ עֵזֶר כְּנֶגְדּוֹ

(2:21) אֱלֹהִים תַּרְדֵּמָה עַל־הָאָדָם וַיִּישָׁן וַיִּקַּח אַחַת מִצַּלְעֹתָיו וַיִּסְגֹּר בָּשָׂר תַּחְתֶּנָּה וַיַּפֵּל יְהוָה

(2:22) וַיִּבֶן יְהוָה אֱלֹהִים אֶת־הַצֵּלָע אֲשֶׁר־לָקַח מִן־הָאָדָם לְאִשָּׁה וַיְבִאֶהָ אֶל־הָאָדָם

(2:23) הַפַּעַם עֶצֶם מֵעֲצָמַי וּבָשָׂר מִבְּשָׂרִי לְזֹאת יִקָּרֵא אִשָּׁה כִּי מֵאִישׁ לֻקֳחָה־זֹּאת וַיֹּאמֶר הָאָדָם זֹאת

(2:24) עַל־כֵּן יַעֲזָב־אִישׁ אֶת־אָבִיו וְאֶת־אִמּוֹ וְדָבַק בְּאִשְׁתּוֹ וְהָיוּ לְבָשָׂר אֶחָד

(2:25) וַיִּהְיוּ שְׁנֵיהֶם עֲרוּמִּים הָאָדָם וְאִשְׁתּוֹ וְלֹא יִתְבֹּשָׁשׁוּ

In chap. 1 there is no relevant variant reading in v. 26a, but in v. 27 there is a variant of the word בְּצַלְמוֹ ("in his image"), which is missing in the Greek LXX. The critical apparatus of the BHS suggest a deletion;[7] it probably is no hint for some earlier Hebrew text not containing בְּצַלְמוֹ as basis of the LXX. The MT is to be preferred. However, the general sense of the verse would not be changed by leaving out בְּצַלְמוֹ, but the reading of that word leads to an emphasis on the fact that it is *God's* image by mentioning it twice and arranging the words one directly after the other, thus even constructing a small chiastic structure within this short phrase, which will be discussed below.

Regarding chap. 2, in v. 18, there is just one minor variant: not including the mappiq of אֶעֱשֶׂהּ ("I will make"), which is in most of the manuscripts. However, inasmuch as the codex Leningradensis reads this word with mappiq, it is maintained in the BHS, although this reading is unusual. The mappiq renders the final *h* a consonant instead of indicating a vowel sound. Additionally, the LXX and the Latin Vulgate know the plural "let us make" (ποιήσωμεν/*faciamus*) instead of the Hebrew "I will make," thus assimilating this verse to Gen 1:26.

While the manuscripts on vv. 21–22 do not contain any variants, the word מֵאִישׁ ("from/out of man") in v. 23 is rendered מֵאִישָׁהּ ("from/out of *her* man") in the Hebrew Samaritan Pentateuch, the Greek LXX (ἐκ τοῦ ἀνδρὸς αὐτῆς), and the Aramaic Targum Onkelos (מִבַּעֲלָהּ). This corresponds to v. 25 reading אִשְׁתּוֹ ("his wife"), thus possibly indicating another assimilation.[8]

In v. 24 there is a major variant in several ancient versions. While the MT reads וְהָיוּ לְבָשָׂר אֶחָד ("they become one flesh"), the Syriac versions, the Samaritan Pentateuch, the Targum Pseudo-Jonathan, the Vulgate, and the LXX all add "the two of them/both" (שְׁנֵיהֶם/תרוויהון/*duo*/οἱ δύο). This might be an assimilation to v. 25, where also the MT reads שְׁנֵיהֶם.[9]

---

7. Rudolph and Elliger, *BHS*, 2.

8. On possible but not forceful reasons for a decision in favor of the מֵאִישָׁה see Tosato, "On Genesis 2:24," 397–98. This will be discussed later in this chapter.

9. In favor of an original reading of the MT including שְׁנֵיהֶם, see ibid., 395–97. He argues against

Finally, the codex Leningradensis B 19^A reads a ו before הָאָדָם ("the man") in v. 25, thus rendering "And the two of them were naked, *and* the man and his woman were not ashamed."

The given variants, although not to be considered as the best readings, yet allude to the fact that subsequent translators and copyists were well aware of the close connection between Gen 2:18, 23–25. and Gen 1:26–27. So we find links between the following verses as given by the variant readings:

2:18 → 1:26   "we will make" instead of "I will make"
2:23 → 2:25   "from/out of *her* man" instead of "from/out of man"
2:24 → 2:25   "the two of them/both" instead of "—"

Even without regarding the variants in other ancient versions than the Masoretic as more authoritative, they point to the other writers' perception of Gen 2:18–25 as internal unit corresponding to Gen 1:26–27.

I.1.1.2.2 Translation

The original text's or even the pericope's meaning is not altered by any of these minor alternatives. That makes a reliable, but tentative translation easier. The following wording is oriented primarily on the MT, but including possible alternatives in brackets.[10]

(1:26ᵃ) And God said, "Let Us make man in Our image, according to Our likeness; and they shall rule [. . .]"
(1:27) And God created man in His own image, in the image of God He created him; male and female He created them.
(2:18) And YHWH God said, "It is not good for the man to be alone; I will make [Let us make] him a helper corresponding to him."
(2:21) So YHWH God caused a deep sleep to fall upon the man, and while he slept He took one of his ribs and closed up the flesh at that place.
(2:22) And YHWH God built into a woman the rib which he had taken from the man, and brought her to the man.
(2:23) And the man said, "This finally is bone of my bones, and flesh of my flesh; this shall be called woman, because this was taken out of [her] man."
(2:24) For this reason a man leaves his father and his mother, and is joined to his woman; and they [the two] become one flesh.
(2:25) And the two of them were naked, the man and his woman, and were not ashamed before one another.

"the doctrine of the *veritas hebraica*" which he calls "in reality, the myth of the *veritas rabbinica*" (ibid., 396; italics given) supporting the variant reading due to its many witnesses, although some of them (like Philo, NT etc.) are dependent on the same source (the LXX). Reasons why it could have been the Rabbis who added (and not deleted) שְׁנֵיהֶם will be given below in this chapter.

10. Rationales as to why translating some words in a concrete way and not another possible rendering, will follow in the following passages concerning literary and linguistic observations.

I.1.1.3 Textual Analysis

I.1.1.3.1 Unity or Discontinuity in Genesis 1–2

Before turning to interesting linguistic features found in the passages of Gen 1 and 2, it is important first to address the subject of unity or discontinuity between Genesis 1–2:3 and 2:4—3:24, specifically 1–2:4a and 2:4b–3:24. Since the late eighteenth and early nineteenth century it has been held that these constitute two independent creation accounts derived from different sources.[11] The most influential and dominant theories are the different versions of the Documentary Hypothesis (Graf-Wellhausen), attributing 1:1—2:4a to a Priestly source, and 2:4b onward to a Yahwist tradition.[12] Yet, primarily Jewish exegetes dared to withstand the mainstream of scholarly interpretation in favor of form critical arguments apparently supporting the hypothesis of discontinuity.[13] In the meantime the number of conservative scholars applying form criticism to demonstrate the literary interrelation and interdependence between chaps. 1–3 is steadily increasing. J. Doukhan's structural analysis of Gen 1–2 is one of the first works clearly supporting the unity of the Eden account by presenting form critical, structural, and linguistic arguments.[14] The articles of Hauser and Garrett further argue in favor of unity and interdependence,[15] with Garrett's concluding that "the *unity* of Gen 1–2 is remarkable."[16] Similarly, Collins investigates linguistic and literary features of the bigger section (Genesis 1–4) and emphasizes concerning Gen 2:4 that

> the structure of Genesis 2:4 argues against dividing the verse. There is a header ('these are the generations of') that marks this as a part of the main plot; then there is an elaborate chiasmus that unites the two pericopes (1:1—2:3 and 2:4–25), inviting us to read them harmoniously. The shift in divine name identifies the cosmic Creator with the covenant God of Israel . . . . These observations about the parts of Genesis 2:4 also show that, whatever their original sources, the parts now function as a literary whole, and thus the sources are unrecoverable. This literary whole invites us to read the two pericopes in a complementary way . . . .[17]

---

11. See e.g., Westermann, *Genesis 1–11 (Ger.)*, 255 who expresses that understanding Gen 1–3 as a unity is very rare among the scholars of his time.

12. For a brief historical review and evaluation of this hypothesis see Doukhan, "Literary Structure," 137–63.

13. Cf. Sarna, *Genesis*, xviii.

14. Doukhan, "Literary Structure," 33–78. Note also the critique of Garrett, *Primeval History*, 194–97 reaffirming most of Doukhan's analysis and concluding: "Thanks especially to Doukhan's work, any reading of Genesis 1–2 as two unrelated texts juxtaposed to one another is impossible." Ibid., 195.

15. See Garrett, *Primeval History*, 188–94; Hauser, "Links," 297–305.

16. Garrett, *Primeval History*, 192; italics given.

17. Collins, *Genesis 1–4*, 229.

The Old Testament Foundation

Further, "it turns out that literary and grammatical considerations supply a better explanation in terms of the overall flow of the narrative."[18] Similarly, Wenham investigates Gen 2:4, recognizing its interesting chiasmus,[19] and finally concludes that this verse "serves both as a title to 2:5—4:26 . . . and as a link with the introduction 1:1—2:3."[20] Indeed, "it could be seen as a chiastic redactional unit connecting Gen 2:5—3:24 and 1:1—2:3."[21] It seems proper to assert that "we should not call these two creation accounts: there is one big-picture creation account, followed by a close-up on the way God created them 'male and female.'"[22] This study follows the modern, convincing rationales in favor of an overall picture, consisting of two harmonious, complementary accounts.

I.1.1.3.2 GENESIS 1:26–27

Regarding linguistic and semantic aspects, Gen 1:26 and 27 have quite a big potential for controversy. A first and much discussed observation is the plural form of נַעֲשֶׂה ("let us") in v. 26. It seems like this use of the first person plural ("let us") refers to the third person singular ("God") mentioned before, but that is not unambiguously clear (cf. also Isa 6:8). In fact, there is a vast debate about the right interpretation of this expression and it is hardly possible to argue by linguistic or semantic facts in favor of one view or the other. However, since the exact interpretation is not substantial for the given topic of this study, a closer scrutiny is omitted.[23] It is, nonetheless, an interesting feature of the story that the first occurrence of the (divine) plural is right at the beginning of the account of the creation of man.

Another important, but unambiguous term in v. 26 is the Hebrew צֶלֶם ("image/statue/model"), which is usually used for statues, models, replicas.[24] It is used here as a

---

18. Ibid., 231.

19. Cf. Wenham, *Genesis 1–15*, 46: (A) Heaven—(B) Earth—(C) Created—(C') Made—(B') Earth—(A') Heaven. This chiasmus is an argument in favor of continuity instead of interruption between Gen 2:4a and b.

20. Ibid., 55. Note also the argumentation of Mathews, *Genesis 1–11:26*, 81–84, 188–91; cf. Soggin, *Genesis*, 48.

21. Stordalen, *Echoes of Eden*, 215.

22. Collins, *Genesis 1–4*, 229.

23. For further comments, theories, and debates about Gen 1:26–27 comprising the problem of "Let Us" as well as the possible meaning of "Image" and "Likeness" see, in addition to the standard exegetical commentaries, the following examples: e.g.: Noort, "Interpretations," 1–18; Clines, "Image," 53–103; Hasel, "'Let Us,'" 58–66; Kline, "Image," 250–72; Mettinger, "Abbild oder Urbild?," 403–24; Miller, "'Image' and 'Likeness,'" 289–304; Fossum, "Gen 1:26 and 2:7," 202–39; Cook, "Image of God," 85–94; Armstrong, *Genesis*, 1–157; Loretz, *Gottesebenbildlichkeit*, 1–173; Hoekema, *Image*, 1–275; Koch, *Imago Dei*, 1–68; Berkouwer, *Man*, 380. See, for a history of the interpretation of "God's image," esp. Mathews, *Genesis 1–11:26*, 164–72.

24. Cf. HALOT/TWOT s.v. צֶלֶם; Num 33:52; 1 Sam 6:5, 11; 2 Kgs 11:18; 2 Chr 23:17; Ezek 7:20; 16:17; 23:14; Amos 5:26; more abstract: Ps 39:7; 73:20. See also Clines, "Etymology," 19–25.

paralleling synonym to the abstract noun דְּמוּת ("likeness/image/form/shape"), the verbal root of which means "to be like/to resemble."[25] That these are used synonymously without the intention to provide some dividing line between certain human faculties may be clear from Gen 5:3.[26] The meaning of man's resembling God as his image is richly discussed in a vast amount of literature and generally tends to emphasize the following aspects to a greater or lesser degree:[27] (1) the image refers to spiritual and mental abilities, which are similar to man's creator; (2) man resembles the physical shape of God; (3) man's function as ruler over the creation on earth makes him a representative (image) of God. These different opinions do not exclude each other, and particularly the וְיִרְדּוּ ("so they may rule") with the vav-conjunctive following the cohortative נַעֲשֶׂה ("let us make") indicates a certain purpose or result of action (cf. Gen 19:20; 34:23; 2 Sam 3:21). Consequently, at least one of the divine tasks or responsibilities of man is ruling over the creation on earth corresponding to the divine pattern. Furthermore,

> although the two concepts are directly juxtaposed, neither here nor in any other Scripture is 'male and female' called part of God's image. The *imago* is relational, but in no way does it require a person somehow to be linked to the opposite sex to reflect God's image fully.[28]

The LXX (as well as the Samaritan Pentateuch and the Vulgate) adds a conjunction by using κατά twice:

בְּצַלְמֵנוּ כִּדְמוּתֵנוּ
In our image according to our likeness

κατ' εἰκόνα ἡμετέραν καὶ καθ' ὁμοίωσιν
According to our image and according to [our] likeness

Thus this phrase echoes the previous verse, thereby possibly emphasizing the fact that, in contrast to the animals which belong to *their* own γένος, humankind belongs to *God's* own γένος:[29]

---

25. Cf. HALOT/TWOT s.v. דָּמָה/דְּמוּת; Clines, *Classical Hebrew*, 2:447–49.

26. Cf. Wenham, *Genesis 1–15*, 30: "The interchangeability of 'image' and 'likeness' (cf. [Gen] 5:3) shows that this distinction is foreign to Genesis, and that probably 'likeness' is simply added to indicate the precise nuance of 'image' in this context."

27. See again the sample of literature mentioned above concerning vv. 26–27. Different commentaries provide brief surveys. Philo is again far from the actual sense of the text and interprets the image as God's "most sacred/ancient word" (λόγου τοῦ ἱερωτάτου· θεοῦ γὰρ εἰκὼν λόγος ὁ πρεσβύτατος; Conf. 147), without elucidating what that practically means (apart from observing the commandments of that word).

28. Beale and Carson, *NT Use*, 58.

29. Cf. Loader, *LXX, Sexuality, and NT*, 27–28; Brown, *Genesis 1:1—2:3*, 41; Rösel, *Übersetzung*, 41–43. Although the Septuagint is deviating from the exact translation of the MT, the same point is made clear by the strong emphasis on *God's* image as unambiguously given in vv. 26–27; 5:1, 3; and 9:6. Furthermore it should be noted that it is this divine *genos*, which most likely is referred to in

τὰ θηρία τῆς γῆς κατὰ γένος καὶ τὰ κτήνη κατὰ γένος καὶ πάντα τὰ ἑρπετὰ τῆς γῆς κατὰ γένος αὐτῶν

The beasts *after their kind* (לְמִינָהּ), and the cattle *after their kind* (לְמִינָהּ), and everything that creeps on the ground *after its kind* (לְמִינֵהוּ)

Proceeding to v. 27 one recognizes a repetition of the divine intention to create man in *God's* image. Moreover it is the realization of the aforementioned plan, since God now does what he previously announced. Interestingly, now there is a definite article with the Hebrew הָאָדָם ("the man") in contrast to the simple, indefinite אָדָם of v. 26. However, since the distinction between male and female is not introduced until v. 27b, we must assume that הָאָדָם is just a concrete reference to the אָדָם of v. 26 (meaning "the aforementioned man"), thus again stressing that there have not been any changes between the stage of planning and the time of modeling man regarding the concrete purpose of God's creative act. It is still the same man to be constructed by God, still resembling the divine image. That is again affirmed by the following emphasis on the man's divine image by using a chiasmus in this short sentence (v. 27a):[30]

(A) He created (וַיִּבְרָא)

   (B) ... God (אֱלֹהִים)

      (C) In his image (בְּצַלְמוֹ)

      (C') In the image [of] (בְּצֶלֶם)

   (B') God (אֱלֹהִים)

(A') He created (בָּרָא)

Considering that the Septuagint version omits בְּצַלְמוֹ ("in his image") in the first part, "probably because of its presence in the second, the omission results in the emphasis in the opening statement of 1:27 falling on the creation of humankind, rather than humankind in the image of God. That qualification becomes a second statement."[31] Beside the fact that, as explained above, the MT is to be preferred as being more reliable/authoritative, particularly the consequence of stressing only the act of creation itself, thereby devaluating the most prominent topic of the special *divine image* in vv. 26–27. makes the Greek variant unsatisfactory.[32] The emphasis clearly lies

---

similar terms in Gen 6:2 calling them "sons of God" (οἱ υἱοὶ τοῦ θεοῦ/בְּנֵי־הָאֱלֹהִים), while the "daughters of men" (θυγατέρας τῶν ἀνθρώπων/בְּנוֹת הָאָדָם) already lost their divine similitude. The Targum Neofiti on Gen 1:27 further supports the idea of creating pairs of the same kind by translating "male and his yoke-fellow/mate he created them" (דכר וזוגיה ברא יתהון; more on this will follow). That has later been used as further support for the monogamy-ideal in Palestine of Jesus' time, cf. Davies and Allison, *Saint Matthew*, 3:10.

30. Cf. Kirchschläger, *Ehe im NT*, 20.

31. Loader, *LXX, Sexuality, and NT*, 28.

32. We have to keep in mind, however, that from the NT perspective, the LXX text most probably has been the one who was more influential, who was more widely read and understood. Yet, to discover the text's original meaning better, the MT is to be preferred as the earlier version. Furthermore, while the LXX was undoubtedly widely used among NT writers, it competed with three other, more literal Greek

upon the aspect that man is created in *God's* image unlike that of the animals before that are created according to *their own* kind.

While v. 27a thus positively stresses the high goal of God's working with man,[33] the second part of the verse as a parallelism elucidates more clearly the concrete way of reaching that aim. Now, for the first time, man is described as being male and female, pointing to the more precise description of their creation in Gen 2:7, 18–25 as well as to their ability to procreate (Gen 1:28).[34] Additionally, the particle אתו with the third person suffix is singular but collective and again alludes to the fact that he created "him" (אתו) as a person not really being singular, but (a collective "combination" of) man and woman. The creational oneness to be investigated in Gen 2:24 is thus foreshadowed in Gen 1:27.[35]

I.1.1.3.3 Genesis 2:18–25

Proceeding to chap. 2 we find the focus more closely on man's creation. The description of God becomes more and more personal, his work now being depicted as an intimate act of creation—creating not only by his (abstract) word, but even "forming" (יָצַר) with his own hands, himself personally "breathing" (נָפַח) into man's nostrils the breath of life, himself "planting" (נָטַע) the great gift for humankind, the wonderful Garden of Eden, and even closely conversing with man, warning him of danger (Gen 2:7–8, 16–17). This growing intimacy in chap. 2 is further expressed by a change of God's

---

translations which, although not emerging in final form until into the Christian era, are believed to have had pre-Christian origins: Aquila, Symmachus and Theodotion. These three are unanimous in retaining the twofold occurrence of "image" in Gen 1:27, in harmony with the MT. This demonstrates the early and widespread dissatisfaction with what seems to be the shortened state of the LXX and support for the view that the *Urtext* behind both MT and these three Greek versions contained the twofold occurrence of "image." (See for these documents Field, *Origenis Hexaplorum*, 10–11)

33. Similarly Davidson, *Flame*, 17; Von Rad, *Erstes Buch Mose*, 37–39.

34. Of course, man is not described as some androgynous, bifacial being as some ancient Jewish comments suggest (e.g., *Gen. Rab.* 8:1; 14:1, 7; 18:1; *Lev. Rab.* 14:1; *midr. Ps.* 139:5; *y. Ber.* 9:7; *b. Ber.* 61a; *'Erub.* 18a; cf. Strack and Billerbeck, *Talmud und Midrasch*, 1:801–2; Zimmermann, *Geschlechtermetaphorik*, 215–19; similarly Philo in *Leg.* 2:13, 19–50; *Her.* 164; *QG* 1:25.) However, it has often been pointed out that "the change from singular to plural in Verse 27 ('in the image of God He created *him*; male and female He created *them.*') is intentional and is meant to indicate a contrast which 'prevents one from assuming the creation of an originally androgynous man.'" Kaye, "One Flesh," 47; cf. Von Rad, *Erstes Buch Mose*, 39; Stuhlmiller, "One Flesh," 4–5; Winter, "Sadoqite Fragments," 79–81; Davidson, *Flame*, 19.

35. While Jesus himself refers to Gen 1:27 in context of marriage (cf. Matt 19:4; Mark 10:6), it is further interesting to notice that Gen 1:27 has been identified already very early in ancient Judaism as belonging to the institution of marriage, as the Targum Neofiti using זוגיה ("spouse") in reference to the female counter part of the דכר ("male") suggests (thus emphasized by Berger, *Gesetzesauslegung*, 523). The Aramaic ברא יתהון דכר וזוגיה thus means "the male and *his spouse/partner* he [i.e., God] created them" (cf. McNamara trans., *Targum Neofiti 1: Genesis*, 55) rather than the simple "male and female" of the Hebrew MT. This seems to indicate a tendency to interpret even the first biblical verse about man and woman in a marital sense.

name from אֱלֹהִים to יְהוָה אֱלֹהִים from Gen 2:4 onward: "*Yahweh-Elohim*, the term for God in this scene, is far more personal than *Elohim*, the term used for God in Genesis 1. Adam is no longer simply a creation of the Creator God; he stands in relation to the 'Lord God.'"[36] Now the author "identifies the cosmic Creator with the covenant God of Israel...."[37] This far more personal description and God's dealing as the "touchable" God who does not shrink away from direct contact with man is beautifully carried out in Gen 2:18–25 (and even in the following story of the Fall of Man).

Now turning to the central passage in Gen 2:18–25 we find in v. 18 a striking contrast to chap. 1, in which everything was "good" (the world and animals) or even "very good" (the man).[38] For the first time since chap. 1, God again speaks or thinks (וַיֹּאמֶר), and for the first and only time in the entire creation account there is something לֹא־טוֹב ("not good"). "Such observation emphasizes the importance of the woman in the mind of God. Divine initiative is the centre stage in this passage [Gen 2:18–25]"[39]—as it was in Gen 1:26–27. The close connection to the brief report in chap. 1 is evident and it seems like Gen 2:18–20 is some kind of introduction, elucidating the urgent necessity for man to have a עֵזֶר.[40] Without the female part as his complement he is not complete, not "very good"—apparently not even God is sufficient to supply man's need of a human partner. The LXX and the Vulgate even render "let us make" (ποιήσωμεν/ *faciamus*) instead of the MT "I will make" (אֶעֱשֶׂה), thus assimilating this verse to Gen 1:26. Another link to the brief report in Gen 1:26–27 is given by the Hebrew word כְּנֶגְדּוֹ ("according to the opposite of him/corresponding him") as a quality of the עֵזֶר complementing the man as his "helper/assistance."[41]

---

36. Scotchmer, "Lessons," 81; italics given. Similarly Moberly, "Serpent," 6: "The use of the personal name of God, Yahweh, could be seen as implying something of God's caring relationship to his people."

37. Collins, *Genesis 1–4*, 229.

38. Generally, the "difference between the two accounts is not due to their dating from different periods or to foreign influences affecting the one and not the other. It arises rather from the fact that the purposes of the two accounts are different." Isaksson, *Marriage and Ministry*, 18. While chap. 1 focuses on the different species of God's creation, chap. 2 focuses particularly on the most important of the created beings: man, male and female. However, as will be shown below, the purpose of chap. 2 certainly is not "to explain in more detail the conditions of human life in a world in which man is the dominant partner. Woman is dependent on man and her task is to help him, help which primarily consists in bearing him children who may carry on his name." Ibid., 19; cf. Pedersen and Møller, *Israel I-II*, 61–62.

39. Mathews, *Genesis 1–11:26*, 212. Similarly, Kirchschläger, *Ehe im NT*, 18–19, states: "Was hier [Gen 2:18–25] geschieht, wird als positiv, ja als für den Menschen zielführend anerkannt. Diese hohe Einschätzung ist konsequent dadurch unterstrichen, daß alles auf Gottes Initiative zurückgeführt werden kann.... In ihrer Idee und Stiftung wird die Institution der Ehe zurückgeführt auf Willen und Tun des Schöpfers."

40. The uncertain and very speculative rabbinical exposition of later times shows this incident in a much darker light reasoned from the later experiences of man's abuse concerning the rights of marriage and divorce: "Reflecting an unhappy reality, *Gen Rab.* 17:4 explains that God did not create woman from the beginning because he knew that man would bring charges against her, and so he waited until expressly asked." Beale and Carson, *NT Use*, 198.

41. HALOT s.v. עֵזֶר; cf. Clines, *Classical Hebrew*, 6:341.

> While this word [עֵזֶר] designates assistance, it is more frequently used in a concrete sense to designate the assistant. (Cf. Gen 2:18, 20 where Eve is created to be Adam's help[er].) As to the source of the help, this word is generally used to designate divine aid, particularly in Psalms....[42]

Similarly TWAT explicates that

> Das Verb 'zr I 'helfen' weckt die Vorstellung des Schutzes, wie das Nomen ᵃzārāh 'Einfriedung' und 'Umrahmung' zeigt. Häufig hat es Gott zum Subjekt und einen Ausdruck zur Bezeichnung der Gläubigen oder des Gottesvolkes als direktes Obj.[43]

It may further be said, especially concerning Gen 2:18, 20, that

> ...ʿezer is a relational term; it designates a beneficial relationship; and it pertains to God, people, and animals. By itself, the word does not specify positions within relationships; more particularly, it does not imply inferiority. Position results from additional content or from context. Accordingly, what kind of relationship does ʿezer entail in Genesis 2:18, 20? Our answer comes in two ways: (1) the word neged, which joins ʿezer, connotes equality: a helper who is a counterpart. (2) The animals are helpers, but they fail to fit ʾadham.... their similarity is not equality. ʾAdham names them and thereby exercises power over them. No fit helper is among them. And thus the narrative moves to woman.... God is the helper superior to man; the animals are helpers inferior to man; woman is the helper equal to man.[44]

Just as Gen 1:27 depicts man as consisting of male and female, so God is now about to create the second part without whom the creation of man cannot be טוֹב מְאֹד. The term כְּנֶגְדּוֹ appears only once more in the entire OT, in Gen 2:20, again referring to the man's help and rather expressing "the notion of complementarity rather than identity. [. . . for] if identity were meant, the more natural phrase would be 'like him,' כָּמוֹהוּ."[45] "The focus is on the equality of the two in terms of their essential constitution. Man and woman share in the 'human' sameness that cannot be found elsewhere

---

42. TWOT s.v. עֵזֶר (translated as "help/support/helper/assistance").

43. E. Lipiński, in: Botterweck et al., TWAT, 6:15.

44. Trible, "Eve and Adam. Genesis 2–3 Reread," 251–52; republished in Kvam et al., Eve and Adam, 432.

45. Wenham, Genesis 1–15, 68; similarly, Kirchschläger, Ehe im NT, 18, says, "Gleichwertigkeit und Ebenbürtigkeit nicht ausdrückliche Identität." Here, again, the LXX seems to link v. 18 with Gen 1:26–27, for it translates כְּנֶגְדּוֹ with κατ' αὐτόν instead of the stronger ὅμοιος αὐτῷ as used for the only other example of כְּנֶגְדּוֹ in v. 20. Cf. Loader, LXX, Sexuality, and NT, 35: "With both κατ' αὐτόν and ὅμοιος αὐτῷ there is an echo in the LXX of 1:26 where the double κατὰ phrases occur and ὁμοίωσιν is used.... Gen 1:26–27 will also have influenced the unexpected choice of the generic ἄνθρωπος ('man/human being') instead of ἀνήρ ('man/male/husband') as the translation of אִישׁ ('man/male/husband') in 2:24. This is all part of the attuning of Genesis 2 to Genesis 1 in the LXX...." See also Rösel, Übersetzung, 69.

The Old Testament Foundation

in creation among the beasts."⁴⁶ The עֵזֶר complementing the man does not connote someone to function as a mere servant of the man.⁴⁷ To the contrary, in the OT it rather alludes to the divine help of God as deliverer of Israel.⁴⁸ Thus the text speaks of a human helper (cf. Eccl 4:9–10), also functioning as representative of God (cf. Gen 1:26–28) in fulfilling the divine command (Gen 1:28; 2:15–17), an instrument of the divine help for the sake of man.⁴⁹ Yet, "to help someone does not imply that the helper is stronger than the helped; simply that the latter's strength is inadequate by itself."⁵⁰ The Hebrew עֵזֶר is simply a "relational term, describing a beneficial relationship, but in itself does not specify position or rank, either superiority or inferiority."⁵¹

Gen 2:21 speaks of תַּרְדֵּמָה, a "deep sleep" caused by God, which indicates not just a usual night's sleep, but a divinely induced sleep (indicated by the hiphil form of נָפַל), which is often closely connected with a divine revelation (closing it up or mostly preparing for it).⁵² The וַיִּישָׁן ("and he slept") may be subordinated to the following verb

---

46. Mathews, *Genesis 1–11:26*, 213. For a brief review of the different opinions concerning the meaning of the hapax legomenon כְּנֶגְדּוֹ see Kvam et al., *Eve and Adam*, 28–29. This term certainly further alludes to homogeny in both partner's personality: "The more a man and a woman have in common even before marriage, the greater likelihood that they will find the companionship marriage should bring and that the union will be a complete success. Conversely, where there are great differences in background, training, attitudes, principles, likes, and dislikes, it is far more difficult to be 'one' in mind and spirit, and thus to find success in the marriage relationship." Nichol and Andreasen, *ABC*, Matt 19:5, 5:454; cf. also Simpson, "Genesis," 500. In the most prominent King James Version the female is described as "an help meet for him." From this expression derived the word "helpmeet" which today just means "spouse/companion." Cf. Schwartz and Kaplan, *The Fruit of Her Hands*, 10–11. But as the Hebrew and Greek texts indicate, she is more than just a companion. She is a person who suits him, made accordingly to his abilities and personality, to fill his lacks and make him whole, to compensate the man's loneliness. She would be "appropriate, that is, to his needs; to complete him . . . it was not God's purpose for him to be alone for long. Loneliness would be detrimental to man's well-being . . . ." Nichol and Andreasen, *ABC*, Gen 2:18, 1:225–26. "Neither Man nor Woman is whole or complete apart from the reunification of their 'flesh' in the sexual relationship of marriage. Sexual drive is the yearning of the incomplete individual for the wholeness which can only be attained through sexual reunion." Stuhlmiller, "One Flesh," 4, referring to Von Rad, *Genesis (1956)*, 82–83 and Zimmerli, *1 Mose 1–11. Die Urgeschichte*, 177–83. Cf. also Hamilton, *Genesis*, 175.

47. Cf. e.g., Rosenzweig, "A Helper Equal to Him," 277–80.

48. Cf. e.g., Gen 49:25; Exod 18:4; Deut 33:7; 2 Kgs 14:26; Job 29:12; Ps 30:11; 54:6; 72:12; 89:20; 107:12; Isa 31:3; 63:5; Jer 47:4; Dan 11:34. Cf. also Wenham, *Genesis 1–15*, 68; Mathews, *Genesis 1–11:26*, 214; Hamilton, *Genesis*, 176.

49. Interestingly, "the verb behind 'ēzer is 'āzar, which means 'succor,' 'save from danger,' 'deliver from death.' The woman in Gen 2 delivers or saves man from his solitude." Mathews, *Genesis 1–11:26*, 222. Perhaps was even meant to save his loyalty by strengthening and encouraging him to secure his loyalty by staying away from the tree of knowledge.

50. Wenham, *Genesis 1–15*, 68; similarly Westermann, *Genesis 1–11 (Ger.)*, 309. Cf. Josh 1:14; 10:4, 6; 1 Chr 12:17, 19, 21, 22.

51. Davidson, "Beginning," 15; cf. Brueggemann, "Flesh and Bone," 541–42; Meyers, *Discovering Eve*, 85; Trible, *Sexuality*, 97–101. For further interpretations of עֵזֶר see Kvam et al., *Eve and Adam*, 28. On the possible Semitic etymology of עֵזֶר supporting the mentioned view of an equal helper see Freedman, "Woman, A Power Equal to Man," 56–58.

52. Cf. Gen 15:12; Job 4:13; 33:15–16; Isa 29:10; 1 Sam 26:12; Wenham, *Genesis 1–15*, 69. Loader, *LXX, Sexuality, and NT*, 37 notes that the LXX uses ἔκστασιν, thereby creating an even greater sense

The Biblical "One Flesh" Theology of Marriage as Constituted in Genesis 2:24

וַיִּקַּח ("and he took"), thus indicating a temporal clause meaning "and while he slept he took" (וַיִּישָׁן וַיִּקַּח)[53] in order to create the man's helper as a new "revelation" of himself (i.e., his image; Gen 1:26–27) to man. The צֵלָע he takes out of Adam could mean "side," not necessarily the more anatomical "rib," as all the other examples in the Hebrew Bible demonstrate.[54] That may again point to the equality of the "help corresponding him" adumbrated in v. 18; she actually is one of his sides, one part of the whole being called "man" resembling the divine image.[55] It particularly may be the very interesting wordplay between the "image" (צֶלֶם) in Gen 1:26–27 and the "rib/side" (צֵלָע) in Gen 2:21 that even more supports the idea of every individual part of the two genders reflecting the divine pattern for him- and herself, but certainly not being perfect before becoming (re-) united as mentioned in Gen 2:24 (לְבָשָׂר אֶחָד, "one flesh").[56] However, the use in the plural form of which God took exactly "one" (אַחַת) rather suggests the translation as "rib," still alluding to similar features.[57]

---

of mystery. The terms in Hebrew and in Greek really seem to prepare the reader for a divine revelation resulting from man's (divinely caused) sleep. On ἔκστασιν ("trance/entrancement/vision/ecstasy/torpor") cf. BDAG/FRI/LSJ/LEH.

53. Cf. NET on Gen 2:21. NET stands for the NET Bible, Version 1.0, Copyright © 2004/2005 Biblical Studies Foundation (included in BibleWorks 8). As is declared by its creators, "the NET Bible™ Learning Environment offers a comprehensive set of free resources available online, including commentaries, articles, word studies, original biblical languages and cross references all integrated into a system that empowers you to carefully study the Word of God and to prepare your teaching lessons quickly." Http://net.Bible.org/home.php. I am well aware of the fact that a deficiency of this version's verse comments is the absence of a concrete author. Nevertheless, it contains many valuable hints and ideas that deserve attention and in some cases even quotation. Furthermore, among the contributors of this Bible version and its annotations are experienced scholars (cf. e.g., http://bible.org/authors) and the critical reviews about this version are very favorable (see http://bible.org/endorse).

54. See Gen 32:32; Exod 25:12, 14; 26:20, 26–27, 35; 27:7; 30:4; 36:25, 31–32; 37:3, 5, 27; 38:7; 2 Sam 16:13; 21:14; 1 Kgs 6:5, 8, 15–16, 34; 7:3; Job 18:12; Ps 35:15; 38:18; Jer 20:10; Ezek 41:5–9, 11, 26; Mic 4:6–7; Zeph 3:19. Cf. on the Hebrew term further BDB/HALOT s.v. צֵלָע. TWOT explains that צֵלָע "is used once for a man's side (Gen 2:21–22) and once for the side of a hill, perhaps a ridge or terrace (2 Sam 16:13; BDB); elsewhere it is an architectural term. It refers to the sides of an object, e.g., the sides of the ark of the covenant (Exod 25:12, 14). It is also employed to describe a location within a building (cf. Exod 26:35). Further it means a side chamber." Its meaning as "side" is also supported by Hamilton, *Genesis*, 178. Brueggemann, "Flesh and Bone," 539 further notes (following Kramer, *The Sumerians*, 149, and Gaster, *Old Testament*, 21–22) that the Hebrew צֵלָע ("rib") could be "derived from a Sumerian usage in which the term used means both 'rib' and 'life' the latter referring to the woman as the mother of life." The ancient rabbis were well aware of the twofold meaning, as Strack and Billerbeck, *Talmud und Midrasch*, 1:802 substantiates.

55. Similarly Mathews, *Genesis 1–11:26*, 213; Kirchschläger, *Ehe im NT*, 43: "Die Vorstellung einer gleichberechtigten, zumindest einer grundsätzlich gleichwertigen Gemeinschaft steht hier ebenso im Vordergrund wie das Verständnis der Ehepartner als Menschen, die einander auch in gegenseitiger Hilfestellung verbunden sind." On the equality of man and woman in Eden see also Luck, *Divorce and Remarriage*, 26–27.

56. Reconsidering the foregoing thoughts about the Hebrew עֵזֶר in Gen 2:18, the close connection between the divine building of the "helper" from man's "rib/side" and the divine "image" of Gen 1:26–27 could further emphasize some kind of a *divine* "assistance/help" as indicated in most of the Old Testament instances using עֵזֶר, cf. esp. TWOT s.v. עֵזֶר.

57. Cf. Davidson, "Beginning," 16–17: "The word ṣēlāʿ can mean either 'side' or 'rib.' Since ṣēlāʿ

Thrice in Gen 2:21–23, once in every verse, the author employed the term לָקַח ("take"), thereby making this verb prominent within this short paragraph on the creational oneness covenant.[58] It may allude to the later usage of "taking a wife" (לָקַח לוֹ לְאִשָּׁה) as "the common idiom for marriage"[59] although vv. 21–23, of course, do not yet speak about marriage. The Hebrew verb בָּנָה ("build") in v. 22 is used only twice concerning God's creative working (here and in Amos 9:6), while the many other instances refer to the usual building of cities, houses, altars, and the temple. It "suggests an aesthetic intent and connotes also the idea of reliability and permanence,"[60] as well as "beauty, stability, and durability."[61] It further "indicates considerable labor to produce solid results. Hence, woman is no weak, dainty, ephemeral creature."[62]

The phrase "he brought her to the man" (וַיְבִאֶהָ אֶל־הָאָדָם) does not allude to some special meaning, as the numerous instances of בוא in the hiphil linked with אֶל, meaning "(to) bring to/before" show.[63] But the exact expression as given in v. 22 only occurs in v. 19, pointing to further concords in vv. 19–23 constructing a parallelism:

---

occurs in the plural in vs. 21 and God is said to take 'one of' them, the reference in this verse is probably to a rib from Adam's side. By 'building' Eve from one of Adam's ribs, God appears to be indicating the mutual relationship, the 'singleness of life,' the 'inseparable unity' in which man and woman are joined. The rib 'means solidarity and equality.' Created from Adam's 'side [rib],' Eve was formed to stand by his side as an equal. Peter Lombard was not off the mark when he said: 'Eve was not taken from the feet of Adam to be his slave, nor from his head to be his ruler, but from his side to be his beloved partner.'" Cf. his references to Westermann, *Genesis 1–11 (Engl.)*, 230; Collins, "The Bible and Sexuality," 153; Keil, *Moses*, 89; Trible, "Depatriarchalizing," 37. See also Mathews, *Genesis 1–11:26*, 216; TWOT s.v. צֵלָע: "This picture [i.e., the woman made of man's 'side/rib'] describes the intimacy between man and woman as they stand equal before God. Since God made the woman, she is responsible to him in worship. She is not a mere extension of man; she possesses a unique individuality in her own right. There is no indication that woman is inferior." This rib rather indicates "a piece of anatomy of great strength and nearest the heart of man." Scotchmer, "Lessons," 82.

58. On the term "covenant" for marriage cf. e.g., Instone-Brewer, *In the Bible*, 1–2; Hasel, "Eheverständnis," 22–28, 33–34; Piper, *Momentary Marriage*, 24, 30, 33–36; Crispin, *Divorce*, 14; Thatcher, *Marriage*, 68–69, 87–95; see Tarwater, *Marriage as Covenant*, 53–75 on the covenant elements given in Gen 1–2 (for a similar purpose see Luck, *Divorce and Remarriage*, 26–46); Hugenberger, *Covenant*, 1–414 deals particularly with this characteristic and consequently titles his dissertation correspondingly.

59. Mathews, *Genesis 1–11:26*, 216; see e.g., Gen 4:19; 6:2; 12:19; 19:14; 20:2–3; 24:67; 25:20; Exod 2:1; Deut 22:13 etc.; cf. Greenberg, "Jewish Tradition," 7, who further points to the fact that there is "no description whatsoever of an actual ceremony, and no explanation of the verb 'take.'" There seem to be no greater procedures required. On the usage of לָקַח לוֹ לְאִשָּׁה see also Clines, *Classical Hebrew*, 1:404.

60. Terrien, "Womanhood," 18; cf. Davidson, "Beginning," 16.

61. Hamilton, *Genesis*, 179.

62. Trible, *Sexuality*, 102.

63. However, there is only one further example of וַיְבִאֶהָ ("and he brought her") in the Hebrew Bible, Gen 24:67, again in a marriage context. In this verse "Isaac brought her [Rebekah] into his mother Sarah's tent, and he took Rebekah, and she became his wife, and he loved her." At least one ancient Jewish commentator, R. Abin, understood this verse as implying that God was the best man of Adam and Eve (see *Gen. Rab.* 18:3; cf. Freedman and Simon, *Midrash Rabbah*, 1:142/fn.2).

The Biblical "One Flesh" Theology of Marriage as Constituted in Genesis 2:24

Gen 2:19–20	Gen 2:22–23
Actor: YHWH God (יְהוָה אֱלֹהִים)	Actor: YHWH God (יְהוָה אֱלֹהִים)
Kind of Work: Formed [animals] (וַיִּצֶר)	Kind of Work: Built [woman] (וַיִּצֶר)
Material: Out of the ground (מִן־הָאֲדָמָה)	Material: Out of the man (מִן־הָאָדָם)
God's Way to Introduce: He brought them to the man (וַיָּבֵא אֶל־הָאָדָם)	God's Way to Introduce: He brought her to the man (וַיְבִאֶהָ אֶל־הָאָדָם)
Man's Reaction: The man called names (וַיִּקְרָא הָאָדָם שֵׁמוֹת)	Man's Reaction: "She shall/will be called woman" (יִקָּרֵא אִשָּׁה)

The similarities are striking, but also certain differences are obvious. Evidently the animals are "formed/shaped" (יָצַר) like the man before in Gen 2:7–8 (cf. also Isa 29:16). The woman, in contrast, is "built" (בָּנָה), just as fathering children leads to "build" one's family (Gen 16:2). It apparently points to the close (blood) relation between the material's origin and the one who is built out of it. Corresponding in this respect is the fact that the animals are shaped "out of the ground" (מִן־הָאֲדָמָה), just like the man (Gen 2:7), while the woman is built "out of the man" (מִן־הָאָדָם). The animals and the woman are by God himself "brought before the man" (וַיָּבֵא/וַיְבִאֶהָ אֶל־הָאָדָם), both times preceding the "calling" (קָרָא) of "names." As investigated in more depth within the section on the literary context, the woman does not actually get a real name at this time of the story (no mentioning of Hebrew שֵׁם), but she is at least called by her generic description: "*'Iššâ* itself is not a name; it is a common noun, not a proper noun. It designates gender; it does not specify person."[64] The animals, in contrast, are given real "names" by their proper nouns (the Hebrew שֵׁם occurs even twice in vv. 19–20). The difference between the naming in vv. 19–20 and v. 23 is further denoted by the different Hebrew verb forms; while v. 20 speaks about the man actively "calling" (וַיִּקְרָא, qal) the animals by name, in v. 23 the woman is only said to be called (יִקָּרֵא, niphal) at some later point of time. Who will call her and when this will happen is not explained at this point of the story, but will be developed soon in Gen 3:20 (again וַיִּקְרָא, qal). The linguistically similar way in relating the creation of woman and animals all the more emphasizes the big difference between each other: only the woman is a worthy partner of the man. This is additionally stressed by the Hebrew wordplay between אִישׁ ("man") and אִשָּׁה ("woman") which further demonstrates their close relatedness through the female's origin. And just like the wordplay with the generic term אָדָם ("man") is an

---

64. Trible, *Sexuality*, 100.

The Old Testament Foundation

allusion to his origin הָאֲדָמָה ("ground") in Gen 2:7, so אִשָּׁה is not to be understood as a real name, but as a sign of affiliation (cf. Gen 3:16–19).[65]

Taking a closer look at Gen 2:23, we find the Hebrew term פַּעַם ("step/pace; foot; time; occurrence"[66]) certainly meaning "this time/now at last"[67] as a happy exclamation that "conveys the futility of the man while naming the animals and finding no one who corresponded to him."[68] Now, finally, he found someone as his own counterpart, eligible to be called "woman" (אִשָּׁה), thus expressing the similarity because of her being "bone of my [man's] bones and flesh of my flesh."[69] As explained above, he is not now giving a name to the woman thus possibly claiming authority over her.[70] The man names the woman not before the Fall (cf. Gen 3:20). Also, the idiomatic construction used here (niphal of קרא with preposition לְ) does not point to the man claiming authority; in every instance where it is used, "the one naming discerns something about the object being named and gives it an appropriate name."[71] The similarity of אִישׁ and אִשָּׁה rather alludes to the striking similarity of both humans and the terms are not to be understood as proper names.[72] Although a common etymological origin is

---

65. Mathews, *Genesis 1–11:26*, 219, further suggests: "The ending –â, indicates feminine gender, but a double entendre has been suggested for the –â, which in Hebrew is sometimes used to indicate direction, 'to' or 'toward.' For the former case the 'man' returns to the 'ground' (*ădāmâ*). In the latter the man moves toward the 'woman' (*'iššâ*) in 2:24, where by marriage he is 'united to his wife' and 'they become one flesh.'" See on this understanding of the suffix of אִשָּׁה as *he locale* also Meier, "Linguistic Clues," 20–21; and on the idea of affiliation similarly Trible, *Sexuality*, 77, 80, 98.

66. Cf. HALOT/TWOT/BDB s.v. פַּעַם.

67. "This noun [i.e., פַּעַם] occurs one hundred seventeen times in the OT, usually meaning 'time, occurrence.' . . . There are numerous expressions for 'time' in which pa'am is one of the elements. For example, 'This is 'at last' (happa'am) bone of my bones' (Gen 2:23)." TWOT s.v. פַּעַם. Clines, *Classical Hebrew*, 6:731–32, similarly, points to a translation of פַּעַם in Gen 2:23 with a temporal meaning: "now/this time/now finally/now at last."

68. NET note on Gen 2:23. Westermann, *Genesis 1–11 (Ger.)*, 314–15, calls it a "jauchzende Bewillkommnung." Rather strange, once more, the interpretation given in *Gen. Rab.* 18:4, where at least R. Judah b. Rabbi says: "At first He created her for him and he saw her full of discharge and blood; thereupon He removed her from him and recreated her a second time. Hence he said: This time she is bone of my bone." Freedman and Simon, *Midrash Rabbah*, 1:142 (emphasis given).

69. Similarly, Reiser, "Verwandtschaftsformel," 3, stresses that this statement is rather a "Verwandtschaftsformel" (kinship formula) than a "Liebeserklärung" (declaration of love).

70. On claiming or expressing authority by giving someone or something a name; see 2 Sam 12:28; 2 Chr 7:14; Isa 4:1; Jer 7:14; 15:16.

71. NET note on Gen 2:23; cf. Gen 3:20; 1 Sam 9:9; 2 Sam 18:18; Prov 16:21; Isa 1:26; 32:5; 35:8; 62:4, 12; Jer 19:6.

72. However, it is worthy of notice that often the circumstances of one's birth led the one naming the newborn to give some special name. That would also be the case with the אִישׁ calling her אִשָּׁה as a hint of her origin/birth, for she is taken of the אִישׁ (cf. Wenham, *Genesis 1–15*, 70). But the actual naming obviously occurs not before Gen 3:20.

doubtful,[73] they represent a wordplay, a paronomasia, and by their like sound again point to the likeness of both's nature.[74]

The man's pleasure at the time the woman is brought by God to him (v. 23) is deeply expressed in his "poetry of Eros,"[75] as it could be called. "The embedded poem is peculiar in the narrative flow and by itself draws attention to the importance of this creative event. The exclamation reflects what the narration has sought to show: the unique compatibility of the man and the woman."[76] For this purpose, several techniques of Hebrew poetry are applied in only five short strophes:

(1) This (זֹאת) finally/this time (הַפַּעַם)
(2) [is] bone (עֶצֶם) out of my bones (מֵעֲצָמַי)
(3) and flesh (וּבָשָׂר) out of my flesh (מִבְּשָׂרִי)
(4) This (לְזֹאת) shall/will be called (יִקָּרֵא) woman (אִשָּׁה)
(5) for from man (כִּי מֵאִישׁ) was taken (לֻקֳחָה) this (זֹאת)

There are two occurrences of parallelism in the lines (2)–(3) and (4)–(5), the paronomasia of אִישׁ and אִשָּׁה in (4) and (5), the hendiadys of "flesh and bone" in (2)–(3), and finally a threefold repetition of the happy proclamation זֹאת ("this") as the frame of this poetic exclamation. Additionally, there is a chiasmus in lines (4)–(5):

(A) This (זֹאת)
  (B) will be called (יִקָּרֵא)
    (C) woman (אִשָּׁה) [for (כִּי)]
    (C') from man (מֵאִישׁ)
  (B') was taken (לֻקֳחָה)
(A') this (זֹאת)

Through this stylistic device again the similarity and (most likely) even equality of man and woman are central, enclosed in the happy repetition of "this," showing the surprise that suddenly even for man has been found a partner.[77] The "poetic formulation of the

---

73. Thus HALOT s.v. אִשָּׁה. TWOT s.v. אנשׁ/אשׁה/אישׁ assumes a common root (אנשׁ) of אשׁה and אנושׁ ("man/mortal person"), but not concretely between אִישׁ and אִשָּׁה. While e.g., Meier, "Linguistic Clues," 22–23, holds that "the phonetic play on the words *'îš* and *'iššâ* is deceptive, for the two words are not genetically related"; (similarly Speiser, *Genesis*, 18), Wenham, *Genesis 1–15*, 70, argues that a common origin could at least be possible (similarly Westermann, *Genesis 1–11 (Ger.)*, 316: "kann offenbleiben"). However, a common origin has not been proved yet.

74. The similarity of generic names may even be indicating their equality in terms of hierarchy as Kirchschläger, *Ehe im NT*, 17–18, suggests. There is another interesting paronomasia given concerning the name of "Eve" which will be investigated in the section on the literary context.

75. Thus Trible, *Sexuality*, 97.

76. Mathews, *Genesis 1–11:26*, 218.

77. The Greek translation of the Septuagint renders the Hebrew זֹאת הַפַּעַם ("this, this time/finally/this is now") with the neuter τοῦτο νῦν ("this now"), thereby referring to the whole event of the woman's creation and not just to the feminine πλευρά ("side/rib"); cf. Mathews, *Genesis 1–11:26*, 218.

traditional kinship formula"⁷⁸ in lines (2) and (3) as later used by Laban, Abimelech, and all Israel, particularly alludes to the same origin, the same family⁷⁹—and perhaps the same God as creator, whose image they should reflect. Just as family bonds by blood relation bind relatives together, so the marriage relation by again becoming "one flesh" binds them inseparably together,⁸⁰ as the next verse more clearly illustrates. Additionally, given the convincing idea that בָּשָׂר ("flesh") also points to man's infirmities,⁸¹ the reference to עֶצֶם ("bone") would be the antonym alluding not only to the complementary material for the human corpus to exist in the given stature, but also to man's "corresponding helper" as necessary complement to his fullness and durable strength:

> It is equally clear that the term *bsr* means weakness, empty of power and meaning. . . . Such an understanding of the term suggests that we are dealing with an assertion that is not concerned simply with physical relationship but includes also psychological dimensions of interaction. The same is true of the other word in the pair. . . . But when it is translated 'bone' we tend to neglect its root meaning of 'power' or 'might.' . . . Thus our two words which conventionally appear in English as physical properties of the body need to be rendered in ways that speak of the functioning of the whole organism. We shall render them 'flesh-weakness' and 'bone-power.'⁸²

Thus, Adam's happy exclamation is also a happy recognition and praise of God's working for his sake. Ortlund, *Whoredom*, 18/fn.10, emphasizes that this expression "suggests the fulfillment of a desire hitherto frustrated," referring for examples to Gen 29:34; 30:20.

78. Wenham, *Genesis 1–15*, 70; cf. Kvam et al., *Eve and Adam*, 30; Reiser, "Verwandtschaftsformel," 3 ("Verwandtschaftsformel"); similarly Brueggemann, "Flesh and Bone," 538–39 ("covenant formula"); Tarwater, *Marriage as Covenant*, 62 ("relational formula"). However, there is no evidence of any marriage oath/vow, as Hugenberger, *Covenant*, 216–39 or Tarwater, *Marriage as Covenant*, 62 claim.

79. See Gen 29:14; 37:27; Judg 9:2; 2 Sam 5:1; 19:13–14; 1 Chr 11:1; (perhaps even Job 2:5); Neh 5:5. Cf. Loader, *LXX, Sexuality, and NT*, 42; Hugenberger, *Covenant*, 162; Berger, *Gesetzesauslegung*, 528, 551; Dunstan, "The Marriage Covenant," 251; Reiser, "Verwandtschaftsformel," 1–3; Baltensweiler, *Ehe im NT*, 20–21; Kaye, "One Flesh," 48–49; Davidson, "Beginning," 17; Collins, *Secrets*, 153; Isaksson, *Marriage and Ministry*, 20–21; Mathews, *Genesis 1–11:26*, 219; Wolff, *Anthropology*, 179. To cut the "naming" of Eve off from the "antique myth of Eve's creation," because they "belong to two different strata, which have at some time or other been brought together in a pseudo-causal relationship by editorial procedures" (Beeston, "One Flesh," 115) is very far-fetched and ignores all the textual hints that allude to far more than just "naming" and the implicit connections to the immediate context. It is almost impossible to argue reasonably in favor of a division between the given unit of verses (vv. 18–25 or at least vv. 23–24). "The terms of Adam's comment [in v. 23] are, of course, drawn from the details of the preceding story." Kaye, "One Flesh," 47–48.

80. Similarly Ryrie, "Biblical Teaching," 178; cf. Kaye, "One Flesh," 48: "This is not the same as kinship in the sense of flesh and blood relationships by common related parentage but is an extension of kinship to bring into relation the contributing families in any marriage which is established. At the same time, however, it is a restriction or definition of the character of the kinship relation in that it defines the man/wife relationship in more exclusive terms than previously existing kinship ties. It is in this sense not kinship, but something beyond kinship, and something which creates further different kinds of kinship patterns."

81. Cf. Hamilton, *Genesis*, 179; Wolff, *Anthropology*, 26–28.

82. Brueggemann, "Flesh and Bone," 533–34. He explains further: "In our verse (Gn 2:23), the poles

These possible deeper aspects of the Hebrew בָּשָׂר and עֶצֶם do not necessarily point to "after Eden" realities, but even more to the pre-Fall status God called "good" (Gen 1:10, 12, 18, 21, 25)—but not yet "very good" (Gen 1:31). The man needs the woman's presence and support to gain his full human strength and a life under perfect (טוֹב מְאֹד; Gen 1:31) conditions. This is not given before the woman's creation as his עֶצֶם and בָּשָׂר.

In v. 24 the happy proclamation continues, but now it seems as being carried on by someone else, using the editorial introduction/comment עַל־כֵּן ("therefore/that is why") speaking about a later reality Adam could not have experienced: parents.[83] The imperfect verb form (יַעֲזָב—"he will leave/forsake") in v. 24 is certainly to be translated as a continuing present tense rather than future, indicating a "repeated, habitual or durative action."[84] However, while the usual translation as "[a man] leaves . . . cleaves . . . becomes . . ." "is flawless, and the sense it yields is quite acceptable,"[85] it must be noted that "the Hebrew imperfect can also be used with a potential force, corresponding to English 'can,' 'may,' 'should,' 'would,' 'could.'"[86] Gen 2:24 would then be rendered as reading: "Therefore a man should/was to leave his father and mother and cling to his wife, and they should/were to become one flesh." Consequently, "the verse can be understood as a description of divine intention rather than of [mere] habitually observed fact."[87] Some English translation (as e.g., the NASB) follow this suggestion and read "*shall* leave . . . *shall* cleave . . . *shall* become . . . ." Hence, Tosato further explains in connection with the introductory עַל־כֵּן that

> there is a whole series of juridical etiologies which link special norms of custom or law to illustrious institutional antecedents in order to provide them with

---

of 'flesh-frailty' and 'bone-power' mean to express the entire range of intermediate possibilities from the extreme of frailty to power. Thus the relationship affirmed is one which is affirmed for every possible contingency in the relationship, as we affirm in the marriage formula, 'in sickness and in health, in plenty and in want.' Here the text says, 'in every circumstance from the extreme of frailty to the extreme of power.' A relation is affirmed which is unaffected by changing circumstances." Ibid., 534–35.

83. On the break between vv. 23–24 see e.g., Wenham, *Genesis 1–15*, 70; Westermann, *Genesis 1–11 (Ger.)*, 317; Von Rad, *Erstes Buch Mose*, 59; NET on Gen 2:24; Baltensweiler, *Ehe im NT*, 45. Kirchschläger, *Ehe im NT*, 18, suggests the comment "darf zugleich als Deutung des Verfassers (und wohl zugleich als ein Bedenken damaligen Eheverständnisses [namely, the editor's reflection]) erkannt werden." See on the "discontinuity [of speakers in vv. 23 and 24] which is insurmountable even on the level of form" and the "double discontinuity (or better, incoherence) of both form and content," also Tosato, "On Genesis 2:24," 392–94 and 393/fn.12.

84. Joüon and Muraoka, *Biblical Hebrew*, 339; consider also the examples given ibid., 338–40. See on the given instance also Wenham, *Genesis 1–15*, 47; the NET note on Gen 2:24. Cf. Gen 10:9; 32:32 (the phrase "to this day" points to characteristic behavior); Num 21:14, 27; 1 Sam 5:5 (again "to this day"); 19:24 (perhaps the imperfect is customary here meaning "were saying"); 2 Sam 5:8.

85. Lawton, "Gen. 2:24," 97.

86. Ibid., 98; see also his reference to Driver, *Tenses in Hebrew*, 41–45, who lists numerous examples of this usage. See on these "modal nuances" of the yiqtol also Joüon and Muraoka, *Biblical Hebrew*, 342.

87. Lawton, "Gen. 2:24," 98. Cf. on this "normative" character of Gen 2:24 (although not due to verbal forms) also Tosato, "On Genesis 2:24," 404–9.

foundations. These etiologies are sometimes introduced, just as in the case of Gen 2:24, by *'al-kēn*. Take, for instance, the etiology concerning the norm of the Sabbath rest.... On the seventh day of creation he [i.e., God] rested; for this reason he ordered that the Sabbath should be observed. The ... argument in Gen 2:24 is similarly structured. God formed the woman by taking her from her husband. In consequence he orders that the man, having left father and mother, should be joined to his wife and be (return to be) one flesh with her."[88]

Concerning the view of a narrator's comment,[89] there are at least two objections to be considered. First, the common practice in narrator's time would not mean for the man to "leave" (עָזַב) his parents, but rather for the woman to leave hers.[90] Yet, the fact that Adam had no parents to talk about, as well as the many other instances with עַל־כֵּן alone in Genesis support the position that we here have to do with a comment of some third person, not a continuation of Adam's exclamation.[91] Furthermore, as second objection, Jesus clearly understands this sentence as explanatory remark from God himself (Matt 19:5). This leads to an interesting understanding: just as man rejoices about God's creation (v. 23), so God is joining this happy proclamation by declaring this final step to the perfectness of creation as being part of the divine pattern for humanity (v. 24). Hence, probably the best alternative is to understand v. 24 as comment of "the Creator, who is regarded as speaking through Moses."[92] If we take this understanding to be true and take into account v. 25 as the narrator's final comment about the innocent state and the beauty of this perfect creation, there are three "witnesses" declaring the creation of humankind and the institution of an even sexual partnership between man and woman to be praiseworthy and completely without any defilement or blemish:[93]

---

88. Tosato, "On Genesis 2:24," 405–6. He refers to the following examples of עַל־כֵּן as introducing a new norm: "Genesis 17 (circumcision). Gen 47:26 (tax on the harvest), Exod 18:13–27 (judicial order), Num 27:1–11; 36:1–12 (inheritance of daughters), 1 Sam 30:25 (division of booty)." Ibid., 406/fn.45.

89. As, for instance, preferred by Ortlund, *Whoredom*, 20: "... with the particle 'Therefore,' intruding the narrator's own parenthetical comment."

90. Against the argumentation in favor of a matriarchal social structure see Jewett, *Man as Male and Female*, 127; Pedersen and Møller, *Israel I-II*, 75–76, 94.

91. Cf. Gen 10:9; 11:9; 16:14; 19:22; 21:31; 25:30; 26:33; 29:34–35; 30:6; 31:48; 32:32; 33:17; 50:11; cf. also Josh 7:26; Judg 18:12; 1 Sam 23:28; 1 Chr 11:7; Esth 9:26.

92. Hagner, *Matthew 14–28*, 548. Similarly Nolland, *Matthew*, 771: "So presumably it is '[God] who said' [ref. to Matt 19:5] because what Scripture says, God says." Cf. also Piper, *Momentary Marriage*, 22 ("He [i.e., Jesus] also believed that Moses was inspired by God, so that what Moses was saying, God was saying."); France, *Matthew*, 717. Roig, "Exegetische Studie," 184, is too superficial in his conclusion ("Jesus [möchte] ihnen [den Pharisäern] zeigen, dass Gott selbst derjenige ist, der hier spricht."), not even considering the above mentioned possibility. Alter, *Biblical Narrative*, 157, introduces the "omniscient narrator" to literary analysis as the source of biblical remarks and thus offers another, slightly differing understanding (attributing v. 25 to God instead of Moses); either way the text supplies enough evidential value concerning the truth it contains, as Deut 17:6 ("on the evidence of two witnesses or three witnesses") makes clear.

93. About the anthropological aspect of sexuality in this context see Domanyi, "Anthropologie und Ethik," 230–31.

v. 23: *Man*	rejoiced	about his woman
v. 24: *God*	declared	"marriage" to be a divinely founded institution/covenant pattern
v. 25: *Narrator*	confirmed	the innocence of their nakedness

It is further noteworthy that there is another connection between vv. 23 and 25 in terms of the protagonists appearance and verbal forms, again emphasizing v. 24 with its particular form, style, and its auctorial (etiological and normative)[94] point of view as its centre and essential expression.[95]

The two significant keywords עָזַב ("leave/forsake") and דָּבַק ("stick/cling/cleave/join/follow"), as well as the phrase וְהָיוּ לְבָשָׂר אֶחָד ("become one flesh") require further investigation. It should be noted first, however, that the vav-consecutive in connection with the perfect verb forms (וְדָבַק/וְהָיוּ) certainly connote the same repeated, habitual or characteristic nuance as the preceding imperfect[96]—or, as Lawton has suggested,[97] the same "divine intention" expressed by the more forceful "shall/should (leave/cleave/become)." The grammar of v. 24, thus, carries the meaning of a common, usual practice not restricted to some ancient (possibly only Edenic) time; it rather is a custom maintained since paradise until at least Moses' time. As Jesus later confirms, it is valid even until his time, again hundreds of years later (cf. Matt 19:5–6). Thus even the grammatical features point to an enduring, normative ideal.

Since it was usual in ancient times for the wo/man to leave her home in order to live with her husband, עָזַב is better translated as "forsake" instead of "leave," for the man usually did not leave his parents regarding the locality;[98] although the dif-

---

94. Cf. e.g., Tosato, "On Genesis 2:24," 390–92, 404–9; he even calls Gen 2:24 a "command." Ibid., 408/fn.56–57. This is further supported by apocryphal and pseudepigraphic usage of this text as well as by the Jewish philosopher Philo in *QG* 1:29 where he speaks about a divine "order/command" concerning Gen 2:24, followed by rabbinic evidence e.g., in *y. Qidd.* 1:1; *b. Sanh.* 57b–58b; *Gen. Rab.* 18:5. (See on these Jewish interpretations the corresponding sections below within the NT chapter: "The Edenic Ideal in Prominent Ancient Jewish Literature").

95. Thus Tosato, "On Genesis 2:24," 395: "In fact, the characters of v. 25 are Adam and his wife, the same as those of v. 23. The initial verbal form of v. 25 (*wayyihyû*) is a *wayyiqtol*, the same as that at the beginning of v. 23 (*wayyōʾmer*)." His conclusion that, due to these and some other observations, v. 24 must be regarded as a (much) later addition (of the post exilic period: ibid., 406), are not convincing. He blends out the possibility of a simply stressed, special remark of another speaker/protagonist in v. 24 (as assumed in the text above), which—in my opinion—is much more likely.

96. On this grammatical possibility with Hebrew qatal forms see Joüon and Muraoka, *Biblical Hebrew*, 333–35: "Sometimes the action, put in the past, is assumed to continue in some way up to the present moment . . . ." Ibid., 333. An interpretation as the rhetorical device called "prophetic perfect" (ibid., 335) could also be possible.

97. See above: Lawton, "Gen. 2:24," 98.

98. In those times it usually was the woman who left her parents to join her husband. Cf. Wenham, *Genesis 1–15*, 70–71; Hugenberger, *Covenant*, 158; Loader, *LXX, Sexuality, and NT*, 39–40; Beeston, "One Flesh," 116–17; Mathews, *Genesis 1–11:26*, 223; Lawton, "Gen. 2:24," 97; Hasel, "Eheverständnis," 22. However, there are examples of both directions of leaving, both of them representing full marriages: (1) Isaac remains at home while Rebekah had to move (Gen 24); (2) Jacob leaves his family, travelling to Laban, and taking his daughters as wives (Gen 29). Meier, "Linguistic Clues," 20–21

ferent Targumim seem to interpret the Hebrew text by their Aramaic translation in just that way: the man leaves (locally) the bed in his father's house.[99] However, of course he did not "forsake" them regarding his filial duties, but what he left or forsook was his primary loyalty; his priorities changed and his wife now became the main person to whom his first obligations were.[100] The narrator is using the stylistic device of hyperbole to emphasize the change of man's priorities for the sake of his wife and a "commonality of concern, loyalty, and responsibility."[101]

---

further suggests that the wordplay between אִישׁ ("man") and אִשָּׁה ("woman") might be the (stylistic) reason for this reversion of directions in Gen 2:24: "But whence this tradition that the direction of departure for forming a new family unit was the converse of contemporary fashion? It is likely that the germ for this conception was the phonetic congruence of the *he locale* with the affix which identified feminine singular nouns: *'iššâ* was the one to whom *'iš* approached.... No other language outside Canaan preserves the grammatical possibility for generating such a word-play in this context." Ibid.

99. Cf. the Onkelos text on Gen 2:24: יִשְׁבּוֹק גְּבַר בֵּית־מִשְׁכְּבֵי אֲבוּהִי ("the man leaves the *bedroom* of his father"); Neofiti: יפרש גבר מדמכיה מן דאבוי ומן דאימיה ("the man separates from the *bed* of his father and of his mother"); Cairo-Geniza: וַיַפְרֵשׁ גְּבַר יַת מִדְמְכֵיהּ מִן אַבוּי ("the man leaves the *bed* of his father"); Pseudo-Jonathan: ישבוק גבר ומתפרש מן בי(ה)(ת)־מדמכיה דאבוהי ("the man leaves separating himself from the *bed* of his father"). It should be noted that מדמוך ("bed") literally means "place for lying down" (CAL s.v. מדמוך; cf. Grossfeld, trans., *Targum Onqelos*, 45: "sleeping abode;" Maher, trans., *Targum Pseudo-Jonathan: Genesis*, 24: "bedroom;" McNamara, trans., *Targum Neofiti 1: Genesis*, 59: "his couch/his sleeping [place];" similarly Beale and Carson, *NT Use*, 60). Although the Hebrew MT is, of course, the more authoritative reading, we may keep in mind the stressing of the bedroom, further confirming a sexual connotation of the one flesh union that encloses the verse (v. 23: "flesh of my flesh"—v. 24: "one flesh"). Beale and Carson, *NT Use*, 60 further suggests that this Aramaic version is influenced by the later culture no more demanding a separation from the man's parents in regard to locality, but of course concerning the sleeping place, which is now to be shared with the newlywed wife. Grossfeld, trans., *Targum Onqelos*, 45/fn.11 adds that "this addition in the Targum is based on the understanding of the Hebrew statement as an injunction against incest with one's parents and sisters. In Rabbinic tradition this interpretation extended to include homosexuality and adultery as well, for which cf. *b. Sanh.* 58a."

100. Cf. Davidson, *Flame*, 44/Davidson, "Beginning," 21: "... for the husband to 'leave' was revolutionary. In effect, the force of this statement is that both are to leave—to cut loose from the ties that would encroach upon the independence and freedom of the relationship." Yet, that does not mean "that a man who abandons his parental clan thereby becomes 'one flesh' with his wife [, which] implies entry into membership of the wife's clan, with all its attendant rights and obligations...." Beeston, "One Flesh," 117. To limit the becoming of "one flesh" strictly to this sole aspect, which is not even clearly implied in vv. 23–24, must be regarded as a very uncertain statement. The text does not require a man to literally leave/forsake his parents or even his whole family clan. Besides, in a more sad sense, the literal meaning of forsaking man's parents likewise came true in man's Eden story. He left his father (God) in order to be loyal to his (fallen) wife. But that, of course, is not the ideal and certainly not what Moses intended in inserting this editorial note. The usage of עָזַב in the other Mosaic and OT instances rather indicates loyalty to God in the first place, loyalty to man or woman in the second.

101. Brueggemann, "Flesh and Bone," 540 (he is referring to Gen 2:23). Cf. Sarna, *Genesis*, 23; Scotchmer, "Lessons," 82–83 explains: "The point is simply this: parents, and all they represent in a patriarchal society, are to be valued less than one's bride or groom. Such is the strength of the tribute that Genesis pays to the marital bond in the Garden of Eden." Similarly Hasel, "Eheverständnis," 22: "Dass erwähnt wird, dass der Mann seine Eltern verlässt, deutet das Gewicht der neuen Orientierung und Verpflichtung an, die ihren Ort nun in der Ehe hat."

The Biblical "One Flesh" Theology of Marriage as Constituted in Genesis 2:24

Since honoring parents is next to honoring God, for a man to forsake them and cling (which is covenantal language [Deut 4:4; 10:20; 30:20], as is also 'flesh of my flesh']) to his wife stresses the supreme sanctity of marriage. In other words, this is not merely descriptive, but rather, in the context of Torah, *constitutes a divine decree.*[102]

While עָזַב indeed can indicate the "leaving" of someone in a literal sense, numerous instances confirm the understanding of v. 24 as referring to (primary) loyalty and the term mostly appears as covenantal language in context of God's working for the sake of his people.[103] It might be meaningful that this verb is used for the first time in Gen 2:24 and then disappears until Gen 24:27 and 28:15, where it reappears in context of the important תּוֹלְדוֹת-train of thought and the loyalty towards God, which commences even in Gen 2:4.[104] Hence, the numerous usages of עָזַב in a covenantal context not only allude to a perception of marriage as a covenant, but also, and most strikingly, as a question of loyalty to the divine creator and his purposes.

It must also be recognized that the text in Gen 2:24 speaks of a "man," not a "boy" or just a "male" who marries: "Adam war ein erwachsener Mann, kein unreifes Kind. Die Aussage, dass ein Mann seine Eltern verlässt, scheint anzudeuten, dass die Ehepartner eine ausreichende Reife und Unabhängigkeit von ihren Eltern besitzen, die bislang für sie gesorgt haben."[105] The physical, mental, and emotional preconditions of an adult are required in order to guarantee a blessed marriage.

Closely connected with this covenantal term is its antonym,[106] the Hebrew word דָּבַק meaning "cling/stick/cleave/join/follow."[107] While it does not by itself convey any

---

102. Beale and Carson, *NT Use*, 197 (italics supplied); cf. Wenham, *Genesis 1–15*, 71; Nolland, *Matthew*, 772. Furthermore, one has to emphasize that "es in unserer Erzählung nicht um eine Rechtssitte, sondern um eine Naturgewalt geht;" it deals with the "urgewaltige Drang der Geschlechter zueinander," Von Rad, *Erstes Buch Mose*, 59–60; cf. Lawton, "Gen. 2:24," 97.

103. Please consider the following examples: Gen 24:27; 28:15; 39:6; Exod 23:5; Lev 19:10; 23:22; 26:43; Num 10:31; Deut 12:19; 14:27; 28:20; 29:24; 31:6, 8, 16–17; 32:36; Josh 1:5; 22:3; 24:16, 20; Ruth 1:16; 2:11, 20; Ps 27:10; 94:14; Isa 1:4, 28; 6:12; 41:17; 49:14; Jer 2:19; 9:12; 16:11; 17:13; 22:9; Hos 4:10; and many more. See also Davidson, "Beginning," 20; Beale and Carson, *NT Use*, 197; Hasel, "Eheverständnis," 22–23; Brueggemann, "Flesh and Bone," 540 adds, "The first part of v. 24 has the language of covenant relations, to abandon (*'azav*) and to cleave (*davaq*). The latter term, when used of interpersonal relations, as in any context, is clearly a covenant term. It is especially used in Deuteronomic contexts in clusters of covenant words to speak about loyalty to covenant partners . . . ."

104. On the significance and importance of the תּוֹלְדוֹת emerging in the Genesis creation account and its relevance for the following Genesis story and the "holy seed" see e.g., Woudstra, "Toledot," 184–89; Habel, *Literary Criticism*, 66–68; Westermann, *Creation*, 24; Westermann, *Genesis 1–11 (Ger.)*, 18–24.

105. Hasel, "Eheverständnis," 22.

106. For עָזַב as antonym of דָּבַק see Clines, *Classical Hebrew*, 2:386.

107. Cf. HALOT/TWOT s.v. דָּבַק; Clines, *Classical Hebrew*, 2:385–86. The TWOT s.v. דָּבַק further elucidates: "dābaq is used quite often in the OT of physical things sticking to each other, especially parts of the body . . . dābaq also carries the sense of clinging to someone in affection and loyalty. Man is to cleave to his wife (Gen 2:24). Ruth clave to Naomi (Ruth 1:14). The men of Judah clave to David their king during Sheba's rebellion (2Sam 20:2). Shechem loved Dinah and clave to her (Gen 34:3) and Solomon clave in love to his wives (1 Kings 11:2). Most importantly, the Israelites are to cleave to the Lord in affection

sexual meaning,[108] even in its figurative usage (as is the case in Gen 2:24) it "retains the idea of physical proximity."[109] Generally, this lemma mostly describes people in their attitude towards someone else (joining or following someone) and is frequently used in context of (covenantal) loyalty, or curse on disloyalty.[110] It signifies a strong personal attachment and,[111]

> applied to the relationship between the sexes in Gen 2:24, it seems clearly to indicate a covenant context, i.e., a marriage covenant . . . . The word *dābaq* especially emphasizes the inward attitudinal dimensions of the covenant bond. It 'implies a devotion and an unshakable faith between humans; it connotes a permanent attraction which transcends genital union to which, nonetheless, it gives meaning.'[112]

---

and loyalty (Deut 10:20; Deut 11:22; Deut 13:4; Deut 30:20; Josh 22:5; Josh 23:8) if his blessing is to be theirs. In Jer 13:11 it is said that the Lord caused the Israelites to cleave to him, and Hezekiah is approved because he clave to the Lord. In these verses parallel words and phrases that describe this proper attitude to the Lord are fear, serve, love, obey, swear by his name, walk in his ways, and keep his commandments. dābaq also means to keep close to someone, and doubtless this sense is included in references admonishing God's people to cleave to him. But God is never the subject of the verb."

108. Cf. e.g., Ruth 1:14; 2:8, 21, 23 and the examples on covenant loyalty in the footnote below. See also Clines, *Classical Hebrew*, 2:385–86; cf. Isaksson, *Marriage and Ministry*, 19–20: "It is clear that it [דָּבַק] had no specific sexual significance. This is probably also the case in Gen 2.24. The verb is used generally to indicate that, by leaving his father and mother and cleaving to his wife, a man forms a new social unit." The Greek LXX translation using προσκολλάω, however, conveys even a sexual notion, as is demonstrated by the use of κολλάω in Sir. 19:2 ("he that cleaveth [κολλώμενος] to harlots [. . .]") or the interpretation of proskolla,w in Philo, *Leg.* 2:49. Similarly Berger, *Gesetzesauslegung*, 529, 532. Greenberg, "Jewish Tradition," 4 anticipates even in "cleaving" what actually is only denoted by the phrase "becoming one flesh," namely: "sensuality, intimacy, interdependency, and a long-term relationship . . . ." Similarly Ortlund, *Whoredom*, 22: "And what does this cleaving look like in life? The language suggests that, physically, the man takes his wife in his arms, so that in the course of normal life their marriage is frequently symbolized, celebrated and refreshed through sexual union. Emotionally, the man fixes upon her alone his deepest affections, under God, with a profound sense of attachment, contentment and fulfillment. And formally or socially, the man lives with his wife in a covenant of strictly inviolable exclusivity, separating him from all others on the earth."

109. BDB s.v. דָּבַק.

110. See on covenantal loyalty e.g., Gen 19:19; Num 36:7, 9; Deut 4:4; 10:20; 11:22; 13:5; 28:21, 60; 30:20; Josh 22:5; 23:8; 2 Sam 23:10; 1 Kgs 11:2; 2 Kgs 18:6; Ps 119:31; Jer 13:11. Cf. G. Wallis, in: Botterweck et al., *TWAT*, 2:84–89; Mathews, *Genesis 1–11:26*, 222; Wolff, *Anthropology*, 181; Hasel, "Eheverständnis," 24–25; Greenberg, "Jewish Tradition," 4/fn.7; Wenham, *Genesis 1–15*, 71: "The use of the terms 'forsake' and 'stick' in the context of Israel's covenant with the Lord suggests that the OT viewed marriage as a kind of covenant." Davidson consents: ". . . applied to the relationship between the sexes in 2:24, it seems to clearly indicate a covenant context, that is, a marriage covenant" Davidson, *Flame*, 45. However, I have to admit that important lexicons (like TDOT and TWOT) do not mention the term "covenant" in their elucidation of דָּבַק. Yet the description of its characteristics and the context of the occurrences of this verb particularly within Deuteronomy hint that it is apparently to be understood just in this way. While Gen 2:24 certainly does not depict a "formal contract," it evidently expresses a most personal inner attitude including a "strong personal attachment" and the necessity of loyalty and faithfulness, thus affirming my perception as argued above (and further throughout this work).

111. Cf. BDB/TWOT/TDOT s.v. דָּבַק.

112. Davidson, "Beginning," 21; referring (by the given quotation) to Collins, *Secrets*, 153, and

Thus, it is closely connected with the foregoing "forsaking" of one's parents, again connoting the significance of changing priorities and one's prime loyalty:

> The language of 'leave' and cleave' appears intended to stress the necessity of a radical change, not of domicile, but of one's preeminent loyalty—a husband is to transfer to his wife the primary familial loyalty which he once owed to his parents.[113]

Finally, the phrase וְהָיוּ לְבָשָׂר אֶחָד ("and they become one flesh") is most important and actually the centre of this study. It occurs only once in the entire Hebrew Bible, so it is impossible to derive some deeper meaning by a study of the wider biblical context. The term בָּשָׂר ("flesh") refers primarily to the flesh of one's body and his whole being; and secondly as synecdoche, it points further to blood relations as given by being of one "flesh and bone."[114]

> The term *bāśār*, 'flesh,' in the OT refers not only to one's physical body but to a person's whole existence in the world. By 'one flesh' is thus connoted 'mutual dependence and reciprocity in all areas of life,' a 'unity that embraces the natural lives of two persons in their entirety.' It indicates a oneness and intimacy in the total relationship of the whole person of the husband to the whole person of the wife.[115]

Brueggemann, "Flesh and Bone," 532–42. Brueggemann notes that "the first part of v. 24 has the language of covenant relations, to abandon (*'azav*) and to cleave (*davaq*). The latter term, when used of interpersonal relations, as in any context, is clearly a covenant term. It is especially used in Deuteronomic contexts in clusters of covenant words to speak about loyalty to covenant partners (Dt 11,22; 10,20; 13,5; Josh 23,8; 1 Kgs 11,2). In the speech of Josh 23 for example, the term suggests an exclusive relationship which asserts the jealousy of the covenant partner and excludes all other relationships. Conversely the term (*'azav*) refers to abandoning one covenant commitment for the sake of another (cf. Jer 1,16; Hos 4,10). The two terms in Gn 2,24 also speak of terminating one loyalty and the embrace of a new one. Thus it substantiates the covenant formula of 2,23a." Ibid., 540; (further referring to Lohfink, *Hauptgebot*, 79 regarding "the cluster of words to which *davaq* is related;" ibid., 79/fn.18a.) Cf. the broader investigation of covenantal characteristics in Davidson, *Flame*, 44–46; Tarwater, *Marriage as Covenant*, 34–93 (on marriage as covenant in Gen 1–2 esp. pp. 53–75).

113. Hugenberger, *Covenant*, 159–60.

114. Meaning "body" cf. e.g., Gen 2:21, 23–24; 6:3, 12, 17, 19; 7:15–16, 21; 8:17; 9:4, 11, 15–17; 17:11, 13–14, 23–25; 40:19; 41:2–4, 18–19 (there are many more examples in the entire Hebrew text; the mentioned ones are just from Genesis). Instances referring to relatives are Gen 29:14; 37:27; Judg 9:2; 2 Sam 5:1; 19:13–14; 1 Chr 11:1. On further instances and their concrete translations as "flesh/body/creature/human being/relative/animal/meat/genitals" see Clines, *Classical Hebrew*, 2:277–80. Interestingly, the LXX translates בָּשָׂר as σάρξ, thereby conveying more sexual connotations since it is (in contrast to the Hebrew בָּשָׂר) not used metaphorically for kinship/family (cf. Loader, *LXX, Sexuality, and NT*, 42). The understanding in NT times (and of NT writers) might thereby have been marked by an even more sexual interpretation. See further HALOT/BDB/TWOT/TDOT s.v. בָּשָׂר; Stuhlmiller, "One Flesh," 4/fn.3; about the peculiar vocabulary regarding expressions with sexual connotations see Davidson, *Flame*, 7–12; Haag and Elliger, *Zur Liebe befreit*, 42–45.

115. Davidson, "Beginning," 22; referring to TWOT/TDOT s.v. בָּשָׂר; Piper, *Biblical View*, 25, 28; Miles and Miles, *Husband-Wife Equality*, 164.

Thus, v. 24 is most closely linked with v. 23, which contains the poetic formulation of the kinship formula, and, of course, with vv. 21–22 which are speaking about the reason why both are so closely tied together. However, besides the close relation in terms of a general similarity being of one genus, namely humankind/human, v. 24 now for the first time mentions further family relations and clearly explains that marriage supersedes any other relationship.[116] Hence, the "flesh" here is also used to describe a new family established by the marital union;[117] but it particularly denotes the sexual union, by which the new blood relation is actually consummated.[118] Finally even the possible result of following the divine command to multiply (Gen 1:28) leads to the "creation" of a new "flesh" as a combination of both parts of the parental flesh.[119]

The Hebrew construction of היה with the ל preposition seems to enclose to a certain degree the content of v. 24 and its different "levels," denoting a sequence of events finally resulting in the climax of "becoming one flesh":

1. Forsake (עָזַב)   [→ father and mother (אֶת־אָבִיו וְאֶת־אִמּוֹ)]
2. Cleave (דָּבַק)   [→ to his woman (בְּאִשְׁתּוֹ)]
3. Become (הָיָה)   [→ one flesh (לְבָשָׂר אֶחָד)]

Just as the previous instances in Gen 1 pointed to a creative act using ל + היה (cf. Gen 1:14–15, 29) or to the enduring change of former conditions (cf. Gen 2:10), the usage

---

116. "These words [. . . of Gen 2:24] refer primarily to the fact that a man's wife is to be first in his affections and that his first duty is toward her. His love for her is to exceed, though certainly not to supersede, a very proper love for his parents." Nichol and Andreasen, *ABC*, Gen. 2:24, 1:227. In the same way Davidson emphasizes: ". . . the paradigm for marriage in Gen 2:24 highlights the element of *exclusivity*. The first of three actions described in this verse is that man *leaves* ('āzab). The verb āzab is a forceful term. It means, literally, 'to abandon, forsake,' and is employed frequently to describe Israel's forsaking of Yahweh for false gods. The leaving of 2:24 indicates the necessity of absolute freedom from outside interferences in the sexual relationship. . . . Just as this freedom was essential in the garden, so it is crucial in all succeeding sexual relationships." Davidson, *Flame*, 43; italics given.

117. Cf. Loader, *LXX, Sexuality, and NT*, 41–42; Hugenberger, *Covenant*, 163.

118. More about this on the next page. Similarly *Gen. Rab.* 18:4: "R. Tanhuma said: When a man takes one of his relations to wife, of him it is said, bone of my bones and flesh of my flesh." Freedman and Simon, trans., *Midrash Rabbah*, 1:143; capitals given.). However, the individuality of the spouses is not lost: "Continuity with the old personality is not broken, but the radical transformation resulting from the intimate personal encounter creates a new self: Individual identity is not absorbed into a mystical oneness but becomes conformed to a common personality of which both partake. Individual will is not lost but each wills what is best for the other . . . ." Batey, "The ΜΙΑ ΣΑΡΞ Union," 279.

119. Yet, seeing the "one flesh" union coming true only by fathering a child is too far from the text in Gen 2:24 (cf. e.g., Von Rad, *Erstes Buch Mose*, 68), where it speaks only about the relationship and loyalty between the spouses. But it may implicitly be included at least when considering the parallel of Gen 1:28. However, sexuality certainly is important even apart from procreation. It is not legitimate only to see it as "subordinated to the intent to propagate children," for "the complete absence of any reference to the propagation of children in Gen 2 highlights the significance of the unitive purpose of sexuality. . . . It does not need to be justified only as a means to a superior end, that is, procreation. The interpretation given by some that husband and wife become one flesh in the flesh of their children is not warranted by the text. Sexual love in the creation pattern is valued for its own sake." Davidson, *Flame*, 49–50; cf. Davidson, "Beginning," 10–11.

in Gen 2:24 may demonstrate that the emphasis of this verse is not merely on the final "one flesh" (בָּשָׂר אֶחָד) union (yet, of course it also is that), but even more on the "new creation," the changing of circumstances for man's life by "becoming" (הָיָה). This would point to the significance of the initial consummation through the sexual union, which is "the indispensable means for the consummation of marriage both in the Old Testament and elsewhere in the ancient Near East."[120]

> In reality the marriage was not consummated until the bride had been conducted to her husband's house and the first act of sexual intercourse had taken place.... The decisive importance attached to sexual intercourse is also clear from the fact that certain marriages, for example, those with women slaves and captives, were clearly arranged without any other real ceremonies than the husband's going in to them (Gen 30.4, Dt. 21.13).[121]

The usage of the "one flesh" terminology certainly does not mean "that following the consummation of the marriage in sexual union or following each successive act of intercourse, the couple reverts to their former state of being two separate fleshes!"[122] As the emphasis of "becoming" may indicate it is, rather, the initial act that leads to the consummation, the first "becoming" of that special union which, of course, comprises more than just sexuality.[123] It further "refers to the entire marital bond,"[124] the "unity

---

120. Hugenberger, *Covenant*, 279; cf. 1 Cor 6:16; Noort, "Interpretations," 12; Tarwater, *Marriage as Covenant*, 63–65; Loader, *LXX, Sexuality, and NT*, 41; Gunkel, *Genesis*, 13; Külling, *Ehe und Ehelosigkeit*, 26, 53; Luz, *Matthäus*, 3:94; Gnilka, *Markus*, 2:74; Crispin, *Divorce*, 12; Davidson, *Flame*, 46; cf. also Stuart, *Exodus*, 509; Zimmerli, *1 Mose 1–11. Die Urgeschichte*, 181; Trible, *Sexuality*, 104; Skinner, *A Critical and Exegetical Commentary on Genesis*, 70; similarly Domanyi, "Anthropologie und Ethik," 245. The "becoming" is, of course, not just the previous "leaving" and "cleaving" as Kaye, "One Flesh," 48 suggests. It is the third stage, assuming that the first two steps are already taken.

121. Isaksson, *Marriage and Ministry*, 25; cf. Neufeld, *Marriage Laws*, 88–90; Stuhlmiller, "One Flesh," 8; Tarwater, *Marriage as Covenant*, 64: "By having sexual intercourse . . . with the woman, the two become husband and wife." (See also references in the previous footnote.) The absence of a marriage vow or any other procedures in this "three steps program" outlined in Gen 2:24 should not pass unnoticed. It tells against those who overemphasizes such cultural, institutional frameworks (like, e.g., Dunstan, "The Marriage Covenant," 251). Westermann, *Genesis 1–11 (Ger.)*, 317–18, for instance, explains that "die beiden Verben ,er verläßt' und ,er hängt an' dürfen keinesfalls als Beschreibungen von Institutionen verstanden werden. . . . Dieser Vers hat seine Bedeutung gerade darin, daß er im Unterschied zu den bestehenden Institutionen und z.T. sogar im Gegensatz zu ihnen auf die elementare Kraft der Liebe von Mann und Frau weist." Similarly Von Rad, *Erstes Buch Mose*, 59–60; Gunkel, *Urgeschichte*, 57 ("an die bürgerliche Institution der Ehe . . . ist nicht zu denken"); Procksch, *Die Genesis*, 30, and Trible, *Sexuality*, 104. However, although there are no procedures given, by taking the steps described in Gen 2:24 she is called "*his* woman" speaking of a new unity of husband and wife, cf. Tosato, "On Genesis 2:24," 402. Thus Gen 2:24 results not just in a temporary sexual union, but strives for a permanent marital union—although independent of any changing, cultural customs.

122. Hugenberger, *Covenant*, 161; similarly Stuhlmiller, "One Flesh," 6; Sarna, *Genesis*, 23.

123. Cf. e.g., Westermann, *Genesis 1–11 (Ger.)*, 318; Wenham, *Genesis 1–15*, 71; Sarna, *Genesis*, 23; Lövestam, "Divorce and Remarriage," 51; Stuhlmiller, "One Flesh," 7; Gnilka, *Markus*, 2:74; Blomberg, "Exegesis," 167; Best, *One Body*, 74–75; Hasel, "Eheverständnis," 27; Domanyi, "Anthropologie und Ethik," 231–32; Crispin, *Divorce*, 12.

124. Scotchmer, "Lessons," 82.

of spiritual, moral, and intellectual facets of the husband and wife,"[125] and "all the rich intimacy of that relationship."[126] Besides, as has only rarely been noticed, the Hebrew אֶחָד ("one") could be understood as contributing to the exceptional quality of that unity, linking it with the *Shema* of Deut 6:4, where it is also used to depict the unity or "oneness" (rather than the numeric "amount" of persons) of the godhead.[127] Thus, the "oneness" of spouses inherently contains characteristics of the divine unity and contributes to the richness of the corresponding NT echoes.

The important aspect of a deeply spiritual, personal intimacy and oneness as well as its very close connection with the sexual union of the two partners is further supported by the Hebrew word used frequently to describe the physical as well as the mental closeness that results in procreation: יָדַע ("know/perceive/learn/realize/understand/experience/be familiar or acquainted with/take care of").[128]

125. Ryrie, "Biblical Teaching," 178.

126. Lawton, "Gen. 2:24," 98.

127. Gulley, "Trinity in the Old Testament," 83–84 explains: "What is this oneness that is attributed to God? Is it more than a *name, uniqueness,* and the *one and only*? There are two words for 'one' in Hebrew (1) *yāḥîd* means unique, such as an only son (Gen 22:2) and an only child (Prov 4:3; Zech 12:10), whereas (2) *'eḥād* means united, such as 'a man will leave his father and mother and be united to his wife, and they will become one flesh' (Gen 2:24). The word *'eḥād* (united) is used in the *Shema*. Millard Erickson observes that the unity of husband and wife is 'not uniqueness, but the unity of diversity. It speaks of union, rather than aloneness.' That's why Duane L. Christensen says, 'The word אחד in the text of the *Shema*' speaks not only of the *uniqueness*, but also of the *unity* of God. The doctrine of monotheism is implicit in this brief creedal statement.' The Hebrew word for 'one' (*yāḥîd*), meaning solitary, or without others, is not used in the *Shema*. So it seems that the *Shema* not only speaks of the uniqueness of God as the only God, but 'refers to the oneness that results from a unity of numerous persons.'" (Italics given; he quotes: Erickson, *Trinity,* 174; Christensen, *Deuteronomy 1:1—21:9,* 145; Whidden et al., *Trinity,* 33–34.)

128. Cf. HALOT/TWOT s.v. יָדַע; Clines, *Classical Hebrew,* 4:99–110, esp. p. 100; see Gen 4:1; 19:33, 35; Num 31:17, 35; Judg 11:39; Judg 21:11; 1 Kgs 1:4; 1 Sam 1:19. Reviewing the central Genesis verse from the New Testament perspective, Son, "Concept," 119 asserts: "It is quite obvious that the 'one body' union denotes something more than the temporary union of two physical bodies in sexual intercourse. It refers to a real and ontological corporate reality created by the sexual union of two unified persons." The Hebrew verb יָדַע usually means "to notice/observe/realize/experience/find out/recognize/know/become acquainted/understand/care about/have judgment" and thereby even refers to "sexual intercourse." Cf. HALOT/TWOT s.v. יָדַע. The Greek verb ἔγνω (ind. aor. act. 3rd p. sg., from the infinitive γινώσκω) in the LXX likewise means "to (come to) know/be quite sure/understand/comprehend/perceive/notice/realize/acknowledge/recognize/learn/discern/sexual intercourse" (cf. BDAG/LEH/FRI/LSJ s.v. γινώσκω) and thus is a perfect translation of the Hebrew verb, comprising the same meanings. Thus the first clearly mentioned sexual union reveals a deep devotion to another person, an unreserved dedication to the other one's personality. It means to become acquainted with his or hers cares and burdens, as well as with joys and happiness. Thus it points to a deep knowledge of one's partner as foundation of a happy marriage. Davidson further asserts that "the word *yādaʿ* in the OT is fundamentally a relational term and often refers not just to objective knowledge but also (and particularly) to existential experience. It implies a deep personal relationship with the one known. The choice of *yādaʿ* here to indicate sexual intercourse emphasizes, as often elsewhere in the OT that in sexual union the man comes to know his wife in the deep intimacy of her being. And the wife shares equally in this sexually intimate knowledge." Davidson, *Flame,* 425. In the same way Sapp concludes that the sexual encounter "provides the most complete, most accurate, and most fulfilling knowledge of one another available to humans." Sapp, *Sexuality,* 21. Thus "marriage is a commitment by a male and a female unity, based on and for the purpose of love that is unique, exclusive, total, and

> 'Becoming one flesh' then focuses on the sexual union of marriage but is by no means limited to it. It incorporates every aspect of intimacy and interdependence which should ideally render the married couple a unified entity at the deepest levels of interpersonal communion.... Marriage is thus seen as two-fold: a commitment of one's fundamental allegiance and an interpersonal relationship culminating in sexual intimacy. The best term to describe this two-fold enterprise is that of a covenant. Divorce then becomes breaking a covenant (Prov 2:17).[129]

There are three steps (or perhaps better: two steps and a resulting consequence) to be taken by the man after God has done his part in bringing the appropriate woman before him. While the first two steps pertain to important attitudes and priorities, the third finally connotes the practical step as the logical consequence in consummating the marriage by becoming "one flesh." These might be considered as the three "pillars" of the Edenic marriage institution, while the previous conditions and circumstances merely contribute to the atmosphere and proper interpretation of God's perfect dealing with man and his purposes in creating a complementary "helper."

> Here are the three strands from which a human marriage covenant is made: 'leaving,' 'cleaving,' 'one flesh.' In this rich simplicity, the narrator is giving us hints towards his understanding of several facts of life, including human sexuality, the foundational importance for the family, the central concept of covenant fidelity, and the fact that covenant relationships belong within an institutional framework.[130]

At the end of the passage in Gen 2:25 there is some kind of a final remark, again enclosing the foregoing depiction, but now rather comprising the whole passage of Gen 2:18–25. It is a note concerning the very atmosphere that surrounded the entire event of creating the woman. Obviously there was nothing "shameful" in the creation of the genders male and female. By concretely referring to the nakedness of man and woman, the erotic "atmosphere" of the preceding verse concerning the "one flesh" union is emphasized and virtually becomes the centre of interest.

The hithpolel form of being "ashamed" (יִתְבֹּשָׁשׁוּ) conveys the reciprocal meaning best to be rendered as "be ashamed in front of each other"[131] or "be ashamed of one another,"[132] while the imperfect may again function as an indicator of a customary state, pointing to a continuing condition.[133] In other words, in spite of their nakedness,

---

permanent. As such, it is endorsed and strengthened by God. In short, and standing for the above, marriage is a 'unity' ('one flesh')." Nies, "Divorce and Remarriage," 1:1.

129. Blomberg, "Exegesis," 167.

130. Atkinson, *To Have and to Hold*, 76–77. These three pillars of God's ideal marriage institution will be developed further in the subsequent chapters on the OT material.

131. Thus HALOT s.v. בּוֹשׁ.

132. Clines, *Classical Hebrew*, 2:132.

133. See Joüon and Muraoka, *Biblical Hebrew*, 338–40. Cf. also Westermann, *Genesis 1–11 (Ger.)*,

man and woman were permanently unashamed, at least before the Fall (cf. Gen 3:7). Most interesting, the Hebrew עָרוֹם used in this verse for "nakedness" is not the same as employed to describe the genital area (עֶרְוָה) elsewhere in the Hebrew OT.[134] עֶרְוָה denotes not just mere nakedness, but also a strong negative moral connotation pointing to some shameful state of conditions,[135] thereby contrasting the innocent עָרוֹם which rather alludes to the (not blameworthy) absence of possessions; "it also indicates exposure, that is, lack of concealment and disguise (Job 26:6) and lack of resources (Amos 2:16)" or bodies only "lightly dressed."[136] In fact, it is this immoral quality which distinguishes the two Hebrew words, as illuminated in the parallelism of Isa 20:4: ". . . young and old, naked [עָרוֹם] and barefoot with buttocks uncovered, to the shame [עֶרְוַת] of Egypt." The use of עָרוֹם instead of עֶרְוַת stresses the same fact as the imperfect verb form of בּוֹשׁ ("ashamed"), thus even constructing a parallelism:[137]

(A) and the two of them were (וַיִּהְיוּ שְׁנֵיהֶם)

(B) naked (עֲרוּמִּים)

(A') the man and his woman (הָאָדָם וְאִשְׁתּוֹ)

(B') and [were] not ashamed [before one another] (וְלֹא יִתְבֹּשָׁשׁוּ)

The Hebrew עֲרוּמִּים ("naked/undressed") and וְלֹא יִתְבֹּשָׁשׁוּ ("not ashamed") are in this verse describing the same condition of moral innocence and perfect sinlessness in contrast to the shameful nakedness of moral failures: "Frequently the nudity indicated by this term [i.e., עָרוֹם] has a symbolic meaning. Adam and Eve's lack of embarrassment at their nakedness suggests innocence (Gen 2:25)."[138] It has been suggested that עָרוֹם further denotes "vulnerability/helplessness."[139] That would also properly introduce the report of the Fall in 3:1–7 where the vulnerable condition of the first human pair is clearly exposed.

253; Wenham, *Genesis 1–15*, 47, 71; NET on Gen 2:25; Davidson, "Beginning," 23.

134. See for the instances and their meaning e.g., Clines, *Classical Hebrew*, 6:555–56.

135. Mostly the shameful nakedness of undressed or not properly/sufficiently dressed persons (Gen 9:22–23; Exod 20:26; 28:42; Lev 18:6–19; 20:11, 17–21; Isa 20:4; 47:3; Lam 1:8; Ezek 16:8, 36–37; 22:10; 23:10, 18, 29; Hos 2:11), but also e.g., a whole country that is not sufficiently "covered," i.e., fortified/protected cf. Gen 42:9, 12. It also appears with a stark immoral aspect devoid of any (obvious) further allusion to any sexual failure (so in Deut 23:15; 24:1; 1 Sam 20:30). Especially Deut 24:1 will be investigated more thoroughly in the subsequent chapters of this study.

136. Cf. BDB/HALOT s.v. עָרוֹם; TWOT s.v. עוּר/עָרוֹם; Clines, *Classical Hebrew*, 6:382. As the parallel usages in the other biblical texts strongly suggest, we may have to assume some kind of a "light dress" even with Adam and Eve already in sinless Eden before the Fall, rather than complete nakedness. Consider especially the texts mentioned in TWOT s.v. עוּר who leave no doubt that the people in these instances were at least lightly clothed with underwear or the like: 1 Sam 19:24; Isa 20:2–4; Mic 1:8; Job 24:7; 26:6; Isa 58:7; Amos 2:16.

137. The other literary, stylistic feature given by the wordplay of עָרוֹם in Gen 2:25 and עָרוּם in the immediately following verse of Gen 3:1 will be dealt with in the next chapter about the literary context.

138. TWOT s.v. עוּר/עָרוֹם.

139. Thus, for instance, Hauser, "Genesis 2–3," 25.

Similarly, the Hebrew בּוֹשׁ ("be ashamed") is stronger than just being embarrassed and refers, rather, to being "unabashed/not disconcerted;" free from guilt and the fear of exploitation, innocent as children.[140]

> The primary meaning of this root [בּוֹשׁ] is "to fall into disgrace, normally through failure, either of self or of an object of trust." . . . the force of bôsh is somewhat in contrast to the primary meaning of the English "to be ashamed," in that the English stresses the inner attitude, the state of mind, while the Hebrew means 'to come to shame' and stresses the sense of public disgrace, a physical state. . . . Fourthly, shame results from imprudent or immoral action. . . . The final use of bôsh is the one which coincides most closely with the common English connotation: a feeling of guilt from having done what is wrong."[141]

The nakedness in Gen 2:25 obviously is without any blemish, no "disgrace," "failure," no wrong "physical state" or "imprudent or immoral action" that would result in "a feeling of guilt from having done what is wrong." Man and woman have not done anything wrong and their mere nakedness is no failure either—the scene is perfectly beautiful and innocent. They need not "be ashamed in front of each other."[142] Also, this innocence of עֲרוּמִּים and וְלֹא יִתְבֹּשָׁשׁוּ is certainly not only referring to sexuality as connoted in the "one flesh" union of v. 24 and possibly the "nakedness" in v. 25, but rather to the entirety of their moral state and level as newly and perfectly created beings.[143]

I.1.1.4 Wider Biblical Context

By closely investigating the literary context and certain connections within the first chapters of Genesis or even the whole Pentateuch and the entire Hebrew Bible, we find as early as from Gen 2:5 onwards already a different perspective, alluding to some historically later point of time. Although man is still sinless in Gen 2:4—2:25, the way it is narrated changes compared to Gen 1:1—2:4 and there are certain hints pointing to the world after leaving paradise. It is a review to the happy conditions initially given in God's perfect creative working, nonetheless already implicitly "predicting" the way and some of the negative consequences of humankind's betrayal.[144]

---

140. Thus Davidson, "Beginning," 23.
141. TWOT s.v. בּוֹשׁ; cf. also TDOT s.v. בּוֹשׁ.
142. HALOT s.v. בּוֹשׁ; similarly Clines, *Classical Hebrew*, 2:132.
143. One has to be careful not to over-emphasize the sexual connotations, for "just as the 'one-flesh' experience applied to more than the physical union, so the concept of nakedness probably connotes more than physical nudity. As Walter Trobisch states it, there is implied the ability 'to stand in front of each other, stripped and undisguised, without pretensions, without hiding, seeing the partner as he or she really is, and showing myself to him or her as I really am—and still not be ashamed.'" Davidson, "Beginning," 23; cf. Trobisch, *I Married You*, 82; Kidner, *Genesis*, 66.
144. A detailed elucidation on this point will follow.

I.1.1.4.1 Gen 2:4–25 Foreshadowing the Fall

There are several interesting observations to be noticed in the narrator's focus on the personal creation story of man and woman in Gen 2:4—2:25 as preparation to the changing conditions after transgression,[145] particularly the central passage of vv. 18–25 as introduction to the Fall.[146]

Post-Fall Elements. In Gen 2:5 the narrator refers to (A) the "shrubs/plants of the field" (שִׂיחַ/עֵשֶׂב הַשָּׂדֶה), he mentions (B) divinely caused "raining" (הִמְטִיר יְהוָה אֱלֹהִים), and knows the man in future (C) "cultivating the ground" (לַעֲבֹד אֶת־הָאֲדָמָה). Younker rightly points out that "the first point this new section [Gen 2:4–6] makes is that there were four things that did *not yet* exist after God had completed the earth and the heavens [cf. Gen 2:1–3]—the shrub of the field, the plant of the field, the man to till the soil, and rain."[147] A word and phrase study reveals that the peculiar terminology employed in this introductory verse to man's and woman's creation already points to (1) the curse of man's working field and God's working for his slavish people (cf. Gen 3:17–18; Exod 9:22, 25);[148] (2) the human's unholy descendants and God's divine working in judgment and deliverance (Gen 6:1–7; 7:4; 19:24;[149] Exod 9:18, 23, 33–34; 16:4), and (3) the expulsion of man from paradise (Gen 3:23).[150]

---

145. Similarly Garrett, *Primeval History*, 189–90; Lawton, "Gen. 2:24," 98.

146. Lawton even recognizes the centre of reversal in Gen 2:24 casting "its shadow over the following narrative, helping to underline the tragedy of the Fall." Lawton, "Gen. 2:24," 98. However, this is not, of course, to be understood in a sense of God creating the woman as Satan's instrument. This section only intends to direct attention and awareness to most interesting literary features which are linking Gen 2:18–25 with several aspects of the seduction story (Gen 3:1–7) and the ongoing narration. As is to be witnessed, there are not just negative implications, but positive ones, too.

147. Younker, *God's Creation*, 52; italics given.

148. More on the peculiar terminology pointing to post-Fall conditions see the footnote after next; cf. Younker, *God's Creation*, 52–58.

149. It is remarkable that the exact verb form of "raining" (הִמְטִיר—hiphil perfect 3rd person masculine singular) in connection with יְהוָה ("YHWH let rain") only occurs in Gen 2:5 and Gen 19:24 (Yahweh rains fire upon Sodom and Gomorrah) thus strikingly pointing to the corruption of humankind as a result of sin (which, of course, is introduced in Gen 3). Furthermore, the first mentioning of rain (beside its "prediction" in Gen 2:5) occurs in context of the worldwide flood (Gen 7:4, 12) and, thus, "rain makes its entrance into the world not as a water source for agriculture but as an agent of God's judgment." Younker, *God's Creation*, 56.

150. I am aware of the divine instruction to "cultivate" (with the same Hebrew verb עָבַד as in Gen 2:5 and 3:23) even before the Fall (see Gen 2:15). But the interesting difference is the object to be cultivated: (a) In Gen 2:5 and 3:23 with exactly the same phrase (לַעֲבֹד אֶת־הָאֲדָמָה) and the same subject (the man) it is the "ground" (הָאֲדָמָה), while (b) in Gen 2:15 it is the "garden of Eden" (גַּן־עֵדֶן) as contrary to the soil of the non-Edenic earth (similarly Younker, *God's Creation*, 54–56). The difference may seem to be small, but it is as significant as the "plants of the field" (עֵשֶׂב הַשָּׂדֶה) pointing not to the "plants yielding seeds" (עֵשֶׂב מַזְרִיעַ זֶרַע) of Gen 1:11–12, 29–30, but expressly to Gen 3:18 (the only other instance in the Hebrew Bible where the expression עֵשֶׂב הַשָּׂדֶה occurs!) and, consequently, to the new conditions of cultivating a cursed nature (this point is also made by Younker, *God's Creation*, 53–54; Cassuto, *Exodus*, 102). Note also the hints given by the phrase עֵשֶׂב הַשָּׂדֶה ("shrub of the field"): ". . . a close reading of the text reveals that the botanical terms of

Genesis 2:5b, therefore, is not saying that no man yet existed after God had made the earth and the heavens. Rather it is saying that no *sinful* man (i.e., one who must work the ground for food) yet existed. Such a man would not exist until after the Fall.... Genesis 2, thus, is setting the stage for what comes later in Genesis 3.[151]

Thus even the "foreword" to the perfect creation of man in v. 7 and finally woman in vv. 18–25 bears the stamps of the worse conditions later to be experienced due to the Fall depicted in Gen 3.

"And YHWH God said." Omitting the obvious links to the Fall as given by the pericope about building Eden and the two important trees (vv. 8–17) standing in the middle of the garden (Gen 2:9; 3:3), we are now turning to the central passage of Gen 2:18–25. There is another hint specifically connecting the creation story of the woman with the curses of sin. In v. 18 it reads וַיֹּאמֶר יְהוָה אֱלֹהִים ("and YHWH God said"). This is worthy of notice, for there are no other occurrences of this seemingly common expression in the entire Hebrew Bible, except in the verses Gen 3:13–14 and 22. That unobtrusively alludes to the fact that, instead of linking Gen 2:18 (and thereby the whole passage (vv. 18–25) which is introduced here) with the "very good" working in Gen 1:26–27, 31, the author discreetly forges links to the final results of the woman's creation as to be seen more clearly by the following table:

יְהוָה אֱלֹהִים וַיֹּאמֶר	Referring to	Reason
Gen 2:18	God himself (cf. 1:26)	To make (עָשָׂה) the woman
Gen 3:13	Woman	The woman made (עָשָׂה)
Gen 3:14	Serpent	The serpent made (עָשָׂה)
Gen 3:22	Man	To prevent becoming immortal

Genesis 1:11, 12 and Genesis 2:5 do not have the identical meaning. The word *siah* ['shrub'] appears only three times in the Hebrew Bible—Genesis 2:5; 21:15; and Job 30:4, 7, while the full expression *siah ha-sadeh* ['shrub of the field'] is unique, appearing only in Genesis 2:5. The contexts of both Genesis 21:15 and Job 30:4, 7 make it clear that the siah is a plant adapted to dry or desert environments.... As such, it is most likely a spiny or thorny plant.... These plants, while essential to the fragile ecosystem of dry, desert regions, are generally classified as intrusive, obnoxious plants by farmers. They are not the type of plant that a farmer of the ancient Near East would deliberately cultivate in his garden, nor where these plants likely included among the species when God planted the garden east in Eden, filling it with 'every tree that is pleasing to the sight and good for food' (Gen 2:9). Thus, one of the plants that did *not yet* exist at the beginning of the narrative of Genesis 2:4b was the thorny xerophyte—the agriculturist's bane." Younker, *God's Creation*, 53 (italics given); cf. also Veith, *Genesis Conflict*, 32–33, adding the assumption that "since Genesis 3:19 states that these plants were used to make bread ... the plants of the second Genesis narrative thus refer to post fall food crops and weeds." Ibid., 33; cf. Younker, *God's Creation*, 54.

151. Younker, *God's Creation*, 55. Of course, Gen 2:5 also says that there was no man at all, but the emphasis is clearly on the *sinful state* which the man (who is not built before v. 7) will finally, unfortunately experience.

Each one of the few instances using the simple, very inconspicuous expression וַיֹּאמֶר יְהוָה אֱלֹהִים refers to another protagonist of the Eden story and finally comprises them all. While the first mentioning is still pertaining to God's perfect work of creation, the others describe the sinful counter-work initiated by the serpent, carried out by the woman, and almost immortalized by the man. While God is the one working to finalize and save his creation in the first and the last instances (Gen 2:18; 3:22), there is the woman along with the serpent tearing down God's perfect work in the middle part (Gen 3:13–14). Already the initial intention, even the first thought or word of God concerning the building of man's helper in Gen 2:18, is thus referring to the downward route to the Fall of Man and his expulsion.[152]

The Helper. Another contextual connection is illuminating here. Regarding the foregoing narration focusing on the tree of knowledge (cf. Gen 2:8–17), the last part of chap. 2, beginning with this crucial v. 18, seems to be God's special dealing for the sake of man. He creates the woman not only as a "helper" in the everyday "business" of Adam cultivating the garden (v. 15),[153] or for the purpose of procreation and ruling (Gen 1:28), but also as a helper in heeding the only prohibition God gave to man: keeping away from the tree of knowledge (vv. 16–17). The close connection between the "problem statement" in vv. 16–17 and the "solution" in v. 18 is sustained by the fact that the only time God is speaking about something not being good are exactly these verses 16–18. Additionally, it is noteworthy that Hebrew צִוָּה ("to command/order") occurs for the first time in Gen 2:16, and the other instances in Edenic context (Gen 3:11, 17) again refer to this single command.[154] In paradise, there apparently is

---

152. Of course, this observance is *not* to be understood as some chauvinistic, sexist attitude of the biblical writer or of me as the exegete. To the contrary, I will explain that it is just another implicit, indirect and seldom recognized feature that the origin of the Fall is not the creation of the woman (as possibly derived from exclusively considering Gen 3:2–6), but retracing the steps to the next instance, her origin is Adam. Also, as Gen 1:27 affirms, both are collectively representing humankind and as such both are created perfect (Gen 1:31) but seduced to become fallen sinners (Gen 3:6). Although the woman is the first one to stretch out her hand to grasp the forbidden fruit, it is also the man with her (Gen 3:6) who eats. It is "to the Hebrew credit that they did not, at least in the literature contained in the Jewish canon of the Bible, interpret the stories of Genesis 2 and 3 (Eve's creation and her part in the first sin in Eden) as a justification for negative attitudes to women. Eve, strangely enough, does not function as any kind of female symbol in the Old Testament. . . . Hebrew women might well have held a secondary place to men in their society, but at least they were not, in the biblical period, considered to be God's unfortunate afterthought. In fact, recent attempts have been made, with some success, to show that the myth of Eve in Genesis 2 and 3 is in no way insulting to woman, but rather depicts her as an equal to Adam, the completion of creation." Clark and Richardson, *Women and Religion*, 29–30.

153. Thus Brueggemann, "Flesh and Bone," 540.

154. Interestingly, the other appearances of Hebrew צִוָּה are concretely contrasting the failure of the first couple: while Eve and Adam were disobedient, Noah heeded what God "commanded" (Gen 6:22; 7:5, 9, 16). Also, both instances (Adam and Noah) instruct concerning food (and, regarding Noah, to bring animals into the ark), and disobedience in both instances would result in death! Thus, the intensity of this verb's meaning becomes even more evident, while the significance of food is also stressed. Please note further that God aggravates especially the procurement and quality of food as a result of disobedience in Gen 3:14, 17–19! Furthermore, in both instances God cares for the necessary

no other "command" of that urgency, no other order worthy to be referred to by this strong expression. This emphasizes the particularity of the following instruction, including the divine understanding of the conditions for man being "not good"—to be perceived most likely in the same respect, namely: "not [yet?] good" regarding man's obedience and faithfulness; he needs assistance—then everything will be "very good." It seems that God creates the "helper" especially in relationship to this command.

Furthermore, the וַיֹּאמֶר יְהוָה אֱלֹהִים is in every instance closely connected with the tree of knowledge. Hence, v. 18 seems to be an intersection between the divinely commanded tasks of man (procreate, rule, cultivate the garden, keep away from the tree; Gen 1:28 and 2:8–17) and the "helper" in these tasks created and introduced in vv. 18–25. Apparently this creational act in Gen 2:18–25, including "marriage" as established in Gen 2:24, should prevent man from losing his high standard of loyalty.[155] One might expect the author would have given literary connections rather pointing to the "very good" ideal of Gen 1:26–27 if God's purpose would have been successful. The fact that he connected it with Gen 3 and the worsening of life's conditions instead is meaningful and significantly tells about the sad failure of the "helper's" mission. This slight link is very discreet, without giving any hints of male-female differentiation or special accusations against womanhood; each one of the protagonists (serpent, woman, man) is to be blamed for his/her individual responsibility. However, the final interrogation and the reaction of God leads to the conclusion that he primarily rebukes the woman for encouraging Adam to become a transgressor instead of supporting him to be loyal:

> We might have expected God to reply to her now [in Gen 3:12–13], 'What! You *too* ate from the tree!?' God does not do so. *Nowhere in this story does God reprimand the woman for eating from the tree!* That is because her cardinal

---

"help": the woman to save Adam (fashioned by God himself), and the ark to save Noah and his family (planned, instructed to be built, and finally closed by God himself). Also, in both instances the protagonists play an important role: while Adam "provides" one of his "ribs/sides," Noah was the one to build the ark and fill it as God commanded. The suggested connection of the "helper" with God's saving purposes thus seems to be quite strong.

155. Please note that Paul in his instructions concerning practical marriage situations also knows a mutual obligation to foster one's spouse's holiness and salvation (1 Cor 7:14, 16; cf. also Eph 5:23–29; similarly Peter in 1 Pet 3:1–2)! In this context of loyalty it is interesting to notice, as Moberly, "Serpent," 4, observed, that the prohibition in Gen 2:17 is "expressed in the [same] emphatic form (לֹא rather than אַל) as in the Decalogue." Also, "the emphatic verbal form used ('You shall surely die:' מוֹת תָּמוּת) is similar to the standard idiom for the death penalty in a legal context [e.g., Exod 21:15–17, Lev 20:9–16, cf. Gen 26:11, Exod 19:12. . . .]." Ibid. Both covenants (marriage in Gen 2:24 and the one of Sinai) have manifold aspects in common, and here (Gen 2–3) the story seems to foreshadow the question or test about loyalty presented later to the people of Israel. (Similarly, ibid., 4–5: "In the light of these detailed points one can see that the situation in 2: 15–17 is surely an exact depiction of the general Old Testament understanding of man, especially Hebrew man, in the world. Man is given the dignity of a responsible role to fulfil, and he is to fulfil it through obedience to God's Torah, his laws given for the guidance of life.")

transgression, and what she was held accountable for, was not her eating the forbidden fruit, but her causing 'her man' to eat![156]

It seems that the absence of God in the garden at the time the woman is tempted[157] has also contributed to the success of the serpent's intention. While God is certainly not to be blamed for his absence, it nevertheless seems that the woman was quite vulnerable particularly at this point in time—and the serpent naturally took advantage of this situation. God made a couple of two persons instead of leaving the man alone, for the purpose of strengthening him to withstand Satan when he would come to tempt him. Two humans would be stronger than one person alone: "And if one can overpower him who is alone, two can resist him. A cord of three strands is not quickly torn apart." (Ecc. 4:12.) The man alone would be almost helpless against this mighty foe; with a "complemental helper" at his side he would be able to resist; and in the presence of God they would as a three-stranded cord be practically invulnerable. The woman's role is thus stressed as to her support in obedience and faithfulness to their divine creator.

Gen 3:1–7 reversing 2:18–25. The last verse of Gen 2 is not just a final remark on the erotic atmosphere (unashamed nakedness, becoming "one flesh") of the story about woman's creation in vv. 18–24. It also is a stepping stone to the next scene (Gen 3:1–7) in which the (unashamed) nakedness and innocence is lost and the humans become aware of their (now shameful) bareness (v. 7).[158] Contrasting Gen 2:18–25 with 3:1–7 it turns out that the very creation of woman is again linked with the sad event of the Fall—and even the first report about the innocence of marriage is foreshadowing the terrible results of the woman's disloyalty. But, as Trible points out,

> this turning point is not totally surprising. A forbidden tree; animals that do not fit; the withdrawal of God; the increasing power and freedom of human creatures—all these aspects . . . now become the occasion for disobedience.[159]

While Gen 2:18–25 richly depicts the innocent beauty of God's image, male and female, the next narrative scene deals with the woman transferring her loyalty to Satan, thereby forsaking the command of God. The man follows her example and becomes disloyal, seduced by his wife. In his way of describing these conditions and events in Eden, Moses apparently contrasts the divine order of loyalty in marriage

---

156. Gellman, "Gender and Sexuality," 328 (italics given).

157. To be deduced from God's sudden arrival in Gen 3:8 "walking in the garden in the cool of the day," leading to a quick hiding of the man and his wife "among the trees of the garden."

158. Mathews makes the same point: "The final verse is transitional, linking the foregoing narrative of creation and marriage to the subsequent narrative of human sin and the consequences of that disobedience . . . ." Mathews, *Genesis 1–11:26*, 224. Cf. Tosato, "On Genesis 2:24," 390, 395; Trible, *Sexuality*, 105.

159. Trible, *Sexuality*, 105. She also recognizes links between Gen 2:18–24 and the comedown or betrayal of ideals in Gen 3:1–7 (see ibid., 105–15).

(Gen 2:18–25) deliberately to the marred results of the serpent's intervention (Gen 3:1–7) by an interesting parallelism:[160]

Gen 2:18–25	Gen 3:1–7
(2:18) External, superhuman initiative: God speaks: s.th. is missing/not good	*(3:1) External, superhuman initiative:* Satan speaks: s.th. is (seemingly) missing/not good
(2:19–22) Effort of persuasion: God cares for man's needs	*(3:2–5) Effort of persuasion:* Satan pretends to care for woman's need
(2:23) Reaching the goal: The man delights in seeing the woman	*(3:6) Reaching the goal:* The woman delights in seeing the tree
(2:24) Editorial note/explanation: 1. Forsaking parents 2. Cleaving to new party (woman) 3. Consummation by physical act (sex)	*(3:6b) Editorial note/explanation:* 1. Forsaking God (the human's father) 2. Cleaving to new party (fruit/serpent) 3. Consummation by physical act (eating)
(2:25) Moral results: Unashamed, innocent nakedness	*(3:7b) Moral results:* Shameful nakedness

Not by specific vocabulary, but by the specific steps that are taken, it becomes clear (or at least a reasonable suggestion) that the serpent succeeds in reversing the perfect work of God.[161] Furthermore, she did well in reversing the intimate, personal relationship with God that was symbolized by the more personal name of God from Gen 2:4 onward.[162] Within the sad and treacherous discussion of Gen 3:1–6 Eve is led to refer to her personal creator by calling him just אֱלֹהִים (vv. 1, 3), omitting the more intimate name of the covenant God יְהוָה. The serpent encourages her by referring similarly to the more remote אֱלֹהִים (v. 5).[163] Consequently,

---

160. Tosato, "On Genesis 2:24," 392 recognizes a chiasmus of the elements Creation of Man (A)/Creation of Woman (B)—Fall of Woman (B')/Fall of Man (A'). He takes this reversion even further concerning the overall context of Genesis 2 and 3, adding: "In fact, this second story [i.e., Gen 3] ends up, on the one hand, with the *'iššâ* who compulsorily returns to *'iš* ... and, so to speak, is reabsorbed by him ... (Gen 3:16, correlated to Gen 2:18–23), and, on the other hand, with *'ādām* who compulsorily returns to and is reabsorbed by the earth ... (Gen 3:17–19, correlated to Gen 2:4b–8)." Ibid.; cf. also ibid., 401.

161. Similarly Moberly, "Serpent," 6 concerning the serpent's speech.

162. See Scotchmer, "Lessons," 81; Collins, *Genesis 1–4*, 229.

163. Scotchmer, "Lessons," 83 concludes handily: "The conversation was subtle and urbane. For the woman it was intoxicating. Like a couple of sophisticates hobnobbing at a party, the woman and the serpent refer to God as *Elohim* (the Creator-God), rather than *Yahweh-Elohim* (the Covenant-God). In doing so, they intentionally objectify the Almighty, depicting their maker as someone remote and official, rather than close and personal. God is no longer Thou, but It. He is now the object of a new discipline, founded by the woman and the serpent: theology, the study of God." Similarly Moberly, "Serpent," 6.

the serpent and the woman discuss theology. They talk about God. Never referring to the deity by the sacred name Yahweh, but only using the general appellation God, they establish that distance which characterizes objectivity and invites disobedience.[164]

An important link between these passages is further given by wordplay in Gen 2:25 and Gen 3:1: Man and woman are עֲרוּמִּים (from עָרוֹם—"naked"), the serpent is עָרוּם ("cunning/crafty"). Both parties are thereby seemingly contrasted as to their "naivety" and innocence, but simultaneously they are (perhaps just randomly) connected by using this paronomasia, even foreshadowing the similarity in character both parties will share at last after betraying the former loyalties.[165] It thus functions as a kind of introduction to the paralleling story of choosing a partner in personal leadership (God exchanged for the serpent) and forming alliances in both sections. Furthermore, this stylistic device seemingly hints to the "knowledge" the first human pair would experience when eating the forbidden fruit, as the serpent promised (Gen 3:5); they would become like their seducer: crafty (in its negative sense) instead of wise (שָׂכַל; v. 6: a positive sense).

Naming/Calling. While the "pedagogical" insertion of Gen 2:19–20 functions as a lesson of God to teach man that there is no adequate complement and helper for him yet, the paronomasia of the Hebrew words חַיָּה ("living animal;" v. 19) and חַוָּה ("Eve;" Gen 3:20) is significant in this respect, especially concerning the content of Gen 2:19–20. Here Adam names the different חַיָּה, but Eve has no name yet—just "a generic identification."[166] She is just called אִשָּׁה ("woman"), corresponding to the male אִישׁ ("man;" both in Gen 2:23) and distinguishing both from the animals which are not man's "flesh and bones." Apparently, since the man does not name the woman as he does with the different animals, Eve is not part of the creation he is to rule in Eden.[167] The woman as man's counterpart rather seems to be on the same level as he is, with unreserved "unity, solidarity, mutuality, and equality"[168] corresponding to the ideal of Gen 1:26–27. Furthermore,

---

164. Trible, *Sexuality*, 109.

165. The interesting moral ambiguity of understanding עָרוּם in a positive way ("prudent/shrewd") or in a rather negative way ("cunning/crafty") is investigated by Moberly, "Serpent," 25 concluding that "the depiction of the serpent ... illustrates the disastrous consequences of a classic misuse (for reasons unstated) of a rather unusual and ambiguous God-given quality."

166. Davidson, "Beginning," 18; see also on the subject of "naming" the woman: Trible, *Sexuality*, 99–100; Hasel, "Equality," 23–24.

167. I share the common opinion that by naming a person one exercises his (or her) authority over him/her. See on this e.g., Wenham, *Genesis 1–15*, 70; Tosato, "On Genesis 2:24," 390–91, 390/fn.4; Doukhan, "Literary Structure," 44/fn.2; Marks, "Biblical Naming," 29–50; Gellman, "Gender and Sexuality," 331; Trible, *Sexuality*, 97, 99–100; Tarwater, *Marriage as Covenant*, 44, 65.

168. Trible, *Sexuality*, 98; cf. p. 100.

Hebrew literature often makes use of an *inclusio* device in which the points of central concern to a unit are placed at the beginning and end of the unit. This is the case in Gen 2. The entire account is cast in the form of an *inclusio* or 'ring construction' in which the creation of man at the beginning of the narrative and the creation of woman at the end of the narrative correspond to each other in importance. The movement in Gen 2 is not from superior to inferior, but from incompleteness to completeness.[169]

After the Fall there is a severe change and the man will henceforth "rule" (מָשַׁל; Gen 3:16) the woman,[170] symbolically illustrated by giving her, for the first time, a proper name: חַוָּה (Gen 3:20).[171] Additionally, the Hebrew text clearly indicates the change by using שֵׁם ("name") in Gen 3:20, while in the creation story of animals and woman (Gen 2:18–23) only the animals are called a שֵׁם (cf. Gen 2:19–20), not the woman.[172]

It seems to be meaningful that the first וַיִּקְרָא ("he called") pertains to God (וַיִּקְרָא אֱלֹהִים) calling day and night (Gen 1:5), the sky (v. 8), the earth and the sea (v. 10). The next time God calls something (וַיִּקְרָא יְהוָה אֱלֹהִים; Gen 3:9) it is the man. Although he is just "calling out to" and not "naming" him, the man is the only living creature "called" by God, while the other living creatures (animals and finally Eve) are called (i.e., "named") by the man, thus subtly establishing a hierarchy—concerning the animals already before the Fall, regarding the woman only afterwards.

---

169. Davidson, "Beginning," 14–15; cf. Muilenburg, "Form Criticism and Beyond," 9–10; Trible, "Depatriarchalizing," 36. Also, "we note, for example, that Adam also was 'derived'—from the ground (v. 7)—but certainly we are not to conclude that the ground was his superior! . . . To clinch the point, the text explicitly indicates that the man was asleep while God created woman. Man had no active part in the creation of woman that might allow him to claim to be her superior." Davidson, "Beginning," 16. He did not father Eve and thus had no right to give her a name. That was allowed to him only after the Fall and God's curse over the woman (Gen 3:16: "Your desire will be for your husband, and he will rule over you."). Finally, the woman is not subordinate only because she has been created after Adam—just like man is not subordinate to all the animals only because he is created at a later point of time (thus Mathews, *Genesis 1–11:26*, 221). Also, "none of Israel's neighbors had a tradition involving a separate account of the creation of the female. In biblical thought the woman is not subsumed under her male counterpart." Hamilton, *Genesis*, 177.

170. While this is probably the correct understanding of the Hebrew term מָשַׁל employed in this instance, it should at least be noted that in some cases it could also mean "to be like," cf. TWOT/HALOT s.v. מׁשׁל; Clines, *Classical Hebrew*, 2:537, 539–40.

171. Whether this new authority is part of a curse against the woman, and as such divinely "ordained" as many commentators claim, or if this simply is an allusion to conditions that will inevitably occur from now on, remains unclear. The text only says what it will be like for the woman henceforth; it does surely not say that it should or must be this way.

172. Trible, *Sexuality*, 100, 133 makes the same point. She further explains that "the verb *call* by itself does not mean naming; only when joined to the noun *name* does it become part of a naming formula. [Further referring to Gen 4:17, 25, 26]." Yet, there are exceptions to the usual "naming formula" (call + שֵׁם + name; cf. e.g., ibid., 99–100) as Gellman, "Gender and Sexuality," 332–33 depicts. He even demonstrates using Gen 16:13 (Hagar calling God by a new name) that naming itself does not in every case mean to exercise power. However, in almost any biblical case it actually does.

I.1.1.4.2 COVENANTAL ASPECTS

Besides the aforementioned aspects concerning primarily the woman's creation, there are further important observations now particularly pertaining to a covenantal relationship between God and man which has been betrayed by eating the forbidden fruit.

"And God said." Taking into consideration a common phrase frequently given in Gen 1, it is interesting that the narrative introduction וַיֹּאמֶר אֱלֹהִים ("and God said") ceases to occur after relating man's perfect creation in Gen 1:26–31.[173] The next time it is employed by Moses is not before Gen 6:13 ("The end of all flesh has come before me; . . . I am about to destroy them with the earth"). Additionally, God's "behold" (הִנֵּה) of Gen 1:29, 31 does not reappear until the same chapter (Gen 6:2, 12–13, 17), now referring to man's corruption and thus constructing a contrasting "observation scene" that contains some more interesting parallels. It looks like God is reevaluating the covenantal conditions and his purpose (cf. Gen 1:26–31) on which he agreed to create and bless humankind:

Gen 1:26–31	Gen 6:11–13
Cause and Perspective: God saw all that he made (וַיַּרְא אֱלֹהִים אֶת־כָּל־אֲשֶׁר עָשָׂה)	*Cause and Perspective:* God saw the earth (וַיַּרְא אֱלֹהִים אֶת־הָאָרֶץ)
Appeal for Others to Evaluate: "Behold" (וְהִנֵּה)	*Appeal for Others to Evaluate:* "Behold" (v. 12: וְהִנֵּה/v. 13: וְהִנְנִי)
Direct Speech of God: "And God said" (וַיֹּאמֶר אֱלֹהִים)	*Direct Speech of God:* "And God said" (וַיֹּאמֶר אֱלֹהִים)
Context: Humankind's *beginning* (בְּרֵאשִׁית; v. 1)	*Context:* Humankind's *ending* (קֵץ)
Judgment Range: All that God made (כָּל־אֲשֶׁר עָשָׂה)	*Judgment Range:* All flesh (כָּל־בָּשָׂר)
Sentence: Very good (טוֹב מְאֹד)	*Sentence:* Corrupt/violent (חָמָס/שָׁחַת)
Consequences: Blessing and fruitfulness	*Consequences:* Curse and destruction

The parallels are obvious. The author is contrasting the initial, excellent creation to the corrupt society living right before the flood. While in Gen 1:26–27 man was created male and female (alluding to the conjugal oneness of Gen 2:24) being in an excellent state (טוֹב מְאֹד, literally meaning "good in abundance/in the highest degree"), in Gen 6 the humans have lost their virtue. They spoil the initial purpose of marriage as an

---

173. The paralleling features and interrelations of וַיֹּאמֶר אֱלֹהִים ("and God said") in Genesis 1 with יְהוָה אֱלֹהִים ("Yahweh God") in the second chapter of Genesis are mentioned above concerning thematic and structural connections of chaps. 1 and 2 cf. esp. Doukhan, "Literary Structure," 42–50 and the critique of Garrett, *Primeval History*, 194–97.

institution to secure faithfulness toward God and become inclined to surrender to apostasy for the sake of female beauty.[174]

"Came before him." Another hint at the connection between marriage and the corruption of humankind, going along with thoughts of the previous section on the woman's creation, is the expression "[God] brought her to the man" (וַיְבִאֶהָ אֶל־הָאָדָם לְאִשָּׁה) in Gen 2:22 and the similar phrase in Gen 6:13 "the end of all flesh came before my [i.e., God's] face" (קֵץ כָּל־בָּשָׂר בָּא לְפָנַי). While the woman (the "female flesh" as contrasted to "all flesh" in Gen 6) is welcomed by Adam after a brief evaluation of her appearance with a happy exclamation of joy, now the final judgment about "all flesh" "comes" (again בּוֹא) before God with deep regret. His creation is no more "flesh of his flesh and bone of his bone" (Gen 2:23), namely: the image of God (Gen 1:26–27) as found initially in the so called "sons of God." To the contrary, they all became corrupt.[175]

"Let us make." Another keyword in this context is the נַעֲשֶׂה ("let us make/do") of Gen 1:26. While in Gen 1:26 it is God who declares his intention to create man in his image and likeness,[176] further occurrences of exactly this Hebrew expression in the Hexateuch speak of God's people promising to keep God's commandments in order to establish the covenant and of single tribes declaring to follow God's words.[177] It points to a strong intention, a deliberate agreement,[178] mostly in context of the human-divine relationship and covenant, as especially Exod 24:7–8 indicates:

> Then he took the book of the covenant and read it in the hearing of the people; and they said, "All that the Lord has spoken we will do (נַעֲשֶׂה), and we will be obedient!" So Moses took the blood and sprinkled it on the people, and said,

---

174. More on this below in the chapter "The 'Sons of God' Going Astray." There is another interesting observation concerning the further verses using וַיֹּאמֶר אֱלֹהִים and the parallels between Gen 1:26–31 and 6:11–13. Beside the destruction of all flesh, Gen 6 also points to a new beginning, a new start of the creation by saving some of the former population. To the same aspect allude the verses in Gen 9:8, 12, 17 as well as Gen 17:9, 15, 19 (the next occurrences of וַיֹּאמֶר אֱלֹהִים): "God said" with the purpose to establish his covenant. Pointing back to the perfect creation of humankind in God's image, he now endeavors to restore this image in man through the means of his divine covenant. The significant and unfortunately mostly sad part of marriage in this connection is significant.

175. Clines, "Significance," 37 puts it thus: "In Gen 6:1–4 ... we find a satanic parody of the idea of the image of God in man. Far from God being present on earth in the person of man as his kingly representative exercising benign dominion over the lower orders of creation, we now have the presence of the divine on earth in a form that utterly misrepresents God ..."

176. It might be interesting to note that some ancient Jewish commentators suggested that God took counsel with "the works of heaven and earth," with "the works of each [creation] day," with "his own heart," or even "with the souls of the righteous" (whoever that should be; see *Gen. Rab.* 8:3, 7). This is far beyond the Text of Genesis 1–2 which only knows of God initiating the creation of man "in his image"—i.e., God's image.

177. See Exod 19:8; 24:3, 7–12 (partly cited above); Num 32:31; Josh 1:16; 9:20; 22:26–27; cf. also (outside the Hexateuch) Neh 5:12; Jer 42:3, 5 (contrast: 44:17, 25).

178. Cf. Joüon and Muraoka, *Biblical Hebrew*, 347.

The Old Testament Foundation

"Behold the blood of the covenant, which the Lord has made with you in accordance with all these words."

Other instances containing this expression almost entirely deal with God's mighty working in connection with his covenant and the plan of redemption.[179] Considering the mentioned parallels to the great Flood, it seems that man had agreed to the conditions of a similar contract in the unwritten context of Gen 1:26–31 and has therefore been equipped with the best opportunities and circumstances to reach the goal as far as God's initiative and creative working is concerned (Gen 2:4—2:25). But he betrayed this trust and the reevaluation of Gen 6:11–13 resulted in the world-wide execution of the penalty named in Gen 2:17, namely death. Consequently, right after the Flood God had to establish a new covenant, again pronouncing the Edenic blessing over the new "first couples" of humankind (Noah and his sons and their wives), again assigning the food they should eat and again referring to the original purpose of God's creation of man in his image; however, the changed conditions are obvious by the permission to shed blood in order to prepare food and the declaration of God's vengeance (cf. Gen 9:1–7). Now, for the first time, the word "covenant" (בְּרִית; Gen 6:18; 9:9, 11, 15, 16) appears in the immediate Flood context. The connections to the institution of marriage as elucidated in the foregoing pages are most interesting and significant.[180]

Tabernacle Terminology. Some scholars recognize a similarity between the meaning of בְּצַלְמוֹ בְּצֶלֶם/בְּצַלְמֵנוּ כִּדְמוּתֵנוּ ("in our image, after our likeness/in his image, in the image [of God]") in Gen 1:26–27 and Exod 25:40 (cf. Exod 25:9), where the tabernacle should be constructed "after the pattern" (בְּתַבְנִיתָם).[181] Additionally, affirming this link between both important "institutions" is the fact that man's צֵלָע ("rib/side") out of which the female "man" was formed, is further used by Moses in the entire Pentateuch only in context of the tabernacle's construction and once as term for Jacob's "side" that has been damaged due to his fight at Penuel.[182] Hence, the seemingly strange use of

---

179. Cf. נַעֲשֶׂה in context of divinely appointed judges (e.g., Judg 11:10; 13:8 2 Kgs 10:5) or prophets (2 Kgs 4:10; 6:15), the ark of the covenant (1 Sam 5:8; 6:2), the "relaunch" of the Passover (2 Kgs 23:22–23; 2 Chr 35:18–19); God's power to save (Ps 60:14; cf. 108:4; contrast: Isa 26:18; Jer 18:12), God's invisible working in the world (Eccl 1:13; 4:3; 8:9, 11, 14, 16, 17; Jonah 1:11).

180. As a final remark regarding the "Let us"-sayings as covenantal language it might be of interest that this type of speech appears for the next time in Gen 11 when planning to build the high tower. In Gen 11:3–4 the people say "let us make bricks" (נִלְבְּנָה), "let us build" (נִבְנֶה), and "let us make" (וְנַעֲשֶׂה), thus establishing a counter covenant between (every) man and his companion (אִישׁ אֶל־רֵעֵהוּ), contrasting the divine "let us make" (נַעֲשֶׂה) in Gen 1:26 (and the divine "building" of the woman in Gen 2:22: וַיִּבֶן). Consequently God speaks "let us come down" (נֵרְדָה; Gen 11:7) to interrupt and destroy this ungodly alliance that would jeopardize the divine covenant of Gen 6–9.

181. See e.g., Wenham, *Genesis 1–15*, 29; NET on Gen 1:26; further aspects by comparison of the creation account with the building of the sanctuary (Exod 25–40) see Kearney, "Creation and Liturgy," 375–87.

182. Check this complete list of occurrences within the five books of Moses: Gen 2:21–22; 32:32; Exod 25:12, 14; 26:20, 26–27, 35; 27:7; 30:4; 36:25, 31–32; 37:3, 5, 27; 38:7. It also appears in the accounts of Salomon's temple (1 Kgs 6:5, 8, 15–16, 34; 7:3) and Ezekiel's vision of the new temple (Ezek 41:5–9,

צֵלָע in the creation story, frequently degraded as part of some ancient myth, rather points to the most important "facility" in ancient Israel's later cult system and the corresponding covenant foreshadowed in the struggle with "Israel" at the Jabbok (Gen 32:25–32). Furthermore, the entire

> Garden of Eden is more than a royal garden. It is the archetype of the tabernacle introduced by Moses, at God's direction, at Mount Sinai. Like the tabernacle, it is bedecked by gold and precious stones (2:12); it is 'served' (the same word as 'to till') by God's priestly representatives on earth; it is designed as a special meeting place for God and his people.[183]

The creation of God concerning man is thus in both instances (Gen 1:26–27; 2:18–25) by terminology and certain attributes and purposes connected with the redemptive work of God that would later be introduced by the tabernacle service for the sake of humankind. God's helping and even saving[184] purposes with the woman being fashioned out of man's צֵלָע amid those reminiscences of the sanctuary are thus also reemphasized.

The connection between the forming of the human after the divine pattern and the link between the woman and the tabernacle connote further significance: both "institutions" (man and the tabernacle) represent divine presence and both are to reveal their divine creator. Additionally, the climactic emphasis of the Sabbath in Gen 2:2–3 as holy institution, and its maintenance along with marriage even out of paradise, both protected by God's most holy laws in Exod 20:8–11, 14, demonstrates to some degree a common importance:

> The literary structural placement of the first wedding ceremony and the first married couple's unashamed sexuality at the climax of the creation account in Gen 2 must be viewed in parallel with the placement of the Sabbath at the climax of the first creation account in 1:1—2:4a . . . these two creation accounts are in a precise literary structural parallelism of seven sections. The narrator has not accidentally paired the Sabbath and the marriage—two institutions continuing in salvation history outside Eden. God actualizes Sabbath holiness by his presence (2:3) and solemnizes the marriage covenant by his presence (2:22–23). By linking these two institutions the narrator implicitly indicates that the marriage relationship is holy like the Sabbath . . . That first Friday night in Eden—the eve of the Shabbat—was their wedding night . . .
>
> The intimacy within the sacred *space* of the Eden sanctuary (2:15–25) is the counterpart to the climax of the first creation account (2:1–3), where the man and the woman experience intimacy within sacred *time*—the Sabbath.

11, 26); cf. Mathews, *Genesis 1–11:26*, 216. The term appears almost exclusively in the temple context.

183. Scotchmer, "Lessons," 81.

184. See above (in this section) my argumentation for the woman as helper in keeping God's commandments.

Sabbath, sanctuary, and marriage intersect in the one-flesh experience of the first couple.[185]

"Out of her Man." Another "covenant link" may be given by the variant reading of Gen 2:23, where the Samaritan Pentateuch, the Aramaic Targumim, and the Septuagint read "out of *her* man" (מֵאִישָׁהּ/מִבַּעֲלָהּ/ἐκ τοῦ ἀνδρὸς αὐτῆς), thus already binding the woman closer to *her* man, reflecting the marital husband-wife relationship.[186] The Hebrew word מֵאִישָׁה appears only once more in the entire Hebrew Bible,[187] where it is used in reference to a somehow reversed case: "They [i.e., the priests] shall not take a woman who is profaned by harlotry, nor shall they take a woman divorced from her husband; for he is holy to his God." (Lev 21:7.) Given the case that the variant rendering would be the more reliable, the literary and linguistic connections supply fascinating insights. First, Lev 21:7 contains a complemental parallelism, not just adding divorce to harlotry, but even more linking the one with the other:[188]

v. 7a:	v. 7b:
Accused: A woman (אִשָּׁה)	*Accused:* A woman (אִשָּׁה)
Elements of Offence: prostituted and deprived of virginity (זֹנָה וַחֲלָלָה)	*Elements of Offence:* cast out of her man (גְּרוּשָׁה מֵאִישָׁהּ)
Sentence/Result: he shall not take (לֹא יִקָּחוּ)	*Sentence/Result:* he shall not take (לֹא יִקָּחוּ)
v. 7c: *Rationale/Reasons for Judgment:* for he is sacred to his God (כִּי־קָדֹשׁ הוּא לֵאלֹהָיו)	

Second, the Hebrew מֵאִישָׁה conveys the Edenic idea of the woman being made "out of the man" (מִן־הָאָדָם) by both times using the particle preposition מִן, at first referring to the still somehow impersonal, more generic "man" (אָדָם), but then to the personally related "husband" (אִישׁ). The text of Lev 21:7 is thus not only hinting that divorce (almost) corresponds to, or perhaps better: is likely to result in, harlotry, thereby

---

185. Davidson, *Flame*, 52–53 (italics given). On the literary structure see Doukhan, "Literary Structure," 35–80.

186. Tosato, "On Genesis 2:24," 398 argues in favor of this variant reading and asserts that "there is strong agreement (both of form and content) between *'iššâ kî mē'išāh* (*with* the possessive pronoun) and *wĕdābaq bĕ'ištô* . . . , i.e., the whole of Gen 2:24 . . ."

187. Beside the concrete form of מֵאִישָׁה, which actually occurs just once, there are only very few examples of the lemmas אִשָּׁה + מִן or אִישׁ usage in the entire OT. And indeed just Gen 2:23 and Lev 21:7 refer to a marital and even normative context. That makes both texts all the more interesting and supports a connection in the mentioned respect.

188. This linkage will reoccur in the New Testament speeches of Jesus as investigated below (see "Jesus about Divorce").

supporting the argumentation of Jesus as given in Matt 5:32 ("I say to you that everyone who divorces his wife, except for the reason of unchastity, makes her commit adultery; and whoever marries a divorced woman commits adultery."). It is also declaring the creational institution to be profaned and made unholy by prostitution, by not being virgin when entering the marital bond, and finally by divorce.[189] To cast out one's wife means, considering the given special terminology, to dissolve the "one flesh" union and separating both "fleshes" again, thus copying the divine act of Gen 2:21 and assigning it to the human sphere of action. That again gives a close connection to the New Testament teaching of Jesus on divorce, who clearly states that it is up to God to unite two fleshes;[190] consequently, it is likewise up to him to separate them again by his divine intervention (and not by man's will) through the death of one spouse (Matt 19:6; cf. Rom 7:2; 1 Cor 7:39). In fact it is not just another flesh that is cast out by divorce, it actually is one's own (Gen 2:21–22; cf. Eph 5:28–29).

Ruth's Cleaving. There are some interesting aspects in the book of Ruth concerning leaving, cleaving, and the separation of partners:

> And they lifted up their voices and wept again; and Orpah kissed her mother-in-law, but Ruth clung (דָּבְקָה) to her. Then she said, "Behold, your sister-in-law has gone back to her people and her gods; return after your sister-in-law." But Ruth said, "Do not urge me to leave you (לְעָזְבֵךְ) or turn back from following you; for where you go, I will go, and where you lodge, I will lodge. Your people shall be my people, and your God, my God. "Where you die, I will die, and there I will be buried. Thus may the Lord do to me, and worse, if anything but death parts (יַפְרִיד) you and me." (Ruth 1:14–17.)

This is a very nice picture of the principles described in Gen 2:24. At first Ruth "leaves" (עָזַב) her "father and mother and the land of her birth" (Ruth 2:11). Then she "cleaves" (דָּבַק; Ruth 1:14) to her mother-in-law, never to "leave/forsake" (עָזַב; v. 16) her until death may finally "divide/separate" (פָּרַד; v. 17) them. The Hebrew terms may indicate that even death will not really "cut off" their sympathies for each other, for the verb פָּרַד only describes a separation concerning location, never regarding the individual affection.[191] Thus פָּרַד differs distinctively from the usual terms used for a man

---

189. Amram, *Divorce*, 109 explains: "The Mosaic law provided that the divorced woman should not marry a priest. This was not because of any stigma cast upon the woman by reason of her divorce, but because of the peculiar sanctity of the priestly office." Therefore, in the ancient Jewish tradition "the marriage with a divorced woman subjected the priest to the penalty of the lash, the punishment being thirty-nine stripes [*m. Mak.* 3:1], and a son born of such a union was not qualified to perform the usual priestly functions [*m. Ter.* 8:1]." Ibid.

190. By the "flame of Yahweh" (שַׁלְהֶבֶתְיָה) mentioned in the Song of Songs (8:6)?

191. See all the examples of פָּרַד as given in Gen 2:10; 10:5, 32; 13:9, 11, 14; 25:23; 30:40; Deut 32:8; Judg 4:11; Ruth 1:17; 2 Sam 1:23; 2 Kgs 2:11; Neh 4:13; Esth 3:8; Job 4:11; 41:9; Ps 22:15; 92:10; Prov 17:9; 18:1, 18; 19:4; Ezek 1:11; Hos 4:14. The only ambiguous examples would be Prov 16:28; 17:9; 19:4; all the others clearly point to a local separation.

divorcing his wife,[192] and has nothing to do with this kind of (emotional) separation. In fact, Ruth declares to cling to Naomi forever, as far as her affections are concerned, even when death may (for a time) separate them.

A similar example is mentioned in 2 Sam 1:23, where Saul and Jonathan are described as beloved/loving each other, unseparated (פָּרַד) in death. Although death of course cut them off, both did not lose their affections between father and son. 2 Kgs 2:11 alludes to the same aspect of פָּרַד: Elijah and Elisha are compelled to separate (פָּרַד), because Elijah had to go up to heaven. Yet their sympathies are not affected. These instances show that it is divine intervention which separates these persons from each other, while the emotions stay untouched. That is a significant feature of the Edenic use of דָּבַק ("cleave"), meaning a remarkable type of clinging to a beloved person, to be separated only by God's initiative.[193]

Covenant Witnesses. At this place, it seems proper to address the perception that marriage without human witnesses is no marriage in a biblical sense. In fact, the Hebrew Bible speaks of only two witnesses of a lawful and proper consummation: (1) the virgin's under-blanket/sheet (הַשִּׂמְלָה; Deut 22:15, 17) as the sign of virginity,[194] and (2) God (יְהוָה; Mal 2:14; 3:5) as the "patron" of this union (cf. Prov 2:17). It is evident from

192. Those would be גָּרַשׁ ("divorce/cast off;" cf. Lev 21:7; Ezek 44:22) and שָׁלַח ("send away/let go;" cf. Deut 22:19, 29; 24:1, 3; Isa 50:1; Jer 3:1, 8; Mal 2:16).

193. Of course, that does not apply to every instance where דָּבַק is used. Even the further usage in Ruth 2:8, 21, 23 refers only to the workers that Ruth is "joining." Nonetheless it expresses the tight closeness which is characteristic of this Hebrew verb, and the important covenantal aspect as explained in the foregoing section concerning the use of דָּבַק as clinging to the Lord.

194. In this context, another interesting (but slightly speculative) observation deserves attention. As already mentioned above (see "Textual Analysis"), the final consummation of the "one flesh" union is particularly given by the physical act of sexual intercourse, thereby (re-) uniting both parts of the human. Now, blood is a very important element within the divine covenant, as esp. Heb 9:18–22 stresses (cf. Zech 9:11; Matt 26:28; Mark 14:24; Luke 22:20; 1 Cor 11:25). The covenants made before the one with Israel in Exod 24:7–8 likewise include blood: Gen 8:20—29:17 (Noah's sacrifice); Gen 17:11 (circumcision; cf. Gen 22: the sacrifice of Isaac). Even the "contract" with Cain is a result from bloodshed (see Gen 4:10, 15). Concerning the covenantal characteristics of marriage, it may be of interest that it would be possible to observe even here some kind of a bloodshed, some "blood of the covenant" (דַּם־הַבְּרִית; cf. Exod 24:8)—as a result of the woman's defloration on the wedding night. This sign is particularly mentioned in Deut 22:17 referring to the "evidence" of the garment/sheet (הַשִּׂמְלָה) that is to be spread before the elders of the city when facing a trial, because of the accusation of not being a virgin at the time of consummating marriage by sexual intercourse. The text euphemistically refers to the blood of the virgin's defloration that should be found on the garment. Apparently, "the physical act of coitus is the primary means of establishing the 'innermost mystery' of oneness, and in the covenant context of this verse seems to constitute the sign of the marriage covenant." Davidson, *Flame*, 46; cf. also e.g., Stuart, *Exodus*, 509; Tarwater, *Marriage as Covenant*, 63–65. One may rightly assume that marriage with its far-reaching significance, aims, and responsibilities also has this covenantal sign, especially when considering the life-giving features of this intimate union—just as the aforementioned covenants have life-protecting features/blessings, partly at the spiritual level (i.e., salvation). ("Redemptive" elements have already been mentioned concerning the woman's role to help Adam fulfilling the divine commandments, esp. the one against touching the forbidden tree. It is interesting that Paul and Peter also know such saving aspects of marriage: 1 Cor 7:14, 16; 1 Pet 3:1–2; cf. also Eph 5:23–29.)

e.g., Gen 4:10; 31:44–52;[195] Deut 30:19; 31:19–28; Josh 22:34; 24:27; Judg 11:10; Ruth 4:7; 1 Sam (6:8); 12:5; Job 16:19; and Ps 89:37 that it is not unusual to have unanimated materials (blood, stone, heaven, earth, altar, song, book, shoe, moon) or/and God himself as a witness (עֵד) or testimony (תְּעוּדָה) for various circumstances, contracts or covenants.[196] Additionally, Deut 19:15 declares that two witnesses are sufficient to make a statement reliable and valid. Furthermore, only these two witnesses (the sheet and God) appear in a judgment context to practically function as real witnesses against adulterers (cf. Deut 22:17–18; Mal 3:5).

The example of Ruth is again most interesting in this respect. While in Ruth 4:9–12 "the elders and all the people" (לַזְּקֵנִים וְכָל־הָעָם; v. 9) are "witnesses" (עֵדִים; vv. 9–11) of Boaz's *intention* to marry Ruth, the practical *"consummation"* is narrated as a private, personal act (v. 13): "So Boaz took Ruth, and she became his wife, and he went in to her" (וַיִּקַּח בֹּעַז אֶת־רוּת וַתְּהִי־לוֹ לְאִשָּׁה וַיָּבֹא אֵלֶיהָ). The result is Ruth's pregnancy (v. 13b). The way this short verse is formulated ties the four steps closely together and lets them even appear as one and the same act: (1) taking, (2) becoming wife, (3) going in to her, (4) becoming pregnant. All these issues are closely related to sexuality; or even more are practically realized by sexual relations, just what Gen 2:24 would call "(to) become one flesh." Hence, a real "witness" of the practical consummation is actually no one but the "garment/sheet" and God himself—the only ones present during this act.

I.1.1.5 Summary and Final Considerations

> With the creation of man the creation account reaches its climax... the acts of creation most germane to human existence—the earth, man's home (vv. 9–13), the sun and moon that determine his life cycle (vv. 14–19)—were described more fully than other less vital aspects of the created order. But now with man's creation, the narrative slows down even more to emphasize his significance.[197]

"Hier ist der Höhepunkt und das Ziel erreicht, auf das alles Schaffen Gottes von V. 1 an angelegt war."[198] Even within this focus it seems to be Gen 2:24 that is the central core of the story: "with this verse the entire preceding narrative 'arrives at the primary purpose toward which it was oriented from the beginning.'"[199] While the holy Sabbath is the climax regarding the divine-human relationship (Gen 2:2–3; Exod 20:8–11)

---

195. Gen 31:44 knows even the covenant itself as witness between two people.

196. Not to forget the non-physical and only temporarily visible rainbow as sign of God's covenant with Noah and all living beings (cf. Gen 9:13).

197. Wenham, *Genesis 1–15*, 27; cf. esp. the catalogue of rationales in Ware, "Male and Female Complementarity and the Image of God," 72.

198. Von Rad, *Erstes Buch Mose*, 37; cf. Davidson, "Beginning," 5; Thatcher, *Marriage*, 77; Beale and Carson, *NT Use*, 197: "... indicated by its extent, special affirmation, and the definite article marking the day number... Gen 1:27 accords the creation of humanity a special status..."

199. Lawton, "Gen. 2:24," 97 citing Von Rad, *Genesis (1972)*, 84–85.

and a necessary requisite of this spiritual covenant (cf. Exod 31:13; Jes. 56:4–7), becoming "one flesh" is the centre of the human-human relationship and corresponding intimacy. The significant patterns concerning marriage within the creation, however, account do not begin and stop with Gen 2:18–25,[200] although v. 24 indeed may be called "a cardinal passage ordaining marriage."[201] Even concerning several further tenets of New Testament theology we recognize that Eden, and particularly Jesus' quote of Gen 2:23–24, is an essential basis.

> Jesus' appeal to the garden (quoting Gen 2:23) as the basis of his teaching on marriage and divorce . . . indicates that the garden established a paradigm for marital behavior. That Eden was viewed by the Hebrews as the model, authoritative experience can be seen also in Jewish literature of the time but especially by Paul, who appeals to its events in speaking of the most profound theological tenets of Christianity (Rom 5:12–21; 1 Cor 15:45) and in offering instructions concerning the propriety of worship (1 Cor 11:2–16; 1 Tim 2:11–15), moral behavior (1 Cor 6:16), and marriage (Eph 5:31).[202]

Already Gen 1:26–30 briefly introduces humankind—and the union of male and female—as a special creation by using the plural form for the first time, saying: "Let Us make man in Our image, according to Our likeness; and let them rule" (נַעֲשֶׂה אָדָם בְּצַלְמֵנוּ כִּדְמוּתֵנוּ וְיִרְדּוּ; Gen 1:26). Also, it is the first time that a created being is described to be male and female (Gen 1:27), nonetheless being *one*—which sounds like an anticipation of Gen 2:24. Thus the *one* God is mentioned in a plural form as well as his human "image" (צֶלֶם; Gen 1:27). The beginning of a very close and communicative relationship is made and the first allusion to the figurative, spiritual sphere of the marital oneness is given.

The report also shows a shifting of the level of God's satisfaction and contentedness by not just declaring the day's work to be "good" (טוֹב; Gen 1:4, 10, 12, 18, 21, 25), but rather "very good" (טוֹב מְאֹד; Gen 1:31). To emphasize this high degree of happiness over his sixth day's creation he even exclaims "behold" (הִנֵּה; Gen 1:31)—apparently inviting any imaginary spectator or reader of the account to have a very close look at the great work God has accomplished on this day. While the creation of the preceding days in Gen 1:4, 10, 12, 18, 21 and 25 are inspected only by God himself and approved by awarding it with a "good" grade, the creation of the sixth day is to be examined by everyone who

---

200. Among modern scholarship it is widely accepted that this text indeed addresses the institution of marriage (cf. Batto, "Institution of Marriage," 629), not just some mutual sexual attraction between man and wife (as argued for instance in the influential commentary of Gunkel, *Genesis*, 13).

201. Sampley, *One Flesh*, 96. Although others declare, "Wir müssen davon ausgehen, dass hier nicht *normativ* über die Ehe geredet wird. So finden wir hier keine bindende Ehegesetzgebung. . . . Ganz unreflektiert wird einfach vorausgesetzt, dass die Einehe der Schöpfungstat Gottes entspricht." Baltensweiler, *Ehe im NT*, 22; Italics given, the depiction of the "creation of marriage" was apparently meant to serve as marriage ideal, for there are no other efforts to introduce some alternative marriage pattern. All deviations are rather estimated as distortion—as the following investigations may demonstrate.

202. Mathews, *Genesis 1–11:26*, 222.

hears this "behold" and anyone who witnesses the greatness of humankind when having a closer look at this wonderful being (cf. e.g., Ps 139:13–16). God obviously is convinced that everyone will share his opinion and pronounce an abundant (מְאֹד; Gen 1:31) *"very good"* regarding man and woman as God's image.

While the first, comprehensive creation account (Gen 1:1—2:3) closes with this proud and joyful remark and the Sabbath as a special blessing for humankind, we find this satisfactory happiness and overwhelming goodness already fading in Gen 2:4—2:25. This passage as a midsection between the creation of the perfect world in Gen 1:1—2:4 and the sudden Fall of Man in Gen 3 represents a close focus on man—virtually the close examination and inspection God invited the reader in Gen 1:31 ("behold!") to carry out. It is most interesting and meaningful that this middle part already describes quite a lot of hints foreshadowing the consequences of what humankind had to experience after transgression. It almost seems as if this close investigation of the human being and the perfect circumstances God so richly provided is inserted for a twofold goal:

(1) The report of Adam in Gen 2:4—2:25 represents a gateway from the perfect (טוֹב מְאֹד; Gen 1:31) conditions at the end of God's working downward to the imperfect conditions at the end of man's and woman's working (Gen 3:1–7). So we find already in Gen 2:5 allusion to the "plants of the field," the mentioning of rain, and the man "cultivating the ground," beside further hints in the way the narrator works with certain Hebrew phrases like וַיֹּאמֶר יְהוָה אֱלֹהִים ("and YHWH God said;" Gen 2:18), all pointing to the expulsion of Eden and the worse conditions man would have to experience outside. Additionally, the focus on the tree of knowledge in Gen 2:8–17 "prepares" the reader to accompany the man on the downward path until Gen 3:6.

(2) The passage of Gen 2:4—2:25 also demonstrates the affectionate, intimate relationship and care God wanted to share with humankind. He did his very best, provided man with the best possible environment and support. He made the woman as man's "helper" to support him in his task of cultivating the ground, but especially in keeping away from the tree of knowledge. She had the representative function of the divine helper (God), working for the sake of man(-kind), by terminology even linked with the redemptive function of the later Israelite tabernacle. Initially she is not subjected, but rather introduced to help man saving his loyalty. Unfortunately she betrayed her trust and the mission failed. But the Fall of Man is not God's fault. It happened *although* God created them perfect—as everyone may and shall affirm (Gen 1:31). The closer look at this "crown of creation" unfortunately reveals the rebellious seed of the great controversy that soon sprang up and bore fruit in Gen 3:6.

While Gen 1:1—2:4 provides a rather cosmic point of view, in Gen 2:5 the perspective changes into a position outside of paradise, looking back into the perfect garden,[203] where the first man in the image of God betrayed his allegiance and loyalty

---

203. As Kaye puts it: "The second account [i.e., Gen 2:4–25] tells the story of ideal in terms of . . . the particular experienced circumstances of the writer." Kaye, "One Flesh," 47.

to Yahweh for the sake of his marriage relation. Later it is again just this relation which leads to another, even deeper fall of man as recorded in Gen 6:1–3. Thus, right from the beginning and even before the actual Fall of Man in Gen 3:6, we find distinctive hints that combine not only the perfect creation of man with apostasy, but even more the special relationship of man and woman as a possible source of disloyalty. Hence, even in this early stage of the rebellion's and the sin's development, Paul's explanation is strikingly appropriate:

> Therefore did that which is good become a cause of death for me? May it never be! Rather it was sin, in order that it might be shown to be sin by effecting my death through that which is good, so that through the commandment sin would become utterly sinful. (Rom 7:13)

Although all conditions were perfect, and thus was the creational marriage ideal of Gen 2:18–25, giving "the relationship between man and woman the dignity of being the greatest miracle and mystery of creation,"[204] one recognizes a subtle seed of disloyalty even in what originally was meant to be a blessing. Consequently, Gen 3 shows the change of loyalties by giving further insights in the way this seed springs up and bears its bitter fruit.

The ongoing story of Gen 3 presents man as being loyal to his sinning wife and therefore disloyal against God. Hereby the initial threefold loyalty between man, woman, and God is broken. Humankind and God are henceforth separated regarding their relationship as well as their locality (by driving man out of the garden, but not by cutting off every way of communication; cf. Gen 3:22–24; 4:6–16, 26). Additionally, the relationship of husband and wife is injured (cf. Gen 3:12). Adam had to decide between his wife and his God, but by choosing the created being rather than the creator, he was not able to save the formerly blessed and unimpaired relationship even with the dear person of his choosing. Henceforth there are thorns and thistles not only with man's work on the ground, but also in the relationship between man, woman, and God. These thorns and thistles, as first alluded to in Gen 2:5, thus are representing the almost omnipotent thorn of Satan (cf. Josh 23:13; 1 Cor 15:55–56), who is constantly working to break any allegiance between God and humankind as well as the loyalty of husband and wife.

All these observations tell much about priorities and exclusivity touching the Edenic oneness ideal. God appears to be more than one person (Gen 1:26; cf. Gen 18:1–2; 19:24), but he is just *one* deity.[205] In the same way the man in Gen 1:27 is explained to be male and female—yet both represent *one* idea: humankind. Both "onenesses" are contrasting each other and are closely connected by the declaration

---

204. Von Rad, *Old Testament Theology*, 1:150; cf. Davidson, "Beginning," 24.

205. I am well aware that Gen 1:26 and 3:22 may not serve as proof texts for the sake of any Trinitarian doctrine. Nonetheless it is an interesting observation, especially in connection with similar aspects concerning humankind, particularly the marriage relation, as given above.

that man is the "image" (צֶלֶם; Gen 1:26–27) of God. The human (marital) relationship between male and female is a special representation of the divine and as such bears a particular responsibility. This responsibility includes the feature of heterosexuality[206] and exclusivity[207] for it is only *one* man and *one* woman who are consummating the first, ideal marriage and there is no hint as to why this relation should or may be broken—if not (under post-Edenic conditions) by the death of a spouse, or by uniting intimately with some other person, thus dissolving the first bond by replacing it with another. Furthermore the creation account and the report about the Fall of Man teach that distinct priorities of loyalty must be given. God is to be at the first position, then comes the spouse; the other way round led to the expulsion from Eden. Hence, the important Edenic patterns concerning the "Edenic ideal," comprise the principle of combining one man with one woman in marriage, both subordinated to one God whose image they are and whom they are to represent in their dominion over the earth and their ability to multiply and thereby create new human beings. The perception of man as male and female, closely connected by the bond of marriage and "built" in the image of God, thus results in far-reaching responsibilities.

Practical consequences for man are further to be derived by the fact that it is God who made a perfect wife for Adam and brought her to him (Gen 2:23), what makes subsequent marriages seemingly claim to be consummated in a similar manner: with highest loyalty to God in view, accepting a partner of his choosing who is similarly loyal to the divine creator and who shares the goal of contributing to the loyal תּוֹלְדוֹת as emerging in the creation story, continued in the whole Genesis account, and finally the entire biblical plan of salvation.

As demonstrated by several aspects of the covenantal language used in different examples of the Hebrew Bible and especially Moses' writings, marriage is a question of loyalty in the highest sense. The first and highest allegiance is the one towards the creator God who made man and his wife. The second loyalty is the one of man regarding his wife who has been brought by God to him for the purpose of complementing him to the wider sense of (again) "becoming one flesh." The parents take the third place of loyalty.

Becoming "one flesh" in the sense of having sexual intercourse is the practical "completion" of the marital union, basing on the previous steps of "leaving" and "cleaving." Also, if the Edenic ideal as investigated in this chapter is understood as a divine marriage "norm"[208]—and according to the New Testament perspective this

---

206. Cf., for instance, Hasel, "Eheverständnis," 20–21; Bruner, *Matthew*, 670–71.

207. Cf. Instone-Brewer, *In the Bible*, 61; Loader, *LXX, Sexuality, and NT*, 42; Beale and Carson, *NT Use*, 198; Daube, *New Testament*, 81; Davidson, *Flame*, 21; Davidson, "Beginning," 22; Mathews, *Genesis 1–11:26*, 222; Tosato, "On Genesis 2:24," 407. More on this in the chapter about polygamy in the OT.

208. Cf. Lawton, "Gen. 2:24," 98; Tosato, "On Genesis 2:24," 404–9. "Gen 2:24 speaks of marriage in a normative way; that is to say, it does not speak of marriage as it was, but rather as it should have been; it explains marriage not as it was practiced (in particular, indiscriminately exposed to polygamy and divorce), but rather as it should have been practiced (in particular, generically linked

study bases on it clearly is (cf. Matt 19:4–6; Mark 10:6–9)—then, perhaps, the other Edenic conditions preceding the central core of Gen 2:24 also deserve attention. This would lead to a construction of altogether eight elements, step by step developing the perfect model:[209]

1. Realizing the need of a partner (Gen 2:19–20);
2. the partner should be a real counterpart, complement, and helper (Gen 2:18, 23);
3. he/she should be created by God;[210] and
4. they should be brought together by divine intervention/providence (Gen 2:22). If that is the case, further steps are:
5. leaving;
6. cleaving; and
7. becoming "one flesh" (all Gen 2:24), not to be separated unless
8. God intervenes again (by the death of the spouse).

Steps 5–7 are not to be made first. They would be the final consummation on the basis of the foregoing conditions (1–4). It actually seems as if in this way "the pattern is established and adjudged good. From then until the close of the biblical corpus it is the assumed norm."[211]

> Having planted, as it were, the originating context of the marriage covenant within the garden, this moral cosmology also sets, more broadly, a defining context and ideal for right conduct outside of it, specifically one that fosters partnership within family and community as well as partnership with the soil from which life emerges and is sustained. The garden, thus, sets the context for kinship and, *mutatis mutandi*, for covenantal service to creation.[212]

The first two chapters of Genesis thus

> provide the interpretive foundation for the rest of the scripture. . . . In particular, the profound portrayal of God's original design for human sexuality at the beginning of the canon constitutes the foundation for the rest of the biblical

---

to monogamy and indissolubility, *wĕhāyû šĕnêhem lĕbāśār ʾeḥād*)." Ibid., 404–5. Gen 2:24 represents "the *hieros logos* of a norm which is generically antipolygamous and antidivorce . . . ." Ibid.; referring to Seeligmann, "Aetiological Elements in Biblical Historiography," 141–69.

209. I am convinced the Genesis text does not intend to insist on the presented gender roles, but simply gives an exemplary structure!

210. Correspondingly, in the world after Eden, this would mean anyone accepting God as his or her creator, being loyal to him. According to 2 Cor 5:17 this especially applies to the "new creation" of Christian rebirth. More on these aspects will follow in the NT chapters.

211. Kinlaw, "Homosexuality," 105.

212. Brown, "Moral Cosmologies," 16.

narrative and discourse on human sexuality and encapsulates the fundamental principles of a theology of sexuality.[213]

Considering the various aforementioned aspects of the "one flesh" union and the fact that it was Moses as "founder" of Israel who bequeathed these contents as a theological "foundation" to Israel, one may acknowledge the importance and significance of a right understanding and good practice of marriage for sake of Israel's blessing. Of course it was not without reason that severe laws concerning sexual misbehavior would follow (cf. e.g., Lev 18; 20), and even curses (cf. Deut 27:20–23) that would seriously injure the people if not faithfully "cleaving" to the Lord and his covenant. As will be investigated in more depth below, the experiences of Israel further demonstrate and emphasize that. In order to spare his people God told them:

> When the Lord your God brings you into the land where you are entering to possess it, and clears away many nations before you, the Hittites and the Girgashites and the Amorites and the Canaanites and the Perizzites and the Hivites and the Jebusites, seven nations greater and stronger than you, and when the Lord your God delivers them before you and you defeat them, then you shall utterly destroy them. You shall make no covenant with them and show no favor to them. Furthermore, you shall not intermarry with them; you shall not give your daughters to their sons, nor shall you take their daughters for your sons. For they will turn your sons away from following Me to serve other gods; then the anger of the Lord will be kindled against you, and He will quickly destroy you. But thus you shall do to them: you shall tear down their altars, and smash their sacred pillars, and hew down their Asherim, and burn their graven images with fire.[214]

It surely is very meaningful that God frequently warns about making a covenant with foreign peoples and immediately turns to the subject of (inter-) marriage.[215] Obviously he regards marriage as a covenant (cf. Prov 2:17; Mal 2:14), and covenants are not to be made with infidels. Yet, just that happened finally to Israel, as 1 Kgs 11:1–10;

---

213. Davidson, *Flame*, 15–16; cf. Davidson, "Beginning," 5, 20; Nichol and Andreasen, *ABC*, Gen. 2:22, 1:226: "The woman was formed for inseparable unity and fellowship of life with the man, and the mode of her creation was to lay the actual foundation for the moral ordinance of marriage." Similarly Kaye, "One Flesh," 49; concerning marriage: Hasel, "Eheverständnis," 18; Von Rad, *Erstes Buch Mose*, 59–60; Schlier, *Epheser*, 263.

214. Deut 7:1–5.

215. See e.g., Exod 34:12–16: "Watch yourself that you make no covenant with the inhabitants of the land into which you are going, or it will become a snare in your midst. But rather, you are to tear down their altars and smash their sacred pillars and cut down their Asherim—for you shall not worship any other god, for the Lord, whose name is Jealous, is a jealous God—otherwise you might make a covenant with the inhabitants of the land and they would play the harlot with their gods and sacrifice to their gods, and someone might invite you to eat of his sacrifice, and you might take some of his daughters for your sons, and his daughters might play the harlot with their gods and cause your sons also to play the harlot with their gods."

Ezra 9–10; and Neh 13:23–30 attest. And even heathen nations recognized the cause of their misfortune, as Hecataeus of Abdera demonstrates:

> As to the marriage and the burial of the dead, [Moses] saw to it that their customs should differ widely from those of other men. But later, when they became subject to foreign rule, as a result of their mingling with men of other nations . . .[216]

While this Greek ethnographer does not explain in detail what has been changed in marital practices, we can reasonably assume that "already, 400 years prior to the rabbinic period, Jewish communities had apparently lost the remains of their distinctive marital practices"[217]—as given in the Edenic ideal and its amplification in the Mosaic laws. Hence, Israel finally lost the covenant's blessing, God's approval and protection.

I.1.2 Everlastingness and Monogamy (Deut 24:1–4 et al)

Before the investigation of the New Testament texts can be processed on a solid basis, it is important to understand whether God designed to give regulations for divorce or for living in polygamy, thus denying a lifelong relationship in (at least) some special cases of a much later time under very different (cultural) conditions. While, due to the limitations of this study, it is not possible to give an extensive treatise on these important (and for our topic in some way even essential) subjects, at least an investigation of the existing research must be provided, presenting my own interpretation of the findings which supports the understanding of marriage as inherently connected with everlastingness and monogamy.[218] At least a brief discussion of these characteristics of the Mosaic legislation seems necessary for two important reasons: (1) to present a firm foundation for interpreting the NT intertextual references particularly concerning Deut 24:1–4 that is brought about by the Pharisees against Jesus; (2) to demonstrate that the divine, Edenic ideal was not essentially injured by the much later divine instructions given through Moses. Although the laws at Sinai take account of different cultural conditions that, of course, were not present in Eden, the original ideal is still discernable (and finally rediscovered by Jesus).

I.1.2.1 Divorce as Unintended Deviation

To begin with, the prominent "divorce" case of Deut 24:1–4 reads as follows:[219]

---

216. Quoted in Diodorus Siculus, Bib. Hist. 40, 3, 8; cf. Satlow, "Rabbinic Views," 612. For a thorough investigation of Hecataeus' statement, its literary aspects and the meaning for Jewish ethnography see Bloch, *Judenexkurs*, 27–41.

217. Satlow, "Rabbinic Views," 612.

218. These interpretations are often closely linked with the New Testament texts and therefore will be deepened and extended in the chapters on the NT passages.

219. For a detailed linguistic outline see Warren, "Did Moses permit Divorce?," 43–45; note also his further grammatical discussion of this passage.

- (24:1) When a man takes a wife and marries her, and it happens that she finds no favor in his eyes because he has found some indecency in her, and he writes her a certificate of divorce and puts it in her hand and sends her out from his house,
- (24:2) and she leaves his house and goes and becomes another man's wife,
- (24:3) and if the latter husband turns against her and writes her a certificate of divorce and puts it in her hand and sends her out of his house, or if the latter husband dies who took her to be his wife,
- (24:4) then her former husband who sent her away is not allowed to take her again to be his wife, since she has been defiled; for that is an abomination before the Lord, and you shall not bring sin on the land which the Lord your God gives you as an inheritance.

This is the first of three texts dealing with the "certificate of divorce" (סֵפֶר כְּרִיתֻת), while the other two occurrences (Isa 50:1; Jer 3:8) only refer to the one stipulated above. Hence, this is not much instruction on any explicit dealing in a case of divorce, and apparently it is not even intended to represent some kind of a "divorce law." One rather finds that "Dtn 24,1–4 einen eher außergewöhnlichen Rechtsfall behandelt und nicht ein eigentliches Ehescheidungsgesetz darstellt; ein solches ist im gesamten Alten Testament nicht zu finden."[220] Furthermore,

> the way in which the bill of divorce is spoken of, however, makes it obvious that it is not being introduced in this injunction but is being taken for granted as an already well known and recognized procedure. [. . . However,] in giving this injunction, he [i.e., Moses] did not wish to introduce divorce as a recognized institution. He assumes that, in accordance with long-standing custom, divorces will occur and he wishes to lay down legal forms and detailed instructions for dealing with them . . . he considers them a necessary evil.[221]

It is evident that vv. 1–3 are the protasis, while v. 4 is the apodosis and as such represents the required dealing if the aforementioned conditions of this concrete, special case are given.[222] It is apparently not dealing with divorce itself, but just with a special case, thereby necessarily referring to a custom that is nowhere else in the laws recognized as legal institution of Israel. "What might especially interest us is therefore incidental. The main point is the prohibition of remarriage to the former husband. Important incidental details are the following: the grounds for divorce, the bill of divorce and the fact that the woman has been defiled."[223]

---

220. Neudecker, "Ehescheidungsgesetz," 350; similarly Beale and Carson, *NT Use*, 196: "Our passage belongs to a series of miscellaneous civil and domestic regulations (21:10—25:19). It is concerned not with divorce laws per se, which the Torah nowhere fully explicates but rather assumes . . . ." Similarly Ryrie, "Biblical Teaching," 179: "In fact the passage only recognizes that divorce was being practiced, but it never prescribes it." Cf. Craigie, *Deuteronomy*, 304–5.

221. Isaksson, *Marriage and Ministry*, 21–22.

222. Cf. also Loader, *LXX, Sexuality, and NT*, 71; Wevers, *Greek Text*, 377; Berger, *Gesetzesauslegung*, 513.

223. Loader, *LXX, Sexuality, and NT*, 71.

The Old Testament Foundation

However, the only reason for a possible divorce is just vaguely stated.²²⁴ Nonetheless, the elements of an offence might be illumined by scrutinizing the expressions in the original text. While many exegetes have already undertaken the work of interpreting the term עֶרְוַת דָּבָר,²²⁵ in context of Deut 24:1–4 we notice that it must refer to some special kind of transgression against the marriage relation. It occurs in only further instance in immediate proximity: Deut 23:15. Isaksson asserts:

> Verse 12 of chap. 23 mentions that there is to be a place outside the camp at which all faeces from the camp are to be buried. This is to be done lest Yahweh, when he walks through the camp, should find ערות דבר (=something exposed). It is clear that here דבר stands for human excrement. It is accordingly a euphemism. Yahweh must not see excrement lying about exposed. The expression is similarly used as a euphemism in Dt. 24. 1 but here it does not stand for human excrement but for the female pudendum.²²⁶

The LXX text in Deut 24:1 only states that any kind of "unseemly, shameful act" (ἄσχημον πρᾶγμα) has been committed, or "the private parts [of the body]"²²⁷ have been exposed. But the Hebrew lemma עֶרְוָה more clearly means "nakedness, genital area (of both sexes)"²²⁸ and might best be translated "the nakedness of a thing."²²⁹

---

224. Considering that v. 3 speaks about the second husband and just tells that he "turns against her" (NASB) or "hate her" (KJV), we have to assume that this is a formula for anything that might be meant by "indecency" in v. 1, since (1) there is no other legislation with reasons or conditions given, and (2) both result in the same "bill of divorce," indicating the fact that both instances deal with the same problem. Cf. on this opinion also Davidson, *Flame*, 394; Gane, "Old Testament Principles," 41; Driver, *Deuteronomy*, 271. It even more seems that this passage is not primarily meant to give any reasons. It rather intends to regulate common practice and to forbid a hasty divorce and remarriage. Grelot argues in the same way and reasons: "The ultimate effect of this legislation is to regulate customs that were common throughout the ancient East, thus giving the Israelites a system adapted on the one hand to their economic and social organization and, on the other, to the fundamental imperatives of faith. . . . Positive law is not the consequence of an ideal principle derived from revelation; it provides the framework for an actual situation determined by the culture of the times." Grelot, "The Institution of Marriage," 42.

225. References will follow, see the other footnotes below in this chapter. On the ancient Rabbinic diversity in interpreting this word see *m. Giṭ.* 9:10. A thorough analysis of the Rabbinic accounts on the understanding and practice of divorce will be given as a background in the discussion of Jesus' speeches.

226. Isaksson, *Marriage and Ministry*, 25–26.

227. Cf. LSJ/BDAG s.v. ἀσχήμων. Philo refers to the reason for divorce as πρόφασις (in *Spec.* 3:30), what either means "valid excuse" or even a "falsely alleged motive/pretext/excuse/pretense," cf. FRI/LSJ/BDAG s.v. πρόφασις. Regarding the usage of the same word in *Spec.* 3:80, Neudecker concludes: "Aus diesen Texten geht hervor, daß das Wort πρόφασις im Gegensatz zu Verleumdung und falscher Anklage steht und das Offenliegende, nicht das Verborgene, betrifft . . . . Mit anderen Worten: ערות דבר wird in der obigen Paraphrase [i.e., *Spec.* 3:80–82] im weiten Sinn (καθ' ἣν ἂν τύχῃ) jedoch mit Berufung auf Tatsachen (πρόφασις) ausgelegt." Neudecker, "Ehescheidungsgesetz," 356/fn.9. For further investigations of Philo's understanding see ibid., 356–60; Loader, *LXX, Sexuality, and NT*, 76–80.

228. Cf. HALOT s.v. עֶרְוָה.

229. Thus e.g., Gane, "Old Testament Principles," 41 (see also pp. 42–49); Driver, *Deuteronomy*, 270; Amram, *Divorce*, 33; Davidson, "Divorce and Remarriage," 5 (see also pp. 6–9); Berger, *Gesetzesauslegung*, 511; Shaner, *Christian View*, 35. The rabbinic interpretation as given by the house of Hillel

Obviously both texts agree and "it is difficult to speak of the LXX as distinctive in substance or emphasis."[230] Also, the texts of Deut 23:15 and Deut 24:1 agree in their general thrust and stylistic (euphemistic) appearance. Additionally, in Deuteronomy one can observe a generally "more periphrastic sexual terminology than in the corresponding portions of Leviticus."[231] Yet, if it should only be dealing with "nakedness" on the woman's part, we have to consider

> A. Isaksson has argued that the phrase means: indecent exposure; the woman has voluntarily or involuntarily, exposed her private parts.... This would certainly make sense in both Old Testament occurrences (Deut 23:14; 24:1), would explain the choice of words ('nakedness of a thing') especially in view of the Israelite abhorrence of nakedness (e.g., Exod 20:26), and in other situations clearly did cause the disgust of the marriage partner (2 Sam 6:12–20; Ezek 23:18). However, it seems so very specific and unusual that it makes this whole law—already subject to unusual circumstances—apply to almost nobody. It seems more likely, therefore, that it is of a rather more general, very probably sexual, nature. Driver suggests 'immodest or indecent behavior.'[232]

Given the fact that adultery results in death-penalty, it would be likely that any other kind of "immorality," respectively sexual dysfunction (impotence, infertility),[233] or at least a "shameful" behavior, might be a legal reason to divorce. Cornes explains that

---

in *m. Giṭ.* 9:10 is invalid (see for more details concerning this debate Neudecker, "Ehescheidungsgesetz," 362–84 and the investigation on the NT backgrounds of Mark 10:2–12 and Matt 19:3–9). Others translate less exactly and even more vaguely "something obnoxious" Beale and Carson, *NT Use*, 196. The conclusion of Ellens, *Sex Texts*, 248 that "the law of Deut 24: 1–4 concerns property issues related to special circumstances of divorce. The law is not about sexual impurity and does not regulate sexual intercourse" apparently concerns the basic category of this law, not the matters involved; for something pertaining to the realm of sexuality is of course spoken of by the vague עֶרְוַת דָּבָר of v. 1.

230. Loader, *LXX, Sexuality, and NT*, 75.

231. Isaksson, *Marriage and Ministry*, 26. "Thus the euphemistic phrase קרה לילה (Dt. 23.11) is used to designate the emission of semen during the night, while in the corresponding injunction Leviticus used שכבת זרע (Lev 15.16). Leviticus often uses גלה ערוה (Lev 18.6–19) to denote sexual intercourse, while Deuteronomy uses שכב עם throughout, possibly combined with גלה כנף (Dt. 22.22, 23.1, 27.20).... While Leviticus speaks of uncovering the nakedness of a father (18.7–8, 20.11), Deuteronomy speaks of uncovering the skirt of a father (23.1, 27.20). Thus here also Deuteronomy avoids directly mentioning the pudendum." Ibid.

232. Cornes, *Divorce and Remarriage*, 133; cf. Isaksson, *Marriage and Ministry*, 25–27; Davidson, *Flame*, 391. He also recognizes an indecent exposure of the private parts. See also Merrill, *Deuteronomy*, 317.

233. The Mishnah also suggests that some kind of infertility is meant in this instance; so *m. Yebam.* 4:11b tells that a man shall prefer a fertile woman; cf. also: *m. Giṭ.* 8:6–7; Craigie, *Deuteronomy*, 304–5; Loader, *LXX, Sexuality, and NT*, 75; Amram, *Divorce*, 99–100. Philo even calls it "intemperate pleasure" (ἡδονῆς ἀκράτορος) to have relations with a barren woman (see *Spec.* 3:34) and recommends divorce if the spouses are not "unable to break through the power of those ancient charms [the habit of familiarity] which by long habituation are stamped upon their souls." *Spec.* 3:35. It is known from more primitive cultures men often are allowed to take another wife besides the first, if it becomes known that the first wife is barren; cf. Thiel, "Marriage," 16–17.

the penalty for adultery in the Mosaic legislation was not divorce but death (Deut 22:22; Lev 20:10; John 8:4–5, cf. Gen 38:24)—or if there was any human doubt in the matter, God's curse of a terrible, wasting disease (Num 5:11–31). For precisely the same reason, 'something indecent' cannot mean pre-marital sex, either while the woman was engaged (Deut 22:23–24) or at any time before her marriage (Deut 22:13–21).[234]

Atkinson further argues:

> It meant rather some other (sexual?) misconduct which was sufficient to justify the withholding of heavy divorce duties which would be needed for a divorce if the wife were not guilty. A. Isaksson, noted that the expression occurs also in Deut 23:14, and so suggests that in Deut 24:1 it refers to the wife's indecent exposure. Calum M. Carmichael, arguing from the formal arrangement of legal material in Deuteronomy, also thinks 'some indecency' refers to the embarrassment caused to the husband by the wife's public behaviour.[235]

However, the exact sort of "transgression" is unfortunately not mentioned, but "something less than adultery must be meant here.... Being guilty of 'something indecent,' however, is more than trivial. It must have sufficient grounds to be alleged as 'something indecent.'"[236] Yet, Merrill suggests that the sin described by עֶרְוַת דָּבָר means, or at least includes, adultery.[237] He argues from Jesus' speech in Matt 19:9 where he refers to the bill of divorce in Deuteronomy and equates "fornication" (πορνεία) with "committing adultery" (μοιχάω),[238] as is obviously the case in the apocryphal book Susanna (v. 63), where no ἄσχημον πρᾶγμα (the עֶרְוַת דָּבָר in the LXX on Deut 24:1) was found.[239] This also accords with the slightly different rendering in the Targum Onkelos on Deut 24:1, where it reads עבירת פתגם ("sentence of sin"), expressly pointing to a "sin" (עבירה) in the sense of breaking a commandment—most likely the seventh.[240] For those who recognize a possible contradiction because adultery is to be punished

---

234. Cornes, *Divorce and Remarriage*, 132–33. Cf. also Cosby, *Sex in the Bible*, 17–20 Nichol and Andreasen, *ABC*, Deu. 24:1, 1:1036–37; Tarwater, *Marriage as Covenant*, 114.

235. Atkinson, *To Have and to Hold*, 103.

236. Kalland, "Deuteronomy," 145; cf. Ryrie, "Biblical Teaching," 181; Davidson, "Scheidung und Wiederheirat," 160.

237. Merrill, *Deuteronomy*, 317. Davidson concurs with him. (See Davidson, *Flame*, 391/fn.52. On the other hand, Merrill holds it possible that this legislation in Deuteronomy is of an older conception, which later was changed [or differently interpreted] and thus became applicable in cases of adultery. Merrill, *Deuteronomy*, 318.)

238. The same point is made by e.g., Sigal, *Halakhah*, 114, who sums up: "In effect, then, Jesus did not abrogate Deut 24:1, he exegeted *'erwat dabar* to mean *porneia*."

239. Cf. Loader, *LXX, Sexuality, and NT*, 75. Besides the explanations given in this passage, a more detailed discussion about similarities and differences between πορνεία and μοιχάω will be presented within the NT section.

240. Cf. CAL s.v. עבירה; Strack and Billerbeck, *Talmud und Midrasch*, 1:314–15; Sigal, *Halakhah*, 110–11; similarly Instone-Brewer, "What God has Joined," 28 asserts that "most Jews recognized that this unusual phrase [עֶרְוַת דָּבָר] was talking about adultery."

by death, it might be asserted that one could understand this instruction as regulating cases of mercy; or as a second procedure if the first (death-penalty) is not executed due to whatever the reason may be.[241]

What that "nakedness of a thing" means exactly, however, cannot be (more) dependably determined due to the "riddle-like quality of the words,"[242] but it must be clear that evident misbehavior in the field of sexuality is meant.[243] So עֶרְוַת דָּבָר might indeed be compared to πορνεία, the word Jesus uses in New Testament times and which also covers a wide range of meaning, also summarized under the term "adultery" in cases of married couples.[244] That also fits the meaningful interpretation of Deut 24:1–4 as given by the prophet Jeremiah (see Jer 3:1–13), who unambiguously points to "her adulteries" (נָאַף) that make her "faithless" (מְשׁוּבָה; v. 8) and finally, after a long period of suffering, urge God to send her away with a certificate of divorce (סֵפֶר כְּרִיתוּת). That is the פֶּשַׁע ("transgression") mentioned in Isa 50:1 as rationale of the same writ. Consequently, the עֶרְוַת דָּבָר in Deut 24:1 most likely is just this kind of sexual misconduct.

Furthermore, considering the above mentioned "more periphrastic sexual terminology" in Deuteronomy compared to Leviticus, עֶרְוַת דָּבָר might indeed be a synonym for the πορνεία Jesus referred to (cf. Matt 5:32; 19:9 etc.; this certainly includes μοιχεύω, which is comprised by the broader term πορνεία). The Hebrew term apparently

---

241. Something very similar is to be witnessed in Deut 27:20–23; there are special curses on sins, which usually entail death-penalty. Also, we find special case laws regarding kings (Deut 17:14–20), although God never intended to set a monarch over Israel (1 Sam 8:7). We find laws against prostitutes bringing their wages to the sanctuary (Deut 23:19), although there should not be even one such woman in Israel (Exod 20:14; Lev 19:29; 21:9; Deut 22:21; 23:18). And finally we have a huge amount of reports concerning unlawful conditions in Israel and Juda even from the times of Joshua and the judges until the Babylonian exile (just for example: Judg 14:1–3; 16:1; 1 Kgs 14:24; Jer 2:20; Ezek 16 etc.). Hence, one must admit that case laws may be given without ignoring the fact that these special ordinances overlap with other laws that might not be executed properly. Furthermore, the death penalty on adultery "was not widely enforced in NT times." Blomberg, "Exegesis," 177.

242. Christensen, *Deuteronomy 21:10—34:12*, 566. Christensen asserts that "the phrase means that the issue at hand, whatever it is, is out in the open for all to see—the woman 'is caught with her pudenda exposed.'" Ibid., 567.

243. That is an almost common assumption of most scholars. Sexual misconduct or "indecent exposure" could be understood to mean "that a wife improperly uncovers herself without physical contact of her sexual body parts with those of another person . . . not covering her arms or head in public or bathing in the presence of one or more adult males other than her husband [. . . or] 'improper conduct with a man other than her husband,' e.g., kissing him, allowing him to fondle her, acting in a lewd or sexually suggestive manner, or otherwise flirting, thereby tempting him to covet her (in violation of the tenth of the Ten Commandments—Exod 20:17; Deut 5:21; cp. Matt 5:28)." Gane, "Old Testament Principles," 45. The more simplistic explanation of possible reasons as given by Josephus ("for any cause whatever, and many such causes happen among men,"—καθ' ἁσδηποτοῦν αἰτίας πολλαὶ δ' ἂν τοῖς ἀνθρώποις τοιαῦται; *A.J.* 4:253), which is possibly reflected likewise in Matt 19: ("for any reason"—κατὰ πᾶσαν αἰτίαν) is generally invalid, for it evidently exceeds the given facts of Deut 24:1 and the solid insights that the expression עֶרְוַת דָּבָר suggests.

244. There are many overlaps in Jesus' speech and the law given in Deut 24. Taking the intertextuality of Deut 24:1–4 and the NT disputes into consideration, we should finally be able to get more detailed allusions about the legal reasons for divorce. We will examine that below in the NT part ("Jesus about divorce") and then draw more concrete conclusions.

reflects the similarly sounding, most unambiguous and strikingly clear formulations in Lev 18 and 20, frequently using גלה ערוה ("uncover nakedness"), thereby evidently referring to illegal sexuality.[245] But any sexuality, apart from the relations with one's own husband, is illegal and tantamount to adultery, thereby again resembling the גלה ערוה of Lev 18 and 20 and breaking the "one flesh" union of the creational ideal in Gen 2:24. Just like "becoming one flesh" is the consummation of marriage, again "becoming one flesh" with another partner than one's own spouse is dissolving/breaking the Edenic bonds of marriage. That is exactly what Jesus is teaching in the New Testament, as will be demonstrated below.

However, regardless of the actual reason for divorce (obviously even if there might not have been a legal reason at all, for death should have been the legal result of any sexual transgression) the man is not allowed to take his former wife again when she had a new relation since.[246] She is characterized as being טָמֵא ("defiled") and it would be an abomination (תּוֹעֵבָה) to take her again. It is very interesting that the woman is called "defiled" already before possibly taking her former husband for a second time. Consequently, she has been defiled either "by the second marriage"[247]

---

245. Most interesting, even the very similar sounding instance in Ezek 23:18 supports this view and thus stands diametrically against the interpretation of the same text by Isaksson; cf. Isaksson, *Marriage and Ministry*, 26–27. Ezekiel says: "She uncovered (גִּלָּה) her harlotries (תַּזְנוּת) and uncovered (גִּלָּה) her nakedness (עֶרְוָה); then I became disgusted (נָקַע) with her . . . ." The whole chapter is metaphorically talking about the unfaithfulness of Israel as Yahweh's wife and frequently mentions different "harlotries" by which "adultery" (cf. vv. 37, 43) is committed. The close similarity to Deut 24:1, where a man is disgusted by "a thing of nakedness" done by his wife, is evident and it might be very likely to assume an equal context of sexual misbehavior, viz., harlotry/adultery. Just like the man in Deut 24:1 does not hand over his wife to the Israelite jurisdiction in order to kill her but is merciful and writes a bill of divorce, so Yahweh circumvents the strict death-punishment by mercifully giving her a "bill of divorce" (cf. Isa 50:1; Jer 3:8); although he later learns that she does not repent (cf. Jer 3:8–10)—and only then he finally considers killing her (cf. Ezek 23:45–49).

246. On the overall aspect and the special topic of prohibiting to retake one's former wife cf. Richter, *Geschlechtlichkeit*, 1:80–83. "Die eigentliche Aussage des oben zitierten Textes ist offenbar, daß eine unter den genannten Bedingungen geschiedene Ehe nicht mehr erneuert werden darf, wenn die Frau inzwischen von einem anderen Mann geheiratet worden ist. . . . Zudem wird dieser eine dritte Ehe nicht untersagt. Sie darf lediglich ihren ersten Mann nicht wiederheiraten. Wodurch erwächst aber die Gefahr, daß das ganze Land sündig wird, wenn diese Frau zu ihrem ersten Ehemann zurückkehren würde? Der Grund für diese auf den ersten Blick fremdartig wirkende Bestimmung dürfte wohl der sein, daß durch sie jeder Art von Zuhälterei ein Riegel vorgeschoben werden soll. (Ohne vorherige 'Entlassung' hatte ein israelitischer Ehemann seine Frau nicht einem anderen Mann überlassen können, weil das Ehebruch mit Todesstrafe gewesen wäre.) Der Text möchte mit der Proklamation der Endgültigkeit einer Ehescheidung, die in dem Augenblick da ist, wo die Frau ihrerseits sich an einen anderen Mann bindet, klare Verhältnisse schaffen." (Ibid., 80–81.) Cf. Isaksson, *Marriage and Ministry*, 22–25!

247. Kalland, "Deuteronomy," 145; cf. also Merrill, *Deuteronomy*, 316, who concerning the defilement of the divorced woman confesses: "Why the remarriage of the original partners was thus described while the divorcée's marriage to a second husband was not is not clear. Most likely it is because the original divorce was not for adultery (otherwise the death penalty would apply) whereas remarriage after an intervening marriage and divorce would be construed as adultery because of the woman's moving from one man to the next and back again. She had thus become an adulteress, and for this reason it was she (and not the act) who was referred to as detestable . . . ." Ibid., 318. Stienstra, *YHWH is the Husband*, 89 confirms: ". . . it seems as if it is indeed the intercourse with another man,

or it just "refers to the woman in relation to her first husband and [is] not a general state brought about by her remarriage."²⁴⁸ Davidson scrutinized this verse and the particular terms concluding that there is a distinctive and cogent linkage between the "defilement" (טָמֵא) in Deut 24:4, the same term in Lev 18 and the unfaithful wife in Num 5:13–14, 20.²⁴⁹ The "defilement" in these closely linked legislations always refers to illicit sexual intercourse with another man than the wife's husband; "the implication of this intertextuality between Deut 24:4, Lev 18, and Num 5 is that in Deut 24:4 the sexual activity of the divorced woman with the second husband is tantamount to adultery or some other illicit sexual intercourse . . . ."²⁵⁰

Philo understands the text similarly. In *Spec.* 3:30 he explains that the woman is defiled by sexual intercourse with a second man, thus claiming that the certificate of divorce is some matter of technical regulation, but actually not really dissolving the partnership in God's view. Thus, again, it is like adultery to remarry if the case of "indecency" has not been the adulterous (and therefore marriage dissolving) πορνεία that Jesus mentioned in Matt 5:32 and 19:9.²⁵¹

But it is very important to notice, that it is not the woman who defiles herself by marrying another husband after the expulsion by the former. A more exact translation of the phrase "she has been defiled" (Deut 24:4) would be "*has been caused* to defile

---

whether it be a second husband or a lover, that renders the woman 'polluted.'" See also Craigie, *Deuteronomy*, 305; Wenham, "Restoration," 36–40.)

248. Christensen, *Deuteronomy 21:10—34:12*, 567. Similarly, the ABC understands the uncleanness as referring only to the ambition of taking the previous husband again: "Consummation of marriage with a second husband made her unclean to her first husband. For him ever to take her again would be to commit adultery. She was unlawful to him (see Jer 3:1)." Nichol and Andreasen, *ABC*, Deu. 24:4, 1:1037.

249. Cf. Davidson, *Flame*, 395–96; Davidson, "Divorce and Remarriage," 11–15. He clearly states that "Leviticus 18 is the only other chapter of the HB [Hebrew Bible] that combines these three terms/ideas [i.e., the words טָמֵא—'defile;' תּוֹעֵבָה—'abomination;' and the idea of bringing defilement upon the land] in one context, and seems undoubtedly to be intertexually connected with Deut 24:4 in the final form of the Pentateuch." Davidson, *Flame*, 395.

250. Davidson, *Flame*, 396; Davidson, "Divorce and Remarriage," 12; cf. also Driver, *Deuteronomy*, 272; Craigie, *Deuteronomy*, 305; Kalland, "Deuteronomy," 146; Keil and Delitzsch, *The Pentateuch*, 3:418. But there is no punishment given for this defilement, since it happens after the official divorce and, therefore, with the (former) husband's consent. However, just these are the words of Christ in Matt 5:32 and 19:9, who calls it "committing adultery" (μοιχάω) to have another (sexual) relationship, even after divorce from the former spouse, if there has not been adultery as reason of divorce.

251. Cf. on this point also Neudecker, "Ehescheidungsgesetz," 357–60. Craigie clearly points out: "If the woman were then to remarry her first husband, after divorcing the second, the analogy with adultery would become even more complete; the woman lives first with one man, then another, and finally returns to the first." Craigie, *Deuteronomy*, 305. That explains the "abomination" in the sight of the Lord. Apparently, leaving one husband and then, finally, cleaving to another one is not as defiling as afterwards returning back to the first and thereby completing the facts of adultery. On the other hand, the first husband is in some way punished, too; he is not allowed to take her again. Thus the act of divorce is even more severe and determines the separation once and for all. Consequently, it demands to examine the cause of divorce very thoroughly; there should be no hasty separations, for they are final and irreversible.

herself" (in the hotpa'al form).[252] Not the woman and not her second husband are the cause of the defilement, but "the ultimate cause, implicit in this rare grammatical form, must be the first husband. The legislation subtly implicates the first husband for divorcing his wife;"[253] and thereby clearly indicates a divine disapproval of this act, finally causing the divorced wife to defile herself—if the reason for divorce has not been adultery anyway.

Again one thing is very evident; it is another confirmation of the fact that an ideal, perfect relationship consists in having not more than one spouse and lasting for a lifetime. Therefore, divorce indeed is merely a compromise. This consideration is strengthened by the fact that there is no further reference or any instruction given on how to write a certificate of divorce[254] or any other detail on how to divorce in a way Yahweh really could "approve." Seemingly he does not approve it in any way, but he merely deals with the established custom and tries to regulate the minimum that seems necessary.[255] In fact, divorce itself is nowhere regulated in the OT; Deut 24:1–4 is just dealing with one matter of a possible *result*![256]

Atkinson emphasizes the same point by discussing different translations and finally concluding that

> the Deuteronomic legislation is a *permission* and not a *prescription*. In other words, this passage does not make divorce mandatory; it does not even encourage or advise men to put away their wives if they are guilty of 'some indecency' (v. 1). It cannot even be said to sanction divorce, though it recognizes that divorces happen . . . .[257]

Furthermore he suggests that this passage simply is meant to prohibit taking a former wife who has meanwhile been married to another man. Thus, the bill of

---

252. Davidson, *Flame*, 396; italics given. Obviously the text emphasizes the same idea later stressed by Jesus: "I say to you that everyone who divorces his wife, except for the cause of unchastity, *makes her commit adultery* . . ." (Matt 5:32; my italics). This is true when not assuming that it is the simple passive form ("she was defiled") without concrete agent; cf. Joüon and Muraoka, *Biblical Hebrew*, 147—what is at least possible, though not probable.

253. Davidson, *Flame*, 396–97; cf. Davidson, "Divorce and Remarriage," 12–13.

254. The only possible hint could be the wording in Hos 2:4 reading "she is not my wife, and I am not her husband." Cf. Davidson, *Flame*, 392: "Such a statement would mean the legal breaking of the marriage covenant just as surely as the death of the marriage partner." But there is no concrete instruction given in the Torah or the entire OT how to formulate and verify the document, and Davidson later makes clear that there is no real divorce between Yahweh and Israel mentioned in Hos 2:4. Ibid., 410.

255. So Kalland concludes, "divorce in the books of Moses . . . appears as a fact of social life; while under certain circumstances it was permitted, it was to be regulated." Kalland, "Deuteronomy," 145; cf. also Merrill, *Deuteronomy*, 316. Cornes asserts: "Again, we need to stress: it was not directly legislated for, it was not encouraged; but it was also not prohibited. Otherwise, it would have been impossible to have a law of this nature." Cornes, *Divorce and Remarriage*, 132.

256. Cf. Nembach, "Ehescheidung," 161; Neudecker, "Ehescheidungsgesetz," 350.

257. Atkinson, *To Have and to Hold*, 102–3; italics given. Cf. Isaksson, *Marriage and Ministry*, 21, 25; Ryrie, "Biblical Teaching," 179: "In fact the passage only recognizes that divorce was being practiced, but it never prescribes it."

divorce should only be an instrument to guarantee and regulate these unwanted cases, it apparently was not meant to legalize it.²⁵⁸ Furthermore, regarding the aspect of a possible remarriage in the investigated law Merrill explains that it is just a hypothetical case and that "the grammatical evidence from the sequence of clauses (*ki* + *waw* conjunctive) does not demand that remarriage here be necessarily sanctioned just because divorce was allowed in the first place."²⁵⁹

Whatever the (sexual) "indecency" as legitimate reason for divorce may have been exactly, it is important to notice that "her husband can forgive her and continue to love her and retain her as his wife. He does not have to submit to pressure to get rid of her . . . ."²⁶⁰ There is no command given that compels someone to divorce whatever the case may be like. Moreover the words "she finds no favor in his eyes because he has found some indecency in her" (Deut 24:1) are meaningful because "the 'indecency' must be the real reason for the breakdown of the relationship, not simply an excuse for divorce on other grounds."²⁶¹

Also Deut 24:1–4 is embedded in the wider context of property and theft,²⁶² thus implying to present legislation against treating women "as mere chattel, to be swapped back and forth at will. . . . The law is aimed, in its final placement within the larger context, to protect the woman from being robbed of her personhood."²⁶³ To sum up, there are many problems in this short paragraph. Deducing a full legal status in these problematic cases is hard to argue—and most probably has not been Yahweh's intention. Other passages supposedly dealing with some kind of divorce support that understanding.²⁶⁴

---

258. Cf. also Nies, "Divorce and Remarriage," 2:2; Davidson, *Flame*, 384; Gane, "Old Testament Principles," 39; Laney, "Deuteronomy 24:1–4," 9. We have especially to keep in mind that we see here a casuistic (case) law, not an apodictic law! Hence, we find a regulation belonging to a special situation (remarriage of formerly divorced spouse), not a general stipulation like "You shall divorce if . . . ." The law does not fully deal with divorce at all (i.e., just secondarily), but only with a special case of remarriage. "The implication is clear: God is in no wise legislating or even sanctioning divorce in this passage. In fact, the whole passage may be expressing tacit disapproval although the divorce is tolerated and not punished." Davidson, "Divorce and Remarriage," 4–5; cf. Neudecker, "Ehescheidungsgesetz," 350.

259. Merrill, *Deuteronomy*, 316; cf. 1 Cor 7:11!

260. Gane, "Old Testament Principles," 39. At least Nembach, "Ehescheidung," 162–63, doubts the thesis that the husband was not under pressure to divorce his wife in order to save the integrity of the land that otherwise might spew them out. He further examines the ancient Jewish law as established in Mishnah and Gemara to support the view that at least in New Testament times some strong reasons to enforce divorce must have been existing; cf. pp. 164–66.

261. Gane, "Old Testament Principles," 39.

262. Cf. Deut 23:16—24:22; cf. Davidson, "Divorce and Remarriage," 3–4.

263. Davidson, *Flame*, 403. He reinforces this aspect by referring to v. 5, dealing with a newly married couple, where the man should "be free at home one year and shall give happiness to his wife whom he has taken." Thus "the law protects against robbing the newly married couple of their intimacy and happiness, and it especially protects the happiness of the wife." Ibid., 403–4; cf. on aspects of protection also Gane, "Old Testament Principles," 50–51 and 40/fn.6c referring to Luck, *Divorce and Remarriage*, 61. See also Beale and Carson, *NT Use*, 196: ". . . perhaps preferably, it [Deut 24:1–4] sought to prevent the woman from being treated as an object in subordination to the man's interests.")

264. The instructions of Deut 24:1–4 obviously deal with Hebrew couples, but there is another

The Old Testament Foundation

Finally, it is the land which Israel is going to inhabit that will be affected gravely by living thus immorally; it is תּוֹעֵבָה ("abomination;" Deut 24:4).²⁶⁵ In the last consequence "the land" would have (by God's command) to "spew" Israel out—just like the pagan nations before them (cf. again Lev 18:24–25). Apparently they will become like pagans if dealing thus carelessly with a matter of that importance. Hence, to be an Israelite meant to share the remarkable characteristic of living with outstanding sexual morals (as given in Lev 18 etc.) a lifelong partnership without divorce—or divorce on reasons of עֶרְוַת דָּבָר only as a tolerated, but never approved exception.²⁶⁶ So the first important aspect of the creational one-flesh union should be clearly defined by affirming that the partnership is to be "everlasting" (i.e., lifelong).²⁶⁷

---

law in Deut 21:10–14 speaking about a type of "mixed marriage" resulting from Israelite military campaigns. While those marriages are generally forbidden, except in case of the heathen partner converting to Yahweh's cult (cf. Exod 34:15–16; Deut 7:3–5; Lev 19:34), the matter in Deut 21:10–14 is somewhat similar. Here a Hebrew man has been granted to take a captive woman by marriage and to release her if he "is not pleased with her" (μὴ θέλῃς αὐτήν/לֹא חָפַצְתָּ; Deut 21:14). Of course the captive woman had to conform to Israelite cult practice and belief, leaving behind her parents and thereby the customs she has been used to live like (this is explained by the rites given in vv. 12–13). The exact reason for separating her is not mentioned. So we have to suppose that the same fact is given as told in Deut 24:1. Furthermore, we recognize that this instruction again intends to protect the wife by forbidding to sell her as slave; cf. also Gane, "Old Testament Principles," 38. Hence, we have not the same case as described in 1 Cor 7:15, for there it is a marriage between an unbelieving and a believing partner, and it is the unbelieving partner who separates. The Christian spouse is not allowed to separate (cf. vv. 12–13)—completely contrary to the Israelite spouse in Deut 21:10–14! Consequently, we also have to assume that the divorce mentioned in Deut 21:14 is also disapproved by God, just as the divorce of Deut 24:1! So it is just briefly mentioned that such divorces happen (Deut 21:14: אִם־לֹא חָפַצְתָּ בָּהּ וְשִׁלַּחְתָּהּ; "if you are not pleased and send her away") and the case is regulated for the benefit of the wife; but it is not approved of. Furthermore, there is only one supposed example of "divorce" in the narratives of the Torah: Gen 21:9–14. Abraham got a child with Hagar, the bondmaid of his wife Sarah. After experiencing a lot of troubles because of this polygamous household, he is commanded by God to do what Sarah tells him, i.e., to send Hagar and her son away. Some scholars hold that as an example for divinely commanded divorce. However, God does obviously not really recognize the relationship between Hagar and Abraham as a marriage; it rather is some kind of an instrumental polygamous relation (for one night) in order to help Sarah (!) getting a child. Therefore, Davidson asserts, "there has never been a valid marriage in God's eyes, and so there was really no divorce, only the dissolving of an illegitimate polygamous relationship." Davidson, *Flame*, 388–89; cf. on a similar event (concerning mixed marriages) also Ezra 9–10; on Ancient Near Eastern backgrounds about Divorce cf. pp. 385–88; Gane here also recognizes "a different kind of case": Gane, "Old Testament Principles," 39/fn.4. Some commentators see a remarriage (after divorce) in the short statement of Gen 25:1: "Then again Abraham took a wife, and her name was Keturah." However, reading Gen 23 it is clear that his first wife, Sarah, had already died and was buried. So there is no remarriage (and, of course, no divorce before), but just a second marriage after the death of the first wife. On further divorce texts in the prophets and their interpretation, altogether referring to the laws investigated above, see Davidson, *Flame*, 410–22.

265. This abomination apparently is due to the same fact of illicit sexual relations mentioned in Lev 18. Here we find the same motivation for the restrictive laws (cf. vv. 24–30). Cf. also Davidson, "Divorce and Remarriage," 14–15.

266. For "if one *hates and* divorces [without the facts of עֶרְוַת דָּבָר], says Yahweh, God of Israel, he covers his garments with violence." Mal 2:16 (my italics) according to the translation of Hugenberger, *Covenant*, 83. (This text will soon be investigated much closer.)

267. So even this supposed divorce-favoring law "points toward the day when such inequalities

I.1.2.2 Polygamy as Cultural Digression

The second significant aspect, also connected with the understanding of the matter of divorce, is the exclusivity of having just one partner at a time. As we recognized by investigating the divorce texts, the intention is to disapprove of the view that wives (and women in general) are to be dealt with as some property to be given away and taken back or hoarded at the will of the husband's "patriarchal" power. So now we have to scrutinize the second aspect of Old Testament legislation that is often held to be interfering with the everlastingness of the original (creational) marriage ideal: polygamy.

As should be evident from the creation account, polygamy is not the ideal kind of relationship; the first "marriage" constituted a connection between one man and only one woman and thus was called "very good."[268] Meanwhile, since that "heavenly" time, some ages elapsed with the world being in a dark state of "apostasy." Thus, although that (heavenly) principle has certainly been well known, some of the old patriarchs commenced to take more than one wife, following the customs of the surrounding culture they lived in.[269] There have been a lot of circumstances and perceptions con-

---

[of bad dealing with women by separating them] will be resolved by a return to the Edenic pattern for marriage." Davidson, "Divorce and Remarriage," 22.

268. Cf. Gen 1:27, 31; 2:18, 22–24. Considering the textual variant in Gen 2:24 discussed in the first chapter about the Genesis creation account, the short adding of "the two of them/both" (תרויהון/ duo/οἱ δύο) in the Syriac versions according to the codex Ambrosianus (1876) and the polyglottam Londinensem (1654), the Samaritan Pentateuch, the Targum Pseudo-Jonathae, the Vulgate, and the LXX, may also point to some later emphasis of the concrete number of partners that belong to the (monogamous) divine ideal—at least emphasized as an interpretative slant in the communities producing these manuscripts. "The two" leaves no room for speculation about possible further spouses for one man, but only *two* (שְׁנֵיהֶם; cf. Gen 2:25) become *one* (אֶחָד). Cf. Instone-Brewer, *In the Bible*, 61; Loader, *LXX, Sexuality, and NT*, 42; Beale and Carson, *NT Use*, 198; Daube, *New Testament*, 81. Isaksson holds it to be "only a stylistic gloss, called forth by the context." Isaksson, *Marriage and Ministry*, 18/fn.1; cf. Gunkel, *Genesis*, Gen. 2:24; Westermann, *Genesis 1–11 (Ger.)*, 253. Loader also notes that in Gen 2:24 the LXX uses the more generic translation ἄνθρωπος for אִישׁ, instead of ἀνήρ, thus possibly again reflecting Gen 1:26–27 and the formation of man (ἄνθρωπος) in the genders male and female (Loader, *LXX, Sexuality, and NT*, 39)—and as such only *two* persons of different genders in this relationship. Hence, "as a third facet of sexual theology found in Gen 1–2, it may be affirmed that the marital form presented by God as paradigmatic for humans from the beginning is a *monogamous* one. In the narrator's description of the first marriage (Gen 2:18–23), the usage of singular nouns and pronouns throughout is significant.... Unmistakably this language denotes a marriage between one man and one woman. In 2:24... the phrase 'a man ['îš]... and... his wife ['ištô],' with both nouns in the singular, clearly implies that the sexual relationship envisioned is monogamous, to be shared between two marriage partners." Davidson, *Flame*, 21; italics given; cf. Davidson, "Beginning," 22; Mathews, *Genesis 1–11:26*, 222; on a similarly conclusion concerning Gen 2:24, but from a different context, also Tosato, "On Genesis 2:24," 407.

269. Remember the story of Esau and Jacob (Gen 26:34–35; 29–30); or (indirectly) Abraham taking his wife's bondmaid (Gen 16). Nonetheless, other important ancestors of the nation Israel like Isaac, Joseph, or Moses himself had not more than one wife. On the other hand, it has obviously been very important for the little family of Abraham and the other patriarchs to secure descendants for the welfare and growth of their tribe. Regarding this issue, Grelot argues: "The importance accorded to the wife's fertility, and to descendants in the masculine line who would ensure the continuance of the tribe and the handing on of the inheritance, explains these legal provisions [i.e., polygamy]: the

trary to the original concept of marriage. Now, dealing with those imperfect conditions, Moses introduced laws to regulate these subjects in an appropriate way:[270]

> And if a man sells his daughter as a female slave, she is not to go free as the male slaves do. If she is displeasing in the eyes of her master who designated her for himself, then he shall let her be redeemed. He does not have authority to sell her to a foreign people because of his unfairness to her. And if he designates her for his son, he shall deal with her according to the custom of daughters. If he takes to himself another woman, he may not reduce her food, her clothing, or her conjugal rights. And if he will not do these three things for her, then she shall go out for nothing, without payment of money. (Exod 21:7–11.)

This passage is written within the context of female Hebrew slaves and their possible relationships to their masters (cf. Exod 21:2–11).[271] If a daughter is sold as slave she shall never be redeemed. But she might become the wife of her master or his son; however, she will have to live her entire life within their home. By reading the text as

---

family comes before the individual and must continue through him. At a later period, Psalm 127:3–5 reminds us that the strength of the family depends on the number of its male members. The custom levirate marriage provided for the extreme in cases in which the husband died without issue: it was a sacred duty for his brothers and nearest relatives to produce a child for him (cf. Gen 36:6–10). The needs met by polygamy are clear, though some passages of the Bible make no effort to hide the difficulties that could arise from it [. . . ; but the good of the tribe is more important than these lesser difficulties." Grelot, "The Institution of Marriage," 40–41. Cf. on the conditions and problems of polygamy also: Richter, *Geschlechtlichkeit*, 84–86. But, as we will see, polygamy is not really approved even in the OT; to the contrary, "although polygamy was practiced in ancient Israel, without exception it is also depicted as an occasion for family trouble." Christensen, *Deuteronomy 21:10—34:12*, 480; cf. Kalland, "Deuteronomy," 132. Hence, instances like that of Jacob are rather failures in family management, and in no way any approval. So the ABC argues that "Jacob's laxity in marriage began with polygamy and ended in concubinage. Though God overruled this for the development of the seed of Israel, He did not thereby place His approval on such a custom." Nichol and Andreasen, *ABC*, Gen. 30:4, 1:392. But, as the case of Hagar demonstrates, God even more intervenes against the (adulterous) extension of monogamy (Gen 21:10–12), even if consummated for the sake of the holy people's welfare.

270. Compare on this hypothesis of "imperfect conditions" Matt 19:7–9! Also, Hoffmann reasons: "In Matthew the dispute (19,4–18) has a theological and hermeneutical function: the original created order is to be the criterion for interpreting the Law, and Jesus' interpretation with the directive it contains is thus shown to be the better exposition of God's will." Hoffmann, "Jesus' Saying about Divorce," 57. Therefore, the laws given here are no instruction about positive exemplars, but rather some means to regulate imperfect conditions.

271. While Kaiser regards this instance as the sale of a bride in terms of a servant; cf. Kaiser, "Exodus," 430. Stuart thinks that "this law assumes the payment to a head of a family of a *combined* contract labor *and* bride price, which would have been in all likelihood a larger sum of money than either payment separately." Stuart, *Exodus*, 482; italics given. The question why he should pay extra for her as servant, Stuart explains by pointing to inheritance rights (pp. 482–83). The son of another woman, therefore, might be able to inherit what the son of the servant-wife cannot. However, beside the fact that polygamy is never recommended, we have nowhere else in the Torah any distinction between wives, but a clear command that the firstborn shall inherit, no matter if he is from the loved wife or the unloved (cf. Deut 21:15–16). That thesis seems to be unprovable just from the evidence of this passage or other related ordinances in the Mosaic legislation. The first, however, may be possible, although it is unclear why she is sold as slave when she is designated to become wife.

given in the translation above, she is married and her husband takes another wife.[272] But still he has to meet these three (marital) duties. So she will not have to miss clothing, food or "conjugal rights"—mostly understood as sexual intercourse—due to her husband's disregard or neglect; thus the importance of sexuality within the bond of marriage would be pointed out clearly.[273] Stuart even sees an "extended paradigmatic range" and assumes that this right to leave the husband (presupposed that the mentioned passage speaks about marriage) would be applicable in "any situation where a woman's marital rights might be denied her . . . ."[274]

But it has to be noted that the translation, and consequently the interpretation of this v. 10, is not plain; "of the three items, one is slightly unclear, one is unclear, and one is very unclear."[275] Furthermore, Propp asserts,

> it is not clear, however, that the subject of v. 10 is technically polygamy, since the law does not consider the maidservant as more than promised (*yʿd*) to become a wife or concubine. *ʾAḥeret* is just another female in the household, whether slave, concubine or wife.[276]

Du Preez, while scrutinizing different opinions, concurs with other scholars that this verse rather has to be translated as follows: "If he takes to himself another woman

---

272. By reading the text as given in the popular translations, it has often been argued that this text proves polygamy to be permitted (e.g., Harrelson, *Ten Commandments*, 60–61; Instone-Brewer, *In the Bible*, 59–61; Nichol and Andreasen, *ABC*, Exod 21:10, 1:613; Durham, *Exodus*, 322; Stuart, *Exodus*, 482–84; Paul, "Maintenance Clause," 49.) But even if the text would have to be understood in that way, it evidently does not meet the ideal of the creation. Nonetheless, e.g., Cosby states: "Deuteronomy considers polygamy an acceptable practice, offering neither encouragement nor condemnation for it." Cosby, *Sex in the Bible*, 13. He also claims that ". . . polygamy is perfectly acceptable in the society proposed by Deuteronomy . . . ." Ibid., 17. However, one has to be careful (as the law about the bill of divorce demonstrated) not to derive a "right" from a regulation dealing with some given infirmities of the contemporary Hebrew society: ". . . if plural marriage is considered to be legitimized simply because the case law mentions its possibility, then it must be concluded that God is sanctioning stealing as well, since the case law in Exod 22:1 likewise considers the possibility of theft. Clearly, case law does not condone all that it treats." Du Preez, *Polygamy*, 66; cf. also Davidson, *Flame*, 191–92. Similarly, prostitution is evidently prohibited (Lev 19:29; Deut 23:17); nonetheless, there is a special law against bringing a harlot's wages to the temple (Deut 23:18)—thus proving for the possible "reality" without legalizing it. Apparently, the passage in Deut 21:15–17 (a man having two wives shall not favor the son of the beloved over the firstborn of the unloved) has to be understood in the same way; regulating, not approving. Just as we saw before in case of divorce (or better: forbidden remarriage) in Deut 24:1–4.

273. By assuring these benefits for every wife, any combating like that of Jacob's wives (cf. Gen 30:1, 14–16) might be reduced. But of course the intercourse would certainly be reduced to the quite "technical" aspect of assuring the possibility to procreate, rather than any kind of remaining love. (The Mishnah even states clearly how often (as a minimum) a man has to lie with his wife (*m. Ketub.* 5:6) and thus regulates the matter even more exactly.)

274. Stuart, *Exodus*, 482. Thus he would present another legal reason for divorce besides the "indecent thing" of Deut 24:1—if this instance is adequate to be taken into consideration in context of divorce (this will be discussed at the end of this study).

275. Propp, *Exodus 19–40*, 201.

276. Propp, *Exodus 19–40*, 200–201; cf. Davidson, "Scheidung und Wiederheirat," 165: "Eine genauere Betrachtung der Lage zeigt, dass dieser Abschnitt weder von Ehe noch von Scheidung spricht."

[instead of the slave girl], he may not reduce her food, clothing, or quarters."²⁷⁷ So this law just guarantees her to be fully supported by her master, even though he refuses to take her as wife. Thus here would be no information given about any dealing with polygamy, what fits to the context in the most reasonable way.²⁷⁸

When examining the text cited above, it is interesting to point out that the four legislating books of the Torah (Exod–Deut) actually do not know the term "concubine" (παλλακή/פִּלֶגֶשׁ).²⁷⁹ While it is present in many other OT books, and thus describes the actual situation in Israel, its absence in the normative laws is all the more conspicuous, and again leads to the conclusion that polygamy was not legalized by Yahweh—and, of course, much less suggested or even recommended.²⁸⁰

The same is to be considered regarding the next passage, apparently dealing with a polygamous marriage:

---

277. Cf. Du Preez, *Polygamy*, 68. The main problem when translating this verse, is the Hebrew word עֹנָה. Since it is a hapax legomenon, it is difficult to interpret this instance reliably. There are different attempts to translate it as "conjugal rights/sexual intercourse" (most common), "oil" (thus indicating one of the basic necessities besides food and clothing; but it could also refer to cosmetics), "responsibility," or "habitation." Ibid. Cf. Davidson, "Scheidung und Wiederheirat," 165/fn.22; Clines, *Classical Hebrew*, 6:501–2 suggests concerning the occurrence of עֹנָה in Exod 21:10 "conjugal rights/pampering (with cosmetics)/her cake(s)/dwelling/oil/ointment." Note also Paul, "Maintenance Clause," 50–53 who argues in favor of translating עֹנָה as "oil/ointments" with reference to several similar ancient near eastern documents stipulating the provision of one's former wife with "food, clothing, and oil" and to Eccl 9:7–8 (equally mentioning food, clothing, and oil as basic necessities of life). Propp, *Exodus 19–40*, 202–3 concluded his evaluation of this difficult term with the statement that it is "an unresolved mystery." Ibid., 203. The only translation that does not lack etymological evidence is "dwelling," since it probably derives from *māʿôn, meʿônāh*, meaning "dwelling/habitation." (See Du Preez, *Polygamy*, 68.) F. J. Stendebach, in: Botterweck et al., *TWAT*, 6:246 similarly holds it possible that עֹנָה is derived from "*māʿôn* 'Wohnung' . . . im Sinne einer Dauerwohnung." Cassuto, *Exodus*, 269 states: ". . . the conditions of her abode (this appears to be the real meaning of the word *ʿōnāthah*, and not as later tradition interpreted it: times of cohabitation)."

278. Cf. Davidson, "Scheidung und Wiederheirat," 165/fn.22; Davidson, *Flame*, 191–92, 409. He investigates this text and recognizes that there are several textual, linguistic and translational problems with the popular translations of these verses. He also concludes that it is not dealing with polygamy, but with a master and his son, who both reject the slave girl, the son taking another wife instead. Hence, the three basic rights mentioned for the benefit of the slave girl are food, clothing, and lodging. And, of course, sexual intercourse is not necessary for a maidservant, but only belongs to the legal wife, who has been chosen instead of her.

279. In Genesis it occurs four times (Gen 22:24; 25:6; 35:22; 36:12); but as we already noticed, there are often narratives given that contain local customs, and which are in no way intending to have any normative effect.

280. Cf. Du Preez, *Polygamy*, 61. Preez further indicates that the Hebrew word for "concubine" does not even have a Semitic origin and is accordingly not pertaining to the Semitic culture. Davidson generally recognizes two "distinct trends" or "rival plans for God's sexual program" of dealing with sexuality after leaving paradise: "Throughout the OT, one encounters these two tendencies: on the one hand, the positive affirmations of sexuality, upholding and amplifying the Edenic pattern, and, on the other hand, the portrayals of departure from the Edenic plan through the exploitation and distortion of God's intent for sexuality." Davidson, *Flame*, 83. Obviously, one kind of exploitation and distortion is polygamy, introduced by the ancient cultures, not by God's original plan for humankind (or at least for the patriarchs and ancient Israel).

> If a man has two wives, the one loved and the other unloved, and both the loved and the unloved have borne him sons, if the first-born son belongs to the unloved, then it shall be in the day he wills what he has to his sons, he cannot make the son of the loved the first-born before the son of the unloved, who is the first-born. (Deut 21:15–16.)

It really seems like this paragraph talks about a situation like that of Jacob with Leah and Rachel (see Gen 30:1, 14–16). And, of course, just for such undesirable conditions the law might be applicable. Yet it is not legalizing, but merely regulating bad circumstances. Although most commentators recognize a polygamous situation,[281] it is not definitely said that the man has both wives simultaneously. It is likely that this passage just deals with a man who had legally two wives, the second not before the first one died. But he loved only one of them; therefore he likes to favor the son of this beloved wife. Regarding the aim of this law, it is likely that it does not intend to primarily regulate some polygamous unhappiness, but rather the maintenance of the inheritance by transferring it to the legal heir, the first-born of the first wife. However, it does not prove a legal status of polygamy; it just intends to regulate affairs of inheritance.[282]

There is another law in Lev 18:18 which apparently speaks about taking two wives, while it has to be guaranteed that the second is not the sister of the first: "And you shall not marry a woman in addition to her sister as a rival while she is alive, to uncover her nakedness." That could mean polygamy is at least regulated, if not even permitted. Harris sums up, ". . . as the very least it forbids this special case of polygamy [i.e., taking two sisters]. This does not mean that polygamy in general is approved—only that its excesses are curbed."[283] But by scrutinizing ancient documents, especially by the interpretation of the Qumran Scrolls,[284] Du Preez concurs with others that just this passage has even been used to confirm the prohibition of polygamy;[285] for there it reads: "And you shall not take a woman as a rival wife to her sister, uncovering her nakedness while her sister is yet alive"—that could refer to just any two women.[286]

---

281. Cf. e.g., Merrill, *Deuteronomy*, 292; Christensen, *Deuteronomy 21:10—34:12*, 480; Kalland, "Deuteronomy," 132–33.

282. Cf. also Davidson, *Flame*, 201–2, who stresses the same point and concludes: ". . . this case law, dealing with the rights of the firstborn, cannot be used to legitimize polygamy any more than can, for example, Deut 32:18 be used to legitimize prostitution because it prohibits the use of prostitute wages for the payment of vows."

283. Harris, "Leviticus," 599.

284. 11QTemple 57:17–19; 66:15–17; cf. Hartley, *Leviticus*, 297.

285. On the Qumran's exegetes' prohibition of polygamy, see also: Instone-Brewer, *In the Bible*, 61–65; similarly Loader, *Dead Sea Scrolls*, 42: "If one understands by sister not a blood relative, but a fellow Israelite, then one could see in this text a prohibition of polygyny." Cf. also pp. 42–45.

286. Du Preez, *Polygamy*, 76–77; cf. Tosato, "The Law of Leviticus 18:18. A Reexamination," 199–214; Archer, *Survey*, 259; Kaiser, *OT Ethics*, 189. Hartley takes another position and, with Sun, "finds Tosato's explanation wanting in light of the use of the term for relationship in the context of this law." Hartley, *Leviticus*, 297; cf. Sun, "Investigation," 119. Rooker at least mentions it, without particularly referring to it. Cf. Rooker, *Leviticus*, 243.

Apparently, the Hebrew expression ("a woman to her sister;" וְאִשָּׁה אֶל־אֲחֹתָהּ) has to be understood as an idiom, just meaning "adding one to another" without any reference to human beings in all the other instances.[287] Consequently, even this instance must not necessarily refer to sisters, but just to the act of "adding one to another;" thus stressing the (prohibited) act of increasing one's wives (i.e., having more than one wife while the first one is still alive). That would also explain the rivalry mentioned in this verse, for it seems to be absurd to assume rivalry only between sisters and not even more between any other women. Hence, this would again prove a strong prohibition against any form of polygamy, instead of just regulating the imperfect custom or even legalizing it only by dealing therewith.

Within the special laws for kings there is one remark about his wives, which could be interpreted as if some (moderate) form of polygamy would be usual. It says, the king "shall not multiply wives for himself, or else his heart will turn away; nor shall he greatly increase silver and gold for himself" (Deut 17:17). Although Israel should generally have no kings (cf. 1 Sam 8:1–9), but only Yahweh as godly king and the priests and prophets as his representatives, here are already ordinances given concerning the new challenges the future kings will have to meet (see Deut 17:14–20). One of these is to deny the increase of wives, for that would lead to pride and apostasy.[288] But the most important reason for this law, particularly addressing the future kings, certainly is the possible refusal of the Torah, and thereby a general acceptance of polygamy as licit practice. Of course, kings would be particularly endangered of conforming to heathen practices. Hence, the final clause of this royal law is very important:

> And it shall be with him, and he shall read it all the days of his life, that he may learn to fear the Lord his God, by carefully observing all the words of this law and these statutes, that his heart may not be lifted up above his countrymen

---

287. Cf. Du Preez, *Polygamy*, 74–79. Davidson points to the other instances using the phrase "a woman to her sister" (וְאִשָּׁה אֶל־אֲחֹתָהּ) in Exod 26:3, 5, 6, 17; Ezek 1:9, 23; 3:13, always meaning "one in addition to another," but never referring to human females. The same with the corresponding expression for "a man to his brother" (אִישׁ אֶל־אָחִיו) in Gen 37:19; 42:21, 28; Exod 16:15; 25:20; 37:9; Num 14:4; 2 Kgs 7:6; Jer 13:14; 25:26; Ezek 24:23; 33:30. Both idioms just mean "adding one to another," without any allusion to human beings. Davidson, *Flame*, 194/fn. 56; cf. also his further argumentation on pp. 195–98. It is right, on the one hand, that the previous verses of Lev 18:18 may hint at the opposite direction (see vv. 6–17), speaking about blood relatives. However, on the other hand, it is very interesting that this verse is located at the "threshold" to another section dealing with final sexual regulations without any connection to relatives (vv. 19–23: no sex during menstruation, no homosexuality, no sodomy). Therefore, the context is not able to clearly allude to family relations as being the central issue in v. 18. It rather seems, these final verses (vv. 18–23) deal with a broader range of sexual laws, the one against polygamy (supposedly v. 18) fitting in the highest sense!

288. As is reported of King Solomon, the breaking of just that command led him to worship pagan Gods and to lead the people of Israel into apostasy (cf. 1 Kgs 11:1–11). Furthermore the people had to suffer high taxes because of the huge growth of his royal court (cf. 1 Kgs 5:2–3, 6–8; 2 Chr 10:4). Also, the generations before the Great Flood were characterized by polygamous lifestyles (cf. Gen 4:19; 6:1–3).

and that he may not turn aside from the commandment, to the right or the left. (Deut 17:19–20.)

If "this law" is understood as the Torah, what would be more plausible than just the few verses to contemplate over and over again, he obviously has no right to exalt himself over his brethren and to claim some special laws regarding polygamy. He would also have to keep Yahweh's ideal of marriage by taking only one wife. Furthermore, "multiplying" principally begins with at least taking a second wife. Hence, the law even could be understood as speaking against any (even moderate) degree of polygamy, thus prohibiting this practice completely.

The question may arise whether the practice of the levirate marriage means to be in some way required by the divine law to take a second wife and start a polygamous partnership, provided that the brother of the childless, deceased husband is married already.[289] To answer this question it is worthwhile to regard the beginning of the instruction: "When brothers live together and one of them dies and has no son . . . ." Usually, the brothers lived together until all had their own families to support:

> 'Dwelling together' means living close enough to share the same pastureland, and that 'this may mean that in biblical times the marriage was obligatory only if the levir's home, where the widow and her future child would reside, was close to that property' . . . .'[290]

Thus, the brother who would have to take up the levirate marriage would be unmarried and therefore not commencing a polygamous relation on God's command.[291]

Finally, one has to keep in mind that the creational ideal, as well as the most examples in the Pentateuch, indicate monogamy as the only appropriate practice. There are Adam and Eve (Gen 2–4), Noah and his wife (7:7, 17), Noah's three sons with

---

289. So e.g., Cosby, *Sex in the Bible*, 12–13 states clearly: "You may imagine how much of a strain such an arrangement [i.e., the levirate] could place upon the surviving brother. He could be forced to acquire a wife he did not want; and if he were already married, he and his wife would have to adjust to the reality of having another woman inserted into their marriage relationship." Although he refers to the possibility of refusal in the next passage, he apparently perceives a "force" upon the surviving brother to marry even a second woman. Kalland asks the same question: "Was the law of levirate marriage an approval of polygamy? Hardly! It was rather an alternate arrangement under specific bounds to make possible the retention of landed property throughout the families of Israel. It had a subsidiary result of protecting widows without children." Kalland, "Deuteronomy," 150. But, despite of these financial and social matters, following Kalland polygamy might have been enforced; although he clearly asserts, with reference to Neufeld, that "among the Jews of postbiblical times there was a tendency to discourage levirate marriage." Ibid.; cf. Neufeld, *Marriage Laws*, 23–55.

290. Christensen, *Deuteronomy 21:10—34:12*, 608; referring to Tigay, *Deuteronomy*, 231. Cf. Gen 38 (Tamar); Du Preez, *Polygamy*, 104; Harris, "Leviticus," 599; Phillips, *Deuteronomy*, 168; Hamilton, "Marriage," 4:567.

291. Cf. Du Preez, *Polygamy*, 104; cf. esp. Davidson, *Flame*, 202, 465–71. Merrill asserts that "a widow whose deceased husband had died without male heir [had to] marry one of his brothers, presumably the next eldest one *who was himself unmarried*." Merrill, *Deuteronomy*, 327; cf. also Hugenberger, *Covenant*, 114–15.

only one wife for each one of them (7:7, 13), Nahor and Milcah (11:29; 24:15), Abram and Sarai (11:29), Isaac and Rebekah (24; 27; 49:31), Hadar and Mehetabel (36:39), Er and Tamar (38:6), Joseph and Asenath (41:45), Amram and Jochebed (Exod 6:20; Num 26:59), Aaron and Elisheba (Exod 6:23), Eleazar and his wife (6:25), and Moses and Zipporah (2:21; 18:2, 5; Num 12:1). Besides, the Mosaic legislation always refers to husband and "wife," not "wives"[292]—just like the Edenic ideal of Gen 2:24 expresses the monogamous character of this union by referring to a man's "wife" (אִשְׁתּוֹ; singular), not depicting any devine intention to create more than one spouse.[293]

These examples clearly agree with the notes given above concerning those laws which are frequently put forward to argue in favor of an Old Testament approval of polygamy. As will be reinforced at other places, this study rejects the widespread idea that God revealed aberrant ways to Moses, himself introducing partnerships so much different from his original, Edenic ideal of monogamy.

I.1.2.3 Summary and Final Considerations

The brief investigations above argue in favor of one lasting, eternal "Edenic ideal," the deviation from which God never intended and correspondingly never approved of—not even in the Mosaic times amid differing cultural, social, and natural conditions compared to the perfect state of the Garden of Eden. Widespread views arguing in favor of mere cultural influences are practically untenable.[294] It is a failure to appreci-

---

292. Another prominent but more general example is stated in the Ten Commandments: "You shall not covet your neighbor's *wife* (אֵשֶׁת; singular)" (Exod 20:17; my italics). Furthermore, Grelot concludes regarding the early biblical family structures and Lamech's "introduction" of polygamy, that "the writer shares the preoccupations of the ancient family law in which polygamy was regarded as licit. Yet on the other hand the account of the creation does not allude to it; on the other [sic.], in the story of the flood Noah and his sons still have only one wife (Gen 6,18)—as if polygamy was introduced only at a later date, during some cultural development tarnished by sin." Grelot, "The Institution of Marriage," 45. "Enoch, as a righteous man in the seventh generation, represents a completion and fulfillment of a life totally dedicated to God. Lamech, as an unrighteous man in the seventh generation, demonstrates the complete corruption of one who lives separated from God. . . . Lamech is listed as a murderer and a polygamist. Both of these actions are clearly antithetical to Gen 1 and 2, where God is the One who not only gives life, but also the originator of the monogamous marital pattern." Du Preez, *Polygamy*, 150. Considering that "seven" frequently is a meaningful number and that these men therefore are at a very prominent position, it may be apparent that here is some kind of an open window, a clear view on the different lifestyles in the holy and the profane lineages of the pre-Flood world (cf. Gen 4:17—16:3; see also ibid., 148–49). That makes the mentioning of Lamech's polygamy all the more important and might even illuminate the reasons for the soon following destructing of the antediluvians in the Great Flood.

293. Cf. Hasel, "Eheverständnis," 24; 'Abot R. Nat. 2; Baltensweiler, *Ehe im NT*, 54/fn.33; similarly Bruner, *Matthew*, 670–71: "If God had supremely intended solitary life, God would have created humans one by one; if God had intended polygamous life, God would have created one man and several women (Chrys., 62:1/382); if God had intended homosexual life God would have made two men or two women; but that God intended monogamous heterosexual life was shown by God's creation of one man and one woman."

294. See e.g., Kaye, "One Flesh," 49–50.

ate the Mosaic instructions for special cases as if they would represent laws that could (for unstated reasons) even exceed the original pattern given much earlier even under perfect circumstances. Only in paradise does one find ideal conditions allowing to establish an ideal pattern for marriage.[295] The times outside of Eden, of course, may require special adaption due to the cultural "failures" distorting that Edenic ideal—but, of course, without altering the ideal itself. Thus

> the legal provision of Moses in Dt. 24 was not intended as a statement of God's purpose for marriage, but as a regrettable but necessary means of limiting the damage when that purpose has already been abandoned. It is a provision to deal with human σκληροκαρδία, not a pointer to the way things ought to be.[296]

To measure the higher ideal by considering these later worse, non-ideal conditions, however, is not permissible. Although the ideal may perhaps seem to be unreachable for sinful humans of subsequent generations, it still remains the divine pattern for a couple to strive for—as far as they are determined to fulfill God's purposes with marriage.[297] Likewise, Jesus affirms this way of seeking God's original intentions by pointing back to the Edenic ideal, not to the Mosaic moderating "clear-up operations" intending to oppose the Israelite husbands' "hardness of heart" (Matt 19:8; Mark 10:5).[298]

Monogamy is not really in question today and most commentators agree that

> polygamy was allowed in Mosaic law, but there were also caveats. . . . Polygamy is nowhere spoken of with approval, and many passages indicate that monogamy is the ideal. There is no evidence that polygamy was widespread in Israel, except perhaps after times of war when the male population was diminished. In the OT, polygamy is almost always related to childlessness and is often associated with problems.[299]

---

295. Cf. Hasel, "Eheverständnis," 18, 21 who calls Gen 2:24 the "Urmuster" for the biblical understanding of marriage; similarly Von Rad, *Erstes Buch Mose*, 59–60; Schlier, *Epheser*, 263.

296. France, *Mark*, 388.

297. Cf. Hagner, *Matthew 1–13*, 126.

298. Besides, as will be discussed in more detail concerning the marriage and prostitution metaphors below (see "Marriage and Prostitution Images"), Kirchschläger, *Ehe im NT*, 46 rightly asserts regarding the everlastingness of the marital bond: "Nur unter diesem Blickwinkel der (zumindest irdischen) Dauerhaftigkeit ist es auch sinnvoll und verständlich, von der Zeichenhaftigkeit der Ehe zu sprechen und damit eine bildhafte Übertragung in den Beziehungsbereich Gott-Mensch vorzunehmen . . . —wie dies aber zweifellos biblisch grundgelegt ist!" Later he adds: "Nur auf Dauer angelegte Ehe kann in diesem Sinn den Anspruch erheben, hier Zeichenfunktion wahrnehmen zu können. Nur in diesem Sinn kann das Zusammenstehen der Ehepartner Gottes nie endende Treue in seiner Zuwendung zum Menschen repräsentieren" Ibid., 50.

299. Instone-Brewer, *In the Bible*, 59; similarly Hasel, "Eheverständnis," 20–21.

The Old Testament Foundation

Furthermore, even in late rabbinic Judaism, "no instance of plural marriage is recorded among the more than two thousand Sages mentioned in the Talmud."[300] "The monogamous family came to be regarded as the ideal."[301]

Divorce is much more discussed, and concerning the special case law of Deut 24:1–4 there exists mostly harmony among scholars that Moses

> could not break completely with the ancient custom [of divorce] but wished to obviate its serious consequences, he tried to limit as far as possible the number of divorces. He sought to do this by (1) only permitting one ground for divorce, (2) forbidding the remarriage of the divorced wife after she had been married to another man in the interim, and (3) requiring the presentation of a bill of divorce. Thus the aim of Dt. 24.1–4 was to regulate the legal aspects of divorce and to try and prevent hasty divorces.[302]

Other scholars agree and present many more reasons, as demonstrated above. In fact, "Deuteronomy 24:1–4 stipulates what is to be done in the event that a divorce took place, but it is not a divorce law."[303] Furthermore, "the purpose of Dt. 24.1–4 is not to give legal sanction to divorces and regulate the divorce procedure but only to forbid a man to re-marry his divorced wife after she has been married to another man in the interim."[304]

> Absicht ist der Schutz der Frau, womit dieses Kasus (wie auch die formalen Parallelen) in die Reihe der Humanitätsgesetze des Dt gehört: damit die Frau nicht leichtfertig entlassen wird, soll der leichtsinnigen Scheidung vorgebeugt werden. Ähnlich geht es in 22,13 [i.e., v. 14] um den Schutz der Frau vor ungerechter Beschuldigung. In Dt 22,28 [i.e., v. 29] und 22,20 [i.e., v. 19] ist sogar ein (jeweils gleichlautendes) Scheidungsverbot ausgesprochen, das mit לֹא־יוּכַל beginnt und daher Dt 24,4a schon rein formal verwandt ist.[305]

Hence, "we cannot interpret these words as meaning that divorce takes place with divine consent and moral sanction."[306] The same is evidently true concerning the monogamous ideal of a relationship between only two spouses. Hence, to sum up briefly, one may fully consent to the final note:

> Without question [Gen] 2:24 serves as the bedrock for Hebrew understanding of the centrality of the nuclear family for the survival of society. Monogamous heterosexual marriage was always viewed as the divine norm from the outset

---

300. Rubenstein, "Jewish Tradition," 7; referring to Moore, *Judaism. Vol. 2*, 122.
301. Rubenstein, "Jewish Tradition," 7.
302. Isaksson, *Marriage and Ministry*, 22.
303. Blenkinsopp, *Isaiah 40–55*, 363.
304. Isaksson, *Marriage and Ministry*, 22.
305. Berger, *Gesetzesauslegung*, 510.
306. Isaksson, *Marriage and Ministry*, 22Cf. Murray, "Divorce," 31–45.

of creation. Mosaic instruction shows considerable efforts to safeguard this ideal against its dissolution . . . .[307]

I.1.3 Ritual Purity of Licit Sexuality (Lev 15:18)

After arguing that even in Mosaic times the enduring ideal for marriage was still the pattern of the Genesis creation (although new cultural problems had to be considered and dealt with—sometimes seemingly covering the original intentions), there is still another research problem left in this context that seemingly mars the overall positive biblical attitude towards sexuality—the supposed impurity attached to legal sexual intercourse according to Lev 15:18.[308] Wenham admits that "the law in Lev 15:18 . . . is one of the most puzzling in the OT. It seems to run counter to the whole tenor of biblical morality."[309] While sexuality in a protected (monogamous, marital) context is depicted as something very positive throughout the Bible, and even as the constituting feature of the divinely ordained institution of marriage (Gen 2:24: "becoming one flesh"), this verse in Lev 15 tends to lead the reader to conclude that sexuality renders one ritually unclean and, therefore, is somehow impure even within a licit, monogamous, marital context. This further results, consequently, in a negative connotation regarding those Old Testament metaphors that deal with the same intimacy between Yahweh and Israel, as well as the NT passages dealing figuratively with the Edenic intimacy between Jesus and his followers (1 Cor 6:16–17; Eph 5:31–32; both echoing Gen 2:24).

The investigation commences with a brief review of the ancient Jewish interpretations of Philo, Josephus, and the few Rabbinic notes on this instance. Then, current scholarly interpretations and a non-defiling alternative of Lev 15:18 and related Old Testament texts will be presented. Finally, adequate conclusions can be drawn from the findings.

---

307. Mathews, *Genesis 1–11:26*, 224.

308. This "impurity" means a ritual defilement, incurred through different circumstances, such as "birth, menstruation, bodily emissions, 'leprosy,' . . . and contact with death" TWOT s.v. טָמֵא; cf. e.g., Lev 11–15 as the chapters most clearly concerned with these kinds of "impurity." See BDB s.v. טָמֵא for more texts. This defilement frequently led to individual social exclusion as long as the uncleanness would exist (cf. Lev 13:46; 15:25, 31; Num 12:15), mostly until evening (see frequently in Lev 11); especially the holy precinct was not be entered by ritually impure persons (cf. Lev 15:31). This uncleanness has, basically, nothing to do with sinfulness, but rather with a state of being "contaminated" by the realm of death (loss of blood, loss of semen, leprosy, carrion etc.)! Cf. also e.g., Countryman, *Dirt, Greed and Sex*, 25–29. The three major aspects of ritual impurity may be summarized as follows: "(1) The sources of ritual impurity are generally natural and more or less unavoidable. (2) It is not sinful to contact these impurities. And (3) these impurities convey an impermanent contagion." Klawans, *Impurity and Sin*, 23. These points apply to the situation examined in this chapter. Point (1) is of special importance, for sexual intercourse would be avoidable—not so the unintended discharges Lev 15 is generally dealing with (more on this, of course, below).

309. Wenham, "Why does," 432.

I.1.3.1 Ancient Jewish Sources

I.1.3.1.1 Philo

Apart from some instances dealing with the institution of marriage in general, Philo did not write very much about the concrete conjugal (sexual) act. That makes it difficult to get reliable information as background of his perception of Lev 15:18. However, there are some hints about his categories of "pure" and "impure" in connection to sexuality that might be valuable.

In *Det.* 102, for instance, he calls only that kind of sexuality "impure" (οὐκ εὐαγεῖς) which is not according to the Jewish law and the purpose of multiplying, thus following the biblical pattern in Lev 18. In the same way he denounces the ancient Sodomites of indulging in "strange/unnatural and impious desires" (ἐκφύλου καὶ ἀσεβοῦς ἐπιθυμίας) when intending to rape the male guests of Lot (*Fug.* 144). Again, when referring to the temptation of young Josephus in Egypt, he speaks about "impurity"[310] only in connection with extramarital and therefore illegitimate sexuality (*Ios.* 44). When speaking about the Ten Commandments, he particularly dwells on further elucidations of the commandment against adultery and thereby refers again to the Mosaic laws as the legitimate instance to declare pure and impure sexual associations (*Spec.* 3:8–82). On the other hand, Philo speaks with respect and honor of having sexual intercourse with one's wife when being confident that the seed will not be shed in vain.[311] Finally, in *Spec.* 3:63 he apparently refers briefly to Lev 15:18, giving a quite clear description of his understanding, albeit devoid of any explanation as to the underlying sense:

> So careful is the law to provide against the introduction of violent changes in the institution of marriage that a husband and wife, who have intercourse in accordance with the legitimate usages of married life, are not allowed, when they leave their bed, to touch anything until they have made their ablutions and purged themselves with water.

Evidently, Philo understands even legitimate intercourse as defiling. Although he generally recognizes different categories of pure and impure sexuality depending on their biblical lawfulness, at this place he interrupts this schematization to interpret (certainly the text of) Lev 15:18 as referring to sexual intercourse, again consequently applying his dualistic morality in order to declare even lawful sexuality to be impure—certainly due to the pleasures involved.

---

310. Here in *Ios.* 44 the antonym καθαρεύω is employed to demonstrate the opposite (lawful) behavior.

311. *Spec.* 3:33: "But if the menstruation ceases, he may boldly sow the generative seeds, no longer fearing that what he lays will perish." The Greek verb employed for "boldly" is θαρσέω and even means "to be cheerful/courageous" (cf. LSJ/BDAG s.v. θαρσέω). Philo obviously tries to encourage husbands to have intercourse with their wives—as long as the purpose of procreation is kept in mind and temperance is maintained.

I.1.3.1.2 Josephus

Proceeding to the second witness of the well-educated representatives of ancient (first century) Judaism, one notices that Josephus clearly, but somehow incidentally, refers to Lev 15:16–18, explaining that he recognizes two ways of a possible defilement: (1) nocturnal emission (corresponding to Lev 15:16–17) and (2) legal, conjugal intercourse (v. 18): "In view of the sacrifices, the law has decreed purifications [... after what sometimes happens to us in bed,] after sexual union with a woman, and from many other causes ...."[312] Shortly hereafter he refers again to v. 18 and elucidates the deeper meaning of the impurity. He apparently understands it as defiling in a moral way:

> Moreover, the law enjoins, that after the man and wife have lain together in a regular way, they shall bathe themselves; for there is a defilement contracted thereby, both in soul and body, as if they had gone into another country; for indeed the soul, by being united to the body, is subject to miseries, and is not freed therefrom again but by death; on which account the law requires this purification to be entirely performed.[313]

Obviously he understood Lev 15:18 as referring to legal sexual intercourse as an element of ritual impurity and defilement.[314] While uniting with the body during sexual intercourse, the soul is apparently "suffering miseries" (κακοπαθέω) and can only by death (θάνατος) be freed from it. These assumptions need a closer investigation.

First we have to recognize that he does not interpret the defilement in the same way many scholars nowadays tend to explain it. There is a huge difference in the basis of the rationale and they are not agreeing although the general tenor is sounding very similar, namely: that conjugal intercourse defiles and that this is the meaning of Lev 15:18. While modern scholars widely agree in perceiving some kind of inherent uncleanness in the legal sexual act itself (whatever it may come from), Josephus is in no way approving of any scholarly explanation given today. He refers to a *moral* problem, basing on the pleasure of the act and the resulting debasement of the soul. The problem for Josephus is not so much the sexual act itself and possibly the "life

---

312. *C.Ap.* 2:198; the addition in square brackets renders the Greek ἀπὸ λέχους as translated by Whiston; Barclay translates "after childbirth"; cf. Josephus, *Against Apion*, 281.

313. *C.Ap.* 2:203 according to the translation of Whiston. Mason renders differently: "It [i.e., the law] gave instruction to wash also after the lawful intercourse of a man and woman; for it supposed that this constitutes a division of the soul (as it passes) into another place. For the soul suffers when it is implanted in bodies and again when it is separated from them at death. Hence it ordered purifications in all such cases." He rather emphasizes the soul's suffering by imparting a part of one's own soul into a new body (the embryo) through the male semen; cf. Josephus, *Against Apion*, 286/fn.817. Cf. on the defilement through sex also *A.J.* 3:263; *Spec.* 3:32.

314. That is reaffirmed in *A.J.* 6:235: "He [i.e., king Saul] saw David's seat was empty, but said nothing, supposing that he had not purified himself since he had accompanied with his wife, and so could not be present."

liquids"[315] that are shed thereby, but the pleasure that is unfortunately indulged in. Furthermore, he approves of legal, conjugal intercourse only for the purpose of procreation and even describes it as "fornication" to have sexual intercourse without the purpose of begetting children (see *C.Ap.* 2:199, 202).[316] So he continues to explicate that men should always govern their desire (κρατεῖν δὲ τῆς ἐπιθυμίας; *A.J.* 4:244), for it is bad to marry with lustful passion (ἐξ ἐπιθυμίας; *A.J.* 4:245). Apparently, the pleasure of sexuality is the *(morally)* defiling element even when practiced only within the "legal" bonds of the wedlock. The only pure and lawful aspect seems to be derived from the purpose to procreate, and just that is the reason for the marriage relation and sexuality at all. However, the way to father those children is defiling and it seems like God obviously made a mistake in connecting pleasure with the act necessary for multiplying. Moreover he is somehow guilty of this defilement, for he even commands that humans should procreate (cf. Gen 1:28).

It is not surprising that Josephus even equates the one who "secretes semen in his sleep" with men "who have sexual relations with a woman in accordance with law [κατὰ νόμον]" (*A.J.* 3:263). While this clearly debases the intimate partnership spouses experience through licit sexual intercourse, he emphasizes, on the other hand, the importance of an affectionate conduct of husbands toward their wives (*A.J.* 4:258; *C.Ap.* 2:201). He endeavors to protect the wives and to urge the husbands to treat their spouses with respect and loving care, but sexuality apparently does not fit that ideal. In his view it seems to be always some kind of an egoistic act, abusing soul and body, defiling both, making the whole creature impure.

Altogether it is not a very happy picture that Josephus is drawing of sexuality in general. On the one hand he knows some sort of "legal" relationship that is founded by God in Eden. But on the other hand he clearly points out that conjugal intercourse is only to be practiced to father children, never just for pleasure. And even though the purpose may be "good" by wishing to get children and by behaving decently in every way, yet it defiles the soul which consequently has to be cleansed in order to extinguish the "miseries."

---

315. Thus argued by Wenham, "Why does," 434 and followed by many commentators.

316. The original Greek phrase (§ 202) reads: τις ἐπὶ λέχους φθορὰν παρέλθοι καθαρὸς εἶναι τότε προσήκει, and means even more: "If someone thus [avoiding procreation] corrupts the marriage bed, the cleanness [of the marital intercourse] passes away." In other words: Such a corruption of the marital intercourse, as to have sex without the purpose of begetting children, is to defile licit intercourse and that finally makes it sinful in God's eyes. Just taking this instance into account could possibly mean that, consequently, sexuality in order to procreate is not defiling. However, his other statements do not clearly support this view; but at least it may be a small hint to better understand his position and intention. Please notice the contrary position presented in Heb 13:4 ("The marriage relation is completely honorable, and the marriage-bed [i.e., sexuality] is pure/undefiled . . . .")—a text that will shortly be dealt with at the end of this study.

I.1.3.1.3 Rabbinic Notes

Concerning the earliest rabbinic notes, the documents we possess today are not older than approximately 200 CE. These are the Sifra as the halakhic interpretation (Midrash) of the book of Leviticus and the Mishnaic tractates, later followed by the Talmudic documents (Mishnah including the traditional Gemara) around 425 AD (the Palestinian or Jerusalem Talmud) and 550 CE (the Babylonian Talmud). It is hardly possible to date the development of special content exactly, albeit we can be certain that some portions reach back until the time before the emergence of rabbinic Judaism that came up after the destruction of the Jerusalem temple in 70 CE. While the date of the ordinances' origin cannot be determined exactly, we nevertheless have to consider that they reflect mainly the Pharisaic part of ancient Jewish halakha. Some influences of the other ancient Jewish religious parties may have been absorbed in the process of establishing rabbinic schools and a firmer, common Jewish doctrine; but the mainstream is, most likely, still somehow Pharisaic in its substance.

The Mishnah has a complete Seder in which all impurities are dealt with: Toharot. Within this major section there are two tractates particularly dealing with genital discharges and the impurities they produce: *Zabim* and *Niddah*. While *Niddah* deals with (generally usual) female discharges, *Zabim* speaks about (unusual) male outflows, but also includes some more instructions concerning female discharges. As is generally well known, the Mishnah is very scrupulous in declaring most exactly what has to be regarded as unclean, for how long, and which rites are to be performed. So it is all the more interesting that there is no clear allusion given concerning the impurity caused by legal, sexual intercourse. The existing ordinances are only dealing with different discharges, their contamination and what becomes in which way unclean. So, for instance, one is only rendered unclean by contamination of semen if it is still wet (*Nid.* 7:1) and being on the same ship with an unclean person is sufficient to defile (*Zabim* 3:1). It is meaningful that the tractate *Zabim* deals only with unusual male discharges outside of sexual intercourse. So even when it is declaring semen to be generally defiling (*Zabim* 5:10), we may assume that a morbid discharge or a nocturnal emission is meant. Only "pollution" (of nocturnal, unintended emission) is declared to be unclean (*Zabim* 5:11), there is nowhere a clear, unambiguous reference to the impurity of usual sexual intercourse.

The Sifra, however, points out that the defiling element in Lev 15:18 is the act of intercourse, not the semen that is shed.[317] While that seems to contradict the immediate context and—as is to be demonstrated below—the content and direction of the entire chapter, Maccoby tries to combine the prevailing scholarly opinion of the defiling semen with this rabbinical view and explains:

> The rabbis concluded, therefore, that this was 'a decree of the King,' for which no human rationale could be found. The rabbis also considered the argument

---

317. Cf. the Sifra on Lev 15:18; see also Maccoby, *Ritual and Morality*, 59.

that, since semen was not the cause of the woman's uncleanness, she ought to be made unclean even by intercourse when no semen was emitted (Sifra). They admitted that this would indeed be a logical conclusion, but it was ruled out by the wording of the text, 'And a woman with whom a man lies with emission of seed (*shikhbat zerʿa*)—they shall bathe in water and be unclean until the evening' (Lev 15:18). Thus the presence of semen is necessary, even though it is not the semen that causes her uncleanness. Her uncleanness is caused by the sexual act, not by the semen, but the sexual act must be a complete one. This is a typical rabbinic argument, in which an apparently redundant phrase is given legal significance, and shown to be necessary in order to counter a logical train of reasoning that would otherwise have been unanswerable.[318]

The explanation that the crucial text in Lev 15:18 simply is "a decree of the king" in order to abandon any further elucidation and resulting debates appears too simplistic and is not helpful for a solid exegesis of this text. But it clearly demonstrates that even the ancient rabbis who were so scrupulous to find possible impurities and adequate purifications had no reasonable rationale for the text of Lev 15:18.[319] Thus they share the problems of ancient writers like Philo and Josephus as well as the challenges of present scholarly research.

I.1.3.1.4 Conclusions

What we finally gained for our investigation of Lev 15:18 is twofold: The general attitude of both well-educated Jewish representatives, Philo and Josephus, is dominated by a strong dualism between body and soul. As Josephus describes it, the soul can only by death (!) be freed from the miseries resulting from the bodily pleasures even of lawful sexual activities. Thus, we cannot expect any good reputation of conjugal intercourse, even though it may serve procreation. The reason why God so inherently linked pleasure with the Edenic instruction to beget children (Gen 1:28) remains unexplained by both authors. They seem to be led by their surrounding intellectual environment, influenced by Hellenistic perceptions like those of Pythagoras and Plato who deeply formed the dualistic attitudes that are very soon found even in Christian thinking and practice—not to forget the inner Jewish advocates of a very ascetic way of life that has been gloriously described by both authors as the highest sense and essence of philosophic Judaism: the Essenes. Furthermore, especially Josephus wrote primarily for educated Romans, rather than for Jews; consequently one must assume that he expressed Judaism in a way intelligible to Roman readers, perhaps describing the facts he was dealing with in a more offensive light.

---

318. Maccoby, *Ritual and Morality*, 59. On the problems of the Sifra's illogical argumentation see also pp. 59–60 and Neusner, *Dual Torah*, 11–192.

319. At least I could not find any further hints at that text or concerning actual practice dealing with ritual sexual impurity within the rabbinic literature.

But one has to acknowledge that Josephus and Philo might reflect some typical Jewish custom of bathing after conjugal intercourse due to some supposed defilement. What we do not know is the source of their perception and the Jewish group(s) they are referring to. Since there has been a great variety of belief and practice in their time, we cannot simply assume that they are speaking of Judaism in general, although their testimony is, of course, valuable to comprehend the "atmosphere" and halakhic streams of Judaism in their time.[320] We have to consider that important and influential groups like the Pharisees and Essenes had many special regulations about purifications and were concerned of impurity where there would be no biblical (Mosaic) ordinance given to denounce some contact or action to be defiling.[321]

The second important aspect that is to be recognized is a result of the first one. We can see that neither Philo nor Josephus support the recent scholarly explanations of the supposed ritual impurity in Lev 15:18. Although both interpret it as the same fact (conjugal intercourse), the rationales for this perplexing statement about defilement are differing widely and the basic assumptions regarding sexuality per se are also completely different and widely contradicted and opposed by today's theologians. Regarding Philo in particular, we even witness that he mainly denounces that sexuality of being "impure" or "polluted" which is not according to the Jewish laws or the purpose of procreation. Especially the last matter might be important for our investigation. Since the purpose of (legitimate) procreation is only maintained when having normal, conjugal intercourse, Philo must have understood the "pollution" of Lev 15:16–17 as deviating from that divine principle, while Lev 15:18 (if understood as referring to sexual intercourse) meets the divine requirements in the "purest" way—but unfortunately defiling corresponding to the bodily pleasure that is (in both author's perception) always disturbing spirituality. So his understanding of the impurity in Lev 15:18 must be the same as Josephus', namely: some kind of a *moral* defilement. But that is not only deviating from recent scholarly attitudes, but it is evidently completely contradicting the overall perception regarding sexuality that is widely shared by theologians today—and it runs counter to the context of the entire chapter Lev 15, which is not dealing with moral failures, but exclusively with ritual (im-)purity. Josephus and Philo, therefore, cannot serve as a positive affirmation of recent scholarly explanations as far as the general perception and the rationale for the defilement is concerned.

Besides, the problems which Philo, Josephus and the ancient rabbis encounter when maintaining the ideal of multiplying according to the Edenic command (Gen 1:28) and at the same time declaring the necessary sexual act as defiling, is very similar to the problems commentators are facing nowadays when trying to explain this antagonism and the resulting tensions, although the respective rationales and the

---

320. While e.g., Josephus glorifies the Essenes, he seems to orientate himself on the sect of the Pharisees. *Vita* 12. And Philo, while highly esteeming the Therapeutae (cf. *Contempl.* 1–90), obviously was not partaking in their way of life (cf. *Spec.* 3:3).

321. Cf. on these over careful practices e.g., Mark 7:2–9 (Pharisees); *B.J.* 2:150 (Essenes).

types of defilement are differing. While these ancient sources clearly demonstrate that the perception of the impurity even of legal sexuality has a long history, it unfortunately does not help us in the purpose of explaining Lev 15:18 and finding a satisfying answer for its supposed impurity. Moreover we notice that even the ancient Rabbinic interpreters had no idea (not even a speculative one) of the intention Yahweh might have had with the precept in Lev 15:18, and thus, naturally, they have been prone to conclude following their own cultural patterns or simply by interrupting any discussion with reference to God's impenetrable omniscience.

I.1.3.2 Current Interpretations and a Non-Defiling Alternative

Now it is necessary to take a closer look at recent investigation and argumentation regarding Lev 15:18, thereby establishing an alternative and, in my view, more adequate understanding of this law. Besides this central text there are two other instances that seem to be connected with it—or at least with the impurity attached to sexuality supposedly spoken of in this verse—namely: Exod 19:14–15 and 1 Sam 21:4–5 Since Lev 15:18 mostly represents the interpretative basis for the other instances that are sometimes viewed as connoting sexual impurity, the following investigation commences with Lev 15:18 and its context, before proceeding to the examination of the few other hints. The main thesis that will be argued is that the text does not speak about sexuality at all, but—as context, structure and other literary features suggests—that it deals with unintended, uncontrollable nocturnal emission of a man who thereby contaminates a woman lying next to him, without any intended, controllable, mutual sexual activity.

To begin with, standard Bible versions such as the NASB usually translate Lev 15:16–18 as follows:

> 16 Now if a man has a seminal emission, he shall bathe all his body in water and be unclean until evening. 17 As for any garment or any leather on which there is seminal emission, it shall be washed with water and be unclean until evening. 18 If a man lies with a woman so that there is a seminal emission, they shall both bathe in water and be unclean until evening.

This English translation gives no direct connection of the last sentence (v. 18) to vv. 16–17, and seems to imply a seminal emission due to normal sexual intercourse with one's wife, at least if one assumes that "to lie with a woman" is to be understood as a sexual relation.[322] But scrutinizing the Hebrew text closer makes one recognize that there is no break between the given sections (vv. 16–17 and v. 18). Even Milgrom, who holds that vv. 18 and 24 refer to sexual intercourse,[323] asserts that

---

322. Similarly Levine, *Leviticus*, 96.
323. See Milgrom, *Leviticus 1–16*, 904.

> the second half of the chapter dealing with discharges from women begins not here [v. 18] but in the next verse. The proof is found in the absence of the relative conjunction *kî*, which would be expected if the verse began a new law. Thus v. 18 is a continuation of vv. 16–17 and still deals with semen. Further proof is supplied by the subscript, v. 32b, which summarizes vv. 16–18 as a single unit with semen as its subject . . . .[324]

This uncleanness is not necessarily connected with the "lying with a woman" in a *sexual* sense. Even more, the Hebrew text does not read "if a man lies with a woman." It just reads thus:

וְאִשָּׁה אֲשֶׁר יִשְׁכַּב אִישׁ אֹתָהּ שִׁכְבַת־זָרַע וְרָחֲצוּ בַמַּיִם וְטָמְאוּ עַד־הָעָרֶב
And a woman, which a man emitting semen lies with, they shall both wash themselves in water, and be unclean until the evening.[325]

It does not necessarily or unambiguously speak about a man approaching a woman for sexual intercourse; it does not contain any of the clear expressions we would otherwise have to expect considering texts like Lev 18:19 or 20:17–18 (". . . approach a woman *to uncover her nakedness*"/". . . *so that he sees her nakedness and she sees his nakedness*"/". . . a man who lies with a . . . woman *and uncovers her nakedness*"), and others that are discussed in the next paragraph. Hence, the given verse could also be understood as describing a man near a woman who has an unintended (nocturnal) emission of semen, without any deliberate sexual intercourse. Before providing textual evidence in favor of this view, there are two linguistic challenges that need to be addressed.

First, the use of the verb שָׁכַב in sexual contexts. This verb, followed by the direct object (שָׁכַב + אֵת), regularly refers to sexual intercourse rather than just physical proximity to another person. While this is mostly undisputed, there is broad textual evidence leading to the conclusion that it is, at least, no absolute rule. The instance in Lev 20:13, for example, demonstrates that this construction is not sufficient to imply sexuality in every case; there it is still necessary to supplement a clarification that "if a man lies with a male" (וְאִישׁ אֲשֶׁר יִשְׁכַּב אֶת־זָכָר) is actually to be understood "*as in lying with a woman*" (מִשְׁכְּבֵי אִשָּׁה), that means: in a sexual sense. Similarly Lev 20:18: ". . . and he *uncovers* her *nakedness*" (וְגִלָּה אֶת־עֶרְוָתָהּ). Lev 20:20 also adds a remark to make sure the reader understands that indeed sexuality is meant (". . . he has *uncovered* his uncle's *nakedness*;" עֶרְוַת דֹּדוֹ גִּלָּה). In Lev 19:20, as well as in Lev 20:11–12, it is again the context providing a clarifying note, that determines the actual incident in view: "there shall be *punishment*" (Lev 19:20); "he has *uncovered* his father's *nakedness*"

---

324. Milgrom, *Leviticus 1–16*, 930. This idea of a literal unit will soon be taken up again to be investigated more closely.

325. Compare the most exact German translations (Elberfelder and Luther) which thus translate this verse and seemingly connect it with the emission of semen referred to within the previous verses. The Targumim and the LXX provide no further insights.

The Old Testament Foundation

(Lev 20:11); or "they have committed *incest*, their *bloodguiltiness* is upon them" (Lev 20:12).³²⁶ As these verses demonstrate, שָׁכַב + אֵת for itself is apparently not sufficient to be immediately associated with sexuality in the reader's mind, but has to be supplemented by unambiguous clarifications.

Further, there seems to be a distinction between שָׁכַב + אֵת compared to a combination of שָׁכַב with the preposition "with" (אֵת + שָׁכַב) concerning the mutuality/consent of the sexual contact. The difference between עִם and אֵת seems to be the force of the action. Mostly, in a situation of mutual consent the preposition עִם is used (to "lie with"); in situations of violence and force it rather is אֵת (to "lay [someone]"). As the investigation of the different instances within the Hebrew Scriptures confirms, it appears uncontradicted that at least שָׁכַב + אֵת, if used in a sexual context, dependably points at some violent force.³²⁷ Now, it seems strange to assume a situation of violently forced sexuality in Lev 15:18—or any verse of Lev 15 at all, since it does not deal with morals, with sin, or punishments, but just with matters of ritual purity. This may lead the reader to the conclusion that this verse actually does not deal with sexuality (or, alternatively, that only forced sex renders the persons involved unclean!); otherwise the construction שָׁכַב + אֵת would evoke (probably unanswerable) questions about the origin and context of this force—and why it appears so suddenly in this verse without any connection to its context.

The different instances using שָׁכַב confirm the conclusion that, in general, the context determines the meaning (frequently *sexuality*, but also often simple, usual *sleeping*: Gen 19:4; 28:11, 13; Exod 22:26; 2 Sam 4:5/7:12 (both שָׁכַב + אֵת!), and very often the *sleep of the dead*: Gen 47:30; Deut 31:16; 2 Sam 7:12; Ezek 31:18; 32:19, 27–30; frequently in 1–2 Kgs and 1–2 Chr), and שָׁכַב, if used in a sexual context, speaks generally about illicit sexual contacts—שָׁכַב + אֵת even about forced illicit sex.³²⁸ Regarding these observations about שָׁכַב, the following points are significant for a better understanding of Lev 15:18:

---

326. Even Lev 15:24, in close proximity of our verse Lev 15:18, does not necessarily imply sexual intercourse (although this is certainly included!), but would also be an adequate depiction of a man lying together with a woman when she suddenly starts to menstruate and thus "contaminates" him, rendering him ritually unclean (more on this verse below).

327. While the story in Gen 19:32–34 with the daughters of Lot "lying (with)" their father demonstrates that both constructions can be used synonymously: וְנִשְׁכְּבָה עִמּוֹ (v. 32); וַתִּשְׁכַּב אֶת (v. 33); שִׁכְבִי עִמּוֹ/שָׁכַבְתִּי אֶמֶשׁ אֶת (both v. 34); וַתִּשְׁכַּב עִמּוֹ (v. 35), other instances leave the impression that עִם indeed implies permission (mutual consent), while אֵת rather denotes force. Cf. the following texts concerning אֵת in a sexual context: Gen 34:2, 7 (please note the remark וַיְעַנֶּהָ: "he humbled her"); 1 Sam 2:22; 2 Sam 13:14 (again: וַיְעַנֶּהָ). See these verses with עִם concerning mutual consent: Gen 30:15–16; 39:7, 12, 14; Exod 22:16; 2 Sam 11:11; 12:24; 13:11. However, there are strong exceptions to this tendency, at least concerning שָׁכַב + עִם: Deut 22:25, 28–29; 2. Sam. 11:4. שָׁכַב + אֵת, on the other hand, seems to permanently convey (at least subliminally, if not openly) a violent force, if used in context of sexuality. Cf. on this also Davidson, *Flame*, 513–14; this grammatical feature is particularly stressed by Sternberg, *Poetics*, 446.

328. Cf. also TWOT s.v. שׁכב; Williams, "שׁכב," 4:102; Davidson, *Flame*, 513/fn.35; see also the verse list of the previous footnote.

1. The entire chapter of Lev 15 does not at all deal with sins (illicit sexuality etc.) and punishments, but just with purity and (ritual) defilement. Therefore, שָׁכַב would be out of place in this context, if meant to denote (illicit) sexual intercourse. "Going in to" or "knowing" one's wife would be the adequate terms to be employed. Hence, the verb שָׁכַב in vv. 18 and 24 (cf. v. 33) seems to present its other meaning: simple sleeping (instead of sex), as the other instances in chap. 15 may confirm (vv. 4, 20, 26; "lying/sleeping [on something]").

2. The verb שָׁכַב is used in v. 18 as well as its parallel v. 24 (on this structure see below) with the direct object marker אֵת, which in general denotes a contact without mutual consent, but rather with force (rape). Nothing at all in the context of these verses would support an understanding of violent sex. It rather implies that here is no mutuality given—simply because there is no sexuality! The incident dealt with emissions from only one person (v. 18: the man; v. 24: the woman) and "forces" the other one (his/her spouse) into the same ritual defilement—of course without mutual consent, just inadvertently. Thus שָׁכַב + אֵת is adequately applied in these verses, but, as it seems, even necessarily without any connection to sexuality (otherwise we would have to expect a strong punishment due to this violent sin, particularly concerning having sex during menstruation (v. 24): Lev 20:18; Ezek 18:6)!

3. On the other hand, as several instances prove, שָׁכַב + אֵת, if not appearing in a sexual context, describes simple lying (mostly sleeping), without any implications regarding mutuality or force, and (taken for itself) completely without any hints at sexuality.[329]

4. While Lev 15:18 and v. 24 use שָׁכַב + אֵת, the summary in v. 33 employs שָׁכַב + עִם as its synonym. That makes clear that the direct object marker אֵת in vv. 18, 24 is not to be overemphasized. It seems there is no deeper sense to be discovered by this particular construction—at least not as a hint concerning (forced) sexuality.[330]

5. If Lev 15:18 really intends to say something about sexuality, one would have to expect a clarifying statement, as in the texts presented above (Lev 18:19; 20:11–13, 17–18, 20), to make that point clear. It would be unreasonable to leave this ambiguous instance, so completely devoid of any contextual hints at sexuality, without any clarification, while entire chapters dealing with sexual transgressions (like Lev 18 and 20) are so explicit in their descriptions even though their context is so unambiguously clear.

---

329. See 2 Sam 4:5; 8:2; and some texts depicting the state of the dead as "lying/sleeping:" 2 Sam 7:12; Ezek 31:18; 32:19, 27–30.

330. This is again to be witnessed concerning Lev 20:11 (שָׁכַב + אֵת) and its parallel in Deut 27:20 (שָׁכַב + עִם).

There is a second issue that seems, for linguistic reasons, to weaken the position that will be presented on the following pages: Num 5:13. There it reads in context of punishment for an unfaithful wife: "If any man's wife goes astray and is unfaithful to him, *and a man has intercourse with her* . . . ." (vv. 12b–13a.) It is evident from the context that "and a man has intercourse with her" refers to sexual intercourse. The Hebrew phrase behind the translation is וְשָׁכַב אִישׁ אֹתָהּ שִׁכְבַת־זֶרַע, exactly the same appearing in Lev 15:18: יִשְׁכַּב אִישׁ אֹתָהּ שִׁכְבַת־זָרַע . . . . ("a man lying with her with emission of semen").[331] The literal meaning of the phrase for itself, however, is ambiguous as to the concrete act—whether unintended nocturnal emission or deliberate sexual intercourse. While the context of Num 5:13 clearly points to an intended transgression of the wedlock, the context of Lev 15:18, to the contrary, rather seems to allude to a man's unintended (nocturnal) emission of semen, which renders him (ritually) unclean, and therefore the woman who lies with him in one bed becomes unclean as well. Just as with the first linguistic investigation on שָׁכַב above, the context (including its further linguistic features) must determine the particular meaning—as will now be further explicated.

To begin with, we have to take a closer look at the structure of the entire chap. 15. Milgrom recognizes two possible structures underlying this chapter, both emphasizing the passage about male and female discharges (vv. 16–24), respectively sexual intercourse (v. 18); his "more meaningful division of this chapter" looks as follows:[332]

(A) Introduction (vv. 1–2a)
   (B) Abnormal male discharges (vv. 2b–15)
      (C) Normal male discharges (vv. 16–17)
         (X) Marital intercourse (v. 18)
      (C') Normal female discharges (vv. 19–24)
   (B') Abnormal female discharges (vv. 25–30)
     [motive: v. 31]
(A') Summary (vv. 32–33)

Milgrom's artificial break within the unit of vv. 16–18 for the purpose of declaring v. 18 and the supposed sexual intercourse to be the center of the chiasmic structure can hardly be supported by the linguistic features that apparently make vv. 16–18 a complete unit. As Whitekettle pointed out (and even Milgrom admitted earlier; see above),[333] the structure of the whole chapter is determined by the following Hebrew terms:[334]

---

331. The only other verse with a very similar wording is Lev 19:20, again dealing with sexuality: "If a man lies with a woman having an emission of semen . . ." (. . . וְאִישׁ כִּי־יִשְׁכַּב אֶת־אִשָּׁה שִׁכְבַת־זֶרַע). As explained regarding Num 5:13 above, the exact meaning of the ambiguous expression must be determined by the context and is not clear enough by itself.

332. Cf. Milgrom, *Leviticus 1–16*, 904–5; similarly Hartley, *Leviticus*, 206; Davidson, *Flame*, 328.

333. Cf. Milgrom, *Leviticus 1–16*, 930; quoted above in the introduction to this section.

334. Whitekettle, "Leviticus 15:18 Reconsidered," 35.

(A) כִּי אִישׁ אִישׁ (v. 2b)
  (B) וְאִישׁ כִּי (v. 16)
    (C) וְאִשָּׁה כִּי (v. 19)
    (C) וְאִשָּׁה כִּי (v. 25)

This structure portrays vv. 16–18 and vv. 19–24 as single, complete units. Nevertheless, Whitekettle tries to define an extra unit of v. 18. He assumes that the אֲשֶׁר of v. 18 should be seen as marker of a particular unit, since it could be understood as a conditional particle. But the fairly rare use of אֲשֶׁר as conditional particle in contrast to its frequent use as relative pronoun can hardly serve as satisfying explanation of a special unit, which appears so suddenly and so unconnected to its context, thus interrupting the underlying order of the entire chapter. There is no need to declare this instruction of v. 18 as a conditional sentence, especially since אֲשֶׁר is used so frequently in the surrounding verses in its usual function as relative pronoun (see vv. 5, 6, 9, 10, 11, 12, 17, 20, 22, 24, 26, 31, 33). There are different allusions pointing to the coherent structure especially of vv. 16–18 and 19–24, which should not so easily be broken up in favor of a rather unlikely semantic possibility.

In particular, considering the vv. 19–24, one finds some kind of repetition, a parallel unit to the passage of vv. 16–18, now concerning (normal) female discharges. Especially the command in the last verse (v. 24), thus corresponding to the last verse of the passage concerning male discharges (vv. 16–18), is very similar to the one investigated: "And if a man actually lies with her, so that her menstrual impurity is on him, he shall be unclean seven days, and every bed on which he lies shall be unclean." It is important to recognize that v. 18 and v. 24 are very closely connected with each other; they reflect the underlying principle in using the same structure, but referring to different (male/female) discharges.

The argument of Whitekettle that v. 18 employs the plural (both man and woman are unclean one day) while v. 24 contains the singular (only the man is unclean seven days)[335] is depending on several matters: (1) The structure is internally somehow reversed (first the plural in v. 19, followed by singulars in the next verses); (2) The whole unit (vv. 19–24) deals with persons contaminated by touching some contaminated material or person and especially the man's possible contamination is constantly emphasized; (3) The impurity is of a different kind: contamination with impure person or material renders unclean for *one* day, contact with impure flow renders unclean for *seven* days; in the man's unit is no such difference given, for the level of impurity obviously is less defiling and not "strong" enough to render persons unclean who just touched thus contaminated materials. However, the most important argument

---

335. Whitekettle, "Leviticus 15:18 Reconsidered," 35–36. His further argumentation (p. 36) that we would have to expect some different kind of wording if just contamination would be meant in v. 18 is the same argument that is applied in this proposal in the opposite direction. If sexuality had been meant, why is there no clear wording given, such as Lev 18:19 or 20:18? Hence, it seems that only the overall context can be really helpful.

regarding the objection that in v. 24 there is only the man called "unclean seven days" and not also the woman he has been contaminated by, is the fact that—contrary to the incident in v. 18—the menstruation lasts longer than one night and the woman perhaps has been unclean already for some days.[336] So she must not be unclean for seven more days, possibly over and over again! She is not rendered unclean anew; only the man becomes (newly) defiled at the time he is "contaminated" by her blood! The following structure regarding the type of contamination, the duration of impurity and the starting point thereof may be helpful to understand the point:

A (vv. 16–17) List of *contaminated material*; unclean until evening; no contamination from material to humans possible; contamination day: X.[337]

   B (v. 18) *Direct contamination* from impure man to woman, unclean until evening, both have *same duration* of uncleanness; contamination day: X (the uncleanness for both *begins always at the same time*, and *ceases always at the same time*).

A' (vv. 19–23) List of *contaminated material or persons*; unclean until evening; contamination from material to humans is possible; contamination day: X or Y.[338]

   B' (v. 24) *Direct contamination* with the defiling flow; unclean for seven days; both have (generally) *same duration* of uncleanness; contamination day: X or Y (the uncleanness for both *may begin at different times*, and therefore *may cease at different times*).

The entire passage (vv. 16–24) is apparently structured according to the type, duration and level of impurity, culminating in the final verse of each unit as the climax with a direct contact to the defiling fluid.[339] Besides the same structural pattern and the resulting similarity of both units (under consideration of different levels/durations of impurity), the given explanations also indicate that v. 24 is not alluding to sexuality, as is frequently argued! Since the only way for v. 24 to mean sexuality would be the sudden commencing of menstruation during intercourse (otherwise both participants would have to die; see Lev 18:19, 26–29), the different duration of the uncleanness points to a simple (possibly unintended) sleeping near each other, thus rendering the

---

336. It is important to notice that, contrary to some Bible translations, the Hebrew text of v. 24 does not exclusively speak about the sudden beginning of the menstruation (thus rendering both persons unclean for the same period, starting at the same day), but about the rather general case "that her menstrual impurity is on him" (וּתְהִי נִדָּתָהּ עָלָיו)—a case that might happen at any time of her menstruation, if she did not duly separate (for whatever the cause may be).

337. X is the first day of the impurity, the starting day.

338. Y is the second to the seventh day of impurity; only possible and applicable in case of female (menstrual) impurity.

339. As we see, the fluid is the cause of uncleanness. However, it does not follow that normal sexual intercourse is defiling due to the fact that semen is involved. It is only the unintended (nocturnal) emission that is spoken of as rendering impure. A simple reason may be the ineffective shedding, the missing of its original aim and sense (this idea will be elaborated below).

man unclean.[340] That would also fit v. 18 as climax of the paralleling unit, not dealing with sexual intercourse, but with simple sleeping near each other and thus being possibly contaminated.

There is another internal hint affirming this structure of connecting v. 18 and v. 24 and thus stressing their similarity or equality; again it is Milgrom, referring to v. 18, who honestly tells: "At the same time, the construction of this sentence has baffled the commentaries. Why is the woman subject if her case does not begin until the next verse? Would not this sentence flow more smoothly if it had read . . . 'If a man has sexual relations with a woman'?"[341]

Reading this verse under consideration of the structure proposed below, thus recognizing the climax of possible defilement in the vv. 18 and 24, there is no question to be answered.

Just like the verses before the high points in v. 18 and v. 24 contain a list of (lifeless) objects to be defiled by *simple contact*, so the respective climax speaks about the (living) object(s) to be defiled by *simple contact* from person to person (cf. v. 17/vv. 20–23). This structure of both blocks is further supported by the unusual fact that, consequently, v. 18 begins with the woman (the word order in the Hebrew text is differing from the way e.g., the NASB reads it: וְאִשָּׁה אֲשֶׁר יִשְׁכַּב אִישׁ)—as living object liable to be defiled—and not with the man, then possibly reading: "If a man has sexual relations with a woman." The woman in this case is to be interpreted as the object to be defiled, just as the man in v. 24 is the object to be defiled the other way round, by the woman. Both instances (vv. 15–18 and 19–24) speak about usual, defiling discharges and consequently list the objects to be defiled at the first position of each explanatory sentence.

Also, if interpreting v. 18 as exclusively referring to sexual intercourse, an important part in the list of possibly defiled "objects" due to nocturnal emissions would be missing: the wife. Obviously, the husband is an element of the women's defilement-list (v. 24); but the wife would be missing in the men's defilement list! Besides, that would not only inexplicably destroy the intention and completeness of the given laws; furthermore it destroys the structure presented by Milgrom and taken over by others, for C and C' would not be reflecting each other. They would not be dealing with the same elements regarding the normal (usual) male/female discharges, since the male does not (and consequently cannot?) defile the woman, as long as there is no sexual intercourse, but just a nocturnal emission; whereas women are always defiling men just

---

340. A menstruating woman had to separate—therefore it would not be easy to be contaminated, unless menstruation occurred suddenly, unexpectedly. However, there are quite a lot of further unusual circumstances in which it would be possible to be defiled, e.g., when it is impossible to separate in cases of illness, war, or just when separation has not been heeded strictly enough to prevent from any contact. But especially in cases of relations with non-Jewish women etc. And we also see in the numerous laws of the Torah that Yahweh provided for those exceptional, unintended cases, possibly in times when some of the given instructions would not be heeded any more (cf. e.g., Deut 17:14–20; 24:1–4; 25:7–10).

341. Milgrom, *Leviticus 1–16*, 930.

by contact with their usual menses. Additionally, the kind (i.e., duration) of impurity is differing in both cases, thus indicating an affiliation to nocturnal emissions (v. 18) or menstruation (v. 24)—but not to an "inverted hinge,"[342] which would only feebly explain an unlikely insertion of an ordinance concerning sexual intercourse, while at the same time adhering to the same kind and lastingness of impurity given in the (completely different) context and demonstrated unity of vv. 16–18![343] The following structure would fit the context, the textual syntax of vv. 18 and 24, and the overall subject much better:

(A) Introduction (vv. 1–2a)
  (B) Abnormal male discharges (vv. 2b–15)
    (C) Normal male discharges defiling the concerned person himself (v. 16)
      (D) Defiling lifeless objects, which <u>do not</u> defile living objects (v. 17)
        (E) *Internal, final Climax*: defiling living objects: wife (v. 18)
    (C') Normal female discharges defiling the concerned person herself (v. 19)
      (D') Defiling lifeless objects, which <u>do</u> defile living obj. (vv. 20–23)[344]
        (E') *Internal, final Climax*: defiling living objects: husband (v. 24)
  (B') Abnormal female discharges (vv. 25–30)
(A') Summary incl. rationale/motive (vv. 31–33)

The various considerations given above support this structure and interpretation. Then there is no need to explain the sudden, unexpected, and rather misplaced insertion of a precept about sexual intercourse, which is usually recognized only once in v. 18, overlooking its similarity to v. 24 and the fact that chaps. 11–17 deal only with uncleanness and purification; sexual regulations are not dealt with until chap. 18, including commandments against sexual intercourse during menstruation (which thus would make Lev 15:24 redundant), using much more concrete terms:

> You shall not approach a woman *to uncover her nakedness* during her menstrual impurity (Lev 18:19).

> If there is a man who lies with a menstruous woman *and uncovers her nakedness, he has laid bare her flow, and she has exposed the flow of her blood* (Lev 20:18).

---

342. Milgrom, *Leviticus 1–16*, 930–31; Davidson and Gane follow that argumentation; cf. Davidson, *Flame*, 329; Gane, *Leviticus/Numbers*, 263. This "inverted hinge" demands the change of כִּי and אִשָּׁה, but does not regard that even v. 17 (also) contains the אִשָּׁה, thus binding together vv. 17 and 18 as a practical interpretation and further application of v. 16. There is no change or break between vv. 17 and 18, not even an inverted hinge. If so, we would also have to expect that inverted hinge in v. 24, thus shifting the sphere of defilement again up to conjugal intercourse. But this evidence is also missing.

343. Cf. again Milgrom, *Leviticus 1–16*, 930; Whitekettle, "Leviticus 15:18 Reconsidered," 35.

344. Please note that the defilement from one unclean object to the other is of another degree (lasting only *one* day: vv. 19–23) than a contamination of the living object through the impure flow itself (lasting *seven* days: v. 24)!

These instances leave not the smallest doubt that it *now* refers to sexual intercourse and not just to lying *near* an unclean person, as Lev 15:18, 24 and the context indicate by pointing to defilements due to a simple *unintended contact*. That it could hardly be deliberate sexual intercourse these verses (i.e., Lev 15:18, 24) are referring to, may be concluded from v. 24, since any deliberate sexual contact during menstruation would have to be punished by "cutting off from among their people" (cf. Lev 18:19, 26–29). The only explanation for yet referring to sexuality would be the sudden beginning of the menstruation during sexual intercourse; but then, again, there would be no intention! Hence, when accepting v. 24 paralleling v. 18, one necessarily has to conclude that v. 18 is also dealing only with an unintended happening, since there is no reasonable way to see any deliberate act in being contaminated by the blood of v. 24. Furthermore, if v. 24 would actually be speaking about sexuality, we would have to expect the pronouncing of the impurity's duration for both participants in that verse, and not just for the man who apparently has newly been contaminated some day after the commencement of the woman's impurity. The entire chapter is seemingly dealing with unintended occurrences. To interpret v. 18 as the only exception, and that without any special introduction, a particular and unambiguous linguistic marker, or another obvious shifting of levels, is very unlikely.

As to the reason why it is only the nocturnal emission that has the potential to defile the woman, in contrast to usual sexual intercourse, this is easily explained by their different aims and results. While sexual intercourse is the instrument to follow the blessing of Gen 1:28, and to experience the mutual intimacy of Gen 2:24, nocturnal emission is completely devoid of such prospects and merely constitutes a rather senseless loss of "life liquids."[345] Furthermore, only thus there is another structural concordance between the male and female defilements in vv. 16–18 and vv. 19–24, since both passages contain such "life liquids" (semen and menstrual blood), both shed *in vain*, without reaching their original aims, namely: pregnancy/procreation. This is surely not applicable to sexual intercourse.[346] It seems evident that semen should not be shed except through conjugal intercourse—yet this must not result in reasoning that procreation is the only adequate aim of sex. Licit sexual intercourse involves much more; it constitutes the marital oneness, the deep intimacy hinted at in Gen 2:24 (the two become "one flesh"), it makes one deeply "know/experience" (יָדַע; Gen 4:1) one's spouse, and is described foremost with its lustful, pleasurable character in many instances, particularly in the Song of Solomon—and even in context of the great longing for children as presented in Gen 18:12: "Sarah laughed to herself, saying, 'After I have become old, shall I have (sexual) pleasure (עֶדְנָה), my lord being old also?'"

---

345. Similarly, although erroneously applied to sexuality: Wenham, "Why does," 434; followed by other commentators who see the senseless loss of these life-giving liquids as rationale for the impurity mentioned in Lev 15:18.

346. Albeit quite a lot of semen is lost anyway, sexual intercourse still moves toward the mentioned aims of intimacy (Gen 2:24) and procreation (Gen 1:28); nocturnal emission never does.

It is significant that, although both were waiting so long for descendants, Sarah nevertheless depicts the sexual act primarily as "having pleasure" and not as "procreating."

Commentators mostly recognize an allusion to sexual intercourse and its (inherent) uncleanness only in v. 18, usually overlooking the similarity (and even actual equality) of v. 24.[347] But if both verses generally belong to the same realm, one has to inquire why the (quality/duration of the) uncleanness of v. 18 is not the same as in v. 24 while both instances are obviously referring to the same cause (act) of impurity.[348] The duration is evidently depending on the kind of discharge, not the kind of act (i.e., sexual intercourse vs. "normal sleeping" beside each other including the resulting contamination). Consequently, the uncleanness itself must depend on the kind of discharge, and not the way one comes into contact with it. The most natural explanation for the similarity of vv. 18 and 24, and yet their different (quality/duration of) uncleanness, is to assume a communication from one spouse to the other through lying in the same bed with each other at the time of nocturnal emission or menstruation—there is absolutely no need to put any *sexual* contact into these verses, particularly when considering the aforementioned very difficult problems that arise when we do this.[349]

The summary of vv. 32–33 is also of considerable importance, because there we find no reference to sexual intercourse, but just an abstract of the other, unambiguous topics:

> This is the law for the one with a discharge, and for the man who has a seminal emission so that he is unclean by it, and for the woman who is ill because of

---

347. An exception would be Milgrom and Hartley who also consider v. 24 as referring to sexual intercourse; cf. Milgrom, *Leviticus 1–16*, 904; Hartley, *Leviticus*, 212. Others like Wenham, Whitekettle, and Davidson do not take this paralleling verse into consideration.

348. That it is not the same "level" of impurity and therefore not the same act as reason for the uncleanness, is to be seen from the fact that the uncleanness in the first instance (seminal emission) continues until evening, while the second (menstrual contamination) lasts seven days. Furthermore, we have to consider Deut 23:10–11 which again speaks about a man's unintended (nocturnal) emission, thus excluding him from the Israelite camp until bathing in the evening. Consequently, in connection with Lev 15:16–17 it points to the fact that the uncleanness is not a result of sexual intercourse. Otherwise we would have to expect further instructions regarding sexual contacts with women in the camp (since even during military campaigns there might have been such intercourse; against Wenham, "Why does," 432), or at least some special type of impurity with a peculiar time of uncleanness due to sexual relations in Lev 15:18 and/or v. 24. (Also, it might be interesting to notice that at least the ancient rabbis understood the "camp" of Deut 23:10 not as referring to a military campaign (v. 9 referring to Israel's enemies for them was a complete ordinance in itself), but to the camp of the Levites and the Temple; cf. Maccoby, *Ritual and Morality*, 62–63. Thus there would not be any connection at all between supposed impurity from sexuality and some military campaign, but it simply shows the necessity of separating (cf. 1 Sam 20:26). However, the context (vv. 9–14) suggests that the text indeed deals with a military campaign against Israel's enemies.)

349. We again have to notice that the previous vv. 16–17 and 19–23 are only dealing with defiling different objects *by contact*. Consequently, the respective climax found at the end of each passage by referring to humans is also indicating that even humans will be defiled *by contact*—simple contact, without the necessity of sexual intercourse.

menstrual impurity, and for the one who has a discharge, whether a male or a female, or a man who lies with an unclean woman.

It clearly alludes to the actual content, namely (as aforementioned in the structural outline above):

(A) Unusual (morbid) male discharges (vv. 2b–15)
   (B) Usual (non-morbid) male discharge: (Noct.) emission of semen (vv. 16–18)
   (B') Usual (non-morbid) female discharge: menstruation (vv. 19–24)
(A') Unusual (morbid) female discharges (vv. 25–30)

Even the order of the chapter's content is echoed in vv. 32–33, thus presenting a precise summary of the given subjects, thereby excluding a sudden insertion of other topics like common sexuality. It really seems that there is no place and no reason to find a short statement about usual, licit sexual intercourse in v. 18. Judging from the given text, its structure, context, and wording in Lev 15, there is generally no ritual uncleanness at all attached to legal sexual intercourse, because it generally does not deal with this kind of incident. What makes sexuality "unclean" is finally stated in chap. 18 of the book of Leviticus, dealing with deliberate actions that violate holy law. Hence, "pure" and "impure" regarding sexuality have to be reasoned by those ordinances;[350] licit sexuality goes out free of any impurity.

Furthermore, considering the consequences, God would evidently disapprove of his own Edenic institution (marriage) with all the negative consequences involved in that perception.[351] It is hardly possible to interpret the ritual uncleanness reasonably, while simultaneously keeping exalted the Edenic ideal of oneness (Gen 2:24: "one flesh") as the great "holistic" feature[352] and the perfect unity approved by God and even used as significant symbolism of his relationship with Israel (resp. Christ and the church: Eph 5:30–32). Transferring these consequences to the spiritual sphere God is using to describe his relationship with Israel, it would mean that the deepest intimacy ("one spirit" with God in 1 Cor 6:16–17) would be defiling the intimate (spiritual) relationship he wants to share with Christians.

In fact, particularly the rationale for rendering participants of conjugal intercourse ritually unclean is the crux of this case for those understanding that Lev 15:18 indeed deals with sexual intercourse.[353] It is mostly explained by the strict separation

---

350. As we have seen above, Philo works in just that way declaring only that kind of sexuality unclean which is against the divine order given in Lev 18 and similar chapters evidently dealing with sexuality and not with uncontrollable discharges.

351. So e.g., Wenham states: "In my commentary on Leviticus (1979) I realised this problem and was therefore unable to see symbolic significance in the uncleanness of sexual intercourse." Wenham, "Why does," 433. Although he tries to give an explanation on pp. 433–34, it is not really satisfying, as Whitekettle demonstrated (see Whitekettle, "Leviticus 15:18 Reconsidered," 32–34).

352. Cf. e.g., as basic idea in Davidson, *Flame*, 1–844; Hartley, *Leviticus*, 211.

353. Cf. e.g., Hartley, *Leviticus*, 210–11: "Since sexual intercourse, above all in the context of marriage, is essential to carry out God's command given to humans at creation, 'Be fruitful and multiply'

of Yahweh from anything related to the "cycle of life and death."³⁵⁴ Therefore, anything like male semen, female blood flow, and, finally, even sexual intercourse itself would be defiling, for it belongs to the realm of procreation. The ineffective shedding of life fluids³⁵⁵ is, at least, a good explanation for the separation demanded by Yahweh regarding the general morbid as well as non-morbid discharges, but concerning the Edenic command to multiply (and that requires sexual intercourse) it only serves as a poor and unsatisfactory explanation, as is candidly admitted by some researchers.³⁵⁶

(Gen 1:28), and his great promise of numerous descendants to Abraham (Gen 15:5), it is baffling that legitimate sexual intercourse renders the participants unclean." Wenham honestly admits: ". . . the law in Lev 15:18 . . . is one of the most puzzling in the OT. It seems to run counter to the whole tenor of biblical morality . . . as Dillmann forcibly pointed out, there is no suggestion that marital intercourse or childbirth (cf. Lev 12) were ever considered sinful in Israel. Indeed it is hard to see how this could be so against the background of Gen 1:28; 9:7." Wenham, "Why does," 432. Cf. also Davidson, *Flame*, 329–32; for a survey of (rather unsatisfying) explanations see Milgrom, *Leviticus 1–16*, 766.

354. Cf. on these opinions e.g., Davidson, *Flame*, 328–31; Whitekettle, "Leviticus 15:18 Reconsidered," 31–41; Maccoby, *Ritual and Morality*, 60, 207; Gane, *Leviticus/Numbers*, 261–62; Harris, "Leviticus," 586; Milgrom, *Leviticus 1–16*, 904–5, 930–31; Stuart, *Exodus*, 427; Durham, *Exodus*, 265; Hartley, *Leviticus*, 210–11. Rooker reasons from 15:31 that vv. 16–18 are just a precaution against any pagan fertility cult within the tabernacle precinct; and that "this demythologizing of sex thus has a polemical role; the legislation does not indicate that sex was sinful and without value"; cf. Rooker, *Leviticus*, 203–4. But he does not directly discuss the aspect of ritual uncleanness perhaps due to sexual intercourse.

355. Wenham, "Why does," 433–34; Hartley, *Leviticus*, 211; Davidson, *Flame*, 331. Another explanation is given by Whitekettle, "Leviticus 15:18 Reconsidered," 39–44, who convincingly criticizes Wenham's argumentation and proves it to be wrong in case of Lev 15:18, since it is too far from the actual setting and biological circumstances of sexual intercourse; cf. Hartley, *Leviticus*, 211. Furthermore, Whitekettle explains the crossing of "functional boundaries" (urination and seminal emission) to be the defiling cause. Whitekettle, "Leviticus 15:18 Reconsidered," 43–44. But, consequently, every act of urination would again render the man unclean, for the "functional boundaries" are crossed again the other way round! Also, if only the crossing of functional boundaries is to be regarded as reason, the woman would again only be defiled by contamination, not by active participation. And that is again contrary to the whole foundation of Whitekettle's argumentation (cf. p. 36). Hartley simply understands the text as some prevention against the introduction of sexual acts in the sanctuary. Hartley, *Leviticus*, 211. This explanation is not really better, since there are other regulations against temple prostitution that are dealing much more clearly with this danger (cf. e.g., Deut 23:18). His second explanation (p. 214) of the law as to control sexual passion is also unsatisfying, for the common Israelite would not have to attend the sanctuary very often, while the priests, on the other hand, would excessively be kept from sexual "pleasure/delight" (עֶדְנָה; Gen 18:12) and thus even from the chance to procreate—intemperance evidently would have to be dealt with in another, more obvious way.

356. Maccoby, for instance, explains: "Some of the discharges that produce impurity are indeed life-diminishing (abnormal discharges of semen or menstrual blood), but they are not enough to substantiate a theory that requires that all life-diminishing discharges defile. Moreover, normal loss of semen hardly comes into the category of life-diminishing discharges. . . . Involuntary loss of semen might be regarded as life-diminishing, but a discharge that produces new life cannot be so regarded." Maccoby, *Ritual and Morality*, 31; cf. Whitekettle, "Leviticus 15:18 Reconsidered," 33, 38; Davidson, *Flame*, 331/fn.102 also points to this fact. Nonetheless Maccoby and Whitekettle share the common view that conjugal sexuality is always defiling Maccoby, *Ritual and Morality*, 30–32, 58–59; Whitekettle, "Leviticus 15:18 Reconsidered," 42–44. Gane, *Leviticus/Numbers*, 261 clearly explicates that "human sexuality and reproduction are not intrinsically impure. The Lord created this facet of life for perfect human beings in a perfect world (Gen 1:27–28; 2:23–25). Made in the image of the holy God (1:26–27), they were designed to continue and participate in, the divine process of creation, thereby

It would be more precise to term it a "deviation from comprehensive life" (instead of "cycle of *life and* death"), since all those elements are defiling that are associated with a loss of life (and not those giving life!): contact with (1) a loss of life-giving blood (menstruation, blood flow after childbirth, morbid discharges . . .); (2) a loss of life-giving semen (nocturnal emission, morbid discharges . . .); (3) disease and death (leprosy, carrion, dead humans . . .). Obviously, sex is not part of any of these categories and as such would be completely out of place in Lev 15—and, in fact, anywhere else. Having licit sex, to the contrary, belongs to the realm of pure life, will usually be life-increasing, in fact, life-giving—having nothing to do with a loss of life-giving fluids, with disease or death. Furthermore, God is never associated with the foregoing categories of deviating from life, he never commands anything that would necessarily result in ritual impurity. But sex is part of the divine plan for human happiness and wholeness—already in sinless paradise (Gen 1:28), where originally absolutely no "deviation from comprehensive life" existed, but where everything was approved of him as being "very good" (Gen 1:31).[357] The state of mortality as the basis of the intriguing theory of the "cycle of life and death" did not yet exist in paradise—but sex did. After the Fall there emerged different "deviations from comprehensive life," as those mentioned above. Sexuality, however, does not belong to this post-Fall state of mortality and disease, but to the Edenic ideal of everlasting life, health, and comprehensive well-being.

I.1.3.3 Further Evidence?

I.1.3.3.1 Exod 19:14–15

In scholarly literature the interpretation of Lev 15:18 is at times linked with the command given at Mount Sinai before Yahweh's glory came down to the mountain top:

> The Lord also said to Moses, "Go to the people and consecrate them today and tomorrow, and let them wash their garments; and let them be ready for the

---

emulating their Creator. So God intended sexuality to be a vital component of holy living (cf. the Song of Songs)." And he finally states: "Marriage is still honorable and the marriage bed remains morally pure (Heb 13:4)." Ibid., 262. His interpretation of Lev 15:18, however, still follows the common opinion of ritually impure sexuality, although it would be only life-giving, and so weakens the previous statements about the positive aspects of sexuality, which are generally right.

357. Attentive readers might respond that having sex, becoming pregnant, and finally giving birth, indeed results in a ritual defilement, namely: blood flow after childbirth (Lev 12). That is right and might be the only exception. Considering Gen 3:16, however, it seems likely that this circumstance could be linked to the changes appearing after the Fall. As this verse instills, birth in paradise would have been without pain—incredible for women nowadays. So why could it not, consequently, also have been without defilement due to some way of avoiding blood flow (e.g., a much better and incredibly fast "healing" process)—similarly incredible for us today? However, it still remains true that sex per se, in the first place, has nothing to do with a senseless loss of semen or blood (although possibly resulting circumstances may have).

third day, for on the third day the Lord will come down on Mount Sinai in the sight of all the people...."

So Moses went down from the mountain to the people and consecrated the people, and they washed their garments. And he said to the people, "Be ready for the third day; do not go near a woman." (Exod 19:10–11, 14–15.)

The expression "do not go near a woman" (אַל־תִּגְּשׁוּ אֶל־אִשָּׁה) is often interpreted as a euphemism meaning "to have sexual relations with a woman."[358] Taking into consideration that the Mosaic legislation is generally unambiguous when speaking about sexuality, we have to assert that this text is conspicuously ambiguous and unclear. It actually is very strange and significant that it does not read, "Do not *lie* with a [better: your] woman," as is formulated frequently in other instances—even within the same book (Exodus), only three chapters away (cf. Exod 22:15, 19)! At least, there are no general euphemistic tendencies detectable in this book that might support the euphemism theory. In fact, the Hebrew שָׁכַב ("lie"), functioning as an indicator of sexual relations in many instance it is used—except another meaning (i.e., simple sleep or the sleep of the dead) is clearly supported by the given context –,[359] is completely absent in the entire passage. Similarly any hint at a man "knowing" (יָדַע; e.g., in Gen 4:1) or "going in to" (אֶל + בּוֹא; usually וַיָּבֹא אֵלֶיהָ, e.g., in Gen 29:23; 30:4; 38:2, 18; Ruth 4:13) his wife is missing. The text only speaks about "approaching/drawing near" (נָגַשׁ). Thus the mere contact is emphasized, not just intimate (sexual) intercourse. It rather speaks about contamination which occurred even by simple contact when coming (too) close to any menstruating woman, because that would make them unable/ineligible to draw near to Yahweh.[360] The Hebrew נָגַשׁ ("draw near"), in fact, nowhere else

---

358. See e.g., Wenham, "Why does," 432; Davidson, *Flame*, 329–30; Gane, *Leviticus/Numbers*, 581 and many others; cf. Koltun-Fromm, "Sexuality and Holiness," 388–94 about the ancient rabbinic interpretation (also referring to sexual abstinence concerning Exod 19:15) as given in 'Abot R. Nat. 2:3; Exod. Rab. 19:3; 47:3; b. Šabb. 87a; Yebam. 62a. (Similarly Philo in *Mos.* 2:68–69, focusing on Moses' continence.) Josephus renders the phrase in Exod 19:15 as possibly referring to sexuality; cf. *A.J.* 3:78. He is deviating from the LXX which is, like the Hebrew text, only speaking about "approaching/coming near" (μὴ προσέλθητε γυναικί; cf. LSJ/BDAG/LEH s.v. προσέρχομαι). Josephus formulates ἀπὸ συνουσίας τῆς γυναικῶν, while this συνουσία literally means just "a being with/social intercourse/society/conversation/communion/intercourse with a teacher/cohabitation" (LSJ s.v. συνουσία), but he uses it also as euphemism for sexual intercourse; cf. e.g., *A.J.* 3:275; 6:235; 19:239; *C.Ap.* 2:203, 234. However, he also knows the more decent and discreet meaning of a social gathering and friendly conversation; cf. *A.J.* 1:167; 5:307; 12:118, 197; 14:454; 15:241; 18:150; *B.J.* 1:489, 570.

359. Cf. on concretely implying sexuality: Gen 19:32–35 (7x); 26:10; 30:15–16; 34:2, 7; 35:22; 39:7, 10, 12, 14; Exod 22:15, 18; Lev 18:22; 19:20; 20:11, 12, 13, 18, 20; Num 5:13, 19; Deut 22:22–29 (5x); 27:20–23 (4x); 28:30. Sleeping with different genital discharges: Lev 15:4, 18, 20, 24, 26, 33. Simple sleep: Gen 19:4; 28:11, 13; 47:30; Exod 22:26; Lev 14:47; 26:6; Num 23:24; 24:9; Deut 6:7; 11:19; 24:12–13; 31:16.

360. Cf. Propp, *Exodus 19–40*, 162–63; he also asserts that the verb used in this instance for "approaching/go near [a woman]" (נָגַשׁ) "may originally have connoted touching." Hence, "this command addressed to the men, might be meant either euphemistically—do not heterosexual intercourse—or literally—to avoid women, lest they spread menstrual impurity." Ibid., 163.

(of 125 instances in the OT!) connotes sexuality and appears in only two instances in context of touching, embracing, or kissing someone (cf. Gen 27:21–27; 48:10)![361] To suppose a sexual meaning just once in the given passage seems too far-fetched for a verb occurring so frequently with another (less intense/intimate) meaning. It is more naturally explained by considering a ritual defilement through simple contamination, possibly by touching, embracing, or kissing a woman. This contamination happens, of course, likewise through sexual contact with a (suddenly) menstruating woman. The intention of Exod 19:15, however, is not only this possible incident, but any way the consecrated men might run the risk of becoming unclean immediately before approaching their holy God. The text is not declaring mere sexual intercourse to be defiling. Hence, it speaks rather generally about "a [namely: any] woman" instead of "your woman/wife."

Of course it is possible that some other uncleanness occurs even without touching women (Lev 12–15), and in order to avoid any impurity due to these other possible defilements, all men were consecrated "for the third day" by washing themselves on the first and second days (and perhaps even immediately) before the Lord's approach. So there would finally just the women be left as the only possibility to be accidentally defiled immediately before meeting Yahweh if a woman suddenly began to menstruate and then touched one of the consecrated men. Consequently there are precautions to be taken by generally separating from women, not just by abstaining from sexual intercourse.

If the time of consecration is to be understood as lasting for three days—from the day when Moses went down from the mountain (v. 14) until the third day of the Lord's appearance (v. 15)—we have to recognize that this time span is not in accordance with the ordinances given in Lev 15:16–24! In fact, the time for consecration would have to last for at least one day (due to the possible uncleanness of seminal emission or contact with something that has been touched by a menstruating woman) or for seven days (if directly contaminated by menstrual blood).[362] Besides the generally blurred

---

361. Cf., for instance, this selection of the occurrences within the Pentateuch: Gen 18:23; 19:9; 29:10; 33:3, 6–7; 43:19; 44:18; 45:4; 48:13; Exod 19:22; 20:21; 21:6; 24:2, 14; 28:43; 30:20; 32:6; 34:30, 32; Lev 2:8; 8:14; 21:21, 23; Num 4:19; 8:19; 32:16; Deut 20:2; 21:5; 25:1, 9. Please note further esp. 2 Sam 17:29 where נגשׁ is used without any sexual connotation and then שׁכב is added to indicate the following sexual contact. As aforementioned within the word study on שׁכב (above), this word for itself is evidently not sufficient to imply sexuality.

362. Cf. Lev 15:16–24. Kaiser reads Exod 19:15 as a command to abstain from sexual intercourse. Yet he does not link it with ritual impurity. For him it is just a sign for the inner purification and preparation (cf. Kaiser, "Exodus," 418; cf. also Nichol and Andreasen, *ABC*, Exod 19:10, 1:596), thus, for Buttrick, marking the beginning of "Sunday clothes;" cf. Rylaarsdam, "Exodus," 974. Propp clearly points out that "a male seminal emission elicited by proximity to a woman would also be ritually defiling." Propp, *Exodus 19–40*, 163. Thus he rather supports the view that it is the seminal emission while lying *near* a woman which is defiling, not sexual intercourse per se. Nonetheless he contemplates about other possible reasons for the required separation in Exod 19:15. Stuart holds the (possible) opinion, that men and women were addressed and should have met Yahweh. Stuart, *Exodus*, 427; cf. also Propp, *Exodus 19–40*, 163. So the command would be pertaining to women as well, guarding

wording, this exact period of three days seems to interrupt any linkage to Lev 15:18 or 24. It could as well be the case that it does not deal with any of the impurities spoken about in Lev 15! It could simply be a time of special consecration for the most holy Lord's approaching, without any particular reference to common ritual impurity—which, of course, would have to be avoided anyway. Even to abstain from legal, conjugal sexuality would be adequate in this context, for the waiting men should be completely consecrated, focusing solely on the Lord's soon arrival.[363]

Another idea would be possible, albeit not that likely: Considering the given ANE cultural setting with its frequent sacralization of sex and (some) women's part therein by serving the deity through prostituting themselves,[364] the precept in Exod 19:15 could also be understood as a precaution for Israel (and their heathen observers) to be sure that no mixing of sexuality and cult would occur—not even as a misunderstanding of the holy things to be witnessed.

It seems that all three possible cases (of understanding the text) do not provide a hint at any impurity attached to licit sexuality, but point to widely differing motivations of keeping a distance to (all) women (not only wives).

I.1.3.3.2 1 Sam 21:4–5

Beside this text in Exodus, a similar occurrence in 1 Sam 21:4–5. is used as rationale for interpreting sexual intercourse in itself as being unclean.[365] There it reads:
And the priest answered David and said, "There is no ordinary bread on hand, but there is consecrated bread; if only the young men have kept themselves from women." And David answered the priest and said to him, "Surely women have been kept from us as previously when I set out and the vessels of the young men were holy, though it was an ordinary journey; how much more then today will their vessels be holy?"

The expression "if only the young men have kept themselves from women" (אִם־נִשְׁמְרוּ הַנְּעָרִים אַךְ מֵאִשָּׁה) again does not necessarily indicate sexual intercourse. It just

---

themselves not to be defiled by some possible male impurity.

363. More on this see below, the passage: "Humble Your Souls" or a Missing Precept?

364. See for a good overview of the ANE cultural setting concerning sex and cult: Davidson, *Flame*, 85–97; about its impact on Israel see further pp. 97–113.

365. Cf. e.g., McCarter, *1 Samuel*, 349; Klein, *1 Samuel*, 213; Bergen, *1, 2 Samuel*, 222; Wenham, "Why does," 432; Maccoby, *Ritual and Morality*, 61–62; Davidson, *Flame*, 334. The text in 2 Sam 11:11, frequently referred to by commentators when interpreting 1 Sam 21:4–5, is again not (primarily) speaking about the issue of sexuality that Uriah is refraining from! He just demonstrates his moral sensibility by not indulging in a comfortable, easy living while "the ark and Israel and Judah are staying in temporary shelters, and my lord Joab and the servants of my lord are camping in the open field." The kind of (comfortable) living obviously is the centre of Uriah's exclamation, not his possible sexual intercourse with his wife that might occur when sleeping in one bed with her! And even if that would have been Uriah's message (what it surely was not!), he might also have been thinking of possible impurities he might be contaminated with, thus being excluded for at least one day (but possibly even up to seven days!) from his campaign (cf. Deut 23:10–11)!

speaks about "protecting/being careful" (שָׁמַר).³⁶⁶ Again it may refer to ritual impurity due to female discharges, just like the previous instance (Exod 19:15) probably indicates. But also any avoidance of sexuality might be possible—evidently without declaring conjugal intercourse to be impure, but simply defining a time of special consecration adequate for the approaching of the Lord, just like the instance in Exod 19:15 might demonstrate.

Furthermore, David refers to what is at times translated as "bodies" of his soldiers, by calling it "vessels" (כְּלִי). If כְּלִי has to be translated as his soldiers' "equipment/weapons," which is most likely,³⁶⁷ it would just point to a ritual defilement of the armors, which had to be purified. But the only defilement imaginable in this case would be a contamination by blood—just like it could have happened in case of having any unintentional contact with (menstruating) women. And even if it is to be understood as the "bodies" of his soldiers, it would again be dealing with ritual impurity by *simple contact*, especially emphasized by using "vessel"—the same term which is used oftentimes within Lev 11–15 when speaking about defilement *by contamination*.

At least, it is very unusual to employ these expressions if it is intended to (1) allude to sexual intercourse, and (2) impurity by sexual intercourse—and not just by contact with an impure (e.g., menstruating) woman. Furthermore, even if Lev 15:18 would refer to impurity due to sexual intercourse, there still is no Mosaic legislation to instruct the priest of requiring sexual abstinence from David's soldiers for *three* days. *One* day would have been enough by contact with semen or anything that has been touched by a menstruating woman; *seven* days would be necessary by direct contamination with menstrual blood (Lev 15:16–24). But *three* days must have been some different time span, without any (concrete) connection to Lev 15:18 (or 24), but much more to Exod 19:15 and the encountering of Yahweh that required this special time of consecration and separation—without any connection to some impurity attached to possible sexual intercourse.³⁶⁸

I.1.3.3.3 "Humble Your Souls" or a Missing Precept?

Another consideration should be mentioned. Some scholars hold that the command to "humble/afflict one's soul" (piel of עָנָה + נֶפֶשׁ; Lev 16:29, 31; 23:27, 32) as regards "be humbled/afflicted [before God]" (pual of עָנָה; Lev 23:29) on the Day of Atonement includes sexual abstinence in context of approaching God. This view is at times supplemented by a reference to the rabbinic opinion mentioned in *m. Yoma* 8:1 listing the following things to abstain from: "On the Day of Atonement it is forbidden to eat and to drink, to wash, to anoint, to lace on shoes, and to hold sexual intercourse." While

---

366. Cf. HALOT and BDB s.v. שָׁמַר; (similarly the LXX: "guarding/defending/preventing;" cf. BDAG/LSJ s.v. φυλάσσω).

367. See BDB/HALOT s.v. כְּלִי and all the other 275 (!) instances containing כְּלִי within the OT.

368. Interestingly, even in Exod 19:15 it is Moses who adds the separation from women to the divine command of consecration that Yahweh had previously given.

it is, of course, possible to have these things included within the rather vague expression "humble/afflict your souls; be humbled/afflicted," they are at least nowhere commanded within the biblical evidence—neither in context of the Day of Atonement, nor in any other comparable instance. While abstinence from food (perhaps including potables) can be witnessed in texts like Ps 35:13 ("I *humbled* my soul *with fasting*"), Isa 58:3 ("Why have we *fasted* and You do not see? Why have we *humbled* ourselves and You do not notice?;" cf. further the parallelism of "hungry" and "humbled" in v. 10), and 2 Sam 12:16–17, the description of what David did immediately after his fasting in 2 Sam 12:20 may further show a possible avoidance of washing, anointing, and (beautiful, comfortable) clothing (instead of simple sackcloth or another humble garment; cf. also Ps 35:13; Esth 4:1; 1 Chr 21:16): "So David arose from the ground, *washed, anointed* himself, and *changed his clothes*; and he came into the house of the LORD and worshiped. Then he came to his own house, and when he requested, they set *food* before him and *he ate*" (italics supplied). Dan 10:3 further hints at the fact that abstinence from food could refer to (only) some special diet, such as avoiding wine, meat, and "tasty food."[369] It seems to be a personal, and therefore to some extent also individual, decision which elements are chosen within one's humbling before God.

What we may generally say about the OT evidence is, at least, that abstinence from sexuality is nowhere commanded and nowhere (not even basically) witnessed by the biblical writers—although it nevertheless would be an adequate preparation to avoid the pleasures of sexuality when even "smaller" pleasures like "tasty food" (Dan 10:3) or comfortable clothing are shunned. It seems to be a fact that all the passages dealing with holy ministries and special events/festivals including the approaching of God at his sanctuary do not give any hints at requirements of sexual abstinence. One would have to expect these in clear terms, if really necessary and demanded. Even if these would exist, the argumentation (compared to Lev 15:18) would still be different: to avoid sexual pleasure in order to humble oneself is far from avoiding sexuality due to a ritual defilement that could be connected with it. To abstain from wine, meat, and "tasty food" as well as wearing sackcloth and shunning washing or ointment has nothing to do with a ritual necessity—it is a personal consecration in times of need, when a human realizes his own miserable, sinful, poor (and therefore: "humble/afflicted") state before the almighty, holy God. One does not avoid these common elements of (a pleasurable) life because they would be impure; the same is true of (the pleasure of) sexuality.

I.1.3.3.4 A New Testament Hint?

Just as an afterthought regarding this subject it might be interesting to take a New Testament statement into consideration. The author of the letter to the Hebrews in 13:4

---

369. Besides, Daniel also refrained from ointment: "I did not eat any *tasty food*, nor did *meat* or *wine* enter my mouth, nor did I use any *ointment* at all until the entire three weeks were completed" (Dan 10:3; my italics).

quite clearly states that honoring the marriage relation and/by keeping the marriage bed undefiled from fornication and adultery obviously not only bears the approval of God, but expressly please(s) him. A more exact translation of this text reveals and emphasizes another meaning, contributing to the impetus of this chapter:

(A) Τίμιος
  (B) ὁ γάμος
    (C) ἐν πᾶσιν
  (B') καὶ ἡ κοίτη
(A') ἀμίαντος
      (D) πόρνους γὰρ καὶ μοιχοὺς κρινεῖ ὁ θεός

(A) Precious/honorable [is]
  (B) the marriage relation
    (C) in all parts/completely,
  (B') and the marriage-bed (i.e., sexuality[370])
(A') [is] undefiled/pure,
      (D) but fornicators and adulterers will be judged by God.

This verse, especially considering the emphasis and focus on the importance of sexuality within marriage by the parallelism of (B)||(B'), stresses in (A)||(A') the purity of sexuality within this divinely ordained (monogamous, lasting) relation, contrasted to illicit sexual relations of fornicators and adulterers (D).[371] It might be applicable as reference to the New Testament understanding of marital sexuality as something that is known to be entirely pure (morally and ritually); and that the author is speaking against those well-known notions of (Hellenistically influenced) first century Judaism that declared sexuality to be impure and not proper for men serving God—as Josephus and Philo might be understood. Corresponding to this perception of Heb 13:4, defilement is received by immorality (that means: illegal sex according to laws like those of Lev 18 and 20), not by licit sexuality (according to Gen 2:24).

I.1.3.4 Summary and Final Considerations

While the investigation of Lev 15:18 among modern scholars mostly led to a discussion about the possible reasons for the impurity attached to legal, conjugal intercourse,

---

370. The Greek term κοίτη is a euphemism for "sexual intercourse/cohabitation/emission;" see BDAG/LSJ s.v. κοίτη.

371. Cf. also the KJV version which is similar: "Marriage is honorable in all, and the bed undefiled: but whoremongers and adulterers God will judge." Here also the contrast between legal (= not defiling) and illegal (= defiling) sexuality becomes strikingly clear. Heb 13:4 apparently declares sexuality within the marriage bonds to be generally pure and undefiled, unlike illegal intimate relationships outside of it. Of course, the defilement of illegal sex is of a moral character and not ritual.

this study aimed to inquire another point: whether it deals with sexuality at all. The baffling problems connected with current interpretations would thus be solved quite easily. Beginning with ancient Jewish evidence, one finds that the earliest Jewish "commentators" Philo and Josephus understood Lev 15:18 as a *(moral)* defilement of conjugal intercourse due to the seemingly unavoidable pleasures. A completely different kind of argumentation is witnessed in their works, not supporting recent scholarly research in its hypotheses. These ancient Jewish scholars were apparently molded by the strong Hellenistic influences of their time and they were aware of the inner Jewish diversity existing not only in Palestine, but also in the Diaspora where both authors were living in the time of their writing (Alexandria and Rome). It also has to be recognized that particularly the field of impurity and purifications has been expanded and intensified by the most influential Jewish groups (esp. Pharisees and Essenes) which distinctively molded the Jewish practice of everyday life (halakha) and to a large extent even the spiritual perception of ancient Judaism. The New Testament frequently criticizes the halakhic "excesses" of that time. Hence, one must not have too much confidence in any interpretation of the Mosaic material so many hundreds of years after its emergence in the establishing process of early Israel. Although Philo, Josephus, and the rabbinic evidence may give us important hints to some common practice in ancient Judaism of the Greco-Roman period, this halakhic understanding and practice is not necessarily adequate to present original, authentic interpretation of Mosaic laws, as already the inner Jewish sectarian diversity of the second century BCE up to at least 70 CE convincingly demonstrates. While the rabbinic tradition generally agrees with the perception of Philo and Josephus regarding the impurity of sexuality, it declares intercourse per se as being unclean, regardless of any seminal emission. The rabbis have no explanation for that law and thus neither support theses of current research, nor do they contradict them. The evidence they provide is altogether very unsatisfactory and not really helpful for a consistent interpretation of Lev 15:18.

Besides these ancient Jewish opinions and their apparent reference to at least some stream of Jewish halakhic tradition and (in Philo and Josephus) the application of a dualistic philosophy, the next step was to reappraise the Old Testament evidence. The center of any scholarly argumentation on sexual impurity of legal intercourse is found in Lev 15:18. The other texts are depending on the interpretation of that short ordinance. What we found is the following evidence that rather supports the perception that the text does not speak about sexuality at all, but just about an unintended, uncontrollable nocturnal emission of semen:

1. There are two distinct, complete units (vv. 16–18/19–24) speaking about usual (non-morbid) discharges of (1) males and (2) females.

2. They are parallel to each other and contain a similar, final climax corresponding to the "highest level" of contamination from (1) man to woman and (2) woman to man.

3. Both units have individual kinds of impurity, rendering both man and woman (the causing person and the contaminated) only in their climax similarly unclean (v. 18: both *one* day, beginning at the *same* day; v. 24: man *seven* days, corresponding to the *seven* days of the woman, but of course possibly *deviating* in the *starting day*!).

4. The paralleling equality of both units is not continually kept up by commentators. On the one hand they, at times, assert the equivalence of v. 18 and v. 24, on the other hand only v. 18 is understood as dealing with sexual impurity, for v. 24 obviously is not (at least not in the same way, i.e., *deliberately, uncontrollable*). The defiling "factor" evidently is the unintended contamination with blood. But that evidence is not consequently transferred to v. 18 (defiling factor would be *unintended, uncontrollable* (nocturnal) seminal emission).

5. The structures of the chapter presented by commentators are mostly inconsistent. While v. 24 is sometimes interpreted as speaking about sexuality, the chiasmic structures are artificially modeled to meet the demands of a special position of v. 18 (excluding v. 24), since otherwise there is no reasonable rationale suddenly to change content, level of impurity, and level of intention (to a deliberate act).

6. The respective climaxes (vv. 18, 24) have different durations of uncleanness, what alludes to the fact that different kinds of impurities are given. The cause of impurity therefore is not intercourse, but contamination with differently defiling substances, thus exactly fitting the context.

7. In both paralleling units we find (1) the cause of impurity as an introduction (v. 16: unintended, uncontrollable seminal emission; v. 19: unintended, uncontrollable menstruation); (2) lists with possible objects to be defiled by this given cause (v. 17: lifeless objects; vv. 20–23: lifeless objects and persons by contact to these objects); (3) direct contamination of another person (both times obviously the spouse) and transfer of the same duration of impurity, which points to the same cause of impurity (v. 18: unintended, uncontrollable seminal emission, one day; v. 24: unintended, uncontrollable menstruation, seven days).

8. If v. 18 would point to sexual intercourse, the woman would be missing in the man's "defilement list" and the parallelism would be destroyed. Furthermore, any allusion of a possible defilement of humans would be missing.

9. The chapter's summary in vv. 32–33 does not contain any allusion to sexuality. To the contrary, it clearly shows that the content of the whole chapter just deals with unintended, uncontrollable discharges and their respective impurities.

10. Until chap. 18, there is no reference to sexuality at all. Finally, chap. 18 contains a lengthy list of sexual impurities that are altogether not to be purified (but to be sentenced to death). The terms "defiling" or "unclean," therefore, are not employed referring to sexuality before that chapter and are only used to describe illegal relationships or improper times of intercourse (i.e., during menstruation).

11. The kind of expression and the word order in Lev 15:18 (as well as in v. 24) are not explicit enough to allude clearly to sexuality, especially when compared to chaps. 18 and 20. To the contrary, it adequately fits the demands of a simple defilement list with an impurity accidentally and inadvertently caused while simply sleeping.

12. The use of the construction אֵת + שָׁכַב in Lev 15:18 (and v. 24), if embedded in a context of sexuality, would result in the conclusion that it speaks about forced sex. Nothing at all in Lev 15 supports this assumption. To the contrary, Lev 15 does not deal with *morality*, sin, and proper punishments, but just with *ritual* (im-) purity. Consequently, other instances of the OT using אֵת + שָׁכַב (without sexual context) must determine the meaning of this expression in Lev 15:18 (and v. 24): Simple, usual *sleep*, as supported e.g., by 2 Sam 4:5—and many others speaking about the *sleep* of the dead (e.g., 2 Sam 7:12; Ezek 31:18; 32:19, 27–30).

13. A textual hint or at least some reasonable explanation for the incomprehensible insertion of an ordinance concerning sexuality within a completely different context and (the resulting) improper structure is still missing.

14. A satisfying explanation for the supposed impurity is still missing, especially under consideration of the Edenic ideal (Gen 2:24; 1 Cor 6:16–17; Eph 5:31–32), the divine command to multiply (Gen 1:28; cf. Ps 127:3), and the usage of terms connoting sexual intimacy in context of Yahweh's relationship with Israel.

15. Finally, it is odd that there is nowhere any concrete, unambiguous ordinance in another (much more adequate) context commanding priests and/or common Israelites to shun the sanctuary at least for one day after having sexual relations with one's spouse. While there are different precautions to be taken that are explicated in detail, there is nowhere any hint at sexuality as a means of preventing a person to approach God.

To sum up, it might be concluded that the whole chapter deals with *unintended* impurities caused by *uncontrollable* bodily discharges and communicated *by contact*. There is no hint given to reason that, all of a sudden, v. 18 is completely different, dealing with impurity *deliberately* caused by a mutual *action* that is *controllable*. Consequently, if Lev 15:18 does not speak about sexual intercourse and thus does not attach any impurity to legal sexuality, there is no other allusion left in the whole biblical (and particularly Old Testament) account to be used as proof text for this most problematic cause of impurity. The texts of Exod 19:14–15, 1 Sam 21:4–5 (and 2 Sam 11:11) as well as the rather general hints on personal consecration perhaps in context of the great Day of Atonement (Lev 16:29, 31; 23:27, 29, 32), have no connection to Lev 15:16–24 and do not point to sexuality as reason for the need of purification and abstinence (from women).

This interpretation not only solves the problem of explaining the impurity, which is not satisfyingly accomplished yet, as most commentators candidly admit. It contributes even more to the initial, Edenic ideal as established in paradise (Gen 2:24), spiritually applied in the Old Testament symbolism, and finally transferred to the "great mystery" of Eph 5:31–32 and the "one spirit" (ἐν πνεῦμα) union of 1 Cor 6:16–17. Similar to these instances, the author of Hebrews defends the purity of conjugal sexuality in Heb 13:4, most likely including any supposed ritual defilement. The holy marriage ideal is used by Yahweh, Jesus, the prophets, and some of the apostles for explaining in figurative as well as in most practical terms the intimacy not only spouses are privileged to experience, but what even more God desires to share with his followers as a spiritual union. And that great holy union is not impure, but "honorable [. . . and] undefiled/pure" (τίμιος [. . . καὶ] ἀμίαντος; Heb 13:4) in its highest and deepest sense.

I.2 Approaching the Spiritual Sphere

I.2.1 Interaction Between the Two Levels

In the accounts of the Pentateuch there are most significant stories concerning sexual transgressions and their specific spiritual impact. By examining these occurrences one may expect to obtain some deeper information about the potential to blur the boundaries between the literal and spiritual spheres that sexuality apparently comprises (or figuratively represents), namely: the relationship between Yahweh and Israel. The given instances unfortunately deal solely with negative aspects, but nonetheless we may be able to draw some more positive conclusions at the end. Thus this section deals with a very meaningful aspect for understanding the responsibility involved in the sexual act of becoming "one flesh." This will be valuable, not only for better interpreting the Old Testament foundation and its spiritual or figurative meaning, but even more to rightly approach the concerned New Testament texts and evaluate their spiritual facets.

Within the Pentateuch there are three, perhaps even four, prominent examples on how God has been dealing with the "wickedness" of man concerning sexual, specifically marital "misconduct." The first chapters of the biblical account and the times of early Israel as related in the Pentateuch are particularly important, because in these times God dealt very distinctively with his "newborn" people, showing the תּוֹלְדוֹת that bears the Messianic seed (cf. Gen 3:5; 12:2–3, 7 etc.) the right way to worship and to follow the divine pattern—in short: Yahweh leads them the way to restore the divine image of Gen 1:26–27. However, there are certain severe deviations endangering the intentions of God. These instances and the manner in which God treats these apostate behaviors tell a lot about the spiritual impact of sins interfering with or derogating the divine ideal. This will widen and deepen the perspective from which sexuality is usually perceived by particularly emphasizing its significance as divine covenant pattern foreshadowed in Gen 2:24.

I.2.1.1 The "Sons of God" Going Astray (Gen 6:1–4)

The first story to be examined, and which has already been referred to in context of the textual analysis of Gen 2, is found in Gen 6:1–4 immediately preceding the deluge. This narrative deserves broader investigation not just because of the manifold problems connected with the "human interpretation" of the "sons of God," but particularly due to the comparable state of this world (and seemingly especially marriage) immediately before Christ's return as Matt 24:36–39 predicts.

The brief passage in Gen 6:1–4 reads:[372]

> (6:1) Now it came about, when men began to multiply on the face of the land, and daughters were born to them,
> (6:2) that the sons of God saw that the daughters of men were beautiful; and they took wives for themselves, whomever they chose.
> (6:3) Then the Lord said, "My Spirit shall not strive with man forever, because he also is flesh; nevertheless his days shall be one hundred and twenty years."
> (6:4) The Nephilim were on the earth in those days, and also afterward, when the sons of God came in to the daughters of men, and they bore children to them. Those were the mighty men who were of old, men of renown.

The short note in Gen 6:2 does not contain any comprehensive explanation about the apparently enormous sin(s) the antediluvians must have committed to justify a punishment as sentenced by God in v. 3. There is just one rather discrete hint given that must serve as the starting point to find an answer about the reason for the great judgment in a worldwide, life-extinguishing flood. It is the remark that "the sons of God . . . took wives for themselves, whomever they chose" (v. 2). Immediately after this short observation the judgment is passed: "Then the LORD said, 'My Spirit shall not strive with man forever, because he also is flesh; nevertheless his days shall be one hundred and twenty years'" (v. 3).

It is evident that there must have been something wrong with the marriages in these times. Since marriage per se is not at all sinful, but even an Edenic institution and as such belonging to a time and state that was not marked by sinfulness, but by entire innocence (cf. Gen 1:26–28; 2:24–25), the actual problem is apparently implied by the short phrase "whomever they chose" (מִכֹּל אֲשֶׁר בָּחָרוּ; v. 2). The first part of the sentence ("the sons of God saw that the daughters of men were beautiful") seems to

---

372. There are only two minor textual variants (concerning v. 3: בְּשַׁגַּם—"because"; v. 4: וְיָלְדוּ—"they bore"), which do not at all alter the sense of the text. The problems we are to encounter do not belong to the realm of linguistic difficulties, but have primarily to do with the interpretation of some obscure expressions in the text. Besides, as Fockner, "Reopening the Discussion," 442–48 and Van Gemeren, "Sons of God," 325–30 demonstrated, the best delimitation of this passage would comprise vv. 1–8. Nonetheless I stop after v. 4, since these few verses are the problematic core that deals with marriage; vv. 5–8 are quite clear and do not need any further probe.

be the basis for the "problem statement" in the second part of the verse. It implies an important difference between the so-called "daughters of men" (בְּנוֹת הָאָדָם) and those termed "sons of God" (בְּנֵי־הָאֱלֹהִים). There must have been something wrong with choosing whomever they wanted, thereby mixing these two distinct groups. Another slight hint at the problem might be the fact that the "sons of God" are actively committing the sin; the "daughters of men" seem to be out of question regarding this particular failure. The "sons of God" are blamed for their bad selection, not the "daughters of men" for giving in to this relationship. It seems the "daughters of men" were expected to accept these marital unions, while the "sons of God" sinned by actively striving for these relationships.

The crucial question at this place is the one concerning the meaning of both group designations. It seems, in case the "sons of God" are correctly and reliably identified, the meaning of their apparently opposite part, the "daughters of men," is a rather easy task, representing a group with qualities contrary to the ones that honor the first company to have a "name" so closely connected with God. However, "there have been innumerable conflicting opinions, with few if any concrete gains;"[373] it seems that "every verse is a source of exegetical difficulty,"[374] so "the mysterious identity of the 'sons of God' continues to humble the expositor,"[375] and the whole passage (Gen 6:1–4) was characterized as one of the most difficult in the entire OT.[376]

There are usually three main strands of interpretation regarding the "sons of God:"[377]

1. Most commentators share the common opinion that these "sons of God" must be some supernatural beings (angels) who once were loyal to God, but gave up their faithfulness for the sake of marrying human women due to their overwhelming beauty.[378]

---

373. Speiser, *Genesis*, 45.

374. Mathews, *Genesis 1–11:26*, 320.

375. Mathews, *Genesis 1–11:26*, 332.

376. Thus Heinisch, *Genesis*, 159; Van Gemeren, "Sons of God," 321; Cassuto, *Exodus*, 269; Spero, "Sons of God, Daughters of Men?," 15.

377. Similarly Mathews, *Genesis 1–11:26*, 325; Sailhamer, "Genesis," 76; Clines, "Significance," 33–34; NET-Bible (2006) on Gen 6:2. Marrs, "Sons of God," 218–19 misses point (3); slightly differing by further subdividing point (3): Spero, "Sons of God, Daughters of Men?," 16 (referring to Rabbi David Tzvi Hoffmann). Spero, "Sons of God, Daughters of Men?," 17–18 himself interprets this reference regarding the mixing of two different groups completely different by suggesting that these two groups were prehistoric humans: homo erectus (Neanderthal Man) and homo sapiens! This seems entirely out of place considering the conceptual framework not only of Gen 6, but rather of Gen 1–11 as a whole, particularly concerning its many connections to God's personal and perfect (finished) creation instead of some kind of an evolution.

378. Henceforth called the "angelic interpretation." This view is shared by e.g., Simpson, "Genesis," 533; Von Rad, *Erstes Buch Mose*, 83–85; Collins, "Sons of God," 259–74, esp. pp. 260–61; Speiser, *Genesis*, 44–45; Skinner, *Genesis*, 139–47; Gunkel, *Genesis*, 55–59; Schüle, *Urgeschichte*, 109–13; Brueggemann, *Genesis*, 71; Sarna, *Genesis*, 45–46; Van Gemeren, "Sons of God," 320–48; Clines, "Significance," 36.

2. A few scholars do not consent to this interpretation, but are convinced that the "sons of God" are the faithful, God-fearing Sethites, while the "daughters of men" are the corrupt, impious Cainites.[379]

3. The third group understands the "sons of God" as a term denoting powerful tyrants, behaving as if they were divine, following the example of Lamech (cf. Gen 4:19, 23–24) in his brutality and in abusing the original marriage ideal (of Gen 1:26–27; 2:23–24) by living in polygamy.[380]

It will be helpful to notice that interpretations (2) and (3) are not completely contrary. It is possible, and the following investigation will further confirm the probability of this idea, that the faithful Sethite "sons of God" were loyal to their divine creator even amidst a world of unfaithful Cainite "daughters of men," but then changed into mighty sinners resp. powerful tyrants (the Nephilim/giants), becoming brutal and sexually abusive, seduced by the beauty of their opponents—and with the "salt of the earth" (cf. Matt 5:13) eradicated, the pre-flood world must have been filled up with the cruelest sins—just as the evil example of Lamech in opposition to Enoch demonstrates (cf. Gen 4:19, 23–24; 5:22–24; Jude 14–16) even a few generations before the divine sentence.[381]

I.2.1.1.1 Objections against the Human Character

Besides the fact that apparently "the continuing dominance of the mythical (or at least angelic) interpretation of the passage [i.e., Gen 6:1–4] has been [based upon] the absence of a satisfactory alternative,"[382] one usually encounters three major arguments put forward in favor of the the angelic interpretation:

Similar Wordings. The supernatural view interpreting the "sons of God" as angels is usually substantiated (concerning the biblical context) by a single argument, namely the angelic "atmosphere" of the same expression appearing in Job 1:6 ("Now there was

---

379. Henceforth called the "human interpretation." This opinion is held by, for instance, Mathews, *Genesis 1–11:26*, 325–32; Heinisch, *Genesis*, 159–63; Pröbstle, "Söhne Gottes," 48–51; Scharbert, *Genesis 1–11*, 79–81; Fockner, "Reopening the Discussion," 446–56

380. Although there is apparently no further allusion to what exactly might have been sinful (except something with the relationships between "daughters of men" and "sons of God") there have been convincing attempts to prove that polygamy has been another cause for the judgment of their wickedness; cf. Du Preez, *Polygamy*, 154–55; Nichol and Andreasen, *ABC*, Gen 6:2, 1:250; Pröbstle, "Söhne Gottes," 50; Heinisch, *Genesis*, 161; Scharbert, *Genesis 1–11*, 79–80.

381. Please notice that both appear as the seventh person in their genealogies, both being described in more detail than any other of the names mentioned in Gen 4–5, thus granting broader insight into the circumstances and lives of their respective lineages, emphasizing the huge difference between Sethites and Cainites.

382. This is a quotation presented in Van Gemeren, "Sons of God," 343 with reference to a work of Meredith G. Kline, but unfortunately without mentioning its title or further bibliographical information in the entire article. Ibid., 346 supports this perception of a lack of alternatives.

a day when the sons of God came to present themselves before the Lord, and Satan also came among them;" cf. 2:1). Some commentators add further verses: Job 38:7, Ps 29:1; 82:6; 89:7; Dan 3:25.[383] These instances, however, are not at all unambiguous and as such unable to identify clearly and distinctly the expression "sons of God" as referring *exclusively* to angels.[384] It rather seems that a more *inclusive* perception is suitable, generally meaning all those creatures that are faithfully serving God, be they angels or humans.[385]

Job 38:7 ("When the morning stars sang together and all the sons of God shouted for joy?") is completely unclear, and the synonymous expression "morning star" (כּוֹכְבֵי בֹקֶר) in Scripture refers to the original God-fearing, pure character of Satan (once he is deciphered from the encoded image in Isa 14:12); the (human-) divine nature of Christ (cf. Rev 22:16: "ὁ ἀστὴρ ... ὁ πρωϊνός;" perhaps also meant in 2 Pet 1:19: "φωσφόρος"), in respect to the elevated, powerful standing of the faithful humans before God according to Rev 2:27–28. "Morning star," therefore, does not exclude the human nature—to the contrary, it is expressly included (again Rev 2:27–28; as image/allusion also in Isa 14:12 literally referring to "the king of Babylon" [v. 4]).

The instance in Ps 29 (v. 1: "Ascribe to the Lord, o sons of God, ascribe to the Lord glory and strength.") does not contain a concrete hint to angelic/heavenly beings and could equally mean the (human) people of God, while Ps 89:7 ("For who in the skies is comparable to the Lord? Who among the sons of God is like the Lord?") through the parallelism of "in the skies" and "among the sons of God" seems to allude more directly to superhuman beings—at least at first glance, for it could also be an example for "a constant switch between heaven and earth. Verse 6 contrasts the heavens with the assembly of the holy ones (earth) and v. 7 follows this pattern by setting those who are in the clouds against the sons of God (earth). In v. 8 the order is reversed."[386]

Ps 82:6 ("I said, 'You are gods, and all of you are sons of the Most High.'") rather alludes to the human sphere (yet without excluding angels), considering vv. 1–5 speaking about unrighteous leaders of Israel,[387] and Jesus' application of this verse in John 10:33–36. Particularly this last instance in Ps 82:6 leads to the conclusion that the one (human beings) does not necessarily exclude the other (angelic/heavenly beings), but it seems to depend upon the respective context. In general, those are described as

---

383. E.g., Heinisch, *Genesis*, 160; Scharbert, *Genesis 1–11*, 79; Collins, "Sons of God," 261.

384. Similarly, Fockner, "Reopening the Discussion," 449/fn.36.

385. This idea also mentioned by Clines, "Significance," 35, and further supported by Fockner, "Reopening the Discussion," 449–50 (p. 449: "... the word בן includes all supportive relationships ... constituting a group of human and superhuman beings which is united through allegiance to God. Such an interpretation not only makes sense of Job and Genesis 6, but also complies best with the rest of the occurrences of this term in the Bible."). So it is important to note that Satan "is not included in the group of the sons of God but mentioned separately since he is not a loyal follower of the Godhead." Ibid., 449/fn.38.

386. Fockner, "Reopening the Discussion," 449/fn.39.

387. Cf. also Fockner, "Reopening the Discussion," 449/fn.39.

"godly/sons of God," "to whom the word of God came" (John 10:35), namely, those living in God's presence and listening to (i.e., heeding) the divine voice. This further fits the context of the last instance in Dan 3:25, certainly speaking of Jesus as the one like "a son of God" (לְבַר־אֱלָהִין) hovering among those humans that are the most faithful to God amid the most trying conditions.

It really seems to depend on the context which kind of creatures are most probably meant. As the following review intends to demonstrate, it becomes evident that the context of Gen 6:1–4 strongly favors the purely human, non-angelic understanding of the "sons of God" and, consequently, the Nephilim.

The Nephilim/Giants. Another objection against the human interpretation is presented by referring to the "giants" (נְפִלִים) in Gen 6:4 as the supposed offspring of the connection between angels and women.[388] However, this verse must rather be understood in a different way, without any cause-result connection between the Nephilim and the offspring of the unholy intermarriages. Firstly, concerning the term נְפִלִים,

> in Num 13:33 the Israelites reported that they felt like mere grasshoppers in the sight of the *nephilim*, which the KJV translates 'giants.' There is reason to believe that this Hebrew word may come from the root *naphal*, and that the *nephilim* were 'violent' ones, or terrorists, rather than physical 'giants.' Since in those days the entire human race was of great stature, it must be that character rather than height is designated.[389]

There are no other references to נְפִלִים in the Hebrew Bible beside those two in Gen 6:4 and Num 13:33. So the immediate context must serve as the main evidence of any interpretation. In Gen 6:4 we find two differing expressions for נְפִלִים, functioning as synonyms: הַגִּבֹּרִים אֲשֶׁר מֵעוֹלָם ("the mighty ones of old"), and אַנְשֵׁי הַשֵּׁם ("men of renown").[390] The Hebrew גִּבּוֹר ("strong/mighty") occurs only four times in the entire Pentateuch, once referring to the mighty God of Israel (Deut 10:17) and thrice to Nimrod (Gen 10:8–9), the "mighty" hunter. He seems to be a reflection of the "mighty men of old" and as such appears immediately after the flood, again in context of the important (human) genealogies. These instances do not allude to some supernatural, superhuman beings as fathers of the נְפִלִים in this verse. Furthermore, the Hebrew text, in fact, merely contains an editorial note telling some historical feature of the time before the flood, certainly intending to help the reader embed the story in its early historical context. The author was apparently sure that his audience was acquainted with those ancient "mighty men" he referred to—please note the definite article in

---

388. See e.g., Collins, "Sons of God," 262.

389. Nichol and Andreasen, *ABC*, Gen 6:4, 1:251; for further discussion and emerging problems of this word's translation cf. Mathews, *Genesis 1–11:26*, 335–39; Sailhamer, "Genesis," 77. A completely strange perception is presented by Skinner, *Genesis*, 147, who holds that this text indicates further mixtures of angels and women begetting giants, instead of using this much clearer instance to interpret the ambiguous one in Gen 6.

390. Cf. Clines, *Classical Hebrew*, 5:723; Marrs, "Sons of God," 222/fn.13.

הַגִּבֹּרִים, instead of an indefinite mentioning as if it was some new piece of information for the reader.[391] Most important, however, is the observation that the Nephilim obviously already existed before the illicit intermarriages occur: "The Nephilim were on the earth in those days, *and also afterward* (וְגַם אַחֲרֵי־כֵן), when the sons of God came in to the daughters of men, and they bore children to them." (Gen 6:4; my italics.) It is not the intermarriage that results in "giants"—these were already present and very well known—but it is just a synchronic historical feature assisting the reader to approach the historical context of that time.[392] The Nephilim did already exist, intermarriage followed afterward.

There are some hints in ancient Jewish literature alluding to the fact that these Nephilim/mighty ones of the antediluvian age seem to have been a rather well-known notion, as as for example, Bar. 3:26–28 confirms:

> There were the giants famous from the beginning, that were of so great stature, and so expert in war (οἱ δὲ γίγαντες οἱ ὀνομαστοὶ οἱ ἀπ' ἀρχῆς γενόμενοι εὐμεγέθεις ἐπιστάμενοι πόλεμον). Those did not the Lord choose, neither gave he the way of knowledge unto them: But they were destroyed . . . .

Much briefer is the remark in Wis. 14:6: "For in the old time also, when the proud giants perished (καὶ ἀρχῆς γὰρ ἀπολλυμένων ὑπερηφάνων γιγάντων), the hope of the world governed by thy hand escaped in a weak vessel, and left to all ages a seed of generation." Other texts like Sir. 16:7 ("the old giants;" τῶν ἀρχαίων γιγάντων), *3 Macc.* 2:4 ("mighty and arrogant giants;" γίγαντες ἦσαν ῥώμῃ καὶ θράσει), and perhaps even Ezek 32:27 ("They do not lie with the fallen warriors of ancient times, who went down to Sheol with their weapons of war . . . .")[393] further support the idea that "giants/mighty ones" is most likely an expression used to describe the brutal, impious (human) generation before the Flood, while instances like Num 13:33, Deut 2:11, 3:11, and Jdt. 16:6 speaking about giants as part even of the life after the Flood may demonstrate that these are most probably not to be understood as some superhuman/angelic-human beasts resulting from intermarriage between human and angelic

---

391. This point is also made by Sarna, *Genesis*, 45; Fockner, "Reopening the Discussion," 452; Hamilton, *Genesis*, 270. It further seems that this verse does not describe a one-time action about a rather short period, but probably circumstances occurring over a long time, as may be pointed out by the usage of the imperfect verb form for "going in" (יָבֹאוּ) in Gen 6:4, which could be understood as frequentative; cf. Clines, "Significance," 35.

392. See also Heinisch, *Genesis*, 162. Clines, "Significance," 35 overlooked this linguistic fact and claimed instead: ". . . Genesis 6:1–4 represents the 'sons of God' as the generation prior to the Nephilim and גִּבֹּרִים." This is untenable in view of the Hebrew text, as Fockner, "Reopening the Discussion," 453–54 demonstrated by highlighting וְגַם אַחֲרֵי־כֵן as a "double disconnection/disjunction:" "Each of the two phrases וְגַם and אַחֲרֵי־כֵן would have independently made clear that the mentioned procreation is not causative for the existence of the Nephilim. It is obvious that the Nephilim were around before the 'going in' of v. 4b took place. This fact has long been ignored. . . . Gen 6.4 brings background information. . . . Far from establishing causality, this phrase actually denies that the existence of the Nephilim was terminated through the 'going in.'" Ibid.

393. Thus also Marrs, "Sons of God," 222/fn.13.

natures, now terrorizing the rest of humanity. These must (simply) have been mighty warriors, "men of renown," just as those mentioned in Num 13:33.

The Contrast between אֱלֹהִים and אָדָם. The third and, in my opinion, weakest of the three arguments in favor of the angelic interpretation, is the idea that the sons of אֱלֹהִים cannot be human because they are contrasted with the daughters of אָדָם in Gen 6:2. This understanding is easily refuted by reference to similar texts in the OT which clearly show that such a contrast is not absolute, but may refer to a subgroup as part of something bigger. In Judg 20:3, for instance, the sons of Benjamin are contrasted to the sons of Israel—of course Benjamin is actually a part of Israel and does not stand outside of it, just as Israel in Jer 32:20 is, of course, also human ("... both in Israel and among mankind"). The same is to be recognized in Judg 16:7 (Samson—man), Ps 73:5 (the wicked—humans), and even in immediate context of our passage: in Gen 6:5–8 Noah is contrasted to (the rest of) humankind.[394] In the same way, we have to understand the sons of אֱלֹהִים as (the pious) part of the more general group of humankind, which is at that time primarily represented by the daughters of אָדָם (the impious part of humanity), by choosing "daughters" rather than "sons" already foreshadowing the problems belonging to the realm of sex(uality) as further stressed in the same verse (Gen 6:2).[395]

I.2.1.1.2 ARGUMENTS IN FAVOR OF THE HUMAN INTERPRETATION

There are some important terminological hints supporting the "human interpretation" of the "sons of God:"[396]

"Spirit," "Flesh," "Generation," and "Seed."[397] Although there are hints that led many exegetes to interpret the "sons of God" as angels (see the previous section), the immediate context as the most important exegetical instrument seems, by further terminological hints, to point rather clearly in another direction. In fact, all the chapters before and even many after Gen 6 do not at all refer to angels, and not more than three narratives in the whole book of Genesis do speak about angels as God's messengers.[398]

---

394. Cf. on these texts also Fockner, "Reopening the Discussion," 450, Keil and Delitzsch, *The Pentateuch*, 130.

395. Besides, otherwise (by again using "sons" (of אָדָם) to denote affiliation) the entire sense of the verse would be destroyed, for then it would point to homosexuality rather than to mixed marriages.

396. See for a concise summary of the arguments hitherto put forward in favor of the human interpretation Van Gemeren, "Sons of God," 334, basing on the larger reviews of Keil and Delitzsch, *The Pentateuch*, 131–38 and Murray, *Principles of Conduct*, 243–49.

397. Van Gemeren, "Sons of God," 326 adds the term אֲדָמָה ("ground/land") occurring in Gen 6:1, 7, 20 as a connection to chap. 5 (there: v. 29). On further slight links between Gen 6:1 and chap. 5 see ibid., 326–29. Fockner, "Reopening the Discussion," 448 notes אָדָם as the "Leitwort" showing "exactly what the verses are about: humanity and what happened to it during that time."

398. Reviewing the text of Genesis we find only three stories quite unambiguously dealing with angels as God's messengers: Gen 19:1, 15 (the two angels visiting Lot in Sodom); 28:12 (Jacob dreaming of the angels on the ladder); 32:2 ("the angels of God meeting Jacob"). The few other instances deal

Besides, it is worth of consideration that the entire Hebrew Bible contains almost no reference to fallen, apostate angels, but merely to good angelic beings working for the sake of humankind, as briefly characterized in Heb 1:14.[399] It is, therefore, besides all the other evidences, unlikely that Gen 6 all of a sudden speaks about disloyal angels. Instead, Gen 6:3 refers quite concretely to the creation account, mentioning God's "spirit" (רוּחַ) only in Gen 1:2 and 6:3 (3:8 is rather to be translated as "wind/cool"), and "flesh" (בָּשָׂר) only in Gen 2:21, 23–24 and 6:3, 12–13, 17, 19. Both Hebrew terms disappear after the creation narrative until Gen 6:3. While in Eden man is created, being perfect, in Gen 6 he is destroyed, being corrupt; both instances take a close scrutiny on the state of man and, finally, come to differing sentences resulting in different consequences (blessing/curse). In particular, the Hebrew בָּשָׂר, which appears first in Gen 2:21, 23–24 and then disappears until Gen 6:3, is of importance. It not only indicates that the text speaks about human beings and not spirits (viz., angels), it further alludes to the far-reaching significance of this term carried on in Gen 17 when God is establishing his covenant with Abraham by the sign of circumcising one's בָּשָׂר (Gen 17:11, 13–14, 23–25).[400] Thus the close linkage between the "seed" (זֶרַע; Gen 3:15; 4:25; 9:9), "generation" (תּוֹלְדוֹת; Gen 2:4; 5:1; 6:9; 10:1, 32), and the "flesh" (בָּשָׂר; Gen 2; 6–9; 17), all summed up under the important topic of establishing and renewing the divine covenant, becomes evident. But within this context God is always dealing with men, never with angels. Especially important concerning the rationale for the flood, these aspects appear just in immediate context of marriage in Gen 2–3 and 6, additionally referring to allegiance (Gen 2:16–17) and the pattern man is molded after (Gen 1:26–27).

"They saw . . . good." There is another connection between 6:2 and 3:6 that seems significant: In both instances the protagonists claim the ability of calling something "good/agreeable/pleasant" by using the divine approval-clause רָאָה . . . כִּי־טוֹב ("[he/she/they] saw that . . . was/is good;" cf. Gen 1:4, 10, 12, 18, 21, 25). Thus Eve claims the

---

with "the angel of the Lord" (Gen 16:7–11; 21:17–18; 22:11–18; 24:7, 40; 31:11–13; 48:16)—another expression for God in his redemptive work for humans (see esp. Gen 31:11, 13: "The angel of God said: . . . I am God.").

399. Cf. Gen 16:7, 9–11; 19:1, 15; 21:17; 22:11, 15; 24:7, 40; 28:12; 31:11; 32:2; 48:16; Exod 3:2; 14:19; 23:20, 23; 32:34; 33:2; Num 20:16; 22:22–27, 31–32, 34–35; Judg 2:1, 4; 5:23; 6:11–12, 20–22; 13:3, 9, 13, 15–18, 20–21; 1 Sam 29:9; 2 Sam 14:17; 19:28; 24:16–17; 1 Kgs 13:18; 19:5, 7; 2 Kgs 1:3, 15; 19:35; 1 Chr 21:12, 15–16, 18, 20, 27; 2 Chr 32:21; Job 33:23; Ps 8:6; 34:8; 35:5–6; 91:11; 103:20; 148:2; Isa 37:36; 63:9; Dan 3:28; 6:23; Hos 12:5; Zech 1:9, 11–14; 2:2, 7; 3:1, 3–6; 4:1, 4–5; 5:5, 10; 6:4–5; 12:8; Mal 3:1. Not even Satan is freely described as an angel (cf. Gen 3:1–4, 13–14; 1 Chr 21:1; Zech 3:1–2; perhaps only in Job 1–2; certainly in Ezek 28:14). (Only Dan 10:13, 20 could be understood as dealing with a mighty angel (note: not מַלְאָךְ but שַׂר!) hindering (most probably) Gabriel in his task for Daniel.)

400. Cf. the instances of בָּשָׂר in Genesis: We witness a greater theme marked by the occurrence of the term בָּשָׂר from *marriage* in Gen 2:21, 23–24, over the *deluge* in Gen 6:3, 12–13, 17, 19; 7:15–16, 21; 8:17; 9:4, 11, 15–17, until the *covenant* with Abraham in Gen 17:11, 13–14, 23–25, followed by rather unimportant familial references (29:14 and 37:27) and Joseph's interpretation of dreams (40:19; 41:2–4, 18–19). Thus, marriage, (the circumstances of) the deluge, and the divine covenant with Abraham are closely connected in Genesis.

divine authority of knowing what is "good" (Gen 3:6) just as the "sons of God" some generations later (Gen 6:2). This failure of perception and understanding pertains only to the human realm as the few other instances in Genesis demonstrate (cf. Gen 40:16; 49:15). It even seems to represents some kind of a pattern regarding the "usual" way to sin (cf. Jas 1:14–15): Just like Eve and the "sons of God" "saw," "desired," and finally "took," so Lot "saw" the beautiful valley of Sodom and Gomorrah and "chose" it (Gen 13:10–11); Achan "saw," and "coveted" and "took" (Josh 7:21); similarly Jesus warns about "looking at a woman with lust for her" (Matt 5:28). All of these examples end up in unfaithfulness/apostasy and, consequently, even in death. But what is important for the present investigation, is the fact that they all refer to human's mistakes concerning a wrong estimation and desire. The same seems to be true in Gen 6:2: Humans declare the "daughters of men" to be "good/agreeable," desiring rather to marry them than to secure their own faithfulness toward God. Thus the story of Adam is repeated, who rather clung to fallen Eve than to keep his own pure, sinless standing before God. These instances (Eve and Adam in 3:6, the "sons of God" in 6:2) are an eloquent introduction immediately pointing to the forsaking of God's authority, claiming to choose for themselves what is "good" and turning into the contrary what God called "forbidden" (cf. Gen 2:17).[401] The horrible results are thus even subtly foreshadowed by just three short Hebrew terms (רָאָה . . . כִּי־טוֹב). Humans without God's guidance are obviously unable to discern what is "good" for their own welfare and incur a curse.

"Sons and Daughters." The immediate context further shows that "sons and daughters" (בָּנִים וּבָנוֹת) is a central object of Gen 5–11, perfectly fitting the general topic of "generation" (תּוֹלְדוֹת), "seed" (זֶרַע), and "flesh" (בָּשָׂר). Gen 5 contains no less than nine references to this phrase, Gen 11 again eight.[402] (The only other occurrence in the entire Pentateuch is Deut 28:41, referring to the consequences of "forsaking" (עָזַב; v. 20) God's covenant.) And just between these two important genealogical chapters of Gen 5 and 11 there is the story of God's dealing with these "sons (of God)" (בְּנֵי הָאֱלֹהִים) and "daughters (of men)" (בְּנוֹת הָאָדָם).[403] The strange note "and daughters were born to

---

401. A connection between Gen 3:1–6 and 6:2 is also mentioned by Scharbert, *Genesis 1–11*, 80–81.

402. Cf. Gen 5:4, 7, 10, 13, 16, 19, 22, 26, 30; 11:11, 13, 15, 17, 19, 21, 23, 25.

403. Please note Fockner, "Reopening the Discussion," 446–47 on the significance of Cain's genealogy preceding the one of Seth and the story of Gen 6:1–4: "The purpose of depicting the descendants of Cain is not so obvious. Usually, when Genesis includes genealogies that have no bearing upon the history of Israel, they are included to indicate the origin of certain nations or peoples with whom the Israelites must deal (10:13–19; 19:37–38; 25:12–18; 36:9–19). However, this is not the case with Cain, since all of his descendants die in the flood and humanity starts anew with Noah. Furthermore, the list given in Gen 4:17–24 is in its form not structured as genealogies usually are. No numbers of years or deaths are mentioned and the repetitive formulas are missing. Also, there is no rhythm in it: it gives some information about Cain, then accelerates to Lamech, dwells there for several verses, and then abruptly comes to an end. Furthermore, it does not cover the same ground as ch. 5, for three generations are missing. So, why is it included in the narrative? What did the author want to communicate? It seems that the intent is not that of a chronicler, but rather of a theologian. Genesis 4:17–24 is critical

them" (Gen 6:1) subtly turns the view to the cause (or further progression) of apostasy. "The sons of God saw," and "took . . . whomever they chose" (v. 2). It should also be noticed that the text says the sons of God "took [as] wives" (Gen 6:2). The phrase "taking [for/as] a wife" (לָקַח לְאִשָּׁה) is a terminus technicus for marriage and occurs in the entire OT only in reference to humans[404]—corresponding to the train of thought in the first chapters of Genesis, which always deal with humans (not angels) and their blessings or curses. So there would not be any proper explanation for punishing *humans* if *angels* were committing this sin of "taking as wives" whomever they (instead of God) chose.[405]

It seems there must have been two distinct human societies on earth before the flood, one of which is described as being "man"-like, the other as "god"-like:

> Such a designation of the men and the women in this summary [i.e., Gen 6:1–2] is in keeping with the earlier description of the origin of the man and the woman. Though the description of the creation of the man and the woman in chapter 1 is clear that both have been created in God's image, chapters 2 and 3 specify that the man was created by the breath of God . . . and that the woman was created . . . from the 'side' . . . of the man. Thus men are called the 'sons' . . . of God—denoting their origin from God—and women are called the 'daughters' . . . of man—denoting their origin from man.[406]

Even the first biblical mentioning of man is closely linked to his origin: "Then God said, 'Let Us make man in Our image, according to Our likeness;' . . . God created man in His own image, in the image of God He created him; male and female He created them" (Gen 1:26–27)—in order to represent God on earth (Gen 1:28).[407] The next reference to this event again alludes to the divine origin of man by stating: "This is the book of the generations of Adam. In the day when God created man, He made him in the likeness of God. He created them male and female, and He blessed them and named them Man in the day when they were created." (Gen 5:1–2) Similarly Luke 3:38 formulates ". . . τοῦ Ἀδὰμ τοῦ θεοῦ"[408] to describe the origin of man. That does not

---

for the rest of the story. . . . The verses inform the reader that from that first murderer originated a part of the population which is in dire contrast to the one presented in ch. 5. The descendants of Cain and the descendants of Adam form two sides of humanity. Cain does not leave the stage of world history—he continues to be active and his legacy of rebellion is perpetuated in his descendants. Humanity is divided into believers and unbelievers."

404. Similarly Fockner, "Reopening the Discussion," 439.

405. Similarly Mathews, *Genesis 1–11:26*, 326–27; Pröbstle, "Söhne Gottes," 48; Heinisch, *Genesis*, 161; Brayford, *Genesis*, 261.

406. Sailhamer, "Genesis," 78.

407. Similarly Clines, "Significance," 37.

408. This may demonstrate how ancient Jews and early Christians might have understood certain expressions that may be difficult to interpret for us today. Concerning these familial differences between humankind and angels, it further seems worthwhile to recognize Jesus' rationale on the abolishment of marriage in Matt 22:30: "In the resurrection they neither marry, nor are given in marriage, but are like angels in heaven." This text evidently presupposes that angels are genderless and therefore

make man supernatural, but rather links him closely to his creator. Consequently, the "sons of God" referred to in Gen 6:2 are not necessarily supernatural, but it expresses a close affiliation to God. In the same way the "sons of the prophets" (בְּנֵי־הַנְּבִיאִים; 2 Kgs 2:3, 15; 4:1; 6:1) were not Elijah's (or Elisha's) literal sons, but simply his followers—the "sons of his divine spirit," so to speak.[409] Remembering the results of the textual analysis on Gen 1:26–27 above, one also has to consider the emphasis on man's γενός resembling the divine image in contrast to the individual "kind" or "family" of animals (cf. Gen 1:25). I made clear that from these verses one could conclude that man is to be understood as belonging to God's "family," bearing his image, likeness and similitude—a wonderful, enduring theme of consideration even outside of Eden (cf. Gen 5:1–3). The expression "sons of God," then, rather describes the divine authority these men initially followed and the image they once bore and reflected, and whom they betrayed by taking wives just as their eyes desired. There obviously something was wrong with these basically legal marriages—and it seems the point one needs to understand is the meaning of "sons of *God*" as an important quality per se prohibiting such mixed relationships with "daughters of *men*." If this is not speaking about a supernatural quality, we have only one alternative left: it denotes affiliation and loyalty to God instead of man.

Now, the idea of interpreting God's followers as "sons of God" is well known in the Hebrew Bible[410] and it outnumbers the three exact wordings of בְּנֵי הָאֱלֹהִים in Job, as well as the other similar occurrences in Psalms and Daniel, by far. In fact, heavenly beings are nowhere else described as "God's children," but the faithful Israelites clearly are: בָּנִים אַתֶּם לַיהוָה אֱלֹהֵיכֶם ("You are the sons of the Lord your God;" Deut 14:1); ". . . Thus says the LORD, 'Israel is My son, My firstborn.'" (Exod 4:22); "Thus you are to know in your heart that the LORD your God was disciplining you just as a man disciplines his son." (Deut 8:5) etc.[411] Therefore, probably the most adequate explana-

---

do not marry as humankind does. Any mixing between angels and human women, therefore, is utterly strange and too far-fetched for early Christians believing Jesus' expositions. (See also Sailhamer, "Genesis," 76.)

409. Also stressed by Heinisch, *Genesis*, 161.

410. A fact completely overlooked by Skinner, *Genesis*, 141–42, thus even [mistakenly] concluding that "the sense of these vv. [i.e., Gen 6:1–2] is perfectly clear."

411. See further: Deut 14:1; 32:6; 2 Sam 7:14; Ps 73:15; Isa 1:2; 43:6; 45:11; 63:16; Jer 3:14, 19; 31:9, 20; Ezek 21:15; Hos 2:1; 11:1; additionally, God's dealing "like a father" in Deut 1:31; Ps 82:6; 103:13; Prov 3:11–12; or the significant names in 1 Sam 8:2 (Abijah—"Yahweh is my father") and 2 Sam 2:13 (Joab—"Yahweh is father"); also, Adam is "from God" ('Αδὰμ τοῦ θεοῦ; Luke 3:38); the Qumran version of Deut 32:8 further shows that it was a well-known idea to identify Israel as the son of God: there it reads בְּנֵי אֱלֹהִים (4Q37/4QDeut) instead of בְּנֵי יִשְׂרָאֵל (MT). Cf. Fockner, "Reopening the Discussion," 450/fn.39; Pröbstle, "Söhne Gottes," 49; Heinisch, *Genesis*, 161; Scharbert, *Genesis 1–11*, 79–80. Consequently Paul later asserts: "For all who are being led by the Spirit of God, these are *sons of God*." (Rom 8:14; my italics.) It is interesting that the (most reliable version of the) LXX translates the הָאֱלֹהִים בְּנֵי in Gen 6:2, 4 as οἱ υἱοὶ τοῦ θεοῦ, while it renders the instances in Job as οἱ ἄγγελοι τοῦ θεοῦ (Job 1:6; 2:1; cf. 38:7: πάντες ἄγγελοί μου [i.e., God]). The Jewish translators in Hellenist Alexandria of the third century BC seemingly acknowledged a difference between both groups.

tion of the Hebrew expression בְּנֵי־הָאֱלֹהִים is to interpret אֱלֹהִים as a genitive of quality, meaning "godly sons."[412]

> Das plötzliche Auftreten der „Söhne Gottes" lässt vermuten, dass der Verfasser dachte, diese Gruppe sei treffsicher zu identifizieren. Der Text aus 1. Mo 3–5 zeigt, dass es sich hierbei um die Linie der Gläubigen handelt, denn das Gegenüber der beiden Linien ist ein prominentes Thema der Kap. 3–11.[413]

The predicted "battle" between the זֶרַע or תּוֹלְדֹת of Eve and the serpent (Gen 3:15) commences already in the first post-Edenic generation: Cain against Abel (Gen 4), and finally the lineage of Cain (cf. Gen 4:17–24) against the זֶרַע (v. 25) of Seth (cf. Gen 4:25—25:32).[414] It becomes apparent that the holy lineage began to betray their trust by taking any wife they desired, even from the unbelieving. Thereby the two classes have been mixed, which should maintain their "enmity" since the expulsion from Eden until the end of time (cf. Gen 3:15; Rev 12 etc.).

> Die Vermischung von Gläubigen und Ungläubigen bewirkte auf lange Zeit gesehen, dass der Einfluss des Guten drastisch abnahm. Die Gläubigen begannen ihre Orientierung zu verlieren. Das Endergebnis wird in V. 5 geschildert: Alles Sinnen der Menschen war böse. Die letzte Konsequenz ihres Handelns war schließlich der Zustand, den Gott mit der Flut beenden musste.[415]

"And God said," "Behold," "Came before him." Further evience in favor of the human interpretation is given by the quite strong allusions to man's creation as becomes apparent when comparing Gen 1:26–31 and Gen 6:11–13. We already saw within the

---

412. Cf. Mathews, *Genesis 1–11:26*, 330; Joüon and Muraoka, *Biblical Hebrew*, 437; Weisengoff, "Impious," 53 confirms as well: "That the Jews considered themselves 'sons of God' is evidenced from the very beginning of their national existence (Deut 14:1; Ps 82:6; Is. 1:2; 30:1; Hos 2:1). This title was the heritage of all men by reason of creation (cf. Is. 43:6), but of the Jews in particular because of their special vocation (Ex. 4:22). Naturally enough, the faithful would be the true, worthy sons of God. So it is not surprising that the just would be proud of this title, which was proof of their loyalty to their heavenly Father (cf. Ecclus. 4:10)."

413. Pröbstle, "Söhne Gottes," 49; cf. generally on this topic also Davidson, *Flame*, 182–84.

414. For further evidences of the close linkage between this account of the pre-Flood conditions and the general separation of Sethites and Cainites, which finally and unfortunately has been broken as described in the narrative, see especially the skillful compilation in Mathews, *Genesis 1–11:26*, 320–21. He also concludes about the cause of the Flood that "human transgression of divinely established boundaries [. . .]" (ibid.) was the reason leading to the miserable state that called for divine intervention; cf. also ibid., 322–39.

415. Pröbstle, "Söhne Gottes," 51. Cf. Nichol and Andreasen, *ABC*, Gen 6:2, 1:250: "These unholy alliances between Sethites and Cainites were responsible for the rapid increase of wickedness among the former. God has ever warned His followers not to marry unbelievers, because of the great danger to which the believer is thus exposed and to which he usually succumbs. (Deut 7:3, 4; Josh 23:12, 13; Ezra 9:2; Neh 13:25; 2 Cor 6:14, 15)." It seems suitable to recognize that certainly not all of Seth's descendants were purely serving God, as Heinisch, *Genesis*, 161 and Fockner, "Reopening the Discussion," 447/fn.31 note. There certainly were some that changed camps. Obviously, not all of Seth's descendants were like Enoch. The contrast between the two lineages rather shows that at some point of time (reaching Gen 6:1–4) neutrality was no option anymore.

investigation on Gen 1–2 in the first chapter above that the narrative introduction וַיֹּאמֶר אֱלֹהִים ("and God said") ceases to occur after relating man's perfect creation in Gen 1:26–31. The next time it appears is not before Gen 6:13 ("The end of all flesh has come before me; . . . I am about to destroy them with the earth"). Additionally, God's "behold" (הִנֵּה) of Gen 1:29, 31 does not reappear until the same chapter (Gen 6:2, 12–13, 17), now referring to man's corruption and thus constructing a contrasting "observation scene" that contains seven interesting parallels resp. contrasts:

1. *Cause and Perspective:* "God saw all that he made" | "God saw the earth"
2. *Appeal for others to evaluate:* "Behold!" | "Behold!"
3. *Direct Speech of God:* "And God said" | "And God said"[416]
4. *Context:* Humankind's beginning | Humankind's ending
5. *Judgment Range:* "All that God made" | "All flesh"
6. *Sentence:* "Very good" | "Corrupt/violent"
7. *Consequences:* Blessing and fruitfulness | Curse and destruction

It looks like God is reevaluating the covenantal conditions and his purpose (Gen 1:26–31) on which he decided to create and bless humankind—and he now (in Gen 6:11–13) decides to "regret" it. This seems to be further connoted by the usage of the expression "[God] brought her to the man" (לְאִשָּׁה וַיְבִאֶהָ אֶל־הָאָדָם) in Gen 2:22 and the similar phrase in Gen 6:13 "the end of all flesh came before my [i.e., God's] face" (קֵץ כָּל־בָּשָׂר בָּא לְפָנַי). While the woman (the "female flesh" as contrasted to "all flesh" in Gen 6) is welcomed by Adam after a brief evaluation of her appearance with a happy exclamation of joy, now the final judgment about "all flesh" "comes" (again בוֹא) before God with deep regret. His creation is no more "flesh of his flesh and bone of his bone" (Gen 2:23), namely: the image of God (Gen 1:26–27) as found initially in the so called "sons of God." To the contrary, they all became corrupt.[417]

---

416. As already pointed out above in context of Gen 1–2, there is another interesting observation concerning the further verses using וַיֹּאמֶר אֱלֹהִים and the parallels between Gen 1:26–31 and 6:11–13. Beside the destruction of all flesh, Gen 6 also points to a new beginning, a new start of the creation by saving some of the former population. To the same aspect allude the verses in Gen 9:8, 12, 17 as well as Gen 17:9, 15, 19 (the next occurrences of וַיֹּאמֶר אֱלֹהִים): "God said" with the purpose to establish his covenant. Pointing back to the perfect creation of humankind in God's image, he now endeavors to restore this image in man through the means of his divine covenant. The significant and unfortunately mostly sad part of marriage in this connection is significant.

417. Clines, "Significance," 37 puts it thus: "In Gen 6:1–4 . . . we find a satanic parody of the idea of the image of God in man. Far from God being present on earth in the person of man as his kingly representative exercising benign dominion over the lower orders of creation, we now have the presence of the divine on earth in a form that utterly misrepresents God . . . ."

I.2.1.1.3 Conclusions

The task of interpreting Gen 6:1–4 as introduction and rationale of the disastrous deluge described afterwards would be much easier with a less ambiguous expression than "sons of God" and "daughters of men." The reason that the author nevertheless decided to select just these terms leads to the conclusion that he had a much more important message to present—much more important than merely depicting antediluvian history. He apparently intended to present a general principle leading to corruption and apostasy not only in this early generation, but most likely as a special danger of his own time—and certainly until the end of all time(s), i. e. this world's history. So it does not wonder that at other places in the books of Moses we find the strongest commands and punishments particularly concerning sexual transgressions (see esp. Lev 18 and 20), clearly stating that there were great sexual sins among the peoples of Canaan resulting in their deadly punishment:

> Do not defile yourselves by any of these things; for by all these the nations which I am casting out before you have become defiled. For the land has become defiled, therefore I have brought its punishment upon it, so the land has spewed out its inhabitants. But as for you, you are to keep My statutes and My judgments and shall not do any of these abominations, neither the native, nor the alien who sojourns among you (for the men of the land who have been before you have done all these abominations, and the land has become defiled); so that the land will not spew you out, should you defile it, as it has spewed out the nation which has been before you. For whoever does any of these abominations, those persons who do so shall be cut off from among their people. Thus you are to keep My charge, that you do not practice any of the abominable customs which have been practiced before you, so as not to defile yourselves with them; I am the LORD your God. (Lev 18:24–30.)

Considering the strictness expressed in this declaration, and the prevailing prominence of such instructions (to avoid sexual immorality absolutely) among the different God-given regulations for ancient Israel, as well as the sole hint in Gen 6:1–4 at sexual relationships as the reason for God's strict judgment, it seems reasonable to assume the unfaithfulness of the "sons of God" just along these terms of sexual ethics, and not regarding any human-angelic mixture nowhere else to be witnessed within the Scriptures. Since there is nothing wrong with licit (male-female) marriage per se, the important ordinance disregarded by those formerly being faithful to God must have been the same that was afterwards so firmly demanded from Israel:

> You shall not intermarry with them [i. e. heathen nations]; you shall not give your daughters to their sons, nor shall you take their daughters for your sons. For they will turn your sons away from following Me to serve other gods; then the anger of the Lord will be kindled against you and He will quickly destroy you. (Deut 7:3–4; cf. Exod 34:16.)

The Flood narrative depicts the most momentous punishment regarding sexual relationships, as regards marriages, and it points to the moral disaster resulting from losing sight of the biblical marriage ideal consisting of two partners being loyal to the same divine authority (cf. Gen 2:18–25; 1 Cor 7:39: μόνον ἐν κυρίῳ; 2 Cor 6:14–18).[418] Sailhamer emphasizes, "just as in [Gen] 2:24, where the author turned briefly to the theme of marriage before moving on to the account of the Fall, so also in 6:1–4, on the eve of the Flood, the narrative turns briefly again to the theme of marriage"[419]—thereby eloquently demonstrating the destructive outcomes of deviations from the creational marriage ideal and the devastating results for one's own ethical standards, as well as the far-reaching influences on the world's moral values. The first chapters of the Genesis story dealing with the world outside of Eden significantly consist of severe attacks on the marriage ideal of Gen 2:23–24. The predicted enmity of Gen 3:15 seemingly appears with distinction in just that respect—and is very successful in the destruction of God's approval concerning humankind, resulting in the death punishment for all but eight souls. Obviously, "die intimste Beziehung auf Erden zeigt Konsequenzen für die intime Beziehung mit Gott. Und umgekehrt . . . Was 1. Mo 6 uns also vermitteln will ist nichts weniger als die Ehrfurcht vor der Ehe."[420] The significance of maintaining the purity of the creational marriage ideal (Gen 2:23–24), including the figurative meaning of Adam's exclamation "bone of my bone and flesh of my flesh" (thus referring to the divine creator as their common father, what consequently makes them "sons *and daughters (!)* of God"), thus becomes evident. It is a question of loyalty and faithfulness to God.[421]

I.2.1.2 Israel's Apostasy at Shittim (Num 25)

Apparently closely related with the foregoing story of the "sons of God" in the pre-Israel times, there is another important judgment story concerning the later "sons of God," Israel,[422] again going astray and thereby distorting the Edenic ideal of marriage,

---

418. Similarly Fockner, "Reopening the Discussion," 451: ". . . the problem depicted in Gen 6.2 is the marriages (וַיִּקְחוּ לָהֶם נָשִׁים) between believers and unbelievers. . . . The motif of men compromising their religious beliefs because of unbelieving women is a widespread phenomenon in the history of Israel [referring to: Gen 24:3; 28:6; Exod 34:16; Deut 17:17; Judg 14:3; 1 Kgs 11:3–4; Ezra 9:11–14; Neh 13:25–26] and it is also the only reading that does justice to all the textual elements of Gen 6.1–8."

419. Sailhamer, "Genesis," 76.

420. Pröbstle, "Söhne Gottes," 51.

421. Finally, once the previous list of arguments and the corresponding interpretation is accepted, we are able to recognize another interesting consideration concerning the sexual/marital immorality resulting in the Flood. We find a noticeable parallel in the last book of the Bible, in John's Revelation, again alluding to "harlotry"—and thus sexual transgressions—resulting in divine wrath (cf. Rev 12–18: the theme of the pure woman and the harlot Babylon). Albeit the images in Revelation are of a figurative nature, the general principle is still maintained: Sexual transgression/intermarriage of formerly faithful servants of God with the unfaithful leads to another destruction of this world—just as it was "foreshadowed" by the story narrated in Genesis 6.

422. To identify Israel as "sons of God" see Exod 4:22–23 ("Thus says the LORD, 'Israel is My son, My first-born. So I said to you, 'Let My son go, that he may serve Me.'"); Deut 8:5 ("Thus you are to

The Biblical "One Flesh" Theology of Marriage as Constituted in Genesis 2:24

intimacy, and allegiance. In Num 25:1–13 Israel is approaching Moab and intends to enter Canaan. But before they are prepared to carry out this purpose they have to demonstrate their ability to overcome the dangerous hazards of the early "sons of God," who went astray by means of false allegiances through their "lust" for intermarriage. That is a meaningful allusion to the spiritual impact of deviations in sexual relations by becoming "one flesh" with those who do not fit the required pattern of Gen 2:23–24. It seems as if such an aberrance prepares a repetition of the Fall in Gen 3:1–7 by again clinging more to a human than to God.

> (25:1) While Israel remained at Shittim, the people began to play the harlot with the daughters of Moab.
> (25:2) And they invited the people to the sacrifices of their gods, and the people ate and bowed down to their gods.
> (25:3) And Israel joined themselves to Baal of Peor, and the Lord was angry against Israel.

The result is a severe plague and Phinehas' faithful intervention (Num 25:4–13; cf. Ps 106:28–31). Interestingly, the Israelite "sons of God" are again led astray by "daughters of men"—now from the people of Moab.[423] Again there are certain levels

---

know in your heart that the LORD your God was disciplining you just as a man disciplines his son."); 14:1 ("You are the sons of the LORD your God."); 32:6 ("Do you thus repay the LORD, O foolish and unwise people? Is not He your Father . . . ?"), and the many other texts mentioned in the section about "The Sons of God Going Astray" above.

423. There even is a connection to the destruction of Sodom, since Moab is a son of Abraham's nephew Lot, fathered immediately after (and as a result of) the destruction (cf. Gen 19:30–38). Thereby the story is even linked to Sodom's fate, which is also based on sexual immorality and corresponding attacks against "sons of God" (cf. Gen 19:4–9).

Also, there is another most interesting connection between the contrast of Israel as the new "sons of God" and Moab as the new "daughters of men" and the pre-Flood contrast of the two competing lines of people in Gen 6. Immediately before the Shittim-account above, Balaam predicts in Num 24:17: "I see him, but not now; I behold him, but not near; A star shall come forth from Jacob, A scepter shall rise from Israel, And shall crush through the forehead of Moab, And tear down all the sons of Sheth." This "scepter" will "crush through the forehead of Moab, and tear down all the sons of Seth." The name of Seth appears here for the first time since its frequent occurrences in Gen 4:25–26; 5:3–4, 6–8 (total: seven times). The parallelism of the "sons of Seth" (בְּנֵי־שֵׁת) with the "foreheads of Moab" (פַּאֲתֵי מוֹאָב) on the one hand may point to the literal meaning of a people with that name possibly settling in the area of Moab (so HALOT s.v. שֵׁת). However, "a connection with II שֵׁת [i.e., Adam's son Seth] is not improbable, but cannot be really explained" (HALOT s.v. שֵׁת; referring to Noth, *Numeri*, 168). I want to briefly present a possible connection. As investigated above (see "The Sons of God Going Astray"), the title "sons of God" in Gen 6:2 is a descriptive, qualifying name of the "sons of Seth" who once have been loyal to their divine pattern (Gen 1:26–27), God, their father. Yet, by succumbing to the temptation of the beautiful "daughters of men," they became an apostate generation, so corrupt that they even had to be destroyed by divine intervention/judgment (Gen 6:11–13). As mentioned already above, that subject reoccurs in exactly the same manner with the later "sons of God" (Israel) and the "daughters of Moab" in Num 25. The divine oracle of Num 24:17, therefore, also functions as an introduction to the intervention of Phinehas in Num 25:6–8, who somehow gives the starting signal to the crushing defeat of the Moabites in Num 25:17–18; 31:1–18, thus fulfilling partly the literal sense of Balaam's divine oracle. But there is more. The title "sons of Seth" in Num 24:17 further points to the Moabites themselves, for they likewise forsook their divine origin and became corrupt, now being enemies of God. Through their father Lot,

The Old Testament Foundation

to be recognized which reflect the Flood story of Gen 6:1–7 as well as the central "covenant pattern" in Gen 2:24 which again is reversed (thus even forging connections to Gen 3:1–7):[424]

1. Lust for sexual relationships (compare בּוֹא ... אֶל, "come in to/have sexual relations with" in Gen 6:4 and זָנָה, "commit fornication," in Num 25:1 with the ideal of וְהָיוּ לְבָשָׂר אֶחָד, "they will be one flesh," in Gen 2:24) with

2. Illicit partners (compare בְּנוֹת מוֹאָב in Num 25:1 and בְּנוֹת הָאָדָם in Gen 6:2 with בְּצֶלֶם אֱלֹהִים, "in the image of God" or וַיִּבְרָא/וַיִּבֶן יְהוָה אֱלֹהִים, "God created/fashioned," in Gen 1:27 and 2:22) which leads to

3. Self pollution (compare חָלַל, "pollute/defile/profane/begin," in Gen 6:1 and in Num 25:1—both in hiphil![425]—with the innocence, לֹא בּוֹשׁ, of Gen 2:25) resulting

---

they are also descendants of the holy lineage (זֶרַע/תּוֹלְדוֹת) that once "forsook" his father's house, "cleaved" to Yahweh in order to "become" God's holy people and "establish" his covenant in the Promised Land (cf. Gen 12:1–5; 19:30–38). As referred to above, this holy genealogy or semen (cf. Gen 3:15) is the main train of thought, the main interest in the book of Genesis and thus contributes to a right understanding of the "sons of God" in Gen 6:2, as well as to the difficult interpretation of the "sons of Seth" in this *Numeri* text. It seems to be very likely to recognize a new generation of apostates and especially spiritual enemies in these "sons of Seth," the "forehead of Moab," thus even more contributing the Christological "atmosphere" of the story in Num 25. Just like the first, literal "sons of Seth" in Gen 6:2 were eradicated from the earth, so the second, spiritual "sons of God" will be eradicated by the Messiah who is here predicted as their executor. This spiritual meaning is taken up in Ps 110, where the Lord again works for his Messiah to "stretch out" his "strong scepter" in order to subdue his enemies (v. 2; cf. Gen 49:10; Rev 12:5). The Messiah will "smite" (מָחַץ; the same in Num 24:17 and Ps 110:5) kings and judge the nations (vv. 5–6). Jesus applies this meaning to himself (Matt 22:41–46; cf. Acts 2:34–36) and thus affirms the Messianic interpretation of the spiritual, figurative meaning not only of Ps 110, but thereby also of the closely connected prediction in Num 24:17. Moab thus functions as metaphor of the apostate generation living in the "day of his wrath" (Ps 110:5), the time immediately before Christ's return, as Jesus foretold (cf. Luke 17:26–30). It is also suspicious that the oracle speaks of the foreheads (פֵּאָה, literally "corner/side"). Here, again, are perhaps two spheres mingled with each other: The literal king David smote the forehead (מֵצַח) of the strongest and most dangerous enemy Goliath (1 Sam 17:49). In the same way the "spiritual, messianic king David," namely Jesus, triumphs over the strongest and most dangerous enemy, Satan, the serpent of Gen 3, whose head shall also be "crushed" (שׁוּף) according to Gen 3:15 (cf. Rev 12:7–9); further he "smites" (מָחַץ) kings "in the day of His wrath" (Ps 110:5), namely, his great, final judgment day (cf. Isa 13:13; Zeph 1:18; 2:2–3; 3:8). Besides, the forehead might also allude to the important command of binding God's words, his laws, "as a sign . . . on your forehead (בֵּין עֵינֶיךָ, literally: "between the eyes")." (Deut 6:8; cf. 11:18.) Just these laws are broken by the seducing influence of the "daughters of Moab" and the "sons of Seth." To sum up, Num 24:17–19 is a messianic prediction, containing a literal fulfillment (cf. Num 25:17–18; 31:1–18) as some kind of a pledge, a partial, advance payment in view of the actual fulfillment in the Christological context of the New Testament events, and the final, eschatological "day of God's wrath" (Ps 110:5) as foreshadowed by the incidents in Num 25. The "sons of Seth" in this context are, just like the "sons of God" in Gen 6, an apostate generation of a people formerly related to the holy lineage of Genesis, once resembling the divine image of Gen 1:26–27, thus once worthy of the name "sons of God/Seth," but now the corrupt enemies of God that someday will be eradicated due to their unfaithfulness concerning their holy heritage.

424. This will be elucidated in more detail below and especially in the table within the final conclusions of this chapter. On the reversion as given in Gen 3:1–7 see above the chapter about "The Edenic Constitution of Marriage—Wider Biblical Context."

425. Although the primary meaning of the hiphil in these cases is "(to) begin," the substantial

in

4. Forsaking Yahweh (similar to "forsaking," עָזַב, one's parents in Gen 2:24) by joining new Gods/allies (compare צָמַד, "join," in Num 25:3 and לָקַח לְאִשָּׁה, "taking [for/as] a wife," in Gen 6:2 with דָּבַק, "join," in Gen 2:24).

5. Finally, in either case God is annoyed (compare חָרָה, "angry," in Num 25:3 and נחם, "regret," in Gen 6:6 with טוֹב מְאֹד, "very good," in Gen 1:31) and intervenes with a severe, deadly judgment. The outcome is ruin and decrease (Gen 6:3–7; Num 25:4–5) instead of growth and increase (Gen 1:28)—thus completing the reversion of the Edenic ideal and fulfilling the prediction of death due to disloyalty/disobedience against God (Gen 2:17; 3:19).

As will further be elucidated below, this outline of the downward path to destruction seems to represent a counter-pattern to the divine ideal stipulated in Gen 2:24.

Turing again to the events at Shittim, we also find different hints referring to sexual rites the Israelites indulged in while worshipping Baal-Peor. While e.g., "[Israel] joined themselves [to Baal of Peor]" (וַיִּצָּמֶד), usually means "commit/attach oneself to," it is "suggested that the notion of being 'yoked' may imply sexual rites.... The rarity of the phrase may be indicative of some technical cultic term, the meaning of which is now lost."[426] Since Baal was the prominent fertility god of Canaan, and sexual rites are significant in this context, it is likely that cultic prostitution is referred to in this instance.[427] Also, the punishment executed by Phinehas concretely alludes to sexual immorality in a ritual context—or, as Budd suggests, to intermarriage as cause of (subsequent) pagan worship.[428] While e.g., Cole recognizes a (brief and incomplete) chiastic structure in vv. 1–3 emphasizing the gravity of the sin of sacrificing to pagan idols,[429] I also see a steady increase of offence until the final climax of "joining" (צָמַד) the Baal of Peor, as Moses' rationale for the death sentence in v. 5 additionally affirms: "Each of you slay his men who have *joined* (צָמַד) themselves to Baal of Peor." The structure, possibly some general type of this kind of apostasy, looks like the following:

Starting point: God blesses Israel (Num 23–24)

(A) Israel dwells (וַיֵּשֶׁב יִשְׂרָאֵל) (Num 25:1a)

   (B) The people is profaned by harlotry (וַיָּחֶל הָעָם לִזְנוֹת) (Num 25:1b)

      (C) The Moabites invite to sacrifice (וַתִּקְרֶאןָ לָעָם לְזִבְחֵי) (Num 25:2a)

   (B') The people eat and bow down (וַיֹּאכַל הָעָם וַיִּשְׁתַּחֲוּוּ) (Num 25:2b)

(A') Israel joins (וַיִּצָּמֶד יִשְׂרָאֵל) (Num 25:3a)

---

meaning of the verb "(to) pollute/defile/profane" is clearly maintained and could even lead to perceive these sentences as pointing to the commencement of a pollution/defilement through illicit sex.

426. HALOT s.v. צָמַד; Budd, *Numbers*, 279; cf. also Cole, *Numbers*, 436–37 and Milgrom, *Numbers*, 212; they all suggest some kind of covenant agreement.

427. Cf. Cole, *Numbers*, 435–36

428. Cf. Budd, *Numbers*, 280; cf. also Cole, *Numbers*, 441.

429. See Cole, *Numbers*, 435.

End point: God curses Israel (Num 25:3b–9)

As (A) and (A') seem to suggest, dwelling (with pagans) leads to joining (these neighbors).[430] (B) until (B') represent apostasy from right worship practices, while the centre and climax (C) even demonstrates the blasphemy of bringing illicit sacrifices, thereby—especially in a Christological context—exchanging God's perfect sacrifice by some own replacement, making worthless the perfect redeemers work.

While "Balaam arose (וַיָּקָם בִּלְעָם) and departed (וַיֵּלֶךְ) and returned (וַיָּשָׁב) to his place, and Balak also went (וְגַם־בָּלָק הָלַךְ) his way" (Num 24:25), only "Israel remained/dwelled" (וַיֵּשֶׁב יִשְׂרָאֵל; Num 25:1)![431] Especially the intensifying particle conjunction גַּם in וְגַם־בָּלָק הָלַךְ all the more emphasizes the fact that something is wrong with Israel's "remaining/dwelling" at Shittim, the name of which is translated by Philo as "the thorns of the passions" (*Somn.* 1:89), only some ten miles east of Jericho, the starting place of the conquest under Joshua.[432] While the enemies leave the stage, Israel remains and virtually awaits the next attack. The author seems to connote that Israel is wrong in this place and should have moved, too.[433] Just like some day before the donkey better understood God's ways than the prophet did (cf. Num 22), so now even the enemies of Israel are better in doing what the Lord wanted Israel to understand. They had to enter the land upon the blessing Balaam just pronounced over them by God's intervention, but they stayed—and certainly "saw," "desired," and finally "took" the women that were presented through Balaam's repeated action (cf. Num 31:16; Rev 2:14). The close connection between Israel's "remaining" and its apostasy ("joining") is further stressed by the usage of יִשְׂרָאֵל in "stages" (A) and (A'), instead of הָעָם ("the people") in (B) and (B'). The similarity to the already investigated instances is striking: Eve stays with the serpent and finally desires and sins; likewise the "sons of God" dwelt

---

430. This is further supported by clear statements in Exod 23:33; 34:12; Deut 7:16; Josh 23:13; Judg 2:3, which all point to the problem of living together with (among/amid) pagans, respectively of letting them live among Israel.

431. Interestingly, in Israel it is only Phinehas who "arises" (קוּם; Num 25:7) to prepare the way for Israel to return home (to the Promised Land). While all the people "bow down" (חָוָה; Num 25:2) Phineas "arises" (קוּם), he "stands up" and "rebels" (cf. HALOT/BDB s.v. קוּם) against the apostasy, thereby making "atonement" in order to "(re-) erect" the broken covenant. As a sign he is granted God's "covenant of peace . . . a covenant of a perpetual priesthood" (vv. 12–13). But for the rest of the people Moses declares in Num 32:14: "You have *risen up* in your fathers' place, a brood of sinners, to increase still further the fierce wrath of the Lord against the Israelites." And while he warns against false prophets that would "arise" (Deut 13:2–3), God predicts that "you [Moses] are about to lie down with your fathers; and this people will arise and play the harlot with the strange gods of the land" (Deut 31:16.) by "raising up/erecting" self made idols (cf. Lev 26:1; Deut 16:22; 32:38).

432. The Hebrew term actually means "acacia trees," probably located near the modern Tell Kefrein/Tell el-Hamaam; cf. Budd, *Numbers*, 279; Levine, *Numbers 21–36*, 282; Ashley, *Numbers*, 516. Josephus connected Shittim with the town Abila of his time; see *A.J.* 4:176; 5:4; i.e., Khirbet el-Kefrein; cf. Ashley, *Numbers*, 516.

433. In the Talmud R. Johanan asserts: "It reads [Num 25:1]: 'And Israel dwelt in Shittim.' Said R. Johanan: Everywhere such an expression is to be found it brings infliction." (*b. Sanh.* 6; cf. Rodkinson, *Babylonian Talmud*, Sanhedrin, 343.)

near the "daughters of men" and took them, now Israel remains in Shittim, desires and takes. And every time morality is widely corrupted as a result. Illicit sexuality and spiritual apostasy are thus closely connected, while the first (evil one-flesh union literally) frequently functions as a powerful key to the last (evil one-flesh union spiritually), as Philo in the given context eloquently elucidates:

> He [i.e., Balaam] knew that the only way by which the Hebrews could be subdued was by leading them to violate the law, he endeavored to seduce them by means of debauchery and intemperance, that mighty evil, to the still greater crime of impiety, putting pleasure before them as a bait; for, said he, "O king [Balak]! the women of the country surpass all other women in beauty, and there are no means by which a man is more easily subdued than by the beauty of a woman; therefore, if you enjoin the most beautiful of them to grant their favors to them and to prostitute themselves to them, they will allure and overcome the youth of your enemies . . . and so, being wholly subdued by their appetites, they will endure to do and to suffer anything. . . . And the lover being, as it were, taken in the net of her [i.e., a damsel's] manifold and multiform snares, not being able to resist her beauty and seductive conversation, will become wholly subdued in his reason, and, like a miserable man, will obey all the commands which she lays upon him, and will be enrolled as the slave of passion. [. . .]" (*Mos.* 295–99.)[434]

Josephus relates about the advice of Balaam:

> ". . . So that if you have a mind to gain a victory over them for a short time, you will obtain it by following my directions: do you therefore set out the prettiest of such of your daughters as are most eminent for beauty, and proper to force and conquer the modesty of those who behold them, and these decked and trimmed to the highest degree you are able. Then send them to be near camp, and give them a charge, that the young men of the Hebrews desire their company, allow it; and when they see they are enamoured of them, let them leave; and if they entreat them to stay, let give their consent till they have persuaded to stop their obedience to their own laws the worship of that God who established them, to worship the gods of the Midianites; and for by this means God will be angry at them." (*A.J.* 4:129–30.)[435]

---

434. He goes on to "illuminate" the silence of the Scriptures by filling it with interesting suggestions from the mouth of God's fallen prophet Balaam: "And let any damsel who is thus prepared for the sport resist, and say, wantonly, to a lover who is thus influenced, 'It is not fitting for you to enjoy my society till you have first abandoned your native habits, and have changed, and learnt to honor the same practices that I do. And I must have a conspicuous proof of your real change, which I can only have by your consenting to join me in the same sacrifices and libations which I use, and which we may then offer together at the same images and statues, and other erections in honor of my gods.'" *Mos.* 298.

435. Trans. of Whiston. See for the entire story, depicting the tactics of the Moabite women even more thoroughly: *A.J.* 4:126–55.

There is more in the text especially alluding to the last mentioned aspect, the false one-flesh union as spiritual apostasy leading to a slavish relationship with a new "lord." The significant verb צָמַד ("join") is further used in the verbal form once to describe the "fastening" of a belt at one's waist (2 Sam 20:8), and the devoting of one's tongue to deceptive speeches (Ps 50:19). The other instances within the Hebrew Bible contain the root צמד as noun (צֶמֶד), and therefore do not necessarily carry the same meaning as the verb. However, they obviously maintain a common basis, referring to a pair of draft animals or to the field that can be worked with such a pair pulling the yoke.[436] The Hebrew צָמַד is unusual in context of people "joining" someone else and thus may demonstrate that Israel was improperly "coupling" with the Baal of Peor, both becoming a strange "pair," pulling the same yoke, walking the same direction.[437]—Or even more: Israel sold herself just like an animal to a new "lord" (בַּעַל), who now leads them new ways, and they have devoted themselves so deeply to his service, that it may be compared to a pair of oxen led by their master. Although the Hebrew verbs דָּבַק and צָמַד are not the same, the similar meaning "to join" is significant. Israel exchanged his former covenant with God in terms of marriage corresponding to the Edenic ideal of Gen 2:24 (דָּבַק "cleaving") with a new "lord" or *"husband"* (both correct translations of בַּעַל!) through a new relation, now rather reflecting the slavish "relationship" between a donkey or an ox "joined/bound" (צָמַד) to his master—or even just a belt "fastened" to their new lord's waist, thereby devoted/compelled to do his will.[438] The ambiguity of the new God's name בַּעַל ("lord/husband") is most interesting in this context, for it more strongly establishes a marital atmosphere around the entire events at Shittim and places Israel even more clearly on the side of adulterers.

---

436. Cf. Judg 19:3, 10; 1 Sam 11:7; 14:14; 2 Sam 16:1; 1 Kgs 19:19, 21; 2 Kgs 5:17; 9:25; Job 1:3; 42:12; Isa 5:10; 21:7, 9; Jer 51:23. Cf. also Levine, *Numbers 21–36*, 283–84.

437. Partly similar: Cole, *Numbers*, 436–37; Budd, *Numbers*, 279. The imagery of 2 Cor 6:14–15 ("Do not be bound together with unbelievers.... What harmony has Christ with Belial") thus becomes all the more meaningful and certainly may even be interpreted by the significant, unusual usage in this instance. The LXX uses the verb τελέω ("finish/complete/consummate/fulfill/perform/carry out;" cf. FRI/LEH/BDAG s.v. τελέω) in Num 25:3, which may mean "'to initiate into the mysteries' (i.e., of the mystery religions, Gnosticism)," thus possibly concealing "some technical cultic meaning now lost" in the Hebrew term. Ashley, *Numbers*, 517; Budd, *Numbers*, 279; cf. LSJ s.v. τελέω. Additionally, it could indicate a sexual union; cf. Ashley, *Numbers*, 517; Sturdy, *Numbers*, 181; Budd, *Numbers*, 279.

438. Merrill and Harrison likewise recognize that there is a "crystal clear" breaking of the covenant through the worship of Baal-peor, although there is no technical vocabulary of covenant in the passage about the apostasy at Shittim; cf. Merrill, *Deuteronomy*, 116; Harrison, *Numbers*, 337. This comparison in the context of the new covenant with Yahweh shortly before entering and conquering Canaan is again representing the spiritual fight they must win in order to possess the Promised Land. Yahweh obviously is warning them to focus on their real enemies as revealed at Shittim, forgetting about the visible enemies that will not be able to overpower Israel by human agencies. Consequently, he also again stresses the negative, injurious spiritual power of sexual sins, especially in a religious context (cf. also 1 Cor 6:15–20).

Returning to the aforementioned chiasmus with its internal climax of pagan worship, the steady increase of "stages of apostasy" is also meaningful:[439] (1) a wrong dwelling leads to illicit mingling by sexual relations, points (A)–(B), followed by (2) giving in to pagan worship practices, points (B)–(C)–(B'); thus (3) joining a foreign "lord/husband," point (A'). The fourth stage of this increase is the final result: (4) annoying Yahweh and severe punishment. Seemingly the actual offence is not the illicit sexuality itself, even though it is with pagans. As is to be seen in the different examples investigated in this chapter, the punishment is always connected with the following paganism and its false worship practices. The deviation from the Edenic ideal prepares the way in each case of these strict judgments.

In this instance, the punishment is of a unique type and very meaningful for further considerations concerning the New Testament perspective of this study:[440] "The Lord said to Moses, 'Take all the leaders[441] of the people and hang them (יָקַע)[442] in broad daylight before the Lord, so that the fierce anger of the Lord may turn away from Israel'" (Num 25:4). It evidently is a punishment that is able to turn the anger away—in other words, to make "atonement" (כָּפַר) for Israel (cf. v. 13). This is very interesting in a Christological context, particularly with reference to the form of this highly efficient punishment/atonement. The only other instance mentioning a hanging up (תָּלָה) as

---

439. Please remember the intertextual, Hebrew connections given above concerning this instance in Num 25 and the significant accounts and patterns in Gen 1–3 (of course esp. 2:24) and 6.

440. As will further be developed, especially by the following observations. Num 25 can be closely linked to the redeeming work of Christ for the sake of his church; the intimacy between Christ and his church in the NT passages that are to be investigated (1 Cor 6:12–20; Eph 5:21–33) is particularly reflected in this account of the Edenic ideal's distortion.

441. The Samaritan Pentateuch and the Targum Onkelos moderate the punishment of "all the leaders" (כָּל־רָאשֵׁי) by paraphrasing that only the guilty must be slain. However, v. 5 points to the same fact. Surely both commands (vv. 4–5) are one and the same, both paralleling each other and thus illumining v. 4 by the more detailed instruction of v. 5. Cf. Ashley, *Numbers*, 517; Keil, *Numbers*, 204–5; Cole, *Numbers*, 439.

442. The exact meaning of the phrase וְהוֹקַע אוֹתָם לַיהוָה, however, is somewhat obscure. Budd suggests, "the punishment is probably similar to that described in 2Sam 21:6, 9 where the Hiphil of יקע is again employed"; cf. Budd, *Numbers*, 279. Additionally, the few other instances using יקע point to "dislocation" (Gen 32:26: Jacob's thigh), the "hanging up" of divinely cursed persons (see above: 2 Sam 21:1–14), and the "alienation" or "disgust" of God towards his people (cf. Jer 6:8; Ezek 23:17–18). Hence, it is always referring to utter divine (dis-) approval, certainly equal to the particular punishment introduced in Deut 21:22–23 and referred to in the NT as crucifixion (cf. Gal 3:13). Similarly, Köhler-Baumgartner explain the employed hiphil form of this Hebrew lemma יקע as "display with broken legs and arms (alt. to impale, break upon a wheel)." HALOT s.v. יקע; cf. Cole, *Numbers*, 438; similarly Milgrom, *Numbers*, 213, 478. The Qumran documents read correspondingly "[im]pale" as the punishment of Num 25:4; cf. 4QNum[b]. The ancient rabbis clearly understood this passage as referring to a "hanging up" of the offenders; cf. *m. Sanh.* 6:4; *b. Sanh.* 4 (on *m. Sanh.* 4:1); 34b; cf. Rodkinson, *Babylonian Talmud*, Sanhedrin, 106. Philo mentions this instance corresponding to the Septuagint translation as "making an example" (παραδειγματίζω) of the offenders (cf. *Somn.* 1:89), thus giving no further insights. However, at another place he describes the punishment as the "slaying" of v. 5, using the Greek ἀναιρέω ("bear away/destroy/kill/slay/abolish/annul;" cf. LSJ/FRI/LEH/BDAG s.v. ἀναιρέω; see *Mos.* 303–4). Thereby he links vv. 5 and 4 as synonymously paralleling each other, following the usual reading of the text.

death-punishment (מִשְׁפַּט־מָוֶת) in the bright sun, especially warning against letting the convict hang longer than sunset, is given in Deut 21:22–23—and that is exactly fitting the punishment Jesus had to suffer (cf. Acts 5:30; 10:39; 1 Pet 2:24) in order to appease the wrath of God (cf. John 1:29, 36; Rom 5:10; Isa 53:12) and the potential curse that once has been executed in the story of 2 Sam 21:1–14, again becoming reality by Jesus' death: "Christ redeemed us from the curse of the Law, having become a curse for us, for it is written, 'Cursed is everyone who hangs on a tree'" (Gal 3:13). Additionally, the plague finally stopped by "piercing" (Num 25:8: דָּקַר) the apostate couple through their bodies by Phinehas (Num 25:7–8), just like Jesus would later be "pierced" (Zech 12:10: דָּקַר) by other zealous Israelites, being regarded as "crushed" by God's curse (Isa 53:3–5; Gal 3:13).

The offence in Num 25:1–3, therefore, must have been very severe, functioning as a foreshadowing of Christ's redeeming act. Thus the underlying offence of Israel "dwelling" at Shittim has, as a principle, apparently much greater significance for the general spirituality of Israel (and consequently the members of the New Testament church, too) than this short narrative initially supposed to contain. This will become evident when investigating a third and last example of God's dealing in context of Israel "forsaking" the divine covenant and "clinging" to another deity. But before turning to this last example, the ongoing story must also be considered.

At first, the Hebrew term used in v. 5 for commanding to "slay/kill" (הֲרֹג) the wicked "is usually used to speak of ruthless violence, murder (as in Exod 5:21)."[443] Thus it expresses even more God's abhorrence of the acts committed by the people. Beside the general execution of those who "joined" Baal of Peor, a plague killed 24,000 people of Israel (v. 9). The whole people bore the curse of what some of them have caused. Just like the story of Achan in Judg 7, this story points to the responsibility of the entire congregation regarding the sin of individuals. That becomes particularly clear in the intervention of Phinehas (vv. 6–13) against the Midianite woman (Cozbi) and the Israelite man (Zimri), both of additional high responsibility due to their noble origin (vv. 14–15).[444] The deed of these offenders has also been of special weight, because they even dared to have intercourse in immediate proximity to the weeping, repenting congregation at the tent of meeting (vv. 6–8), possibly even in the entrance of just this most holy tent to have sacral sex inside of it. So Allen translates v. 6 considering different textual problems and concludes that it would be possible to understand it as follows: "Then a certain Israelite man brought *the* Midianite woman to *the tent [of God]* right before the eyes of Moses and the eyes of all the congregation of Israel; *and*

---

443. Allen, "Numbers," 917.

444. The Midianite woman (Cozbi) certainly was one of the "daughters of Moab" (v. 1), because they were a mixed population in this territory; cf. Ashley, *Numbers*, 516, 520. See esp. Num 22:4, 7: "Chs. 22–24 highlighted Moab's attempt to overthrow Israel; Midian played a minor role in these chapters. Here the reverse is true—Midian is the chief actor, with Moab taking a supporting role." Ibid., 516; cf. Gane, *Leviticus/Numbers*, 718.

they were sporting at the entrance of the Tent of Meeting."[445] Thus the offense would be much more serious, entering the holy precinct and exercising pagan worship practices by sexual actions right before Yahweh and his holy assembly. Additionally, the Midianite woman is identified with the definite article in the Hebrew text. She might have been "a pivotal player," perhaps even the high priestess of Baal Peor; that would well explain the stark action of Phinehas against just that couple.[446] Further,

> the word *qebah* appears elsewhere only in Deuteronomy 18:3 where it refers to the stomach of a sacrificial animal. This adds another ironic ritual twist to the story. The Midianite woman, who is likely in the process of enticing the Israelite, man to participate in a sacrifice to her gods (cf. Num 25:1–2) is publicly brought as if she were a sacrifice (hiphil of *qrb*; 25:6) and is slain by an Israelite priest while his people are assembled at the sanctuary.[447]

To sum up, Num 25 "is a pivotal section in the theology of the Torah"[448] embedded in masterpieces of Christological and even eschatological foreshadowing.

> Ever since the deaths of Nadab and Abihu in Lev 10 the priestly account operates with something of a priestly triumvirate with Aaron at its head, and with his sons Eleazar and Ithamar as assistants. As the material in Num 1–4 makes clear there are always functions for the sons. The death of Aaron (Num 20) and the promotion of Eleazar created a gap which Phinehas readily fills, and which the story justifies. Viewed in this light the story can be seen, along with the investiture of Eleazar in Num 20, as evidence of God's continuing commitment to the priestly leadership, despite its failures.[449]

These facts allude to God's merciful purposes, working for atonement although Israel freely joined another "Lord." He does not easily give up his "marital bond" to his people, but he intends to forgive Israel as far as there are the smallest signs of repentance and corresponding actions. He even uses apostasy to reveal his plans concerning

---

445. Allen, "Numbers," 918; italics given; cf. on the possibility of a sanctuary context also Budd, *Numbers*, 280; he points to a similar Arabic word meaning "camp sanctuary;" similarly Cole, *Numbers*, 440–42; Ashley, *Numbers*, 520–21. However: "Although one cannot eliminate the cultic connection out of hand, if the site were the tabernacle, the words *tent of meeting* would probably have been used (as in v. 6), and the evidence for another shrine is not convincing. The translation *tent* is vague, but our knowledge of the meaning of the word [i.e., קֻבָּה; v. 8] is vague as well." Ibid., 521; cf. Levine, *Numbers 21–36*, 287–88.

446. Cf. Allen, "Numbers," 920; cf. vv. 14–15—both have been important persons. Furthermore, Allen even suggests that the "weeping" (בֹּכָה) of the congregation rather means engaging in sexual play, for the word indicates that as euphemism e.g., in Gen 26:8 and Exod 32:6; cf. ibid., 919. He concludes that "the issue was so blatant, so outrageous, so unspeakable . . . that the ancients had to hide the meaning somewhat in code words." Ibid.

447. Gane, *Leviticus/Numbers*, 719.

448. Allen, "Numbers," 922.

449. Budd, *Numbers*, 282; on the priesthood and Eleazar's eligibility by executing divine punishment cf. also Cole, *Numbers*, 440–41; Milgrom, *Numbers*, 214, 217.

the continuity of the priesthood, granting an everlasting bond immediately after the gravest transgression, enclosing the entire story in an overwhelming marital, messianic, Christological atmosphere.

I.2.1.3 The Golden Calf (Exod 32)

Very similar in many respects to the foregoing story at Shittim is the next report, chronologically placed even before the one in Numbers. Yet, it is not as obviously linked to illicit sexuality, and thereby to a spiritual deviation from the Edenic ideal, as are the stories discussed above; therefore, it is put after the clearer events in the plains of Moab (Num 25). This section now deals with Exod 32 and the story of Israel's apostasy with the golden calf. There are several significant similarities and far-reaching topics agreeing with the story in Num 25 which makes a closer examination necessary in order to complete the investigations about the Shittim story:[450]

Exod 32	Num 25
(32:1) *Long Dwelling:* "Moses delayed to come down"	(25:1) *Long Dwelling:* "Israel remained at Shittim"
(32:1) *New Orientation:* Turning to Aaron, intending to worship new God(s)	(25:1) *New Orientation:* Turning to Moab's daughters, seduced to worship new god(s)
(32:1) *Forsaking previous Leader:* "Make us gods that will go before us … this Moses, the man who brought us up from the land of Egypt, we do not know what has become of him."	(25:3) *Forsaking previous Leader:* "Israel joined (צָמַד) themselves to Baal" ("joined" like a pair of oxen or horses, led in their master's yoke)
(32:2–6, 8, 19) *Worshipping Idols:* Sacrificing, eating, bowing down	(25:2) *Worshipping Idols:* Sacrifices, eating, bowing down
(32:1, 4) *One Concrete God:* The people turn to "gods" (אֱלֹהִים) but worship only *one* god having *one* image.	(25:2–3) *One Concrete God:* The people turn to "gods" (אֱלֹהִים) but join only *one* god having *one* name.
(32:2–6) *Organized by Apostate Prophet:* Unfaithful Aaron (cf. Exod 7:1; Num 12:2; Mic 6:4)	(31:16) *Organized by Apostate Prophet:* Unfaithful prophet Balaam (Num 22:8–9 etc.)
(32:6, 25) *Sexually connoted Activities:* "They rose up to play (צָחַק)"/"were out of control (פָּרַע)"	(25:1) *Sexual Activities:* "They played the harlot (זָנָה)"
(32:7, 9) *God becomes Angry:* "*your* people, whom *you* brought up from the land of Egypt"/"they are an obstinate people"	(25:3) *God becomes Angry:* "The Lord was angry against Israel"
(32:7–10) *God intends to Destroy:* "Let Me alone, that My anger may burn against them, that I may destroy them"	(25:4–5) *God intends to Destroy:* "Take all the leaders of the people and hang them"/"Each of you slay his men who have joined themselves to Baal"

---

450. In addition, Exod 32 is the final chapter about the account of God making a covenant with Israel (Exod 24–32) and as such is even more valuable to be examined considering the basic goals of this whole chapter.

Exod 32	Num 25
(32:10, 27–28, 35) *Punishment:* Who: Everyone How: Kill (הָרַג) Executioner: Faithful Levites God's action: Plague (נָגַף) Result: 3,000+ killed	(25:4–5, 9) *Punishment:* Who: Leaders How: Hang up (יָקַע)/Kill (הָרַג)[451] Executioner: Faithful judges God's action: Plague (מַגֵּפָה) Result: 24,000+ killed
(32:11–14, 26–28, 31–35) *Twofold Priestly Atonement:* Moses: Bloodless intercession Levites: Killing all the offenders Result: God's curse remains	(25:4, 7–8, 9) *Twofold Priestly Atonement:* Phinehas: Bloody "intercession" Judges: Hanging up the leaders Result: God's curse stopped
(32:28–29) *Priestly Blessing:* Levites blessed for their strict, faithful, and bloody judgment	(25:12–13) *Priestly Blessing:*[452] Phinehas and his descendants blessed for strict, faithful, and bloody judgment
(32:13–14) *Persuasive Argument:* Past/early history of Israel: –Covenant with Abraham, Isaac, Israel –Sign: The blood of circumcision (cf. Gen 17:11, 13–14)	(25:4) *Persuasive Argument:* Future/late history of Israel: –Covenant with Abraham's spiritual descendants (cf. Gal 3:29) –Sign: The blood of Jesus' crucifixion (cf. Matt 26:28; Heb 12:24)
(32:30–35) *Messianic Perspective:* Moses is willing to die for Israel's sake Purpose: Save Israel God's response: Not acceptable Success: Not all are killed, but curse still remains	(25:4) *Messianic Perspective:* Jesus died for Israel's sake Purpose: Saved (spiritual) Israel God's response: Acceptable Success: No repentant believer is killed, curse (Deut 21:23) is abolished (Gal 3:13)

Skipping a reiteration of all the similarities in both chapters as mentioned in this table above,[453] I just want to highlight some major aspects contributing to the main subject of the Edenic covenant ideal and the consequences of its distortion. A first important connection is given by the sexual play the Israelites are seemingly engaged in both instances. While the vocabulary in Num 25:1 is very clear, Exod 32:6 is somehow

---

451. It is unclear whether the command to "slay/kill" in Num 25:5 is referring to the previous mentioned leaders (v. 4), or to the men subordinate to the judges of the different tribes (v. 5). But it is likely that in v. 4 God speaks to Moses and consequently Moses passes the command on to the judges in v. 5. That's also the way Philo understands it; cf. *Mos.* 303–4. The hanging up of the leaders may have been executed right after slaying them.

452. This similarity between Phinehas' and the Levites' choosing as the Lord's priestly class is also observed by Gane, *Leviticus/Numbers*, 719.

453. Beside the agreements between Exod 32 and Num 25 there are further connections to the Flood story in Gen 6 and even the reversion of the Edenic covenant ideal in Gen 3:1–7: (1) Long, peaceful dwelling; no visible danger (2) Proximity to ungodly "elements" (the serpent; pagans/"daughters of men/Moab") (3) New Orientation by seeing and desiring; (4) Forsaking previous ally (Yahweh); (5) Joining new ally (the serpent; pagans/"daughters of men/Moab"); (6) Obedience to their new rules (taking the desired object (fruit/women); pagan worship). Please remember also the more detailed list of similarities between Num 25, Gen 6, and Gen 1–2 (see above on "Israel's Apostasy at Shittim") which, in several details, is also applicable here.

ambiguous, for it only relates that the people "rose up to play" (וַיָּקֻמוּ לְצַחֵק). Yet vv. 7 and 25 reinforce the suspicion that it is a euphemism of sexual activity; there it reads they "have corrupted themselves" (שִׁחֵת) and "they were out of control" (פָּרֻעַ), thereby becoming "a derision among their enemies."[454] These expressions seem to allude to more than just a golden image and some "chaste/decent" adoration. Philo interprets the scene as follows:

> Then, having fashioned a golden bull, in imitation of the animal held most sacred in that country, they offered sacrifices which were no sacrifices, set up choirs which were no choirs, sang hymns which were very funeral chants, and, filled with strong drink, were overcome by the twofold intoxication of wine and folly (ἀφροσύνης). And so, revelling (κωμάζοντες) and carousing the livelong night (παννυχίζοντες), and unwary of the future, they lived wedded to their pleasant vices (ἡδέσι κακοῖς), while justice, the unseen watcher of them and the punishments they deserved, stood ready to strike. (*Mos.* 2:162.)

He further describes the multitude being "full of anarchy and wickedness" (ἐμπιπλαμένου τῶν ἐξ ἀναρχίας κακοπραγιῶν).[455] It is very likely that Israel assimilated itself to pagan worship practices of the surrounding Canaanite fertility cults, including their sexual activities, thus foreshadowing the events at Shittim, with which the story has so much else in common.[456] The golden calf most likely was no Egyptian god, for there are no deities known in that imagery; it rather must have been the well known Canaanite god Baal, who was also widely known in the Nile Delta at the time Israel lived there.[457] And since sexuality was one of the main aspects of Baal worship, it is probable that "the verb translated 'to play' suggests illicit and immoral sexual activity which normally accompanied fertility rites found among the Canaanites who worshiped the god Baal."[458] In the same way the other

---

454. The Hebrew words used for these three descriptions, have the following (additional) meanings: צָחַק, translated as "to play," also means "to joke/amuse oneself/play around with;" שָׁחֵת ("become corrupt") also means "become spoiled/ruined/wiped out;" and פָּרַע ("out of control/naked") meaning "hang loose/let go/run wild/ignore/neglect/spreading depravity." Cf. HALOT s.v. צָחַק/שָׁחֵת/פָּרַע; further sources/dictionaries consulted and cited below. The KJV even translates v. 25 as follows: "Moses saw that the people were naked; for Aaron had made them naked unto their shame among their enemies."

455. *Mos.* 2:163; trans. by Yonge, which in this instance renders the Greek κακοπραγιῶν ("misadventures/failures/wickednesses") a bit more concretely.

456. It is likely that even Paul understood that instance as referring to sexual play; cf. Rosner, "Temple Prostitution," 346–47 investigating 1 Cor 10:7–8 in connection with 1 Cor 6:12–20.

457. Cf. Davidson, *Flame*, 97. Philo interprets the golden calf as an image of "the most sacred animal in that district" (*Mos.* 2:162), certainly referring to the area Israel dwelled in while Moses was on Mount Sinai (cf. § 161). Thus he would also affirm the assumption that they made an image of Baal, although he speaks of "Egyptian inventions" they were imitating in their worship practices (cf. § 161).

458. Davidson, *Flame*, 98; Davis, *Moses*, 285. Stuart, on the other hand, assumes an Egyptian bull cult; cf. Stuart, *Exodus*, 663; cf. also Allen, "Numbers," 915, who considers the "Egyptian bull-god Apis." However, in either case "there is little doubt that Israelites of all times believed that it was Yahweh, and no other god, who had delivered them from Egypt. In other words, Yahweh was now being represented by an idol...." (Stuart, *Exodus*, 665; cf. Exod 32:4: "And they said, 'This is your

expressions seem to share a distinctive sexual connotation and thus point to a sexual context of this apostasy story.⁴⁵⁹

While some commentators do not identify the Hebrew verb צָחַק ("play/indulge in revelry") as indicating sexual debauchery, but rather "singing and dancing with abandon,"⁴⁶⁰ others also interpret it as alluding to drunken, immoral orgies and sexual play.⁴⁶¹ Generally, "the root describes untrammeled behavior" and is somehow reflecting the עֲנוֹת of v. 18 mostly meaning "singing" but also possibly connoting "to have sexual intercourse," considering the "Canaanite goddess of violence and sex, 'Anat(u) [. . .], whose name was regionally pronounced 'Anot . . . ."⁴⁶² Further, in Gen 26:8 and 39:14, 17 the same verb צָחַק rather clearly points to "sexual play."⁴⁶³ However, the sexual dimension is, at least, not to be excluded at any of these instances (Gen 26:8; 39:14, 17; Exod 32:6).⁴⁶⁴

---

god, O Israel, who brought you up from the land of Egypt.'") It seems to be more likely that they chose the prominent Canaanite Baal than the Egyptian bull, just because the Egyptian goddesses obviously have not been as strong as the one who delivered them. And since the god who freed them from the Egyptian slavery led them to Canaan, it suggests itself to mold the invisible deliverer after the Canaanite pattern of Baal.

459. Thus Davidson, *Flame*, 98–99.

460. E.g., Stuart, *Exodus*, 666–67 (quotation on p. 667); cf. Exod 32:19.

461. Cf. Kaiser, "Exodus," 478. In the same way Allen and Budd identify the Hebrew verb צָחַק in Exod 32:6 as speaking of sexual playing; they also connect it with the Baal worship at the plains of Moab in Num 25; cf. Allen, "Numbers," 915; Budd, *Numbers*, 275, 281; cf. also Cole, *Numbers*, 440. The few instances where this lemma is used indicate firstly (mainly) a simple "laughing" (cf. Gen 17:17; 18:12–13, 15; 19:14; 21:6; Judg 16:25; Ezek 23:32), and secondly (more ambiguous) a violent (cf. Gen 21:9; 39:14, 17) or affectionate (cf. Gen 26:8) kind of intercourse—whether sexual (possibly in Gen 39:14, 17; Exod 32:6) or non-sexual (likely in Gen 21:9; 26:8). The LXX uses the Greek παίζω ("play/sport/jest/joke/amuse oneself (amorously);" cf. LSJ/LEH/BDAG s.v. παίζω) thus exactly translating the Hebrew term without giving new insights.

462. Propp, *Exodus 19–40*, 553, 557. "The roots 'ny and ṣḥq may well overlap in meaning; Tg. Onqelos, for instance, translates both with məḥayyəkîn 'making sport.' But precisely what activity is described? The main possibilities are sexual intercourse and singing . . . the former interpretation . . . chimes with Hosea 2. Yahweh proposes to 'seduce' Israel, i.e., regain their allegiance, by leading the nation into the wilderness, where she will 'ny 'as in her youth-days, and like the day of her ascent from the land of Egypt' (Hos 2:17). Yahweh will then espouse Israel: 'You will call me 'my man' (i.e., husband) . . . and I will betroth you to me forever . . . and you will *know* [יָדַע] Yahweh' (both carnally and covenantally) (Hos 2:18, 21–22). This leads to an outbreak of fertility, also described by the root 'ny Hos 2:23–24). . . . Overall, however, . . . 'singing' is the most probable understanding of 'annôt in Exod 32:18 (cf. Vg *vocem cantantium*)." Ibid., 557; italics given. I suggest "singing" does not necessarily exclude "having sexual intercourse"—both are frequently and closely combined in pagan worship practices like those of the Canaanite fertility rites (Baal worship etc.).

463. Cf. Sarna, *Exodus*, 204; R. Bartelmus, in: Botterweck et al., *TWAT*, 7:740–41. Durham, *Exodus*, 422, taking for granted the sexual connotation of צָחַק, recognizes another significant aspect: "The contrast with the ritual and the communion meal of chap. 24, which may originally have immediately preceded the narrative of 32:1–6, is devastating and must not be lost with the insertion of the instruction narrative of chaps. 25–31. The celebration of an obligating relationship in Exod 24 becomes in Exod 32 an orgy of the desertion of responsibility."

464. Thus R. Bartelmus, in: Botterweck et al., *TWAT*, 7:740.

Kaiser further argues that the summarizing verb in v. 7, translated as "have corrupted themselves" (שִׁחֵת) "renders the same verb found in Genesis 6:12 for the apostasy or corruption in Noah's day."[465] This Hebrew term is actually very prominent and important in the prelude to the flood, appearing no less than five times alone in Gen 6 (vv. 11–13, 17), again referring to men who once have been called the "sons of God," but who fell into apostasy. That is particularly meaningful, for it might give an insightful hint to the kind of corruption we are dealing with in this instance, and it further ties the three instances investigated in this chapter more closely together. Also, it seems to be some kind of foreshadowing to the (death) penalty God is about to execute. Just like the wicked antediluvians had to die, so the wicked men of Exod 32 and Num 25 are doomed to be killed. And in all three instances God is visibly present, which makes the offense even more serious.[466] Additionally, all three apostasies lead to a restoration of the divine covenant and a reaffirmation of the initial purpose (Gen 1:26–27 and the [spiritual] ideal of Gen 2:23–24) by blessing a group of loyal "priests" (Noah and family, Levites, Phinehas and family) representing the divine image through performing God's will.

Turning to the second term summarizing Israel's actions at the foot of Mount Sinai, פָּרַע ("were running wild/out of control") might convey:

> The people had cast off all restraint; 'they were running wild and ... out of control' (v. 25). The exact word used twice in this verse (*pr'*) is found in the warning of Proverbs 29:18: 'Where there is no revelation [i.e., message from or attention to the word of God], the people cast off all moral restraints [i.e., they become ungovernable]' (pers. tr.). The idea of the verb 'to cast off all restraints' is that of losing or uncovering. It would appear that there was a type of religious prostitution connected with the people's worship of the golden calf.[467]

"The root *pr'* presumably includes the activities denoted above by *ṣiḥēq* (v 6) and *'annôt* (v 18)."[468] Although sexual connotations are certainly included in the wild behavior connoted by this Hebrew term, it is not the case that פָּרַע clearly, or at least primarily, alludes to sexual activities; it rather summarizes a "letting go" or general neglect of all moral restraints.[469] Sexuality may, of course, be included. What is more

---

465. Kaiser, "Exodus," 478.

466. Before the flood he was "present" in form of the paradise garden and the angels standing at the doors; in Exod 32 he was visible in the clouds and fire at the mountain top, as well as (also Num 25) through the pillars of clouds and fire by day and by night.

467. Kaiser, "Exodus," 480.

468. Propp, *Exodus 19–40*, 562.

469. The other occurrences of פָּרַע point to "drawing away [from work]" (Exod 5:4); "uncovered [head]/wild [hair]" (Lev 10:6; 13:45; 21:10; Num 5:18; Ezek 44:20); "long hair/locks" (Num 6:5; Deut 32:42; [Judg 5:2?]); "unrestrained [behavior/due to lack of visions]" (2 Chr 28:19; 29:18); "neglect [counsel/discipline]" (Prov 1:25; 8:33; 13:18; 15:32; Ezek 24:14); "avoid [false path]" (Prov 4:15). The Septuagint translates this Hebrew term with the verb διασκεδάζω, meaning "to scatter abroad/reject"; cf. LSJ/LEH s.v. διασκεδάζω, thus reflecting the Hebrew expression without concretely pointing to possible sexual connotations. See on the word's meaning esp. T. Kronholm, in: Botterweck et al.,

important for the overall topic of this chapter, however, is the fact that Israel obviously gave up all divine restraints that signified their covenant loyalty and allegiance to Yahweh. They "forsook" him, now "cleaving" to another "Lord" (בַּעַל), demonstrating this new union (oneness) by conformity to his cultic practices, certainly including sexual play—thereby somehow establishing a counter/competitive "one flesh" covenant with their new master. Again, the close relation to Num 25 becomes evident. It is even possible to identify a higher, overall chiastic structure connecting the stories of Exod 32 and Num 25, enclosing several occurrences of discontent and insubordination:[470]

(A) *Apostasy* (The Golden Calf; Exod 32)
  (B) *Discontent* (Taberah/quail; Num 11)
    (C) *Insubordination—Individuals* (Miriam and Aaron; Num 12)
      (D) *Open Rebellion—Israel* (The Twelve Spies; Num 14)
    (C') *Insubordination—Individuals* (Dathan and Abiram; Num 16)
  (B') *Discontent* (Snakes; Num 21)
(A') *Apostasy* (Shittim; Num 25).

This structure, as well as the table of agreements above, reaffirms the close connection between both instances of apostasy, including the same cult (Baal), severe punishment due to the gravity of immorality (idolatry and sexual depravity), and the choosing of a special group to uphold the true, divine worship (Levites/family of Phinehas) in Israel's future. Also, the first apostasy marks the beginning of the travel, the second marks the end of it—the golden calf is the first apostasy right after leaving Egypt, the Moabite women are the last one, right before entering Canaan. The accounts indicate that Israel did not change, at least not entirely, although they had had 40 years to learn obedience and faithfulness.[471] This is even more emphasized by the intensifying insertion of the interesting קום that plays an equally prominent role within the apostasy at Shittim, as mentioned above. In Exod 32 Israel "*rose up* to play" (וַיָּקֻמוּ לְצַחֵק; v. 6) after commanding Aaron to "*rise up* to make a God" (קוּם עֲשֵׂה־לָנוּ אֱלֹהִים; v. 1). While Israel in Shittim "sits down" (וַיֵּשֶׁב יִשְׂרָאֵל; Num 25:1) neglecting to arise and leave the place of temptation and only Phinehas "*arises*" to stop the apostasy, here at Sinai the people work even actively in the wrong direction. At Shittim they were passively welcoming the beautiful temptations. At Sinai they even "*stood up*" to introduce them, and they "*arose* to play" with them, thereby becoming a derision among

TWAT, 6:757–60; cf. Clines, *Classical Hebrew*, 6:772–73.

470. Based on the outline of Budd, *Numbers*, 281.

471. Yet it is not exactly clear at which stage of time the events at Shittim took place. But reasoning from the hint in Num 26:63–65 and the reports about the preparations for the conquering of Canaan following immediately after chap. 25, one may conclude that the end of the 40 year period has been reached and the experiences at Shittim were some kind of a final, and unfortunately unsuccessful test of the next generation's loyalty and resistance against temptation, apostasy and the resulting evils. Some commentators suggest that the plague of Num 25:9 killed the last survivors of the old generation thereby preparing the way to enter Canaan shortly thereafter (see e.g., Ashley, *Numbers*, 515).

those, who "*stand up*" (בְּקָמֵיהֶם; v. 25) against Israel. Even Moses is commanded by God to "*stand up*" (קוּם) and "go down" (יְרֵד) to "your [i.e., Moses'] people" (עַמְּךָ; all in Deut 9:12; cf. Exod 32:7), telling them that God now became their enemy (cf. Deut 9:13–14; Exod 32:8–10)—rhetorically demonstrated by no more calling Israel his (God's) own people, thus reflecting the choice of Israel in Exod 32:1. As a last and considerably sad detail, it must be said that Israel thereby unfortunately "stood" in the traditional line of this world's first offender and rebel, Cain, the first one to "*rise up*" against his brother (Gen 4:8). Similarly, Israel *rose up* against their divine covenant partner, Lord, father, and husband, "forsaking" their originally very close relationship.

All these details contribute to the dangerous atmosphere of apostasy at Sinai and Shittim. The apparent links between both stories can hardly be denied[472] and they further allude to the great significance and importance of these instances as instructive and educational "lessons" to function as fundamental theological principles demonstrating the vast impact of a deviation from the Edenic ideal applied to the spiritual sphere of the relationship between Yahweh and Israel.

I.2.1.4 Summary and Final Considerations

The three significant examples investigated above contain several similarities that connect them with each other under the main subject of the literal one-flesh union (i. e., sexuality/the marital bond) and its interaction with the spiritual one-flesh union (the divine covenant between God and man) as to be seen most clearly when deviating from the Edenic ideal (Gen 1:26–27; 2:23–24). This ideal is a matter of allegiance in its highest sense and, as such, closely related to the divine covenant between believers and God. That concept was presented, first, through literal and literary connections as investigated in the section about the creation narrative, and is now especially emphasized by these three experiences of the former and the later "sons of God." It seems that the Edenic ideal functions somehow as a protective wall against a deviation in literal as well as spiritual respects, while the "same-flesh" foundation and the intervention of God as described in Gen 2:18–23 is alluding to the necessity of belonging to the same "divine family" of God, being of his "flesh and bone" (Gen 2:23) reflecting his "image and likeness" (Gen 1:26–27), worthy to be called "sons/children of God" (Gen 6:2). That evidently was the way God would have it with Israel, his own dear people that he called "my son, my firstborn" (בְּנִי בְכֹרִי; Exod 4:22).

The meaningful stories in Gen 6, Exod 32, and Num 25 thoroughly depict the gradual development from "simple failures" over dangerous relationships to grave apostasy. First, there is an unsound "dwelling" in proximity of paganism ("daughters of men/of Moab"); second, losing sight of the spiritual leader (God/Moses) and a new

---

472. That is further affirmed by Davidson, *Flame*, 99; cf. Wenham, *Numbers*, 184–85. There are not only strong parallels to the story at Moab's borders, but also to the (sexually) wicked times before the Flood, as Kaiser suggests; cf. Kaiser, "Exodus," 478.

turning toward an alternative (Baal/Aaron). The next step, working mostly as impetus and motivation for rejecting God at the first two stages, is sexual attraction and corresponding activities (seeing, desiring, and taking). However, it is significant that the sexual intercourse itself (and even the resulting intermarriage) is not the reason for God's judgments, but the most serious spiritual decline that follows almost immediately. The deviation from the Edenic ideal thus functions as a turning point—somehow even as a point of no return—and a springboard up to a new level of "forsaking" God and "cleaving" to a new "lord." This affinity between marriage resp. sexuality (the literal one-flesh union) and worship resp. individual lifestyle (the spiritual one-flesh union) seems to be programmatic throughout the entire Old Testament. The author of the early Edenic report about the creational oneness devoted the biggest part of his account to this ideal and its early distortions (altogether: Gen 1:26–31; 2:4—3:24), thus illustrating already right at the beginning of the Torah what the reader of Israel's history through the ages would have to expect.[473]

Deviations from the original one-flesh ideal are apparently a special device of Israel's enemies in order to attack God's "firstborn son" most efficiently, particularly regarding their spirituality. Hence, beside Gen 6 and Exod 32, Num 25 "presents a formative encounter with Baal worship, a miniature of the disaster that would one day engulf and destroy the nation."[474] This kind of apostasy "by participation in the debased, sexually centered Canaanite religious rites of Baal worship . . . would become the bane of Israel's experience in the land."[475] This Baal cult "from this point on [was] a constant temptation to the Israelites, eventually becoming one of the key reasons for the subjugation, destruction, and captivity of Jerusalem, Judah, and Israel . . . ."[476] It is not surprising that these examples are found at so vital points of Israel's (or man's) history: the flood as the world's restart with changed conditions, the golden calf shortly after receiving the Ten Commandments and the official consummation of the covenant at Sinai, and the events at Shittim shortly before conquering Canaan.

As these instances demonstrate, God is constantly trying to educate his people by punishing them severely, but at the same time he reaffirms his divine covenant by appointing proper priests to make atonement for his people.[477] The fact that Israel sinned

---

473. Please consider the stories of Samson (Judg 16), David and Bathsheba (2 Sam 11–12), Solomon and his thousand wives (1 Kgs 11:1–4), and nothing less than three entire chapters in the Proverbs dealing with matters of adultery and prostitution (Prov 5–7). Furthermore, there are again and again references to prostitutes, temple whores and polygamy throughout the OT (1 Kgs 14:24, 15:12; 2 Kgs 23:7; Hos 4:14). It has been one of the worst failures of Israel to indulge in different deviations from the Edenic ideal.

474. Allen, "Numbers," 914. On the more general topic of "sexuality as danger to boundaries" (including the human-divine realm) further affirming the negative power of sexual misconduct see Frymer-Kensky, "Law and Philosophy," 95–99.

475. Allen, "Numbers," 914

476. Cole, *Numbers*, 435.

477. On this kind of "divine education" see Prov 3:11–12; Heb 12:7–11. The punishments in form of destruction, plagues, and curses cf. Gen 7; Exod 32:27–28, 35; Num 25:4–5, 9. On the priesthood

so seriously even after the long period of education in the wilderness explains the strict and Christological most significant punishment by hanging up the responsible leaders as a warning and a sign of shame, divine disgrace and curse (cf. Deut 21:32). Also, only by the "bloody intercession" of Phinehas is the curse abandoned and the people saved. That he slay the apostate couple while they were apparently having sexual intercourse, and that the Hebrew text especially emphasizes the detail that he "pierced . . . the woman through her abdomen" (הָאִשָּׁה אֶל־קֳבָתָהּ), further stresses the sexual and procreative aspects of Gen 2:24 that are distorted by this illicit union.[478] The other Christological aspects mentioned above additionally point to the far-reaching responsibility of one's dealing with sexuality and its spiritual facets as illustrated in Num 25.

There is an important underlying pattern that demonstrates not only God's disapproval of sexual sin and apostasy, but also illustrates his appointed means of mediation and purification, even foreshadowing the events of Jesus' redeeming act on the cross of Calvary. That is reaffirmed by Moses' prominent speech shortly before his death and the conquering of Canaan in Deut 4:18. In this "farewell address" the righteous and just commandments of Yahweh are clearly contrasted to the worship of Baal-peor; the incident at the borders of Moab thus serves as counterexample to the true and most holy worship of Yahweh. Even the law as condition of the covenant is contrasted to this negative experience, thereby also reflecting the breaking of the commandment tables due to the events in Exod 32 (see v. 19). The reputation of Israel as God's holy people is again emphasized and God declares his intention to exalt them over all the peoples of the earth—when being faithful to him. Thus, the severity and weightiness of a deviation from the Edenic ideal of allegiance in literal as well as spiritual respects, its close relatedness to complete apostasy and false worship, as well as the far reaching responsibility of the individual member's behavior, are positively highlighted.

Corresponding to the importance of the Shittim experience and the future dangers, Moses receives a divine prediction shortly before his death, foretelling that "this people [Israel] will arise (קָם; cf. Exod 32:6) and play the harlot (זָנָה; cf. Num 25:1) with the strange gods of the land, into the midst of which they are going, and will forsake (עָזַב; cf. Gen 2:24) Me [Yahweh] and break My covenant [. . .]" (Deut 31:16). Finally, "narrative, poetry, and prophetic utterance from the rest of the HB [i.e., Hebrew Bible] will make evident the extent of this apostasy and will refer repeatedly to the incident of Baal-Peor."[479] This instance, linked with the breaking of the covenant through worshipping the golden

---

cf. Gen 8:20—29:3; Exod 32:11–14, 28–29; Num 25:10–13.

478. The LXX renders the Hebrew קֳבָתָהּ as τῆς μήτρας αὐτῆς ("her womb"), thus also stressing the female "organ in which offspring are formed." FRI s.v. μήτρα; cf. BDAG/LSJ. "The words *qubbâ* (tent) and *qᵒḇāṯāh* (stomach) were probably used together because of their similar sounds. Later Jewish interpretation held that Phinehas found the two in the act of sexual intercourse and pierced both of them through their sex organs [. . .]—the punishment fits the crime!" Ashley, *Numbers*, 521. Similarly Milgrom, *Numbers*, 215.

479. Davidson, *Flame*, 102. He refers to the texts in Josh 22:16–18; Ps 106:28–31; Ezek 20:21–26 and Rev 2:14. Cf. also Hos 9:10.

calf and the distortion of God's image (Gen 1:26–27) by the "sons of God" in the times before the flood, is an alarming example of the spiritual decline that will be the outcome of "forsaking" (עָזַב) the marriage-like covenant with God in order to exchange it for a slavish relationship by "joining" (צָמַד) some other "lord" (בַּעַל). Although God is strict in his judgments, "even over the most distorted practices and abhorrent abominations, God's forgiving and empowering grace still prevails."[480] That is evident from his almost joyful declaration in Num 25:10–13, the blessings in Gen 8:21–22 and Exod 32:29, and particularly his irreversible resolution to bring his people into the Promised Land, whatever the obstacles may be. One of the biggest obstacles certainly is the deviation from the Edenic covenant ideal, in literal as well as spiritual respects, as the ongoing history of Israel until the exile so eloquently demonstrates.

Finally, it is not appropriate to presume that

> It is apparent from this absence of any use of the phrase ["one flesh"], and the presence of extensive discussion of the nature of marriage and of the appropriate legislative framework within which marriage can operate in Israelite society, that there is no fundamental theological or moral concept which is expressed by this phrase which was important in Israel's thinking throughout the entire span of its history.[481]

The use of different aspects of the Edenic marriage "covenant" frequently referred to in the Old Testament as metaphor of the covenant between God and Israel clearly alludes to the fact that it actually was very important.[482] Yet, it is not the phrase בָּשָׂר אֶחָד ("one flesh") that is used in the OT Scriptures, but the three respective "pillars" which are comprised thereby: (1) forsaking; (2) cleaving; (3) becoming. As explained within the textual analysis of Gen 2:24, the "one flesh" union is the result of these foregoing steps, and corresponds spiritually to the institution of the covenant, requiring the same three steps or pillars for its actual consummation. The translation or transfer of the Edenic ideal (Gen 2:24) to the spiritual sphere of Israel's relationship with Yahweh would consequently look like the following:[483]

---

480. Davidson, *Flame*, 175.

481. Kaye, "One Flesh," 49.

482. Cf. further the tradition of Gen 2:24 in Jewish history as outlined by Berger, *Gesetzesauslegung*, 528–33.

483. The biblical references are mostly given in the investigations above. If not, they are attached as footnotes in the table below.

The Old Testament Foundation

	Literal Level (Gen 2)	Spiritual Level (Exod 24)[484]	Distortion (Num 25; Exod 32)[485]
Initiator	God	God	Lust/Sin/Satan
Who	Man	Israel/Humankind ("sons of God")	Israel/Humankind ("sons of God")
Familial Attributes	Human Pattern for Woman (כְּנֶגְדּוֹ)	God's Firstborn Son (בְּנִי בְכֹרִי) His Image & Likeness (בְּצַלְמֵנוּ כִּדְמוּתֵנוּ)	Creator of Idols Servant/Slave [486]
Pillar (1)	Forsake [parents] (עָזַב)	Forsake [false gods] (עָזַב)	Forsake [God] (עָזַב)[487] Profane [self] (חָלַל)
Pillar (2)	Cleave (דָּבַק)	Cleave (דָּבַק)	Join/Bind (צָמַד)
Pillar (3)	Be(come) One Flesh (הָיָה לְבָשָׂר אֶחָד)	Accept Divine Word[488] (עַל כָּל־הַדְּבָרִים)	Play the Harlot (זָנָה)
To Whom	Woman	God	Baal/Idols ("daughters of men")
Familial Attributes	"Bone of my bones, and flesh of my flesh" (מֵעֲצָמַי וּבָשָׂר מִבְּשָׂרִי) (עֶצֶם)	Creator/Father/Divine Pattern for Man (בְּצַלְמֵנוּ כִּדְמוּתֵנוּ)	Man's Creation[489] (מַעֲשֵׂה יְדֵי אָדָם) Lord/Master (בַּעַל)
Establishing Act[490]	Sexuality	Sacrificing	Sacrificing

484. Of course, Exod 24 is not the only chapter that contains information about the making of a covenant (cf. e.g., Gen 8–9; 15–17 etc.), but it is the most important example regarding information about the formal making of the most important Old Testament covenant between Yahweh and the people of Israel. On ancient Jewish interpretations of the Sinai-covenant as marriage between God and Israel see Zimmermann, Geschlechtermetaphorik, 208–14.

485. In this table Num 25 functions as prime example and pattern of the deviation/distortion from the Edenic ideal on the spiritual as well as the literal level. As explained throughout the foregoing investigations of this chapter, it comprises the significant aspects of the other pivotal examples (Gen 6; Exod 32) in the best and fullest way, thereby additionally employing skilful stylistic devices, somehow summarizing the previous apostasies.

486. Deut 4:28; 27:15; Ps 115:4; Isa 2:8.

487. See e.g., Deut 28:20; Judg 10:13; 1 Sam 8:8; 1 Kgs 11:33; 2 Kgs 22:17; and many more.

488. See Exod 24:8 (cf. Eph 5:26; John 1:1–3, 14 and 6:48–63, etc.).

489. Ps 115:4; Deut 4:28; cf. Deut 27:15; Isa 2:8.

490. When accepting the hint I have mentioned within the section about the wider biblical context of Gen 2:24 and its "covenantal aspects," there is another accord given between these three levels, directly related to the "establishing act:" The "Blood of the Covenant" (דַּם־הַבְּרִית) as given by defloration (concerning literal level) and the sacrifice (concerning spiritual level/distortion). Although there is no text that unequivocally proves that Eve's blood was shed (the first blood is at least to be assumed around the "garments from skin for Adam and his wife" in Gen 3:21), not even that Adam and Eve had sex before leaving the garden (the first hint in Gen 4:1), Deut 22:17 demonstrates that, at least in the time of the Pentateuch's writing down, the blood of the defloration was recognized as a formal sign of the marriage's "consummation."

Spiritual Result	Unveiled Seeing (וַיִּהְיוּ שְׁנֵיהֶם עֲרוּמִּים) Knowing (יָדַע)[491] Blessing (וַיְבָרֶךְ אֹתָם)	Unveiled Seeing Communal Meal[492] Blessing[493]	Communal Meal Anger/Curse/ Corruption
Spiritual Sign	Lovingkindness/ Faithfulness	Lovingkindness/ Faithfulness[494] (חֶסֶד וֶאֱמֶת)	Obstinacy (קָשָׁה) Rebellion (מָרָה)[495]
Formal Result	"One Flesh" (בָּשָׂר אֶחָד)	Covenant (בְּרִית)	Breach of Covenant Apostasy
Formal Sign	Garment[496]	Circumcision[497] Sabbath[498] The Commandments[499]	Breaking of Command-ment Tables Execution (יָקַע)
Long term outcome (cf. Deut 28)	Life Procreation Prosperity	Life Growth/Procreation Prosperity	Death Plague/Perishment Decline

I.2.2 Marriage as Model of the Divine Covenant

Basing on the findings of the previous chapter, this section will now investigate the concrete imagery related to a marital covenant between Yahweh and his chosen people, Israel. The aim is to reaffirm the aforementioned line of reasoning and to explore further the significance of Gen 2:24 which "is indicated by its use as a common metaphor for God's relationship to Israel."[500] In particular, covenantal aspects and possible facets to be considered as enrichment for the literal sense of (human) marriage are important, thereby preparing the way for the investigation of both spheres (literal and spiritual) in the following chapters on the New Testament echoes. At first, I will briefly (as a survey) depict the major OT instances using metaphors related to marriage. Then I will, second, investigate in more detail the concrete covenantal aspects connecting the figurative and the literal spheres, pointing to marriage as a model of the divine covenant (and vice versa).

---

491. Cf. e.g., Gen 4:1, 17, 25.

492. Cf. also Gen 26:29–31; 31:46, 54.

493. For instance: Deut 10–11. Frequently elsewhere in the Old Testament on being faithful to the covenant.

494. Exod 34:6; 2 Sam 2:6; Ps 25:10; 61:8; 85:10; 86:15; 89:15; Prov 3:3; (20:28).

495. E.g., Deut 9:24.

496. Deut 22:17.

497. Gen 17:7–14.

498. Exod 31:13–17.

499. Deut 6:8; 11:8.

500. Beale and Carson, *NT Use*, 197.

I.2.2.1 Marriage and Prostitution Images

While the prostitution symbolism is mentioned several times already within the Pentateuch, explicit allusions to the marriage symbolism do not occur before the application of that imagery by the prophet Isaiah. The warnings against spiritual prostitution of Israel are closely linked with the imagery of a marriage between Yahweh and his people. And "obwohl die Vorstellung von ehelicher Liebe zwischen Gott und Israel im Pentateuch nicht ausdrücklich erwähnt wird, scheint sie latent vorhanden zu sein."[501] Gane, for instance, recognizes elements of a marriage relation within the consummation of the covenant at Sinai and asserts:

> After the wedding at Sinai, where God proclaimed the covenant vows (Ten Commandments) with awesome splendour, Israel said "I do," and they built a house (sanctuary) together, there was a journey through the wilderness of real life. Whatever happened, they were in it together.[502]

The warnings against breaking the covenant by taking foreign wives and finally "playing the harlot with their gods" (וְזָנוּ אַחֲרֵי אֱלֹהֵיהֶן; Exod 34:15–16) is in close relation to the "jealousy" (קַנָּא; Exod 20:5) of God.[503] Even in the Ten Commandments God points to this jealousy as an individual sign of his intimate relationship with Israel:[504]

> The marriage metaphor of Yahweh has very early roots, as seen in the language of jealousy in the Decalogue and other parts of the Pentateuch. The whole language of "jealousy," which is central to the picture of God in the Pentateuch, has the connotation of marriage. The concept of jealousy is already linked with spiritual whoredom in the Pentateuch and Judges. Sinai can be seen as

---

501. M. Weinfeld, in: Botterweck et al., *TWAT*, 1:808; cf. Stienstra, *YHWH is the Husband*, 178–86. Baltensweiler, *Ehe im NT*, 32 simply presupposes a "hieros gamos" between Yahweh and Israel.

502. Gane, *Leviticus/Numbers*, 471. Cf. e.g., rab. Numeri 12:8/Exodus 23:5; Batey, *Nuptial Imagery*, 16–17: "The further attempt to rationalize the concept of Israel as married to the Lord was introduced by citing Exodus 31:18, 'And he gave to Moses, when he had made an end (*kekallotho*) of speaking with him on Mt. Sinai, the two tables of the testimony.' By a slight variation in vocalization, which was the method for much rabbinic exegesis, *kekallotho* (when he had made an end) was read *kekallatho* (as his bride). The resulting meaning was given: 'When Yahweh had made (Israel) as his bride, while speaking to Moses on Mt. Sinai, he gave Moses the two tables of the testimony.' Moses, who represented the agent of the Lord, was responsible for the purity and consecration of the people. The tables of the testimony were the marriage document delivered into the possession of Israel as evidence of the choice and obligation laid on her. The marriage symbol was a metaphor of the personal encounter effecting a covenant bond." On ancient Jewish interpretations of the Sinai-covenant as marriage between God and Israel see Zimmermann, *Geschlechtermetaphorik*, 208–14.

503. Similarly M. Weinfeld, in: Botterweck et al., *TWAT*, 1:808; Stienstra, *YHWH is the Husband*, 178–86, 226–30; cf. also Ortlund, *Whoredom*, 30.

504. Exod 20:4–5: "You shall not make for yourself an idol, or any likeness of what is in heaven above or on the earth beneath or in the water under the earth. You shall not worship them or serve them; *for I, the Lord your God, am a jealous God* . . . ." Cf. on this characteristic as indicating marriage also Instone-Brewer, *In the Bible*, 2, 34–35.

the point at which God marries his people, and Leslie W. Pope finds a reference to God collecting his bride and bringing her to him in the wilderness.[505]

As was noted in the previous section, the wilderness experience indeed contains some of the most striking reports on God's behaviour as "jealous husband" of his precious bride (cf. e.g., Exod 20:5; 34:14; Deut 5:9). In fact,

> 'the divine sentiment of jealousy/zeal is the supreme marital emotion within the covenant bond' and shows how the motif of divine marital jealousy is particularly highlighted in the Baal of Peor episode of Num 25, where Phinehas is represented as the only human in Scripture to reverberate with the emotion of divine jealousy in his swift response to Israel's spiritual harlotry.[506]

Additionally, it is possible and likely to recognize some kind of an ancient "marriage formula" in declarations like the following: "I will take you [Israel] for my people, and I will be your God; and you shall know (יָדַע) that I am the Lord your God" (Exod 6:7); "I will make my dwelling among you, and my soul will not reject you. I will also walk among you and be your God, and you shall be my people." (Lev 26:11–12; cf. Ezek 37:27); "You shall be my people, and I will be your God." (Jer 30:22; cf. Ezek 36:28). These wordings contain clear similarities to legal marriage declarations in ancient Canaan; God apparently wishes to establish a covenant with Israel that greatly reflects and equals the one between a husband and his wife.[507]

---

505. Instone-Brewer, *In the Bible*, 34–35; cf. also M. Weinfeld, in: Botterweck et al., *TWAT*, 1:808; Ortlund, *Whoredom*, 27–40; Stienstra, *YHWH is the Husband*, 177–86; Sohn, *Divine Election*, 44.

506. Davidson, *Flame*, 114; referring to Balorda, "Jealousy of Phinehas," 57–69, 78–86, quotation on p. 82. Davidson further asserts: "In this chapter the Hebrew *qn'* is employed four times, and the verbal form of this Hebrew root appears only here in the Pentateuch." Davidson, *Flame*, 114. Thus the most significant events at Shittim are even more emphasized.

507. Thus Kirchschläger, *Ehe im NT*, 24–25, 47–48; cf. Instone-Brewer, *In the Bible*, 12–13. for legal records of ancient Near Eastern marriage covenants resembling the wordings given above. Similarly Davidson, *Flame*, 378, who follows Instone-Brewer. Also, M. Weinfeld, in Botterweck et al., *TWAT*, 1:808 supports this view. Furthermore, Paul seems to affirm this understanding in Rom 11:2 by declaring that God formerly "knew" Israel and never intended to dissolve this close relationship. He is using the same verbal root ([προ-] γινώσκω) employed in the Greek OT to express the Hebrew יָדַע ("know/experience"), which is the well known euphemism for marital intimacy (cf. e.g., Gen 4:1). Paul similarly refers to God's free choice (as the instances quoted above, cf. additionally Deut 7:6–8) in selecting Israel for his own people (see the entire context of Rom 11:2). Besides, note the similarities in the stories of Abraham and Israel compared to the steps in Gen 2:24. Gen 12:1–3 is conspicuously reflecting the three important stages of Gen 2:24, although not using the same terminology: being called by God, Abraham had first to *forsake* his country, his relatives, and his father's house (Gen 12:1); he even had to separate from his nephew Lot (Gen 13:1–12) in order to be exclusively God's own, chosen person. Second, he had to *cleave* to God, being led by him into a land that he did not know until that time (v. 1). And finally, third, he would *become* a great nation, being blessed by God with procreation (v. 2; cf. 1:28) and an everlasting covenant (Gen 17:7–14). Similar steps are taken by Israel in the Exodus; called out from Egypt, *forsaking* their past experiences as members of a pagan nation, *cleaving* to God in his working for their deliverance, being led by him into a country they did not know yet, with the purpose of finally *becoming* a great nation under God's divine blessing. These "Edenic pillars" are the foundation of God's own people, the only nation exclusively "chosen to be a people for His own possession" (Deut

Turning to some of the major metaphors appearing in the later prophets, it is worthwhile to have a look into the imagery depicted by Isaiah. In chap. 54 he describes God as maker (עָשָׂה), redeemer (גָּאַל), and husband (בָּעַל) of Israel (v. 5). She (Israel) is a wife once married in her youth, presently being rejected, grieved (v. 6), and infertile like a widow (vv. 1–4). But God loves her. He "called" (קָרָא) her like a "forsaken" (עָזַב) wife. In v. 7 he explains that he "forsook" (עָזַב) her for only a short moment, thereby elucidating that he was the one to make her an infertile widow, a forsaken wife who once was married by him in her youth. Remembering his promise of Deut 30:3–4, he now begins to "gather" her and makes her an object of his special interest to be blessed with prosperity (cf. vv. 8–10; Isa 60:15–16). Of special interest considering the previous section on three significant examples of apostasy somehow related with the Edenic ideal, is v. 9 referring to the times of Noah. Additionally, v. 10 speaks of the "covenant of my [i.e., God's] peace" (בְּרִית שְׁלוֹמִי) closely connecting this prophetic speech with the passage about Shittim and "my [i.e., again God's] covenant of peace" (בְּרִית שָׁלוֹם) granted to Phinehas and his descendants in Num 25:12–13.[508] Just like God re-established his covenant at Shittim through the atoning work of Phinehas, so Yahweh is now about to enter anew the close "marital" relationship with his people, reversing the former "forsaking" of his Israelite bride:

> It will no longer be said to you, 'Forsaken,' [עָזַב] Nor to your land will it any longer be said, 'Desolate;' But you will be called, 'My delight is in her,' And your land, 'Married' [בָּעַל]; For the Lord delights in you, And to Him your land will be married [בָּעַל]. (Isa 62:4–5.)

Here, again, important terminology is employed, alluding to the Edenic ideal of Gen 2 and its deviation in Gen 3:1–7, as well as the theologically most significant instance of reversing the divine covenant by "joining" the בַּעַל at Shittim and, most likely, at Sinai, too. This contrast between Yahweh and Baal in terms of a marital covenant is further mentioned by Jeremiah:

> 'Behold, days are coming,' declares the Lord, 'when I will make a new covenant with the house of Israel and with the house of Judah, not like the covenant which I made with their fathers in the day I took them by the hand to bring them out of the land of Egypt, My covenant which they broke, although I was a husband [בָּעַל] to them,' declares the Lord (Jer 31:31–32).

The prophet explains that God evidently was Israel's בַּעַל during their march in the wilderness. The marital covenant's consummation certainly happened on Mount Sinai as described in Exod 24.[509] The adulterous breach occurred immediately while

---

7:6) to grant them "loving-kindness and faithfulness" (cf. Exod 34:6; 2 Sam 2:6; Ps 25:10, etc.) within an everlasting covenant (cf. Exod 19–24; 31:12–18 etc.) that reflects the Edenic "one flesh" ideal of Gen 2:24.

508. More about this will follow in the next paragraph about covenantal aspects.

509. See the table comparing the "covenants" of Gen 2, Exod 24, and the apostasies of Num 25, Exod 32, and Gen 6 in the table of the conclusions of the previous chapter. See also e.g., Thompson,

still dwelling at Sinai in Exod 32. And even after decades of training in being faithful to Yahweh they again broke the covenant while dwelling at Shittim (Num 25), right before God's "taking the bride home" to Canaan. There, through the seductive influence of the "daughters of Moab," they exchanged their בַּעַל of Sinai for the בַּעַל of Peor. That characteristic of unfaithfulness sadly remained all through the ages, hence God declares: "My people have forgotten Me days without number. How well you prepare your way to seek love! Therefore even the wicked women you have taught your ways" (Jer 2:32–33). "As for your adulteries and your lustful neighings, the lewdness of your prostitution on the hills in the field, I have seen your abominations. Woe to you, O Jerusalem! How long will you remain unclean?" (Jer 13:27).

In Jer 3:1, God even applies the law of Deut 24:1–4 to the present situation of the relationship between him and Israel or Judah. Interestingly, the prophet does not state that God divorced his wife. He only refers to the land's pollution as result of the adultery and even harlotry with other gods,[510] leaving open whether he would take Israel back or forsake her permanently. As Isaiah above confirmed, the Lord finally agrees to give her another chance, again loving her with "everlasting lovingkindness" (חֶסֶד עוֹלָם; Isa 54:8). Instead of divorcing her, God only "forsook" (עָזַב) her "for a brief/insignificant moment" (בְּרֶגַע קָטֹן; Isa 54:7). Remembering their "marriage" in the youth of Israel, God declares:

> 'I passed by you and saw you, and behold, you were at the time for love; so I spread My skirt over you and covered your nakedness [עֶרְוָה]. I also swore to you and entered into a covenant with you so that you became Mine,' declares the Lord GOD. (Ezek 16:8.)

Ezekiel further describes that Jerusalem (i.e., Israel/Judah) behaved like an unfaithful wife devoted to harlotry (Ezek 16). "Nevertheless, I [i.e., God] will remember my covenant [בְּרִית] with you in the days of your youth, and I will establish [קוּם] an everlasting covenant with you." (Ezek 16:60.) The outcome will be that Israel "knows" (יָדַע) Yahweh (v. 62). However, before this "everlasting covenant of peace" can be established, the former "heart of prostitution" (לֵב הַזּוֹנֶה; Ezek 6:9)[511] must be exchanged for "a new heart and a new spirit" (לֵב חָדָשׁ וְרוּחַ חֲדָשָׁה; Ezek 36:26; cf. 18:31), instead of "stone" (אֶבֶן) the new heart is of "flesh" (בָּשָׂר). In other words, Ezek 36:26 declares Israel not to be of "one flesh," since it consists of stone (as heart) and flesh (as body). By God's divine working, through imparting his divine spirit (v. 27), the heart of stone becomes one of flesh, combining two parts of flesh to "one flesh" as a complete whole—thereby

---

Jeremiah, 580.

510. Cf. the "introduction" of the prostitution metaphor even in the Pentateuch, and its subsequent extension: Exod 34:15–16; Lev 17:7; 20:5–6; Num 15:39; Deut 31:16; Judg 2:17; 8:27, 33; 1 Chr 5:25; 2 Chr 21:11–14; Ps 73:27; 106:39.

511. The Hebrew verb זָנָה ("commit fornication/play the harlot") used in Ezek 6:9 as figurative description of Israel's "heart/character/mentality" also appeared in Num 25:1 alluding to the literal as well as the spiritual prostitution of Israel at Shittim. On the verb conveying both spheres cf. Ashley, *Numbers*, 516; Bird, "'To Play the Harlot,'" 75–94.

reflecting the Edenic ideal of Gen 2:23–24 and foreshadowing Paul's application in 1 Cor 6:16–17, where he again points to the partaking in the holy spirit as making up the human-divine "one flesh/one spirit" relation.

Finally, the most striking application of the marriage metaphor is given in the life and message of the prophet Hosea. He even had to practically represent the harlotry of Israel by taking for himself a harlot and her children as picture of God's ruined relationship with Israel (see Hos 1). He is not divorcing her, although she is unfaithful. He even more intends to be merciful with Judah and Israel, once more granting prosperity and fertility (Hos 1:7; 2:1–3, 16–25; 11). Yet, the almost omniscient curse of Israel's "harlotry" is to be witnessed throughout the entire book of Hosea,[512] and God finally sighs: "My people are hung up [תְּלוּאִים] in turning from me. Though they call them to the One on high, none at all exalts Him."[513] The Hebrew תָּלָא ("hang up") thus might here be used figuratively "to describe Israel's moral inability to detach itself from apostasy."[514] Once more it alludes to the most devastating experience at Shittim, where the leaders of the apostasy had to be "impaled/hung up" (יָקַע) before the Lord in order to obtain atonement for Israel (cf. Num 25:4). Obviously, Israel again "joined" the Baals, repeating the sin of their fathers at Shittim, thus figuratively "hanging up" themselves according to the punishment on that kind of unfaithfulness. They "forgot" (שָׁכַח; Hos 2:13) Yahweh, thus reversing the former privilege of intimately "knowing" (יָדַע; cf. e.g., Ezek 34:27, 30; 37:28) him.[515] No matter how faithful and merciful God is and ever will be, Israel apparently is not able to change her "heart of harlotry" (Ezek 6:9) without divine aid through judgment (Hos 2:8–15; 3:3–4), repentance, and conversion (vv. 9b, 18; 3:5). Then God will finally be called Israel's בַּעַל ("husband") and גֹּאֵל ("redeemer;" Isa 54:5).

I.2.2.2 The "Covenant of Peace"

I.2.2.2.1 HUMAN-DIVINE "MARRIAGE"

The בְּרִית שָׁלוֹם appears at only five instances within the Hebrew Bible: Num 25:12; Isa 54:10; Ezek 34:25; 37:26; and Mal 2:5. At first we will have a look at Isaiah's and Ezekiel's hints at this covenant; afterwards it will be easier to understand the basic

---

512. Cf. e.g., Hos 1–3; 5:3; 6:10; 7:4; 9:1.

513. Hos 11:7. Yet, "with few alterations to the MT text (and/or revocalizations), however, one could read the words of the verse in the following way: 'Then my people will tire of turning away from me; and on the Most High they will call; all together they will surely exalt him.' The sense which results from this construction is different: the verse becomes a transition toward the expectation of renewal to the covenant..." Stuart, *Hosea-Jonah*, 180–81—the covenant God wants to establish as introduced in chap. 2.

514. NET on Hos 11:7.

515. So Stuart affirms: "Israel forgot Yahweh: that is the essence of the indictment. How can she remain his wife if she doesn't even remember that she is married to him? In 4:6 and 13:4–6 שׁכח 'to forget' functions as a precise antonym of the covenantally important verb ידע 'to know.' Thus Israel's forgetting placed her outside the covenant." Stuart, *Hosea-Jonah*, 52–53. This covenant breach of Israel was contractually indeed tantamount to literal "adultery," also resembling the "forsaking" (עָזַב) of former relations in order to cleave to some new person (Gen 2:24).

similarities between Isaiah, Ezekiel, the story of Phinehas in Num 25, and the most interesting connections to the message of Malachi.

In Isa 54:10 it speaks about the firm covenant of God with his people: "'For the mountains may be removed and the hills may shake, but my lovingkindness will not be removed from you, and my *covenant of peace* will not be shaken,' says the Lord who has compassion on you" (italics supplied). This verse, as well as its context, speaks about God's continual, marital faithfulness to his dear people Israel. The prophet introduces God as the "husband/ruler" (בַּעַל; v. 5) and "redeemer" (גֹּאֵל; ibid.) of Israel, the "God of the entire earth" (אֱלֹהֵי כָל־הָאָרֶץ; ibid.). He is a God that would never leave his dear wife Israel (vv. 6–10). These four main qualities appearing in this passage seem to be closely connected to what one may understand as the foundation of that close relationship between God and Israel, explained in the climax of the prophet's speech (v. 10): God's "lovingkindness" (חֶסֶד; v. 10) as expressed through his "covenant of peace" (בְּרִית שָׁלוֹם; ibid.).[516] As we will see, the other instances mentioning this special covenant will also stress these features and thus embed this covenant in the context of marriage as well as of redemption—both aspects going closely together.

The next two instances are to be found in Ezek 34:25 and 37:26 dealing with God's granting Israel another king David as the true shepherd of Israel, reestablishing the sanctuary amongst his people, and speaking in terms of marriage that thus God's "dwelling place will be with them; and I will be their God, and they will be My people" (Ezek 37:27). There are significant similarities in these three (marriage, shepherd, and king) metaphors resulting in a new covenant, apparently indicating a pattern of God's working and the final blessing as an outcome of this special covenant:

---

516. Please note the close connection between these two terms emphasized through the beautiful parallelism of Isa 54:10:

(A) For the mountains may be *removed* (מוּשׁ)
 (B) and the hills *may shake* (מוֹט),
(A') But My lovingkindness will not be *removed* (מוּשׁ) from you,
 (B') And My covenant of peace *will not be shaken* (מוֹט)

Just as the terms "mountain" (הַר) and "hill" (גִּבְעָה) are interchangeable (A+B), so are the terms "lovingkindness" (חֶסֶד) and "covenant of peace" (בְּרִית שָׁלוֹם); they will not be removed (twice מוּשׁ), and not even shaken (twice מוֹט). God's faithfulness basing on his lovingkindness and expressed through his covenant of peace with Israel is steadfast.

Ezek 34:23–31 (Messianic Shepherd)	Ezek 37:16–28 (Messianic King)	Isa 54 (Messianic Husband)
(vv. 23–24) *One Leader:* Messianic David:[517] Shepherd (רָעָה) Servant (עֶבֶד) Prince (נָשִׂיא)	(vv. 24–25) *One Leader:* Messianic David: Shepherd (רָעָה) Servant (עֶבֶד) Prince (נָשִׂיא) King (מֶלֶךְ)	(vv. 5, 8, 10) *One Leader:* Maker (עָשָׂה) Redeemer (גָּאַל) Husband (בַּעַל) Compassionate One (רָחַם)
(vv. 11–22) *God's Work:* Gather (קָבַץ) Deliver (נָצַל) Lead out (יָצָא) Feed (רָעָה) Judge (שָׁפַט)	(vv. 21–25) *God's Work:* Gather (קָבַץ) Deliver (יָשַׁע) Bring out (לָקַח) Live (יָשַׁב) Cleanse (טָהֵר)	(vv. 4–10) *God's Work:* Gather (קָבַץ) Deliver (גָּאַל) Call out (קָרָא) Marry (בַּעַל) Feel Compassion (רָחַם)
(v. 23) *One People:* (Implicit: Israel and Judah)	(vv. 16–22) *One People:* Israel and Judah	(passim) *One People:* (Spiritual) Israel, Zion, Jerusalem
(v. 24) *One God:* "I will be their God" (אֶהְיֶה לָהֶם לֵאלֹהִים)	(vv. 23, 27) *One God:* "I will be their God" (אֶהְיֶה לָהֶם לֵאלֹהִים)	(v. 5) *One God:* "God of all the earth" (אֱלֹהֵי כָל־הָאָרֶץ)
(v. 25) *One Covenant:* Peace (בְּרִית שָׁלוֹם)	(v. 26) *One Covenant:* Peace (בְּרִית שָׁלוֹם) Eternal (בְּרִית עוֹלָם)	(v. 10) *One Covenant:* "My Peace" (בְּרִית שְׁלוֹמִי) Eternal Grace (חֶסֶד עוֹלָם; cf. vv. 8–10)
(vv. 25–31) *Blessing:* Peace Fertility Deliverance (נָצַל)	(vv. 25–26, 28) *Blessing:* Peace Fertility Sanctification (קָדַשׁ)	(vv. 11–17) *Blessing:* Peace Fertility Righteousness (צְדָקָה)
(vv. 26, 30) *Presence:* God's Hill God is with them	(vv. 26, 28) *Presence:* God's Sanctuary God's Dwelling Place is with them	(vv. 5–6) *Presence:* Called to be God's Wife
(vv. 30–31) *Relationship:* ". . . The house of Israel, are my people . . . and I am your God."	(v. 27) *Relationship:* "I will be their God, and they will be my people."	(v. 5) *Relationship:* "Your husband is your maker . . . and your redeemer . . . ."
(vv. 27, 30) *Experience:* Knowing (יָדַע)	(v. 28) *Experience:* Knowing (יָדַע)	(v. 13) *Experience:* Taught by the Lord (לִמּוּדֵי יְהוָה)

These three instances referring to the eternal "covenant of peace" are evidently very similar.[518] In each of these passages God, or the messiah to come, is depicted by

---

517. Of course, that is the messianic, godly David, for in Ezek 34:11–16 it is God himself who declares his intention to be the shepherd of his people. All these metaphors are more-or-less alluding to the future messianic kingship and respective qualities revealed in the coming, eternal king of Israel—thus even foreshadowing Rev 21:1–4 as the ultimate fulfillment of these wonderful promises (more about this see below within the NT part: "Nuptial Imagery").

518. Another instance could even be Gen 9:8–17 with its covenant promise of everlasting peace, i.e., the declaration of God never again to destroy the world by a flood; cf. Block, *Ezekiel*, 302; further

a main quality (shepherd, king, husband). At the same time, they have most aspects in common and obviously describe one and the same messianic figure as initiator of one and the same covenant. It seems the "covenant of (my) [i.e., God's] eternal peace" in fact means "covenant of (my) [i.e., God's] eternal atonement"—obtained by the atoning sacrifice of the messianic sufferer in Isa 53 who is immediately preceding the prophetic "introduction" of this covenant in Isa 54; hence:

> 'No weapon that is formed against you will prosper; and every tongue that accuses you in judgment you will condemn. This is the heritage of the servants of Yahweh, and their righteousness is from me,' declares the Lord. (Isa 54:17).

Ezekiel's prophetic view of the restored and united kingdom under this one great servant, shepherd, prince, king, judge, and God is nothing else than a most striking prediction of the messiah's life and death, thus even more closely linking these passages with the New Testament reports and its imagery.

The description of this special covenant of peace particularly in Ezek 34 "offers one of the fullest explications of the Hebrew notion of *šālôm*. The term obviously signifies much more than the absence of hostility or tension. It speaks of wholeness, harmony, fulfilment, humans at peace with their environment and with God"[519]—thus depicting the beautiful imagery of a future restoration of the Edenic conditions. The Edenic climax of creating man and woman as a complementary unit becoming "one flesh" fits this context in the best way and again alludes to the similarities of both covenants, the marriage covenant and the one of שָׁלוֹם. God's purposes for marriage, consequently, are considerably high and utterly glorious. The important initial steps of "gathering," "delivering," and "leading/bringing/calling out," further confirm that "Ezekiel's vision of the restoration is always presented in terms of past realities and past experiences. The original exodus from Egypt provides the paradigm for the new exodus from among the nations."[520] One of the next steps, and of course the most important one, is the making of the covenant and the living together like a married couple,[521] thus resembling again the steps taken by man and woman in Gen 2:18–25.

Batto, "The Covenant of Peace: A Neglected Ancient Near Eastern Motif," 187–211. Thus, beside the text of Num 25, even the apostasy in Gen 6:2 and its "atonement" through cleansing the world by a flood would, at least partly, belong to the context of the "covenant of peace." That would again foreshadow the new cleansing of the earth in God's final judgment and the fulfillment of the "covenant of peace"-promises in Rev 21:1–4 (see below the chapter "Nuptial Imagery").

519. Block, *Ezekiel*, 303.

520. Block, *Ezekiel*, 420.

521. So especially in Ezek 37 "emphasis is laid on the restored temple towering over the people as the capstone of the new divine-human constitution that time would not decay. It would be a material symbol to the world of the special relationship between God and the people consecrated to him (cf. Lev 20:26). . . . The unit [i.e., Ezek 37] in its closing verses clearly paves the way for the vision of chaps. 40–48. In its latter part it also wants to draw together positive strands from chaps. 34 and 36, as well as from chap. 28. The message of new life and of the fulfillment of covenant ideals is both repeated and developed along fresh lines." Allen, *Ezekiel 20–48*, 194, 196. These important strands in Ezekiel's visions further developed from this "covenant of peace" illumine and much more emphasize the deeper

In addition, although not by exact terminology, the usage of the marriage metaphor in Hosea 1:11—12:25 seems to be likewise referring to this special "covenant of peace," as the corresponding comparison of the main elements as given above may demonstrate:

Subject	Content	Reference
One Leader	"One Head" (רֹאשׁ אֶחָד)	Hos 1:11
God's Work	Gather (קָבַץ) Lead up (עָלָה) Allure (פָּתָה) Bring (הָלַךְ) away Speak kindly (דָּבַר עַל־לִבָּהּ) Betroth (אָרַשׂ)	Hos 1:11; 2:14, 19–20
One People	Israel and Judah	Hos 1:11
One God	"My husband"/"My God"	Hos 2:1, 16–17, 23
One Covenant	Marriage	Hos 2:16–20
Blessing	Peace and Fertility	Hos 2:18, 21–22
Presence	Led out to be God's wife	Hos 2:15–23
Relationship	"I will say, 'You are My people!' And they will say, 'You are my God!'"	Hos 2:23; cf. v. 1; 1:11
Experience	"You will know (יָדַע) the Lord"	Hos 2:8, 20

These descriptions of the divine "covenant of peace" closely reflect the Edenic covenant ideal. There, also, God (in respect to the messiah Jesus Christ; cf. Eph 3:9; Col 1:16) is the initiator and leader of the events that happen. He works for the sake of man, leading the process of building the woman, bringing her to him, thereby "marrying" the first couple.[522] They become "one flesh" (Gen 2:24) calling each other "my

---

significance of the most similar/equal marriage bond as its literal pattern. A certain similarity between the covenant granted to Phinehas (Num 25:12–13), the Lord's covenant with king David (including its messianic perspectives), and the covenant made at Sinai is also briefly mentioned by Gane, *Leviticus/Numbers*, 720 regarding its covenantal "framework."

522. Even the language used especially in Hos 2:14 is very passionate: "'Seduce' (מפתיה) means to romance, entice, allure (cf. Exod 22:5 [16]; Hos 7:11). To 'romance her' (דבר על לבה) is a tender expression, used of courtship (Gen 34:3) and winning back love (Judg 19:3), and also kind, considerate favor not necessarily involving romantic intentions (Ruth 2:13)." Stuart, *Hosea-Jonah*, 53; cf. Andersen and Freedman, *Hosea*, 272. It reminds one of the "declaration of love" in Deut 33:3, where it is confessed about God: "Indeed, He loves the people [חָבַב]; All Your holy ones are in Your hand, And they followed in Your steps." Davidson explains that "this verse contains the only occurrence of *ḥābab* in the HB, a verb that in Aramaic means 'love' or 'make love' and here in Hebrew may contain an allusion to the intimate relationship between Yahweh and his people established at Sinai, parallel to that of a husband's love for his wife." Davidson, *Flame*, 115. It further is "the most common term used in later rabbinic tradition for the love between husband and wife." Ibid., 115/fn.122; cf. Satlow, *Jewish Marriage*, 234–35; see also Jer 11:15; 12:7 (יָדִיד "beloved"). In addition, the three groups of animals in v. 18 are exactly reflecting the three groups of animals mentioned in Gen 1:30 (cf. Andersen and Freedman, *Hosea*, 281; Stuart, *Hosea-Jonah*, 58) thus alluding even more to the basic pattern and the entire "atmosphere" of the Genesis creation account. "What Hosea has in view, therefore, is a restoration of the

woman" and "my man" (אִישִׁי; Hos 2:16! Cf. Gen 2:23; 3:6, 16).[523] This union is specially blessed in matters of fertility (Gen 1:28)—and heavenly peace existed anyway:

> It was peace and rest which humanity lost through sin (Gen 3:15; 4:8) and which the Mosaic covenant promised as a result of obedience (Lev 26:6). But in spite of Israel's disobedience, the prophets envisioned a coming restoration of peace and all the other characteristics of life before the fall. This will come to pass in the Messianic Age with the restoration of the ideals of life as it was lived in Eden....[524]

Close communion and even unveiled viewing of each other were given (Gen 2:25), and the final experience also was יָדַע (cf. Gen 4:1, 17, 25), resulting in procreation.

> The verb 'to know' also has covenant connotations, and in this passage the betrothal is a covenant. The attributes in vv 21–22 are the attributes of Yahweh in covenant-keeping. To live in the covenant is to know Yahweh. The verb 'to know' in 2:22 is as climactic as it is in 6:3, where it is the end result of returning to Yahweh. The knowing of Yahweh, which is the climax of the betrothal, is matched by the titles which the husband receives in marriage in v. 18, in which the wife calls the husband 'îšî (the first title in 2:1–25).[525]

It is through יָדַע that man and woman become "one flesh" and may multiply;[526] this even more contributes to an understanding of the one flesh union as consisting

---

creation order—a paradise regained." Garrett, *Hosea, Joel*, 92. Furthermore, the "parallel passage" of Ezek 34 as investigated in the table above also contains a special covenant with the animals to ensure a peaceful living (cf. Ezek 34:25, 27) thus again reflecting the Edenic state and its representation as alluded to within the covenant between God and Noah; cf. Gen 9:2; somehow similar also, Andersen and Freedman, *Hosea*, 281.

523. Especially the renaming of the Lord by calling him henceforth only אִישִׁי ("my man/husband") and not בַּעְלִי ("my man/husband/lord/pagan deity Baal") anymore, describes a future time in Israel when the original covenant pattern as introduced in Eden and reestablished at Sinai and Shittim will be the valid and binding basis of the relationship between Yahweh and Israel, finally forsaking any relation to the counter-god Baal: "Both of these words can mean 'husband,' אִישׁ referring to husband as 'man' in the sense of marriage partner, and בַּעַל connoting more the lordship, ownership, and legal right of the husband in relation to a wife ('master'). The point of this oracle is based, however, not on that distinction, but on the fact that בַּעַל means 'Baal,' the god, as well as 'husband, lord, master.' Israelites in the new age of restoration will simply never use the word בַּעַל in *any* of its meanings. Baal worship will not exist, *a fortiore*, because even the very word בַּעַל will be unknown (v 19 [17])." Stuart, *Hosea-Jonah*, 57; italics given; (similarly Garrett, *Hosea, Joel*, 91–92; Andersen and Freedman, *Hosea*, 278–79; Davidson, *Flame*, 116–17).

524. Cooper, *Ezekiel*, 303. Cf. also ibid., 349 on further elements of Edenic origin to be restored according to the visions of Ezekiel.

525. Andersen and Freedman, *Hosea*, 284. "The covenant [of Hos 2:18] is ... not made *with* God's people, but is imposed *on behalf of* God's people on all living creatures, with peace as a purpose." Stuart, *Hosea-Jonah*, 58; italics given. That is, of course, true. Nevertheless, it also concerns Israel immediately, for it is the preparation for the betrothal and marriage in the subsequent verses. It rather seems to be an extensive, full covenant with all living creatures. God is about to make *tabula rasa* in order to restore the ideal Edenic patterns.

526. Cf. Num 31:17: וְכָל־אִשָּׁה יֹדַעַת אִישׁ לְמִשְׁכַּב זָכָר ("every woman *known* of a man *by lying* with a

of close physical as well as spiritual/mental intimacy. The corresponding spiritual offspring, implicitly or even explicitly alluded to in the investigated metaphors, most certainly is the one foretold in Isa 53:10 as the descendants of God's messiah (cf. Isa 54:13; Ezek 34:29; Hos 1:10).

> In all likelihood, a people more numerous than ethnic Israel per se is envisioned as benefiting from this covenant, as the contextual ambiguity of the word להם "for them" [v. 18] suggests. Hosea has already prophesied the existence of a new kind of Israel, very different from the one he knew in the eighth century BC (2:1–3 [1:10—12:1]).[527]

The chronologically first reference to the בְּרִית שָׁלוֹם is given in Num 25:12. Comparing both instances (Isa 53–54 and Num 25) it is significant that the same covenant's blessing is granted to the descendants of the messiah (literally, the suffering "servant" of God) as predicted in Isa 53:10–12 and likewise to the descendants of the priestly Phinehas in Num 25:13. In both texts the bloody atonement through a "servant of the Lord" is the centre and represents the "legal" basis for granting the covenant's eternal blessing. Further messianic/Christological aspects of the Shittim story and the atoning act of Phinehas have already been addressed in the previous chapter, but it might be worthwhile to reconsider the fact that Phinehas pierced the offending couple through their lower abdomen (קֵבָה; v. 8), thereby primarily "destroying" the area which is necessary to multiply. Perhaps, this incident may be transferable to the spiritual sphere of Isaiah and the "godly offspring" mentioned in Mal 2:15, thereby contrasting the זֶרַע אֱלֹהִים (Mal 2:15) with the evil seed (also זֶרַע) of the serpent (see Gen 3:15).

The two opposing seeds of Gen 3:15 and God's concrete predictions to them are further significant. He says to the serpent "you will bruise his [i.e., the woman's seed's] heel" (וְאַתָּה תְּשׁוּפֶנּוּ עָקֵב; Gen 3:15). That figurative "bruising" seems to reflect the real, practical "piercing" (Heb דָּקַר) of the heel of the special, messianic descendant, since the teeth are the serpent's only weapon in this picture of a man killing a serpent by treading on its head.[528] Now it is the priestly Phinehas piercing (דָּקַר; Num 25:8) through the abdomen of Zimri and Cozbi, thereby figuratively "bruising" the "evil seed" of Gen 3:15, while finally the "godly seed" (Gen 3:15; cf. Mal 2:15), will at least

---

male"); the following verse expresses the same fact: וְכֹל הַטַּף בַּנָּשִׁים אֲשֶׁר לֹא־יָדְעוּ מִשְׁכַּב זָכָר ("but all the girls who have not *known* a man *by lying* with a male"); cf. on this also Clines, *Classical Hebrew*, 4:100. Stuart, *Hosea-Jonah*, 60 adds: "Since Hebrew ידע is the most common OT euphemism for cohabitation, i.e., the consummation of the marriage in this case (e.g., Gen 4:1; Num 31:18; 1 Kgs 1:4), Yahweh and the new Israel will this time live together as man and wife. While the term can have sexual overtones, its use here suggests not sex but metaphorically 'intimacy' in a covenant sense. Eschatological Israel will know Yahweh, but not other lovers, in the intimacy of a consummated marriage of permanent faithfulness."

527. Stuart, *Hosea-Jonah*, 58.

528. However, it must be noted that the Hebrew terms שׁוּף ("bruise/crush;" Gen 3:15) and דקר ("pierce;" Num 25:8) are not the same, and not synonymous. Yet, they are congruent regarding their practical meaning and result, as explained above.

be pierced in his heel—that means, not with (lasting) death as result—just like the messianic prediction of Zech 12:10 (also דָּקַר) additionally confirms (cf. John 19:34).

I.2.2.2.2 THE MARRIAGE COVENANT IN MALACHI

Further attesting an implicit connection between the subjects of the "covenant of peace," Phinehas' atoning act of piercing at Shittim, and the evil/holy "seed," is the last occurrence of the בְּרִית שָׁלוֹם (although with a minor deviation) most significantly placed in context of the "anti-divorce" speech of Mal 2. In v. 5 the prophet speaks against the Levites who broke the divine "covenant of life and peace" (בְּרִיתִי הַחַיִּים וְהַשָּׁלוֹם; cf. vv. 1–9); then he turns to the intermarriage of Israel and Judah with pagan nations (vv. 10–12), before he finally and most severely addresses the "covenant breach" concerning literal marriages in vv. 14–17. Malachi speaks of a "godly seed" (זֶרַע אֱלֹהִים; Mal 2:15) fathered by those who are faithful to their spouse and who possess at least "a remnant of the Spirit" (שְׁאָר רוּחַ; ibid.):[529]

> The prophet's allusions to the creation of male and female (Gen 1:27) and the divine prescription for human marriage as "one flesh" . . . , (Gen 2:24) intimate that the 'godly offspring' Yahweh seeks are those who faithfully maintain this divine ideal for marriage.[530]

Perhaps Malachi intended to contrast the "covenant of peace" that was broken by the Levites in Mal 2:1–9 to the "marriage covenant" between Yahweh and Israel that was broken by spiritual adultery (vv. 10–12; perhaps also to be understood as literal intermarriage), and finally the covenant breach by individual Israelites and their wives in vv. 13–17: (1) The *Levites* broke their covenant of peace with God by deviating from true instructions (cf. vv. 6–8). (2) *Israel and Judah* broke the covenant with God by spiritual adultery, through "marriage with a foreign God's daughter" (certainly also

---

529. Similarly, Isa 53:10–11 speaks about "justified seed" (זֶרַע/צָדֵק) as a result of the "guilt offering" (אָשָׁם), Isa 54:13 mentions "sons taught of the Lord [having] much peace" (וְכָל־בָּנַיִךְ לִמּוּדֵי יְהוָה וְרַב שְׁלוֹם בָּנָיִךְ), and Ezekiel knows about "establishing [קוּם] a renowned planting place" (וַהֲקִמֹתִי לָהֶם מַטָּע לְשֵׁם; Ezek 34:29). They seemingly allude to similar ideas of godly offspring. Concerning the "spirit" Shields, "Malachi 2, 10–16," 80–81 even suggests to interpret the Hebrew רוח as denoting "moral character, so that those who have רוח are those who are morally upright, who obey the law of Yahweh. This also makes good sense of the repeated exhortation to guard one's own רוח in verses 15 and 16." However, the more exact translation "spirit" naturally conveys this meaning of conformity to God's will who gave his spirit for just that purpose (see Ezek 36:27).

530. Hill, *Malachi*, 246. Similarly Taylor and Clendenen, *Haggai–Malachi*, 353: "An entirely different (and preferable) interpretative path is taken by those who consider *ʾeḥād*, 'one,' in the initial clause to be part of the predicate and the Lord (from v. 14) to be the understood subject of *ʿāśâ*, 'make.' The verse would allude then to Gen 2:24 and the original divine intention for marriage. As v. 10 argues filial unity against treachery on the basis of God's covenant with Israel at Sinai, so here Malachi more pointedly argues against marital treachery on the basis of the marital 'one flesh' relationship, which was set forth in the account of the original paradigmatic couple"; cf. also Hugenberger, *Covenant*, 148–67; Davidson, "Scheidung und Wiederheirat," 175; Kaiser, "Divorce in Malachi 2:10–16," 75.

literal intermarriage followed). (3) *Individual Israelites* broke their personal covenant by divorcing the wives of their youth. The prophet's message in this entire chapter is in each of these cases the same, thus connecting the three accuses: entire Israel is imbued with covenant breach. Perhaps there is even a "line of infection" given: from the false instructions of the Levites the apostasy spread over all Israel and Judah, and led even to disloyalty at the most personal level, the marriage of individual Israelites. Thus Malachi would closely connect and compare both covenants, the spiritual covenant of Yahweh with his people and the literal of the marriage bond of Gen 2:24. It almost seems like breaking the first results in breaking the second and vice versa, thus presenting a causal connection.

The significance of Mal 2 is further emphasized by God's remarkable exclamation, "I hate Divorce" (שָׂנֵא שַׁלַּח; v. 16),[531] and the twofold warning not to deal treacherously against the wife of one's youth (vv. 15–16).[532] Of particular interest concerning the foregoing observation about the "godly seed" born by those who possess רוּחַ is further the fact that with both warnings there is the רוּחַ mentioned as important rationale, immediately referring to the זֶרַע אֱלֹהִים of v. 15. Twice the phrase וְנִשְׁמַרְתֶּם בְּרוּחֲכֶם ("take heed to your spirit") occurs (vv. 15–16), and it might well be alluding to the spirit of Yahweh (רוּחִי) who makes Israel "take heed" (תִּשְׁמֹרוּ) of his

---

531. Although in the text of Mal 2:15–16 "as it stands, the syntactical and exegetical problems are legion." Taylor and Clendenen, *Haggai-Malachi*, 350; cf. Isaksson, *Marriage and Ministry*, 27 etc. This translation actually seems to be the correct one, despite criticisms like those of Schreiner, "Mischehen-Ehebruch-Ehescheidung. Betrachtungen zu Mal 2,10–16," 207–18. It is widely favored nowadays as the best variant going well with the consonantal text (cf. Rudolph, "Zu Mal 2,10–16," 85–90) as well as the immediate context and the basic messages of Mal 2; cf. e.g., Berger, *Gesetzesauslegung*, 529; Amram, *Divorce*, 30–31; Instone-Brewer, *In the Bible*, 55; Kirchschläger, *Ehe im NT*, 57; Dautzenberg, "Φεύγετε τὴν πορνείαν," 278; Verhoef, *Haggai, Malachi*, 262–63, 278–79; Smith, *Micah-Malachi*, 319–20, 323; Hill, *Malachi*, 221, 249–50; Collins, "The (intelligible) Masoretic Text of Malachi 2:16," 38–40; Hays, *Moral Vision*, 363; Jones, "Note," 683–85; Turner, *Matthew*, 459. Some translate "If he hates so as to divorce" (Taylor and Clendenen, *Haggai-Malachi*, 357, 361) or similarly (e.g., Hugenberger, *Covenant*, 76: "'If one hates and divorces [merely on the grounds of aversion],' says Yahweh, God of Israel"; cf. Shields, "Malachi 2, 10–16," 83), thereby clinging to the same deeper sense, namely God regards divorce as violence/sin (see v. 16b; cf. e.g., ibid., 84–85; Hugenberger, *Covenant*, 76; Instone-Brewer, *In the Bible*, 56–57; at this point there exists great harmony among researchers). Even the later rabbis with their evidently very lenient attitude towards admissible reasons for divorce (cf. *m. Giṭ*. 9:10) understood Mal 2:16 as meaning, "I hate divorce, says Yahweh, the God of Israel" (*p. Qidd*. 1:58c:16; *Gen. Rab.* 18:5; cf. Strack and Billerbeck, *Talmud und Midrasch*, 1:312, 805). That is most significant, for in the same context (*p. Qidd*. 1:58c:16) it is said that divorce is a privilege granted only to Jews, not to the nations; cf. *Gen. Rab*. 18:5; see on this topic also Strack and Billerbeck, *Talmud und Midrasch*, 1:312, 805; Amram, *Divorce*, 135–36, 140–41; Lehmann, "Basis for Divorce," 265.

532. As Shields, "Malachi 2, 10–16," 85 concludes his investigations on the difficult text of Mal 2:16, he suggests on a slightly different understanding of the Hebrew text that "the faithlessness which Malachi seems to be addressing here is a situation where »hatred« was considered sufficient cause for divorce." Winter, "Sadoquite Fragments," further asserts: "The restriction is here on ethical grounds; no general prohibition of divorce is intended nor is the marriage state understood to be based on eternal principle." Jesus' permission of divorce in cases of πορνεία (Matt 5:32; 19:9) is, therefore, no contradiction to the exposition of Malachi.

ordinances (Ezek 36:26–27).[533] So "the verb translated 'guard' yourself (šmar, 'watch, guard, keep') in its basic form (qal) is used in 2:7 of the priest's responsibility to tend or 'preserve' the divine revelation and in 2:9 of 'following' instructions."[534]

Thus, once more the texts containing information about the בְּרִית שָׁלוֹם are closely connected, for the reference to taking heed through "the instrument" of the spirit in Ezek 36:27 immediately precedes the overwhelming view of restoring entire Israel to new life by the divine רוּחַ (Ezek 37:5–6, 9–10, 14), thus preparing the way to reunite Israel and Judah (Ezek 37:15–22), to anoint the messianic king as their leader (vv. 22–25), and establish the eternal "covenant of peace" (v. 26) with God dwelling among Israel (vv. 26–28), cleansing and sanctifying them (v. 23, 28; see also the table above). To sum up, people who have רוּחַ apparently do not divorce, at least not because of "hatred."[535] Thus the Edenic covenant pattern functions as everlasting bond not only in its literal sense (marriage), but to the same degree and far-reaching responsibilities as well as privileges concerning the human-divine covenant.[536]

The Malachi text is all the more meaningful when taking into consideration the particular placement of this late reference to the בְּרִית שָׁלוֹם and the זֶרַע אֱלֹהִים. It is not only the combination of these most meaningful terms and their links to the other passages connected with marriage, sexuality, and procreativity as investigated above. It moreover is the link to the new era dawning at the time of Malachi, the new era of the "new" covenant and the appearance of the divine messiah. Only a short time and the מַלְאַךְ הַבְּרִית ("angel/messenger of the covenant;" Mal 3:1) would come. With this "name," respectively in this mission, he appeared only once before, in Judg 2:1. There the מַלְאַךְ־יְהוָה came up from Gilgal and pronounced the sentence of covenant breach over Israel (Judg 2:1–3). Gilgal was the place they had renewed their covenant with the Lord under Joshua right after passing over the Jordan and right before the

---

533. There are altogether not more than three other verses containing the terms רוּחַ and שָׁמַר: Job 10:12; Eccl 11:4; Ezek 36:27. While the first two are without theological significance, the last one is all the more meaningful in this context: "I will put My Spirit within you and cause you to walk in My statutes, and you will be careful to observe My ordinances."

534. Taylor and Clendenen, *Haggai–Malachi*, 358.

535. But perhaps because of adultery as Jer 3:8 about God's (allegorical?) divorce demonstrates (see below)? On the allegorical quality of the statement in Jer 3:8 see Ryrie, "Biblical Teaching," 180. Cf. Instone-Brewer, *In the Bible*, 37–38, 42–43 who accepts the literal understanding of the text but suggests: "Perhaps it should not be said that God divorced Israel, but instead that God *suffered* the divorce, because, although he is the one who carried it out, he was forced into it. Israel had broken everyone of the marriage vows, including the most obvious, faithfulness. She was committing constant and multiple acts of adultery, which had resulted in illegitimate children." Ibid., 38; italics given.

536. Further, please note that "if as seems likely the third person *lô* ('to it') refers back to the marriages that were being dissolved, then the function of the 'spirit' in view was in giving life not to the men but to their marriages, witnessing to the union and filling them with the divine presence. What may be in view, then, is not a threat but a reality that was being neglected. Marriage is not only a union of flesh that can be dissolved but one of the divine Spirit, who 'remained,' maintaining a unity that survived human efforts to sever it. . . . That is, in spite of the men's treachery there was yet a remnant of the spiritual bond." Taylor and Clendenen, *Haggai–Malachi*, 355.

beginning of the conquering of Canaan. There they were circumcised and celebrated the Passover (Josh 5:1–10), thus being prepared to enter the land victoriously. Correspondingly, the שַׂר־צְבָא־יְהוָה ("leader of the host of the Lord;" v. 14) appeared, revealed himself as a divine person (v. 15; cf. Exod 3:5), and thereby encouraged the people to carry out the first conquest being assured that God would be with them. Evidently, for a considerable period of time the angel of the Lord remained at Gilgal, thus demonstrating that he still would be with Israel. Finally, however, he reappears, now as "angel/messenger of the Lord," again revealing his divinity,[537] declaring the covenant to be broken and God's protection and blessing to be withdrawn.

In Mal 3:1 the same messenger is introduced by יְהוָה צְבָאוֹת ("the Lord of warfares") thereby connecting this instance more closely with the military incidents at Gilgal and Bochim, and, of course, the holy covenant that Israel once renewed (Gilgal) and soon broke (Bochim). Consequently, the appearance of this special, and evidently divine[538] messenger in the given context is very impressive and must be of great importance. Considering the context, it points to repeated covenant breach that brings him on to the scene for the sake of his holy "covenant of life and peace" (Mal 2:5) which has been broken by the Levites (Mal 2:1–9) obviously forgetting about their inheritance and responsibility due to the righteous and atoning deed at the introduction of this covenant for the priesthood following Phinehas (Num 25:12–13). Furthermore, the covenant of Israel's exclusivity is broken by marrying "the daughter of a foreign god" (Mal 2:11; cf. vv. 10–12). And finally, even the marriage "covenant" is broken by "dealing treacherously"[539] against one's wife, thus refusing to "take heed of the spirit" (vv.

---

537. By speaking of God in the first person: "*I* brought you up out of Egypt and led you into the land which *I* have sworn to your fathers; and *I* said, '*I* will never break *My* covenant with you....'" (Judg 2:1.)

538. There is a considerable discussion about the meaning of מַלְאָךְ as human or divine (re: "angelic") being. I favor the divine interpretation, first, because of the immediate context, second, due to the wider context. Mal 3:1 further explains that just this "messenger" will come "to *his* temple, the Lord" (אֶל־הֵיכָלוֹ הָאָדוֹן). The parallelism of v. 1 obviously equating Lord (אָדוֹן) and messenger (מַלְאָךְ), as well as "to his temple" (אֶל־הֵיכָלוֹ) and "behold he is coming" (הִנֵּה־בָא) is most naturally interpreted in this way and makes it difficult to understand it as allusion to only some human or (created/non-divine) angelic person. It seems to be the best and most natural reading of the text. Similarly Verhoef, *Haggai, Malachi*, 289 or Taylor and Clendenen, *Haggai–Malachi*, 385: "These relative clauses probably should be understood as alluding to the question in 2:17 to which the Lord is responding, 'Where is the God of justice?' If our understanding is correct, then this is one of those enigmatic Old Testament passages in which God and his unique angel/messenger ('the angel of the LORD') are spoken of as if they are one and the same (Gen 16:7–14; 18:1 19:1; 22:12; Exod 3:1–6). From a Christian perspective its meaning is elucidated only in the New Testament through the coming of Jesus, God's Son, the Sent One (John 3:17; 3:34; 4:34; 5:23–24, 30, 36–38; 6:29, 38–39, 44, 57; 7:16, 18, 28–29, 33; 10:36; 12:44–45, 49; 13:20; 14:24; 17:3, etc.)." Cf. Hill, *Malachi*, 269.

539. Instone-Brewer, *In the Bible*, 57 further explains that the word "treacherous" implies "the breaking of a treaty. It occurs only forty-three times in the OT, and is used overwhelmingly for violations of covenants, as S. Erlandsson [in TDOT s.v. 'Bāghadh'] summarizes: 'It is used when the OT writer wants to say that a man does not honor an agreement, or commits adultery, or breaks a covenant or some other ordinance given by God.' It is used for those who break the Sinai covenant, for those who break a betrothal covenant, and for those who break a marriage covenant." (Cf. Exod 21:8; 1 Sam

13–16). Again the different spheres of "marriage covenants" are blurred, thus reflecting the proverb: "[She] leaves the companion of her youth, and forgets the covenant of her God." (Prov 2:17.) It is "God's covenant" that is broken by (literal) adultery, as even the Joseph story affirms (see Gen 39:9). So it is God who first appears as this special covenant's witness (Mal 2:14) on the day of consummation, and who finally reappears to witness against the transgressor of this holy bond (Mal 3:5).[540]

Furthermore, Mal 4:5–6 speaks about the "great and terrible day of the Lord" that is soon to come, pointing to the work of reconciliation that the (figurative) prophet Elijah will perform in the times of the New Testament events (cf. Matt 11:14; 17:12; Luke 1:17).[541] The great "day of the Lord" will reveal the distinction between "one who serves God and one who does not serve Him" (Mal 3:18).—And the rejection of just that distinction is exactly what Israel is accused of in the previous context of divorce in Mal 2:17: "You have wearied the Lord with your words. Yet you say, 'How have we wearied Him?' In that you say, 'Everyone who does evil is good in the sight of the Lord, and He delights in them,' or, 'Where is the God of justice?'" This reproof on disdaining God's righteous judgment is the final remark following the lengthy reproach for breaking the holy marriage covenant by divorce (vv. 10–16). The wording, "Everyone who does evil is good in the sight of the Lord, and He delights in them," is conspicuously ironic and in context of divorce most likely could have been some contemporary argumentation even demanding divorce in certain occasions reasoning that God would have it thus. Yet, since God here makes it clear that he "hates divorce" (v. 16),[542] the evil they pronounce "good in the sight of the Lord" (v. 17) must be closely related to a divine ordinance that could thus be misunderstood dealing with something concerning divorce. And since the only instruction mentioning anything about divorce is Deut 24:1–4, it seems likely to assume some Israelite halakha about "proper divorce" that has been far from the "righteous judgment" of the Lord that he will reveal once more when his "great and terrible day" will come (cf. Mal 3–4). It might be a hint to an early stage of the doctrine which Jesus is later again confronted

---

14:33; Ps 119:158; Jer 3:20; 9:2.) Thus these covenants are, again, closely combined with each other.

540. All these observations clearly contradict the view that "the O.T. concept ברית is quite incompatible with what marriage meant at this period [i.e., Malachi's time]." Isaksson, *Marriage and Ministry*, 31; cf. Kraetzschmar, *Bundesvorstellung*, 168, 240; Torrey, "The Prophecy of Malachi," 9. At least theologically, if not historically, it seemingly always has been a covenant with responsibility and holiness similar to that between Yahweh and Israel. Hence, even God calls the marriage between himself and Israel a covenant (Ezek 16:8)—and as I argue in this chapter, this is the "covenant of peace," of being reconciled with God (Rom 5:10; 2 Cor 5:20).

541. At least as a first part in NT times, to be repeated in an eschatological frame.

542. As the NET note on Mal 2:16 rightly asserts, does שָׂנֵא appear "to be a third person form meaning 'he hates,' ... unless one emends the following word to a third person verb as well." Then it could be translated as: "He [who] hates [and] divorces her ... is guilty of violence"; cf. Shields, "Malachi 2, 10–16," 81–85. However, "it is possible that the first person pronoun אָנֹכִי ('I') has accidentally dropped from the text after כִּי and if one restores the pronoun, the form שָׂנֵא can be taken as a participle and the text translated, 'for I hate' (so NAB, NASB, NRSV, NLT)." NET on Mal 2:16.

with, where the Pharisees tell him that "Moses *commanded* [ἐντέλλομαι] to give her a certificate of divorce and send away"—and that even for possibly arbitrary reasons (κατὰ πᾶσαν αἰτίαν; Matt 19:3). The second part of this study is thought to investigate such considerations more thoroughly, but nevertheless one has to recognize that especially in the book of Malachi certain important lines are converging that touch our concern regarding the Edenic ideal of the marriage covenant and God's working for its apology and defense.

The messianic foreshadowing to the great day of the Lord soon to come in New Testament times and finally in the eschatological last day events, may serve as a last consideration in this respect. The announcement of God's vindicating intervention is a pivotal part of Malachi's message and thus corresponds to the climax of Balaam's prophetic speech in Num 24:17, where he predicts that "a star shall come forth from Jacob, a scepter shall rise from Israel, and shall crush through the forehead of Moab, and tear down all the sons of Seth." A possible interpretation of the apocalyptic symbols has already been given above; now I just want to reemphasize its close connection to the messianic Psalm 110 and Mal 3–4. While the immediate, literal part of Balaam's prophecy was fulfilled by Phinehas' atoning act and the correspondingly granted "covenant of peace" in Num 25, the deeper, spiritual meaning is taken up and carried on in paradigmatic messages like those of Ps 110 and Mal 3–4: The messiah will come to rule, judge, and destroy the evil according to the first prediction on the work of the holy seed in Gen 3:15. Most impressively it is, on the one hand, the significant "covenant of peace" that appears in this context, and on the other hand, it is the Edenic ideal of the marriage covenant which is also to be vindicated by the Lord's action. The close, although primarily metaphorical, connection between both covenants is not only some stylistic device employed by the biblical writers. It seemingly conveys and even emphasizes the similar structure and like holiness of both covenants, which sometimes are even synonymously used in a parallelism like that of Prov 2:17 or short declarations like Gen 39:9 and Mal 2:14.[543]

I.2.2.2.3 DIVORCE IN THE PROPHETS

Of special interest to the topic of divorce is the text of Jer 3:1–13 as an illustration of God's dealing with the case law in Deut 24:1–4. God is determined to forgive his wife and take her back as soon as she is ready to enter the renewed covenant. "'For I hate divorce,' says the Lord, the God of Israel." (Mal 2:16.) He patiently waited for Israel to repent and even "thought, 'After she has done all these things she will return to me'" (Jer 3:7), but she did not. Therefore, finally, "for all the adulteries of faithless Israel, I

---

543. The translation of Mal 2:14 as "she is your companion and your wife by covenant" (NASB) of the Hebrew phrase וְהִיא חֲבֶרְתְּךָ וְאֵשֶׁת בְּרִיתֶךָ could also be translated as "and she is your companion and the woman of the covenant," possibly alluding to the holy covenant between Yahweh and his people which is thereby affected; cf. the note of the German Elberfelder Bible.

[i.e., God] had sent her away and given her a writ of divorce" (Jer 3:8; cf. Isa 50:1)⁵⁴⁴—at least for a short period (Isa 54:7–8), but never permanently. It rather seems to be a half-hearted decision. Israel is sent away without full consent and approval of God—but it is an important act among the efforts to finally win her back.⁵⁴⁵ These aspects still remain, even when interpreting Jer 3:8 and Isa 50:1 as mere allegory.⁵⁴⁶

A last, most significant fact is the actual reason for divorce that made God send her away. "Her adulteries" (נַאֲפָה) make her "faithless" (מְשׁוּבָה) in the sight of God (Jer 3:8). That is the פֶּשַׁע ("transgression") mentioned in Isa 50:1 as rationale of the certificate of divorce. Consequently, one has to assume that the only, unfortunately ambiguous reason for divorce given in Deut 24:1, the עֶרְוַת דָּבָר ("thing of nakedness"), is just this kind of misbehavior. Although the death penalty is the appropriate punishment in those cases (cf. Lev 20:10), and God even thought about this way of dealing with her (Ezek 23:43–49), he prefers temporal separation—thus clinging to the hope of finally seeing her repent and return to him (Jer 3:7–13; cf. Hos 2:6–8 etc.). Then, finally, he would renew his covenant with the formerly adulterous, apostate Israel, never to send her away any more (see Isa 62:4–5; Jer 31:31–32; Ezek 16:60–62).

All these different considerations on covenantal qualities jointly demonstrate the further theological and particular messianic-Christological range of the deeper spiritual features underlying the Edenic marriage-covenant ideal. Thus they will prove to be a profound preparation for the investigation of the very similar application of the Edenic marriage metaphor in the New Testament and particularly in the letters of Paul.

I.2.2.3 Summary and Final Considerations

The marriage pattern constituted in Gen 2:24 is a highly adequate metaphor for the relationship between Israel and Yahweh, because "die Beziehung [des Vasallen zum Lehnsherrn und] der Frau zum Ehemann lassen keinen Platz für doppelte Loyalität und sind deshalb passende Bilder für die Loyalität in einer monotheistischen Religion."⁵⁴⁷ It is also true that "die Bundestreue Gottes in der Bundestreue der Ehepartner sichtbare Gestalt [findet]"⁵⁴⁸ and that "marriage becomes the ultimate paradigm for the relation-

---

544. Also referring to "her treacherous sister Judah" in Jer 3:8, the prophet "points to the nation's fundamental flaw: it was not so much a breaking of die divine *law*, as it was a failure in *relationship* with God, from which all other calamities flowed." Craigie et al., *Jeremiah 1–25*, 56; Italics given.

545. That reminds one of Paul's instruction in 1 Cor 7:11, where he likewise demands Christians not to divorce, and if they are separated, they should endeavor to reconcile. However, Paul is not speaking about cases of adultery but rather about various unmentioned personal conflicts.

546. Cf. Ryrie, "Biblical Teaching," 180: "The question of Isa 50:1 is either a rhetorical one presupposing a negative reply or it should be understood as an allegory like Jer 3:8. If these illustrations are pressed to make God a divorcee, then perhaps he was also a polygamist, since he married both Israel and Judah. Nor should such poetical and metaphorical language be pressed into the service of determining the exact meaning of πορνεία in legal passages in Matthew's gospel."

547. M. Weinfeld, in: Botterweck et al., *TWAT*, 1:808; cf. Hasel, "Eheverständnis," 33–34.

548. Pöhler, "Sakrament," 261.

ship between God amd the Jewish people."⁵⁴⁹ However, "elsewhere in the ANE texts, the deity never is depicted as a 'husband' of, or in covenant relationship with, his people, but the Bible clearly portrays Israel's God entering into covenant relationship with his people and often utilizes the imagery of a husband-wife relationship."⁵⁵⁰

Both covenants (husband-wife and Israel-Yahweh) are very special. God wanted Israel to be distinguished from all the surrounding peoples, exclusively belonging to Yahweh as their real בַּעַל ("husband/lord" cf. Isa 62:4–5; Jer 31:31–32), not to any counter(feit) בַּעַל like that of Shittim. The covenant he wished to (re-)establish would be a "covenant of peace" (Num 25:12; Isa 54:10; Ezek 34:25; 37:26) and life (Mal 2:5) closely related to the (literal) marriage covenant and depicted in corresponding language, structure, and similar blessings, responsibilities, and holiness. The Edenic covenant ideal and the one flesh union by "knowing" (יָדַע)⁵⁵¹ the Lord are paradigmatic for what God designed to obtain with his individually chosen people (Deut 7:6). This close union would be as prosperous in any possible respect as the blessing pronounced over the first pair in Eden (Gen 1:28). Also, Israel would be elevated "high above all the nations of the earth" (Deut 28:1) just like Adam and Eve were meant to rule over the earth (Gen 1:28), if they would only reflect the divine image (Gen 1:26–27) so that finally even "the nations will know [יָדַע] that I am the Lord who sanctified Israel" (Ezek 37:28). All the peoples of the earth would יָדַע the Lord by Israel's instrumentality, so that at last "the earth will be filled with the knowledge of the glory of the Lord, as the waters cover the sea." (Hab 2:14; cf. Isa 11:9). Thus, finally, God's purpose with the Edenic couple would be fulfilled by the promises of a covenant so similar to the one consummated in Eden by the first man and woman.

The deviations as investigated regarding the apostate "sons of God" (Gen 6:2; the Sethites) foreshadowing the sad experiences of the later "sons of God" (Israel) at Sinai (Exod 32) and particularly at Shittim (Num 25), therefore, are all the more significant and represent more than just a metaphorical, figurative "adultery." The covenant between Israel and Yahweh actually is a marital relationship and bears all the hallmarks of the corresponding Edenic pattern. God indeed was betrayed with other "men" like the Baal of Peor. It is more than just a metaphor, although not every aspect of the literal sphere is perfectly "compatible" and as such transferrable to the spiritual level. That means, what humankind experiences as (at least) partly physical relationship, is completely spiritual in the believer's relationship with God. There is, for instance, in no way any sacralisation of sex,⁵⁵² neither in Israel's worship service nor in the per-

549. Greenberg, "Jewish Tradition," 5.

550. Davidson, *Flame*, 113. Cf. M. Weinfeld's comment in Botterweck et al., *TWAT*, 1:807: "Die Vorstellung von einem Bund zwischen einer Gottheit und einem Volk ist uns in anderen Religionen und Kulturen unbekannt," although "es ist nicht unmöglich, daß einige alte Völker Bünde mit ihren Göttern hatten."

551. See again Num 31:17; Ezek 34:27, 30; 37:28; Hos 2:8, 20.

552. Similarly Davidson states *Flame*, 117: "Sexuality is rescued from the land of the enemy and restored by God to its place of value and dignity and holiness as in the beginning [i.e., Gen 2], and at

sonal, conjugal intercourse. But the Hebrew euphemism יָדַע serves in both spheres as appropriate expression for the intimate "knowledge" one obtains about the other person. Just as the first couple could unveiled, uncovered "know" each other (Gen 2:25), so the covenant partners of the human-divine relationship should at least endeavour to be acquainted with one another in this depth; so that, finally, "one who joins himself to the Lord is one spirit with Him" (1 Cor 6:17). Hence, to sum up:

> Ihren tiefsten Ausdruck findet die Wertschatzung der Ehe im Alten Testament darin, daß sie als Metapher für das Verhältnis Jahwes zu seinem Volk dient. Die Ehe als tiefste Form irdischer Lebensgemeinschaft kann somit die Treue Gottes veranschaulichen. . . . Es ist zudem jeweils ein Bund, der ohne Übereinstimmung der Partner nicht lebensfähig ist, der sich nicht auf Zwang gründen läßt, der immer wieder neu Ereignis werden muß. Das gilt von Jahwe und seinem Volk wie von Mann und Frau.[553]

I hoped to succeed in demonstrating that the metaphor of the marriage covenant is more than "but another figure of the Covenant imagery."[554] In fact, marriage is used "in bevorzugter Weise als ein Modell und als ein Bild für das Verhältnis Gottes zu seinem Volk."[555] It is a holier and much more far-reaching covenant than the relationship between a shepherd and his sheep or a king and his servants. While the most metaphors elucidate what God *does* for his people, the marriage metaphor rather elucidates what God *is* (or at least wishes to *be*) for his people. That makes a great difference and alludes once more to the meaningful, most significant pattern established in Eden.

Through the covenant of peace and eternal atonement by divine, messianic intervention, the experience of Shittim can be reversed by exchanging the name of the evil בַּעַל for the holy, Edenic אִישׁ as Hosea predicts (Hos 2:16; cf. Gen 2:23–24; 3:6, 16). Then, finally, Israel may "dwell securely" (וְיָשְׁבוּ לָבֶטַח; Ezek 34:28)—unlike the dangerous "dwelling" (also יָשַׁב) at Shittim (Num 25:1).[556] They would be granted a relationship with God as close as the marital communion and intercourse. They may even יָדַע the

---

the same time, by the use of obvious metaphor, no room is left for a literalistic sexual view of divine-human cohabitation that would lead to the divinization or sacralization of sex." Cf. Frymer-Kensky, "Law and Philosophy," 90–91.

553. Richter, *Geschlechtlichkeit*, 1:74.

554. Dunstan, "The Marriage Covenant," 246.

555. Kirchschläger, *Ehe im NT*, 24.

556. As mentioned above, the long "dwelling" at Sinai and Shittim led the people to "forsake" God, breaking the divine covenant by "joining" another "husband/Lord." The same problematic nature of the New Testament's covenant people is depicted in Jesus' parable of the ten bridesmaids (see Matt 25:1–13). Again it is the long delay (cf. Exod 32:1), the dwelling amidst pagan apostasy (cf. Num 25:1; Gen 6:1–2) that results in the "lukewarmness" (Rev 3:16) of some members of the New Testament church, falling asleep and forgetting about the preparation for the bridegrooms arrival. Yet, just as God did not forsake his "wife" Israel in the long run, refusing to reject her permanently and rather wishing to pardoned her by demonstrating the marital blessings that await her (cf. Hos 2; Isa 54; 62:4–5; Jer 31:31–32; Ezek 16:60–62; Mal 2:16), so Jesus is not forsaking his church, as particularly the message of the book of Revelation affirms.

The Old Testament Foundation

Lord and by his blessing bring forth זֶרַע אֱלֹהִים ("godly offspring;" Mal 2:15; cf. Isa 53:10), thus continuing the holy תּוֹלְדוֹת or זֶרַע once commenced in Eden (Gen 2:4; 3:15), established by the formerly faithful בְּנֵי־שֵׁת/בְּנֵי־הָאֱלֹהִים ("sons of God/Seth;" Gen 6:2; Num 24:17), carried on by Noah and Abraham, down to the marriage of God with Israel at Sinai (Exod 24): "Yahweh seeks 'the seed of God,' descendants of Abraham, Isaac, and Jacob who love him, obey him, and hold fast to him (Deut 30:19–20) and those who love justice, hate wrongdoing, and act faithfully (Isa 61:8–9)."[557]

Through periods of separation and judgment due to adulterous apostasy, the way of the human-divine conjugal relationship led to the final confirmation of the eternal covenant of peace and atonement—through Christ's atoning blood on the cross where the זֶרַע of the serpent (Gen 3:15) would "pierce" (דָּקַר; Zech 12:10; Num 25:8) him for a short time. Just as the leaders of the "adultery" at Shittim had to be hanged (Num 25:4) in order to obtain atonement and stop the divine curse (Num 25:8), so the messiah had to "hang before the Lord" on the cross being cursed by God (Deut 21:23) in order to redeem the church, his bride, from the curse of adulterous apostasy (Gal 3:13). The holiness of the marital union, exemplified by the paradigmatic transfer and consequent application of the Edenic ideal on the spiritual level, impresses and even imprints the significance of the marriage covenant on both spheres the literal as well as the spiritual.

---

557. Hill, *Malachi*, 247.

II

The New Testament Echoes of the Edenic Ideal

WHILE THE FIRST PART of this study dealt with the Old Testament foundation that must necessarily be considered when approaching the New Testament center of this treatise, in this second part we are now focusing on this study's core.

At first, it will be valuable to take a look into the ancient Jewish literature and its specific perceptions contributing to a thorough understanding of different religious opinions within Judaism concerning our topic in NT times. Subsequently, the texts to be scrutinized as center of the New Testament theology regarding the Edenic ideal and its far-reaching significance are Jesus' and Paul's sayings when referring to the Edenic marriage ideal as given in Gen 2:24. The main passages are found in the context of Jesus' speeches about divorce and adultery. Those are Matt 5:32; 19:3–9, Mark 10:2–12, and Luke 16:18. Paul's references are primarily 1 Cor 6:12–20 and Eph 5:21–33. While there are also some minor links to the Edenic ideal in further passages of the New Testament which will be investigated in the final section of this chapter, the texts given above are the core and center, not only of this chapter, but of the entire study. Hence, these texts are to be scrutinized very thoroughly in the following parts, beginning with Jesus' teachings and then proceeding to Paul's amplifications.

II.1 The Edenic Ideal in Prominent Ancient Jewish Literature

The different parts of this chapter all focus on the creational oneness, the "marriage" ideal as given in Gen 1:27; 2:18, 20–25 and its specific recapitulation and interpretation by the most important and influential Jewish authors of the New Testament times. Those are first Philo and Josephus, along with the writings given in post-biblical Jewish literature. Regarding Philo and Josephus, at first their general attitude toward sexuality and marriage will be investigated to understand better their individual interpretations of the Edenic story and to emphasize possible specific perceptions of the established creational oneness ideal in their time and religious setting.[1] Regarding the other non-biblical works, I will focus solely on the particular reflections of the creation of the woman and the understanding of Gen 2:24. Thus, the following survey shall serve as a wider historical and literary background to be considered when investigating the New Testament texts on the creational marriage ideal and its theological aspects in the next section of this chapter. It will finally lead to a more profound comprehension of the unique character of the New Testament's approach, which is almost nowhere following the other ancient Jewish interpretations.

II.1.1 Philo

The well known Jewish philosopher Philo of Alexandria, in contrast to Josephus, is very eloquent in describing theological conceptions underlying God's working and the Holy Scriptures. He was a Jew of the Diaspora, in close contact to the Hellenists in Egypt and constantly trying to justify the Jewish belief as a worthy alternative, a "Mosaic philosophy."[2] While he is called "the apex of Jewish allegorical interpretation in Greek," he also "is an early example of a Platonic way of thinking, usually called Middle Platonism."[3] He frequently writes about the relation between spirit and body (the mind and the senses), always trying to show the hazards of letting carnal passions grow or even reign.[4] The sharp dualism he represents, of course, also affects his attitudes toward marriage and sexuality. While he interprets marriage per se as some kind of slavery,[5] he consequently regards even conjugal intercourse as problematical and further thinks that adultery is "the greatest of all violations of the law" (*Decal.* 121), due to the pleasure involved in it (see *Spec.* 3:8; *Decal.* 122).

Generally, Philo does not exempt any kind of "sound" pleasure, but calls it generally bad or at least inferior to "virtue" and therefore in some way depraved (cf. e.g., *Sacr.* 1:21; *Spec.* 2:1), although he even refers to some supposedly "useful" passions

---

1. See the tables in the Appendix for the passages in Philo and Josephus dealing with sexuality and marriage.

2. Cf. Kuntz and D'Evelyn, *Ten Commandments*, 12.

3. Hoek, "Philo's Thoughts," 64. "His genius took up biblical interpretations of earlier days, of which only early fragmentary evidence has otherwise survived, created new explanations, and coated both with a heavy layer of Platonic thought." Ibid.

4. "In several passages Philo describes the body as 'earthlike' (e.g., in *Leg.* 1:32), made of matter, disorderly and irrational, exercising power and making it difficult for the mind to subdue it. The life of the man is, therefore, an unending struggle between mind and body. In *QG* 3:10 Philo describes the soul of the wise man, when in the body, as in 'a land which is not his own.' The bodily passions, though they may become our helpers, are in fact our enemies, and we are constantly afflicted from within by pleasures, desires, sorrows and fears." Williamson, *Philo*, 284. Esp. in context of Eden see *Leg.* 2:25–30; *Opif.* 165–66.

5. See esp. *Hypoth.* 11:14–17. §17: "Instead of a free man unconsciously [when marrying] he becomes a slave" (ἀλλ' ἕτερος λέληθε γεγονώς, ἀντ' ἐλευθέρου δοῦλος).

(cf. *Leg.* 2:5, 8).⁶ However, he supports thinking in distinctive black-and-white categories, promoting an ascetic lifestyle. On the other hand, however, he knows blessed marriages, even though there will be, of course, the "pleasure" of sexuality. But when he is talking of a "blameless" marriage that is "exceedingly praiseworthy" (οὐ μόνον ἀμέμπτους ἀλλὰ καὶ σφόδρα ἐπαινετοὺς εἶναι τοὺς γάμους), then it is the one holding fast to modesty while hoping for children (*Spec.* 1:138). The praiseworthy aspect of marriage is the aim of procreation, thus fulfilling the divine command of Gen 1:28.⁷ However, while Philo honors this purpose of the marriage relation, he simultaneously demands a strictly decent way of conjugal living, without too much sexual pleasure.⁸

That is even more sustained by the fact that Philo discredits infertile women as those who do not deserve any sexual intercourse at all, for the manly seed would be shed in vain (*Spec.* 3:34).⁹ On the other side, he acknowledges some kind of (sexual) "pleasure in accordance with nature" (ἡ κατὰ φύσιν ἡδονή) as far as it is not immoderately indulged in (*Spec.* 3:9).

Philo does not really differentiate between a sinless state before the Fall of Man and the sinful conditions afterwards. It is to be noticed that certain sentiments of his time and his understanding of the human nature are unreservedly transferred to the Edenic state of things.¹⁰ He even claims that "nothing in creation lasts for ever, [. . . therefore]

---

6. Especially *Leg.* 2:8 is worthy of quoting: "There is also another class of assistants, as I have already said, namely, the passions: for pleasure also is an assistant, co-operating towards the durability of our race, and in like manner concupiscence, and pain, and fear, biting the soul, lead it to treat nothing with indifference. Anger, again, is a defensive weapon, which has been of great service to many people, and so too have the other passions in the same manner." Here Philo candidly admits some valuable traits of different passions, even sensual pleasure, but just for certain higher purposes like e.g., procreativity. Otherwise "every passion is open to and deserving of blame." *Spec.* 4:79; (cf. likewise §§ 80, 84, 95).

7. *Praem.* 139: "They [the husbands] will see too the women whom they took in lawful wedlock for the procreation of true-born children . . . ." Cf. also *Virt.* 199; *Det.* 102; *Ios.* 43; *Spec.* 3:11.

8. Cf. e.g., again *Spec.* 1:138. The Greek expression χρὴ λογιζομένους καὶ ἄνδρας καὶ γυναῖκας σωφροσύνης seems to support this opinion for that rather means: "It is necessary for the man and the woman to consider *self-control*" right after talking about bringing forth "first fruits" whilst hoping for "a number of children." See also *Spec.* 4:79 (temperance).

9. This topic obviously is very important for Philo. The seed should never be shed in vain, therefore Yahweh set apart the times of menstruation, in which the couple would not be allowed to have intercourse. They would otherwise violate "the law of nature" (νόμον φύσεως) and waste the precious seed. *Spec.* 3:32. Consequently, he recommends divorce in cases of infertility (*Spec.* 3:34–35) "lest the gratification of the senses be considered more desirable than progeny." Amram, *Divorce*, 100. Hence, Philo claims: "But those who sue for marriage with women whose sterility has already been proved with other husbands, do but copulate like pigs or goats, and their names should be inscribed in the lists of the impious as adversaries of God. For while God in His love both for humankind and all that lives spares no care to effect the preservation and permanence of every race, those persons who make an art of quenching the life of the seed as it drops, stand confessed as the enemies of nature." *Spec.* 3:36.

10. To get an impression of his more general views about Eden it is helpful to read his three main works about creation and the garden: De Opificio Mundi, Legum Allegoriae, and Quaestiones et Solutiones in Genesim. *Leg.* 1 is about Gen 2:1—2:17, *Leg.* 2 about Gen 2:18—13:1. QG refers to Gen 2:4—6:13.

it was unavoidable that the first man should also undergo some disaster." (*Opif.* 151.)[11] It almost seems to be divinely designed that man should fall into sin; it seems to be "natural."[12] Furthermore, Philo perceives evident corruption even in the first, Edenic pair: "It was the more imperfect and ignoble element, the female, that made a beginning of transgression and lawlessness, while the male made the beginning of reverence and modesty and all good, since he was better and more perfect."[13]

Here we find a positive distinction between the sexes and their qualities.[14] Since Philo is referring to the natural conditions as given by the creator, one must assume that even in paradise before the Fall Eve is held to be imperfect (cf. *QG* 1:25, 37),[15] while "the first man, who was altogether adorned with virtue" (§ 18), is absolutely perfect.[16] However, that imperfection does not affect the outward appearance of the woman, for she is "most shapely and very charming" (*QG* 1:28).[17] Philo also elucidates that the Genesis text about the "helpmeet"

> refers to partnership, and that not with all persons but with those who wish
> to help and bring mutual profit even though they may not be able (to do

---

11. Trans. by Yonge.

12. Sexuality, however, for Philo, is "natural" only when serving one purpose: "The first bridal pair, the man and the woman ... came together in mutual intercourse *to procreate* their like." *Virt.* 199; italics supplied.

13. *QG* 1:43. He even talks about savage beasts, which man has to fear. Ibid., 23; thus he further introduces post-fall elements into the sinless state of the Eden story.

14. Yet, Philo explains that God in the beginning of the creation (cf. Gen 1:26) made the human being "after the (Divine) image was an idea or type or seal, an object of thought (only), incorporeal, *neither male nor female*, by nature incorruptible." *Opif.* 134; my italics. Already in Gen 2:7, however, he introduces male/female features in combination with a corruptible (real) human body. Ibid. For a more detailed investigation of "the single creation of man" see Tobin, *Creation*, 56–101.

15. It is not surprising that Eve is imperfect even in paradise. Philo's general perception of women throughout his writings is so clearly a negative one that, of course, the prototype, the mother of all women, has to be imperfect in her very nature. On the imperfection of most women in Philo's works see e.g., *Spec.* 1:108; *Virt.* 115; *Congr.* 180; *Gig.* 29; esp. *Legat.* 39; *QG* 1:33, 37, 43 etc.; cf. also Sly, *Women*, 81–82, 207; Taylor, "Virgin Mothers," 41–46; Hoek, "Philo's Thoughts," 75: "Strong women do appear in his [Philo's] writings but they happen to have lost their essential features as women. Only by denying their femininity can they gain credit in his pervasively male world view."

16. But even the first man is interpreted in different ways by Philo. He introduces a "heavenly man" (in God's image) of Gen 1:27 and an "earthly man" (created from the dust of the garden) in Gen 2:7 (see *QG* 1:8; cf. Tobin, *Creation*, 136). The man who is placed in the garden of Eden is, of course, the earth-like man; cf. *QG* 1:8. "There are two different reasons given for this. First, since the garden is a sensible reality, only the earthly, sense-perceptible man could be placed there.... The second reason ... is that only the 'molded man' is in need of teaching and instruction." Tobin, *Creation*, 136. Apparently even the man of Eden (that is the second man in Philo's interpretation of the creation account; Gen 2:7) has some "deficiencies" in his earthly, non-divine nature, contrasting the first man (Gen 1:27) of divine nature/image. Hence, real perfection is only given until Gen 2:3, as the exclamation of God in Gen 1:31 proves. With the creation of the earthly man we might notice the beginning of imperfection, while the creation of Eve is the prelude to passion, transgression, iniquity, and finally death.

17. Yonge translates even more to the point: the woman is "of a form so far more beautiful, and endowed with such excessive life and grace."

so). For love is a strengthener of character not more by usefulness than by union and concord, so that to every one of those who come together in the partnership of love the saying of Pythagoras can be applied, that 'a lover is indeed another self.' (*QG* 1:17)

He reemphasizes that aspect of the ideal counterpart by referring to their "complete similarity in body and soul" (*QG* 1:23).[18] But that similarity obviously is no equality, as Philo interprets Gen 2:21 and the aspect of creating the woman from the man's rib and not from earth (cf. *QG* 1:27).[19] Although Philo in *Leg.* 2:21–22 explains that the "rib/side" (πλευρά) stands for many positive powers, the woman is still lesser qualified than the man. She is "second, both in rank and power"[20] (*Leg.* 2:24) since God took by the rib "one of the many faculties of the mind, the faculty of sense-perception" (τοῦ νοῦ δυνάμεων μίαν ἔλαβε τὴν αἰσθητικήν; *Leg.* 2:35). And while the wife is described as "taking the rank of a servant" (*QG* 1:29) and the husband as "having the authority of a master" (ibid.), yet the "man should take care of woman as of a very necessary part of him; but woman, in return, should serve him as a whole." (*QG* 1:27). That service is corresponding to the one she previously yielded to her parents—whom she is now leaving by marriage according to Gen 2:24; consequently the husband is "figuratively to take care of woman as of a daughter" (*QG* 1:27).[21] The spheres of practical service are also divided by a word of Gen 2:22, where

> the harmonious coming together of man and woman and their consummation is figuratively a house. And everything which is without a woman is imperfect and homeless. For to man are entrusted the public affairs of state; while to a woman the affairs of the home are proper. The lack of her is ruin, but her being near at hand constitutes household management. (*QG* 1:26)

The "exchange" of families by leaving the parents and clinging to the spouse necessarily needs an "the most extreme exaggeration in partnership, so that he may endure to abandon even his parents." (*QG* 1:29.) This new communion is meant "for the sake of the woman" and the man is to "control and still his desires, being fitted to his spouse alone as if to a bridle." (Ibid.).

---

18. Batey further asserts: "Philo understood the woman's creation to be from a half (πλευρά) of Man's body and even speculated concerning which half of Man's bilateral body was taken. This seemed logical to him since 'truly our sides are twin in all their parts and made of flesh' (*QG* i. 25; *Leg.* II, 19–20)." Batey, *Nuptial Imagery*, 32.

19. Here (*QG* 1:27) Philo goes on explaining that this inequality should be expressed by taking only younger wives, "since those who marry wives more advanced in years than themselves deserve blame, as having overturned the law of nature." (Trans., Yonge.)

20. According to the translation of Yonge, who more concretely renders the Greek τὸ δεύτερον ("the second"). Colson translates "*next to* it alike in order and in power . . . " (my italics).

21. Philo further explicates: "She . . . should worthily give the same honour to her husband which she has previously given to her parents; for the husband receives his wife from her parents, as a deposit which is entrusted to him; and the woman receives her husband from the law." *QC* 1:27; (trans. Yonge).

In his allegorical interpretation of the creation account and other topics, Philo equates the man (Adam) with the mind and the woman (Eve) with the senses.[22] But "this is only the beginning and it gets steadily worse, particularly, for the woman. Sense-perception, which is neutral in itself and necessary for the mind to function in the body, becomes fully entangled in sensuality and sexual pleasures."[23] Philo completely rejects the meaning of the Hebrew בָּשָׂר which rather points to "integrated humanity" and replaces it with the Platonic sense of σάρξ in opposition to πνεῦμα or νοῦς. Accordingly negative is his interpretation of the "one flesh" story in Gen 2:24:

> For the sake of sense-perception the Mind, when it has become her slave, abandons both God the Father of the universe, and God's excellence and wisdom, the Mother of all things, and cleaves to and becomes one with sense-perception and is resolved into sense-perception so that the two become one flesh and one experience. (*Leg.* 2:49.)

> But when Scripture says that the two are one flesh, it indicates something very tangible and sense-perceptible, in which there is suffering and sensual pleasure, that they may rejoice in, and be pained by, and feel the same things, and, much more, may think the same things. (*QG* 1:29.)

The creational "one flesh" union obviously is no sacred, holy oneness, considering that passion is the foundation of all evil as Philo declares over and over again in all his writings.[24] But particularly the fact that "it is not the woman that cleaves to the man, but conversely the man to the woman, [that is] mind to sense-perception" (*Leg.* 2:50), makes it even more precarious, because "when that which is superior, namely Mind, becomes one with that which is inferior, namely sense-perception, it resolves itself into the order of flesh which is inferior, into sense-perception, the moving cause of the passions." (Ibid.) The woman, symbolizing the outward senses, "overpowers" the mind, symbolized by Adam, and thus creates a new "one flesh" union of a worse,

---

22. He does this at different places (see *Cher.* 57, 60; *QG* 1:37; *Her.* 53, 231 etc.), but especially in *Leg.* 2–3 (e.g., 2:14, 38 etc.). In *Opif.*, he particularly elucidates the connection between the sensual woman and the man's misfortune: "Pleasure does not venture to bring her wiles and deceptions to bear on the man, but on the woman, and by her means on him. This is a telling and well-made point: for in us mind corresponds to man, the senses to woman; and pleasure encounters and holds parley with the senses first, and through them cheats with her quackeries the sovereign mind itself . . . " (165).

23. Hoek, "Philo's Thoughts," 73. So Philo e.g., teaches: "In a word we must never lose sight of the fact that Pleasure, being a courtesan and a wanton, eagerly desires to meet with a lover, and searches for panders, by whose means she shall get one on her hook. It is the senses that act as panders for her and procure the lover. When she has ensnared these she easily brings the Mind under her control." *Opif.* 166. Cf. Benjamins, "Paradise," 95.

24. He recognizes only one good "marriage" consisting of a union between virtue (ἀρετή) and reason (νοῦς): *Abr.* 101–2; cf. *Congr.* 12. The physical union entailing bodily pleasure is disgusting to him: "And the marriage in which pleasure (ἡδονή) unites people comprehends the connection of the bodies (σωμάτων κοινωνίαν), but that which is brought about by wisdom is the union of reasonings which desire purification, and of the perfect virtues; and the two kinds of marriage here described are extremely opposite to one another." *Abr.* 100; cf. Dautzenberg, "Φεύγετε τὴν πορνείαν," 280.

passionate nature. "For Philo the identity of two persons has allegorical significance for revealing the nature of the abstract unity existing between Mind and Sense. The unity ideally should result in Mind, as the superior force, assimilating unto itself the faculty of sense."[25]

Although this allegorical type of explanation may not be compared to a literal analysis of the creation account, it is meaningful as to the general thrust of Philo's thought and perception, in which the "woman becomes for him [the man] the beginning of a blameworthy life" (*Opif.* 151). That touches not only the Edenic story, but even more the distinctions between male and female, as well as the (principally negative) interpretation of sexuality and the legal, conjugal "oneness" because the "desire for fellowship with the other . . . begat likewise bodily pleasure, that pleasure which is the beginning of wrongs and violation of law, the pleasure for the sake of which men bring on themselves the life of mortality and wretchedness in lieu of that of immortality and bliss." (*Opif.* 152.) Philo here talks about Adam's first glance at Eve, and he immediately interprets it as sexual tension and successive iniquity and transgression.[26] For him it must be marriage and the corresponding sexuality that is pronouncing "misfortune" (κακοδαίμονα) over humankind.[27] Consequently,

> love is the origin of his [the man's] ill-fortune: Love brings together the divided halves of the original androgynous man, created 'after the image,' and sets up a desire for fellowship. This aspect of love is a valuable one, but the desire for fellowship also sets up a desire for bodily pleasure, which is the root of wrong and of mortality.[28]

Whether these views echo his own opinion about the sexes and sexuality or if he is primarily employing Platonic sentiments in order to win readers and salvage at least a part of the creation account even for a non-Jewish audience, cannot be answered ultimately. However, the fact that such ideas are scattered so far among all his works, even in context of completely different topics, rather leads to the conclusion that it is his own thinking, doubtlessly influenced by Platonic thought, but exemplifying his own convictions regarding divinely ordained "natural" conditions concerning man, woman, and sex.

---

25. Batey, *Nuptial Imagery*, 32.

26. Thus there is no harmony between Philo's perception and the account in Eph. 5:29–33, as Batey, "The ΜΙΑ ΣΑΡΞ Union," 273 incorrectly suggests. There is no pure "love" in Philo's description, but mere sexual drive leading to sensual iniquity rather than creative, pure, and blessed unity.

27. "Woman's introduction to the scene was, as we saw, the beginning of all misfortune. . . . The allegory concentrates on the hapless senses, which woman exploits and also embodies and which are virtually identical with sensuality and wrongly directed sexuality. The issue of procreation disappears, and attention turns entirely to bodily pleasures, for which there is no positive role in Philo's system." Hoek, "Philo's Thoughts," 73. The woman is responsible for all the bad qualities humankind henceforth encountered and struggled with. Cf. ibid., 73–74; Sly, *Women*, 216.

28. Benjamins, "Paradise," 95.

II.1.2 Josephus

Leaving Philo and turning to the Jewish historian Josephus, we find that he gives no new insights about his special Jewish perceptions of the creation account. He just shortly explains the Jewish understanding of the world's origin without further elucidating the process; he is merely summing up the first three chapters of Genesis (see *A.J.* 1:27–51).[29] So we have only his general perceptions to draw some conclusions form. We might begin with an important statement at the siege of Jerusalem in the Jewish War (66–70 AD) with Josephus appealing to the inhabitants of Jerusalem to confess their sins and take a subordinate role to the Roman headship:

> Indeed, what can it be that has stirred up an army of the Romans against our nation? Is it not the impiety of the inhabitants? Where did our servitude commence?... As for you, what have you done of those things that are recommended by our legislator! And what have you not done of those things that he has condemned! How much more impious are you than those who were so quickly taken! You have not avoided so much as those sins that are usually done in secret; I mean thefts, and treacherous plots against men, and adulteries. You are quarrelling about rapines and murders, and invent strange ways of wickedness. Nay, the temple itself is become the receptacle of all, and this divine place is polluted by the hands of those of our own country; which place has yet been reverenced by the Romans when it was at a distance from them, when they have set aside many of their own customs to give place to our law.[30]

Here one prominent "impiety" (ἀσέβεια) of Jerusalem's inhabitants, which is evoking the divine wrath, is adultery (μοιχεία). The accumulation of various sins in that realm[31] results in the Roman siege and finally the destruction of the "wicked" city and even the temple towards the end of the war.

He also argues against pagan practices of sexuality that, in his opinion, resemble the lifestyle of the heathen's immoral gods (cf. *C.Ap.* 2:244–46, 270–77). He explains that as the Gods are, so will the man be; the deities are the patterns which men will strive for. "And why not, when even the eldest, the king, could not restrain his urge for sex...?" (*C.Ap.* 2:246). That pagan sexuality is abhorrent for every Jew, because it comprises (cf. *C.Ap.* 2:270–77):

1. Raping (lit. φθορά, "corrupting") virgins and then marrying them.
2. Adultery, unfortunately favored by Roman law in being slightly punished by only fining the transgressor.

---

29. The only further references to Adam are in context of time tables (see *A.J.* 8:62; 10:148), besides the immediate story after the Fall (Gen 4) as related in *A.J.* 1:52–83 and a short note (without new information) in *A.J.* 3:87. Eve is nowhere mentioned except the brief explanation on Gen 1–3 as given above.

30. *B.J.* 5:395–402 according to the translation of Whiston. The new translation of Mason was not yet published at the time this study was written.

31. Notice the plural form: μοιχείας (adulteries).

3. "Lying with males" as an "unnatural and impudent" (τῆς παρὰ φύσιν καὶ [ἄγαν] ἀνέδην) lust.

4. Further "sodomitical practices" of men and Gods, typified as "absurd and unnatural pleasures" (τῶν ἀτόπων καὶ παρὰ φύσιν ἡδονῶν).

Concerning the peculiar Jewish laws Josephus gives some interesting explanations. He teaches that it simply is "advantageous for both states and households that children be legitimate"—and for that reason Moses forbade adultery (A.J. 3:274). His rationales are just that Moses (as God's representor) abhors such unrighteousness (ibid.), without giving deeper explanatory insights.

The purpose of marriage is retraced to the initial blessing in paradise, where the first relation was thought to "fill the earth" (Gen 1:28). Therefore, "the only sexual intercourse recognized by the law is the natural intercourse with a woman, and that only if it is with the intention of procreation." (C.Ap. 2:199).

> It [the law] gave orders to nurture all children, and prohibited women from causing the seed to miscarry and from destroying it. But if it were to become evident, she would be an infanticide, obliterating a soul and diminishing the [human] race. Thus, not even if someone were to approach a stillborn fetus at childbirth would he be fit to be pure at that time. (C.Ap. 2:202.)

Apparently, according to Josephus' perception, the first marriage in paradise has been introduced just to fulfill the divine command of procreation. Therefore any infanticide, whatever the way of accomplishing it, would be against the will of Yahweh, for it "diminishes the human race." To have sexual intercourse without the purpose of begetting children is nearly equated with fornication, and always "the soul, by being united to the body [through sexual intercourse], is subject to miseries, and is not freed therefrom again but by death." (C.Ap. 2:203.)[32] Thus, of course, even legal sexuality is abasing and perhaps even depraving humankind.

Josephus continues claiming that men should always govern their desire and marry only free virgins (A.J. 4:244), "for thus the dispositions of your children would be free and directed towards virtue, if they should not happen to be born from shameful marriages nor from coming together in a passion that is not free." (A.J. 4:245).[33] The pleasure of sexuality is not good, even when practiced only within the "legal" bonds of the wedlock. Real lawfulness seems to derive from the purpose to procreate, and the marriage relation is just the basis of sexuality at all. However, he emphasizes the importance of an affectionate conduct of men toward their wives:

---

32. Trans., Whiston.

33. In this paragraph he also tells that one shall not marry harlots, obviously contradicting the opinion of Philo who approves that, as long as they have changed their way of life (cf. *Spec.* 1:102).

> ... For it is fair and just that in taking her to bear children, he should have regard for her wishes, and that he should not in pursuing only his own pleasure disregard what is pleasing to her. (*A.J.* 4:258.)
>
> A woman, it says, is inferior to a man in all respects. So, let her obey, not that she may be abused, but that she may be ruled; for God has given power to the man. (*C.Ap.* 2:201.)

Obviously he endeavors to protect the wives and to urge the husbands to treat their spouses with respect and loving care. In that point Philo is concurring with Josephus, and both are also agreeing on the general corruption of sexual pleasures, even in conjugal relations.[34] Thus the blessed, creational ideal is marred to a certain degree, while both authors at the same time declare the divine working as being faultless—despite the fact of becoming "one flesh."

II.1.3 Post-Canonical Jewish Literature

The third group of witnesses to the early Jewish interpretation of the creational ideal of oneness (that is to say, the creation of male and female as well as the constitution of "marriage") comprises the Old Testament Apocrypha, the Pseudepigrapha, and the Qumran literature. It is surprising that there are only a few allusions to the creation of both male and female, while quite a number of texts are concerned with the creation of Adam only.[35] The passages that are speaking about both sexes in context of marriage are: Tob. 8:6; *Jub.* 2:14; 3:1–7; 8; *2 En.* 30:8–18; *Sib. Or.* 1:22–37; *Apoc. Mos.* 7:1; 40–42; *L.A.B.* 32:15 and only a few texts of Qumran. *Apoc. Mos.* is not useful for the investigation of the creational ideal, since it only deals with the conditions after the Fall.[36] And the short passage in **Liber antiquitatum biblicarum** (32:15) just declares:

> Rejoice, O land, over them that dwell in thee, for in thee is the knowledge of the Lord which buildeth his stronghold in thee. For it was of right that *God took out of thee the rib of him that was first formed*, knowing that out of his rib Israel should be born. And thy forming shall be for a testimony of what the Lord hath done for his people.

---

34. A detailed analysis of their perception regarding the supposed impurity of conjugal sexuality was given in the corresponding chapter above (see "Ritual Purity: Ancient Jewish Sources").

35. As Van Ruiten, "Early Jewish Literature," 34 lists them, those would be (of Apocrypha and Pseudepigrapha): Ben Sira 15:14; 16:17—17:24 (esp. 16:26, 17:1); 17:25—18:14; 33:7–13; (33:10, 13); 36:26; 40:1–11 (40:11), 27; 49:16; Wisdom of Solomon 2:23–24; 7:1–6; 9:1–3; 10:1–2; 15:7–13; Sibylline Oracles 3:24; Pseudo-Philo, Liber Antiquitatum Biblicarum 13:8–9; 26:6; 32:15; (37:3); 4 Ezra 3:4–11 (esp. 3:4–7); 4:30; 6:45–46, 53–54; (7:62–74, esp. 7:70); (7:116–31); 2 Baruch (4:1–7); 14:17–19; 48:42–47; Greek Life of Adam and Eve 33:5; 35:3; 37:3; Latin Life of Adam and Eve (Vita Adae et Evae) 13:2–3; 2 Enoch 44:1; 65:2; Greek Apocalypse of Ezra 2:10–11.

36. The text of "Joseph and Aseneth" will also be omitted, since it does not contain any hint at Gen 2:24, but only deals with marriage per se.

It is not even clear if the allusion with the rib is really pointing to Eve, rather than to Adam, "he that was first formed [out of thee, i.e., the land]." So here we also find no insights concerning the Edenic types. Hence, only the following texts can serve as basis for this third group of witnesses for the New Testament milieu.

Tobit 8:6 reads as follows:

> Thou madest Adam, and gavest him Eve his wife for an helper and stay: of them came mankind: thou hast said, It is not good that man should be alone; let us make unto him an aid like unto himself. (KJV)

The second part of this statement ("thou hast said . . .") is almost a verbatim quotation of God's declaration in Gen 2:18 as given in the LXX version of the text. The author (and/or translator) of the book of Tobit apparently intended to give an exact wording of the Genesis text, only changing κατ' αὐτόν (LXX) into ὅμοιον αὐτῷ (Tob. 8:6) what is in no way deviating from the original meaning. Again the phrase "Eve his wife an helper and stay" (βοηθὸν Ευαν στήριγμα τὴν γυναῖκα αὐτοῦ) reflects the terminology of Gen 2:18, where there occurs βοηθός ("helper"). Apparently στήριγμα ("a support/helper") just repeats that description, again without changing the content. That the next verse (Tob. 8:7) speaks about taking the "sister" not "for lust but uprightly" (οὐ διὰ πορνείαν . . . ἀλλ' ἐπ' ἀληθείας) on the one hand indicates that the author possibly is emphasizing the similitude of the creational patterns for both husband and wife by referring to the spouse as "sister" (ἀδελφή). On the other hand, the topic of sexuality is plainly introduced and any improper "fornication" (πορνεία) is excluded right at the beginning of the marriage relation.[37] The divine influence in "pairing" spouses together (cf. Gen 2:22; see below rabbinic perceptions) is indicated by Tob. 6:18, where it says that "she is appointed unto thee from the beginning" (cf. also Tob. 7:12). The man's response in Edenic manner is "being cleaved" (ἐκολλήθη; v. 19) to her (cf. Gen 2:24: προσκολληθήσεται; both 3rd pers. passive of (προσ-) κολλάω).[38] While there are no new interpretative hints, one may assert that

---

37. Baltensweiler recognizes "eine Abkehr von dem rein sexuellen Verständnis der Ehe. . . . Hinter der lauteren Gesinnung [i.e., the 'uprightly' (ἐπ' ἀληθείας)] ist nach dem Zusammenhang das Wissen um die Schöpfungsordnung Gottes zu verstehen." Baltensweiler, *Ehe im NT*, 37. Tosato, "On Genesis 2:24," 408/fn.53 further asserts that "from Tob. 8:6–7 it is clear that Gen 2:18–24 acts as a normative matrimonial model."—In order to wed his fiancée he turns to the Genesis story as the normative foundation of the intimate relationship he is about to commence.

38. Cf. also Sampley, *One Flesh*, 60. He further stresses the similarities to the crucial passage in Eph 5:21–33: "Κολλάω is the verb used here as in Gen 2:24 and in Eph 5:21–33 in the context of marriage. Of special interest is the relationship that exists in Tobit 6:19 between the phrases 'he loved her very much, and his heart cleaved unto her' and the same relationship that exists in Eph 5:21–33 where the love of Christ for the church is spoken of in conjunction with the use of the OT verse that speaks of a man leaving his father and mother and cleaving to his wife (Gen 2:24). Already in Tobit, there is the conjunction of Gen 2:24 and love that is so pronounced in Eph 5:21 ff. In Eph 5:23, Christ is spoken of as the head of the church αὐτὸς σωτὴρ τοῦ σώματος. . . . In Tobit 6:18, Raphael is portrayed as saying that Tobias' marriage to Sarah will save her: καὶ σὺ αὐτὴν σώσεις." These aspects of the NT text will further be developed in the following chapters below (see esp. the section about "Paul's Spiritual Application").

The use of Genesis 2–3 by the author of Tobit makes it clear that according to him the rules that apply to Adam and Eve in Genesis would apply also to Tobit and Sara, because all "seed of men" came out of Adam and Eve. Adam and Eve, as the first married couple, seems [sic.] to function as example for all married couples after them. Marriage is anchored in the Creation. It stresses the fact that Tobias does not take Sara for lust (Tobit 8:7a), but that he is acting according to the order of Creation.[39]

The book of **Jubilees** is more detailed in its description of man's creation and the couple's oneness. The author of the book is only slightly deviating from the story in Gen 2:[40]

> And the Lord said unto us: 'It is not good that the man should be alone: let us make a helpmeet for him.' . . . He brought her to him, and he knew her, and said unto her: 'This is now bone of my bones and flesh of my flesh; she shall be called [my] wife; because she was taken from her husband.' Therefore shall man and wife be one, and therefore shall a man leave his father and his mother, and cleave unto his wife, and they shall be one flesh. In the first week was Adam created, and the rib—his wife: in the second week He showed her unto him . . . .[41]

Obviously the one-flesh union is an important aspect in this representation of man's origin. In contrast to the biblical account here the oneness is mentioned twice, thereby strongly emphasizing it.[42] Furthermore, Adam's first sexual relations with his wife (v. 6: "and he knew her"), perhaps as "the fulfillment of Adam's desire evoked by his observing the animals to find a partner and helper for himself,"[43] are clearly mentioned before the Fall (v. 20)—actually even before the first pair entered paradise (vv. 9–12).[44] Also, "here too [as in Tobit] marriages are preordained *ab aeterno*"[45]—for Adam and "the rib, his wife" are created at the same time, while she is showed to him only when God decided to do so (*Jub.* 3:8). Tobit further presupposes a monogamous and indissoluble ideal of marriage, basing on the creation story.[46]

---

39. Van Ruiten, "Early Jewish Literature," 39.

40. For a table comparing the wording of both accounts (*Jub.* 3:1–7 and Gen 2:18–24) see Loader, *Enoch, Levi, Jubilees*, 237–38.

41. *Jub.* 3:4–8. Quotations are from the translated version of Charles, *Pseudepigrapha*.

42. Similarly Loader, *Enoch, Levi, Jubilees*, 243–44.

43. Thus Loader, *Enoch, Levi, Jubilees*, 242; Anderson, "Reflections," 128.

44. The same point is made in Kvam et al., *Eve and Adam*, 43, 51 and Anderson, "Reflections," 129. Loader, *Enoch, Levi, Jubilees*, 240 further notes a positive evaluation of sexuality in the description of Adam observing the sexual difference between the "male and female" animals in *Jub.* 3:3 right before the Lord is saying that "it is not good that the man to be alone."

45. Tosato, "On Genesis 2:24," 408/fn.54; italics given.

46. Cf. again Tosato, "On Genesis 2:24," 408/fn.54.

In the book of **Sirach** the separation of this close union is described as "cutting her off from your flesh" (ἀπὸ τῶν σαρκῶν σου ἀπότεμε αὐτήν; Sir. 25:26), thereby interpreting the marital oneness to be of the closest kind that could be imaginable.[47] Dissolving it means "cutting off" one's own "flesh." Nevertheless, divorce is made an easy decision: "If she does not go as you direct [εἰ μὴ πορεύεται κατὰ χεῖράς σου]—cut her off from your flesh" (ibid.). There is no further illustration of any special meaning concerning this one flesh union; yet it is illuminating that the creation of male and female, including the sexual undertones, is placed right before the entering of paradise (cf. *Jub.* 3:8–9)—and thereby it is in its beginning kept out of it.[48]

In the **Sibylline Oracles** it is again the loneliness of the man that causes God to create the woman (cf. *Sib. Or.* 1:26–37).[49] Apart from this, there is not much similarity between the Genesis account and the portrayal thereof in *Sib. Or.*; no exact quotation can be found. So it might also not be surprising that it is the desire of Adam for conversation and his prayer that made God create Eve. It is Adam's initiative that stands at the beginning of Eve's life:

> But in that fertile field of Paradise
> He longed for conversation, being alone,
> And prayed that he might see another form
> Such as he had. And forthwith, from man's side
> Taking a bone, God himself made fair Eve,
> A wedded spouse, and in that Paradise
> Gave her to dwell with him.
> . . . with wise words
> Spontaneous flowing answered he in turn
> For God had care for all things. For the mind
> They darkened not with passion, nor concealed
> Their nakedness, but with hearts far from evil
> Even like wild beasts they walked with limbs exposed.
> (*Sib. Or.* 1:33–39, 42–47)

---

47. Dautzenberg, "Φεύγετε τὴν πορνείαν," 279 further asserts concerning Sir. 25:26: "Die Ehe wird unter dem Einfluß von Gen 2,24 c als somatische Einheit verstanden, die Auflösung dieser Einheit hat, wie die Wahl des Bildes vom 'Abschneiden' verrät, dramatischen und die Integrität des Mannes bedrohenden Charakter. D. h. unter einem patriarchalischen Vorverständnis werden 'die beiden' so εἰς σάρκα μίαν, daß die Frau in die σάρξ des Mannes aufgenommen wird."

48. Van Ruiten, "Early Jewish Literature," 48 explains: "Moreover, the author considers the Garden of Eden as the prototype of the Temple. Since it was not permissible to enter the city of the Temple a certain period after having sex, the first sexual contact between Adam and Eve does not take place in the garden of Eden, but before they enter." However, it was not sex, but the impurity of childbirth, which hindered the person from entering the temple. And the text more clearly points to just this kind of impurity; the period of 40 days for Adam and 80 days for Eve to wait before entering paradise (*Jub.* 3:8–9) strongly alludes to the Levitical law in Lev 12:2–5 (male: 7+33 days; female: 14+66 days of purification before entering the temple). The sexual undertones are, of course, still maintained.

49. Translation and paragraphing according to Terry, *Sibylline Oracles*.

Since it is Adam's wish to have a partner to converse with, they are consequently speaking "wise words."—"The mind they darkened not with passion," but, to the contrary, their hearts were "far from evil." The a- and even anti-sexual tendencies are evident:

> The aspect of sexuality is completely disconnected from the creation of men. It enters the life of the first couple only with regard to the curse, after eating from the Tree of the Knowledge of Good and Evil. The spiritualization in OrSib 1:35–37 of the nakedness can be seen in the same line. . . . Finally, sexuality is disconnected from the creation of Adam and Eve. Before the eating from the Tree of Knowledge, they seem to have a sort of Platonic relationship. Only after this does sexuality enter their life.[50]

While sexuality is, again, kept out of paradise, also the sin and seductive influence of Eve is kept outside for the sake of a blameless partnership inside the holy garden.[51] Not before the eating from the Tree of Knowledge they come to know sexuality and only then they are blessed (or requested) to multiply and increase (cf. *Sib. Or.* 1:53–59, 70–72). Hence, in the Sibylline Oracles we find no "creational ideal" referring to the one-flesh union at all. Here the creational oneness is a relationship solely consisting of oral conversion with no flesh involved in it.

The last text to be investigated is **2 Enoch** 30:17—31:1. The many unclarities concerning dating, authorship, religious and philosophical backgrounds,[52] and even the translation of the passage belonging to our topic, make it necessary to be very careful with conclusions. Hence, I will try to only briefly give an impression of the few remarks somehow dealing with Gen 2:24.

In *2 En.* 30:17–18 God "took from him a rib, and created him a wife, that death should come to him by his wife."[53] Obviously, the last part of the verse is very meaningful. According to the author of *2 En.*, it is God who not only tempts Adam, but who even more creates the woman with the clear intention to bring death over him! Again this event is (seemingly) taking place outside the garden, since God creates Eden not before *2 En.* 31:1. Additionally, the picture of the spouse's communion is further darkened by the fact that nowhere is an allusion to the loneliness of Adam and his desire to have an equal partner, a help or a support.

> As a consequence, the man does not recognize Eve as part of himself, and nothing is said of a special union of man and woman. This can be seen to be

---

50. Van Ruiten, "Early Jewish Literature," 54.

51. Cf. Van Ruiten, "Early Jewish Literature," 54: "Eve is not created so that sin and death might come to Adam or to humankind. Eve is created as a partner equal to Adam. Although later on in the story she is the one who persuades Adam to eat from the fruit of the Tree of Knowledge, it is the serpent who is seen as the first responsible. He is in fact the only who is to be cursed, whereas the curse on Adam and Eve is lightened very greatly because it is connected with the blessing of God."

52. Cf. Charles, *Pseudepigrapha*, 425–30.

53. This translation according to Charles, *Pseudepigrapha*, 450; NN, *Henoch*, 28.

in one line with the omission of the command to be fruitful from Genesis 1. The marital relationship between Adam and Eve is left out.... The point of the story of the creation of Eve is that she has brought death to Adam: "So that death might come to him by his wife" (3:17g).[54]

That assumption that Eve had sexual relations with Satan (2 *En.* 31:6: "... he [i.e., Satan] entered and seduced Eva") cannot clearly be derived from the text. It just says that Eve has been "corrupted" or "seduced" by the devil, what might point to sexuality as well as to any other kind of (moral) corruption by seducing her to disobey the divine command through eating from the forbidden tree. Howsoever, the image of Eve is blackened, there is no good quality at all, and even God is playing Adam a nasty trick in creating Eve. Thus Adam was only "five and half hours in paradise" (2 *En.* 32:1)! Consequently, we cannot obtain any illuminating information concerning the creational ideal, for it simply is reversed to the contrary. It is no ideal; it is a threatening danger—even right in front and inside of Eden.

As a final note, the passage in 1 Esdras 4:20, 27 should be mentioned. It is not of the same class as the previous texts, since it is not concerned with the Edenic conditions, nor interpreting the creation account, but rather using it for a contemporary discussion about the most powerful force in a man's life:

> Then the third, that is Zerubbabel, who had spoken of women and truth, began to speak: Gentlemen, is not the king great, and are not men many, and is not wine strong? Who then is their master, or who is their lord? Is it not women? Women gave birth to the king and to every people that rules over sea and land. From women they came; and women brought up the very men who plant the vineyards from which comes wine. Women make men's clothes; they bring men glory; men cannot exist without women. If men gather gold and silver or any other beautiful thing, and then see a woman lovely in appearance and beauty, they let all those things go, and gape at her, and with open mouths stare at her, and all prefer her to gold or silver or any other beautiful thing. *A man (ἄνθρωπος) leaves (ἐγκαταλείπει) his own father, who brought him up, and his own country, and cleaves (κολλᾶται) to his wife.* With his wife he ends his days, with no thought of his father or his mother or his country. Hence you must realize that women rule over you!
>
> Do you not labor and toil, and bring everything and give it to women? A man takes his sword, and goes out to travel and rob and steal and to sail the sea and rivers; he faces lions, and he walks in darkness, and when he steals and robs and plunders, he brings it back to the woman he loves. *A man loves his wife more than his father or his mother.* Many men have lost their minds because of women, and have become slaves because of them. Many have perished, or stumbled, or sinned, because of women. And now do you not believe me? (1 Esd 4:13–28 (RSV); my italics.)

---

54. Van Ruiten, "Early Jewish Literature," 59.

The New Testament Echoes of the Edenic Ideal

In vv. 20 and 25 (italicized above) this text clearly echoes Gen 2:24. It does not, however, shed any new light on the ancient Jewish interpretation of Gen 2:24, but at least it demonstrates its possible presence in the minds of individuals discussing the powerful force of love in man's life, as is beautifully written in Song 8:6–7: "For love is as strong as death, Jealousy is as severe as Sheol; Its flashes are flashes of fire, The very flame of Jahweh."

II.1.4 The Qumran Scrolls

Surprisingly, in Qumran there are only very few allusions to Gen 1–3 and most of them do not refer to marriage in respect to the one flesh union of Gen 2:24. One of these few hints is given in CD 4:20—25:2, which reads as follows:

> The Shoddy-Wall-Builders who went after 'Precept'—Precept is a Raver of whom it says, 'they shall surely rave' [Mic 2:6]—they are caught in two: fornication, by taking two wives in their lifetimes, although the principle of creation is 'male and female He created them' [Gen 1:27] and those who went into the ark 'went into the ark two by two' [Gen 7:9]. Concerning the Leader it is written 'he shall not multiply wives to himself' [Deut 17:17].[55]

Although it is clear that this passage is against polygyny,[56] it cannot be derived from it that the Qumran people would generally reject divorce and remarriage (even while the former, divorced wife was still alive), since CD 13:17–18 stipulates that the permission of the "bishop" (*mebaqqer*) is prerequisite for divorcing a wife and remarriage *after* divorce is not regarded as polygyny.[57]

While another text in 4QInstruction[a]/4Q415 2:II:4 apparently speaks of marriage as a covenant ([. . . ברית קוֹדֶשׁ—"hol[y] covenant"), IX:8 (בה המשל רוחה—"her spirit make to rule over her") may allude to Gen 1:27 in combination with 3:16, emphasizing the dominion of the husband over his wife.[58] Another fragmentary phrase in XI:11 may perhaps point to Gen 2:24 ([. . . וֹאם נפרדה בהריתכה קח מֹוֹלדיה—"If she is

---

55. Trans. by Wise. See for a discussion of this text esp. Loader, *Dead Sea Scrolls*, 110–19; also Martínez, "Man and Woman," 99–109; Collins, *Divorce*, 82–84; in context of Jesus' understanding of πορνεία: Sigal, *Halakhah*, 135–40; cf. 11QT 57:17–19.

56. Cf. Winter, "Sadoquite Fragments," 78; Loader, *LXX, Sexuality, and NT*, 81; Loader, *Jesus Tradition*, 65; Berger, *Gesetzesauslegung*, 521, 524; Instone-Brewer, *In the Bible*, 61–65, 138; Niederwimmer, *Askese und Mysterium*, 47–48; Meier, *Marginal Jew IV*, 88–91; Beale and Carson, *NT Use*, 59, 198; Zimmermann, *Geschlechtermetaphorik*, 335, 337, 358; Lövestam, "Divorce and Remarriage," 50; Sanders, *Jesus and Judaism*, 258; Baltensweiler, *Ehe im NT*, 55–57; Davies and Allison, *Saint Matthew*, 3:10; Martínez, "Man and Woman," 109; Turner, *Matthew*, 459/fn.4; Luz, *Matthäus*, 3:93/fn.24.

57. Cf. Vawter, "Divorce and the NT," 534/fn.9; Instone-Brewer, *In the Bible*, 65–72; Loader, *Dead Sea Scrolls*, 115–18; Loader, *Jesus Tradition*, 65; Steudel, "Ehelosigkeit bei den Essenern," 123–24; Meier, *Marginal Jew IV*, 90–91; against Fitzmyer, "Matthean Divorce Texts," 218–21 and Martínez, "Man and Woman," 109.

58. Thus also Loader, *Dead Sea Scrolls*, 300–302.

divided [?] when she is pregnant for you, take the off[spring of her]"), denoting the separation from one's parents through marriage, or the separation of Adam's flesh (his rib) for the purpose of the divine act of "building" Eve.[59]

A little bit more interesting appears 4QInstruction[b]/4Q416 2:III:21 saying: "From the mystery that is to come while in your relations with her together, walk with the helper of your flesh" ([. . .] מרז נהיה בהתחברכה יחד התהלך עם עזר בשרכה). The sexual encounter of the spouses is here called a "mystery/secret" (רז) and the wife is referred to with the term "helper" (עזר) and "your flesh" (בשרכה), just as it occurred in Gen 2:18, 20 and 2:24; consequently, the text continues in the next column (IV:1) with a quotation of Gen 2:24: את אביו וֹ֯אֵת אמו ודֹ֯בָ֯ק באשתו והיו לבשר אחד) "his father [and] his mother and clin[g to his wife and they shall become one flesh]"—but, again (as in 4QInstruction[a]/4Q415 2:IX:8), only to proceed to Gen 3:16 and the husband's dominion.[60] No further exposition of Gen 2:24 is given, only the occurrence of a synonym (שאר—"flesh/relative") for בָּשָׂר ("flesh") is to be found in IV:5 ([. . .] ואתה ליחד עם אשת חיקכה כי היא שאר ערותכה)—"and you shall be made into a unity with the wife of your bosom, for she is the flesh of [your] nak[edness]"). The last text in 4QMiscellaneous Rules/4Q265 2:VII:12, echoing *Jub.* 3:8, only alludes to Gen 2:23 (עֶצֶם מֵעֲצָמַי, "bone of my bones") carrying the fragment [. . . ועצם מעצמיו ("bone [of his bones . . .]"). Altogether, however, it seems that the Qumran material does not render any new insights for the investigation of Gen 2:24.

II.1.5 Rabbinic Perceptions

The rabbinic material may present a last view of Jewish interpretations of Gen 2:24. Yet it has to be considered that even the earliest rabbinic material (Mishnah and Tosefta) is not older than the second century AD; and the Tannaitic stratum therein, which is regarded as going back beyond the destruction of the temple in 70 AD, is not easily identified and interpreted.[61] But even the discussions of the following centuries may be able illuminate a little bit the basic interpretative tendencies.

Generally, the creation account has been respected very highly by the ancient rabbis. *M. Ḥag.* 2:1 even teaches that it should not be taught about the creation before two students, except they are savants who earned insights by their knowledge.

---

59. Cf. Loader, *Dead Sea Scrolls*, 303, 309.

60. Cf. Loader, *Dead Sea Scrolls*, 306–9.

61. About the problems of obtaining authentic Pharisaic material of the time the Jewish sects existed (i.e., before 70 AD) see esp. Sanders, *Palestinian Judaism*, 59–84; Müller, "Datierung," 551–87; Rivkin, *Revolution*, 125–27; Neusner, "Rabbinic Traditions," 297–302; Neusner, *From Politics to Piety*, 90; Green, "What do we really know," 409; Deines, *Pharisäer*, 538–40; Gehring, *Religionsparteien*, 615–21. However, "in certain cases the verbal agreement between the form in which a general command or counsel, a gnomic saying or exhortatory observation, spoken by Jesus, is expressed in the Gospels, and paradigmatic statements found here and there in late Jewish literature is so striking that it is far from unreasonable to assume the existence of common sources." Winter, "Sadoqite Fragments," 71.

Otherwise the precious teachings from the first chapters of Genesis would not be adequately appreciated. Although "no aspect of Genesis 1–3 escapes scrutiny and rabbinic comment; [and] no gap in the story line goes unfilled,"[62] this section focuses only on the rabbinic perceptions about the central passage of Gen 2:24 and the "one flesh" concept. Further aspects like the rabbinic teachings on adultery, divorce, remarriage etc. will be investigated within the exegesis on Jesus' sayings below. To begin with,

> Rabbinic interpretation of Genesis 2:24 is interesting in a number of respects. First, the Rabbis are almost entirety pre-occupied with the question of whether or not the verse implies a matriarchal kind of society or whether it casts into question the patriarchal pattern with which the Rabbis were so familiar in Israel. Secondly, they very rarely, if ever, take an interest in the question of the meaning of the term 'one flesh.' The absence of any serious consideration of the term 'one flesh' by the Rabbis fairly reflects the attitude of the rest of the Old Testament in so far as the term does not occur again.[63]

It has also to be pointed out that the rabbis were much more concerned with legal matters than with theological ideas. Hence, there is more information about right and wrong, and less about the deeper meaning of Gen 2:24.[64] Nevertheless, there are also some interesting hints to several aspects the rabbis understood as being implied in the expression "one flesh" and the steps to consummate this intimate union.

The Complemental Helper. There was a significant perception properly formulated by Rabbi Chijja ben Gamda (third century AD) who said that he who has no wife "is incomplete;" and Rabbi Eleazar ben Pedath (died ca. 270 AD) adds: "Any man who has no wife is not [yet] a human being."[65] It is evident that "in Judaism, and from the very moment of origins of the Jewish people, marriage was considered to be the ideal state,"[66] and "sex, in the context of marriage, was of positive value . . . celibates were

---

62. Kvam et al., *Eve and Adam*, 69.

63. Kaye, "One Flesh," 49. Beale and Carson, *NT Use*, 60 (referring to Strack and Billerbeck, *Talmud und Midrasch*, 1:802–3) emphasize that "later rabbinic discussion seems to have focused primarily on what this principle [i.e., becoming 'one flesh' in Gen 2:24] meant in the context of extended families often living together."

64. This became already clear in the investigation above of the textual variants of Gen 2:24 (see "The Edenic Constitution of Marriage—Text and Translation"). The expansion in an Aramaic version, the Targum Neofiti ("a man leaves *the bed* of his father and mother"), seems to be understood by the rabbis in a strictly legal sense; cf. Grossfeld, trans., *Targum Onqelos*, 45/fn.11. At least their comments on this text esp. in *b. Sanh.* 58a–b and *Gen. Rab.* 18 point in that direction and have nothing to say about the quality or theology of the marriage relationship.

65. *B. Yebam.* 63a; *Gen. Rab.* 17:2; cf. Strack and Billerbeck, *Talmud und Midrasch*, 1:802 (if not referred to another translation, I am working with the sources in ibid., vols. 7–8). Others translate the declaration of R. Eleazar b. Pedath as ". . . is no proper man" (see Kvam et al., *Eve and Adam*, 83). Cf. also Beale and Carson, *NT Use*, 59, 198. Winter, "Sadoquite Fragments," 83 further adds that "the rabbis of a later age [similarly] used [Gen 1:27; 5:1–2] in their exegetic exercises to prove the advantage of marriage over celibacy."

66. Greenberg, "Jewish Tradition," 3.

frowned upon, even if they were considered among the greatest scholars .... The sexual urge was considered a basic and normal need that required satisfaction."[67] The ancient Jewish rabbis believed that

> an unmarried man dwelt without good, help, joy, blessing, and atonement, and was not a proper man. Some teachers maintained that God's image was present only after marriage and the uniting of male and female into one whole Man ... the wife was the source of man's wholeness, peacefulness, and happiness."[68]

Consequently, it is not surprising that even an obligation to marry was formulated, closely combined with "the very first biblical commandment" to procreate (Gen 1:28) as "a fundamental obligation of the marriage partners."[69] Nevertheless, even the pleasure of sex alone was a positive value, even if no pregnancy could be expected (because of an already existing pregnancy, infertility, the immaturity of a minor, or the finished menopause).[70]

Further concerning the Hebrew עֵזֶר כְּנֶגְדּוֹ ("a helper as his counterpart/who corresponds him;" Gen 2:18) the Talmud knows an interesting interpretation of the same rabbi Eleazar, who said: if he deserves it, she helps him, if not, she is against him.[71] That is further elucidated by the following explanation: "It says כנגדו, and we pronounce it כְּנֶגְדּוֹ: does he deserve it (is he worthy), then she is corresponding to him (complementing him, כְּנֶגְדּוֹ), does he not deserve it (is he unworthy), then she is a scourge (כְּנֶגְדּוֹ = מְנַגַּדְתּוֹ who scourges him)."[72] However, basically it may be asserted that

> typical of rabbinic teachings is the idea that men and women alone had in themselves only partial existence and that only in sexual union can a person find the fullness of the divine image in which Man was created. It was often stated that a man's wife was the source of his wholeness, peace, and blessings.[73]

---

67. Greenberg, "Jewish Tradition," 6; referring to *b. Yebam.* 63ab; *Qidd.* 29b; *Ketub.* 63a; *Soṭah* 4b.

68. Batey, "The MIA ΣΑΡΞ Union," 272; referring to *Gen. Rab.* 8:9; 17:2; 22:2; *b. Yebam.* 63a; *Šabb.* 25b. See Kvam et al., *Eve and Adam*, 83.

69. Greenberg, "Jewish Tradition," 5, 7; quotations from p. 7. Cf. *b. Qidd.* 29ab, 30a; *Ketub.* 67b; *Yebam.* 62b, 113a; *Pesaḥ.* 113b; Rubenstein, "Jewish Tradition," 7, 11. Note esp. the following: *b. Yebam.* 63b: "It was taught: R. Eliezer stated, He who does not engage in propagation of the race is as though he sheds blood; for it is said, Whoso sheddeth man's blood by man shall his blood be shed, and this is immediately followed by the text, And you, be ye fruitful and multiply. R. Jacob said: As though he has diminished the Divine Image; since it is said, For in the image of God made he man, and this is immediately followed by, And you, be ye fruitful etc. Ben 'Azzai said: As though he sheds blood and diminishes the Divine Image; since it is said, And you, be ye fruitful and mutltiply." (Trans. Epstein.)

70. See Rubenstein, "Jewish Tradition," 11, 14; referring to *midr. Pesaḥ.* 72b; Tos'fot RiD (R. Isaiah di Trani) to *Yebam.* 12b; Feldman, *Marital Relations*, 162.

71. *B. Yebam.* 63a.

72. *B. Yebam.* 63a; cf. *Gen. Rab.* 17:3, 11d.

73. Stuhlmiller, "One Flesh," 5. Cf. Greenberg, "Jewish Tradition," 7; *b. Yebam.* 63a; *Gen. Rab.* 17; *Kohelet Rab.* 9:9; Batey, "The MIA ΣΑΡΞ Union," 272.

Leave. The first step mentioned in Gen 2:24 is the "leaving" of one's father and mother. This has been a point of dispute among ancient Jewish scholars, while they rather speak about the proselyte "leaving" his home and his parents; the question central to this matter was the determining of whom the phrase "one's father and mother" (Gen 2:24) meant.[74]

Be Joined. The divine intervention for the sake of the first marriage (Gen 2:22: God brought her to the man; Gen 2:24: the man responds by accepting and cleaving to her) led several rabbis to the conclusion that, since God completed his work on creating the earth within six days, his work ever since consists of pairing men and women to become married couples (one flesh);[75] and this work is as difficult to perform as the miracle at the Red Sea.[76] Raba (died 352), for example, held that every man has his own wife allocated by God who chooses the proper woman for a man.[77] Similarly, Rab (died 247) said that the Torah, the prophets, and the Hagiographa harmoniously prove that a man's wife comes from Yahweh.[78] He further taught that forty days before the forming of a child in its mother's womb (i.e., the time of conception), a heavenly voice goes out from heaven and speaks: The daughter of so and so is meant for so and so.[79] Nevertheless, on the human's part, "great care had to be taken in selecting a mate.... All measures of compatibility were to be considered: character, background, values, the extended family, even genetic makeup. Wealth, however, was not to be a consideration, but mutual desire was a requisite."[80]

Become One Flesh. R. Jehudah, for instance, said: "It reads further, 'and they become one flesh;' and with this the verse associates them to be equal in every respect."[81] This equality is firstly meant in respect of the human nature, not to have intercourse with an animal, for thus it is impossible to become "one body."[82] This is further elucidated

---

74. Cf. *b. Sanh.* 58a.

75. Cf. *midr. Pesiq.* 11b; *Sam.* 5:13:31b; *Gen. Rab.* 67:3; 68:43b; *Lev. Rab.* 8:110b; *Num. Rab.* 3:139d; *b. Mo'ed Qaṭ.* 18b; *Soṭah* 2a; Strack and Billerbeck, *Talmud und Midrasch*, 1:803–4; Baltensweiler, *Ehe im NT*, 50; Greenberg, "Jewish Tradition," 6.

76. See *midr. Pesiq.* 11b; *Gen. Rab.* 67:3.

77. *B. Mo'ed Qaṭ.* 18b. Cf. Lehmann, "Kirchliche Feier," 281.

78. *B. Mo'ed Qaṭ.* 18b; referring to the following interesting biblical texts: Gen 24:50: "The matter [Isaac's servant finding Rebekah] comes from the LORD." Judg 14:4: "His [i.e., Samson's] father and mother did not know that it was of the Lord." Prov 19:14: "A prudent wife is from the Lord." These texts, as well as the rabbinic interpretation thereof, are most interesting concerning Jesus argumentation against the Pharisees' lenient view of divorce.

79. *B. Soṭah* 2a; cf. *b. Mo'ed Qaṭ.* 18b; Abrahams, *Studies*, 69.

80. Greenberg, "Jewish Tradition," 5–6; referring to *b. Soṭah* 2a/*Qidd.* 41a/*Ketub.* 102b.

81. Rodkinson, *Babylonian Talmud*, Sanhedrin, 171.

82. See *b. Sanh.* 58a; *y. Qidd.* 1:58c:8; *Gen. Rab.* 18:5; cf. Barth, *Ephesians 4–6*, 727; Berger, *Gesetzesauslegung*, 532; Sampley, *One Flesh*, 55–56. Baltensweiler cites *b. Yebam.* 63a stating that "R. Eleazar hat gesagt: Was heisst, was geschrieben steht Gen 2, 23: Diese ist endlich einmal Bein von meinem Gebein und Fleisch von meinem Fleisch? Das lehrt, dass Adam allem Vieh und Wild beigewohnt hat; aber sein Sinn beruhigte sich (wurde befriedigt) erst, als er der Eva beiwohnte." Baltensweiler, *Ehe im*

by Rabbi Eleazar's comment on Gen 2:23a ("This finally is bone of my bones, and flesh of my flesh") who thought that "this teaches that Adam had intercourse with every beast and animal but found no satisfaction until he cohabited with Eve."[83] Homosexuality is likewise excluded by the phrase in Gen 2:24, for it says "he will cling to his *woman*."[84] Most interestingly for our topic is the fact that even a divorced woman is still identified as the own "flesh" of her former husband. So it is said: "'Do not withdraw from thy flesh,' said Isaiah [58:7]; this Rabbi Jacob bar Aḥa interpreted to mean 'Do not withdraw help from thy divorced wife.'"[85]

Further admonitions concerning the being of "one flesh" declare intercourse with one's own wife in an unnatural manner is worthy of the death-penalty (at least for Noachides); the natural way of sex is at the place of the woman's body, where they can represent "one body."[86] Concerning monogamy at least Judah ben Bathyra realized: "Hätten Adam, dem ersten Menschen, zehn Frauen zugestanden, so hätte Gott sie ihm gegeben. Aber Gott gab ihm nur eine Frau. So sei denn auch mir genug an der einen Frau, die mir zusteht."[87]

Generally, there was no doubt that "(to) become one flesh" (Gen 2:24) meant the sexual union and that marriage is actually consummated through sex, basically without the necessity of certain marriage procedures. Hence, in *m. Qidd.* 1:1 it is stipulated that "in three ways a woman is acquired . . . through money, writ or intercourse." Greenberg and Ilan consequently point out: "What these three methods have in common is a certain privatism for the marriage partners: a man initiates, and a woman consents. Technically, in each instance marriage can be effected in the absence of any sort of control or sanction by community."[88]

> This text [*m. Qidd.* 1:1] posits intercourse as a valid marriage form—equivalent in all aspects to the writ—which may be interpreted as the wedding contract. Rabbinic literature is elsewhere critical of this marriage form (*b. Qidd.* 12b), but in the relatively old Mishnaic tradition, it is presented as fully legitimate.[89]

NT, 36/fn.9; referring to Strack and Billerbeck, *Talmud und Midrasch*, 3:71. Barth, *Ephesians 4–6*, 727/fn.455 points to the omission of this rabbinical statement in Ginzberg, *Legends*, "perhaps because it is too preposterous to be taken seriously."

83. *B. Yebam.* 63a; cf. Batey, "The ΜΙΑ ΣΑΡΞ Union," 272.

84. *Y. Qidd.* 1:58c:8; cf. *Gen. Rab.* 18:5.

85. Cf. *Gen. Rab.* 17:3; see Amram, *Divorce*, 110; Batey, "The ΜΙΑ ΣΑΡΞ Union," 272. For some brief rabbinic opinions about the sexual act of Adam and Eve see Kvam et al., *Eve and Adam*, 89.

86. Cf. *b. Sanh.* 58b; *y. Qidd.* 1:58c:8; *Gen. Rab.* 18:5.

87. From *'Abot R. Nat.* 2 as quoted in Baltensweiler, *Ehe im NT*, 54/fn.33. Similarly, note the comment of Bruner, *Matthew*, 670–71: "If God had supremely intended solitary life, God would have created humans one by one; if God had intended polygamous life, God would have created one man and several women (Chrys., 62:1:382); if God had intended homosexual life God would have made two men or two women; but that God intended monogamous heterosexual life was shown by God's creation of one man and one woman."

88. Greenberg, "Jewish Tradition," 8.

89. Ilan, "Premarital Cohabitation," 256. For an ancient document (dated August 131 AD)

Isaksson similarly points out concerning the Mishnaic legislation that

> (1) ... A wife can be acquired by three means: by money, by a document, and by sexual intercourse (*m. Qidd.* 1:1). (2) Certain marriages, for example, leviratical marriages, were entered into simply by the man having sexual intercourse with the woman (again *m. Qidd.* 1:1). (3) If the wife committed adultery, the husband was not allowed to forgive her but was compelled to divorce her.... The husband was also forbidden to re-marry his wife after he had divorced her on the ground of her adultery. Directly the wife had intercourse with another man, her husband was forbidden to have intercourse with her. (Cf. *m. Sota* 1:2; 5:1; *Yebam.* 2:8; *Giṭ.* 4:7.) (4) When a divorced man and a divorced woman had been alone together, it was assumed that sexual intercourse had taken place and the school of Hillel therefore demanded a fresh divorce (*m. Giṭ.* 8:9). (5) The wife had a right to divorce if her husband was impotent or denied her her conjugal rights ... (*m. Ned.* 11:12; *Ketub.* 5:5–6).[90]

These facts represent the perception of consummating marriage through sexual intercourse—even completely without any sanction and official approval by the community. Correspondingly one breaks this bond through sexual relations with another partner than one's own spouse—without any official document. The same is expressed in *Gen. Rab.* 18:5 declaring the first man having sexual relations with a prostitute to be her husband thenceforth, while she having sex with another man afterwards would actually be committing adultery; and since that is even said of gentiles, we have to assume that it functioned as universal (namely Edenic) law. Therefore,

> BerR 18 [i.e., *Gen. Rab.* 18] legt Gen 2,24b.c nicht (nur) als eine Ordnung aus, auf die sich Partner und Partnerin beim Eheschluß willentlich verpflichten, sondern als eine Grundordnung, die für jeden Sexualverkehr gilt, unabhängig von der Intention von Mann und Frau, die stärker ist als von Menschen getroffene vertragliche Abmachungen.[91]

---

witnessing that a Jewish couple "officially" lived together already before their marriage contract was drawn up see the entire article ibid., 247–64. Cf. also Greenberg, "Jewish Tradition," 8 about the legitimacy of sex as an act of "acquisition" and the later rabbinic criticism of this method carrying "the taint of licentious behavior." The rabbinic intention was "to bring them more in line with community norms;" therefore "we see that control over procedures of marriage was legally shifted from parties of the first part onto the community ... ." Ibid. The same was happening to the Christian church, as will be mentioned in more detail at the end of this study.

90. Isaksson, *Marriage and Ministry*, 40–41; cf. also Kirchhoff, *Sünde*, 163–65.

91. Kirchhoff, *Sünde*, 164. This perception of being married without contract is close to the ἄγραφος γάμος, found in Greek papyri from Egypt where instances are related "of couples living together as man and wife in what is termed as 'unwritten marriage' (ἄγραφος γάμος), which was sometimes later converted by a written contract into ἔγγραφος γάμος." Lewis, *Greek Papyri*, 130; cf. Wolff, *Marriage*, 1–128; referred to in Ilan, "Premarital Cohabitation," 252, 263. "Although such a marriage was mocked by the rabbis for its leniency, it was in reality just as strict and binding as that promoted by the rabbis themselves." Ibid., 263.

Conclusions. In general, "apocryphal and intertestamental literature provide noteworthy examples of indebtedness to and interpretation of Gen 2:24."[92] Philo is more explicitly elucidating the supposed intentions and allegorical meanings of the creation account than Josephus or any of the other authors of pseudepigraphic and apocryphal literature. Both Josephus and Philo are positively bearing witness in favor of the Jewish ordinances as given in the Mosaic laws. They do not doubt the validity of any of them, even in times of strong Hellenistic and Roman influences. They also acknowledge the significance of the creational marriage ideal, although both declare that sexuality is detrimental to sound spirituality. The contradiction to the divine blessing for being "fruitful and multiply" (Gen 1:27–28) is not cleared up. The "escalating" use of Edenic typologies by Philo in his *Legum Allegoriarum* once more emphasizes the importance and special estimation of that Edenic pattern, thus corresponding to the biblical use of the marriage ideal—although, of course, differing widely in the interpretation thereof.

The few occurrences (or many omissions) of the "one flesh" union in post-canonical Jewish literature may be interpreted in a twofold manner: (1) one must clearly assert that the creational oneness is a meaningful theme; although (2) the one-flesh union is not widely and not uninhibitedly dealt with. The apocalyptic focus of these documents could reasonably explain the lack of interest in broader developing Gen 2:24 and marriage.

> All texts stress the marital relationship between Adam and Eve. Sometimes they refer to their sexual union (*Tobit*, *Jubilees*), sometimes their union is depicted as being totally asexual. In the latter case, sexuality is connected with the events that take place later in the Garden. In the *Sibylline Oracles*, sexuality starts with the curse on man and woman, although this curse is connected with a blessing.... As far as the sexual union is concerned, in the *Book of Jubilees* they have intercourse before they enter, in the *Sibylline Oracles* after they leave the Garden.[93]

It is only the author of Tobit who places the one-flesh union into paradise, but simultaneously explains that it is not meant to satisfy lust. One finds in all of these ancient sources that Gen 2:24 has consistently been interpreted as referring primarily to sexuality. Consequently, the rather "dangerous" implications are defused by embedding the plot and the sexual allusion in the explanation of the union outside of paradise,[94] or (at least) by adding some comment in regard to the "right attitude" to-

---

92. Sampley, *One Flesh*, 57.

93. Van Ruiten, "Early Jewish Literature," 61–62.

94. Similarly Ginzberg, *Legends*, 5:134/fn.134, recognized that several Jewish pseudepigraphic works (as well as quite a lot of early church fathers) "presuppose that not only the birth of the children of Adam and Eve took place after the expulsion from paradise (Gen 4: 1–2, 25), but that the first 'human pair' lived in paradise without sexual intercourse." The reason for this "sex-free" interpretation may be correctly assumed by Anderson, "Reflections," 121, who points Eden's "function as a metaphor for the world-to-come." But it should not pass unnoticed that Eden also functioned as an example of an ideal world, without any blemish—and sex more and more became such a stigma in the Hellenistic

ward (negative) sexual desire. That reminds one of the problems exegetes even nowadays encounter when interpreting Lev 15:18; and perhaps there is a close connection given. The supposed impurity attached even to lawful, conjugal intercourse (although the intention to procreate may be given), must have been evoking corresponding effects in the perception of the Edenic ideal within the creation story.

The ancient rabbis discuss the Edenic marriage ideal only briefly and demonstrate certain interpretations or perceptions that partly reappear in the short discussion of the Pharisees with Jesus. The disputes are, however, concentrating much more on legal aspects and practical considerations than on the interpretation of the theological substance of Gen 2:24 and its context.[95]

II.2 Concrete NT References to the Edenic Ideal

Keeping in mind the foregoing investigation about Jewish thinking concerning the Edenic ideal and specific perceptions about man and woman in Eden as provided by intertestamentary and contemporary Jewish literature, we may now turn to the central New Testament echoes of Gen 2:24.

While Jesus refers to the Edenic ideal in order to respond to questions about divorce, Paul applies the concept to elucidate some points of the marriage relation itself, as well as its spiritual, figurative level. Thus we have at least a small variety of contexts and purposes in which the creational ideal has been used. That should enable us to get some more and deeper insights from the usage of the Genesis text, certainly going beyond the first inquiries on marriage, sexuality, and divorce. Without giving further thoughts on content or theology beforehand, as a next step the selection of appropriate texts and their textual analysis has to be discussed. Then we might proceed to investigate the New Testament passages themselves thoroughly as intended in the following sections.

II.2.1 Jesus about Divorce (Matt 5:32; 19:3–9; Mark 10:2–12; Luke 16:18)

There are two major instances in which Jesus speaks about the creational (marriage covenant) ideal, both in response to (explicit or implicit) questions on divorce. It should be possible to draw a line between the inquiry of the Pharisees testing Jesus'

---

times of the Pseudepigrapha and the early church fathers. For Rabbinic Judaism, however, "the act of human procreation was not simply an acceptable act, it was a commanded act. It is the subject of the very first command God gives men and women [. . . Gen 1:28]. It should come as no surprise, then, that in rabbinic exegesis the Garden was the location of humankind's first sexual encounter." Ibid., 122. For more Jewish material regarding the "sexual consummation in the garden" see ibid., 123–29. It is not discussed here, because it is too far from this chapter's aims.

95. Similarly, Sampley asserts: "It is curious, in light of the variety of interpretations of Gen 2: 24 in other writings, that its usage in the Talmud is so clearly restricted to halakhic decisions." Sampley, *One Flesh*, 55.

moral attitude toward licit reasons of divorce in Matt 19:3–9 and Mark 10:2–12. The other part accordingly consists of Jesus' explanation and elucidation of the everlastingness and strict interpretation of the divine commandments in Matt 5:32 and Luke 16:18. Before starting the investigation of these Gospel accounts, a thorough scrutiny of the historical backgrounds will be helpful to comprehend better the situation presented by Matthew, Mark, and Luke. Some observations from the subsequent sections (esp. the textual analysis) will already be integrated in order to demonstrate its strong coherence.

II.2.1.1 Historical Context

First, it is important to observe that Mark 10:2–12 and Matt 19:3–9 parallel each other, being embedded in the same narrative setting, the Pharisaic inquiry. The texts of Matt 5:32 and Luke 16:18 are placed in context of discussions about the everlastingness of the law and, as such, refer with only a very short remark to the case of adultery in order to reaffirm that the seventh commandment still has its validity and everlasting legal force.[96] The most important and fundamental literary context is evidently the Edenic marriage ideal, which has already been investigated thoroughly in the first part of this treatise and in the chapter about "The Edenic Ideal in Prominent Ancient Jewish Literature." Now in this section, therefore, the extra-biblical Jewish material directly related to the Gospel passages will be investigated to grant a glance at the (probable) historical situation illuminating Jesus' discussion with the Pharisees. The wider biblical (i.e., NT) context will be skipped at this place, since it will be explored in the subsequent chapters. Some results from the following textual analysis are already presupposed in this section for the purpose of more closely connecting the historical context with the given textual features.

---

96. It is true that Luke 16:18 seems to be an "Einzelspruch in einer losen Spruchkette." Baltensweiler, *Ehe im NT*, 60; cf. pp. 79–80; Shaner, *Christian View*, 37; Gilmour, *St. Luke*, 287; nevertheless it may not be overlooked that this verse fits the surrounding context quite well and is not incidentally inserted at this place of Luke's report. Please note the following structure surrounding the statement of Luke 16:18: (1) Parable against the love of money (vv. 1–13); (2) Transitional explanation/hinge between 1 & 3 (v. 14); (3) Clarification concerning the dignity and holiness of the gospel (vv. 15–16); (4) Clarification regarding the high standards (the law) of the gospel (v. 17); (5) Clarification concerning a special, much discussed issue of the law as emphasis of the foregoing declaration (v. 18); (6) Parable on the practical obligations of the gospel (vv. 19–31). The statement concerning marriage and divorce, therefore, is intentionally given at this place and conveys a concrete purpose, especially considering the audience (Pharisees) that evidently had problems with Jesus' interpretation of marriage (Mark 10:2–12; Matt 19:3–9). The shifting to marriage in v. 18, therefore, is very reasonable (against Baltensweiler, *Ehe im NT*, 79–80).

II.2.1.1.1 The LXX as Basis of the Debate

As a supplement to the OT foundation, a table comparing the LXX Genesis texts and their echoes within the synoptics will provide an overview of the rather slight deviations.[97]

Gen 1:27; 2:24 (LXX)	Mark 10:6–8a	Matt 19:4b–5
καὶ ἐποίησεν ὁ θεὸς τὸν ἄνθρωπον κατ' εἰκόνα[98] θεοῦ ἐποίησεν αὐτόν	ἀπὸ δὲ ἀρχῆς κτίσεως	ὁ κτίσας ἀπ' ἀρχῆς
ἄρσεν καὶ θῆλυ ἐποίησεν αὐτούς	ἄρσεν καὶ θῆλυ ἐποίησεν αὐτούς ((ὁ θεός))·	ἄρσεν καὶ θῆλυ ἐποίησεν αὐτούς; ...
ἕνεκεν τούτου καταλείψει <u>ἄνθρωπος</u> τὸν πατέρα αὐτοῦ καὶ τὴν μητέρα αὐτοῦ	ἕνεκεν τούτου καταλείψει <u>ἄνθρωπος</u> τὸν πατέρα αὐτοῦ καὶ τὴν μητέρα ((αὐτοῦ))	ἕνεκα τούτου καταλείψει <u>ἄνθρωπος</u> τὸν πατέρα [–] καὶ τὴν μητέρα [–]
καὶ προσκολληθήσεται πρὸς τὴν γυναῖκα αὐτου	(καὶ προσκολληθήσεται πρὸς τὴν γυναῖκα αὐτοῦ),	καὶ (προσ-)κολληθήσεται [–] τῇ γυναικὶ αὐτου
καὶ ἔσονται <u>οἱ δύο</u> εἰς σάρκα μίαν	καὶ ἔσονται <u>οἱ δύο</u> εἰς σάρκα μίαν·	καὶ ἔσονται <u>οἱ δύο</u> εἰς σάρκα μίαν.

These three accounts are matching each other almost exactly[99] while "the differences are inconsequential."[100] The deviations in comparison to the Hebrew MT text are in accord with the LXX pattern, which uses ἄνθρωπος instead of ἀνήρ to translate the Hebrew אִישׁ and which inserts the οἱ δύο as emphasis of the monogamous ideal, where the MT is silent.[101] Loader correctly asserts that the οἱ δύο derives mainly from LXX influence, not necessarily by the intention to reemphasize monogamy in the times of

---

97. The sign [–] means a word is missing in comparison to the LXX Genesis pattern. Single round brackets mark words or phrases that perhaps belonged to the original and occur in many NT manuscripts, but which are not part of the Greek NA²⁷ text. Words in double round brackets indicate terms that are very unlikely to be authentic, but which are supported by at least some evidence. Words in italics are deviations, mostly due to the narrative flow. The underlining indicates words that are differing from the Hebrew MT text.

98. The Hebrew doubling בְּצַלְמוֹ בְּצֶלֶם ("according to his [i.e., God] image, according to the image [of God]") is not exactly rendered in the Greek LXX. There it is simplified by only reading κατ' εἰκόνα ("after the likeness/image [of God]").

99. Cf. Nolland, *Matthew*, 771, 773.

100. Davies and Allison, *Saint Matthew*, 3:11.

101. Concerning the LXX "Vorlage" note Loader's comment: *LXX, Sexuality, and NT*, 81: "The use of ἄνθρωπος ('man') in LXX instead of ἀνήρ ('male/man/husband') and the presence of οἱ δύο ('the two') will have made the link with Gen 1:27 easier and so enhanced the sense that the coming together in some way inaugurates a restored unity which corresponds to an original unity. It remains speculative whether there is some influence from the myth of the androgyny here. There is, in any case, an argument that they belong together because they originate from one. As in the LXX the focus is unity of two rather than their commonality which Hebrew achieves through its pun. Certainly the focus lies on the coming together as fulfilling God's purpose in creation. The use in the LXX of σάρξ ('flesh') also throws the emphasis strongly on the aspect of sexual union, rather than on kinship of flesh." Cf. also Berger, *Gesetzesauslegung*, 551.

the NT.[102] Teachings like those of the Qumran sect may indicate that polygamy was despised in Jesus time at least with some sectarians.[103] Also, "Jesus' justification of the doctrine of the indissolubility of marriage clearly assumes it to be self-evident that marriage is monogamous."[104] Furthermore, προσκολληθήσεται ("be joined/cleaved/united/caused to stick")[105] in this passive form, might have led the reader to understand it as true passive and not as deponent, thus pointing to God as the one who takes the initiative to pair a couple,[106] just as the rabbinic teachings (see above) confirm.[107] Thus, Jesus' conclusion in Mark 10:9 and the exactly matching reading in Matt 19:6 (ὃ οὖν ὁ θεὸς συνέζευξεν ἄνθρωπος μὴ χωριζέτω) emphasizes even more God's authority in joining the pair, while man, consequently, forces his way into the divine realm if he dares to separate what the most holy God in his wisdom has "caused to stick together."[108]

> The link between Gen 1:27 and 2:24 may have also contributed to this understanding, for it speaks of the action of God in creating male and female. Then Gen 2:24 could be heard as indicating that the oneness restores what was God's intention in creation and therefore is not to be undone, that is, uncreated.[109]

According to these considerations the active part of God in both respects "joining" and "become one flesh" is clearly emphasized in Jesus' speech of Mark 10:8b–9 and Matt 19:6, including the sexual overtones of the one flesh union.[110]

---

102. Cf. Loader, *LXX, Sexuality, and NT*, 80–81; similarly Dautzenberg, "Φεύγετε τὴν πορνείαν," 280.

103. See CD 4:20—25:2. Cf. on this interpretation (as speaking against polygamy): Winter, "Sadoquite Fragments," 78; Loader, *LXX, Sexuality, and NT*, 81; Berger, *Gesetzesauslegung*, 521, 524; Instone-Brewer, *In the Bible*, 61–65, 138; Beale and Carson, *NT Use*, 59, 198; Sanders, *Jesus and Judaism*, 258; Baltensweiler, *Ehe im NT*, 55–57; Davies and Allison, *Saint Matthew*, 3:10; Martínez, "Man and Woman," 109; Turner, *Matthew*, 459/fn.4; Luz, *Matthäus*, 3:93/fn.24. Consider also the teaching of rabbi Judah ben Bathyra (100 AD) who said that Adam got only one wife from God, not many; if it would be according to God's will, he would have given him more than Eve; therefore, a man should life monogamously (quoted in Baltensweiler, *Ehe im NT*, 54/fn.33 from 'Abot R. Nat. 2).

104. Isaksson, *Marriage and Ministry*, 126. He further explains: "On the basis of a polygamous conception of marriage it cannot be maintained that a man commits adultery by divorcing one or two of his wives and taking a third or a fourth." Ibid.

105. Cf. BDAG/LEH s.v. προσκολλάω.

106. Thus also Loader, *LXX, Sexuality, and NT*, 81; Roig, "Exegetische Studie," 185.

107. Please note also the apocryphal evidence from the book of Tobit: γάρ ἐστιν μεμερισμένη πρὸ τοῦ αἰῶνος ("for she is destined for you from eternity;" Tob. 6:18). Cf. Loader, *LXX, Sexuality, and NT*, 82/fn.11; Fitzmyer, *Advance*, 85.

108. This "sticking together" might even be a more adequate translation of the Greek (προσ-)κολλάω, since it more clearly points to the literal sense of "sticking/gluing" something together in order to create a new unit; cf. BDAG s.v. προσκολλάω; similarly Roig, "Exegetische Studie," 185.

109. Loader, *LXX, Sexuality, and NT*, 81, cf. pp. 85–86; cf. Berger, *Gesetzesauslegung*, 548. Besides, "the role which the passive form προσκολληθήσεται ("be joined") appears to have played in the argument would support a textual decision that it was part of the original and later omitted." Loader, *LXX, Sexuality, and NT*, 82.

110. Loader asserts: "That should not surprise us since the allusion is to God's creation and

There are some important developments that prevailed in Jesus' time and which further contribute to the understanding of the given discussion. First, the death penalty on adultery was about to be abolished, or was already abolished in his days.[111] Even when the Jews actually sentenced to death, they were unable to execute freely according to their own judgment, but had to persuade the Roman authorities that capital punishment would be adequate in the given case; the Jewish Sanhedrin alone was not authorized to kill the accused.[112] Hence, cases of divorce must have been more common than one may assume for the times when the Torah was just established and death would have been the proper execution on this kind of iniquity. Second, the understanding of Deut 24:1–4 was certainly influenced by the LXX translation of the Hebrew text, since the Septuagint was widely read by the Greek speaking Jews—even in Palestine, where not all the people could rightly understand the Old Testament Hebrew anymore. Third, it could even be possible that the LXX renders the translation of a Hebrew variant extant in the time of Jesus, because the fixing of the proto-Masoretic text was probably not finished until the second century CE. For these reasons it will be worthwhile to consider briefly the Septuagint rendering as a background to the accounts of Mark and Matthew.

Turning to Deut 24:1–4 in the LXX, "the complex protasis of the Hebrew of Deut 24:1–3 is retained in the LXX with minor variations. In both Hebrew and LXX, Deut 24:1–4 constitutes a single conditional sentence with 24:4 as the apodosis."[113] Hence, these "minor variations" are rather incidental, but are nevertheless somehow distinctively influential for the NT accounts of the divorce debate. A matter of influence may be a different understanding of the Greek καὶ ἔσται as "and it shall be/apply" (imperative) or "and it will be/happen/occur" (future). In either case one could interpret the instance as mandatory commandment: "Der griechische Leser muß das ἔσται also entweder jussivisch verstehen—dann liegt ein Scheidungsgebot für bestimmte Fälle

---

creativity. It does add a theological dimension to the widely held assumption in the world of the time that sexual intercourse really does create something which is much larger than the act itself or something of sheer physicality (which . . . Paul also assumes occurs even when it is contrary to divine will; 1 Cor 6:12–20). The use of the LXX helps reinforce this by the more directly sexual connotations of its language and indirectly by the passive προσκολληθήσεται ('be joined')." Loader, *LXX, Sexuality, and NT*, 82.

111. Cf. Davidson, "Divorce and Remarriage," 8–9; Davidson, *Flame*, 655 (referring to Charles, *Divorce*, 21–22); France, *Matthew*, 210–11; perhaps to be concluded from b. Sanh. 41a.

112. See the typical example of the legal proceedings as to be witnessed in Jesus' case: Matt 27:1–26 (par.). The emotive behavior given in the case of Stephanus (Acts 7:54–58) was not legal (cf. also Albright and Mann, *Matthew*, 335); they were only allowed to arrest the accused person (see e.g., Acts 9:1–2) and then prosecute him before the legal Roman authorities. Note esp. John 8:31: "So Pilate said to them, 'Take Him yourselves, and judge Him according to your law.' The Jews said to him, 'We are not permitted to put anyone to death.'" Although they judged according to their own law that he would have to die, they were not allowed to execute him.

113. Loader, *LXX, Sexuality, and NT*, 71; cf. Wevers, *Greek Text*, 377; Berger, *Gesetzesauslegung*, 513.

vor, oder mindestens futurisch—dann sieht er darin eine sichere Erwartung, wird also mindestens daraus schließen können, daß Ehescheidung positiv erlaubt ist."[114]

Thus Deut 24:1 became a concrete divorce law mandatorily commanding divorce in cases of ἄσχημον πρᾶγμα (i.e., עֶרְוַת דָּבָר).[115] That obviously is the case in Matt 19:7 ("Why then did Moses *command*"), and is further supported by Mishnaic evidence for the understanding of Hebrew כָּתַב as "he shall write" (cf. *m. Soṭah* 4:1–5).[116] However, "such a construction would be difficult, because one would expect an indication of a new protasis in 24:2,"[117] and not just a continuation of the foregoing prerequisites for the final prohibition in v. 4. Jesus, however, "will never *require* divorce, even in the case of marital unfaithfulness. Thus Jesus' overall approach to divorce and remarriage is even more conservative than any of the Jewish parties in his day."[118]

II.2.1.1.2 Josephus and Philo about Divorce

From the life of Josephus we may catch a brief statement of his putative perception of the licit reason to divorce, the עֶרְוַת דָּבָר or ἄσχημον πρᾶγμα as interpreted in his own life. Josephus himself has been divorced three times and married four times.[119] He separated from his second wife without mentioning any reason. The third wife he divorced because he was "not pleased with her behavior" (τὴν γυναῖκα μὴ ἀρεσκόμενος αὐτῆς τοῖς ἤθεσιν; *Vita* 426). His next wife, to the contrary, had a character that "excelled many women, as her subsequent life demonstrated" (ἤθει πολλῶν γυναικῶν διαφέρουσαν ὡς ὁ μετὰ ταῦτα βίος αὐτῆς ἀπέδειξεν; *Vita* 427). Evidently, for him the ἦθος of a woman was crucial and the corruption of which was reason enough to divorce her, even though she was the mother of three children (*Vita* 426). However, at another place he outlines his own view of Deut 24:1–4 and clearly explains that, "one who wishes for whatever reason—and many such arise among human beings—to be divorced from a woman who is living with him, let him confirm in writing that he will never cohabit with her . . . ." (*A.J.* 4:253.) This "for *whatever* reason" (καθ' ἀσδηποτοῦν

---

114. Berger, *Gesetzesauslegung*, 514.

115. Loader, *LXX, Sexuality, and NT*, 71–72, 80, 84; cf. Berger, *Gesetzesauslegung*, 513–14; similarly *A.J.* 4:253 ("let him"). Berger explains: "Das ἐνετείλατο in Mk 10,4 [i.e., v. 3] ist vom griechischen Text her durchaus zu rechtfertigen. Auch im LXX-Text beginnt die eigentliche Vorschrift erst mit V. 4 (οὐ δυνήσεται), aber durch καὶ γράψει wird eine Zwischenbestimmung eingefügt.—Freilich kann man auch aus dem hebräischen Text ein eigenständiges Gebot herauslesen, wenn man diesen Satz isoliert sieht; er würde dann dem im Dt üblichen Aufbau folgen: והיה + כי + Nebensatz + Waw + Verb im Hauptsatz. Allein—aus dem Zusammenhang des MT ist dies nicht zu rechtfertigen." Ibid., 514.

116. Cf. Instone-Brewer, "Jewish Divorce Certificate," 235/fn.25; Rodkinson, *Babylonian Talmud*, Hagiga, 6.

117. Loader, *LXX, Sexuality, and NT*, 72.

118. Beale and Carson, *NT Use*, 59; italics given.

119. His first wife he lost in Jerusalem during the siege (cf. *B.J.* 5:419), so it is no divorce in a juridical sense. The second wife he took on command of Vespasianus, but she soon left him. *Vita* 415. His third and fourth wives are now described in *Vita* 426–27.

αἰτίας; *A.J.* 4:253) seems to reflect the same perception demonstrated in Matt 19:3 ("for *every* reason"—κατὰ πᾶσαν αἰτίαν) and possibly indicates the prevailing legal understanding of the special Deuteronomic case law in the New Testament times.

Concerning Philo, we do not know whether Philo himself was married and how he possibly dealt with divorce in his own life,[120] but there is at least a short treatment of the brief instruction about a divorced woman in his writings. In *Spec.* 3:30–31 he interprets the law of Deut 24:1–4 and states:

> Another commandment is that if a woman after partaking from her husband for any cause whatever marries another and then again becomes a widow, whether this second husband is alive or dead, she must not return to her first husband but ally herself with any other rather than him, because she has broken with the rules that bound her in the past and cast them into oblivion when she chose new love-ties in preference to the old. And if a man is willing to contract himself with such a woman, he must be saddled with a character for degeneracy and loss of manhood. He has eliminated from his soul the hatred of evil, that emotion by which our life is so well served and the affairs of houses and cities are conducted as they should be, and has lightly taken upon him the stamp of two heinous crimes, adultery and pandering. For such subsequent reconciliations are proofs of both. The proper punishment for him is death and for the woman also.

Philo literally speaks of "any pretense/pretext happening" (καθ' ἣν ἂν τύχῃ πρόφασιν),[121] thus possibly slightly insinuating that the cause for a divorce may actually (and perhaps frequently?) not be significant enough to release a woman.[122] However, in the subsequent argumentation he seemingly accepts the reason as of sufficient weight—or he perceives the remarriage consequently as violation of the seventh law—and therefore proceeds to accuse the woman as the instrument of iniquity, being adulterously violating her first marriage bond; at least by having relations with a new husband. The blaming of having "broken with the rules that bound her in the past and cast them into oblivion when she chose new love-ties in preference to the old" indicates that she finally is somehow guilty of leaving her husband and finding a new one.[123]

---

120. See Gehring, *Religionsparteien*, 314–20 on the few biographical backgrounds we know about Philo; cf. on more general aspects e.g., Williamson, *Philo*, 1–314.

121. Cf. LSJ/BDAG s.v. πρόφασις.

122. Beale and Carson, *NT Use*, 196, referring to the law of Deut 24:1–4 in general, further notes: "It does, however, raise the question of how serious this displeasure could have been if he then remarries her. In any case, there is nothing to suggest that the grounds of the divorce are improper, since no financial restitution is involved." Amram, *Divorce*, 34 understands the Philonic phrase "under any pretence whatever" as prescriptive, not descriptive, and thus concludes that "Philo held, the wife could be divorced by the husband at his will, and his right to divorce her did not depend upon the Deuteronomic Law, but was an ancient customary right." That obviously is much more than the text in Philo actually says and could (as suggested above) be understood right to the contrary.

123. Berger suggests that Philo—similar to Jesus' interpretation—virtually understands the certificate of divorce as of no value when judging remarriage as adultery: "Wenn also trotz des Scheidbriefes

Hence, it is the former husband who can be accused of being bare of "that disposition which hates iniquity" if he considers taking her back again.

Compared to the conclusions we drew from the gospels' reports, Philo and Josephus are more lenient compared to Jesus' interpretation of Deut 24:1–4. They rather support the Pharisees' perception—although, however, at least in the case of Philo this is only partly true, since he also alludes to a stricter view when interpreting Deut 22:13–15 with its assembly of the elders to judge about the desired divorce as a precaution against too thoughtless divorces.[124] Therefore, it seems correct to assume that Philo's "for any cause whatever" must rather be understood "as meaning for whatever reason within the parameters of allowable grounds."[125]

II.2.1.1.3 Rabbinic Teachings on Divorce

Generally, the rabbinic material tells much more about why and how to divorce, when and how to remarry etc. than the Old Testament does. First, there is the tractate *Giṭṭin* dealing with the bill of divorce. In additional, there are some more instructions within the other sections of the Seder about "women" (*Našim*). I will give a brief summary on issues that may be interesting in order to catch the "atmosphere" regarding divorce that possibly prevailed in the time the Pharisees brought up the discussion with Jesus.[126]

The two most influential Pharisaic schools of Hillel and Shammai were disputing about the interpretation of the עֶרְוַת דָּבָר in Deut 24:1. The founders of these schools most likely lived shortly before and within the Herodian era and their teachings were well known among Palestine Jews, especially Pharisees, of Jesus' time. No other Pharisaic or later Rabbinic school was more influential than these two streams of tradition.[127] Therefore, it is fully justified to presume that the most important background for the halakhic discussion about the legal reasons for divorce is to be found in the rabbinic doctrines of this early, Tannaitic stratum; "ein Großteil der bezüglich des Neuen Tes-

---

die Ehe noch besteht, ist die Entlassung der Frau Veranlassung zum Ehebruch." Berger, *Gesetzesauslegung*, 519–20; cf. Heinemann, *Bildung*, 318–19. Yet, Philo is not clear whether the "having violated her former ties which she forgot, and having chosen new allurements in the place of the old ones" refers to some incident (namely adultery) leading to divorce, or if he thus refers to the remarriage.

124. Similarly Sigal, *Halakhah*, 132.

125. Sigal, *Halakhah*, 135.

126. Yet, as already mentioned above, it has to be considered that even the earliest rabbinic material is not older than the second century AD and the Tannaitic stratum therein, which is regarded as going back beyond the destruction of the temple in 70 AD, is not easily identified and interpreted. Some mainstreams of ancient discussions, however, may be regarded as reaching back into the NT time. Further, "in certain cases the verbal agreement between the form in which a general command or counsel, a gnomic saying or exhortatory observation, spoken by Jesus, is expressed in the Gospels, and paradigmatic statements found here and there in late Jewish literature is so striking that it is far from unreasonable to assume the existence of common sources." Winter, "Sadoqite Fragments," 71.

127. See e.g., Neusner's table on the amount of pericopes derived from the schools of Hillel and Shammai. Neusner, "Rabbinic Traditions," 299.

taments aufgeworfenen Probleme erhält, was die Position Jesu und die seiner Gegner betrifft, von hier sein spezifisches Gepräge."[128] Thus "the question the Pharisees raise clearly reflects the intra-Pharisaic debate between the proto-rabbis Shammai and Hillel."[129] However, even though the influential teachers Shammai and Hillel lived earlier than Jesus, the subsequent development of further traditions is not easily dated and has to be considered with reservations as to the concrete time of their emergence.

Reasons for Divorce. The well known debate referred to above between the schools of Shammai and Hillel (and R. Aqiba) about the admissible reasons that allowed a man to release his wife is rendered in the Mishnah as follows:

> The house of Shammai say, "A man should divorce his wife only because he has found grounds for it in unchastity, since it is said, *Because he has found in her indecency in anything* (Deut 24:1)." And the house of Hillel say, "Even if she spoiled his dish, since it is said, *Because he has found in her indecency in anything.*" R. Aqiba says, "Even if he found someone else prettier than she, since it is said, *And it shall be if she find no favor in his eyes* (Deut 24:1)." (*M. Giṭ.* 9:10.)[130]

These views must have been prominent not only among the Pharisees, but also among the rest of the Jewish people of Jesus time. So we learn that Gamaliel I., the famous student and successor of the great Hillel, has been largely respected by all the people (Acts 5:34) and he is directly confronted with the early Christian "sect" (cf. Acts 5:34–39). Since the debate about admissible reasons was primarily a school-intern discussion, at least the secondary intention might have been to identify the halakhic position of Jesus, whether he would tend to one of the inner-Pharisaic positions, either Shammai or Hillel,[131] while Rabbi Aqiba later developed the doctrine of Hillel further. Both Hillel and Rabbi Aqiba considered עֶרְוַת and דָּבָר as two individual reasons for divorce and thus reasoned that a wife is to be released for any reason whatever, may it be for the reason

---

128. Neudecker, "Ehescheidungsgesetz," 384–85; cf. Strack and Billerbeck, *Talmud und Midrasch*, 1:303–21; Turner, *Matthew*, 460–61; Kirchschläger, *Ehe im NT*, 56; Isaksson, *Marriage and Ministry*, 122; Ryrie, "Biblical Teaching," 183; Kaye, "One Flesh," 51; Instone-Brewer, *In the Bible*, 134.

129. Blomberg, "Exegesis," 164.

130. *M. Giṭ.* 9:10; Italics given. Besides, infertility would be an appropriate reason to divorce (see *m. Giṭ.* 8:6–7; *b. Yebam.* 64a; or even more *m. Yebam.* 6:5: an infertile woman regarded as "whore"). Just like Philo and Josephus repeatedly emphasize, the offspring is the chief goal of any marriage. Therefore infertility is a distinctive blemish that also functioned as an important and legal reason for divorce; cf. Craigie, *Deuteronomy*, 304–5; Loader, *LXX, Sexuality, and NT*, 75; Baltensweiler, *Ehe im NT*, 39; Abrahams, *Studies*, 77. Concerning the "spoiling of his dishes" as legal reason for divorce notice: "Wir dürfen nicht vergessen, dass das Kochen zu den obersten Pflichten einer Ehefrau gehörte. Im Anbrennenlassen der Speisen kommt nicht so sehr die Unfähigkeit der Frau zum Ausdruck, als vielmehr ihre absichtliche Missachtung des Mannes. So konnte die Frau also gleichsam «passiven Widerstand» leisten." Baltensweiler, *Ehe im NT*, 38.

131. These inner-Pharisaic controversies and the effort to become acquainted with Jesus' position regarding the controversial points is to be seen also in further instances of the NT reports; cf. Gehring, *Religionsparteien*, 533–38.

of דָּבָר ("anything"), or for the reason of עֶרְוַת ("shame/nakedness").¹³² While Shammai's focus was on the עֶרְוַת and as such did not sanction "any matter" divorces, "the Hillelite 'any matter' divorce very quickly became the most common procedure"¹³³ and "was also considered to be the most righteous form."¹³⁴ The עֶרְוַת as legal basis to divorce was understood as illicit sexual relation or, in a wider sense, as anything that violated given customs and moral standards (*m. Ketub.* 7:6), namely:

> [Concerning the Mosaic laws:] If she gives him something to eat that is not tithed, if she lies with him during her menses, if she does not separate the dough, or violates an oath. [. . . Concerning Jewish customs:] If she goes out with her hair uncovered, if she is spinning on the street or talking with everyone. Abba Scha'ul says: Also if she insults her begetter in his presence. R. Tarfon says: Even a loudly crying woman. (And what is a loudly crying woman? She is one who speaks in her house and her neighbors hear her talking.) (*M. Ketub.* 7:6.)

> A woman eating on the street, gulping down something to drink on the street, breastfeeding [her child] on the street, then she shall be divorced, as R. Meir [around 150] said of these. (*B. Giṭ.* 89a.)

> That is a godless man, who sees his wife going out with uncovered hair, and how her heart is jolly with her slaves and neighbors, and how she is spinning on the street and bathing with men. To release this one [by divorce] is required by law. (*T. Soṭah* 5:9.)¹³⁵

Further reasons could be the damaging of the husband's reputation ("anything offensive to the husband"¹³⁶), not honoring the husband, seemingly possessing a "bad character," infertility, when the wife becomes mentally incapacitated, or the case that the marriage was consummated under certain requirements and the wife is not able to meet them.¹³⁷ If the husband's job or his illness incurs unreasonable adverseness,

---

132. Cf. s. Deut. 24:1; Strack and Billerbeck, *Talmud und Midrasch*, 1:314–15; Instone-Brewer, "What God has Joined," 28: "The Hillelite rabbis wondered why Moses had added the word 'thing' or 'cause' when he only needed to use the word 'immorality.' They decided this extra word implied another ground for divorce—divorce for 'a cause.' They argued that anything, including a burnt meal or wrinkles not there when you married your wife, could be a cause! The text, they said, taught that divorce was allowed both for adultery and for 'any cause.'"

133. Beale and Carson, *NT Use*, 196; cf. Instone-Brewer, "What God has Joined," 28: ". . . a few decades before Jesus, some rabbis (the Hillelites) had invented a new form of divorce called the 'any cause' divorce. By the time of Jesus, this 'any cause' divorce had become so popular that almost no one relied on the literal Old Testament grounds for divorce."

134. Instone-Brewer, *In the Bible*, 115; on the different reasons see ibid., 85–132, on the "any matter" divorces esp. pp. 110–17. It is strange, however, that it is Hillel who formulated with such a harshness, for he "was a teacher noted for his tender humaneness." Abrahams, *Studies*, 71. Yet, he "gave the husband the legal right to divorce his wife for any cause," even though he might be understood as using a metaphor (cf. ibid.).

135. Cf. *y. Soṭah* 1:17a:32; *b. Giṭ.* 90a.

136. Amram, *Divorce*, 33.

137. See *m. Ketub.* 7:7; *t. Ketub.* 7:4; *y. Ketub.* 11:34b:52; *Yebam.* 63b (the law requires to separate

the wife has to be divorced or may herself demand to be released (cf. *m. Ketub.* 7:9–10).¹³⁸ Also, impotence, domestic violence, or apostasy of the Israelite husband could represent sufficient grounds for the woman to demand divorce.¹³⁹ Additionally there are some instances about oaths that a man could demand from his wife, but which would degrade her. In order to protect the wives against these bad vows, the Mishnah required the man to release her with her dowry.¹⁴⁰ "Das Ganze macht aber durchaus den Eindruck, als ob es sich schließlich nur um einen Kniff der Männerwelt gehandelt habe, auf diese Weise ein bequemes Ehescheidungsmittel in die Hand zu bekommen."¹⁴¹ Finally, at least in Talmudic times, any divorce was valid; even if it later turned out that the divorce was performed on a false and actually invalid basis—without entailing a penalty (cf. *b. Giṭ.* 90a).¹⁴²

Just as a short note, there is a big problem hidden in the perceptions of the above mentioned עֶרְוַת, as well as in the more lenient attitude of Hillel and Aqiba permitting divorce practically for any reason (דְּבָר). Considering Deut 22:13–19, there is a severe punishment given on falsely blaming a virgin of not being decent.¹⁴³ The amount the accuser had to pay in order to redeem his bad accusation was enormous (v. 19: 100 shekels of silver; cf. v. 29 on rape: "only" 50 shekels of silver!). Consequently, if the practices of R. Hillel or Aqiba would have been acceptable to Yahweh, no man would ever had to argue that his bride was no virgin, for the risk he thereby ran would have

---

a bad wife, for Prov 22:10 tells: "Drive out the scoffer, and contention will go out, even strife and dishonor will cease."); *Gen. Rab.* 17:11d; *Lev. Rab.* 34:131d. Cf. Strack and Billerbeck, *Talmud und Midrasch*, 1:316–18; Rubenstein, "Jewish Tradition," 8. Note also Sir. 25:25–26: "Give the water no passage; neither a wicked woman liberty to gad abroad. If she go not as thou wouldest have her, cut her off from thy flesh, and give her a bill of divorce, and let her go" (KJV). Concerning infertility "A Boraitha states that if a couple have lived together for ten years and no children are born to them, the husband ought to give his wife a Bill of Divorce, for the object of marriage has been defeated [*b. Yebam.* 64a], and Mark Samuel held that the Court will compel him to divorce her [*b. Ketub.* 77a]. His opinion prevailed, although this practice soon fell into abeyance. The Rabbis continued to urge divorce in such cases, but did not compel the couple to separate if they preferred to dwell together as man and wife in spite of the childlessness of their union." Amram, *Divorce*, 99. See on infertility also Instone-Brewer, *In the Bible*, 91–93; on insanity also Abrahams, *Studies*, 75–76.

138. Cf. also *t. Ketub.* 7:11; *y. Ketub.* 7:31d:22; *b. Ketub.* 77a; Baltensweiler, *Ehe im NT*, 37; Amram, *Divorce*, 54–62. See as well Instone-Brewer, *In the Bible*, 85–90 for women's rights to divorce.

139. See on these further reasons Amram, *Divorce*, 63–77.

140. Cf. *m. Ketub.* 5:5; 7:1–5; *t. Ketub.* 7:1–6.

141. Strack and Billerbeck, *Talmud und Midrasch*, 1:318.

142. "Rabha, a distinguished Babylonian Amora (299–352 CE), on being asked whether a man may divorce his wife if he finds her guilty neither of unchastity nor of any other objectionable conduct, answered, 'Where a man has violated a virgin the Torah forbids him to divorce her; and if he does so he will be compelled to take her back again; but in the case about which you inquire, whatever the husband has done, is done.' If he divorces her without cause he cannot be compelled to take her back again.' 'But,' continues Rabha in answer to a further question, 'if his wife is living under his roof and he is harboring designs against her to divorce her (though he may exercise his right under the law), read, of him, the words of Scripture, "Devise not evil against thy neighbor, seeing he dwelleth securely by thee."' [Prov 3:29]." Amram, *Divorce*, 38, citing *b. Giṭ.* 90a.

143. And additionally, as Ryrie, "Biblical Teaching," 179 notes, on hatred as reason of divorce.

been too serious and certainly too expensive. It just would have been sufficient for him to blame her for spoiling the dishes or for being not attractive enough in order to divorce her without any payment and penalty. So the actual reason for divorce rather must have been something else, something indeed referring to עֶרְוַה; thus being comparable to the accusation put forward in Deut 22:13–19, which—most interestingly—provides a concrete reason for divorce (in case of the death penalty of Deut 22:20–21 not being executed) that generally is overlooked in discussions about the עֶרְוַת דָּבָר of Deut 24:1, although being placed within the immediate, preceding context.

How to Divorce. There are several instructions given in the Mishnah about the way the bill of divorce had to be written and transmitted (see *m. Giṭ.* 1:1—8:4).[144] To sum up briefly, there were three steps to be taken:

> (1) A legal document was prepared. A man's complaint must be clearly stated. This required him to thus indirectly affirm that his wife was not adulterous.... This was rough on the male pride and placed a check on irresponsible charges against his wife. (2) It was delivered to her (an emancipation proclamation). This was done formally, with witnesses, so that her freedom could not be contested. She could go and become another man's property and her place in society was secured. (3) She was released with appropriate provisions to reach her father's house in safety. (Gen 21:14; Deut 15:13.) This probably also involved his loss of her dowry.[145]

The bill of divorce would look as follows, at least the Maimonides form of medieval Judaism (ca. 1013–1103):

> On the ... day of the week and ... day of the month of ... in the year ... since the creation of the world (or of the era of the Seleucidae), the era according to which we are accustomed to reckon in this place, to wit, the town of ... do I ... the son of ... of the town of ... (and by whatever other name or surname I or my father may be known, and my town and his town) thus determine, being of sound mind and under no constraint; and I do release and send away and put aside thee ... daughter of ... of the town of ... (and by whatever other name or surname thou and thy father are known, and thy town and his town), who hast been my wife from time past hitherto; and hereby I do release thee and send thee away and put thee aside that thou mayest have permission

---

144. On matters like the material of the certificate, who was to write and how to transmit etc. see Strack and Billerbeck, *Talmud und Midrasch*, 1:303–11; Amram, *Divorce*, 142–55, 171–91. On the concrete divorce proceedings (comprising 101 steps!) notice especially ibid., 192–204.

145. Nies, "Divorce and Remarriage," 2:2. The later developments were not for the good of the divorced wife. While the bill of divorce initially protected the woman not to be charged of adultery when taking a new husband, it more and more became a stigma: "Through male rationalizations it came to be thought that a woman had to be corrupt if a man could not life with her. Thus, the bill of divorce lost its social thrust in improving a woman's lot in the marital enterprise and became a license for a husband to dump his wife at his whim." Ibid.

and control over thyself to go to be married to any man whom thou desirest, and no man shall hinder thee (in my name) from this day forever. And thou art permitted (to be married) to any man. And these presents shall be unto thee from me a bill of dismissal, a document of release and a letter of freedom according to the law of Moses and Israel.

... the son of ... a witness

... the son of ... a witness.[146]

As soon as the woman received this bill, she was released and the man was henceforth not able to annul it (*m. Giṭ.* 4:1; cf. also 8:1). However, there is an exception regarding the mental state in which the bill was written.[147] Furthermore, it is interesting to witness that it is not possible for a man to divorce his wife and to additionally prohibit her to marry some other special person (*m. Giṭ.* 9:1). Thus, the power of the husband over his (former) wife ceased with the signing and delivering of the document. The woman probably was subject to her parents again, but she generally has been free to marry whomsoever she desired: "The Mishnah, which unlike the Old Testament certainly does legislate directly for divorce, says: 'The essential formular in the bill of divorce is: 'Lo, thou art free to marry any man'" (*m. Giṭ.* 9.3)."[148] The act was publicly made known or approved by witnesses, so anyone could know that she from now on was allowed to remarry as she wished: "The 'note of separation,' or 'note of cutting,' completely dissolved the marriage."[149] There were no legal rights or claims of her former husband in relation to her anymore. Nevertheless, "her privilege ... was not entirely unrestricted, her [re-] marriage to certain persons being forbidden by law,"[150] as the next paragraph will demonstrate.

Remarriage. It was usual to remarry after divorce, for

> der Jude, der sich von seiner Frau scheidet, sucht nicht in erster Linie die Freiheit vom Ehejoch. Das wäre modern gedacht. Sondern er will die Ehe. Ehe ist ja für den Gottesfürchtigen ein Pflichtgebot.... Normalerweise denkt jeder, der seine Ehe auflöst, automatisch an Wiederverheiratung.[151]

---

146. Thus given in Amram, *Divorce*, 157–58, referring to *m. Giṭ.* 3:2; 4:2; 8:5; 9:1, 3–5, 7–8; *m. Yad.* 4:8; *Yebam.* 3:8; 14:1. Similarly exemplified (in German) by Strack and Billerbeck, *Talmud und Midrasch*, 1:311–12.

147. Cf. *m. Giṭ.* 7:1. Concerning the mental state when dealing with women in general note *m. Nid.* 6:14: "Said R. Joshua, 'before you repair the affairs of the foolish women, repair those of the intelligent ones.'" Obviously there is a discrimination given that applies to more than just divorce.

148. Cornes, *Divorce and Remarriage*, 134; cf. Amram, *Divorce*, 106; Instone-Brewer, *In the Bible*, 118–21.

149. Nichol and Andreasen, *ABC*, Deut 24:2, 1:1037. Davidson emphasizes the clarity and protective elements of the bill of divorce, declaring with Instone-Brewer that "there is no equivalent to the divorce certificate in any ancient Near Eastern culture outside Judaism." Davidson, *Flame*, 392–94; citation on p. 393; Instone-Brewer, *In the Bible*, 32.

150. Amram, *Divorce*, 106–7.

151. Baltensweiler, *Ehe im NT*, 62. Similarly Isaksson, *Marriage and Ministry*, 107: According to

Correspondingly, the many situations and cases of divorce had to be regulated. The Mishnaic legislation knows a kind of "doubtful engagement" and of "doubtful divorce" that impugned the right to (re-)marry freely.[152] Also, if a man remarried his former wife he generally had to divorce her and a child would be a bastard (*m. Yebam.* 4:12.).[153] But there are even some special regulations about situations in which it would be possible to remarry one's former wife:

> [If] he (1) gave her a writ of divorce and (2) then took her back, [if] then she (3) exercised the right of refusal against him and (4) married someone else and (5) was widowed or divorced—she is permitted to go back to him. [If] she (3) exercised the right of refusal and (2) he took her back, [if] he [then] gave (1) her a writ of divorce and she (4) married someone else and (5) was widowed or divorced, she is prohibited from going back to him. This is the general rule: In a case of a writ of divorce following the exercise of the right of refusal, she is prohibited from returning to him. In a case of exercise of the right of refusal after a writ of divorce, she is permitted to go back to him.
>
> She who exercises the right of refusal against a man [1] and was remarried to another, who divorced her [2]—[and who went and was assigned to yet] a third man, and she exercised the right of refusal against him, [and who went and was assigned to yet] a fourth, who divorced her, [and who went and was assigned to yet] a fifth, and she exercised the right of refusal against him—any of the men from whom she went forth with a writ of divorce—she is prohibited from going back to him. [And any of the men from whom she went forth] by exercising the right of refusal—she is permitted to go back to him.[154]

Particularly concerning Jesus saying about remarriage in Matt 5:32, it is interesting to note that according to the rabbinic tradition of *m. Soṭah* 5:1 the wife is not allowed to marry her lover with whom she committed adultery and betrayed her (former) husband.[155] Also, she is generally prohibited of marrying the messenger deliver-

---

"the contemporary Jewish concept ... a man was bound to marry and beget children. The requirement that a man should marry was indeed not a binding *halakah* at this period but a *derek eres*, a custom which should be followed [*m. Yebam.* 6:6]. And according to the O.T. (Ex. 21.10) and the Mishnah (*Ketub.* 5.5–6) husband and wife are bound by a command to have sexual intercourse." See also Strack and Billerbeck, *Talmud und Midrasch*, 2:372–73; Instone-Brewer, *In the Bible*, 117.

152. See *m. Yebam.* 3:8: "What is the case of doubt concerning betrothal? [If] he threw her a token of betrothal—it is a matter of doubt whether it landed nearer to him or to her—this is a case in which there is doubt concerning betrothal. And a case of doubt concerning a writ of divorce? [If] one wrote the writ of divorce in his own hand, but there are no witnesses to attest the document—[if] there are witnesses to attest the document, but it is not dated—[if] it is dated, but it [contains the attestation of] only a single witness—this is a case in which the divorce is subject to doubt." There are also some special instructions on how to prove the death of one's spouse in order to be allowed to marry a second time; cf. *m. Yebam.* 15:1—16:7. On "divorces coupled with conditions" cf. also Amram, *Divorce*, 165–70.

153. For further comments on when a child is a bastard also: *m. Qidd.* 3:12–13; 4:8.

154. *M. Yebam.* 13:4–5. On some further directions concerning the possibility to take the previous wife back again see also: *m. Giṭ.* 4:7–8; on reconciliation cf. also Amram, *Divorce*, 78–88.

155. Cf. *m. Yebam.* 2:8; Instone-Brewer, *In the Bible*, 121; Amram, *Divorce*, 107 adds: "At Jewish

ing the bill of divorce,[156] to marry a priest (cf. Lev 21:7), or to remarry within three months.[157] Further it is recommended for a man not to marry a divorced woman, at least not a divorcee from the neighborhood.[158] And in *b. Giṭ.* 90b Rabbi Meïr (about 150 AD) teaches: "He who marries her that is divorced from her husband because of her evil conduct [i.e., the "unseemly thing" (עֶרְוַת דָּבָר; Deut 24:1) of her going out with her hair unfastened and spin cloth in the street with her armpits uncovered and bathe with the men, or just bathing in the same place as the men], is worthy of death; for he has taken a wicked woman into his house."[159] Yet, "the moral law, which always sought to inculcate principles of righteousness, recommended the gentle treatment of the divorced woman, and especially praised him who supported and comforted her."[160]

Adultery. The rabbis' understanding of "adultery" is apparent from their interpretation of the seventh commandment ("You shall not commit adultery") and the death-penalty on adultery in Lev 20:10. The Sifra on Lev 20:10, for instance, teaches that the law applies to "a man" (אִישׁ) and the wife of another "man"—therefore minors (i.e., a boy under the age of nine years and a day) are not to be considered, as well as the wife that is not married to an Israelite man.[161] If these conditions are given, it does not matter whether it is the woman or the man who commits adultery, but the sinner has to be "found lying" (Deut 22:22) by two or three witnesses (cf. Deut 17:6; 19:15).[162] It

---

law the mere suspicion of adultery was enough to prevent the marriage."

156. *M. Yebam.* 2:9. Notice the explanation of Amram, *Divorce*, 107–8: "Inasmuch as the validity of the divorce depended upon his testimony alone, which was accepted in lieu of the usual proof by two witnesses, there was a strong temptation for him, if he felt so inclined, to forge a Get [i.e., the bill of divorce] in the absence of the husband, and by making the statement that it was written and attested before him, divorce her, and then marry her himself." Similarly, she is not allowed to marry the judge who initiated her divorce due to his legal validation of her oath. *M. Yebam.* 2:10. "The reason in these cases was to prevent falsehood and self-interest from vitiating the acts of the parties; but if the circumstances were such that the reason no longer existed, the prohibition against such re-marriage was removed. So that where more than one messenger brought the Get, or a court of three judges sustained the vows of the woman, anyone of the messengers or of the judges could marry her after she had been divorced." Ibid., 108.

157. Cf. *m. Yebam.* 4:10; this period of three months is meant to ascertain the paternity if it turns out that the woman is pregnant.

158. Cf. *s. Deut.* 24:2; *b. Giṭ.* 90b; *Pesaḥ.* 112a; *t. Soṭah* 5:9.

159. Cf. Amram, *Divorce*, 38. On further regulations concerning reconciliation and remarriage see ibid., 78–88.

160. Amram, *Divorce*, 110.

161. See *s. Lev.* 20:10 (368a); Rodkinson states: *Babylonian Talmud*, Sanhedrin, 160: "The rabbis taught: It reads [Lev 20.10]: 'And if there be a man'—'man' means to exclude a minor, 'Who committeth adultery with a man's wife'—'man's wife' means to exclude the wife of a minor (whose marriage is not considered). 'With his neighbor's wife' means to exclude those people who live with their wives in common." Cf. Kirchschläger, *Ehe im NT*, 67. On the age to be regarded as adult see *m. Nid.* 5:6 (boys at the age of 13, girls with 12 years). But in matters of sexuality the age could be lower: *m. Nid.* 5:4; *Yebam.* 10:6; *b. Sanh.* 55b: Boys could marry by sexual intercourse at age nine, girls even at age three!

162. See *s. Lev.* 20:10; *Deut.* 22:22; see on further details Strack and Billerbeck, *Talmud und Midrasch*, 1:296.

is to be recognized further that "the old Synagogue" understood "adultery" as given only if a married or betrothed person was involved; sexual intercourse with a single person was not "adultery" but "harlotry."[163]

Finally, it goes unpunished to have extra-marital sexual intercourse (1) with a wife or a betrothed woman of a gentile, (2) with a Jewish minor who is younger than 9 years and a day, (3) if the "adulterer" himself is a minor (younger than 12 for girls and than 13 for boys), or (4) if no witnesses are present to testify the adulterous act committed after receiving a first warning.[164] While a woman was called an "adulteress" when the foregoing conditions applied and even if she was thinking of another man while having sexual relations with her own husband,[165] a man was not necessarily an "adulterer" in these cases, for he could acquire more than one wife to live with them in polygamy; and that took place, for example, by sexual intercourse (*m. Qidd.* 1:1) with another unbetrothed, unmarried Jewish woman who must have been at the age of at least 3 years and a day (*m. Nid.* 5:4).[166] If according to these definitions "adultery" occurred, "Jewish law *required* divorce in the case of adultery (*m. Yebam.* 2:8; *m. Sota* 5:1), whereas Jesus only permits it."[167]

Conclusions. Finally, to sum up particularly concerning the rabbinic teachings on the admissible reasons to divorce, we may conclude that, at least in the Mishnaic period, there was no marriage, "die nicht kurzerhand vom Manne in völlig legaler Weise durch Aushandigung eines Scheidebriefes hätte gelöst werden können. Und daß es später nicht anders gewesen ist, beweist *Giṭ* 90a."[168] That is exactly the center

---

163. Strack and Billerbeck, *Talmud und Midrasch*, 1:297.

164. Cf. Strack and Billerbeck, *Talmud und Midrasch*, 1:297.

165. See on this Baltensweiler, *Ehe im NT*, 115–16: "Instruktiv ist ein Passus, der folgendermaßen lautet: Unsere Lehrer haben gesagt: Wenn eine Frau mit ihrem Ehemann allein ist und er wohnt ihr bei, und sie richtet ihr Auge auf einen andern während des Beiwohnens, so gibt es für sie keinen Ehebruch, der grösser wäre als dieser . . . ." Cf. Strack and Billerbeck, *Talmud und Midrasch*, 1:301.

166. Strack and Billerbeck, *Talmud und Midrasch*, 1:297; cf. Ilan, "Premarital Cohabitation," 256.

167. Beale and Carson, *NT Use*, 24; italics given.

168. Strack and Billerbeck, *Talmud und Midrasch*, 1:319–20; cf. Roig, "Exegetische Studie," 186–87 referring to Gnilka, *Markus*, 71. The same is not true as to the wife: "A woman may be divorced with or without her will, but a man only with his will." *B. Yebam.* 14:1; cf. Abrahams, *Studies*, 70. Inquiring how the Jews of Jesus' time understood the clear response of Malachi concerning the careless and indifferent dealing with divorce in Israel, it must be asserted that the warning of Malachi "wurde seines eigentlichen Sinnes beraubt. Es wurde gewöhnlich so ausgelegt: In Israel habe Gott die Scheidungsmöglichkeit gegeben, nicht aber bei den andern Völkern; dort hasse er die Scheidung!" Baltensweiler, *Ehe im NT*, 37; cf. *y. Qidd.* 1:58c:16; Strack and Billerbeck, *Talmud und Midrasch*, 1:312. The coarseness and rudeness of this erroneous interpretation is obvious. However, at least *b. Giṭ.* 90b "acknowledges the great sorrow that divorce brings to God." Stein, *Mark*, 456/fn.5. By referring to Mal 2:13–14. R. Eleazar teaches: "Over him who divorces the wife of his youth, even the Altar of God sheds tears. Rabbi Yoḥanan (199–279 CE) said, 'he who putteth her (his wife) away is hated of God.'" Amram, *Divorce*, 38; cf. Abrahams, *Studies*, 69. Thus, "the voice of Malachi re-echoed in many dicta of the Talmudic moralists, who condemned the practice of hasty and groundless divorce which the law allowed." Amram, *Divorce*, 31; similarly, Abrahams, *Studies*, 69. On rabbinic limitations of the husband's originally absolute, unlimited right to divorce see also Amram, *Divorce*, 41–53; Instone-Brewer, *In the*

of the Pharisees' inquiry referring to "any reason whatever." However, as was to be seen above in context of the rabbinic teachings on Gen 2:24, they hold that it was God who with great efforts worked the "miracle" of pairing husband and wife.[169] Hence, it is a contradictory attitude to assume that God works marriages and it is up to man to separate so easily what God achieved with so much difficulty. This is just the point Jesus is stressing in his aphorism of Mark 10:9 and Matt 19:6b: "Therefore, what God has joined man shall not separate."[170] Thus, the background for the disputes in the gospels is evidently clear. It is the עֶרְוַת דָּבָר of Deut 24:1 and the Pharisaic interpretation thereof as elucidated above.

II.2.1.2 Text and Translation

II.2.1.2.1 THE GREEK TEXT

At first, the main texts of Matthew and Mark have to be investigated. I will provide a synoptical composition of both quite similar passages, arranging the sentence order according to the longer account of Mark and marking greater differences between corresponding statements by underlining, while minor (rather individual stylistic) deviations are written in italics. Square brackets enclose major, important textual deviations in the Greek documents. Subsequently I will criticize and discuss the Greek standard text of the NA[27] version, finally giving my own translation of both passages.

Bible, 81–84. Also, further support even for one's divorced wife is recommended or even demanded by some rabbis; cf. *Gen. Rab.* 17:3; Batey, "The ΜΙΑ ΣΑΡΞ Union," 272; Amram, *Divorce*, 110.

169. Cf. *midr. Pesiq.* 11b; *Sam.* 5:13:31b; *Gen. Rab.* 68:43b; *Lev. Rab.* 8:110b; *Num. Rab.* 3:139d; *b. Soṭah* 2a. Esp. *b. Mo'ed Qaṭ.* 18b referring to the following interesting biblical texts: Gen 24:50: "The matter [Isaac's servant finding Rebekah] comes from the LORD." Judg 14:4: "His [i.e., Samson's] father and mother did not know that it was of the Lord." Prov 19:14: "A prudent wife is from the Lord." These texts, as well as the rabbinic interpretation thereof, are most interesting concerning Jesus argumentation against the Pharisee's lenient view of divorce. Further: Ps 68:6 in *b. Soṭah* 2a.

170. Cf. Baltensweiler, *Ehe im NT*, 50–51: "Wenn die Rabbinen nämlich sagen, die Eheleute seien von Gott zusammengefügt, dann stellen sie diese Aussage in ihrem eigentlichen Gewicht sofort wieder in Frage, indem sie eine Ehescheidung als etwas Selbstverständliches und Erlaubtes ansehen. Bei Jesus aber ist gerade die Tatsache des Eingreifens Gottes der Grund dafür, dass die Ehe nicht geschieden werden soll." Not even for mutual consent, although, "if the parties agreed to be divorced, the Rabbis could not oppose any objection, because the mutual consent of the parties was the highest moral ground for divorce." Amram, *Divorce*, 39–40.

Mark 10:2–12	Matt 19:3–9
(v. 2) Καὶ προσελθόντες Φαρισαῖοι ἐπηρώτων αὐτὸν εἰ ἔξεστιν <u>ἀνδρὶ</u> γυναῖκα ἀπολῦσαι, πειράζοντες αὐτόν.	(v. 3) Καὶ προσῆλθον αὐτῷ Φαρισαῖοι πειράζοντες αὐτὸν καὶ λέγοντες· εἰ ἔξεστιν <u>ἀνθρώπῳ</u> ἀπολῦσαι τὴν γυναῖκα αὐτοῦ <u>κατὰ πᾶσαν αἰτίαν</u>;
(v. 3) ὁ δὲ ἀποκριθεὶς εἶπεν αὐτοῖς· τί ὑμῖν ἐνετείλατο Μωϋσῆς;	---
(v. 4) οἱ δὲ εἶπαν· <u>ἐπέτρεψεν</u> Μωϋσῆς βιβλίον ἀποστασίου γράψαι καὶ ἀπολῦσαι.	(v. 7) λέγουσιν αὐτῷ· τί οὖν Μωϋσῆς <u>ἐνετείλατο</u> δοῦναι βιβλίον ἀποστασίου καὶ ἀπολῦσαι [αὐτήν];
(v. 5) ὁ δὲ Ἰησοῦς εἶπεν αὐτοῖς· πρὸς τὴν σκληροκαρδίαν ὑμῶν <u>ἔγραψεν</u> ὑμῖν <u>τὴν ἐντολὴν ταύτην</u>.	(v. 8) λέγει αὐτοῖς ὅτι Μωϋσῆς πρὸς τὴν σκληροκαρδίαν ὑμῶν <u>ἐπέτρεψεν</u> ὑμῖν ἀπολῦσαι τὰς γυναῖκας ὑμῶν, ἀπ' ἀρχῆς δὲ οὐ γέγονεν οὕτως.
(v. 6) ἀπὸ δὲ ἀρχῆς κτίσεως ἄρσεν καὶ θῆλυ ἐποίησεν αὐτούς·	(v. 4) ὁ δὲ ἀποκριθεὶς εἶπεν. οὐκ ἀνέγνωτε ὅτι ὁ κτίσας ἀπ' ἀρχῆς ἄρσεν καὶ θῆλυ ἐποίησεν αὐτούς;
(vv. 7–8a) ἕνεκεν τούτου καταλείψει ἄνθρωπος τὸν πατέρα αὐτοῦ καὶ τὴν μητέρα [καὶ προσκολληθήσεται πρὸς τὴν γυναῖκα αὐτοῦ], καὶ ἔσονται οἱ δύο εἰς σάρκα μίαν·	(v. 5) καὶ εἶπεν· ἕνεκα τούτου καταλείψει ἄνθρωπος τὸν πατέρα καὶ τὴν μητέρα καὶ κολληθήσεται τῇ γυναικὶ αὐτοῦ, καὶ ἔσονται οἱ δύο εἰς σάρκα μίαν.
(vv. 8b–9) ὥστε οὐκέτι εἰσὶν δύο ἀλλὰ μία σάρξ. ὃ οὖν ὁ θεὸς συνέζευξεν ἄνθρωπος μὴ χωριζέτω.	(v. 6) ὥστε οὐκέτι εἰσὶν δύο ἀλλὰ σὰρξ μία. ὃ οὖν ὁ θεὸς συνέζευξεν ἄνθρωπος μὴ χωριζέτω.
(v. 10) Καὶ εἰς τὴν οἰκίαν πάλιν οἱ μαθηταὶ περὶ τούτου ἐπηρώτων αὐτόν.	---
(v. 11) καὶ λέγει αὐτοῖς. ὃς ἂν ἀπολύσῃ τὴν γυναῖκα αὐτοῦ καὶ γαμήσῃ ἄλλην μοιχᾶται <u>ἐπ' αὐτήν</u>.	(v. 9) λέγω δὲ ὑμῖν ὅτι ὃς ἂν ἀπολύσῃ τὴν γυναῖκα αὐτοῦ μὴ ἐπὶ πορνείᾳ καὶ γαμήσῃ ἄλλην μοιχᾶται.
(v. 12) καὶ ἐὰν αὐτὴ ἀπολύσασα τὸν ἄνδρα αὐτῆς γαμήσῃ ἄλλον μοιχᾶται.	---

Mark 10:11–12	Matt 19:9	Matt 5:32	Luke 16:18
καὶ λέγει αὐτοῖς·	λέγω δὲ ὑμῖν ὅτι	ἐγὼ δὲ λέγω ὑμῖν ὅτι	
ὃς ἂν ἀπολύσῃ τὴν γυναῖκα αὐτοῦ	ὃς ἂν ἀπολύσῃ τὴν γυναῖκα αὐτοῦ	πᾶς ὁ ἀπολύων τὴν γυναῖκα αὐτοῦ	Πᾶς ὁ ἀπολύων τὴν γυναῖκα αὐτοῦ
	μὴ ἐπὶ πορνείᾳ	παρεκτὸς <u>λόγου πορνείας</u>	
καὶ γαμήσῃ ἄλλην μοιχᾶται <u>ἐπ' αὐτήν</u>·	καὶ γαμήσῃ ἄλλην μοιχᾶται.	ποιεῖ αὐτὴν <u>μοιχευθῆναι</u>,	καὶ γαμῶν ἑτέραν <u>μοιχεύει</u>,
καὶ ἐὰν αὐτὴ ἀπολύσασα τὸν ἄνδρα αὐτῆς		καὶ ὃς ἐὰν ἀπολελυμένην	καὶ ὁ ἀπολελυμένην ἀπὸ ἀνδρὸς
γαμήσῃ ἄλλον μοιχᾶται.		γαμήσῃ, μοιχᾶται.	γαμῶν <u>μοιχεύει</u>.

The New Testament Echoes of the Edenic Ideal

As these tables contrasting the different reports shall demonstrate, there are some interesting deviations in the accounts of the three evangelists.[171] While there are no contradictions, we find some additional remarks in either version that are worthy of further consideration. But beforehand, the Greek text itself must be criticized by investigating further variants in the different documents that make up the NA[27] text. Omitting an extensive, detailed report about the concrete documents that contain this or that reading, I will refer only to the main uncertainties and the reasons why to choose which rendering.

Mark 10:2–12. Beginning with the account of Mark, the first textual "problem" occurs in v. 2, where some documents do not contain the words (καὶ) προσελθόντες (οἱ) Φαρισαῖοι. Thus, the introduction of v. 2 only reads [καὶ] ἐπηρώτων αὐτόν, with the αὐτόν pointing back to the ὄχλοι of v. 1, and not to the special group of Pharisees. The Pharisees, however, principally appear more often with their religious party's name within the account of Matthew, while Mark rather speaks about the people in general.[172] Furthermore, "inasmuch as the impersonal plural is a feature of Markan style, the words προσελθόντες Φαρισαῖοι are probably an intrusion from Matthew."[173]

> The fact that the MSS vary in how they express this subject lends credence to this judgment.... Further, the use of an indefinite plural (a general 'they') is a Markan feature, occurring over twenty times. Thus, internally the evidence looks rather strong for the shorter reading, in spite of the minimal external support for it. However, if scribes assimilated this text to Matt 19:3, a more exact parallel might have been expected: Matthew has καὶ προσῆλθον αὐτῷ Φαρισαῖοι (..., 'then Pharisees came to him'). Although the verb form needs to be different according to syntactical requirements of the respective sentences, the word order variety, as well as the presence or absence of the article and the alternation between δέ and καί as the introductory conjunction, all suggest that the variety of readings might not be due to scribal adjustments toward Matthew.[174]

---

171. For another table pointing out the agreements of Matt 5:31–32 and 19:7–9 see Turner, *Matthew*, 460. Cf. also Kirchschläger, *Ehe im NT*, 60–61; on a reconstruction of Matt 5:27–32 in the same order and structure of the previous antitheses of the Sermon on the Mount even more stressing the renewal concerning the perceptions about marriage, divorce and adultery see ibid., 65.

172. Cf. Pickup, "Pharisees," 94–95: "In four out of five such instances [where Mark speaks only about scribes], Matthew identifies Mark's scribes as Pharisees;... it is quite apparent that Matthew gives more emphasis to the Pharisees as opponents of Jesus than he does to the scribes.... At any rate, it appears that the author of Matthew tried to identify Jesus' opponents as Pharisees every opportunity that he could.... He recognized (as did the author of Mark) that a number of the scribes from Jerusalem were affiliated with the Pharisaic party, and he presumed that the scribes who acted in concert with the Pharisees in opposing Jesus' halakha were Pharisaic scribes."

173. Metzger, *Greek NT*, 88. Cf. NET on Mark 10:2; Baltensweiler, *Ehe im NT*, 44. Lohmeyer, *Markus* (on Mar. 10:2).

174. NET text critical note on Mark 10:2. Similarly, Metzger, *Greek NT*, 88: "The fact that the Matthean passage is not absolutely parallel (προσῆλθον αὐτῷ Φαρισαῖοι) and the widespread and impressive support for the longer reading led ... to retain the words in the text."

While the text of v. 3 is certain, v. 4 again contains another reading for the phrase ἐπέτρεψεν Μωϋσῆς. Another document family (*f¹*) reads ἐνετείλατο instead of ἐπέτρεψεν, thereby reflecting the verb Jesus used in v. 3. The sense, however, may only be partly changed, for ἐντέλλω ("to give or leave instructions/command/order/give orders") and ἐπιτρέπω ("allow/permit, order/instruct") could be used as synonyms.[175] In the LXX it is the Greek ἐντέλλομαι which is used to express the Hebrew צוה ("order/direct/appoint/command"), while ἐπιτρέπω is very rare (only in Gen 39:6; Esth 9:14; Job 32:14) and has no concrete Hebrew equivalent. Both can express "authorise" as well as "command." Yet, ἐπιτρέπω conveys a more voluntary overtone (cf. e.g., Gen 39:6), while ἐντέλλω simply is a command denoting a certain necessity to do accordingly. Since the majority of texts reads ἐπέτρεψεν, it will likewise be used in my exegesis, but under special consideration of its more demanding qualities.

Proceeding to v. 5, there is a minor variant without any real alteration of the meaning. Some document families (*f¹.¹³*; Syrus Sinaiticus, Peshitta; some old Latins and Vulgate) have καὶ ἀποκριθεὶς ὁ instead of ὁ δέ. The sense, however, is in no way changed, for καὶ ἀποκριθεὶς ὁ Ἰησοῦς εἶπεν αὐτοῖς· ("and answering Jesus said to them") and ὁ δὲ Ἰησοῦς εἶπεν αὐτοῖς· ("but Jesus said to them") is basically the same.

In Mark 10:6 we again find a slight deviation, now concerning the word αὐτούς. Several manuscripts exchange it with ὁ θεός (D; W; few old Latins), while others add ὁ θεός after the αὐτούς (A, Θ, Ψ, *f¹.¹³*, old Latins and Vulgate, Majority text, all Syriac documents). It seems likely that "the insertion of ὁ θεός as the subject of ἐποίησεν must have seemed to copyists to be necessary lest the uninstructed reader imagine that the previously mentioned subject (Moses) should be carried on."[176] "Thus, both on internal and external grounds, the most probable wording of the original text here lacked ὁ θεός."[177] However, the meaning is in either case again unaltered: ἄρσεν καὶ θῆλυ ἐποίησεν (αὐτούς) [ὁ θεός] ("male and female [God] he created (them)").

The quotation from Gen 2:24 in the Greek text of v. 7 contains several variants, including a major omission. The first textual difficulty is that several witnesses (few old Latins and some single manuscripts of the Vulgate, cf. D) add an (seemingly superfluous) αὐτοῦ after τὴν μητέρα, thus assimilating it to the preceding πατέρα αὐτοῦ and to the LXX on Gen 2:24. Concerning the omission of the larger phrase καί προσκολληθήσεται πρὸς τὴν γυναῖκα αὐτοῦ ("and he will join his wife") it is unclear whether it represents an assimilation to the Matthean or Genesis text inserted by later copyists, or if it inadvertently fell out by a copyist's failure (the eye of the scribe passing from καί to καί).[178]

> Further, the form of the longer reading is identical with the LXX of Gen 2:24, but different from the quotation in Matt 19:5 ... The significance of this is

175. Cf. BDAG s.v. ἐντέλλω and ἐπιτρέπω.
176. Metzger, *Greek NT*, 88; cf. NET on Mark 10:6.
177. NET text critical note on Mark 10:6.
178. Metzger, *Greek NT*, 88–89.

that Matthew's quotations of the OT are often, if not usually, directly from the Hebrew—except when he is following Mark's quotation of the OT. Matthew in fact only departs from Mark's verbatim quotation of the LXX in 15:4 and 19:19 ... (and in both places the only difference from Mark/LXX is the dropping of σου ...). This might suggest that the longer reading here was not part of what the first evangelist had in his copy of Mark. Further, the reading without this line is harder, for the wife is not explicitly mentioned in v. 7; the casual reader could read 'the two' of v. 8 as referring to father and mother rather than husband and wife. (And Mark is known for having harder, shorter readings that scribes tried to soften by explanatory expansion. . . .)[179]

Nevertheless, most manuscripts have the clause and so it has been included in the NA[27] text using square brackets indicating doubts as to its authenticity. That seems to be a reasonable compromise.

Verses 8–10 are clear, but vv. 11 and 12 are uncertain. Few witnesses (W and a few Syrus Sinaiticus documents) confuse the order, omit the final ἐπ' αὐτήν,[180] and set the woman as subject separating her husband at the first place, followed by the example of a man divorcing his wife. But that does principally not alter content and meaning, it only stresses the possibility of a woman divorcing her husband even a little bit more than the reverse order in the main documents (as given in the table above). Furthermore, others (A, D, Θ, f^{13}, Majority text, all Latins, Syriac Peshitta and the edition of Thomas von Harkel) read γυνή instead of αὐτή in v. 12, thereby by no means altering the meaning. Additionally, some (D, (Θ), (f^{13}), old Latin) read καὶ ἐὰν ἐξέλθῃ ἀπὸ τοῦ ἀνδρὸς καὶ ἄλλον γαμήσῃ ("and if she goes out of her husband and marries another") instead of καὶ ἐὰν αὐτὴ ἀπολύσασα τὸν ἄνδρα αὐτῆς γαμήσῃ ἄλλον ("and if she divorces her husband and marries another"). At first glance both seem synonymous and it is possible that this is the intended meaning. Yet, the alternative text is not unambiguously pointing to the fact that the woman divorces. It rather seems that "she goes out" because she has been sent away by her husband, and not because she divorced him.[181] Thus, the only instance referring to the woman's possibil-

---

179. NET text critical remark on Mark 10:7; cf. Metzger, *Greek NT*, 89; Loader, *LXX, Sexuality, and NT*, 79/fn.2. See also Berger, *Gesetzesauslegung*, 549 who argues in favor of the shorter reading and notes that without this insertion according to the Greek text it would also be possible to understand it as referring to the woman leaving her parents (since the generic term ἄνθρωπος can mean both genders). The omission of this phrase "would also emphasize even more strongly the becoming one flesh, which without the 'joining' would carry the full weight in describing the union, perhaps even more strongly emphasizing the sexual aspect." Loader, *LXX, Sexuality, and NT*, 80.

180. Fitzmyer noticed: "V. 11d as given above includes the *ep' autén*; it thus specifies that the divorce and subsequent marriage are an act of adultery 'against her.' This would seem extraordinary from the Jewish point of view. Indeed, this is probably the reason why it is omitted in some mss. The phrase *ep' autén* is almost certainly a Marcan addition made in the light of what is to be said in v. 12. It is an explicative addition, which makes Jesus' words express the fact that adultery against a woman is something now to be considered." Fitzmyer, *Advance*, 85.

181. This feature as a possibility to interpret this short phrase is widely overlooked, as e.g., the lacking scrutiny of Baltensweiler, *Ehe im NT*, 67 demonstrates. It is generally considered in such a

ity of divorcing her husband would disappear and make way to more "compatibility"[182] and agreement with the parallel accounts only speaking about "a divorced woman" (ὁ ἀπολελυμένην ἀπὸ ἀνδρός/ἀπολελυμένην; Luke 16:18/Matt 5:32) whom to marry would mean to commit adultery (against the former wedlock).

While Matt 5:32, Matt 19:9; and Mark 10:11–12 read the middle (or passive)[183] form of μοιχᾶται (ind. pres. 3rd pers. sg.), only Luke 16:18 renders the active form μοιχεύει (ind. pres. act. 3rd pers. sg.: "he/she commits adultery"). A reasonable and most likely synoptical agreement between the different verbal forms is reached by accepting the variant reading "and if she goes out of her husband and marries another" instead of "and if she divorces her husband and marries another" in Mark 10:12, thus leaving out the (unlikely?) option of this single text alone speaking about the woman's possibility to divorce her husband.[184] The usage of the verbs μοιχᾶται and μοιχεύει in their individual contexts of the paralleling passages seem to affirm that, since they all literally speak about marrying another man's divorced wife (or the man who actively divorced his former wife himself marrying someone else) as an act of adultery, never about a man being the object of divorce and remarriage. Hence, the woman is always the passive part being "adultered"[185] (i.e., adultery committed against her) by the action of the first husband who divorces her in combination with the second husband who subsequently marries her, thereby breaking the first "one flesh" union.

Yet, there are several witnesses, although not in exact harmony with one another, that affirm the decision of the NA[27] text to leave the note about the woman's intervention untouched (W, a few Sinai Syriacs, some Coptics, A, B, C, L, D, (Θ), Δ, Ψ, f[3], Majority text, most Latins and Vulgate, Syriac Peshitta, and the edition of Thomas von Harkel). And it may even be a plausible explanation that "wenn wir berücksichtigen, dass sich Markus an Heidenchristen und Matthäus an Judenchristen wandte, können wir verstehen, warum der eine diesen Grund erwähnt und der andere nicht."[186] By considering also Josephus' remark on the active divorce of Salome about the time of Jesus, a divorce on the woman's part at least seems to be possible somehow, even if it was unusual and basically illegitimate, generally representing no Jewish custom, as Josephus particularly emphasized.[187] Altogether, however, this strange and

---

close relation to the other variants that the possibility of differing meanings is easily left out. Yet, this reading is the only one being completely in harmony with the other paralleling texts.

182. Shaner, *Christian View*, 37 even speaks of this variant reading as "making the verse more Jewish" (by again putting the woman to be a rather passive object).

183. The mode best to be accepted (middle or passive) in the given instances will be discussed at the end of this section right before presenting the final translation.

184. However, Fitzmyer explains that v. 12 is "introduced to suit the contingencies of Gentile Christian communities in areas where Roman and Greek law prevailed and where a woman was permitted to divorce her husband." Fitzmyer, *Advance*, 85; cf. Baltensweiler, *Ehe im NT*, 67; Collins, *Sexual Ethics*, 25. That would be a reasonable explanation for this unusual case.

185. More on this non-extant English word to describe the Greek passive mode see the footnote of the next occurrence below.

186. Roig, "Exegetische Studie," 190.

187. Josephus explains: "She [Salome] sent him [Costobarus] a bill of divorce and dissolved her

unusual reading with the woman as the active initiator of divorce seems uncertain. Yet, in the translation below it will be retained due to the manuscript evidence speaking in favor it.

Matthew 19:3–9. Verse 3 contains three small deviations, at least two of them do not at all alter the meaning, in fact not even the style. The first is the insertion of a οἱ, thus reading προσῆλθον αὐτῷ <u>οἱ</u> Φαρισαῖοι. Others also insert a second αὐτῷ after λέγοντες. The third deviation, changing the sense just slightly, is ἀνδρί instead of ἀνθρώπῳ, thus referring rather to one's "husband" instead of the more generic term "man." The Greek ἀνδρί most likely is an assimilation to the Markan text, while "a few significant MSS (א* B L Γ 579 [700] 1424* *pc*) have neither noun. As the harder reading, it seems to best explain the rise of the others."[188] The reading of ἀνθρώπῳ in many important manuscripts may have served as clarification to give the following αὐτοῦ an antecedent.[189]

In verse 4 quite a lot of manuscripts add αὐτοῖς (C, W, Θ, *f*[1.13], Majority text, old Latins and Vulgate, all Syriacs, all middle-Egypts) after ὁ δὲ ἀποκριθεὶς εἶπεν and also many texts read ποιήσας (א, C, D, (L), W, Z, *f*[13], Majority text, old Latins and Vulgate, all Syriacs) instead of κτίσας (affirmed by B, Θ, *f*[1], a single Latin (e), Coptics, and Origen).

> However, it is easier to suppose that copyists changed the word κτίσας (which is supported by several excellent witnesses) to ποιήσας, thus harmonizing it with the Septuagint text of Gn 1.27 (which is quoted in the immediate context), than to suppose that ποιήσας was altered to suit the Hebrew word used in Gn 1.27 (ברא, which means "created").[190]

The κολληθήσεται ("join/bind closely/unite/cling/attach") of v. 5 is rendered in many manuscripts (א, C, K, L, Z, Γ, Δ, some of *f*[1]) as κολληθήσεται ("stick/adhere

---

marriage with him, though this was not according to the Jewish laws; for with us it is lawful for a husband to do so; but a wife, if she departs from her husband, cannot of herself be married to another, unless her former husband put her away. However, Salome chose to follow not the law of her country, but the law of authority [ἀπ' ἐξουσίας], and so renounced her wedlock; and told her brother Herod, that she left her husband out of her goodwill to him." *A.J.* 15:259–60; trans. Whiston. Fitzmyer elucidates further: "... we know that divorce was envisaged as a possibility at least for Jewish women living in the military colony at Elephantine in Egypt in the fifth century BC. A number of Aramaic marriage contracts from that place mention it explicitly. But the evidence for such a practice in Palestine itself is meager indeed, almost nonexistent." Fitzmyer, *Advance*, 85–86; cf. Kremer, "Jesu Wort," 53: "Charakteristisch für die Mk-Wiedergabe ist, daß unter Umständen auch eine Frau ihren Mann entläßt. Das war in Palästina zur Zeit Jesu kaum möglich und spiegelt eher die Verhältnisse in der hellenistisch-römischen Welt wider." Similarly Baltensweiler, *Ehe im NT*, 66–67; cf. also Instone-Brewer, *In the Bible*, 72–80; Fitzmyer, *First Corinthians*, 289–90; Lövestam, "Divorce and Remarriage," 48/fn.3 Frankemölle, however, mentions even Palestinian evidence of a wife's active divorce: Frankemölle, "Wiederverheiratung," 31–33; similarly Ilan, "Divorce Bill," 195–202. See further on the topic of women's rights to divorce esp. Schweizer, "Scheidungsrecht," 294–300; Brooten, "Scheidung," 65–80; Brooten, "Debatte," 466–78.

188. Text critical note of the NET on Matt 19:3.

189. Cf. NET on Matt 19:3.

190. Metzger, *Greek NT*, 38; similarly Blomberg, "Exegesis," 165/fn.20. Furthermore, "one could also put the question mark after 'female,' and make the rest of the sentence a statement, but the simple co-ordination of εἶπεν ... καὶ εἶπεν favors treating both clauses alike." Ibid., 166/fn.21.

closely/be faithfully devoted/join"),[191] thus assimilating the word to the terminology of the LXX on Gen 2:24. If the insertion in Mark 10:7 indeed is an assimilation to Matt 19:5, then the original LXX quotation using κολληθήσεται must be the earlier reading. However, the sense is not altered, again. But it seems to me more likely that the early writers rather used the LXX wording of that quotation.

In v. 6 the word order of σὰρξ μία is reversed in very few manuscripts (only ℵ, D 579), without any change of the meaning at all. Again only very few witnesses (D, old Latins) read εἰς ἕν between συνέζευξεν ἄνθρωπος, thus emphasizing the oneness of the formerly *two* fleshes. However, the evidence for this nice insertion is too small.

Turning to v. 7 we find an omission in many documents leaving out the αὐτήν at the end of the verse (ℵ, D, L, Z, Θ, some of *f*¹, Old Latins and Vulgate). The shorter reading may be assimilation to the Markan parallel, but "since it is attested in early and diverse witnesses . . . and since the parallel verse (Mark 10:4) already departs at many points, the shorter reading seems more likely to be original."[192] It is hardly possible to retrace whether it is an insertion or the original term; accordingly it is kept in square brackets in NA²⁷.[193]

After the introductory λέγει αὐτοῖς in v. 8 some add ὁ Ἰησοῦς, and in v. 9 some deleted the ὅτι; both in no way altering the verses' sense. The last textual criticism is addressed to the last part of v. 9. Here a few documents have ποιεῖ αὐτὴν μοιχευθῆναι (cf. Matt 5:32) instead of γαμήσῃ ἄλλην μοιχᾶται, but the evidence is rather weak. It is assumed that "the phrase ποιεῖ αὐτὴν μοιχευθῆναι ('makes her commit adultery' [i.e., when she remarries]) has come into several witnesses (including B C* *f*¹) from [Matt] 5.32, where it is firm."[194] Likewise, the "excepting clause" μὴ ἐπὶ πορνείᾳ is rendered by several witnesses (including B, D, *f*¹, *f*¹³ 33) as παρεκτὸς λόγου πορνείας, again assimilating the sentence to the one of Matt 5:32.[195] Finally, "the short reading of 1574, καὶ γαμήσῃ ἄλλην, has been conformed to the prevailing text of Mk 10.11."[196] On the last major deviation in v. 9 concerning a possible adding of καὶ ὁ ἀπολελυμένην γαμῶν (or γαμήσας) μοιχᾶται at the verse's ending (cf. B, C*, W, Z, Θ 078, *f*¹·¹³ 033, Majority text, old Latins and Vulgate, Peshitta), the committee deciding about the Greek NT text of the United Bible Societies further explains:

> Although it could be argued that homoeoteleuton (μοιχᾶται . . . μοιχᾶται) accounts for its accidental omission from ℵ D L 1241 *al*, the fact that B C* *f*¹ *al* read μοιχᾶται only once (at the conclusion of the combined clauses) makes it

---

191. Cf. BDAG s.v. κολλάω and προσκολλάω.
192. NET text critical note on Matt 19:7.
193. Cf. Metzger, *Greek NT*, 38.
194. Metzger, *Greek NT*, 38.
195. Similarly interpreted as scribal assimilation to Matt 5:32 in Baltensweiler, *Ehe im NT*, 67.
196. Metzger, *Greek NT*, 38.

more probable that the text was expanded by copyists who accommodated the saying to the prevailing text of [Matt] 5.32.[197]

Evidently, the text of Matt 5:32 has manifoldly influenced the copyists' work regarding Matt 19:9. It will be worthwhile to continue the textual analysis by turning to just that passage at first, finally proceeding to the last text in Luke 16:18.

Matthew 5:32. As referred to before, the text of Matt 5:32 is very firm. The only deviation worth mentioning is a variant for ὃς ἐὰν ἀπολελυμένην γαμήσῃ reading ὁ ἀπολελυμένην γαμήσας (thus B, poss. a few Sahidic documents and Origen). But the text of B "seems to have been substituted for the reading of the other uncials (ὃς ἐὰν ... γαμήσῃ) in order to make the construction parallel to the preceding participial clause (ὁ ἀπολύων)."[198] Some manuscripts even omit the whole phrase (D, some single old Latins (a; b; k), some of Origen, Greek and Latin manuscripts according to Augustine), what may be due to "pedantic scribes who regarded them as superfluous, reasoning that if 'everyone who divorces his wife, except on the ground of unchastity, makes her an adulteress [when she remarries],' then it would go without saying that 'whoever marries a divorced woman [also] commits adultery.'"[199] Hence, the Greek text as it stands in the NA²⁷ should be considered as the most reliable.

Luke 16:18. There are three rather unimportant variants in the second part of the Greek verse of Luke 16:18. Some add a πᾶς before ὁ ἀπολελυμένην, while the early 𝔓⁷⁵ omits the ὁ before ἀπολελυμένην.[200] A few of D, the Sinai and Cureton Syriac texts, the Peshitta, and a single Boharitic manuscript also omit the ἀπὸ ἀνδρός; and perhaps it might even "represent the more original form of the saying."[201] However, even καὶ (ὁ) [πᾶς] ἀπολελυμένην (ἀπὸ ἀδρὸς) γαμῶν μοιχεύει is still loyal to the common meaning: "And (the) [every] woman being divorced (from husband) marrying commits adultery."

II.2.1.2.2 Translation

The following tables contain my own translation of the Greek text including possible deviations at least in round brackets (rather likely reading) and double round brackets ((unlikely reading)).[202] Square brackets enclose insertions that are added only to make the text better understandable in English. Underlining and italics again mark the differences between the individual accounts (cf. the table above).

197. Metzger, *Greek NT*, 38–39.
198. Metzger, *Greek NT*, 11.
199. Metzger, *Greek NT*, 11.
200. On the text of 𝔓75 (late second or possible early third century) cf. Comfort and Barrett, *Earliest NT Manuscripts*, 551.
201. Fitzmyer, *Advance*, 83.
202. For another, slightly differing comparison and translation of the verses containing the "exception clauses" see e.g., Shaner, *Christian View*, 51–52, 55–57.

At this place, a brief discussion of the significant verbal forms of μοιχεύω and μοιχάω (both meaning "to commit adultery") in Mark 10:11–12; Matt 5:32; 19:9; and Luke 16:18 has to be inserted. It is noticeable, although passing unrecognized by almost every commentator,[203] that μοιχάω is nowhere used in its active mode, but only as μοιχᾶται (indicative present middle or passive, 3rd person sg.). Yet, modern translations generally render it as simple active: "(he/she) commits adultery." The deeper meaning of the verbal form is thereby lost. Unfortunately, it is not easy to decide whether this verbal form was meant as middle or passive,[204] and it is also difficult, in either case, to maintain adequately its particular meaning in an English translation.

However, I suggest that μοιχᾶται be understood in every instance as middle, since it always refers to the causer of the divorce as *the actively acting person* (the object),[205] who *in his own interest* divorces and remarries. The divorced spouse as *the passive subject* is nowhere referred to by μοιχᾶται. While in most cases it is the husband who commits μοιχᾶται, in the only instance Jesus mentions a woman as the causal agent of divorce (Mark 11:12), he again uses μοιχᾶται, now in reference to this woman. Hence, it is independent from gender, but dependent on the *active* causer of divorce and remarriage.

The middle further stresses the (unjust) behavior of the divorce's causer, since

> in general, in the middle voice the subject *performs* or *experiences the action* expressed by the verb in such a way that *emphasizes the subject's participation*. . . . Perhaps the best definition is this: 'The middle calls special attention to the subject . . . the subject is acting in relation to himself somehow.' The difference between the active and middle is one of emphasis. The active voice emphasizes the action of the verb; the middle emphasizes the actor [subject] of the verb. 'It, in some way, relates the action more intimately to the subject.'[206]

The special functions of the middle voice particularly allude to[207] (1) a behavior with a strong self-interest (indirect-reflexive); (2) an act that directly affects oneself

---

203. Two exceptions would be Luck, *Divorce and Remarriage*, 105–10 and Fitzmyer, *Advance*, 84.

204. BDAG s.v. μοιχάω understands all forms of μοιχάω in these texts as passive, explaining: "'Cause to commit adultery,' in our lit. (as well as LXX; PsSol 8:10) only pass." Others, however, are somehow reserved to follow this interpretation and hold the middle to be the proper decision; cf. Schwyzer, *Griechische Grammatik*, 235.

205. Cf. for a similar instance John 8:4 (μοιχευομένη), where the woman is evidently actively involved, for her own interest. The middle, therefore, is the right choice.

206. Wallace, *Exegetical Syntax*, 414–15 (italics given); first quotation from Robertson, *Grammar*, 804; second citation from Dana and Mantey, *Manual Grammar*, 157. Wallace, *Exegetical Syntax*, 415 further explains concerning the middle of the New Testament Greek: "For Koine Greek, the term *middle* has become a misnomer, because it inherently describes that voice that stands halfway between the active and the passive. Only the direct middle truly does this (in that the subject is both the agent and receiver of the action). Since the direct middle is phasing out in Hellenistic Greek, the term is hardly descriptive of the voice as a whole." This leads to an even stronger emphasis of the active behavior.

207. See for this short summary of particular functions esp. Bornemann and Risch, *Griechische Grammatik*, 210–12; Mehrlein et al., *Ars Graeca*, 205–6; for more details cf. Wallace, *Exegetical Syntax*, 414–30.

(direct-reflexive; the subject is the direct object: the adulterer breaks *his own* marriage bond); (3) an intensification of the verb's active meaning (intensive middle); (4) a person (subject) that *causes* an act for his (i.e., the same subject's) self-interest (causative middle; cf. Matt 5:32: "*he makes/causes her* . . . "); (5) the subject allows something to be done for or to himself (permissive middle); (6) the middle even emphasizes acts affecting one's own *body*[208] (as is certainly the case with adultery through *sexual* relations!). These grammatical features obviously much more illuminate Jesus' estimation of the causer's behavior! They point to the fact that the "subject intimately participates in the results of the action"[209] and thus adequately emphasize the divorce's causer's responsibility for the results of his action, namely: adultery due to his previous act of releasing resulting in remarriage.

This general understanding of the direction of active behavior and passive suffering is further emphasized by the two special clauses in Mark 10:11 (μοιχᾶται ἐπ' αὐτήν; "he commits adultery *against her*"[210]) and Matt 5:32 (ποιεῖ αὐτὴν μοιχευθῆναι: "he makes (i.e., causes) her *to be adultered*").[211] This last instance (Matt 5:32) uses the other Greek verb (μοιχεύω), which elsewhere in our texts always refers to the husband as the actively acting object. But here, describing the woman as the passively suffering subject, it is clearly used as passive (infinitive aorist). Thus, even in case of the (former) wife remarrying another man, it is the causer of the divorce who solely bears the responsibility for the subsequent adultery (by remarriage) and is rebuked as the one to be blamed.[212] The woman who remarries goes out free, she is not the adulterer—that is her (former) husband.

---

208. Cf. esp. Bornemann and Risch, *Griechische Grammatik*, 210–11.

209. Young, *Intermediate Greek*, 134; cf. Wallace, *Exegetical Syntax*, 442/fn.15.

210. On "against her" as the best translation of ἐπ' αὐτήν see BDAG s.v. μοιχάω § 1b; Stein, *Mark*, 458.

211. Thus ("to be *adultered*") the translation of the passive form μοιχευθῆναι in Fitzmyer, *Advance*, 84 and Lövestam, "Divorce and Remarriage," 53; another possibility would be "adulterized" (thus Luck, *Divorce and Remarriage*, 106). It means that she is passive in the act of adultery which is on the one hand committed by her new spouse (according to Luke 16:18b), but on the other hand actually her former husband is responsible for that adultery (*he makes her* to be adultered [by the new partner]; see BDAG s.v. μοιχεύω § bβ; cf. Lövestam, "Divorce and Remarriage," 61). He is the one to be blamed, the one responsible for the adultery, irrespective of the fact who of both former spouses will be the first to enter a new (sexual/marital) relationship. On the passive form see also Baltensweiler, *Ehe im NT*, 61; his translation as "zum Ehebruch verführt werden" (ibid., 65) is misleading, for then it would still be the woman who actively commits adultery although being seduced, but that is not what the text and particularly the passive form intends to say (similarly wrong is Turner, *Matthew*, 459: she "is made an adulteress;" or Shaner, *Christian View*, 41, 44, 46: "she is being made a committer of adultery"). It rather is adultery committed *against* her (she being completely without active responsibility), as Fitzmyer, *Advance*, 84 rightly asserts. A similar error happened to Lohmeyer, *Markus* concerning the interpretation of ἐπ' αὐτήν (Mark 10:11) as "er buhlt *mit ihr*"—indicating that she would also be actively involved, and not just the suffering, passive object.

212. Similarly the translation of BDAG s.v. μοιχεύω § bβ; cf. Shaner, *Christian View*, 44; Luck, *Divorce and Remarriage*, 107: ". . . his act of divorcing makes her adulterized. In other words, it [i.e., the text with its peculiar grammatical features] seeks to identify her husband as an adulterer."

The English translation, however, is only able to render "he/she commits adultery;" but one has to keep in mind the distinct quality of a strong self-interest in this behavior and Jesus' emphasis thereof. In the following tables I try to maintain this feature by adding the short insertion [for him-/herself] in square brackets.

Mark 10:2–12	Matt 19:3–9
(v. 2) And (Pharisees) came up asking him whether a *husband* is permitted to release[213] [his] *woman*, testing him	(v. 3) And Pharisees came *to him*, testing him and saying: "Whether (a *man*/husband) is permitted to release his *wife* for any/every reason?"[214]
(v. 3) But answering he said to them, "What did Moses command/instruct you?"	---
(v. 4) They said: "Moses permitted[215] writing a certificate of divorce and releasing."	(v. 7) They said to him: "Why then did Moses command/instruct *to give* [her] a certificate of divorce and to release (her)?"
(v. 5) But Jesus said to them: "Because of your hardness of heart he wrote you this commandment.	(v. 8) He said to them *that* "Because of your hardness of heart Moses permitted you to release your wives, but from the beginning it has not been this way."
(v. 6) But from the beginning *of creation* male and female he ((God)) made them.	(v. 4) And he answered and said: "Have you not read that *he who created* from the beginning made them male and female?"
(vv. 7–8a) 'Therefore a man will leave his father and the ((his)) mother, (and will *cleave*/be *cleaved* to his wife) and the two will be/become one flesh.'	(v. 5) And he said: "'Therefore a man will leave the father and the mother and will *join*/be *joined* to his wife, and the two will be/become one flesh'?
(vv. 8b–9) So they are no longer two, but one flesh. Accordingly, what God has joined together, man[216] shall not separate."	(v. 6) So they are no longer two, but one flesh. Accordingly, what God has joined together, man[217] shall not separate.
(v. 10) And in the house the disciples began asking him about this again.	---

213. The Greek ἀπολύω is the terminus technicus for what nowadays is called "divorce" (cf. e.g., Blomberg, "Exegesis," 165; more references will follow) and connotes a special legal act of "releasing" someone from his charge/dept/state, as will be discussed in the next section on the textual analysis in more detail. I cling to the translation with "release" because of this legal quality.

214. It should be noted that there are basically two possibilities of translating the Greek κατὰ πᾶσαν αἰτίαν ("for any reason"): (1) "Is it allowed for every reason whatsoever to divorce?" or denoting (2) "Is there any reason at all allowing divorce?" As Luz, *Matthäus*, 3:92/fn.19 rightly asserts, "läßt sich die Alternative sprachlich nicht entscheiden, aber die erste Möglichkeit passt besser zur mt Ausnahmeklausel in V. 9."

215. Conveying a mandatory overtone; cf. the textual criticism on Mark 10:4 above.

216. It should be noted that "man" is not meant in its gender connotation, but rather as denoting "human" (Greek: ἄνθρωπος) as contrary to God. Thus also Piper, *Momentary Marriage*, 162; Loader, *Jesus Tradition*, 95; Hays, *Moral Vision*, 351.

217. See previous footnote.

Mark 10:2–12	Matt 19:3–9
(v. 11) And he said to them: "Whoever would release his wife and would marry another [woman], commits adultery [for himself] <u>against her</u>;	(v. 9) But I say to you: Whoever would release his wife, except for unlawful sexual intercourse, and would marry another [woman] commits adultery [for himself]."
(v. 12) and if she releases her husband/((she goes out from her husband)) [and] would marry another [man], she commits adultery [for herself]."	---

Mark 10:11–12	Matt 19:9	Matt 5:32	Luke 16:18
And he said to *them*:	"But I say to you:	"But I say to you *that*	
"Whoever would release his wife	Whoever would release his wife,	everyone releasing his wife,	"Everyone releasing his wife
	except[218] for unlawful sexual intercourse,	except for <u>a word of</u> unlawful sexual intercourse,	
and would marry another [woman], commits adultery [for himself] <u>against her</u>;	and would marry another [woman], commits adultery [for himself]."	makes her to be adultered,	and marrying another [woman] <u>commits adultery</u>,
and if she releases her husband/((she goes out from her husband))			
[and] would marry another [man], she commits adultery [for herself]."		and *whoever* would marry <u>a released [woman]</u>, commits adultery [for himself]."	and *the one* marrying <u>a [woman] released from her husband</u>, commits adultery."

II.2.1.3 Textual Analysis

Comparing the anecdotes of Mark and Matthew, we find that the sequences are not exactly matching each other, although, by rearrangement, a general agreement is obtained.[219] Nevertheless, as frequently given in the synoptic gospels, there are some

---

218. The fact that the Greek μὴ ἐπὶ [πορνείᾳ] (Matt 19:9) and παρεκτὸς [λόγου πορνείας] (Matt 5:32) are pointing to a legal exception ("except in cases of/under conditions of…") of the foregoing basically absolute rejection of divorce, is presently generally undoubted; cf. Kirchschläger, *Ehe im NT*, 72–73. The mostly Roman-Catholic attempts to interpret these expressions with an inclusive sense meaning divorce is always prohibited and even adultery as legal reason to divorce is "excepted" are untenable (see on a discussion and rejection of this view e.g., Baltensweiler, *Ehe im NT*, 89–91; Isaksson, *Marriage and Ministry*, 129–30; Greeven, "Aussagen," 111–12).

219. As Amram, *Divorce*, 36 puts it: "The parallel passages in which the opinion of Jesus is quoted, vary somewhat in phraseology, but practically they are alike." Similarly Blomberg, "Exegesis," 173:

minor deviations in the way the disputation is narrated, and particularly in the generosity or scantiness regarding the provided information. To begin with literary features of the given pericopes, one recognizes that Mark 10:2–12 is composite, consisting of a first part (vv. 2–9) with a "pronouncement-story or *Streitgespräch*" that ends up in the apophthegm of v. 9; and joined to this pronouncement story is a "dominical saying, addressed to the disciples later on in the house (vv. 10–12) . . . . This brings it about that there are here in Mark 10 two sayings of Jesus about divorce."[220] The second is "similar to and related to . . . Luke 16:18 and Matt 5:32"[221] and basically stresses the same point, as the table above demonstrates. At the same time, Matt 19:3–12 "offers the first in a series of three pronouncement or controversy stories, as Jesus begins journeying to Jerusalem under the shadow of the cross [. . . and] emerges in as occasional a setting as any in the epistles."[222]

Mark is more exactly situating the discussion; while Matthew seems to report about a single event entirely in context of the Pharisees' testing inquiry,[223] Mark elucidates that there are at least two situations, one with the Pharisees and one at home with Jesus' disciples. His report is placed "within the framework of the catechetical middle part of the gospel about the true Christian way of life (8.27–10.45) . . . ,"[224] thus stressing the significance of the Edenic ideal for Christian lifestyle, while Matthew's account "falls at the beginning of the second subsection of the larger section on the

---

"Whichever explanation is adopted, Matthew and Mark are not to be viewed as contradictory." Cf. Instone-Brewer, *In the Bible*, 161–67 demonstrating that "even the longer accounts in Mark 10 and Matthew 19 were abbreviated because a verbatim account would be inappropriately long." Ibid., 161. There are no contradictions but rather deliberate omissions concerning little aspects that were not of great importance to the author. For an interesting paraphrase "putting it all together" see ibid., 175–77.

220. Fitzmyer, *Advance*, 84; cf. Kremer, "Jesu Wort," 53; Baltensweiler, *Ehe im NT*, 43, 45–46, 59. On the term "Streitgespräch" also Meier, *Marginal Jew IV*, 102.

221. Fitzmyer, *Advance*, 85.

222. Blomberg, "Exegesis," 162.

223. The Markan explanation that the Pharisees came to "test" him (v. 2) "indicates that this was not a sincere theological question but an attempt to entrap Jesus (cf. 2:16, 18, 24; 7:5; 8:11; 12:13). . . . If this is true, the Pharisees' testing Jesus 'across the Jordan' may have involved less a desire to learn Jesus' theological position on the issue of divorce and remarriage than an attempt to ensnare him in a statement that would have angered Herod." Stein, *Mark*, 455. Similarly, Baltensweiler, *Ehe im NT*, 84; cf. Instone-Brewer, *In the Bible*, 160–61; France, *Mark*, 390; Blomberg, "Exegesis," 164: "John the Baptist's reaction to Herodias' divorce and remarriage got him executed (Matt 14:3–12), and Jesus' own previous teaching on the topic may have suggested to some that he was abrogating the Law of Moses (5:31–32). He was obviously in as much a Catch-22 situation as later in 22:15–22 when asked about paying taxes. Whatever his reply, someone stood ready to condemn him." Beale and Carson, *NT Use*, 198 further suggest: "The Pharisees might be attempting to ensnare him politically in light of recent high-profile divorces [. . .], to gather further evidence of his unorthodox views, and/or to marginalize him socially by getting him to defy popular opinion." (On the last suggestion, also Ryrie, "Biblical Teaching," 183.)

224. Farla, "The Two," 69.

climax of Jesus' mission [i.e., the passion] . . . each time his teaching embraces important implications for discipleship . . . ."[225] Furthermore, in Matthew's passage

> the form of the dialogue within vv. 3–12 follows the rabbinic *proem midrash* known as *yelammedenu rabbenu* ("let our master teach us"). An initial question designed to trap Jesus (v. 3) receives a preliminary answer (vv. 4–6). The Pharisees then pose a counterquestion (v. 7) to which Jesus gives a counter-reply (v. 8), preparing the way for his solemn, climactic pronouncement (v. 9). Matthew characteristically abbreviates and combines together two separate discussions (vv. 3–8, 9–12; cf. Mark 10:10) by then appending Jesus' later interchange with his disciples: their objection (v. 10) and his reply (vv. 11–12).[226]

The genre in both is a simple report about a debate between representatives of the Pharisaic sect and Jesus. Matthew is stricter in emphasizing that the challenge is directed concretely against Jesus; he writes προσῆλθον αὐτῷ (they came *to him*) immediately followed by the πειράζοντες αὐτόν (testing *him*).[227] Mark is slightly more lenient in omitting the more concrete αὐτῷ and by setting the πειράζοντες αὐτόν at the end of the verse as some kind of a belated, but nevertheless alerting remark.

> The language [i.e., the use of πειράζοντες] echoes 16:1 and resumes the temptations of Jesus illustrated classically in 4:1–11. Already before any words are spoken, Matthew's narrative cautions his readers against expecting a calm consideration of every aspect of marriage and divorce. The context is polemical; Jesus' reply will have to avoid the trap, whatever other issues it may leave untouched.[228]

Thus, even within the introduction it already becomes clear that Jesus encounters a trap basing on Deut 24:1, not an open debate about the theological concept of marriage (including divorce) with all its implications, consequences, and distortions.

Matthew further stresses the personal familiarity and relatedness of the woman that is to be released by speaking about τὴν γυναῖκα αὐτοῦ instead of the shorter Markan γυναῖκα. Yet, this is compensated by Mark's more personal ἀνδρί in contrast to Matthew's ἀνθρώπῳ. However, there also exists textual evidence for the same ἀνδρί in the Matthean text, although one has to assume that it is a later assimilation to Mark. As investigated above, others do not contain either noun; thus the hints about the closer connection of man and woman in both texts are indeed approximately balanced.

Most significantly, we find that the "inner core" of the Pharisees' question in Matthew is the actual reason for divorce: κατὰ πᾶσαν αἰτίαν ("for every reason");[229] while

---

225. Blomberg, "Exegesis," 162.

226. Blomberg, "Exegesis," 163.

227. While "πειράζοντες, a telic participle, can mean 'test' or 'tempt' [. . . it] almost always carries the latter sense when evil people are its subject." Blomberg, "Exegesis," 163.

228. Blomberg, "Exegesis," 163.

229. "Matthew's added words κατὰ πᾶσαν αἰτίαν, 'for any cause,' however, can be taken in two

The Biblical "One Flesh" Theology of Marriage as Constituted in Genesis 2:24

Mark seemingly focuses on the inquiry whether divorce is allowed at all, stressing the basic Christian attitude by omitting any reference to the legitimate exception(s).[230] Accordingly, only Matthew refers to the exception clause μὴ ἐπὶ πορνείᾳ ("except for unlawful sexual intercourse;" Matt 19:9)[231] or παρεκτὸς λόγου πορνείας ("except for *a word of* unlawful sexual intercourse;" Matt 5:32). This is the concrete response to the Pharisees' inquiry about the Deuteronomic law, by Jesus' Greek terminology even more exactly echoing the Hebrew עֶרְוַת דָּבָר ("a word of nakedness/a sexually unlawful thing") than the ἄσχημον πρᾶγμα ("shameful/unseemly thing") in the LXX.[232] Mark may be more detailed in describing the situational context providing two places (in public/at home) and two groups of inquirers (Pharisees/disciples), but Matthew

---

ways, i.e., 'for every reason whatever' (i.e., Hillel's position) or 'for any reason (at all).' If the grammar is ambiguous, the context favors the former alternative." Hagner, *Matthew 14–28*, 547. Furthermore, there is no hint pointing out that the inquiry refers to "any kind of indecency, however minor" (Beale and Carson, *NT Use*, 58); it actually refers to "every reason" in its literal sense as the rabbinic discussions mentioned above (see "Historical Context") may emphasize more clearly.

230. Beale and Carson, *NT Use*, 198 add rightly: "In the first century the primary question surrounding divorce in the public mind concerned what constituted valid grounds. Since it would make little sense to ask Jesus if divorce itself was lawful when everyone assumed that it was, the Pharisees' question is almost certainly truncated [in Mark's report], the intent of it being this: is it lawful to divorce for any matter (the view that was dominant and considered more righteous) or only for indecency . . . ? Jesus' response, even in its obviously abbreviated and minimal form, can hardly be what they expected." See further about possible reasons why only Matthew presents the exception clause Luck, *Divorce and Remarriage*, 154–56, who primarily holds "that Mark eliminated the exception clause for the sake of brevity." Ibid., 154.

231. It should be noted, as Wenham, "Syntax of Mat. 19.9," 17 points out, that the syntax of Matt 19:9 "is without parallel in the Gospels. It is unique in that it contains two verbs, ἀπολύσῃ, γαμήσῃ, with an exception, μὴ ἐπὶ πορνείᾳ, sandwiched between them. . . . The combination of two verbs and an exception is unique." Also, Matthew introduces Jesus' saying with the authoritative λέγω δὲ ὑμῖν, "[jene] feierliche Wendung, die uns an die Sätze der Bergpredigt erinnert . . . , also an Situationen, wo Jesus seine ganze Autorität einsetzte, um den wahren Geist des Gesetzes zu offenbaren." Roig, "Exegetische Studie," 188. That stresses the special character of this much discussed clause. Furthermore, as Blomberg, "Exegesis," 173 asserts, there is no contradiction between the seemingly absolute prohibition in Mark and the exception in Matthew: "Whichever explanation is adopted, Matthew and Mark are not to be viewed as contradictory. [Matt 19,] v. 9 must be understood as implying or at least not excluding Mark 10:12. This observation makes it strange to see how adamantly some writers insist that μὴ ἐπὶ πορνείᾳ must be interpreted so as not to be a true exception to Jesus' 'no divorce' statement in Mark 10:11. This leads them to reject the very natural harmonization which assumes that Mark simply implies the exception which Matthew makes explicit, presupposing the universal acknowledgment in Jewish and Greco-Roman circles that adultery provided grounds for divorce." (See on such a necessary harmonization also Matt 16:4 and Mark 8:12; cf. ibid., 174.) For a summary of 12 different interpretations of the exception clause see Collins, *Divorce*, 199–205; further Keener, *. . . and Marries Another*, 28–31; and Luck, *Divorce and Remarriage*, 92–103.

232. However, it must be noted that the Greek λόγος, of course, also conveys the meaning "a thing" (cf. BDAG s.v. λόγος [§ 1e]) and thus also corresponds to the Greek πρᾶγμα (cf. BDAG s.v. πρᾶγμα [§ 3]). But the semantic range is, nevertheless, more congruent between the Greek λόγος and Hebrew דָּבָר. Similarly noticed by e.g., France, *Matthew*, 209–10; Collins, *Divorce*, 188; Hays, *Moral Vision*, 356; Keener, *. . . and Marries Another*, 28.

evidently is more precise in retaining the actual centre of the Pharisees' request. That does not mean, however, that Mark did not know the exception.[233]

Another interesting observation concerning the literary style are the verbs Mark and Matthew use to formulate the question of Jesus or the Pharisees about what Moses "commanded" (ἐντέλλω) and the answer referring to what Moses "permitted" (ἐπιτρέπω). In Mark, it is Jesus who draws attention to the Mosaic instructions, while Matthew skips the question of Jesus and jumps directly to the answer of the Pharisees, now (certainly for literary requirements) reformulated as a question to Jesus. In Mark 10:3, Jesus speaks about Moses "commanding/instructing" (ἐντέλλω)—leaving open whether he refers to (A) the *instruction/commandment* of Gen 1:26–27; 2:24;[234] (B) to a commandment demanding *divorce* (Deut 24:1); or to (C) the commandment demanding the *certificate of divorce* (Deut 24:1).[235] In Matthew (19:7), to the contrary, the Pharisees use ἐντέλλω referring to Deut 24:1–4 and thus obviously select the wrong one of the two possibilities implied by ἐντέλλω, as Jesus' answer points out; he "dismisses this text [Deut 24:1] as being inadequate . . . , and refers to the beginning of the Creation."[236] The change of the verbs in Mark compared to Matthew is easily explained:

> Mark's account has to have the words this way because Jesus was responding to the question 'Is it lawful for a man to divorce his wife?' It would be inappropriate for Jesus to respond with 'What did Moses allow?' because anything the Law said was regarded as a command. In Matthew the Pharisees use 'command;' but they could equally well have said 'allow?' It is therefore significant in Matthew that the Pharisees speak about Moses' command, and that Jesus answers that Moses 'allowed' them to divorce.[237]

---

233. Compare for a similar incident Paul's different depiction of the possibilities to dissolve the marriage bond: In Rom 7:1–3 and even 1 Cor 7:39 it seems he knows no exception at all, every marriage lasts until the death of one spouse; in 1 Cor 7:15, to the contrary, he speaks about the possibility of dissolving a mixed marriage (believer-unbeliever)—while he at the same time does not mention Jesus' exception clause (in case of "harlotry"), which certainly was well known to him (cf. his reference to the "instruction of the Lord" about divorce in 1 Cor 7:10).

234. Farla, "The Two," 69 explains that "from the contradiction between [Mark 10, vv.] 5–9 and 4, Gen 2.24 is given the character of a *commandment* sent by God." (My italics.)

235. See on the possibility of (B) and (C) e.g., Berger, *Gesetzesauslegung*, 541. It should be noted that, following (C), the "hardness of heart" also refers to the certificate—and that is rather unlikely. In fact it seems like Jesus implies the creation story (A), while the Pharisees think of Deut 24:1 (B). Beale and Carson, *NT Use*, 24 considers the possibility that "Jesus is deliberately turning Deuteronomy's 'if clause' into a command to reflect a distorted use of the text by certain Jewish leaders in his day."

236. Farla, "The Two," 69. However, Jesus does not contradict Deut 24:1 by pointing to Gen 1:26–27 and 2:24, as will be argued in more detail below in this section. Deut 24:1 simply is not able to demonstrate any ideal pattern. The event in Gen 1:26–27 and 2:24, to the contrary, definitely is.

237. Instone-Brewer, *In the Bible*, 143. He adds: "There was only one situation in which the early rabbis thought that Moses 'commanded' divorce. This was the case of adultery, as dealt with in Deuteronomy 24:1–4. In early Judaism it was generally considered necessary to divorce a wife even if she was only suspected of adultery. . . . The Pharisees introduced this teaching about compulsory divorce on the grounds of adultery at this point in order to counter Jesus' argument that God wants marriage to be life-long. They were saying, in effect, that the Law 'commands' divorce in some situations, and

The Biblical "One Flesh" Theology of Marriage as Constituted in Genesis 2:24

The answers about the Mosaic instruction (Mark 10:4; Matt 19:8) is similar, both using ἐπιτρέπω ("permit"),[238] although with a certain mandatory overtone, as alluded to in the textual analysis of the respective verses above.[239] The ensuing debate in Mark illuminates that Jesus apparently understood the Edenic narration by referring to what Moses "instructed" and not the Deuteronomic law that he much later "commanded"— for a special exceptional case. Matthew arranges his report in a different sequence order and sets it at the beginning, thus again more stressing the ideal Jesus evidently intended to reemphasize. That fits the concrete context much better, since in Matthew the actual question is about the reasons for divorce, not just divorce in general. Jesus' aphorism in Mark 10:9 and Matt 19:6b finally is exactly the same in both accounts: ὃ οὖν ὁ θεὸς συνέζευξεν ἄνθρωπος μὴ χωριζέτω ("accordingly, what God has joined man shall not separate").[240] Thus, although differing in details of narrative art/style and certain emphases, the important message (the "zenith"[241] of the pronouncement) remains the same in both accounts, both times argued by the Edenic ideal concluding in favor of the same everlastingness of the wedlock that is further dwelt upon in the four paralleling texts of Mark 10:11–12, Matt 19:9, Matt 5:32, and Luke 16:18:

> Es hat sich gezeigt, dass das ganze Streitgespräch in V. 9 [of Mark 10] seine Spitze findet. Auf diesen Höhepunkt hin ist es angelegt, und in diesem Vers müssen wir das eigentliche Anliegen der Perikope sehen. Es geht um die Grundlage, auf der erst ein Eherecht aufgerichtet werden kann. Jesus will, dass seine Gegner in den menschlichen Ordnungen die göttliche Ordnung sehen. Diese Ordnung heisst: Gott hat zusammengefügt.[242]

The important verb συζεύγνυμι used in this "climax" of Matt 19:6 and Mark 10:9 literally means to "yoke together,"[243] thus reflecting the close relationship of both

---

so marriage cannot be regarded as lifelong. This reply also brought Jesus back to the Text in Deuteronomy 24:1 about which the Pharisees wanted to ask Jesus." Ibid.

238. Berger suggests, "das ἐπέτρεψεν ist Verteidigung der Pharisäer. Ein Parallelbeispiel ist Philo, Spec Leg II,232: Das Gebot Dt 21,18ff, daß die Eltern einen unbelehrbaren Sohn töten müssen, wird, weil es Philo unbequem ist, nur als Erlaubnis hingestellt (ähnlich verteidigt Augustinus Moses für Dt 24,1ff in Ad Luc et c Faust 19,26); . . . ." Berger, *Gesetzesauslegung*, 541.

239. In Mark 10:3 Jesus asks: What did Moses *command* you? According to the textual analysis, it could also be read ἐνετείλατο ("command/order") in v. 4; hence we may assume a more forceful interpretation of the basically more lenient ἐπέτρεψεν ("permit/order") in the NA[27] text of v. 4.

240. The Greek relative pronoun ὃ in the accusative neuter singular form stresses the fact that it is a new unit to be regarded as one entity (singular), no more existing of two parts (plural; cf. Roig, "Exegetische Studie," 186). Similarly Berger, *Gesetzesauslegung*, 547–48: "Die beweisende Kraft von Gen 1,27 liegt darin, daß Gott sie als *einen* Mann und als *eine* Frau geschaffen hat. Die Zweiheit von je einem Mann und je einer Frau wird dann, so lehrt das folgende Zitat, zur Einheit zusammengefügt." (Italics given; cf. Baltensweiler, *Ehe im NT*, 58–59.)

241. Thus Blomberg, "Exegesis," 172.

242. Baltensweiler, *Ehe im NT*, 51.

243. BDAG s.v. συζεύγνυμι.

partners who henceforth pull the same yoke in their lives, striving for the same goals.²⁴⁴ This yoke image further implies a common master joining and leading the pair—and that should, of course, be YHWH, the Lord (cf. 1 Cor 7:39). It is also resembling the rare Hebrew צָמַד of Num 24:3, where Israel "yoked" itself to the "lord" (Baal) of Peor, and the being "unequally yoked together" (ἑτεροζυγοῦντες) of 2 Cor 6:14.²⁴⁵ Furthermore, it is the "yoke" (ζυγός) that is used by Jesus in Matt 11:29–30 to illustrate how the faithful believer is "bound" and "led" when following his "master" (or companion/coworker?) Jesus Christ. Hence, it seems proper to suggest that this "yoking" in Matt 19:6 and Mark 10:9 denotes a special divine component (or responsibility against God about whom to join), and, as Jesus explains, a divine working for the sake of the human marriage:

> The antithesis between ὁ θεός and ἄνθρωπος highlights the basis of Jesus' rejection of divorce: it is a human decision (that of the husband, who had the right to make such a decision on his own, rather than that of a legal officer) attempting to undo the union which God has created. God's act is expressed as a fait accompli by means of the simple aorist συνέζευξεν.²⁴⁶

Another very meaningful observation concerning philological features—especially considering the corresponding usage in 1 Cor 7:10–11 as will be investigated below—is the usage of the verbs for expressing "to release/divorce" (ἀπολύω) and "to separate/divide" (χωρίζω). It is conspicuous that in the discussion about divorce both Jesus and the Pharisees in every instance speak about ἀπολύω when referring to the legally valid divorce: Matt 5:31–32; 19:3, 7–8, 9; Mark 10:2, 4, 11–12; Luke 16:18 (twice). Apparently it is a well defined terminus technicus, as such even setting aside the Greek ἐξαποστέλλω ("send away/send off/send out/dispatch") used in the LXX version of Deut 24:1 for the equivalent Hebrew שָׁלַח ("give free/let go/send away").²⁴⁷ Thus

---

244. Similarly Blomberg, "Exegesis," 169; Roig, "Exegetische Studie," 186. Kirchschläger, *Ehe im NT*, 29 puts it thus: "Im Vordergrund steht nicht das negative Moment des Jochs als Zeichen von Unterdrückung und Zwang, sondern das Moment des Miteinander-unter-einem-Joch-Stehens, also: des Gemeinsam-bemüht-Seins um dasselbe Ziel . . . sie können aus dem Joch nicht ausbrechen, denn sie bilden ein Gespann."

245. In this context it might be meaningful to consider that the Aramaic translation of Gen 1:27; 5:2; and 35:9 in the Targum Neofiti repeatedly uses וזוגיה ("yoke/pair/spouse/[. . .]") as counterpart to the נשא ("man/person"); cf. CAL s.v. נשא/וזוגיה. This indicates that the "yoke" or "yoking" in reference to a person in ancient Judaism also denotes the marital bond. The Greek συζεύγνυμι is also commonly used to convey the meaning of marriage in the Greek world; cf. the ancient Greek sources referred to in BDAG/LSJ s.v. συζεύγνυμι (esp. Xenophon Oec. 7:30: νόμος συζευγνὺς ἄνδρα καὶ γυναῖκα; similarly Berger, *Gesetzesauslegung*, 537; Baltensweiler, *Ehe im NT*, 45; Rodríguez, "Konfessionsverschiedene Ehen," 217–18). Further it is most interesting that the Aramaic זוג is a loan-word from the Greek.

246. France, *Mark*, 392.

247. It is strange, but ἐξαποστέλλω is actually nowhere in the NT used in context of divorce. It indeed seems to be no longer in usage (as meaning divorce), being replaced by ἀπολύω as terminus technicus. Cf. about ἀπολύω further Benoit et al., *Les Grottes*, 104–9, 243–54; Isaksson, *Marriage and Ministry*, 95; Baltensweiler, *Ehe im NT*, 64; Blomberg, "Exegesis," 165. Similarly, Shaner, *Christian View*, 39, states: "In classical Greek ἀποστασίου δική is used to describe an action against a freedman for forsaking

Jesus' rather strange usage of χωρίζω instead of ἀπολύω (or even ἐξαποστέλλω) is all the more interesting. This χωρίζω is used only twice in the gospels, both times in the same context and at the same position: Matt 19:6 and Mark 10:9. It occurs only immediately after the quotation of Gen 2:24 as the "ultima ratio" on the discussed topic: "Accordingly, what God has joined together, man shall not separate (χωριζέτω)." Hence, it is all the more significant that in the given context Jesus does not speak about ἀπολύω (divorce), but even more about χωρίζω (separation), although, of course, the second simply forms a better antonym to "join" (κολλάω).[248] While the first one rather refers to the legal act, the last one indicates a separation not necessarily equal to the greater meaning of becoming or being legally "divorced," although that is of course *included*.[249] Thus Jesus not only condemns divorce, but he also disapproves of separation which might not necessarily result in legally valid divorce.[250] Any action against the close joining of God in "one flesh" seems to contradict the creational will of God. The fact that Jesus introduces this differing expression at just this point of the discussion concerning "ἀπολύω," immediately following the citation of the "one flesh" maxim of Gen 2:24, seems to introduce first allusions to an emphasis of sexuality in marriage and

---

his προστάτης ('defender,' 'guardian') and choosing another (Demosth., 25,65; cf. 35,48). In the papyri ἀποστασίου συνγραφή means a deed of cession (V.G.T. 69);" cf. pp. 42–43; Taylor, *St. Mark*, 418.

248. Cf. Instone-Brewer, *In the Bible*, 140; Collins, *Sexual Ethics*, 27 ("The language of 'separation' produces a direct and vivid contrast to the language of Gen 2:24, which speaks of 'joining' and 'becoming one.'").

249. Cf. BDAG s.v. ἀπολύω: "(1) As legal term, to grant acquittal; (2) to release from a painful condition; (3) to permit or cause someone to leave a particular location; (4) to grant a request and so be rid of a pers.; (5) to dissolve a marriage relationship; (6) to make a departure from a locality." Χωρίζω: "(1) to cause separation through use of space between . . . ; (2) to separate by departing from someone." The emphasis of χωρίζω clearly is on separation by departing/through space in between, while with ἀπολύω it is on the legal act (divorce). This differentiation seems to be meaningful, especially in context of Paul's exposition of the "command of the Lord" (1 Cor 7:10). Baltensweiler, *Ehe im NT*, 45 and Collins, *Divorce*, 15–19 seem to be wrong in overlooking the difference between the Pharisees' inquiry concerning ἀπολύω and Jesus' answer regarding χωρίζω, thus suggesting legal divorce supported even by 1 Cor 7:10. To the contrary, as the discussion of 1 Cor 7:10 below (see "Paul on Marital Separation/Celibacy") will demonstrate, the term χωρίζω is not necessarily a "terminus technicus" of divorce; cf. Greeven, "Ehe nach dem Neuen Testament," 381; Fitzmyer, *First Corinthians*, 293. However, Baltensweiler, *Ehe im NT*, 45 at least admits that the understanding as mere "Ehetrennung" would be possible as well. Also partly agreeing concerning the different connotations is Blomberg, "Exegesis," 169: "But the shift in verbs may suggest that Jesus is forbidding people to do that which would rupture a relationship at any level, even far short of full-fledged divorce." (Similarly Greeven, "Ehe nach dem Neuen Testament," 381/fn.2.) My understanding of a primarily physical separation is further supported by the terminology used in Gen 2:24 (which clearly is echoed here) to denote the (even physical) closeness expected by marriage partners: the Hebrew דָּבַק ("cleave/cling/stick") used in Gen 2:24 in a figurative sense still "retains the idea of physical proximity." BDB s.v. דָּבַק.

250. Similarly Luck, *Divorce and Remarriage*, 137: "Jesus does not use the normal and technical term for divorce here, but instead uses the word *chorizo*, which is well translated 'sunder.' In all the uses of this word in the New Testament it never is used as a synonym for divorce. Jesus does not deny the right to *divorce a spouse*, he merely says it is wrong to *sunder a marriage covenant*." (Italics given.)

corresponding consequences on unsound (sexual) separation even within the marital bond, as interpreted by Paul in 1 Cor 7:10–11 in more detail (see below).²⁵¹

Regarding these explanatory, concluding, or summarizing final remarks of Jesus, it is noticeable that only Matthew knows the exceptive clause (παρεκτὸς λόγου πορνείας/μὴ ἐπὶ πορνείᾳ). Considering that Matthew is naturally more interested in sound, well founded answers to prevailing, contemporary theological discussions of Palestinian Judaism and that this gospel was primarily written for informed Jewish communities, it is almost requisite to expect more detailed hints about inner Jewish peculiarities.²⁵² Just as this account frequently identifies the rather vague "people" (ὄχλοι) more specifically as "Pharisees" or "Sadducees," it is most natural for the author to include the real, inner core of the Pharisees' inquiry, for divorce in general was not subject in theological debates at that time.

Corresponding to the matter in question (Deut 24:1–4), Jesus' interpretation of different divorce cases has in every instance the man as its actively acting subject and the woman as the passively treated object (except Mark 10:12, but the causal agent is dealt with equally). The Greek verbs are properly applied to point out this feature, thus resembling the "atmosphere" of the Deuteronomic law (and basically the rest of the Mosaic instructions). While Mark and Matthew explain that the husband "commits adultery [for himself/in his own interest] (against her)" (μοιχᾶται [ἐπ' αὐτήν]; Mark 10:11–12; Matt 5:32; 19:9), or the releasing husband "makes her to be adultered" (ποιεῖ αὐτὴν μοιχευθῆναι; Matt 5:32), only Luke (16:18) employs the active verb form, but then with reference to the husband as the acting subject: "he commits adultery" (μοιχεύει; twice). Thus the NT passages not only apply and quote exactly the Edenic pattern of Gen 1:27 and 2:24 (see the LXX table above), but also echo the pattern of the Deuteronomic case law, thereby evidently claiming to interpret the two important matters of עֶרְוַת דָּבָר as well as the "defilement" of the woman referred to in Deut 24:4.²⁵³

Any broader discussion about what the term πορνεία may imply exactly seems to be superfluous, for it generally comprises all "unlawful sexual intercourse"²⁵⁴ and

---

251. At this place I want to reemphasize that becoming "one flesh," of course, comprises more than just sexuality. Yet, the sexual oneness seems to be the climax and the particularity of this significant union. While I can share great portions of my life (time, home, money, convictions, aims, ambitions etc.) with good friends, the physical union through sex is something that distinguishes the marital relationship from all other forms of intercourse that is possible with others. It seems as if Jesus is mainly speaking about this intimacy, while he does not lose sight of the other aspects necessary for a oneness in wholeness.

252. Similarly Blomberg, "Exegesis," 173.

253. More on these points see the conclusions-chapter.

254. See BDAG/THA/LSJ s.v. πορνεία; Hauck and Schulz, "πορνεία," 579–95; cf. Wenham, "Syntax of Mat. 19.9," 18; Dautzenberg, "Φεύγετε τὴν πορνείαν," 284–98; Hays, *Moral Vision*, 355; Luz, *Matthäus*, 1:362–63; Isaksson, *Marriage and Ministry*, 132–35; Blomberg, "Exegesis," 176–78; Davies and Allison, *Saint Matthew*, 1:529–31; Hagner, *Matthew 1–13*, 124–25; Nolland, *Matthew*, 245; Roig, "Exegetische Studie," 189; Dunn, *Theology*, 690; Lövestam, "Divorce and Remarriage," 58; Sigal, *Halakhah*, 117–25. The case in Thatcher, *Marriage*, 262–63 (similarly, Crispin, *Divorce*, 29) suggesting that this exception of "porneia" may "on the revisionary view . . . be seen as a general category

The Biblical "One Flesh" Theology of Marriage as Constituted in Genesis 2:24

therefore evidently includes "adultery,"[255] as e.g., Sir. 23:23 indicates: ἐν πορνείᾳ ἐμοιχεύθη ("in/by πορνεία she is adultered").[256] The laws to be applied here are those in context of the Deuteronomic case law: the Levitical instructions.[257] Furthermore,

---

of destructive behavior, not confined to a single, sexual offence" (p. 263) is too far-fetched and not supported by ancient terminological or cultural understanding. It rather seems to be Jesus' focus on the particular meaning and significance of sexuality for (the constitution and break up of) marriage, although further reasons for divorce may exist, as will be argued in the corresponding chapter below (see "Further Legitimate Reasons for Divorce"). For an overview of different interpretations of πορνεία see e.g., Hays, *Moral Vision*, 354–55.

255. Cf., for instance, Schlatter, *Matthäus*, 180, 572; Roig, "Exegetische Studie," 189. But the term obviously refers to much more, as Albright and Mann, *Matthew*, 65 admit: "πορνεία quite certainly means adultery here, and generally is used of illicit sexual relations . . . ." Luz, *Matthäus*, 1:363 further explains: "Vielmehr bedeutet πορνεία an unserer Stelle [d.i., Matt 5:32] sexuelle Bträtigung der Frau außerhalb der Ehe, d.h. faktisch Ehebruch. . . . Erklären muss man höchstens, warum προνεία und nicht μοιχεία dasteht. Dafür gibt es drei Gründe: 1. In der biblischen Sprachtradition wird der Stamm μοιχ- eher von Männern, der Stamm πορν- eher von Frauen gebraucht. 2. Beide Stämme meinen nicht Verschiedenes, vielmehr ist μοιχεία eine spezifische Form von πορνεία, so daß beide Wörter auch synonym auftreten können. 3. Doppeltes μοιχεία/μοιχεύω ware unschön." Furthermore, "adultery" in its broader sense of illicit sexual relations with someone else than one's own spouse corresponds exactly to the usage of the Greek ἄσχημον πρᾶγμα (LXX Deut 24:1 for the Hebrew עֶרְוַת דָּבָר) in the apocryphal book *Susanna* (1:63), where she is praised "because there was no ἄσχημον πρᾶγμα found in her." In that story, this ἄσχημον πρᾶγμα clearly indicates adultery. Cf. Berger, *Gesetzesauslegung*, 515: "Daraus ist zu folgern, daß zur Zeit des NT dieser Ausdruck in Dt 24,1 als Ehebruch verstanden wurde, und zwar trotz der Vieldeutigkeit auch des griech. Ausdrucks, denn ἄσχημος kann sowohl Schande als auch Scham (Lev 18,7ff LXX) bedeuten."

256. Yet it is to be considered that πορνεία can also denote simple sexual "lust" (cf. Isaksson, *Marriage and Ministry*, 133; Ryrie, "Biblical Teaching," 186), as is the case e.g., in Tob. 8:7: "I take not this my sister for lust [διὰ πορνείαν] but uprightly."

257. As the NT references to πορνεία may affirm: Acts 15:20, 29 (context of Levitical laws, summarized by keywords!); 21:25; 1 Cor 5:1; 6:13, 18; 7:2 (even polygamy!); 2 Cor 12:21; 1 Thess 4:3 (concretely contrasting πορνεία to sanctification! Cf. exactly the same context and contrast in Lev 18 (laws against sexual immorality = πορνεία) and Lev 19–21 (sanctification and holiness in everyday life). On the meaning of πορνεία for the New Testament church considering Acts 15; Matt 19; and Lev 17–18 see further e.g., Davidson, "Divorce and Remarriage," 7–8, 21. Cf. on Acts 15:20, 29 also Baltensweiler, *Ehe im NT*, 92–93. Generally on the meaning of πορνεία in NT and classical Greek see e.g., Dautzenberg, "Φεύγετε τὴν πορνείαν," 284–98; on the different interpretations of πορνεία among NT scholars cf. Isaksson, *Marriage and Ministry*, 128–36. Against the interpretation of πορνεία as referring solely to prohibited (namely incestuous or mixed) marriages basing merely on 1 Cor 5:1 (incest) and Heb 12:16 (Gentiles) as put forward by Baltensweiler, "Ehebruchsklauseln," 340–56; cf. Baltensweiler, *Ehe im NT*, 87–102; Ryrie, "Biblical Teaching," 188–89, or Fitzmyer, *Advance*, 97, see Isaksson, *Marriage and Ministry*, 129–30: "Even if we assume that the regulations in the Apostolic decree reflect those in Lev 18, it is an unjustified limitation of the meaning of πορνεία to assume that in this decree it refers only to marriages forbidden by Jewish law. Lev 18 indeed mentions not only marriages in forbidden degrees but also homosexuality and sexual intercourse with animals. Even in the Apostolic decree it is therefore reasonable to assume that πορνεία is being used of unchastity in general and not only of those forms of marriage forbidden by Jewish law." Furthermore, as Wenham, "Syntax of Mat. 19.9," 18 asserts: "In effect this [dissolution of forbidden marriages] makes Jesus give grounds for nullity rather than divorce." "According to Jewish law, no divorce was necessary when a marriage involved an incestuous relationship of the first degree. In that case the marriage was regarded as a nullity. . . . Accordingly no divorce was necessary, even if the convert [concerning proselytes] was a partner in a marriage forbidden by Jewish law." Isaksson, *Marriage and Ministry*, 130–31. Similarly Sigal, *Halakhah*, 124; Loader, *Jesus Tradition*, 71. However, what is

Jesus obviously intended to leave the semantic range that broad, for otherwise (possibly by using the term μοιχεία, "adultery") exegetes could tend to interpret it in a more narrow way, for instance by dropping cases of sodomy (zoophily), pederasty or incest.[258] Particularly the contemporary Jewish perception of adultery would stand in the way of the broader meaning the term "adultery" would evoke nowadays, as is to be seen from the rabbinic evidence (see the corresponding section about the historical context above) that granted the husband much more freedom without calling every extra-marital sexual intercourse "adulterous." Additionally, only πορνεία really fits the indistinct, obscure Hebrew עֶרְוַת דָּבָר and thus functions as the best term to interpret the challenging case of Deut 24:1.

II.2.1.4 Summary and Final Considerations

It clearly seems the matter "under attack" in the debate between Jesus and the Pharisees or Jesus and "the people" in all of the investigated texts is the interpretation of Deut 24:1.[259] This is particularly demonstrated in Matt 5:31–32, where Jesus introduces his explanation regarding divorce by unambiguously referring to Deut 24:1; then, similar to the other instances in the Sermon on the Mount, he deepens the people's understanding of the official doctrine by presenting his own interpretation ("You have heard that . . . ; but I say to you . . . ;" Matt 5:21–22, 27–28, 31–32, 33–34, 38–39, 43–44), thereby doing away with wrong perceptions, reestablishing the original, divine intention. The Pharisees in Matt 19 and Mark 10 likewise wanted Jesus to reveal and defend his own standpoint concerning the inner-Pharisaic debate about the legitimate reason(s) for divorce: would he prefer and support the Shammaite or the Hillelite view?[260] There is no intent to start a comprehensive discussion about problematic conjugal situations like, for example, domestic violence (including rape) which are likely to be subject to other Mosaic laws and ultimately allowing divorce;[261] the gospel passage is obviously not

---

overlooked is the fact that Jesus is interpreting the ancient law of Deut 24:1 without necessarily having in mind the possible proto-rabbinic norms. It is not possible to simply assume that he would not include Lev 18 in his understanding of πορνεία, just because the juridical cases were managed differently. It is much more likely to perceive the original broad range of the term, of course including the prohibitions of Lev 18, otherwise there would a lot of important meanings be missing.

258. Similarly Keener, . . . *and Marries Another*, 31; Lövestam, "Divorce and Remarriage," 56–57. Nolland, *Matthew*, 245–46 further explains: "No NT document invests in trying to give precision to πορνεία. The point of rendering 'rwt as πορνεία here is likely to be no more precise than to insist that an adequate basis for divorce will involve serious moral failure, specifically in the sexual area." Similarly Crispin, *Divorce*, 34.

259. This is widely acknowledged, see e.g., Collins, *Sexual Ethics*, 29.

260. Similarly Niederwimmer, *Askese und Mysterium*, 16; Instone-Brewer, "What God has Joined," 28: "The Pharisees wanted to know where Jesus stood. 'Is it lawful to divorce your wife for any cause?' they asked. In other words: 'Is it lawful for us to use the 'any cause' divorce?'" See further the investigations above about the "Historical Context" regarding the rabbinic teachings.

261. Certainly likewise applying in cases of domestic violence was Exod 21:24–27 (the Lex Talionis): When even slaves were to be freed when losing (only) a tooth due to the violence of their Hebrew

"intended to cover all possible scenarios."²⁶² The given passages are Jesus' response to, and interpretation of, legal reason(s) to divorce as seemingly given in Deut 24:1 by the obscure עֶרְוַת דָּבָר.²⁶³ Therefore, it also is inappropriate and simply wrong to assume that "Jesus himself . . . explicitly abolish[ed] this rule [Deut 24:1], once he had asserted in the presence of any other Jew that marriage was quite indissoluble."²⁶⁴ To the contrary, "He wasn't rejecting the Old Testament—he was rejecting a faulty Jewish interpretation of the Old Testament. He defended the true meaning of Deuteronomy 24:1."²⁶⁵

In particular, Matt 5:32 ("everyone who releases his wife, except for a word of unlawful sexual intercourse, *makes her* to be adultered") is closely reflecting the Deuteronomic law.²⁶⁶ In Deut 24:4, also, it is the first husband who *makes her* unclean, in-

---

master, how much more must *free* wives have had the right to be released. See Instone-Brewer, *In the Bible*, 100–101; Luck, *Divorce and Remarriage*, 35–36, 38–39 (this way of reasoning corresponds to "the most commonly employed" ancient Jewish exegetical technique, the so called Qal Vahomer (from minor to major; Instone-Brewer, *Techniques and Assumptions*, 17). Especially in cases of rape perhaps also applying: Deut 22:26 (equal to murder). At least a divorce with the right to remarry must have been applying, since a Hebrew wife was more worth than a foreign captive (cf. Deut 21:14). Consider also the explicit marital rights of Exod 21:10–11; cf. Beale and Carson, *NT Use*, 199; Instone-Brewer, "What God has Joined," 28–29. More in this in the corresponding chapter below, "Further Legitimate Reasons for Divorce."

262. Beale and Carson, *NT Use*, 61; cf. p. 199, cf. Kaye, "One Flesh," 52: "Jesus' remark about the singular condition for divorce is of a . . . particular kind." See esp. Blomberg, "Exegesis," 162–63 pointing to further instances where Matthew preserves seemingly exceptionless absolutes, which no one would dare to interpret thus strictly literally: Matt 19:21; ("If you wish to be complete, go and sell your possessions and give to the poor, and you will have treasure in heaven; and come, follow me."); 9:15; 13:57 ("A prophet is not without honor except in his hometown and in his own household."); 5:22 ("But I say to you that everyone who is angry with his brother shall be guilty before the court; and whoever says to his brother, 'You good-for-nothing,' shall be guilty before the supreme court; and whoever says, 'You fool,' shall be guilty enough to go into the fiery hell."); 5:28, 39; 5:41 ("Whoever forces you to go one mile, go with him two"); cf. also Luke 14:26 ("If anyone comes to Me, and does not hate his own father and mother and wife and children and brothers and sisters, yes, and even his own life, he cannot be My disciple."); more on this in the last, concluding chapter ("Further Legitimate Reasons for Divorce"). See for another example in Paul's writings Rom 7:1–3 and 1 Cor 7:39 compared to 1 Cor 7:15: While Rom 7:1–3 and 1 Cor 7:39 knows no divorce, but only a binding claim until one's spouse's death, in 1 Cor 7:15 he actually refers to an exception. In Rom 7 and 1 Cor 7:39 he simply was focusing on a theological principle he wanted to apply in his argumentation, he was not developing a theology of marriage or divorce. The same has to be assumed in Jesus' speech within the gospels. Finally, "the incident recorded in the book of Ezra [see Ezra 9–10] clearly refutes any dogmatic assertion that divorce was only allowed for sexual misconduct." Crispin, *Divorce*, 31.

263. Similarly e.g., Berger, *Gesetzesauslegung*, 512–13; Instone-Brewer, *In the Bible*, 187; Davies and Allison, *Saint Matthew*, 3:9; Hagner, *Matthew 14–28*, 547; Roig, "Exegetische Studie," 183; Sigal, *Halakhah*, 111, 114–17. Ryrie, "Biblical Teaching," 184 is again overlooking the significant agreements between Matthew's exception clauses and Deut 24:1 in structure, terminology, and content.

264. Thus Isaksson, *Marriage and Ministry*, 127.

265. Instone-Brewer, "What God has Joined," 28.

266. See also Vawter, "Divorce and the NT," 534; Mahoney, "Divorce Clauses," 166; Blomberg, "Exegesis," 165; France, *Matthew*, 206; Hays, *Moral Vision*, 356; Luz, *Matthäus*, 1:359; Instone-Brewer, *In the Bible*, 156–59; Davies and Allison, *Saint Matthew*, 528; Nolland, *Matthew*, 244–45; Sigal, *Halakhah*, 111; Collins, *Divorce*, 188; cf. Berger, *Gesetzesauslegung*, 517–18 (for differing reasons).

dicated by the hothpaal form (הֻטַּמָּאָה) of טָמֵא ("unclean/defiled/profaned"):[267] "She has been defiled." The ritual defilement must be the result of the actions that took place in Deut 24:1-2 by writing the βιβλίον ἀποστασίου and particularly the subsequent marriage to another man.[268] Hence, it is not said (either in Deut 24:1-4 or in the NT echoes) that she is already defiled by her "thing of nakedness" (עֶרְוַת דָּבָר/ἄσχημον πρᾶγμα), but by the following events. The עֶרְוַת דָּבָר of v. 1 is something actively incurred by the wife and her own action, but seemingly only punctual at a specific point of time—perhaps a single misconduct that makes her "find no favor in his [her husband's] eyes" (Deut 24:1). It is a single דָּבָר, not plural דְּבָרִים. The defilement alluded to in v. 4, in contrast, is permanent in its nature and is passively incurred by the wife, "transmitted" by the actions that took place after her own misbehavior of עֶרְוַת דָּבָר. "She has been defiled" (הֻטַּמָּאָה) by the first husband's initiative to release her and the following permanent clinging to someone else. It is also important to consider that the defilement is not "universal," it is "valid" only in regard to her first husband. In other words, her first husband makes her defiled against himself.

That is evidently tantamount to Jesus' interpretation: The first husband, by divorcing her, causes her to become defiled by exposing her to the necessity of (or by neglecting to protect her from) marrying someone else.[269] The only exception for the man not to become the "defiler" is the only licit reason for divorce mentioned in this passage: πορνεία. But in these cases of a λόγος πορνείας (Matt 5:32), the absence of a sentence pronouncing her "defiled" through עֶרְוַת דָּבָר is again conspicuous—as is the whole law, for it seems to intersect with (and even contradict) the ordinance about the death-penalty on adultery (Lev 20:10). According to Deut 24:1-4, and that is the issue in question, the woman is not necessarily defiled by עֶרְוַת דָּבָר, but she will be if her husband refuses to reconcile and thus "exposes" her to remarriage.[270] In any of

267. Cf. Davidson, "Divorce and Remarriage," 13; HALOT s.v. טָמֵא. If not assuming that it is the simple passive form ("she was defiled;" cf. Joüon and Muraoka, *Biblical Hebrew*, 147) without concrete agent pointed out.

268. Cf. Wevers, *Greek Text*, 379: "The point is that as far as the first husband is concerned, his former wife is now defiled by remarriage. Such a marriage is by definition a βδέλυγμα before the Lord." See also Loader, *LXX, Sexuality, and NT*, 73.

269. Kremer similarly interprets Matt 5:32: "Vorausgesetzt ist, daß eine entlassene Frau, die damals nicht allein bleiben konnte, durch einen Scheidebrief nicht von ihrem Mann getrennt wird und deshalb ihr Geschlechtsverkehr mit einem anderen Ehebruch ist. Daher gilt: ‚Und wer immer eine Entlassene heiratet, begeht Ehebruch'; denn er verkehrt mit einer Frau, die Eigentum eines anderen ist." Kremer, "Jesu Wort," 56. Instone-Brewer, "What God has Joined," 28 explains similarly concerning the seemingly absolute statement of Jesus "whoever [re]marries ... commits adultery" (Matt 5:32; cf. Luke 16:18) that "the fact that they said 'any divorced person' instead of 'virtually all divorced people' is typical Jewish hyperbole—like Mark saying that 'everyone' in Jerusalem came to be baptized by John (Mark 1:5). It may not be obvious to us, but their first readers understood clearly what they meant." Of course, there are legitimate reasons for divorce and, consequently, not every single remarriage results in "adultery."

270. Cf. Kirchschläger, *Ehe im NT*, 66 interpreting Matt 5:27-32: "Die Ausstellung des Scheidebriefes führt zu Ehebruch, da sie zum Eingehen einer neuen Beziehung provoziert. Deshalb ist diese Praxis ebenso auszumerzen wie das Auge, das zur Sünde verführt." Similarly Baltensweiler, *Ehe im NT*, 68 on Matt 5:32: "Der Mann begeht selbst nicht mehr den Ehebruch, vielmehr trägt er die Schuld an dem

the invested cases it is the man who bears the responsibility and who is to blame for releasing his wife, and that might indicate some unfair and unjust releasing Jesus is referring to. The only acceptable reason is πορνεία ("unlawful sexual intercourse")—and that simply is, according to the detailed instructions of Moses (cf. e.g., Lev 18; 20), any sexual activity with someone else than her husband—and that, again, is in any form tantamount and equal to what otherwise is called "adultery."

Returning to Jesus' interpretation and the usage of the passive verb form regarding the woman (in Matt 5:32a), it is most important to note that she is not called an adulteress even in case of marrying a new partner. If not released because of πορνεία, she is the one being "adultered" by her first husband's irreconcilable refusal (that exactly is also comprised by Jesus' charge against σκληροκαρδία—"hardness of heart") and releasing; she is the one becoming "defiled" for *him* by *his* action, not to anyone else by her own reorientation. Thus, even in cases of divorce without πορνεία, at least the one who is passively separated ("sent away;" Deut 24:1) may not be prohibited from taking a new partner (perhaps until the former spouse had sexual relations with someone else and thus provides the licit reason of πορνεία, as some have suggested).

Although, of course, both shall reconcile, as Paul explains referring to a word of the Lord in 1 Cor 7:10–11 (if both are Christians), this ideal is not contradicting Jesus' speech in the gospels. In Jesus' saying we find two concrete offences: (1) πορνεία and (2) irreconcilability (σκληροκαρδία), while Paul is not speaking about πορνεία, strict irreconcilability (σκληροκαρδία), and not even about ἀπολύειν (divorce).[271] Hence, if the divorcing partner is irreconcilable, the subsequent remarriage is no sin for the released partner—whatever the reason of divorce may have been.[272] It is no sin in cleaving to a

---

Ehebruch, den die Frau begehen wird, wenn sie sich wieder verheiratet. Dann wird sie nämlich die immer noch bestehende erste Ehe brechen." He adds consequently: "Indem nun der Mann seine Frau mit einem Scheidebrief fortschickt, geht er sozusagen das Risiko ein, dass sie sich wieder verheiratet. Und dann—aber im Sinn von V. 32 a erst dann!—wäre der Ehebruch perfekt. Die Verantwortung des Mannes wird in dem Sinn festgehalten, dass er es ist, der die Frau in den Ehebruch treibt." Ibid., 69; cf. Vawter, "Divorce and the NT," 530; Shaner, *Christian View*, 41, 46; Hagner, *Matthew 1–13*, 125. However, Blomberg, "Exegesis," 174–75, suggests with some linguistic support that the phrase "[he] makes her to be adultered" rather indicates the metaphorical sphere corresponding to the OT use of "adultery" as reference to Israel's unfaithfulness: ". . . divorce itself, except when it is for sexual sin, is metaphorical adultery—faithlessness to the person to whom one promised permanent loyalty . . ." Thus divorce is "adultery" even without necessarily demanding remarriage of one of the former spouses.

271. A more detailed argumentation will follow in the section dealing with 1 Cor 7 below (see "Paul on Marital Separation/Celibacy").

272. Similarly, Loader, *LXX, Sexuality, and NT*, 73: ". . . our passage [i.e., Deut 24:1–4] does not assume anything illegitimate about the second marriage." Cf. also Stein, *Mark*, 458. Against the opinion of Wenham, "Syntax of Mat. 19.9," 19, who assumes every remarriage to be adulterous (cf. also Heth and Wenham, *Jesus and Divorce*, 134; Heth, "Divorce in Matthew 19:3–9," 147), even when one's former spouse already committed adultery and thus broke the marriage bond; further against this artificial construction Blomberg, "Exegesis," 165/fn.19; Holwerda, "Jesus on Divorce. An Assessment of a New Proposal," 119. Hagner, *Matthew 1–13*, 125, adds: "The conclusion is drawn by some interpreters that while divorce may be allowable for the Christian, on the basis of this passage [i.e., Matt 5:31–32] remarriage is prohibited because it involves adultery. A divorce without the possibility

new partner, but it evidently has been a ("one-time act of") sin committing πορνεία (עֶרְוַת דָּבָר),²⁷³ or releasing motivated by σκληροκαρδία without the firm basis of one's spouse having committed deliberate, intentional,²⁷⁴ and possibly regular unlawful sexual intercourse (thereby representing "divorce" in Jesus' sense; cf. Matt 19:9; Mark 10:11).²⁷⁵

It may generally be asserted that the final clauses on divorce and remarriage, diverse as they are in the synoptic accounts with their differing textual witnesses, all point to one and the same feature Jesus is evidently stressing: a formal divorce, even including the βιβλίον ἀποστασίου of Deut 24:1, is worthless and trifling.²⁷⁶ Just as the marriage is consummated by no formal, outward means, by no concrete procedures that would be evident in the biblical text about the marriage's Edenic establishment, but only by "becoming one flesh" (Gen 2:24; Matt 19:5; Mark 10:8),²⁷⁷ so it is with di-

---

of remarriage is, however, in the context of this discussion really only a separation and not a divorce. Moses allowed divorce *and* remarriage . . . .'." (Italics given.) France, *Matthew*, 211-12 adds rightly: "Modern discussions of divorce in the light of Jesus' teaching sometimes suggest that Jesus recognized the necessity of divorce after adultery, but forbade remarriage. But such a view does not fit the Jewish context, where divorce consisted of the provision of a certificate which explicitly granted the right to remarry: the standard wording, according to *m. Giṭ.* 9:3, was, 'You are free to remarry any man.' Without that permission it was not divorce. Divorce and the right to remarry are thus inseparable, and the Jewish world knew nothing of a legal separation which did not allow remarriage. There is nothing in Jesus' words, here or in the Mark and Luke parallels, to suggest that he intended to initiate any such provision. His condemnation of remarriage as adultery is simply on the grounds that the divorce (unless for adultery) was not legitimate and so the original marriage remains valid in the sight of God."

273. Blomberg, "Exegesis," 174, explains concerning the sin of committing πορνεία: "Jesus claims that the offending person 'commits adultery.' Not one of the textual variants in this verse or in 5:32 uses the nouns 'adulterer' or 'adulteress' (μοιχός, μοιχαλίς), leaving the interpretation 'becomes an adulterer/-ess' particularly misleading. Even if one divorces for unbiblical reasons and remarries, such a person does not enter into an ongoing adulterous relationship. The commission of adultery is a one-time act. Nor does the present tense of μοιχᾶται lend support to the notion of continuous adultery. In the indicative mood, present tenses are not always progressive. The form of a pronouncement story leads one to expect as its climax a proverbial statement, which will employ gnomic or timeless verbs, not ones that emphasize ongoing action."

274. "Deliberate" and "intentional" is meant to exclude forced, passively "suffered" sexuality like rape, what certainly is not meant by Jesus' πορνεία.

275. Similarly Blomberg, "Exegesis," 172: "To be sure, Christians too can divorce because of hardheartedness, but they sin when they do." On the point of regular/repeated actions against the marriage see also Keener, *. . . and Marries Another*, 32-33, who suggests that "it is also possible that persistent misconduct, rather than a single act of adultery, is in view."

276. Cf. Baltensweiler, *Ehe im NT*, 63: "Auch die Frau ist Subjekt der Ehe. Auch *ihre* Ehe, d. h. der vom Mann mit ihr geschlossene Ehebund, kann nicht einfach gelöst werden. Der Mann, der eine Entlassene heiratet, bricht ihre erste Ehe, die fortbesteht trotz der Scheidung." (Italics given.) Similarly Isaksson, *Marriage and Ministry*, 126: "Jesus' argument for the indissolubility of marriage is then that the sexual union is of such importance that the unity which thereby comes into existence cannot be dissolved by the legal formality of writing out and handing over the bill of divorce to the wife. A marriage consummated by sexual union still exists, even after the legal contract has been annulled." Cf. also Heth, "Divorce in Matthew 19:3-9," 147; Albright and Mann, *Matthew*, 65; Instone-Brewer, "What God has Joined," 28; Meier, *Marginal Jew IV*, 107; Lövestam, "Divorce and Remarriage," 52, 63.

277. See also as an example Deut 21:13: The man has to "come in to" the woman in order to make her his married "wife" (תָּבוֹא אֵלֶיהָ וּבְעַלְתָּהּ וְהָיְתָה לְךָ לְאִשָּׁה; v. 13). This is similar to the instance of Ruth becoming the wife of Boaz through sexuality (Ruth 4:13) or the man who seduced an unbetrothed

vorce: The "one flesh" union is only dissolved (better: broken) by "becoming one flesh" with some other person (or of course by the death of one spouse).[278] Formal contracts or certificates are insignificant in this special, most individual realm:

> As sexual intercourse was an essential element in creating a psychosomatic union, so sexual intercourse can destroy that unity. Just as there is an assumption that a union is created in this way, so there is an assumption that such a unity is broken in this way . . . because it was widely believed that something was created and uncreated by sexual intercourse which had an ontic quality. Adultery does not just create a potential crisis; it creates something new and destroys the old.[279]

Yet, there seems to be a way back, as the marriage metaphors of the OT and also, as an extra-synoptical account, John 8:1–11[280] demonstrate. "Following Yahweh's example, divorce even in these situations [i.e., Exod 21:10–11; Matt 19:9; 1 Cor 7:10–16] is not mandatory, and reconciliation and forgiveness are much to be preferred."[281] John chap. 8 further depicts the case of an adulteress who possibly fell into a trap so that the Pharisees were able to catch her while committing adultery (v. 3). Jesus finishes the trial by telling her: "I do not condemn you, either. Go. From now on sin no more" (v. 11). Adultery is no "cardinal sin" in its modern sense, superseding all the other possible sins. In fact, irreconcilability is, according to Jesus' explanation, tantamount to adultery ("he [i.e., the irreconcilable husband] makes her to be adultered;" Matt 5:32). It is also not necessarily a "point of no return," although it has the overwhelming

---

virgin and therefore has to regard her as his legal wife (Deut 22:28–29). Cf. also e.g., Isaksson, *Marriage and Ministry*, 126; Crispin, *Divorce*, 13.

278. This is also confirmed by ancient Jewish convictions as, for example, in *m. Soṭah* 5:1; *Yebam.* 2:8; *Ketub.* 3:5. Further stressed by France, *Matthew*, 210.

279. Loader, *LXX, Sexuality, and NT*, 86. Note also Stuhlmiller, "One Flesh," 5, about the deep significance of the sexual one flesh union: "In reference to the 'one flesh' expression, Josephus states that in sexual intercourse the souls of each are shared with each other and that this mingling of souls brings them into a common oneness. Philo referred to the 'one flesh' of marriage as unity in which both partners share all experiences and even think alike. Rabbi Eleasar, referring to Gen 2:23, comments that the 'one flesh' expression refers to more than sexual intercourse; it depicts a phenomenon that remains even after divorce. It is clear, then, that the terminology, context, and traditional interpretation of these verses point beyond covenantal ideas (though these may have been present in the traditions embodied in this passage)." He is referring to less significant covenantal ideas differing from those propagated in this study based on just that Edenic ideal of Gen 2:24. However, he is rightly recognizing that there is no such thing as "casual sex"; cf. Smedes, *Sex for Christians*, 28; Atkinson, *To Have and to Hold*, 77–98.

280. I am well aware of the textual problems associated with this passage (John 7:53—58:11), which is not contained in various important early documents. I follow, however, the remarks of Metzger, *Greek NT*, 187–88 concerning its historical veracity: "The evidence for the non-Johannine origin of the pericope of the adulteress is overwhelming. . . . At the same time the account has all the earmarks of historical veracity. It is obviously a piece of oral tradition which circulated in certain parts of the Western church and which was subsequently incorporated into various manuscripts at various places."

281. Beale and Carson, *NT Use*, 199.

potential to become just that marital catastrophe;[282] she is not told to leave her husband, but only to resist and avoid adultery in the future.[283]

Furthermore, since "Jesus answered that Moses did not 'command' divorce, but he 'allowed' it, the implication is that even in a case of adultery, divorce is not mandatory."[284] As alluded to in Matt 18:15–17 immediately before the account of the divorce debate, any Christian sinner should be reproved at least thrice before expulsion from the church—and pardon in response to *honest* repentance must even be obtainable as often as it is needed (Matt 18:21–22)—that generally applies to adulterers as well.

> [Jay Adams] would treat marital offences with the guidelines of Matt 18:15–18. If the offending party ultimately does not respond to the loving confrontation of the entire Christian congregation, then he or she should be treated as an unbeliever, which makes divorce and remarriage for the victimized party possible via 1 Cor 7:15. Jesus' words in Matt 18:17 ("let that person be to you like a Gentile or tax collector") probably cannot bear that much freight, but Adams' instincts are good. Just as excommunication is a counsel of despair, a measure of last resort, after everything else one can possibly think of has been tried, but nevertheless a necessary procedure in certain instances, so too with divorce.[285]

These Christian principles should be considered when dealing with cases of adultery, irreconcilability, and impending divorce; at least it clearly corresponds to Yahweh's (and thus Jesus') behavior against Israel's unfaithfulness as already pointed

---

282. Against e.g., Isaksson, *Marriage and Ministry*, 25: "As was clear from our comparison with other O.T. passages, it [i.e., Deut 24:1–4] is a rule regulating the relationship between a man and his divorced wife, in accordance with the view that a wife who has had sexual intercourse with some other man, irrespective of the circumstances under which it occurred, must not have intercourse again with her former husband." This is a rule that actually cannot be derived from any OT ordinance, not even when assuming sexuality as the "legal act" of consummating marriage, as it is accepted in this treatise. Particularly the legislation for cases of rape does not justify this erroneous view (cf. Deut 22:25–27), for only the man is to be punished, the woman is without sin and it is "as if her first man was murdered" (v. 26)—she is not figuratively "divorced" and thus prohibited from remarriage with him according to Deut 24:4.

283. Please note that the case in Deut 24:1–4 included several elements that only together made up the "uncleanness" (v. 4) of the woman, making it impossible for her to return to her (former) husband: (1) marriage, (2) man recognizes "עֶרְוַת דָּבָר," (3) she loses favor, (4) he divorces, (5) she leaves his house, (6) she marries another man, (7) that man dies | or: (7) she is hated again by the new husband, (8) she is again divorced, (9) she again leaves the house, || *then* she is made unclean for her former husband and remarriage with him would be "an abomination before the LORD" (v. 4). But only steps (1) and (2) are initially given in case of adultery due to the woman's misconduct and sin. Steps (3)–(5) depend on the husband's decision, and steps (6)–(9) are even including another man's decision. Therefore, it is unwise to assume the uncleanness and the corresponding prohibition of taking her back even after step (2), although the following points may easily occur shortly after the woman's sin. But, nevertheless, the man is in no way compelled to refuse the restoration of the original "one flesh" union with his fallen wife before steps (3)–(6) are performed. Not before fulfilling the Edenic pattern by also "forsaking" the former family and authority (in this case: the first husband), and permanently "cleaving" to the new partner, the new, counter-relationship is established and the "point of no return" crossed.

284. Instone-Brewer, *In the Bible*, 143.

285. Blomberg, "Exegesis," 194; Adams, *Marriage*, 57–59.

out in the OT metaphors as well as in John 8:1–11. "From the beginning of creation" (ἀπὸ δὲ ἀρχῆς κτίσεως; Mark 10:6)[286] there should be no reason at all that necessarily leads to divorce or separation, but rather forgiveness and grace leading to reconciliation, restoration, and henceforth life-long faithfulness. Therefore, "divorce must always be recognized as failure, as an admission of defeat, but the conditions of a fallen world may in certain cases suggest that divorce is preferable to 'business as usual.'"[287]

To all these considerations the rationale used by Jesus as explanation for Moses "granting" divorce fits in the highest sense. It really is the (first) husband's σκληροκαρδία ("hardness of heart") that makes him irreconcilable, even if עֶרְוַת דָּבָר, as regards πορνεία, took place. Although the LXX text of Deut 24:1 could be (mis-)understood as a mandatory commandment in cases of a deed of unlawful sexual intercourse, it evidently is not according to the Hebrew text of this passage and Jesus' proper interpretation thereof in the gospels. The entire structure, the whole pattern, as well as the terms used by Jesus in response to the concrete inquiry on Deut 24:1, reassures the fact that he is obviously elucidating the right perception and application of the Deuteronomic law. There is no New Testament alteration of possibly outdated Old Testament instructions, there is—as to be observed throughout the gospels and especially the Sermon on the Mount in the context of which the exception clause of Matt 5:32 appears—generally nowhere an exchange of OT laws for NT ordinances. Similarly, Jesus is not playing the Edenic ideal off against the Mosaic instruction,[288] he rather reveals the original idea behind it, which was covered up by the customs of Judaism in Jesus' times (particularly Pharisaism, as the introduction to the debate on divorce may demonstrate),[289] and reaffirms the last-

---

286. Taking into consideration that it was Jesus himself who created in the beginning (see John 1:3; Rom 11:36; 1 Cor 8:6; Col 1:16; Eph 3:9; Heb 2:10), he is actually speaking about himself as the one who not only established marriage, but who now also tries to reestablish the holiness he indissolubly linked to the Edenic marriage covenant ideal. His authority in not only referring to the Edenic ideal, but also in interpreting the Deuteronomic law is thus even more emphasized. Farla, "The Two," 69, adds: "By means of the, especially in Wisdom literature, well-known introductory formula ἀπὸ δὲ ἀρχῆς κτίσεως both Genesis texts [Gen 1:27 and 2:24] become characterized as descriptions of God's will since the time of the Creation."

287. Blomberg, "Exegesis," 192.

288. That would have been tantamount to a blasphemous act; cf. *m. Sanh.* 10:1; *b. Sanh.* 99a; Strack and Billerbeck, *Talmud und Midrasch*, 1:805. The Pharisees certainly would have arrested Jesus and brought him to trial, or immediately would have killed him, if they had understood him attacking Moses' divine authority, and not just (as argued above) interpreting Deut 24:1–4 by focusing on the Edenic ideal as the most important background to understand all of God's purposes with the marital institution.

289. Thus I am also arguing against the reasoning of Gane, "Old Testament Principles," 47–48: "Thus, Jesus says that whereas Moses allowed divorce for indecent exposure without illicit sexual relations. He permits divorce only if illicit sexual relations take place"; cf. also ibid., 58; Davidson, "Divorce and Remarriage," 8. That is against the general thrust especially of the Sermon on the Mount, where Jesus (only) rediscovers God's ideals, although he uses the term "but." "Just as in the other 'But I say unto you' sayings of Matthew 5, Jesus is not changing or adding something new to the Law, but showing the true and deeper meaning that is already contained in the Law, which had been distorted by later misinterpretation." Davidson, "Divorce and Remarriage," 13–14, 21; cf. also Nembach,

ing validity and significance of the first and only divine, biblical "marriage pattern" given in Gen 2:24.²⁹⁰

The concrete reference to the Edenic ideal, and thus the enhancement and emphasis of the earliest covenant ideal of humanity's history, may allude to the everlasting ideals God established for humankind within the creation process. If God "sticks" to this covenant ideal introduced in Gen 2:24, as the investigation of the Old Testament marriage metaphors and significant judgment stories proved, then spouses may not "forsake" this ideal for whatever reason—except deliberate, intentional, and regular actions of one spouse occur that destroy the exclusive marital "one flesh" union. Only in those cases Yahweh himself would dare to separate Israel (Jer 3:8), but without any σκληροκαρδία and with the determined purpose to regain the lost partner (Isa 54:6–8). God's intention is the final establishment of the בְּרִית שָׁלוֹם, a covenant of marital faithfulness, intimacy, fruitfulness, and all that the meaningful, most significant Hebrew term שָׁלוֹם comprises. His idea(l) for the literal marriage is by no means smaller. To the contrary, it should exemplify the divine sphere, thus compelling spouses to behave as affectionate, loving, and reconcilable as God behaves—even in cases of עֶרְוַת דָּבָר/πορνεία, for σκληροκαρδία is a sign of people not devoted to Yahweh and the ideal of his holy covenant and "should be defined broadly as the calloused attitude of humanity in its fallen state against the standards of God. In the context of marriage and divorce, it will refer to a stubborn unwillingness to be faithful to the marriage covenant."²⁹¹

Some scholars point to another significant quality of the statement concerning σκληροκαρδία in Mark 10:5 asserting that "es wäre unvereinbar mit dem biblischen Gottesgedanken, wenn Gott der Verstockung des Menschenherzens weder mit Zorn noch mit Liebe, sondern mit—Nachgeben begegnete."²⁹² "Das Ganze ist also nicht als

---

"Ehescheidung," 170; Gehring, *Religionsparteien*, 531–33. Jesus is constantly pointing back to the already given (Mosaic) ideals and clothes them with a new (i.e., the original) meaning. The same happens by referring to the Edenic marriage ideal in Matt 19 and Mark 10. However, the allusion to the ideal (Gen 2:24) does not necessarily exclude divorce (Deut 24:1–4), but it restricts this practice seriously and demands reconciliation whenever possible.

290. Similarly Hasel, "Eheverständnis," 18: "Die Tatsache, dass 1. Mose 2,24 nicht weniger als dreimal im Neuen Testament erwähnt wird ... macht deutlich, dass der Schöpfungsbericht, wie er von Jesus und Paulus verstanden wurde, für das biblische Eheverständnis grundlegend ist."

291. Blomberg, "Exegesis," 171; cf. Instone-Brewer, *In the Bible*, 144–46; France, *Mark*, 391; Exod 9:12; 10:20, 27; 11:10; 14:8; Deut 2:30; 10:16; Jer 4:4; 2 Chr 36:13; LXX-version. As Berger, *Gesetzesauslegung*, 538, concerning the Jewish tradition summarizes, does σκληροκαρδία convey the following meanings: "1. Hartherzigkeit bezeichnet 'Abfall', und zwar den von der Ordnung der Natur und besonders in Bezug auf sexuelle Gebote. 2. Im Zusammenhang mit Gesetzen des Moses bezeichnet Hartherzigkeit den Abfall des Volkes zum Götzendienst an das goldene Kalb. ..."; cf. also Berger, "Hartherzigkeit," 1–47. "Die Begriffsgeschichte des Wortes σκληροκαρδία zeigt, daß es sich hier um ein spezielles Überhören von Gottes Gebot handelt. Das Scheidungsgebot ist also eine nur menschliche Satzung, die dem Ungehorsam gegen Gottes Schöpfungs- bzw. Dekaloggebot korrespondiert. Die Juden stehen also nicht erst mit der Tötung Jesu, sondern ‚rückwirkend' schon seit dem Sinai auf der Seite der Ungerechten." Berger, *Gesetzesauslegung*, 552. Cf. also Baltensweiler, *Ehe im NT*, 48–49 who sums up: "Es ist das Unvermögen gemeint, die Offenbarungen des göttlichen Heilsplanes zu erkennen und zu verstehen."

292. Greeven, "Aussagen," 114.

ein Resignieren des Moses zu verstehen, sondern so, dass Mose die Vorschrift gegeben hat «auf eure Herzenshärtigkeit hin». Die Herzenshärtigkeit «ist das Ziel, das er treffen will, nicht der Ort, von dem er herkommt.»"[293] Therefore, the law is not giving way to the lenient attitude of ancient Israel regarding divorce; it rather is a commandment *against* divorce by regulating this distortion of the ideal in order to check the spread of this unholy custom:[294]

> Mit andern Worten: Jedesmal, wenn ein Jude vor mindestens zwei Zeugen einen Scheidebrief ausstellt, ist er gezwungen zu bezeugen, dass er die von Gott eingesetzte Ordnung bricht. Schuldhaftes Verhalten soll aus der Anonymität und Heimlichkeit herausgezogen und vor Gott und Welt festgehalten werden. Die Worte «auf eure Herzenshärtigkeit hin» bekommen direkt den Sinn «zum Zeugnis gegen euch über eure Herzenshärtigkeit».[295]

Thus, by Jesus' shrewd answer concerning the Pharisees' σκληροκαρδία, "their question is exposed as stubborn disbelief; their androcentric marriage moral contradicts God."[296] The common interpretation of Jesus declaring Deut 24:1 to represent a Moasic "concession" due to (and in favor of) man's hardness of heart is therefore to be rejected.[297]

To sum up, the answer Jesus is giving in response to the Pharisees inquiry concerning a divorce κατὰ πᾶσαν αἰτίαν ("for any/every reason") evidently is a rejection of almost any possible rationale. Even the licit reason on basis of Deut 24:1 and its reference to a punctual, possibly "accidental" (i.e., committed in a weak and frail

---

293. Baltensweiler, *Ehe im NT*, 48; basing on Greeven, "Aussagen," 115; cf. Greeven, "Ehe nach dem Neuen Testament," 377–78. Niederwimmer, *Askese und Mysterium*, 14/fn.5 is against this interpretation, calling it "künstlich," but without seriously considering the rationales given in Greeven, "Aussagen," 114–15 and Greeven, "Ehe nach dem Neuen Testament," 377.

294. As was investigated on Deut 24:1–4 above (see "Divorce as Unintended Deviation"). Jesus follows this OT principle and interprets the purpose of Deut 24:1–4 rightly. Cf. also Stein, *Mark*, 456; Beale and Carson, *NT Use*, 199; Luck, *Divorce and Remarriage*, 138–39; similarly Piper, *Momentary Marriage*, 160; Lövestam, "Divorce and Remarriage," 49; France, *Matthew*, 212, 714, 719–20 ("troubleshooting legislation").

295. Baltensweiler, *Ehe im NT*, 48, almost verbatim echoing the reasoning of Greeven, "Aussagen," 115; Greeven, "Ehe nach dem Neuen Testament," 377–78. The same point is supported by Pesch, *Freie Treue*, 25 (again with reference to the mentioned proposal of Greeven).

296. Farla, "The Two," 68.

297. This erroneous interpretation is advocated e.g., by Shaner, *Christian View*, 39 ("Divorce was only a compromise law allowed because man was unable to obey the higher morality of God;" similarly Beale and Carson, *NT Use*, 60), Roig, "Exegetische Studie," 188 (referring only to Gnilka, *Markus*, 72), Davidson, "Scheidung und Wiederheirat," 160 ("Moses Entgegenkommen gegenüber der 'Herzenshärtigkeit' Israels . . ."), Piper, *Momentary Marriage*, 161 ("God's will about divorce in Genesis 1–2 is not the same as his will expressed in Deuteronomy 24."), Hays, *Moral Vision*, 350 ("a concession to 'your hardness of heart'"), Collins, *Sexual Ethics*, 31 (". . . this concession was not in accord with God's creative will."), Countryman, *Dirt, Greed and Sex*, 174 ("Jesus abolished one part of Scripture, the divorce law, on authority of another, the creation accounts."), Loader, *Jesus Tradition*, 68, 101, 106–7 ("The treatment of Deuteronomy 24 appears to indicate that the provisions it assumes are so much a concession for sinners that they should not be contemplated." P. 101), Collins, *Divorce*, 96, Friedrich, *Sexualität und Ehe*, 133–34, Kleinschmidt, *Ehefragen*, 213, and Luz, *Matthäus*, 3:94–95.

condition) עֶרְוַת דָּבָר/πορνεία is only "permitted" due to the irreconcilable "hardness of heart" on the part of the unforgiving partner. The ideal is reconciliation as Paul later reemphasizes (1 Cor 7:10–11). In cases of permanent, unchangeably determined irreconcilability of one spouse, remarriage is no sin.[298] The only sins mentioned are πορνεία and σκληροκαρδία resulting in a defilement of the released person and applying only to the former spouse (Deut 24:4), not to anyone else.

II.2.2 Paul's Spiritual Application (Eph 5:21–33; 1 Cor 6:12–20)

While Jesus responded to the Pharisees' inquiry about divorce according to Deut 24:1–4, Paul is focusing more concretely on the Edenic ideal of Gen 2:24, especially the meaningful "one flesh" union, in its spiritual realm. There are two echoes in two letters to two different churches, referring to a differing context. While the first deals with a close connection of literal and spiritual sphere in sexual intercourse and the influence on body and spirit (1 Cor 6:16–17), the other passage again compares literal and symbolic spheres, but now taking the spiritual level as example for instructions on the most practical, literal level (Eph 5:29–32).[299]

The delimitation of both passages is determined by their individual contexts and it seems proper to set the boundaries as close as possible to the central quote (or echo) of Gen 2:24. In the first letter to the Corinthians, that would be 1 Cor 6:12–20; the

---

298. Cf. generally on this point also Luck, *Divorce and Remarriage*, 144–47, 158.

299. In this study the authorship of Paul is assumed for the letter to the Ephesians. Similarly to the arguments of Son, "Concept," 107–8/fn.2, this includes the following reasons: First, the Baur tradition of the nineteenth century is open to serious questions based on the doubtful literary presuppositions involved concerning style, vocabulary, and theological perceptions. "It often does not fully consider . . . changing circumstances or subject matter, the use of nonauthorial pre-formed traditions, and the use of the amanuensis in Paul's letters." Ibid. Second, the majority of congruent concepts, of vocabulary, and style with other (undoubted) letters of Paul are estimated too lightly. That will also become evident in the corporate investigation of the two central passages Eph 5 and 1 Cor 6–7. Third, many of the early Christian Fathers support Paul's authorship. Among them are Clement of Rome, Ignatius, Hermas, and Polycarp. Finally, the results obtained by the exegetical study of Eph 5:21–33 are not essentially altered even by completely omitting any reference to a concrete author. On further literature criticizing the Baur tradition see e.g., Ellis, *Documents*, 320–29; Ellis, *Christ and the Future*, 212–41; Höhner, *Ephesians*, 2–61; Son, *Corporate Elements* 5–6/fn.9. Also, Barth (in his *Ephesians 1–3*) argues through line-by-line examination of vocabulary, style, parallels with and distinctions from the undisputed Pauline corpus, its use of the Old Testament, and its dialogue with orthodox and heretical Judaism, that Paul was almost certainly the author. The traditionalist view assuming Pauline authorship is further supported by scholars that include Ezra Abbot, Asting, Gaugler, Grant, Harnack, Haupt, Hort, Klijn, Johann David Michaelis, Percy, Robinson, A. Robert, Feuillet, Roller, Sanders, Schille, Schlier, Schmid, Scot, Westcott. (For the concept of Ephesians dictated by Paul with some interpolations from another author e.g., Albertz, Benoit, Cerfaux, Goguel, Harrison, Holtzmann, Murphy O'Conner, Wagenfuhrer.) It is reasonable, therefore, that "von zahlreichen Exegeten . . . der Eph auch noch in jüngster Zeit als genuiner Brief des Paulus aufgefasst [wird]," since the author of "Eph die theologischen Grundgedanken des Apostels sehr genau gekannt und verarbeitet hat." Sellin, *Epheser*, 57. Please note further the comprehensive discussion about the letter's author in Schlier, *Epheser*, 22–28, who also concludes that this letter was written by Paul. Ibid., 27–28.

subject of endangering one's spirituality or glorifying the Lord by the "instrument" of one's body in reference to sexuality is commenced with vv. 12–13 as introduction, and it ends with v. 20 as preparation for turning to the more general topic of marriage in chap. 7. Thus the passage encloses the theological reflection of Gen 2:24 as its central part (vv. 16–17). In the letter to the Ephesians the most proper delimitation seems to be Eph 5:21–33,[300] perhaps even commencing with v. 19,[301] thus starting with the first of two admonitions regarding headship and love as introduction to the interpretation of the Edenic ideal, and ending with a reference to both subjects in v. 33. Further arguments in favour of these limits will appear within the textual analysis.

II.2.2.1 Historical Context

In this section I will briefly outline historical backgrounds of both churches that may be relevant for the particular passages investigated afterwards.

II.2.2.1.1 Ephesians

Concerning the Ephesian church it seems likely to reckon with a "entstehenden christlichen Milieu bescheidenen Umfangs in städtischer Umgebung [. . .], das er [i.e., the author], überzeugt von der Überlegenheit des eigenen Standpunkts, mit seinen massiven Entgegensetzungen christlichen und heidnischen Lebensstils zu stützen sucht."[302]

The author speaks to "Heidenchristen und möchte zur sozialethischen Gestaltung ihres 'Hauswesens' in heidnischer Stadtumgebung aus dem Geist christlichen Glaubens beitragen."[303] Although it is almost impossible to define them definitely, we have to assume that there were different Gnostic tendencies in Ephesus that led to a distortion of Christian principles, particularly concerning the union of body and spirit as emphasized by the imagery in the examined passage.[304] Concerning the loving unity between husband and wife in our passage (5:21–33), with the man as the head of

---

300. Cf. e.g., Theobald, "Heilige Hochzeit," 230–32 using the same delimitation. Baltensweiler, *Ehe im NT*, 218–19 differs slightly by commencing with v. 22 instead of 21, even though he admits that the (especially terminological) connections are of a very close nature.

301. Considering that Eph 5:21 starts with the participle of "subjecting" (ὑποτασσόμενοι) that equals the participle constructions of vv. 19–20 (λαλοῦντες/ᾄδοντες/ψάλλοντες/εὐχαριστοῦντες; all present active nominative masculine plural, the Ὑποτασσόμενοι of v. 21 differs only concerning its mode: passive instead of active), it clearly seems as if Paul in v. 21 is still continuing the exhortation of vv. 19–20 (similarly, Sellin, *Epheser*, 437). This should be kept in mind, although these verses (19–20) do not have to be investigated within the passages delimitation in order to get its full meaning. Hence, they will be left out in the textual and literary criticism.

302. Theobald, "Heilige Hochzeit," 243.

303. Theobald, "Heilige Hochzeit," 244.

304. See e.g., Schlier, *Epheserbrief*, 272–79; Schlier, *Epheser*, 265–76 (esp. on the hieros gamos concept); Fischer, *Tendenz und Absicht*, 176–200; cf. Theobald, "Heilige Hochzeit," 244–46; Batey, *Nuptial Imagery*, 26, 33, 70–76; Batey, "Jewish Gnosticism," 121–27.

the wife (v. 23), Paul might be applying an ancient perception the Ephesians were possibly already familiar with, interpreting it as particularly Christian in its deeper sense:

> Plutarch, ein Vertreter des Liebespatriarchalismus, vergleicht in Praecepta Coniugalia 142 E das Verhältnis des Mannes zu seiner Frau mit dem der ψυχή zum σῶμα, Musonius Rufus [13 a] fordert für die Ehe umfassende Gemeinsamkeit/κοινωνία zwischen den Ehepartnern... Dagegen war Gen 2,24c in Sir. 25,26... so verstanden worden, daß die Frau zum ‚Fleisch' des Mannes gehört. Der Eph versteht die Aussage betr. die somatische Einheit von Mann und Frau von Gen 2,24c unter der gleichen patriarchalischen Voraussetzung...[305]

Of course, in promoting wifely subordination, this author [of Ephesians] is not attempting to introduce a radically new mode of behavior. Instead, he appears to be seeking to set out a specifically Christian rationale for what was already a fundamental expectation for female conduct.[306]

II.2.2.1.2 CORINTH

As was the case in all the churches of Asia Minor, Greece and Italy, the church of Corinth consisted of former Jews and heathens.[307] The city was inhabited by a lot of different ethnic groups (freedmen, colonists, veterans), all carrying their own cults with them,[308] so that a variety of different religious perceptions and ideas existed in the mixture of Corinthian culture.[309] Concerning the topic of slavery in 1 Cor 6–7, "the imagery derives from the slave auction, familiar to Corinthians because Corinth was a major center for slave trafficking."[310] Many researchers assume that temple prostitution and cultic meals including the consumption of meat from animal offerings for idols were well known cultural institutions; some even claim that "die Sexualriten der Aphroditenverehrung brachten in der damaligen Zeit eine Versexualisierung des Lebens mit sich, von der schwer zu sagen ist, ob sie durch die heutigen Verhältnisse überboten wird."[311] Following these ideas it would not be surprising that "there were

---

305. Dautzenberg, "Φεύγετε τὴν πορνείαν," 281–82; see on Musonius Rufus' and Plutarch's attitudes toward marriage esp. Hering, *Haustafeln*, 247–60. Cf. Beattie, *Women and Marriage*, 79; Müller, "Haustafel," 292–98.

306. Beattie, *Women and Marriage*, 79.

307. Cf. 1 Cor 7:18; 8:10; 10:27, 32; 12:2, 13.

308. Cf. Kirchhoff, *Sünde*, 71; Schrage, *1. Korinther*, 1:27–28.

309. See for a variety of ancient sources depicting the historical city of Corinth: Murphy-O'Connor, *St. Paul's Corinth*, 1–192.

310. Garland, *1 Corinthians*, 239.

311. Thus, for instance, Baltensweiler, *Ehe im NT*, 159–60 and (probably copied by) Domanyi, "Anthropologie und Ethik," 238. Besides, it is generally held that the majority of church members were basically of the lower classes, and thus possibly used to have contact with prostitutes in their daily affairs, while the wealthy members may have had female servants that frequently were regarded as prostitutes; Paul apparently has to deal with resulting liberal perceptions concerning values of sexuality still

libertines who clearly thought that the individual's sex life was of little importance as regarded his or her religious life. The satisfaction of sexual needs was placed on the same level as the satisfaction of the need of food and drink."[312] Yet, "we do not have evidence of sacral prostitution at Corinth in the Roman period"[313]—apart from the only ancient statement mentioning temple prostitutes in Corinth (Strabo 8:6:20) speaking of more than 1,000 Hetaerae[314]—if this brief account is reliable.[315] In fact, we do not have any conclusive evidence that sacred prostitution in antiquity existed at all.[316] However, there were at least certain places like public baths (thermae/balnea) and taverns offering opportunities to engage freely in extramarital sex and prostitution with (mostly female) slaves serving in those establishments and at temple feasts,[317] even though this kind of sexual activity would not be sacral in its character.[318] However, "auf jeden Fall galt Korinth in der ganzen Antike als Hochburg des Dirnenwesens, was für eine Hafenstadt nicht ungewöhnlich ist."[319] It is not surprising, therefore, that this topic is addressed in the letter to the Corinthians, although it is most probable that it is not referring to cultic prostitution, but rather to profane sexuality. Also, there is no group known that would claim, "Sexualität sei ein moralisch irrelevanter Bereich, und [die] ihre Promiskuität philosophisch-theologisch gegenüber Kritikern

---

maintained even after becoming members of the Christian faith community. Cf. Kirchhoff, *Sünde*, 100; she concludes her investigations stating: "Es bestätigt sich, daß die paulinischen Adressaten keine libertinistischen Gegner waren, sondern Christen, die die Konsequenzen, die ihre Zugehörigkeit zur christlichen Gemeinde für die Wahl ihrer Sexualpartnerin haben sollte, (noch) nicht gezogen hatten." Ibid., 101.

312. Isaksson, *Marriage and Ministry*, 104 referring to 1 Cor 6:12–20; cf. Lietzmann and Kümmel, *An die Korinther I-II*, 27–28.

313. Loader, *LXX, Sexuality, and NT*, 95; cf. Zeller, *1. Korinther*, 32–33 (pointing to further sources supporting this position); Conzelmann, "Aphrodite," 152–66; Kirchhoff, *Sünde*, 42–47; Beale and Carson, *NT Use*, 713; Schrage, *1. Korinther*, 13; Rosner, "Temple Prostitution," 347–48. Prostitutes, however, were usually present at temples feasts, and Paul may refer to just those situations (thus, ibid., 348–51; Beale and Carson, *NT Use*, 713).

314. Cf. Rosner, "Temple Prostitution," 347–48.

315. Against its full reliability cf. Budin, *Sacred Prostitution*, 165–67.

316. For a monograph devoted to the aim of refuting the existence of sacred prostitution in antiquity see Budin, *Sacred Prostitution*. For a bief summary of ancient examples of cultic prostitution see Zimmermann, *Geschlechtermetaphorik*, 707.

317. Cf. e.g., Kirchhoff, *Sünde*, 46–47. She further asserts: "Kultprostitution, die zudem für Griechenland sehr ungewöhnlich wäre, lässt sich somit für den Aphroditekult in Korinth nicht wahrscheinlich machen. Es bestand lediglich ein indirekter Zusammenhang zwischen den verschiedenen in Korinth ansässigen Kulten und der (profanen) Prostitution, insofern die Heiligtümer viele Männer anzogen, die wiederum potentielle Kunden der Prostituierten waren." Ibid., 47. The same point makes Rosner, "Temple Prostitution," 348–51.

318. Similarly Rosner, "Temple Prostitution," 341: "Of the two alternatives, sacred or secular prostitutes, the former is the more specific hypothesis and thus must bear the burden of proof; if the evidence for sacred prostitution is weak, then we may safely assume Paul is opposing secular prostitution. At least this seems to be the approach of the majority of modern commentaries, which customarily dismiss cultic prostitution before concluding that secular prostitution is in view."

319. Zeller, *1. Korinther*, 33.

verteidigt haben. Für gnostische, stoische und jüdische Gruppen ist weder eine solche Argumentation noch eine entsprechende Praxis belegt."[320]

However, "schon damals wandten sich grosse Kreise des Volkes angewidert von diesem Treiben ab und drohten, ins andere Extrem zu fallen."[321] Correspondingly, "sexual abstinence was widely viewed as a means to personal wholeness and religious power."[322] It must be assumed that both views abstinence and carelessness in sexual matters were present in the Corinthian church of Paul's time, as the contrasting perceptions in 1 Cor 6:12–13 and 7:1–2 may indicate.[323]

These brief notes demonstrate that the historical backgrounds of the letters to the Ephesians and to the Corinthians lack certainty and themselves raise more questions than they are able to answer. Nevertheless, these considerations at least may grant a slight impression about possible and probable circumstances given in the particular historical situations. However, due to the sparseness of the historical information it is not possible to obtain more precise conclusions concerning our textual investigations.

II.2.2.2 Text and Translation

II.2.2.2.1 THE GREEK TEXT OF 1 COR 6:12-20

Before dealing with textual variants, the Greek NA[27] text should be given to start with:

(12) Πάντα μοι ἔξεστιν ἀλλ' οὐ πάντα συμφέρει· πάντα μοι ἔξεστιν ἀλλ' οὐκ ἐγὼ ἐξουσιασθήσομαι ὑπό τινος.

(13) τὰ βρώματα τῇ κοιλίᾳ καὶ ἡ κοιλία τοῖς βρώμασιν, ὁ δὲ θεὸς καὶ ταύτην καὶ ταῦτα καταργήσει. τὸ δὲ σῶμα οὐ τῇ πορνείᾳ ἀλλὰ τῷ κυρίῳ, καὶ ὁ κύριος τῷ σώματι·

(14) ὁ δὲ θεὸς καὶ τὸν κύριον ἤγειρεν καὶ ἡμᾶς ἐξεγερεῖ διὰ τῆς δυνάμεως αὐτοῦ.

(15) οὐκ οἴδατε ὅτι τὰ σώματα ὑμῶν μέλη Χριστοῦ ἐστιν; ἄρας οὖν τὰ μέλη τοῦ Χριστοῦ ποιήσω πόρνης μέλη; μὴ γένοιτο.

---

320. Kirchhoff, *Sünde*, 76.

321. Baltensweiler, *Ehe im NT*, 160.

322. Hays, *First Corinthians*, 114; cf. Garland, *1 Corinthians*, 263. See esp. Domanyi, "Anthropologie und Ethik," 234–35 who lists several plausible reasons why some Corinthians may have concluded that sexuality is always unholy: (1) Jesus and Paul were not married; (2) there would be no marriage in heaven according to Matt 22:30; (3) Sexuality is contrary to a life in the Holy Spirit; (4) being married to a non-Christian is no real marriage and should be dissolved. Oster, "Archaeological Evidence," 60–64 further asserts that Egyptian cults practiced at Corinth (e.g., the one of Isis) included sacral celibacy and were possibly used as pattern for sexual abstinence demanded by some Corinthians in 1 Cor 7:1; he suggests that it is "the type of religious behavior that is transferred so easily from one religion to another" (p. 64; cf. also Collins, *First Corinthians*, 253; also referred to in Garland, *1 Corinthians*, 265).

323. Similarly Baltensweiler, *Ehe im NT*, 160; Isaksson, *Marriage and Ministry*, 104; Farla, "The Two," 75; Domanyi, "Anthropologie und Ethik," 234–35.

(16) [ἢ] οὐκ οἴδατε ὅτι ὁ κολλώμενος τῇ πόρνῃ ἓν σῶμά ἐστιν; ἔσονται γάρ, φησίν, οἱ δύο εἰς σάρκα μίαν.

(17) ὁ δὲ κολλώμενος τῷ κυρίῳ ἓν πνεῦμά ἐστιν.

(18) Φεύγετε τὴν πορνείαν. πᾶν ἁμάρτημα ὃ ἐὰν ποιήσῃ ἄνθρωπος ἐκτὸς τοῦ σώματός ἐστιν· ὁ δὲ πορνεύων εἰς τὸ ἴδιον σῶμα ἁμαρτάνει.

(19) ἢ οὐκ οἴδατε ὅτι τὸ σῶμα ὑμῶν ναὸς τοῦ ἐν ὑμῖν ἁγίου πνεύματός ἐστιν οὗ ἔχετε ἀπὸ θεοῦ, καὶ οὐκ ἐστὲ ἑαυτῶν;

(20) ἠγοράσθητε γὰρ τιμῆς· δοξάσατε δὴ τὸν θεὸν ἐν τῷ σώματι ὑμῶν.

While vv. 12 and 13 are clear, in v. 14 there are two minor deviations concerning the verb ἐξεγείρω ("awaken/raise (up)/bring into being/elevate").[324] Instead of ἐξεγερεῖ (ind. fut. act. 3rd pers. sg.: "he will awake/raise up;" including 𝔓[46c1], ℵ, C, D³, K, L most minuscules and most versions) some documents have ἐξήγειρεν (ind. aor. act. 3rd pers. sg.: "he has awoken/risen up"; including 𝔓[46c2], B[424c] 1739, Origen) or ἐξεγείρει (ind. pres. act. 3rd pers. sg.: "he awakes/rises up;" including 𝔓[11.46*], ℵ, D*, P 69 88). Although

> the witnesses are fairly evenly divided as to the tense of the verb . . . The context makes the future necessary as the correlative of καταργήσει in ver. 13 (compare also the parallel in 2 Cor 4.14). The aorist ἐξήγειρεν (which involves an interpretation that applies it to baptism) appears to have arisen from mechanical adaptation to the preceding ἤγειρεν.[325]

It seems best to leave the verb form given in NA[27] thus fitting context and general sense in the best way.

Some manuscripts introduce v. 15 with the ἢ ("or"), or read ἡμῶν ("our [bodies]") instead of ὑμῶν ("your [bodies]"), not at all altering the meaning of the sentence. But other deviations concern the verb ἄρας (verb part. aor. act. nom. masc. sg. From αἴρω: "taking"). In some documents the final ς fell out and thus they render instead the particle ἄρα ("so/then/consequently/you see")[326] or also add an ἢ combined as ἢ ἄρα ("or consequently"); but that seems to be a scribal error, disturbing the flow of the sentence, making it more uneven: "(Do you not know that your bodies are members of Christ?) *Or* [shall I] *consequently* make the members of Christ [into] members of a prostitute?" Yet, the sense is again unaltered.

In v. 16, as indicated by square brackets in the NA[27] version, only the introductory ἢ ("or") is uncertain, but the evidence is basically strong, including the manuscripts 𝔓[46], D, K, L, Ψ 6. However, it is rather a matter of style and not contributing to the meaning of the verse.

Verses 17–18 are firm, but in vv. 19–20 there again are minor variants. Some read the plural τὰ σώματα ("[your] bodies") instead of the singular τὸ σῶμα ("[your] body") in v. 19, thereby not at all changing the sense. Yet, it does not fit the singular τῷ

---

324. Cf. BDAG s.v. ἐξεγείρω.

325. Metzger, *Greek NT*, 486–87.

326. Cf. BDAG s.v. ἄρα.

σώματι ὑμῶν in v. 20 which is evidently parallel to the τὸ σῶμα ὑμῶν of v. 19. It seems more reliable when considering the context to hold fast to the singular form.

In v. 20, there are two uncertainties, the first minor variant regarding the Greek δή ("indeed/now/then/therefore")[327] which is exchanged for ἄρατε (verb imperat. aor. act. 2nd pers. pl. from αἴρω: "take!/lift up!"), thus reading "glorify, lift up God in your body" emphasizing the aim of glorification by paralleling "glorify" and "lift up." The textual evidence, however, is meager: Seemingly the original version of 1505, 1611, (Vulgate); those are further weakened by 2495 *ℵ and the Latin Irenaeus which completely omit a possible δή or ἄρατε. The second and major deviation concerns a possible addition at the end of the verse. There C³, D², a note in Ψ 1739/1881, the Majority text, single manuscripts of the Vulgate, as well as the complete Syriac tradition have καὶ ἐν τῷ πνεύματι ὑμῶν, ἅτινά ἐστιν τοῦ θεοῦ ("and in your spirit, which is of God"). This is an interesting variant, particularly because it represents a parallel to vv. 13b and 19, thus enclosing the whole passage with the general goal of glorifying God through the spirit as exemplified on the literal (bodily) sphere. Yet, that these words may be only gloss could be concluded "from the decisive testimony of the earliest and best witnesses in support of the shorter text ($\mathfrak{P}^{46}$ ℵ A B C* D* F G 33 81 1739* it vg cop$^{sa, bo, fay}$ eth Irenaeus^{lat} Tertullian Origen Cyprian al)."[328]

II.2.2.2.2 Translation

To sum up, we may assert that the Greek text of the NA²⁷ should not be altered. Hence, the following translation bases on the text given above, again including possible variants in single or double round brackets to indicate the probability of the textual deviation.

(12) All things are permitted to me, but not all things are profitable. All things are permitted to me, but I will not be mastered by anything.

(13) Food is for the stomach and the stomach is for food, but God will do away with this and that. Yet the body is not for unlawful sexual intercourse, but for the Lord, and the Lord is for the body.

(14) But God raised the Lord, and will also raise us up through His power.

(15) Do you not know that your ((our)) bodies are members of Christ? [Shall] I now take the members of Christ and make them members of a prostitute? May it never be!

(16) (Or) do you not know that anyone joining himself to a prostitute is one body [with her]? For he says [or: it says/it is said], "The two will be/become one flesh."

(17) But the one joined to the Lord is one spirit [with Him].

---

327. Cf. BDAG s.v. δή.
328. Metzger, *Greek NT*, 488.

(18) Flee unlawful sexual intercourse. Every [other] sin that a man commits is outside the body, but the one committing unlawful sexual intercourse sins against his own body.

(19) Or do you not know that your body is ((or: bodies are)) a temple of the Holy Spirit who is in you, whom you have from God, and that you are not your own?

(20) For you have been bought with a price: therefore glorify ((or: glorify, lift up)) God in your body ((and in your spirit, who is of God)).

II.2.2.2.3 The Greek Text of Eph 5:21–33

For this passage the Greek NA²⁷ standard text will again be mentioned firstly, subsequently starting discussing possible textual deviations and suggesting a tentative translation.

(21) Ὑποτασσόμενοι ἀλλήλοις ἐν φόβῳ Χριστοῦ,

(22) αἱ γυναῖκες τοῖς ἰδίοις ἀνδράσιν ὡς τῷ κυρίῳ,

(23) ὅτι ἀνήρ ἐστιν κεφαλὴ τῆς γυναικὸς ὡς καὶ ὁ Χριστὸς κεφαλὴ τῆς ἐκκλησίας, αὐτὸς σωτὴρ τοῦ σώματος·

(24) ἀλλὰ ὡς ἡ ἐκκλησία ὑποτάσσεται τῷ Χριστῷ, οὕτως καὶ αἱ γυναῖκες τοῖς ἀνδράσιν ἐν παντί.

(25) Οἱ ἄνδρες, ἀγαπᾶτε τὰς γυναῖκας, καθὼς καὶ ὁ Χριστὸς ἠγάπησεν τὴν ἐκκλησίαν καὶ ἑαυτὸν παρέδωκεν ὑπὲρ αὐτῆς,

(26) ἵνα αὐτὴν ἁγιάσῃ καθαρίσας τῷ λουτρῷ τοῦ ὕδατος ἐν ῥήματι,

(27) ἵνα παραστήσῃ αὐτὸς ἑαυτῷ ἔνδοξον τὴν ἐκκλησίαν, μὴ ἔχουσαν σπίλον ἢ ῥυτίδα ἤ τι τῶν τοιούτων, ἀλλ' ἵνα ᾖ ἁγία καὶ ἄμωμος.

(28) οὕτως ὀφείλουσιν [καὶ] οἱ ἄνδρες ἀγαπᾶν τὰς ἑαυτῶν γυναῖκας ὡς τὰ ἑαυτῶν σώματα. ὁ ἀγαπῶν τὴν ἑαυτοῦ γυναῖκα ἑαυτὸν ἀγαπᾷ·

(29) Οὐδεὶς γάρ ποτε τὴν ἑαυτοῦ σάρκα ἐμίσησεν ἀλλὰ ἐκτρέφει καὶ θάλπει αὐτήν, καθὼς καὶ ὁ Χριστὸς τὴν ἐκκλησίαν,

(30) ὅτι μέλη ἐσμὲν τοῦ σώματος αὐτοῦ.

(31) ἀντὶ τούτου καταλείψει ἄνθρωπος [τὸν] πατέρα καὶ [τὴν] μητέρα καὶ προσκολληθήσεται πρὸς τὴν γυναῖκα αὐτοῦ, καὶ ἔσονται οἱ δύο εἰς σάρκα μίαν.

(32) τὸ μυστήριον τοῦτο μέγα ἐστίν· ἐγὼ δὲ λέγω εἰς Χριστὸν καὶ εἰς τὴν ἐκκλησίαν.

(33) πλὴν καὶ ὑμεῖς οἱ καθ' ἕνα, ἕκαστος τὴν ἑαυτοῦ γυναῖκα οὕτως ἀγαπάτω ὡς ἑαυτόν, ἡ δὲ γυνὴ ἵνα φοβῆται τὸν ἄνδρα.

Some witnesses insert Ἰησοῦ before Χριστοῦ in v. 21; others read κυρίου or θεοῦ instead. But the most important manuscripts render the text as given above, therefore it should be preferred.

In v. 22 "several early witnesses (𝔓⁴⁶ B Clement½ Origen Greek mss^(acc. to Jerome) Jerome Theodore) begin the new sentence without a main verb, thus requiring that the force of the preceding ὑποτασσόμενοι be carried over."[329] The witnesses "for the shorter reading (in which the verb 'submit' is only implied) are minimal . . . , but significant and early. The rest of the witnesses add one of two verb forms as required by the sense of the passage (picking up the verb from v. 21)."[330] They have ὑποτασσέσθωσαν or ὑποτάσσεσθε after ἀνδράσιν or γυναῖκες. The shorter reading is preferred, although "the text virtually begs for one of these two verb forms, but the often cryptic style of Paul's letters argues for the shorter reading."[331] It "accords with the succinct style of the author's admonitions," while the other readings are explained "as expansions introduced for the sake of clarity, the main verb being required especially when the words αἱ γυναῖκες stood at the beginning of a scripture lesson."[332] However, in basically any English translation the verb is inserted for better understanding.

Some manuscripts reverse the word order of ἐστιν κεφαλή in v. 23; others expand the αὐτός ("he [is]") and read καὶ αὐτὸς ἐστιν ("and he is"), both without altering the sense.

The ὡς ("[here:] as") in v. 24 is omitted in only very few documents (B, few of Ψ, Old Latin b, and in Ambrosiaster). Best evidence is given in favor of this Greek conjunction.

The paragraph of vv. 25–27 contains only one minor deviation in v. 25 with some manuscripts inserting a ὑμῶν (F, G, Old Latins, some Vulgate editions, and the Syriac tradition) or ἑαυτῶν (D, Ψ 0278, Majority text, and a few others) after τὰς γυναῖκας, thus reading "husbands, love *your* wives" or "the husbands shall love *their* wives." The reading of the NA²⁷ is to be preferred.

In v. 28, some important witnesses (including ℵ, Ψ 0278, 1739, 1881, Majority text, Peshitta) do not contain the καὶ, which is indicated by square brackets in NA²⁷.

In v. 29 D² and the Majority text read κύριος instead of Χριστὸς, thereby, of course, referring to one and the same person: Jesus Christ.

A major variation occurs in v. 30. While the text as it stands is basically clear, many manuscripts—including ²ℵ, D, F, G, (K), Ψ 0278, (seemingly also) 0285, (a marginal note in) 1739, Majority text, Old Latins incl. Vulgate, the Syriac tradition, and Irenaeus—add another sentence: ἐκ τῆς σαρκός αὐτοῦ καὶ ἐκ τῶν ὀστέων αὐτοῦ ("out of his flesh and out of his bone"). Thus the quote of Gen 2:24 in the subsequent verse is enlarged by a partial quote of Gen 2:23, and the connection to 1 Cor 6:15 ("members of Christ") and 1 Cor 6:16–17 ("one flesh") becomes even closer. Yet, Metzger explains that

---

329. Metzger, *Greek NT*, 541.

330. NET note on Eph 5:22.

331. NET note on Eph 5:22. On the consequences resulting from the omission or the insertion of the verb cf. Miletic, *One Flesh*, 27–28.

332. Metzger, *Greek NT*, 541.

> Although it is possible that the shorter text, which is supported by early and good witnesses (including 𝔓⁴⁶ ℵ* A B 33 81 1739* cop^(sa, bo)), may have arisen by accidental omission occasioned by homoeoteleuton (αὐτοῦ ... αὐτοῦ), it is more probable that the longer readings reflect various scribal expansions ...³³³

The evidence for the shorter reading is, however, not overwhelming. Most Western witnesses, as well as the majority of Byzantine MSS, the Latins and the Syriacs are strong witnesses of the larger version. Furthermore, the explanation for the omission of the second part of v. 30 "occasioned by homoeoteleuton (αὐτοῦ ... αὐτοῦ)" is very reasonable, while the differing word order of the addition in contrast to the LXX pattern of Gen 2:23 weakens the assumption that it is only a "scribal expansion." At least, it is by no means evident that,

> on intrinsic grounds, it seems unlikely that the author would refer to the physical nature of creation when speaking of the 'body of Christ' which is spiritual or mystical. Hence, as is often the case with OT quotations, the scribal clarification missed the point the author was making; the shorter reading stands as original.³³⁴

To the contrary: in vv. 23 and 29, Paul explicitly refers to the physical nature by speaking about the church as Christ's "body" and spouses as consisting of one "flesh." He uses a literal, visible fact of affiliation between husband and wife (implicitly referring to Gen 2:23) and then shifts from the literal to the spiritual sphere, speaking about the "members" of Christ's body—what would be somehow incomplete without another (now explicit) reference to the Edenic pattern (Gen 2:23). The addition seems almost necessary in order to strengthen the basis of Paul's comparison which reaches its climax in the immediately following verse by quoting from Gen 2:24.

Only a few manuscripts omit the τόν and τήν in v. 31, therefore they are put in square brackets in the NA²⁷. The LXX pattern has both of them, so it could be a scribal emendation. Verse 32 contains a single minor variant concerning the second εἰς, which is omitted in only a handful of documents (including B, K *pc*, Tertullian, Cyprianus, Epiphanius). Verse 33 is clear. The alternative readings in vv. 31–32 are without influence on sense and meaning of the text.

II.2.2.2.4 Translation

Finally, the translation of the Greek text reads:

(21) Becoming subject to one another in the fear of ((Jesus)) Christ ((or: the Lord)).
(22) The wives, to your own husbands, as to the Lord.

---

333. Metzger, *Greek NT*, 541; cf. Best, *Ephesians*, 550; cf. Lincoln, *Ephesians*, 351.
334. NET note on Eph 5:30.

(23) For the husband is the head of the wife, as Christ also is the head of the church, he himself [being] the savior of the body.
(24) But as the church is subject to Christ, so also the wives to the husbands in everything.
(25) Husbands, ((shall)) love the ((their)) (your) wives, just as the Christ also loved the church and gave himself up for her,
(26) so that he might sanctify her, having cleansed her by the washing of water in (with) the word,
(27) so that he might present to himself the glorious church, having no spot or wrinkle or anything like that; but that she is holy and blameless.
(28) Thus the husbands owe (also) to love their own wives as their own bodies. He who loves his own wife loves himself;
(29) for no one ever hated his own flesh, but nourishes and cherishes it, just as the Christ ((or: the Lord)) also does the church,
(30) because we are members of his body (, out of his flesh and out of his bone).
(31) Therefore a man will leave (the) father and (the) mother, and will be cleaved to his wife, and the two will be/become one flesh.
(32) This mystery is great; but I am speaking with reference to Christ and (to) the church.
(33) Nevertheless, each individual among you also is to love his own wife even as himself, but the wife [must be careful] that she fears the husband.

II.2.2.3 Textual Analysis

The textual analysis of the passages under investigation will start with the text of Ephesians, for there we find an important hermeneutical argumentation presented by Paul as evidence to compare literal and spiritual levels legitimately, drawing conclusions from one sphere to the other. In First Corinthians he again applies the same "rules" of interpretation using the same Old Testament pattern (Gen 2:24) in a similar context: interaction between spirituality and the physical nature through intimate (sexual) relationships.

II.2.2.3.1 EPHESIANS 5:21–33

This text is "one great simile: the relationship between husband and wife is like the relationship between Christ and the church."[335] The entire passage contains an interesting and illuminating kind of argumentation. While the author at first draws conclusions from spiritual conditions and applies them to literal, everyday situations, it seems as if he suddenly becomes aware that his way of reasoning might be obscure to his readers. Most significantly, he only uses a short, final reference

---

335. Osiek, "Bride of Christ," 384; cf. Schlier, *Epheser*, 253.

to Gen 2:23–24 in order to support his position sufficiently. There are two hypotheses he presents as his starting point concerning the subject of the "Haustafel"—the family life, especially between husbands and wives. The evidence he uses in favor of his argument goes throughout the entire passage as his special train of thought, culminating in the climactic quotation of Gen 2:24. The thematic structure can be presented as follows:[336]

Basis: Being Subject to One Another in the Fear of Christ (v. 21)[337]

    Hypotheses: Reasoning from Spiritual to Literal level (vv. 22–29)

        Headship

            (A) The headship of Christ as pattern for the headship of husbands. (Vv. 22–23a)

                (B) The church as Christ's <u>body</u> [indicating the wife as the husband's body]. (V. 23b)

            (A') The headship of Christ over the church as pattern for the headship of the husbands over their wives. (V. 24)

        Love

            (C) Husbands shall *love* their wives, as Christ *loves and glorifies* the church. (Vv. 25–27)

                (B') Husbands shall *love* their wives as their own <u>bodies</u>. (V. 28)[338]

---

336. Batey, "Jewish Gnosticism," 124 or Batey, "The ΜΙΑ ΣΑΡΞ Union," 270 recognizes the same three main parts (sovereignty/love/unity); also Lambrecht, *Collected Studies*, 299 is very similar in his outline. For another structure using differing emphases see e.g., Theobald, "Heilige Hochzeit," 231–32. He also recognizes the climax of the passage in the quotation of Gen 2:24. Another differing outline oriented on the respective subject/sphere (human spouses and Christ-church) is given by Sampley, *One Flesh*, 104; here, again, Gen 2:24 (including v. 32a) represents the centre, for it is combining both spheres. Similarly Son, "Concept," 111 outlines the literary structure according to the comparative particles (ὡς, καθὼς, οὕτως) employed in Eph 5:21–33 and arranged concerning the husband-wife and Christ-church relationship. Farla, "The Two," 72 is again slightly differing, but basically agrees concerning the main parts.

337. Please note that a similar basis is already established at the beginning of the chapter (Eph 5:1–2): "Therefore *be imitators of God, as beloved children*; and *walk in love, just as Christ also bloved you and gave Himself up for us*, an offering and a sacrifice to God as a fragrant aroma." (Compare esp. with Eph 5:25.)

338. As Beattie, *Women and Marriage*, 77 rightly notes, the Greek ὡς ("as") "may bear a number of connotations here: taken in a comparative sense, wives are to defer to their husbands in the same manner as they defer to Christ; in the temporal sense, they should submit to husbands for as long as they submit to Christ, that is to say, submission to her husband is the particular form a woman's service to Christ ought to take. Probably both ideas are present here." There may even be a third connotation, esp. concerning v. 28, referring to the deeper reason of the command ("why?"), as Batey asserts: "(1) The husband is to love his wife *as being* his own body, since husbands and wives become one flesh by virtue of their union in marriage (vs. 28b). (2) Because the wife is one body or one flesh with her husband, he should love and care for her as he would his own flesh (vs. 29a). In fact, he who loves his wife loves his own self, or better the single personality which together they compose." Batey, *Nuptial Imagery*, 30–31.

(C') Husbands shall *nourish and cherish* their wives, as Christ the church. (V. 29)

EVIDENCE: Proving from Literal to Spiritual Level (vv. 30–33)

Unity

(D) We are members of his body [, his flesh and bone]. (V. 30)

(B") Quotation from Gen 2:24. (V. 31)

(D') This "great mystery" interpreted as referring to Christ and the church. (V. 32)

RESULT: Approved as Applicable (v. 33)

[FURTHER CONSEQUENCES: Children-Parents/Slaves-Masters (6:1–9)]

The combining instrument of both hypotheses on (1) *Headship* and (2) *Love* is the (3) *Unity* in the sense of a close affinity as given by the Lord's body (B) and the husbands' bodies (B').[339] The "king's evidence" is the "climactic quotation"[340] of Gen 2:24 (B") that evidently combines and closely connects the literal and spiritual spheres which here in the whole paragraph are contrasted and assimilated; although the Genesis text originally knows nothing about headship, this (almost allegorical) proof-text method adequately corresponds to an established interpretative pattern in the NT.[341] Paul uses the spiritual

---

339. This is even more confirmed in Paul's saying: "But I want you to understand that Christ is the head of every man, and the man is the head of a woman, and God is the head of Christ." (1 Cor 11:3.) This verse obviously is very similar to the instance investigated above and stresses the affinity between God, Christ, man and woman, again in context of headship. His rationale on these conditions (man above woman) is further interesting for our topic: "For a man ought not to have his head covered, since he is the image and glory of God; but the woman is the glory of man." (v. 7.) This is a short echo of Gen 1:26, "Then God said, 'Let us make man in our image, according to our likeness....'" While Paul uses the LXX rendering of "image" (εἰκών), he exchanges the "likeness" (ὁμοίωσις) for the "glory" (δόξα) of God. Now, "as the context shows, he uses δόξα to mean 'reflected splendor.' He intends to convey more than just the idea of resemblance or likeness; rather he means likeness due to the derivation of being. Man who has been created in the image of God reflects the divine nature of his creator. Woman is a reflection of that reflection, for she has been taken from man. Dependence of being has implicitly within it the idea of headship and the honor which is due." Batey, *Nuptial Imagery*, 22–23. Consequently, again, the central theme in this passage is not headship, it is unity and affinity. (By the way, the secondary connotation of Greek κεφαλή denoting "source" [cf. LSJ s.v. κεφαλή] is obviously left out, only the meaning "authority" remains; cf. Beattie, *Women and Marriage*, 78.)

340. Thus Beattie, *Women and Marriage*, 81, who further explains that Gen 2:24 "is the basis upon which the author's analogy between Christ and the church and husband and wife must rest." Ibid. Similarly Schlier, *Epheser*, 262; see also the structure of Bailey, "Foundation," 39, with the quotation of Gen 2:24 in its centre.

341. Cf. e.g., Sampley, *One Flesh*, 112: "Within 5:21–33, Gen 2:24 is used to reinforce both of the admonitions [i.e., submission and love] found in the Haustafel." However, in this work it is assumed that the rationale of vv. 31–32 is used in a twofold way: (1) to support the author's general linkage of husband-wife and Christ-church by anatomical comparison. Just as the Edenic ideal speaks in terms of anatomy, so Paul applies this language and justifies this by concrete reference to Gen 2:24. (2) The impact of Gen 2:24 cited in Eph 5:31 is primarily concerning the role of the husbands "to love their own wives as their own bodies" (v. 28). Similarly Miletic, *One Flesh*, 19: "The majority of scholars who

The Biblical "One Flesh" Theology of Marriage as Constituted in Genesis 2:24

sphere to argue in favor of his hypotheses concerning the literal sphere. Then, in order to prove the legitimacy of his reasoning, he reverses the way of arguing and proves in the opposite direction, from literal to the spiritual level.[342] The result of his short "test" is the approval of the kind of reasoning in his previous hypotheses, which now are summarized in v. 33 by turning again to the literal sphere as the goal he wanted his arguments to support. Thus "there is a divine relationship viewed as human, which at the same time forms and gives meaning to the human sphere."[343] In the following admonition (in 6:1–9) he further builds on this foundation, repeatedly transferring and applying divine expectations or conditions of the human-divine relationship to the literal sphere and the conditions of interpersonal relationships.[344]

---

raise the question agree that the literary impact of Gen 2.24 can be discerned only in the address to husbands.... The injunction for subordination (5.22–24) is usually not perceived as related to the text of Gen 2.24 (Eph 5.31)"; cf. Schnackenburg, *Epheser*, 259–62; Son, "Concept," 113–14. As became apparent in the scrutiny of the creation account, there initially is no submission, headship, or any other form of hierarchy discernable in the beginning (Gen 1–2), but perfect equality prevailed. Not before the Fall in Gen 3 we hear of naming and submission, with Adam the "ruler" (מָשַׁל) of Eve. This concrete mentioning would not have been necessary, if this state of things had already existed before. Consequently, it is necessary to likewise suppose the quotation in Eph 5:31 as referring primarily to the immediately preceding argument in its entirety (vv. 21, 25–30; husbands shall love their wives as their own flesh), not to the aspect of dominion (vv. 22–24). Nevertheless, the citation additionally supports the σῶμα image of the previous verses and thus at the same time functions as final rationale of the complete image prevailing in vv. 21–33. The verses 31–32 mainly serve as evidence to justify the author's way of argumentation (from spiritual to literal and vice versa) and are not meant to be a pattern applied in every respect to the foregoing reasoning. In this context, Sampley's observation concerning a certain NT pattern of reasoning by OT quotations deserves attention: "There is an identifiable pattern in the NT whose elements include: (1) a statement that women should be submissive, and (2) a reference to Torah as a means of supporting the concern with the subordination of women. In the first element, the verb is consistently ὑποτάσσομαι and is always related to women. It is in the second element that the author has freedom to adapt the form to his own purposes, but there is a common element that sets some limits to that freedom: the reference ought, in some way, to ground the subordination in Torah. The author is at liberty to choose whatever verse or allude to whatever story in the law that would best serve his needs at the moment." Sampley, *One Flesh*, 97; cf. pp. 97–100; Miletic, *One Flesh*, 20. Hence, even while the OT pattern evidently is not speaking about headship and submission, the author is at liberty to apply the pattern completely to one part of his argumentation and to alter its meaning to further support the other hypothesis. Although Gen 2:24 is actually no valid proof for submission, the underlying assumption of quoting Gen 2:24 to justify switching between spiritual and literal spheres is still given, and therefore is rightly applied by Paul to a statement that has no direct bearing on Gen 2:24.

342. On this "shifting" of spheres cf. also Köstenberger, "The Mystery," 85.

343. Batey, "Jewish Gnosticism," 124; cf. Batey, "The MIA ΣΑΡΞ Union," 271: "The author closes with the postscript that his mind is primarily preoccupied with ecclesiology, but the ethical implications for Christian marriage are also valid."

344. Even though "the headship shared by Christ and husband is not identical,... it is capable of comparison." Batey, *Nuptial Imagery*, 21. Of course there are not all qualities of this relationship to be transferred without proper interpretation and application. The basic pattern, however, is apparently applicable to both spheres: "While the author admits that he is bent on ecclesiology, the ethical implications are valid, and therefore a husband should love his wife as himself and a wife should respect her husband." Ibid., 65. Similarly, as "Christ is the origin (ἀρχή) of the church, he is also the goal and destiny (τέλος) toward which she should grow. As the church individually and collectively approaches maturity, that

> Instructions to this end [i.e., conduct in marriage] are interwoven by way of analogy with reflections on the relationship between Christ and the church. In this way, the author's idealized vision of marriage comes to function as an image of the bond between Christ and his people.... At the same time, the analogy bestows divine sanction upon a socially conservative, hierarchical version of the marriage partnership, and gives the teaching an air of permanence which Paul's provisional instructions lack."[345]

It is most important to acknowledge that this way of "proving" and "sanctioning" the previous hypotheses is only possible when the Edenic covenant ideal of Gen 2:24 is indeed transferable to (or even more the pattern of) the covenant between Yahweh and Israel in the Old Testament. As investigated thoroughly in the first part of this treatise, this idea may be regarded as fully justified by all the evidence given in God's working for the sake of Israel. As demonstrated in the chapters about the spiritual sphere in the Old Testament above, all the steps necessary to speak of a marital relationship between Yahweh and Israel are given, and even exact terminological evidence supports this perception. What Paul is doing now in Eph 5:22–33 and 1 Cor 6:12–20 is simply a consequent application of this most important OT pattern transferred and applied to the NT church.[346] Thus "Eph 5 presents a renewal, or rather, a Messianic transformation, of the prophetic marriage imagery used in the OT to describe the covenant between Yahweh and Israel."[347] Significantly, Paul does not dwell largely on his "masterpiece" of evidence as given in the figurative interpretation of Gen 2:24, but takes it for granted that the reader is well aware of the meaningful consequences that may be derived from the Edenic covenant pattern.[348] "According to the author of

---

is, becomes transformed into the likeness of Christ, it grows toward 'the measure of the stature of the fullness of Christ' (Eph 4:13–16; cf. Col 2:19)." Ibid., 25–26. Thus, the entire church should finally reflect the "image and likeness of God" as the goal of Gen 1:26 states in reference to man. Hence, the levels "individual believer" and "church" are also interchangeable within the given image.

345. Beattie, *Women and Marriage*, 77.

346. On the "hieros gamos" between Christ and the church according to OT patterns see especially Sampley, *One Flesh*, 34–51. He sums up: "It is in v. 26b that the reader first encounters an indication that the author of Ephesians is undertaking a correlation of Christ with YHWH and of the church with Israel. In so doing the author has adumbrated, by means of these slight references, the history of YHWH's relationship with Israel. The author of Ephesians has adapted the YHWH-Israel hieros gamos for his purposes in speaking of Christ and the church. This connection not only ties Christology into the history of Israel and her understanding of YHWH, but also links ecclesiology with that same history. By his development in vv. 26–27, the author makes clear a positive continuity between the history of Israel and the history of the church, between YHWH's action for Israel and Christ's action for the church." Ibid., 133; (see also pp. 153, 162); cf. Kirchschläger, *Ehe im NT*, 25, 40; Richardson, *NT Theology*, 257; Best, *One Body*, 172; Best, *Ephesians*, 559–60; Lincoln, *Ephesians*, 362–63; Osiek, "Bride of Christ," 387–92; Lincoln, "OT in Ephesians," 31; more general on the hieros gamos metaphor: Zimmermann, *Geschlechtermetaphorik*, 62–104.

347. Barth, *Ephesians 4–6*, 739.

348. For Philo, as was investigated above (see "The Edenic Ideal in Prominent Ancient Jewish Literature"), the Edenic ideal is also rich in spiritual implications: "Both Philo and Ephesians agree that the 'one flesh' doctrine is useful to communicate the nature of a spiritual reality; love is the dynamic

Ephesians marriage is a reflection of the paradigm relationship that subsists between Christ and his church."[349] Also,

> in order to explicate the quality of Christ's love the author presupposes the image of the church as the Bride of Christ (5:25–27). The Bride image seems to have been so familiar to his readers that he feels no need to state it directly, but the cumulative effect of his language leaves little doubt that this is his intention.[350]

The same applies to 1 Cor 6:15–20, as will be demonstrated below. But beforehand, another step should be the comparison of Paul's quotation of Gen 2:23–24 and the LXX rendering thereof for the purpose of gaining some further hints on possible emphases. A table contrasting the different sequences reads thus:

Gen 2:23–24 (LXX)	Eph 5:30–31 (incl. the addition)
(v. 23) [. . .] ὀστοῦν ἐκ τῶν ὀστέων μου καὶ σὰρξ ἐκ τῆς σαρκός μου	(v. 30) ὅτι μέλη ἐσμὲν τοῦ σώματος αὐτοῦ ἐκ τῆς σαρκὸς αὐτοῦ καὶ ἐκ τῶν ὀστέων αὐτοῦ
(v. 24) ἕνεκεν τούτου καταλείψει ἄνθρωπος τὸν πατέρα αὐτοῦ καὶ τὴν μητέρα αὐτοῦ καὶ προσκολληθήσεται πρὸς τὴν γυναῖκα αὐτοῦ καὶ ἔσονται οἱ δύο εἰς σάρκα μίαν	(v. 31) ἀντὶ τούτου καταλείψει ἄνθρωπος [τὸν] πατέρα καὶ [τὴν] μητέρα καὶ προσκολληθήσεται πρὸς τὴν γυναῖκα αὐτοῦ καὶ ἔσονται οἱ δύο εἰς σάρκα μίαν

The quotation of Gen 2:24 is almost exactly matching the LXX pattern,[351] only departing from the introduction (ἀντί instead of ἕνεκεν)[352] and the first sequence by twice omitting αὐτοῦ as well as (most likely) the definite articles τόν and τήν. In the uncertain addition to v. 30 the sentence order given in the LXX is confused, mention-

---

which creates unity; the male quality is the dominant force which transforms the female quality into his likeness. Sympathetic harmony results from this unity and ethical implications for domestic living are suggested." Batey, *Nuptial Imagery*, 33.

349. Sampley, *One Flesh*, 157; similarly Beattie, *Women and Marriage*, 77.

350. Batey, *Nuptial Imagery*, 65. Similarly Schnackenburg, *Epheser*, 255–57; cf. Son, *Corporate Elements* 97–98: "Paul applies Gen 2:24 to the church as the bride of Christ and compares the unity between Christ and the church to that of 'one flesh' effected through marriage. The basic idea is twofold: (1) The church is the body of Christ, and (2) Christ is the head of that body. The 'head' in this passage denotes Christ as the bridegroom of the church."

351. It is further to be considered that "Paul's deviations from the modern LXX editions do not demonstrate that he quoted inaccurately. As the other citations of Gen 2:24 in the NT show, several Greek texts were in use during the time of NT." Barth, *Ephesians 4–6*, 721. On the citation's exactness cf. also Lincoln, "OT in Ephesians," 32; Sellin, *Epheser*, 454–55.

352. Beale and Carson, *NT Use*, 827 deem this change of the introduction to be important: "Although both expressions [ἀντὶ τούτου and ἕνεκεν τούτου] mean 'on account of this,' Paul's alteration is significant because it shows that he intended the phrase to carry its meaning within the context of his own argument. . . . He did not leave it out (as he might have done had he thought it unimportant), nor did he simply repeat it because it was part of the biblical text (as we might assume if he had reproduced it verbatim from the LXX). For Paul, the phrase made a clear, logical connection between his statement that Christians are members of Christ's body (5:30) and the phrase 'the two shall be one flesh' (5:31)."

ing at first the "flesh" and then the "bone." But the altered kind of ordering the four significant elements of v. 30 is not without reason and seemingly reflects a chiasmus that stresses the instrument or parameter of Paul's evidence in the entire argumentation (i.e., (B) and (B')):

(A) μέλη ("Members")
   (B) σῶμα ("Body")
   (B') σάρξ ("Flesh")
(A') ὀστᾶ ("Bones")

The addition in Eph 5:30b thus seeks to establish more clearly the close affiliation between the church and its "head" Jesus Christ (v. 23; cf. Eph 1:22–23), thereby strengthening the evidence Paul uses to prove his preceding argumentation. Particularly the paralleling elements μέλη and ὀστᾶ, both appearing in the plural, establish more firmly the theological perception Paul uses frequently elsewhere to elucidate the manifold parts of each individual member of the church in serving Christ.[353] The σάρξ of Gen 2:24, embedded in the chiasmus of v. 30, finally serves as crucial evidence in favor of the σῶμα he used as rationale in vv. 23, 28 by so closely combining both in this parallelism, obviously using them interchangeably.[354] Thus Paul prepares the way to cite Gen 2:24 suddenly rounding off his reasoning.[355]

The entire passage may further be described as a chiastic inclusio in which the following aspects are enframing the central subject of the Edenic ideal as its theological foundation and core:[356]

353. See e.g., Rom 6:13, 19; 12:4–7; 1 Cor 6:15–20; 12; Eph 4:25 etc.

354. Cf. Son, *Corporate Elements* 87–88. It further seems like, on intrinsic grounds, it is important to interpret the "addition" in v. 30b as authentic material, indeed being significant for the entire argumentation of Eph 5:22–33. Also, if it would have been only a "scribal expansion," one would have to assume that the scribe quoted the LXX more exactly, and not in the given way, creating a parallelism by reversing the sentence order. The omission rather seems to be a scribal mistake: "The addition may be said to fit the present context since its words are drawn from the verse immediately preceding that quoted in v. 31, v. 30 is difficult to explain without them and they provide a referent for τούτου in v. 31. They could have been omitted by homoeoteleuton αὐτοῦ . . . αὐτοῦ." Best, *Ephesians*, 550; cf. Lincoln, *Ephesians*, 351. However, even a possible "lack of textual authenticity need not preclude the truth of their [i.e., the additional words in v. 30b] content." Barth, *Ephesians 4–6*, 722.

355. Similarly Beale and Carson, *NT Use*, 828; cf. Sampley, *One Flesh*, 90: "Furthermore, there is in 5: 21–33 itself evidence that Gen 2: 24 is playing a role even before it is cited in v. 31. . . . it is often conceded by modern scholarship that v. 29a—'For no man ever hates his own flesh'—reads 'flesh' (σάρκα) instead of the just mentioned 'bodies' (σώματα) of v. 28a or 'himself' (ἑαυτῶν) of v. 28b in view of the upcoming quotation from Genesis. . . . Internal evidence confirms the suggestion that the author of Ephesians is offering his interpretation of Gen 2: 24 before he actually quotes it." Loader, *LXX, Sexuality, and NT*, 108 and Schnackenburg, *Epheser*, 258–59 make the same point.

356. Cf. also Sampley, *One Flesh*, 147: "Verse 33 completes the literary form of the unit 5: 21–33 by a chiasmus incorporating the entire passage: wives (vv. 22–24), husbands (vv. 25–30) and husbands (v. 33a), wives (v. 33b)." Additionally, this short "summary" of the preceding unit (vv. 21–32) in v. 33 is qualified to silence all questions about the extent of the quotation in v. 31. As explained by the author in v. 33, it was his purpose to provide OT evidence comprising both topics: love as well as fear/submission (similarly ibid.; Miletic, *One Flesh*, 112)—although Gen 2:24 originally does not speak about hierarchy.

(A) φόβος: Fear Husbands (vv. 21–25)

  (B) ἀγαπάω: Love Wives (vv. 25–29)

    (C) [Quote:] Being One Flesh (vv. 30–32)

  (B') ἀγαπάω: Love Wives (v. 33a)

(A') φοβέω: Fear Husbands (v. 33b)

There are two pillars emphasized by Paul: Fear and Love. The roles of husbands and wives are clear, although according to the introductory v. 21 "all familial relations are governed by mutual submission in the fear of Christ."[357] The wives' part primarily is to "fear,"[358] and the husbands' part is to "love."[359] Taking the spiritual sphere into consideration to which the author is frequently referring, we recognize the two central pillars on which the entire divine-human covenant in the Old and New Testament is based on: For humankind to *fear* God, and for God to prove his *love* for humankind.[360] Significantly, "it is not persons but *relationships* and therefore *interactions* that are compared"[361] in this paragraph of Ephesians.—However, unlike the OT pattern who

---

357. Sampley, *One Flesh*, 158.

358. Lambrecht, *Collected Studies*, 300 rightly notices concerning "fearing" one's husband: "Of course, already in the Old Testament 'to fear' is not necessarily a negative concept. Fearing God contains reverence and love. Yet if by the translation of this vocabulary by 'reverence' or 'respect' one wants to deny any nuance of fear, this most probably goes against the intention of the author. The Christians 'fear' Christ in a religious way; analogously the author demands from the wife to 'fear' her husband." Best, *Ephesians*, 559 explains further that "φοβέομαι ranges in meaning from suggesting terror to respect and reverence. As it denotes here [i.e., Eph 5:33] the wife's reaction to her husband's love it can hardly lie in the area of terror; yet reverence would not be an exact rendering, for her attitude includes obedience and submission. φόβος is a normal element in all authority structures (cf Rom 13.3, 4, 7; 1 Pet 2.18; Eph 6.5), though if the controlling authority acts unreasonably it may degenerate into terror; in our case the controlling authority is directed by love." ". . . the wife's fear is her appropriate response to her husband's headship exercised in self-sacrificial love." Lincoln, *Ephesians*, 385.

359. It is important to recognize that the most natural antonym of the wives' role to "be subject" (v. 21–24) or to "fear" (v. 33) would be the husbands' part to "rule"—but that is not the case here. This is very striking and it reveals the "Besondere der christlichen Mahnung: überhaupt nicht 'beherrschen', sondern 'lieben'!" Schnackenburg, *Epheser*, 258. Barth, *Ephesians 4–6*, 732 interprets: "Only the husband is put under a blunt 'must.' That which he 'must' do is 'to love his wife,' not to tame or dominate her, according to Eph 5:33a. The application for the woman is soft and friendly: 'may she [be enabled to] fear her husband' (5:33b)." Similarly Christ does obviously not intend to simply "rule" the church, but to lead it by convincing and even compelling unselfish love (cf. vv. 25, 28: "*just as* Christ loved" (καθὼς καὶ ὁ Χριστὸς ἠγάπησεν) and "*thus/in this manner* the husbands owe to love" (οὕτως ὀφείλουσιν [καὶ] οἱ ἄνδρες ἀγαπᾶν); cf. on this also Schlier, *Epheser*, 254–55. Further derived from the Christ-church pattern is the following, very positive, appeal: "Wives, let your fallen submission be redeemed by modeling it after God's intention for the church! Husbands, let your fallen headship be redeemed by modeling it after God's intention for Christ. Therefore, headship is not a *right* to control or to abuse or to neglect. (Christ's sacrifice is the pattern.) Rather, it's the *responsibility* to love like Christ in leading and protecting and providing for our wives and families." Piper, *Momentary Marriage*, 80; italics given. Thus, the apostle's exhortation rather is a precaution against the abuse often present in his times, as well as in our times. See on a very good interpretation of these headship and submission topics: Ibid., 73–103.

360. Similarly Best, *Ephesians*, 559.

361. Osiek, "Bride of Christ," 384; italics given.

additionally expects man to love God,[362] "what is surprising [in Eph 5:21–33] is the failure to summon the wife to love her husband."[363]

Batey appropriately sums up concerning the relation of fear and love between Christ and the church:

> Though sovereign, the love of Christ is also sacrificial—freely giving itself for the church's welfare.... The free acceptance of divine love, which wills that which is best for the church, brings about a unanimity of will and purpose without making the church servile. To surrender herself to a Lord who loves her with sacrificial love is the way to liberation. The dialectic between freedom and submission is adequately conveyed by the Bride image, for the church accepts in faith the will of her Lord who wills for her authentic life. The unity of the church is not, therefore, to be maintained by uniformity or conformity to external and objective measures of religion however they may appear. The unity of the church is primarily gained through dedication to that one Lord through whom the divine love has become known.[364]

While these "roles" become apparent in this text, another aspect should not be passed by unnoticed: the aim of glorification and, finally, salvation. As (C) and (C') above demonstrate, even the "tasks" of Christ and the husband are similar: While Christ's loves is expressed in purifying, glorifying, and sanctifying the church (vv. 25–27), the husband is correspondingly to care for his wife, nourishing and cherishing her—certainly not merely in a physical sense, but also concerning the wife's spiritual needs. This again supports the idea of (one of) the marriage's aim(s), namely, to assist in one's spouse's salvation:[365]

> Dieses Schöpfungsverhältnis Adams und Evas, das in sich schon das Erlösungsverhältnis Christi und der Kirche grundlegend birgt und in sich darauf verweist, wird in jeder Ehe von Mann und Frau nach dem Willen Gottes aktualisiert. Damit wird in jeder irdischen Ehe als solcher—unabhängig etwa vom Bewußtsein der Ehepartner über diese Verhältnisse oder der Zustimmung anderer zu solcher Auslegung—nicht nur der Schöpfungswille Gottes vollzogen, sondern in seinem Vollzug auch jener in ihm verborgene Erlöserwille, nicht nur das Schöpfungsverhältnis Adam-Eva nachbildend entfaltet, sondern auch

---

362. See especially the central theme of loving God in the book of Deuteronomy: 6:5; 10:12; 11:1, 13, 22; 13:4; 19:9; 30:6, 16, 20.

363. Best, *Ephesians*, 559.

364. Batey, *Nuptial Imagery*, 68–69.

365. Cf. 1 Cor 7:14, 16 (see below about "Mixed Marriages and Singleness" for a discussion of these verses), remember also the first appearance of this idea in the investigation of Gen 2:17–18, 24 in the first chapter above (see "The Edenic Constitution of Marriage")! Please note also the possible connection of Eph 5:26 ("washing of water with the word") with Christian baptism (see e.g., Schlier, *Epheser*, 256–58). See also Peter's brief hint in 1 Pet 3:1–2.

und eigentlich jenes in ihm vorgesehene Erlösungsverhältnis Christus-Kirche nachbildend durchgeführt.³⁶⁶

Finally, it seems like there is only one term that may be regarded as a meaningful keyword: μυστήριον (v. 32).³⁶⁷ The complete sentence reads τὸ μυστήριον τοῦτο μέγα ἐστίν³⁶⁸ and alludes to God's wisdom as demonstrated in his plan of redemption, which was concealed until Christ's appearance, now being revealed through the preaching of the gospel. Especially Eph 3:3–11 illuminates and concretely defines this meaning as foundation of virtually any μυστήριον mentioned within the New Testament.³⁶⁹ It is the mystery of the gospel (τὸ μυστήριον τοῦ εὐαγγελίου; Eph 6:19; cf. Col 2:2; 4:3), the good news Paul is speaking about when referring to a great and significant τὸ μυστήριον.³⁷⁰ This term "in Ephesians usually connotes a truth that was

---

366. Schlier, *Epheser*, 276.

367. Some even understand κεφαλή ("head") as keyword, since in classical Greek it is not used as image for authority (cf. LSJ s.v. κεφαλή); yet, in the LXX it is frequently used in the literal and metaphorical sense, thus resembling the Hebrew ראש ("head/beginning/chief;" cf. HALOT s.v. ראש); cf. Batey, *Nuptial Imagery*, 24. The sense of the Pauline use, however, is clear right from the beginning, for even v. 21 formulates the topic as dealing with ὑποτάσσω ("submitting"); and the Old Testament background for the following use of images is likewise evident.

368. The Greek τοῦτο ("this") apparently refers to the immediately preceding quotation of Gen 2:24; cf. e.g., Sampley, *One Flesh*, 90–91; Soden, "ΜΥΣΤΗΡΙΟΝ," 194; Dibelius, *Kolosser, Epheser, Philemon*, 95; Beale and Carson, *NT Use*, 828; Lambrecht, *Collected Studies*, 301; Best, *Ephesians*, 553. Slightly differing is Baltensweiler, *Ehe im NT*, 220, 229–33 who recognizes the "great mysterion" in vv. 28b–32, thus applying the τοῦτο only to the passage in Ephesians and the interpretation of the "mystery" hidden in the author's description, partly leaving out the more general, far-reaching Edenic pattern; yet he actually recognizes the citation of Gen 2:24 as the inner core of the mysterion: pp. 230–32. But it particularly refers to the last part of this verse reading "the two will become one flesh" as Köstenberger, "The Mystery," 86–87 and Lincoln, *Ephesians*, 380 convincingly demonstrate by pointing to this phrases' more explicit association with the preceding and following flow of argumentation. The μέγα ("large/great") in Eph 5:32 means "being relatively superior in importance" (BDAG s.v. μέγας: 4b) and does not allude to the greatness of darkness surrounding the "mystery," but to its significance; cf. Sampley, *One Flesh*, 87; Schnackenburg, *Epheser*, 261; Best, *Ephesians*, 554; Lincoln, *Ephesians*, 380; Sellin, *Epheser*, 455; Schlier, *Epheser*, 262; 1 Tim 3:16. As the second part of the verse further explains, Paul just wanted to emphasize that there is more than just one application (namely marriage) of this meaningful Edenic ideal; he stresses the ability of applying it even to spiritual realms (similarly Sampley, *One Flesh*, 87–88; Baltensweiler, *Ehe im NT*, 232).

369. Cf. the complete list of instances: Matt 13:11; Mark 4:11; Luke 8:10; Rom 11:25; 16:25; 1 Cor 2:1, 7; 4:1; 13:2; 14:2; 15:51; Eph 1:9; 3:3–4, 9; 5:32; 6:19; Col 1:26–27; 2:2; 4:3; 2 Thess 2:7; 1 Tim 3:9, 16; Rev 1:20; 10:7; 17:5, 7. On a survey of different understandings and applications of the term μυστήριον in ancient Judaism, Hellenism, Qumran, and Pauline literature see Köstenberger, "The Mystery," 79–94.

370. See esp. Rom 11:25; 16:25; 1 Cor 2:1, 7; 4:1; (13:2; 14:2; 15:51;) Eph 1:9; 3:3–4, 9; 5:32; 6:19; Col 1:26–27; 2:2; 4:3; 1 Tim 3:9, 16; Rev 10:7. There even is a counter-μυστήριον, a false gospel given: 2 Thess 2:7; Rev 17:5, 7! Theobald, "Heilige Hochzeit," 233 rightly calls it the "Heilsgeheimnis." Similarly Dunn, *Theology*, 463 explains: "The mystery of God's purpose previously hidden from the ages and the generations had now been revealed in and as Christ (Col 1.26–27)." Cf. also BDAG s.v. μυστήριον (esp. §1b). The wrong interpretation as holy "sacramentum" due to the Latin translation of the Vulgate "has in the meantime been completely abandoned." Farla, "The Two," 74. Loader, *LXX, Sexuality, and NT*, 109 explains: "The use of the word, 'mystery,' τὸ μυστήριον, suggest that the author is conscious of the

previously hidden but has now been revealed," therefore, mere "marriage can hardly be seen as a previously hidden 'mystery.'"³⁷¹ It rather stresses the union between Christ (Yahweh) and his church (Israel) as intended throughout this world's history.³⁷² More to the core of this "mystery" it is "only the paradoxical principle of 'two becoming one flesh'"³⁷³ that is thus emphasized here, as it was in 1 Cor 6:17.

> So marriage is like a metaphor or an image or a picture or a parable or a model that stands for something more than a man and a woman becoming one flesh. It stands for the relationship between Christ and the church. That's the deepest meaning of marriage. It's meant to be a living drama of he covenant-keeping love between Christ and the church. . . . All of this underlines what Paul calls a 'profound mystery'—that marriage, in it's deepest meaning, is a copy of Christ

---

striking nature of the metaphor and of its existence in tradition and teaching as a way of explaining the relationship with Christ, but its primary context is the use elsewhere in Ephesians (1:9; 3:3; 4:9; 6:19) to describe the unfolding or revelation of God's purpose in Christ. The emphasis on sexual union in Gen 2:24 conveyed by the loss of the pun, אִישׁ אִשָּׁה (*ish-ishshah*; man-woman), the translation of לְבָשָׂר אֶחָד by εἰς σάρκα μίαν ('one flesh'), and the focus on oneness from two-ness, may well lie behind the τὸ μυστήριον ('the mystery') here"; cf. also Lincoln, *Ephesians*, 380–83. Note also Sampley, *One Flesh*, 92–96 further asserting: "Uniquely connected with the use of μυστήριον in chaps. 1 and 3 was the notion that the mystery had to do specifically with God's purpose in uniting all things, both in heaven and on earth, in Christ. In broad scope, that unification was seen in chaps. 1 and 2 to focus upon the joining of Jew and Gentile in the church. In 5:21–33, the focus is upon marriage and the concern for unity again comes to the fore as it did with the earlier occurrences of μυστήριον, in chaps. 1 and 3. The content that the author inserts within the Haustafel form speaks in different ways for the unity that should subsist between husband and wife as well as between Christ and his body, the church." Ibid., 95.

371. Köstenberger, "The Mystery," 86–87; similarly Best, *Ephesians*, 554 who further explains that "since outsiders might misunderstand the sexual language, it must be veiled; cf Philo Cherub 42–43; CH 1.16." That would be the case by using the more discreet "cling/join" (προσκολλάω) in Gen 2:24 (Eph 5:31). The spiritual meaning of this formerly revealed "mystery" is now disclosed by Christ.

372. Cf. Schlier, *Epheserbrief*, 262; Greeven, "Aussagen," 123–24; Ortlund, *Whoredom*, 147–48; Lincoln, "OT in Ephesians," 32–33; Friedrich, *Sexualität und Ehe*, 95; Kleinschmidt, *Ehefragen*, 85–86; Schnackenburg, *Epheser*, 261: "Das »große Geheimnis« liegt für den Verf. [i.e., Verfasser] also nach seinem Verständnis der Schriftstelle nicht in der Ehe als solcher, sondern im Verhältnis von Christus und Kirche." Köstenberger, "The Mystery," 87, 90 further explains: "The structure of Eph 5:22-33 indicates a shift in emphasis from the marital union to the church as the 'body of Christ' in 5:28a–32, thus making Christ and the church the most natural referent of μυστήριον. Note that the immediate antecedent of the Gen 2:24 quotation is the clause 'for we are members of his body,' which gives the reason for Christ's nurture of his church. One would expect Paul to continue this train of thought through the Gen 2:24 quotation. . . . In the union between Christ and the church also, 'the two' become 'one flesh.' It is this spiritual union itself that Paul calls a 'mystery,' not the typological correspondence between marriage and the relationship between Christ and the church." Similarly Lincoln, *Ephesians*, 381: "It is most likely, then, that here in 5:32 the term has the same Christ-event in view, highlighting the aspect of it which has been central in this passage, namely the intimate union between Christ and his Church." Cf. Sampley, *One Flesh*, 90–96. The understanding of Niederwimmer, *Askese und Mysterium*, 153 as denoting the myth of the androgyn man in the beginning of creation (following some ancient Jewish notions), is wrong and completely unsupported by the immediate context or any other hint within the biblical scriptures.

373. Köstenberger, "The Mystery," 90/fn.40.

and the church. . . . 'As God made man in his own image, so He made earthly marriage in the image of His own eternal marriage with his people.'[374]

In this context it is all the more meaningful that he introduces his own interpretation of this "great mystery" by the phrase ἐγὼ δὲ λέγω ("but I say"), thus representing the only occurrence of this prominent phrase outside the Sermon on the Mount (cf. Matt 5:22, 28, 32, 34, 39, 44). Thereby he closely connects the "Verkündigung vom Anbruch der Gottesherrschaft,"[375] the "inaugural speech" of Jesus' gospel work, with the great mystery of the Edenic ideal and likewise introduces a new meaning as contribution or contradiction of prevailing Jewish perceptions.[376] Evidently Paul perceives the gospel—or at least an important part of it—in the creational covenant union.

> The divine truth that once had been hidden but now in the train of Christ's coming and work, is revealed, is God's oneness with His people as realized to a far greater degree than in the OT. While God's faithful love for his wayward people was revealed through the prophets, it was Jesus Christ who took on human flesh and redeemed the Church as his own body on earth. This body, he would nurture (cf. Eph 5:30: 'for we are members of His body'). Paul, a 'steward of God's mysteries (cf. 1 Cor 4:1), was the herald of the μυστήριον.[377]

That may further strengthen the position that the Edenic marriage covenant ideal serves also as ideal for the human-divine covenant, obliging both parties (man and God) to keep the conditions and enjoy the privileges established in Gen 2:24. Thus this keyword even supports the previous observation concerning the two pillars of the eternal covenant and "helps one to think of marriage in relation to God's larger purposes," for "the primary application of the latter passage is to God's plan of restoration 'in Christ' as worked out in the marriage relationship."[378] The redemptive purposes or characteristics of a marriage relation according to the models in Gen 2:17–18, 24 and Eph 5:23–32 thus becomes even more obvious (cf. also 1 Cor 7:14, 16; 1 Pet 3:1).

Wider Biblical Context. There are some special phrases in the given passage that need further investigation regarding their wider literary context. While the extra-biblical accounts pertaining to the given topic have already been dealt with, now only the biblical context will be considered. To begin with, the text of Ephesians 5 is placed amid

---

374. Piper, *Momentary Marriage*, 75–76, quoting Bromiley, *God and Marriage*, 43.

375. Kirchschläger, *Ehe im NT*, 30.

376. Cf. on this also Smith, *Tannaitic Parallels*, 28; Sampley, *One Flesh*, 87–89; Best, *Ephesians*, 555; Lincoln, *Ephesians*, 382; Lincoln, "OT in Ephesians," 33. Niederwimmer, *Askese und Mysterium*, 153 further states: "Das betonte ἐγὼ δὲ λέγω εἰς . . . κτλ. lässt vermuten, daß der Verfasser sich mit dieser seiner Deutung im ausdrücklichen Gegensatz zu einer anderen Deutung der Schriftstelle befindet." He perceives this "Gegensatz" in the allegorical character of Gen 2:24 as presented here in Ephesians. This is basically true—yet it is no "Gegensatz" to the original understanding of Gen 2:24, for the initial meaning regarding marriage is still present, but now on another level, the spiritual realm.

377. Köstenberger, "The Mystery," 91.

378. Köstenberger, "The Mystery," 93; cf. Schlier, *Epheser*, 277.

various most practical admonitions that commence even in chap. four and which turn to the more spiritual sphere from Eph 6:10 onwards dealing with the "armor of God." The beginning of the investigated passage (Eph 5:21) marks also the starting point on a discussion about the Christian household (the "Haustafel") including issues like the one scrutinized in Eph 5:21–33 about the Christian marriage, further the behavior against children and slaves (Eph 6:1–9). While the second part is almost immediately following the quotation of Gen 2:24, it does not seem to be relevant for the interpretation of the first part on the marital "order."

The "Bond of Peace." The introduction of chap. four is apparently closer to the "message" of Eph 5:31–32, for in vv. 4–6 the most prominent "keyword" is "one" (εἷς/μία/ἕν). The entire passage of vv. 1–16 is dealing with the church as "body" of Christ and the responsibility of living accordingly holy. It speaks about the different callings and the order of offices and tasks as members of Christ and thus partly resembles the content of Eph 5:21–33. But there is more, particularly in Eph 4:3; there it speaks about keeping the ἑνότητα τοῦ πνεύματος ἐν τῷ συνδέσμῳ τῆς εἰρήνης ("oneness/unity of the spirit in the bond of peace"). Although it is not the Greek διαθήκη ("covenant"), even the σύνδεσμος τῆς εἰρήνης ("bond/fetter of peace") may be regarded as a possible echo of the significant Old Testament "covenant of peace" (בְּרִית שָׁלוֹם/διαθήκην εἰρήνης) which so prominently appeared in the context of God's (and Phinehas') zealous working for the sake of establishing God's great, blessed covenant according to the Edenic "covenant norm" of Gen 2:24.[379] Furthermore, the mentioning of "being zealous/eager/hasting" (σπουδάζω; Eph 4:3) is most interesting in this context, although it is not described by the Greek ζῆλος or ζηλόω as given in the LXX version of Num 25:11–12 as basis of God granting the "covenant of peace." Yet, the reflection or echo is further strengthened, even if not by exact terminology, for the structure is matching the OT pattern: By "zealous effort" preserving the "unity" in the "bond of peace" a certain (soteriological?) oneness is reached and God blesses his holy people by using them as his instruments ("members").

Eph 4:4 further connects the "unity" through the "bond of peace" with the marital "bond" in the central text of Eph 5:31–32 and even the instance of 1 Cor 6:16–17, for it immediately speaks about ἓν σῶμα καὶ ἓν πνεῦμα ("*one* body and *one* spirit"), thus more concretely interpreting the ἑνότης ("oneness") of v. 3. The close similarity especially to 1 Cor 6:16–17 is evident, and consequently the following verses (Eph 4:5–6) may be regarded as an allusion to the necessary steps to be taken in order to obtain that important "oneness" of v. 3: The overall basis is εἷς κύριος, [to cleaved to through/by the means of] μία πίστις, [and] ἓν βάπτισμα in the name of εἷς θεὸς

---

379. Another reflection of that covenant could perhaps be found in Heb 13:20, speaking about the "God of *peace*" who "*brought up* . . . the *great Shepherd* of the sheep through the *blood* of the *eternal covenant*." These elements are meaningful when considering the OT pattern of the "covenant of peace" as investigated thoroughly within the first part of this study. Seemingly, the author of Ephesians and Hebrews (most likely Paul) was well aware of this significant Old Testament image and employed it in similar contexts (marriage and God's working through his eternal covenant).

καὶ πατὴρ πάντων. Through these important elements a new kinship is established, reflecting the one of Gen 2:24, and by "baptizing them in the name of the Father and the Son and the Holy Spirit" (Matt 28:19) the new ἑνότης officially begins by even "naming" the "newborn child" of Christian faith, thus expressing the New Testament kind of a human-divine "kinship formula."[380]

After establishing this close, familial unity through the "oneness in the bond of peace," the individual Christian is regarded as a "member" (μέλος) of Christ's "body" (σῶμα), which is the church (cf. Eph 5:23, 30). Now he has the name of his new Father, the Son, and the Holy Spirit, being connected by the בְּרִית שָׁלוֹם and led by the "great shepherd" (Heb 13:20; cf. Ezek 34:23–24; 37:24–25).[381]

"Having Cleansed Her by the Washing of Water." This line seems to closely reflect the divine washing of God's bride Israel as depicted in Ezek 16:8–9:[382]

---

380. Similarly Dunstan, "The Marriage Covenant," 251.

381. Further, another phrase, not that prominent, is *"Spotless Members."* The Greek μέλος ("member") occurs only eleven times in the LXX, five times within the Pentateuch, all in context of ordination and inauguration of the priests, or concerning the holy burnt offering (see Exod 29:17; Lev 1:6, 12; 8:20; 9:13). The remaining ones appear in context of different lamentations over the personal situation (Judg 19:29; Job 9:28) or the entire Israelite people (Mic 2:4; Ezek 2:10; 24:6). Interestingly, the only instance in the gospels using μέλος is within Jesus' speech on the everlastingness of marriage in Matt 5:27–32. It is even used twice in vv. 29–30, thus indirectly (when considering the image as used by Paul) linking the marital "bond" with each church member's responsibility of living a faithful live. In Paul's letters, too, this term frequently appears as an image of the individual church member's charge to live a holy life of useful service for the Lord by responsibly working for him, being his sanctified "instrument." Cf. Matt 5:29–30; Rom 6:13, 19; 7:5, 23; 12:4–5; 1 Cor 6:15; 12:12, 14, 18–20, 22, 25–27; Eph 4:25; 5:30; Col 3:5. The understanding of individuals forming a common body was a prominent metaphor in ancient literature; cf. BDAG s.v. μέλος; see e.g., Aristotle Pol. 1253a 20–29; cf. Ar. 13:5; Ath. 8:1. The Greek σπίλον ("spot/stain/blemish") of Eph 5:27 appears only twice in LXX and NT, here and in 2 Pet 2:13. The instance in second Peter speaks about so called false brethren being but σπίλοι καὶ μῶμοι ("stains and blemishes") "having eyes full of adultery" (v. 14) and following "the way of Balaam, the son of Beor" (v. 15). This connection, of course, is most interesting and significant. Again there is a close linkage introduced between the spiritual adultery of the apostasy at Shittim and the idea of a holy marriage covenant between Yahweh and Israel (respectively, Jesus and the NT church) as given in Eph 5:27–32. Further meaningful is the fact that Peter apparently knew the letters of Paul as he explicitly states only some paragraphs below (2 Pet 3:15), possibly applying the ideal of Eph 5:27 as stark contrast to the traitors in the church Peter is addressing his second letter to.—And perhaps it even is the same Ephesian church Peter is writing to, for, at least, they previously received a letter of Paul (2 Pet 3:15) encouraging them to "be diligent to be found by Him in peace, spotless and blameless" (σπουδάσατε ἄσπιλοι καὶ ἀμώμητοι . . . ἐν εἰρήνῃ; v. 14), just as investigated above concerning Paul's admonitions in Eph 4:3 (σπουδάζοντες . . . ἐν τῷ συνδέσμῳ τῆς εἰρήνης) and 5:27 (μὴ ἔχουσαν σπίλον . . . καὶ ἄμωμος). The harmony of no less than four significant terms immediately preceding Peter's reference to Paul is more than just conspicuous, and therefore we may assume a close connection between the underlying perceptions of both instances. The same idea of being ἄσπιλος is further fostered in 1 Tim 6:14; Jas 1:27, and 1 Pet 1:19, all referring to the holiness of Christ and the responsibility of his church to live correspondingly until his appearing. A final connection is further given between the "washing of water" in Eph 5:26 and Ezek 16:9 ("I bathed you with water, washed off your blood from you and anointed you with oil") indicating that the cleansing is a preparation for the marriage of Yahweh and Israel (Ezek 16:6–13), respectively Christ and the church (Eph 5:25–32). (Similarly Beale and Carson, *NT Use*, 826; Beattie, *Women and Marriage*, 79–80; cf. Instone-Brewer, *In the Bible*, 45.)

382. Thus also Zimmermann, *Geschlechtermetaphorik*, 351–53; Thatcher, *Marriage*, 77.

"Then I passed by you and saw you, and behold, you were at the time for love; so I spread My skirt over you and covered your nakedness. I also swore to you and entered into a covenant with you so that you became Mine," declares the Lord GOD. "Then I bathed you with water, washed off your blood from you and anointed you with oil."

As God had to purify Israel, wash and dress her in order to make her a beautiful bride, whose "'fame went forth among the nations on account of your beauty, for it was perfect because of My splendor which I bestowed on you,' declares the Lord GOD" (v. 14). Similarly, the church's fame is to go forth among the nations as being the purified bride of Christ—purified through the word of God (Eph 5:26: "by the washing of water in (with) the word"), and affirmed by the outward sign: baptism in water (cf. Titus 3:5).[383]

"Nourish and Cherish." Christ's work of "nourishing and cherishing" (ἐκτρέφει καὶ θάλπει) the church (Eph 5:29) is, according to Paul's elucidation, the pattern for husbands to do likewise with their wives.[384] It is interesting to recognize that the Greek verb ἐκτρέφω occurs only twice in the entire New Testament, here and in Eph 6:4. The second mentioning refers to the fathers' responsibility of "bringing up" their children "in the discipline and instruction of the Lord." The same meaning is implied in the Septuagint usages of this verb, frequently referring to "keeping alive" (Gen 45:7, 11; 47:17), and particularly to "growing up/bring up" with the basic meaning of a general support concerning all the necessities of life for the benefit of someone weaker than the provider himself,[385] only rarely referring to mere simple feeding/nourishing (1 Kgs 11:20; perhaps also 2 Sam 12:3). "Cherishing" (θάλπω) is paralleling this verb, but it rather emphasizes the fact of caring like "a nursing [mother] *tenderly cares* for her own children" (1 Thess 2:7). Apart from this instance in 1 Thess 2:7, the Greek θάλπω appears only four times in the LXX version of the OT, particularly pointing to the mother's warmth (Deut 22:6; 1 Kgs 1:2, 4; Job 39:14). The literary background of these two rare verbs thus illuminates that Paul speaks about the parental care of Jesus for his church and likewise of husbands for their wives, supporting them in all of life's necessities, tenderly caring for them and educating them with motherly warmth and love.[386]

---

383. More on this "Nuptial Imagery" and the outward signs in the corresponding chapters below (II.3.2 and III.1). On baptism as the symbol alluded to also Thatcher, *Marriage*, 77; similarly Bailey, "Foundation," 29.

384. Cf. Beale and Carson, *NT Use*, 826, 828; Schnackenburg, *Epheser*, 262–63; Lincoln, *Ephesians*, 374, 389; Son, "Concept," 114: "Correspondingly, husbands are to love their wives sacrificially (5:25, 28) as (καθώς) Christ loved the church and gave himself up for her." Similarly Lambrecht, *Collected Studies*, 302–3 or Farla, "The Two," 75: "They [the Christian husband and wife] must give form to their marriage with the ideal of Christ's love for the Church as an example."

385. Cf. 2 Sam 12:3; 1 Kgs 12:8, 10; 2 Kgs 10:6; 2 Chr 10:10; Ps 22:2; Job 31:18; Hos 9:12; Jonah 4:10; Isa 23:4; 49:21; similarly Schlier, *Epheser*, 260.

386. Cf. Lincoln, *Ephesians*, 379–80. Dunstan also affirms: "And speaking of husbands, St Paul says in Ephesians that the quality of their love for their wives, and the purpose of it, are determined by the

II.2.2.3.2 1 Corinthians 6:12–20

In this passage, which is a hinge unit containing "the seeds of many ideas that sprout and blossom in the rest of the letter."[387] The first verses contain several parallelisms in a very similar form and structure.[388] Verses 13–14 are a closer investigation of the πάντα μοι ἔξεστιν ("all things are permissible to me") in v. 12, which seems to be a common cultural notion in Corinth[389] immediately refuted by a Pauline response.[390] This erroneous slogan as the title and basis of the following instructions "could express in a nutshell their moral and theological positions. Carried to an extreme, this maxim would appear to legalize every behavior and every object and could explain the problems besetting the congregation, from the case of incest to the incidents of eating idol food."[391]

Paul answers to this slogan by introducing his own "maxim," again closely combining sexuality and its spiritual influence through the instrument of the body. A possible outline could look as follows:

---

love which Christ the bridegroom has for the Church his bride. Thus there are, in one context, the passion of Christ, a doctrine of marriage, and the nuptial symbolism of the divine bridegroom and the Church his bride. This conjunction is not accidental. . . . So the first commandment of the marriage covenant is a mutual subjection in love, a mutual care so lasting and so deep as to seek ultimately the perfection of the beloved. The quality and the purpose of this love are those of Christ for the Church . . . ." Dunstan, "The Marriage Covenant," 245–46, 248. These different meaningful elements further emphasize the significance of the given passage. Furthermore, here is another parallel given to the chapter of Ezek 16, where God nourishes his bride (v. 13), after having washed her in water (v. 9). On this similarity see also Zimmermann, *Geschlechtermetaphorik*, 352.

387. Garland, *1 Corinthians*, 220. He further asserts: "This passage stands at the juncture of two types of material, oral reports (5:1—6:11) and written responses (7:1) and serves as a hinge unit. Paul may have chosen to discuss the topic of sexual intercourse with prostitutes at this point in his letter because it allowed him to draw to a close his previous arguments and to lay a thematic foundation for what follows. It continues the moral vein of the preceding sections while setting the stage for what is to come." Also, Collins suggests a large inclusio between 6:12 (πάντα μοι ἔξεστιν ἀλλ' οὐ πάντα συμφέρει) and 10:23 (πάντα [μοι] ἔξεστιν ἀλλ' οὐ πάντα συμφέρει): "Within that complex the thoughts Paul develops in 6:12–20 provide a theological-anthropological basis for his response to a variety of considerations on sexual relationships in ch. 7." Collins, *First Corinthians*, 241. Similarly, Kaye, "One Flesh," 52 who calls it an "introductory paragraph for the following material."

388. Cf. Kirchhoff, *Sünde*, 107–8; see also Bailey, "Foundation," 31; Garland, *1 Corinthians*, 229: Food is for the belly/The belly is for food; God destroys the belly/God destroys food; The body is for the Lord/The Lord is for the body; God raised the Lord/God will raise us (our bodies).

389. Although the wide-spread perception of a Corinthian slogan (a thinking of members in the Corinthian church) is a nice explanation to avoid exegetical problems that would arise when trying to interpret the meaning of these rather strange statements (cf. e.g., Fitzmyer, *First Corinthians*, 261, 263), it cannot be denied that it "is frequently ignored . . . that Paul does not include any indicator that he is introducing a citation here in contrast to the instances elsewhere in the letter where he introduces citations from the Corinthians, from other literature, or from a hypothetical dialogue." Garland, *1 Corinthians*, 226. Hence, "it is more plausible that Paul cites a familiar notion about freedom found in the Corinthian culture and recasts it in Christian terms than that he parrots the arguments of sensualists in the church to repudiate them." Ibid., 228; cf. pp. 225–28.

390. Similarly Niederwimmer, *Askese und Mysterium*, 75; Loader, *LXX, Sexuality, and NT*, 88: ". . . in 6:12 . . . Paul cites and then counter-asserts immediately." Cf. also Külling, *Ehe und Ehelosigkeit*, 17; Garland speaks of "counterstatements introduced by ἀλλά." Garland, *1 Corinthians*, 225.

391. Garland, *1 Corinthians*, 225–26.

HYPOTHESIS: Universal Claim of a Corinthian Slogan (v. 12)

> (A) Πάντα μοι ἔξεστιν: All things are permitted to me
>> (B) ἀλλ' οὐ πάντα: but not all things are *profitable*
> (A) Πάντα μοι ἔξεστιν: All things are permitted to me
>> (B') ἀλλ' οὐ . . . τινος: but I will not be *mastered* by anything.

INVESTIGATION: Special Application judged by a Pauline Maxim (vv. 13–14)

> (C) Food is for the stomach and the stomach is for food.
>> (D) But God will do away with this and that.
>>> (E) Yet the body is not for unlawful sexual intercourse, but:
> (C') [The body is] for the Lord, and the Lord is for the body.
>> (D') But God raised the Lord, and will also raise us up through His power.
>>> (E') [Large dwelling on influence of unlawful sexual intercourse: vv. 15–20]

After (E) there is a break, a thematic change away from the preceding cultural "slogans" which apparently deal with perishable (D), merely earthly aspects of live. (E) marks the beginning of a new topic, now introducing an imperishable (D') subject (C') contrasting the spiritually rather unimportant theme of (C) to the most important fact of spiritual peril through a false dealing with matters of sexuality. Correspondingly, (E') marks the long dwelling on the evidence about the influence of unlawful sexual intercourse.

The underlying, general topic apparently is the spiritual (dis-) agreement and (im-) proper fitting of certain elements. The cultural notions as perhaps exemplified by the slogans (A) and (C), are judged by their practical consequences and finally are disapproved by Christian standards. Both subjects (food and prostitution) evidently belong to the realm of ancient pagan worship practices (cf. 1 Cor 10:23–31).[392] The introductory slogan postulating that "anything goes" (A) is kept in check by Paul's immediate response that "anything" (A) may actually be unprofitable (B) or enslaving (B'). This is an anaphorical parallelism emphasizing the problematic nature of statement A and closely connecting the parts (B) and (B'); this stylistic device results in understanding (B') as a special case of (B), that means, even if something is "profitable" (συμφέρω) it should not be "mastering" (ἐξουσιάζω).[393] The concrete claim of (C) is answered with considerable effort, turning to the greater spiritual norms which function as maxims in Christian behavior, thereby refuting the possible idea underlying the brief notes in this passage:

---

392. Loader notes: "By association [in 1 Cor 6:12–14] Paul is probably also implying that in the world to come sexual appetite will play no role . . . , that in the age to come people neither marry nor are given in marriage but are like the angels." Loader, *LXX, Sexuality, and NT*, 89. These two aspects, food and marriage, are also combined in Jesus' prediction and comparison of the time shortly before his return with the days of Noah (Matt 24:37–39; Luke 17:26–27). These topics indeed seem to be the main concerns among humankind and Paul consequently turns against a bad practice concerning these problematic issues.

393. Cf. Kirchhoff, *Sünde*, 108–9; Schneider, *Antithese*, 77.

'Just as food is meant for the stomach and the stomach for food, so also the body is meant for sexual activity and sexual activity for the body. Furthermore, since God will one day destroy both the stomach and the body, is not what we do with our bodies now of no moral consequence?' The two slogans in 6:12 and 6:13 were supposedly combined to justify the belief that Christians were free to do whatever they please in the body.[394]

It is meaningful that Paul continues his argumentation by again employing the Edenic ideal as his most significant pattern. He basically repeats the procedure of Eph 5:21–33, firstly presenting two hypotheses, (A) and (C), on rather earthly matters, before turning to the evidence of his sayings by means of spiritual truths. The lengthy proving of his argumentation's legitimacy in vv. 15–20 finally centers in the most significant echo of Gen 2:24 and its impact even in context of illicit intimacy. Here, again, another narrative (argument-)structure can be observed, which even exceeds the previous one in its artful performance, thus giving the following topic much more prominence:[395]

PROBLEM/RATIONALE on vv. 12–14:

(A) μέλη Χριστοῦ (v. 15a) *[or:]*

   (B) πόρνης μέλη (v. 15b)

EVIDENCE:

(B') σάρκα μίαν with a harlot through κολλάω (v. 16) *[or:]*

(A') ἓν πνεῦμα with the Lord through κολλάω (v. 17)

---

394. Garland, *1 Corinthians*, 230; quotation from Rosner, *Paul*, 129.

395. Another outline, strictly oriented on the three blocks of argumentation introduced by οὐκ οἴδατε ὅτι ("do you not know"), could look like the one of Garland, *1 Corinthians*, 224:

1. Question: Do you not know?
  (A) Statement about relationship to Christ: Your bodies are members of Christ (15a).
    (B) Statement about sexual intercourse with a prostitute: Will you make the members of Christ as members of a prostitute?
    (C) Response: Never!
2. Question: Do you not know? (explaining previous response)
    (B') Statement about sexual intercourse with a prostitute: The one who joins himself to a prostitute becomes one body with her (16b). Scriptural proof: The two shall become one flesh (16c).
  (A') Statement about relationship to Christ: The one who is joined to the Lord is one spirit with him (17).
    (C') Response: Flee *porneia*!
      (D) Explanation: Sexual sin is an attack on the body.
3. Question: Do you not know?
  (A") Statement about relationship to Christ: Your body is a temple of the Holy Spirit, whom you have from God.
  (A'") Statement about relationship to Christ: You are not your own; you were bought with a price.
    (C") Response: Glorify God in your bodies!

Similarly Kaye, "One Flesh," 53. Kirchhoff, *Sünde*, 106–7. gives another differing structure: Introduction (v. 12), part one (vv. 13–14), part two (vv. 15–17), part three (vv. 18–20). Bailey, "Foundation," 33 presents a chiastic structure of 1 Cor 6:13c–20 with v. 16b in its centre.

Solution/Result:

(C) Φεύγετε τὴν πορνείαν (v. 18a)

Problem/Rationale on vv. 15–17:

(D) Universal Claim (of a Corinthian Slogan?[396]): πᾶν ἁμάρτημα ... ἐκτὸς τοῦ σώματός ἐστιν (v. 18b)

(E) Special Quality (Singular): ὁ δὲ πορνεύων εἰς τὸ ἴδιον σῶμα (v. 18c)

Evidence:

(E') Special Quality (Singular): τὸ σῶμα ὑμῶν ναὸς τοῦ ἐν ὑμῖν ἁγίου πνεύματός ἐστιν (v. 19)

(D') Universal Claim: ἠγοράσθητε γὰρ τιμῆς (v. 20a)

Solution/Result:

(C') δοξάσατε δὴ τὸν θεόν (v. 20b)

How:

(B") ἐν τῷ σώματι ὑμῶν (v. 20c)

[and:]

(A") καὶ ἐν τῷ πνεύματι ὑμῶν (v. 20d)

Very similar to the investigated passage in the letter to the Ephesians, the train of thought is again the close link between σάρξ and πνεῦμα, closely connected through

---

396. It should be recognized that unit (D) (πᾶν ἁμάρτημα ὃ ἐὰν ποιήσῃ ἄνθρωπος ἐκτὸς τοῦ σώματός ἐστιν) could be another Corinthian slogan. There is again a universal claim introduced by the Greek πᾶν and it again could lead to letting go any moral restriction. Hence, if not viewed as special harmatological remark (whatever a proper interpretation would be), it might resemble the universal claim of v. 12 (πάντα μοι ἔξεστιν); cf. e.g., Murphy-O'Connor, "Corinthian Slogans," 391–96; Collins, *First Corinthians*, 248; Klauck, *1. Korintherbrief*, 48. Please consider also the NET note on this issue: "It is debated whether this is a Corinthian slogan. If it is not, then Paul is essentially arguing that there are two types of sin, non-sexual sins which take place outside the body and sexual sins which are against a person's very own body. If it is a Corinthian slogan, then it is a slogan used by the Corinthians to justify their immoral behavior. With it they are claiming that anything done in the body or through the body had no moral relevance. A decision here is very difficult, but the latter is to be preferred for two main reasons. (1) This is the most natural understanding of the statement as it is written. To construe it as a statement by Paul requires a substantial clarification in the sense (e.g., "All *other* sins ..." [NIV]). (2) Theologically the former is more difficult: Why would Paul single out sexual sins as more intrinsically related to the body than other sins, such as gluttony or drunkenness? For these reasons, it is more likely that the phrase in quotation marks is indeed a Corinthian slogan which Paul turns against them in the course of his argument, although the decision must be regarded as tentative." However, as Dautzenberg, "Φεύγετε τὴν πορνείαν," 273, asserts, "Diese Lösung ist aber wohl doch zu glatt und mehr durch die theologische Anstößigkeit von V. 18 b als durch Signale im Text nahegelegt. Dessen gedankliche Entwicklung läßt sich ohne eine solche Annahme verstehen." Similarly Barrett, *First Corinthians*, 150: "This attractive explanation is not entirely satisfying, because Paul's reply seems to accept the general proposition, and make an exception to it (cf. verses 12–13), which leaves us with the original problem." Obviously, the interpretation of v. 18b is closely connected to the understanding of vv. 12–13.

the almost "metaphysical device" of sexuality[397] and embedded in chiastic parallelisms. Again the term μέλη is most prominent, again as emphasis of the individual role of each church "member"[398] and his responsibility to be careful in keeping himself as an "instrument of righteousness" (Rom 6:13).[399] Again the Edenic ideal of Gen 2:24 serves as authoritative pattern and norm for earthly and heavenly relationships, although now the concrete application is slightly different. Again he basically expects the church members to be acquainted with the common Christian principles he is elucidating (once more?), as the threefold οὐκ οἴδατε ὅτι (vv. 15–16, 19) indicates. It

397. Similarly Dautzenberg, "Φεύγετε τὴν πορνείαν," 275, explains concerning the special quality of πορνεία exceeding all other sins (v. 18b; if understood as Pauline declaration): "Das eigentlich Entscheidende, was Pl [i.e., Paul] sagen wollte, liegt doch darin, daß die Hurerei im vollen Unterschied von anderer Versündigung den Leib dadurch verdirbt, daß sie ihn unter die ἐξουσία der in der entfesselten sinnlichen Leidenschaft wirkenden Sündenmächte durch organische Verbindung mit ihrer Repräsentantin, der πόρνη, stellt." Quoting Bachmann, 1. Korinther, 247–48; cf. Balz, Christus in Korinth, 63; Loader, LXX, Sexuality, and NT, 93. He further asserts: ". . . der Christus und die porné repräsentieren schon nach V. 15–18a zwei entgegengesetzte Welten, daher komme der πορνεία nach V 18 bc eine sie von den anderen Lastern unterscheidende 'valeur destructive à répercussion métaphysique' zu. . . . Sie [die porneia] wird in dieser Paränese als dämonischer Machtbereich verstanden, welcher dem Bereich des Kyrios konträr gegenübersteht und das menschliche σῶμα anders betrifft als die übrigen Sünden." Dautzenberg, "Φεύγετε τὴν πορνείαν," 275–76; (see also pp. 283–84, 291–92). This is a result of "his understanding of a person's sexuality [. . . as] inseparable from his considering the person as a whole. σῶμα 'body' refers to the integrated whole with a focus on the bodily aspect, but not to body as in any way separable from soul or spirit." Loader, LXX, Sexuality, and NT, 91. Beale and Carson, NT Use, 713 considers "the intended permanence of sexual relationships to highlight the uniqueness of the sin of porneia in 6:18b" and generally concludes "Paul's reflections on the nature of the bond established in sexual relations via Gen 2:24 are intended to impress upon the Corinthians a high view of the body and behavior involving the body. Throughout the paragraph Paul seeks to demolish Corinthian notions about the transience and consequent insignificance of the body." Ibid., 713–14. ". . . sexual sin, unlike other sins, involves one's very body in a union with others and is a sin against self as well as others. It involves the whole self and thus is dangerous and deadly to one's spiritual well-being, for it puts one into the hands and mastery of someone other than the Lord." Witherington, Conflict and Community, 169. For another allusion to "sexuality as danger to boundaries" (human-animal, human-divine) see e.g., Frymer-Kensky, "Law and Philosophy," 95–99.

398. Son further points to the feature that the single "body" of a church "member" might likewise refer to the "spiritual body" of the entire church: "1 Cor 6:13–20 contains two statements that probably allude to the church as the body of Christ. The first occurs in verse 15, 'Your bodies are members of Christ.' Understood in the light of 1 Cor 12:12, 27, this statement is almost the same as saying, 'You are members of Christ' or 'You are members of the body of Christ.' The second assertion occurs in verse 17, 'He who joins himself to the Lord becomes one spirit with him' (1 Cor 6:17). 'One spirit with him [the Lord]' is a direct parallel to 'one body with her [a harlot]' (6:16) and it probably means either 'spiritual body' or the 'corporate Body of Christ created by the Holy Spirit.' If so, it alludes to the church as the body of Christ." Son, Corporate Elements 88; cf. p. 98.

399. In his specific application of the one-flesh concept even to a harlot, Paul "affirms that the union of a man with Christ or with a harlot is of a comparable character, but these two unions are incompatible, i.e., one is not merely physical and the other spiritual. Union with Christ is personal and involves the whole man; other interpersonal relationships are to reflect the new personality created in Christ." Batey, Nuptial Imagery, 34. This "incompatibility" of μέλη Χριστοῦ and πόρνης [μέλη] in v. 15 represents an oxymoron (a syntactic connection of two semantical apparently disagreeing terms); that results in stirring up negative emotions of disapproval and thus prepares for the clear μὴ γένοιτο (v. 15c) as well as for the argumentation that is to follow; cf. Kirchhoff, Sünde, 113.

seems like Paul is extending his theological interpretation of Gen 2:24 in Ephesians, now in response to a Corinthian slogan that had the potential to tear down almost any Christian principle: πάντα μοι ἔξεστιν.

There are several contrasting pairs. The first two, (A)–(B)/(B')–(A'), are the rationale of the foregoing argumentation (vv. 12–14) and simultaneously the introduction to the bigger, underlying problem that is dealt with in the next block.[400] (B) and (B') is a consequent application of what might almost be called the "one flesh equation:" two individualities become one new unity by κολλάω ("joining"),[401] implying "that the man and the prostitute are wedded together even if there are no wedding vows."[402] This echo of at least two steps of Gen 2:24 again functions as Paul's "masterpiece" of evidence and since the Jewish tradition generally interprets the "cleaving" and the "one flesh" union of Gen 2:24 in a sexual sense, it is "nicht ungewöhnlich, wenn Paulus in 1Kor 6,16 den Sexualverkehr mit einer Prostituierten ausgehend von Gen 2,24 beurteilt."[403] Paul's application of Gen 2:24 in 1 Cor 6:16–17, therefore, "is in full agreement with the interpretation given of these words in the divorce pericope in Mt. and Mk."[404] and points to the "mutual exclusiveness" of the two alternatives (vv. 16–17).[405] The strong rhetoric intentions, however, must also be considered. Paul deploys the impressive figure of Gen 2:24 to demonstrate almost excessively how detestable it is for a Christian, whose body and spirit belongs to the Lord (1 Cor 6:19–20), to "cleave" to a prostitute. He strongly emphasizes that "der Geschlechtsakt ist nicht etwas Peripheres, Indifferentes, er ist nicht nur rein physischer, sondern auch ein psychischer

---

400. On the subsequent rationales and the paralleling pairs similarly Kirchhoff, *Sünde*, 107–8.

401. Although in 1 Cor 6:16–17 the κολλάω ("joining") is used twice in the participle present passive form (ὁ κολλώμενος), it is unambiguously clear from the context that it must be understood as deponent (cf. Loader, *LXX, Sexuality, and NT*, 87, 90), for here it is an active deed of the man deciding whom to join, perhaps even against God's will. Thus this echo is slightly differing from the possible interpretation of Jesus' speech in the gospels (divine passive; cf. e.g., Stein, *Mark*, 456), although both closely follow the passive form of the LXX pattern.

402. Garland, *1 Corinthians*, 234; he further explains: "They may regard their union as only a temporary liaison—he to gain sexual release, she to gain a living—but it is more entangling than that; neither is free from the other when they part company." Ibid.; cf. Smedes, *Sex for Christians*, 28; Atkinson, *To Have and to Hold*, 77–98. Similarly, Kirchhoff, *Sünde*, 164: "'Anhängen' bedeutet wie in . . . BerR 18 [i.e., *Gen. Rab.* 18] 'sexuell verkehren'; doch sagt der Text mit Gen 2,24, daß es nicht möglich ist, die Handlung auszuführen, ohne daß der Mann sich an die Frau bindet und eine eheliche Beziehung entsteht. . . . Eine vertragliche Übereinkunft, wie sie der Scheidebrief darstellt, kann das göttliche Handeln (συνέζευξεν [Mark 10:9]) nicht rückgängig machen bzw. außer Kraft setzen." Cf. also CD 4:21. Külling, *Ehe und Ehelosigkeit*, 26 explains: "Der Apostel versucht darzulegen, dass der Verkehr mit der Dirne ein vollumfänglicher Vollzug jener Verbindung ist, die Gott für Mann und Frau angeordnet hat. Dazu dient ihm das Zitat aus Gen 2,24, dessen Schlussteil er gemäss dem Wortlaut der LXX wörtlich zitiert." (The attempt of Piper, *Momentary Marriage*, 31 to explain this fact away, is not convincing and contradicts the clear meaning of the text as it stands.)

403. Kirchhoff, *Sünde*, 165; cf. Dautzenberg, "Φεύγετε τὴν πορνείαν," 278, 282.

404. Isaksson, *Marriage and Ministry*, 106; cf. 110–11.

405. Thus Beale and Carson, *NT Use*, 713.

Akt, er umfaßt die ganze Person und hat weitgehende Konsequenzen für das Leben."[406] It seems he almost overstretches this image, rightly applying the basic fundamentals of Gen 2:24, but leaving out its deeper concerns as would be completeness ("leaving" the previous familial environment) and permanency ("cleaving" with the aim of becoming "one flesh" not just for "one night," but constantly, with all its other related aspects concerning personality and sharing live's burdens).

Both considerations, (A)–(B)/(B')–(A'), are followed by a result (C) which is the starting point for the next pair of arguments, (D)–(E)/(E')–(D'). This pair, most interestingly, responds to both Corinthian slogans of vv. 12–13 by presenting two contrary Christian principles, the first in context of a universal claim,[407] (D)/(D'), and the second as a special, singular quality thereof, (E)/(E'). Both are even a contrast to the universal claim of v. 12 (πάντα μοι ἔξεστιν) and to the special application in v. 13. The Pauline maxim of vv. 13–14 is thus affirmed twice: (1.) by the theological foundation of the Edenic ideal, (A)–(B)/(B')–(A'), and (2.) by the harmatological evidence given in (D)–(E)/(E')–(D'). This by elaborate stylistic devices firmly tied package of an "Edenic" doctrine results in the final conclusion, (C') comprising (B") and (A"), on the entire passage (vv. 12–19) as given by the overall Christian principle of glorifying God in body and spirit (v. 20); that is: in the entire human being—thus further reflecting the Edenic ideal of representing God's image (Gen 1:26–27).[408] This is an important Pauline principle or maxim that is also used elsewhere.[409]

Especially concerning vv. 19–20 it is further interesting to note that the Greek σῶμα could also be understood as a corporative term comprising the entire church (cf. 1 Cor 3:16; Eph 2:21–22)[410] as a representation of the divine image (Gen 1:26–27), being

---

406. Friedrich, *Sexualität und Ehe*, 35.

407. It should again be considered that it is more likely to assume a Corinthian slogan behind πᾶν ἁμάρτημα ὃ ἐὰν ποιήσῃ ἄνθρωπος ἐκτὸς τοῦ σώματός ἐστιν (v. 18b), again immediately refuted by a Pauline maxim (ὁ δὲ πορνεύων εἰς τὸ ἴδιον σῶμα ἁμαρτάνει)—although he did not use the ἀλλ' οὐ of v. 12 and 10:23. However, others support the opinion that "it is best . . . to regard this difficult clause as reflecting Paul's own position, in which he offers another explanation why they should flee *porneia*." This is basically not unreasonable, for "the δέ (*de*), unlike the ἀλλά (*alla*) in 6:12, does not function as a contrastive particle but expresses an exception: 'Every sin a man commits outside his body with the exception of the immoral man who sins against his own body' . . . If 6:18a was a slogan, the response in 6:18b is hardly an adequate refutation." Garland, *1 Corinthians*, 236; cf. Rosner, *Paul*, 144; Kirchhoff, *Sünde*, 176–88. The last argument is very weak, for it rather seems that Paul uses just a single, but very prominent example to refute the entire universal hypothesis of v. 18b. It is not necessary that he deals extensively with that topic when he is able to provide at least one instance to prove the hypothesis to be invalid; and his selection of the one argument is very appropriate, since he is generally talking about sexuality.

408. This idea means that the aim of the "image of God" in Gen 1:26–27 is only reached by "glorifying God in body and spirit" (1 Cor 6:20). I guess this understanding is natural. Of course, man is only able to represent the divine image when he does everything (in body and spirit) to glorify God. Hence, both texts point to one and the same great human-divine goal.

409. See e.g., Rom 6:6–13; 12:1–7.

410. Similarly, for instance, Conzelmann, *1. Korinther*, 136; Ellis, *Paul's Use*, 90–91. While the primary understanding surely is the individual singular, in a distributive sense (cf. Zeller, *1. Korinther*, 227; Kirchhoff, *Sünde*, 182–83), since Paul clearly refers to "one's own body" in v. 18, it is nevertheless

bought by an expensive price (1 Cor 6:20), thus "leaving" the world behind, "joining" Jesus Christ (v. 17),[411] becoming "one spirit" and even "one body" (vv. 17, 19) with him.[412] So the steps (Gen 2:24) and the aim (Gen 1:26–27) of the Edenic ideal are fully presented in this paragraph about the relationship between the Christians of Corinth and their "husband" Jesus Christ. Further, by employing terms that are frequently used in association with slave trading (ἀγοράζω and even σῶμα),[413] Paul makes clear that Christians simultaneously are Christ's "slaves," his "members" (μέλος), to serve his purposes.[414]

Finally, there are two "Sinnlinien" indicating the main theme of the passage, marked by a sequence of closely related terms that occur throughout 1 Cor 6:12–20.[415] The first one is dealing with the physical body and applies the words κοιλία, σῶμα, μέλος, and σάρξ. The second line consists of those terms referring to fornication and prostitution: πορν-, πορνεία, πόρνη and πορνεύω. Furthermore, the entire passage is again enframed by an inclusio. Verses 12–14 and 20 concretely refer to the principles that are discussed or elucidated in between (vv. 15–19) and which centre in the Edenic echo of vv. 16–17. Paul's special interpretation and application of Gen 2:24 thus matches the similar stylistic patterns of Eph 5:21–33 and again allude to the very close connection between salva-

---

possible to perceive a certain interchangeability between the individual church member and the church as a whole: "In addition, although Paul changes the plural σώματα (6: l5) to the singular σῶμα (6:19), he retains the plural ὑμῶν and ἐν ὑμῖν. For this reason, Shedd concludes that it is difficult to know whether τὸ σῶμα in 1 Cor 6:19 refers to the corporate body (i.e., of Christ) or to the individual bodies of believers. This passage is probably a particular application of the general conception of the church as the temple to the individual believer and, as such, it demonstrates that a certain oscillation exists in Paul's thought between the corporate and the individual." Son, *Corporate Elements* 123–24. Similarly Barrett, *First Corinthians*, 151: "When the unity and purity of the church are at stake Paul recalls that the church is the shrine in which the Spirit dwells; when the unity and purity of the moral life of the individual are threatened, he recalls that the Spirit dwells in each Christian, who ought not therefore to defile the Spirit's shrine."

411. Please note that 1 Cor 8:3 is also hinting at this intimate union with Christ, possibly illuminating the central meaning of the Greek κολλάω ("join"): "But if anyone *loves* God, he is *known* by Him." (My italics.) This "known" (γινώσκω) is interesting, being the same as used e.g., in Gen 4:1 as translation of the Hebrew יָדַע, the euphemism for sexual intimacy. Similarly, Gal 4:9 speaks of "knowing God," and "being known by God" in connection with leaving false "gods" and the "elements" of this world: "But now that you have come to know God (γνόντες θεόν), or rather to be known by God (γνωσθέντες ὑπὸ θεοῦ), how is it that you turn back again to the weak and worthless elemental things (τὰ ἀσθενῆ καὶ πτωχὰ στοιχεῖα), to which you desire to be enslaved all over again?"

412. Eph 2:15–18 seems to further develop this image of the corporate Christian church (now concerning Jews and Gentiles) by using similar terminology, reminding about the particular keywords of 1 Cor 6:16–17 (one body—one flesh—one spirit): ". . . so that in Himself He might make the two [i.e., Jews and Gentiles] into *one new man (ἕνα καινὸν ἄνθρωπον)*, thus establishing peace, and might reconcile them both in *one body (ἑνὶ σώματι)* to God through the cross, by it having put to death the enmity . . . for through Him we both have our access in *one Spirit (ἑνὶ πνεύματι)* to the Father." (My italics.) Note the similar keywords: one man—one body—one spirit. It seems, by winning the Gentiles to accept the "one flesh" pattern with Christ, they are incorporated into his unified body, merging into Christ's "one flesh/body/spirit system"—his New Testament church.

413. See about these terms and their distinct association with slave trading esp. Zeller, *1. Korinther*, 228; Arzt-Grabner et al., *1. Korinther*, 241; Conzelmann, *1. Korinther*, 136–37.

414. Cf. e.g., Arzt-Grabner et al., *1. Korinther*, 241.

415. Cf. Kirchhoff, *Sünde*, 108; Egger, *Methodenlehre*, 103–8.

tion, sanctification, and resurrection, possibly endangered by injuring the "one spirit" union through becoming "one flesh" with a harlot. All these perceptions remind one strongly of the Old Testament passages about apostasy through "joining" God's enemies and sexually "becoming one flesh" with them; especially regarding harlotry in a cultic context or in its spiritual application as "forsaking" Yahweh.[416]

Wider Biblical Context. There are some special phrases in the given passage that need further investigation regarding their wider biblical context:

"All things are permitted." Apart from the double mentioning of the Greek πάντα μοι ἔξεστιν in 1 Cor 6:12, it reappears only once in a very similar form in 1 Cor 10:23, again doubled as parallelism. There, again, it is mentioned twice, but in a more general way, omitting the personal pronoun μοι[417] and slightly departing from the responses given in chap. 6:

1 Cor 6:12	1 Cor 10:23
(A) Πάντα μοι ἔξεστιν	(A) Πάντα ἔξεστιν
(B) ἀλλ' οὐ πάντα συμφέρει	(B) ἀλλ' οὐ πάντα συμφέρει ·
(A) πάντα μοι ἔξεστιν	(A) πάντα ἔξεστιν
(B') ἀλλ' οὐκ ἐγὼ ἐξουσιασθήσομαι ὑπό τινος.	(B') ἀλλ' οὐ πάντα οἰκοδομεῖ·
(A) All things are permitted *to me*,	(A) All things are permitted,
(B) but not all things are profitable.	(B) but not all things are profitable.
(A) All things are permitted *to me*,	(A) All things are permitted,
(B') but *I will* not *be mastered by* anything.	(B') but not all things *edify*.

By comparing these very similar phrases it is reaffirmed that only the first parts (A) are the original Corinthian slogan, while the second parts, (B)/(B') are Paul's brief responses to keep the devastating, far-reaching consequences in check. He judges by altogether three important principles; first of all, emphasized by double mentioning, the "profitability" (συμφέρω) of anything. Secondly, it is important not be "mastered" (ἐξουσιάζω) by anything,[418] and thirdly it should "edify/build up" (οἰκοδομέω).

416. But now, for the first time, it is even used in relation to the individual church member becoming "one" (spirit) with God, while in the Old Testament metaphors God is always married to the whole people of Israel, never to individuals, cf. Theobald, "Heilige Hochzeit," 220/fn.1; Westermann, *Jesaja*, 299. Thus, certain individualization can be asserted here; Yahweh seeks loyalty to his covenant not only in the whole congregation, but in every individual member.

417. The insertion of the Greek μοι may hint at the more personal rhetorical context of chap. 6, thus rather emphasizing the more personal understanding of σῶμα in 1 Cor 6:19–20 (cf. v. 18: "the immoral man sins against *his own* body;" my italics) instead of the corporative perception (namely, the entire church)—which, nevertheless, has merit!

418. Interestingly, ἐξουσιάζω reappears only in 7:4, there referring to one's own spouse "being master" over one's own body through sexual intercourse. This connection is meaningful, since thereby even 6:12 implies sexuality. Garland, *1 Corinthians*, 233 explains: "Also left unstated throughout this discussion [i.e., 6:12–15] is Paul's assumption that a person is not a combination of incompatible parts, spirit and body, held together in an unpleasant tension. As a consequence, sex is something that involves the whole self in surrender to another (7:4). In his discussion of sexuality in marriage, Paul claims that the wife does not have authority over her own body but the husband does, and the husband

Besides the more general meaning of these principles, we may assume some special applications concerning marriage, since it is used within the rhetorical introduction to the topics of prostitution and marriage in 1 Cor 6–7. Furthermore, it is most interesting that "all" (πᾶς/πᾶσα/πᾶν) in combination with "permit" (ἔξειμι) occurs in only one further instance within the Greek New Testament, and nowhere in the LXX. This last instance is Matt 19:3, the Pharisees' inquiry whether it is "permitted" to release one's wife for "any" reason (εἰ ἔξεστιν ... ἀπολῦσαι ... κατὰ πᾶσαν αἰτίαν). Of course, there is no brief immediate response as it was possible for Paul while writing a letter. Yet, the synoptic view of the debate and Jesus' answers to that question allude to that fact that even in this case a concrete "exception clause" is given, thus resembling the pattern taken up by Paul in a similar (i.e., marital) context:

(A) εἰ ἔξεστιν ... ἀπολῦσαι ... κατὰ πᾶσαν αἰτίαν (Matt 19:3)

  (B) μὴ ἐπὶ πορνείᾳ (Matt 19:9)

  (B') παρεκτὸς λόγου πορνείας (Matt 5:32)

While the historical background in Paul's letter to the Corinthians is the pagan cult, prostitution (perhaps somehow affiliated with the temple), and the eating of meat offered to heathen gods (cf. 1 Cor 10:14–33), the context of Jesus' response is a distorted view on the Edenic marriage institution within the great Jewish religion. Paul's introduction to his reflection of the Edenic ideal by taking up the same pattern that is enclosing Matt 19:3–9 and the similar subject both are dealing with, connects both instances in the following respects:

1. False assumption concerning "anything is permitted/lawful" transmitted by distorted religious perceptions (Matt 19:3; 1 Cor 6:12).

2. Brief exception clauses basing on Christian principles as (at least partially) refuting responses to the initial hypothesis or inquiry (Matt 19:9; 1 Cor 6:12).

3. Emphasis of the Edenic covenant ideal (Gen 2:24) as the only valid norm (Matt 19:5; 1 Cor 6:16).

4. Emphasizing the fact that God is involved when becoming "one flesh" (Matt 19:6; 1 Cor 6:13–20).

5. Rejection of human standards concerning sexuality, divorce, and πορνεία (Matt 19:8–9; 1 Cor 6:15–20).

Considering the foregoing aspects, we must assume that the marital covenant ideal of Gen 2:24 is something that is easily "misunderstood" or even willfully distorted when dealt with in context of false or unfaithful religions. That concerns not only pagan practices, but also Jewish perceptions—and certainly Christians as well.

---

does not have authority over his own body but the wife does. Is the same true for sexual relations with a prostitute? Does he wish to imply that the Christian comes under the power of the prostitute who becomes his 'unlawful lord' ... ? Sexual intercourse entails the joining together of persons with all their spiritual associations and is not simply the coupling of bodies."

"Φεύγετε τὴν πορνείαν." Paul's appeal to "flee sexual immorality" (1 Cor 6:18) occurs in the same jussive form only two more times within the New Testament, once even in the same letter: φεύγετε ἀπὸ τῆς εἰδωλολατρίας ("flee from idolatry;" 1 Cor 10:14). While this on the one hand reaffirms the underlying context of pagan idolatry endangering Christian principles, in the last instance of Matt 10:23 Jesus tells his disciples to "flee" into another city, if the present Jewish town does not accept their evangelistic efforts. He even speaks about "persecution" (διώκω). The examples of φεύγετε in the Septuagint and all further imperative forms of φεύγω in the NT additionally affirm the context of fleeing from a most certain threat of being spiritually and physically injured.[419] At all times it is God, Jesus, or a prophet speaking in God's name who points to the most likely losing of one's life should the warning not be heeded. Also, we find again a close connection between the dangers of pagan idolatry and the similarly threatening influence of false perceptions within the Jewish religion of Jesus' time.

Another close literary connection is given to *T. Reu.* 5:5 using the same terminology (φεύγετε τὴν πορνείαν; "flee fornication"). "Even though the individual words are not uncommon, the specific injunction occurs only in these two places in ancient Greek literature (along with quotations of 1 Cor 6:18 in the church fathers)."[420] As *T. Reu.* 4:8 indicates, the OT pattern-story behind the warning is the Joseph account in Gen 39 who "fled" (ἔφυγεν; LXX) from Potiphar's wife and thus contrasts the fornication of Judah in the preceding chapter (Gen 38).[421]

Bought to be God's Temple. The Greek phrase ἠγοράσθητε γὰρ τιμῆς (1 Cor 6:20) has at least two significant parallels: 1 Cor 7:23 (τιμῆς ἠγοράσθητε) and Rev 14:3–4 (οἱ ἠγορασμένοι ἀπὸ τῆς γῆς/ἠγοράσθησαν . . . ἀπαρχὴ τῷ θεῷ). In all of these instances men are "bought" (ἀγοράζω) by the blood of the lamb (Rev 5:9) being valued a "great price" (τιμῆς), even regarded as "firstfruits" (ἀπαρχή). They are undefiled, chaste, and following the lamb (Rev 14:4). This is clear cultic language, preparing the way to Paul's final maxim in 1 Cor 6:19: τὸ σῶμα ὑμῶν ναὸς τοῦ ἐν ὑμῖν ἁγίου πνεύματός ἐστιν οὗ ἔχετε ἀπὸ θεοῦ, καὶ οὐκ ἐστὲ ἑαυτῶν ("Your body is a temple of the Holy Spirit who is in you, whom you have from God, and you are not your own"). Particularly in the letters to the Corinthians Paul speaks about this meaningful temple, personifying it with the body of the individual believer: τὸ σῶμα ὑμῶν ναὸς τοῦ . . . πνεύματός ἐστιν. He introduces this term (or phrase) in 1 Cor 3:16–17, again asking his audience: Οὐκ οἴδατε ὅτι . . . ? Evidently they should be well aware of their high calling,[422] but seemingly their practical lives as well as many of their perceptions do not correspond with the Christian standard. It somehow is a "cultic metaphor" of the one-flesh and one-

---

419. Cf. Jer 4:6; 28:6; 30:25; 31:6; Zech 2:10; Matt 2:13; 24:16; Mark 13:14; Luke 21:21; 1 Tim 6:11; 2 Tim 2:22.

420. Beale and Carson, *NT Use*, 714.

421. Cf. on this linkage further Beale and Carson, *NT Use*, 714.

422. Cf. Son, *Corporate Elements* 122–23; Isaksson, *Marriage and Ministry*, 105–6; Weiß, *Der erste Korintherbrief*, 84.

spirit union of 1 Cor 6:16–17, in which this body of the individual church member is described as a "member of Christ" being "one spirit" with him. This union is established by the indwelling Spirit of God, imparted by "joining" (v. 17) him through the purchasing work of Christ (v. 20).

In 2 Cor 6:16 this "temple of God" is contrasted to idolatry in a most significant context, which has already been spoken of several times: The warning of not being "unequally yoked together with unbelievers" (ἑτεροζυγοῦντες ἀπίστοις; 2 Cor 6:14). One may rightly assume that Paul there is also speaking about marriage, and especially about the dangers of marrying idolatrous unbelievers, for there actually is no closer "bounding/yoking" of two people than the intimate marriage relation, establishing even a "one flesh" union.[423] Therefore he explains:

> Do not be bound together with unbelievers; for what partnership have righteousness and lawlessness, or what fellowship has light with darkness? Or what harmony has Christ with Belial, or what has a believer in common with an unbeliever? Or what agreement has the temple of God with idols? For we are the temple of the living God; just as God said, 'I will dwell in them and walk among them; and I will be their god, and they shall be my people. Therefore, 'come out from their midst and be separate,' says the Lord. 'and do not touch what is unclean; and I will welcome you. And I will be a father to you, And you shall be sons and daughters to Me,' Says the Lord Almighty. Therefore, having these promises, beloved, let us cleanse ourselves from all defilement of flesh and spirit, perfecting holiness in the fear of God. (2 Cor 6:14—17:1.)

Resembling his argumentation around the Edenic ideal in 1 Cor 6:12–20, Paul again uses contrasting pairs to support his position against mingling with unchristian elements, thus preventing to perhaps finally become "instruments of unrighteousness" (Rom 6:13) and πόρνης μέλη (1 Cor 6:15):

APPEAL:

[πιστός]   — ἄπιστος: ἑτεροζυγέω   ("Unequally yoked")

RATIONALE/ARGUMENTATION:

δικαιοσύνη — ἀνομία: μετοχή   ("Sharing/Participation")
φῶς   — σκότος: κοινωνία   ("Fellowship")
Χριστός   — Βελιάρ: συμφώνησις   ("Agreement")
πιστός   — ἄπιστος: μερίς   ("Part/Sharing")
ναός θεοῦ   — εἴδωλον: συγκατάθεσις ("Agreement/Union")

---

423. Please remember the Aramaic translation of Gen 1:27; 5:2; and 35:9 (Targum Neofiti), where repeatedly זיווה ("yoke/pair/spouse/[...]") is used as expression for Adam's and Abraham's "wives." This indicates that "yoke" or "yoking," when applied to human persons, strongly denotes marriage—at least in Judaism after the times of the Targumim. For another investigation supporting 2 Cor 6:14 as dealing with marriage see Rodríguez, "Konfessionsverschiedene Ehen," 201–26.

As the first and introductory "appeal," the only negative expression of this passage (ἑτεροζυγοῦντες; v. 14) is the central idea of the subsequent pairs, the title and headline of the following argumentation. Hence, the subsequent pairs are different facets depicting more clearly the two contrary elements and the deeper meaning of "yoking."[424] The Greek verbs ἑτεροζυγέω ("[to] yoke unequally") or ζυγέω ("[to] yoke") do not occur in any other instance within the entire Scriptures (LXX or NT), while the noun ζυγός ("[the] yoke") appears very frequently in context of animals or men under a literal or figurative yoke (e.g., slavery; 1 Tim 6:1). Additionally, only once in the Greek Bible is the adjective ἑτερόζυγος used, in Lev 19:19, again referring to animals being unequally coupled—in context of breeding.[425] Similarly, the rare Hebrew verb צָמַד ("yoke"), strangely enough, appeared in context of the Baal of Peor instance in Num 25:3, likewise referring to paganism and the "yoking" of Israel to a counter-God (see above), just like the contrast between Christ and Belial[426] in the centre of the five pairs in 2 Cor 6:15 above. Now Paul again promises bad results when being "yoked" with an "unequal" partner, who is following some other lord (Belial/Baal). Further it creates a linguistic connection to Matt 19:6 and Mark 10:9 by using the same Greek verb συζεύγνυμι, to describe the way both are henceforth "yoked together."[427] It seems highly permissible to assume or even suppose allusions to the marital bond in 2 Cor 6:14–16,[428] although that might not be Paul's only (or primary) message.[429]

---

424. This is also supported by Martin, *2 Corinthians*, 190–91: "The passage itself is a self-contained entity composed of a statement (6:14a) followed by five antithetical questions (6:14b, c, 15a, b, 16a). Each of these questions is designed to enforce the thrust of the admonition of 6:14a not to 'become yoke-mates with unbelievers.'" Similarly, Thrall, *Second Corinthians (I)*, 472.

425. Cf. LSJ s.v. ἑτερόζυγος "coupled with an animal of diverse kind;" cf. also Thrall, *Second Corinthians (I)*, 472–73.

426. It may be interesting to consider that this Belial (or Beliar) is referred to in context of immoral sexuality already in the pseudepigraphic *T. Sim.* 5:3: "Beware, therefore, of fornication, for fornication is mother of all evils, separating from God, and bringing near to Beliar." Thus it may again be assumed that Paul implies a sexual connotation. Cf. on this point in context of 1 Cor 6:12–20 also Garland, *1 Corinthians*, 235; Dautzenberg, "Φεύγετε τὴν πορνείαν," 291: "Die Assoziation Belial—Unzucht ist nicht auf die Testamente der Pariarchen beschränkt. Nach CD IV 15–17 ist die Unzucht das erste der drei Netze Belials, mit welchen dieser Israel fängt." See further on the traps or "nets of Belial" as referred to by the Qumran sect Sanders, *Jesus and Judaism*, 257–58; cf. Berger, *Gesetzesauslegung*, 553–54: "Unzucht, Reichtum, Befleckung des Heiligtums" (see CD 4:15, 19). On a broader view of the "yoke of Beliar" see *Liv. Pro.* 4:7: ". . . under a yoke of Beliar . . . they become beasts, seizing, destroying, killing, and striking." Please remember further the spiritual/divine component of the yoke-metaphor as presented by Jesus in Matt 11:29–30.

427. Cf. BDAG/FRI/LSJ/THA s.v. συζεύγνυμι.

428. Thus also Rodríguez, "Konfessionsverschiedene Ehen," 218, further referring to the same usage in Josephus (*A.J.* 6:309) and *3 Macc.* 4:8.

429. "Any action that would cause believers to link up with the world in thought or act (through indifference or connivance) must be avoided. Specifically, marriage (1 Cor 7:12–15) was one source of possible mismating. (This is the commonest understanding of 6:14a, though probably it is too narrow . . . .)" Martin, *2 Corinthians*, 197. Cf. Thrall, *Second Corinthians (I)*, 473: "Doubtless he does have in view the contraction of a marriage between a believer and an unbeliever, but he might be thinking also of . . ."

It is close contact with unbelievers that he forbids. He may not have intended, for example, to cancel what he had said in 1 Cor 7.1–16 about the maintenance of mixed marriages, but only to warn against such unions in the future. But he could have been aware that some of his ethical advice in the earlier letter had been received too lightly, so that he now thinks a stronger tone to be necessary.[430]

Considering the general background of pagan worship services in 2 Cor 6:14—17:1, the admonition further resembles the one in 1 Cor 6:12–20 regarding (cultic?) prostitution and the corresponding injury of the Spirit's temple (cf. 1 Cor 6:19/2 Cor 6:16). The verbal tense and mode of the sentence's beginning also support the idea that the Corinthians were only one step away from engaging in idolatrous partnerships, thus debasing their body who is the Holy Spirit's temple;[431] the close connection to Paul's first, urgent warning regarding the very similar topic in 1 Cor 6:12–20 against unchristian, immoral partnerships, therefore, becomes even more apparent.

The contrasting pairs are enclosed by a small inclusio referring to believers and unbelievers[432] in v. 14a and 15b, thus preparing the way to continue another level of argumentation by using the "temple of God" image in the following verses. Paul's concluding rationale in 2 Cor 7:1 speaking to the "beloved" (ἀγαπητοί) and inviting them to be cleansed from all defilement of flesh and spirit further connects this instance with Eph 5:26–27 (Christ sanctifying and cleansing the church) and reflects 1 Cor 6:11 ("you were washed, you were sanctified, you were justified in the name of the Lord Jesus Christ and in the Spirit of our God") as well as 1 Cor 6:20 ("glorify God in body and in spirit").[433] Also, in 1 Thess 4:3 the same author again strengthens and thus reaffirms the close connection of sanctification and sexual morality: "For this is the will of God, your sanctification; that is, that you abstain from sexual immorality; that each of you know how to possess his own vessel in sanctification and honor, not in lustful passion, like the Gentiles who do not know God." His final rationale or conclusion is very similar to the aforementioned instances: "Consequently the one who rejects this is not rejecting human authority but God, who gives his Holy Spirit

---

430. Thrall, *Second Corinthians (I)*, 473.

431. Μὴ γίνεσθε (v. 14): "do not get into/become" (present imperative): they actually seem to be under a constant threat of becoming involved—or even are already entangled. Cf. on this understanding also Martin, *2 Corinthians*, 195–96.

432. See for a deeper investigation of the term "unbeliever" (ἄπιστος) in this context: Rodríguez, "Konfessionsverschiedene Ehen," 207–17.

433. Furthermore, just this "having cleansed her by the washing of water" (Eph 5:26) is a strong reflection of OT marriage patterns and belongs to the realm of the bride's preparation for marriage as Ezek 16:8–9 indicates: "'Then I passed by you and saw you, and behold, you were at the time for love; so I spread my skirt over you and covered your nakedness. I also swore to you and entered into a covenant with you so that you became mine,' declares the Lord GOD. 'Then I bathed you with water, washed off your blood from you and anointed you with oil.'" Obviously God is preparing the marriage with Israel by washing her; therefore: "In Ezekiel, as in Ephesians, the washing with water is directly related to the act of the husband's purifying his bride." Sampley, *One Flesh*, 42; cf. pp. 61, 66–76). Cf. also Song 4:7 ("You are altogether beautiful, my darling, And there is no blemish in you.").

to you" (v. 8). It is again the Holy Spirit dwelling in the temple of the Christian's body which is injured through unlawful sexuality.

Finally, Paul again employs the temple image in Eph 2:21, now referring to the New Testament church in general as God's temple. As will became apparent in the final synoptic overview of the investigated passages of Ephesians and Corinthians in the concluding chapter, the church as a whole (the "body") and the individual church member as a single unit (the "member") are used interchangeably. Besides, in Rev 3:12 the faithful Christian is called a "pillar" (στῦλος) in God's temple, and in Rev 21:22 "the Lord God the Almighty and the Lamb are [. . . the] temple."—Since God is spirit (John 4:24), the Christian will be his temple by "joining" (κολλάω) him, thus becoming "one spirit" and "one flesh [i.e., body/member: σῶμα/μέλος]" with him (1 Cor 6:15, 17, 19); and the entire church is his temple through the indwelling Spirit of God.

II.2.2.4 Summary and Final Considerations

While Jesus is teaching about the literal sphere of marriage, Paul prefers the spiritual level. Nevertheless he draws conclusions for the literal realm, the everyday life, deriving practical Christian principles from spiritual truths to be used in response to important inquiries or problems of two important ancient churches.

Compared to 1 Cor 6:12–20, the text in Ephesians 5 seems to focus more on what Jesus was and still is willing to invest in order to reach his goals with the church. The images are more general in their nature, mostly speaking about the whole New Testament church, turning to the individual only within the practical application on the required behavior of husbands and wives. Christ is introduced as the supreme head of the church. Yet he is the one who perfectly cares for all the needs of his church and who will finally succeed to present his "glorious church" being "cleansed by the washing of water in the word." She will be "holy and blameless," "having no spot or wrinkle or anything like that."[434] Thus, the church members will rightly be called μέλη . . . τοῦ σώματος αὐτοῦ, ἐκ τῆς σαρκὸς αὐτοῦ καὶ ἐκ τῶν ὀστέων αὐτοῦ—the μυστήριον of the gospel being revealed and practically exemplified by their "cleaving" to the Lord, being "one flesh" with him.

> The character of the 'one flesh' union sustained by Christ with the church is personal and permanent. The personal love of God made known in the cross encounters man through the kerygma, the one Spirit, and the community of the faithful (Eph 2:17–22) and shapes man individually and collectively into the 'likeness of God in true righteousness and holiness' (Eph 4:24). The whole

---

434. Batey rightly asserts: "The love for the church showed by Christ and the Father has been the motivation for her election before the foundation of the world to be holy and blameless (Eph 1:4–6, 12). This image offers a clue for understanding the tension between election and freedom which exists in Ephesians and elsewhere in the New Testament. A bride chosen by a young man and his father usually maintained the freedom to accept or refuse their proposal. The church, which has been created and elected in love to be the fulfillment of the divine purpose for the universe (Eph 1:9–10), may also reject this purpose and continually must be encouraged not to jeopardize her calling (Eph 4:1, 22, 23)." Batey, *Nuptial Imagery*, 27.

man is involved in the relationship, but individual identity and continuity are not broken or swallowed up in a mystical *henosis*.

Christians as imitators of Christ (Eph 5:1–2) are the historic continuation of his Body or personality (σῶμα). As each individual encounters and surrenders himself to the power of Christ's personality, so all become conformed to a single 'Body' characterized by love.[435]

This "one flesh mystery" of Ephesians is the starting point of the topic in first Corinthians six. While also shortly referring to the redemptive work of Jesus Christ and the Holy Spirit by washing, sanctifying, and justifying (1 Cor 6:11), the concrete echo of Gen 2:24 is even shorter and the spiritual consequences are even greater. He seems to take it for granted that his Corinthian audience is already familiar to some degree with the corresponding theological perceptions of Ephesians 5, or perhaps different correct ideas about the Edenic ideal. Paul now applies the Edenic covenant norm as a pattern to judge certain Corinthian perceptions, the quite influential slogans possibly prevailing even within the Christian church. He clearly disapproves of the pagan practices behind these impressive ideas and lifts the Christian standard even higher by explaining that instead of partaking in practices associated with idolatry, the individual Christian and the church as Christ's "body" should be a temple of the Holy Spirit. Consequently, the individual church member's responsibility is forcefully emphasized by the significant application of the Edenic pattern in 1 Cor 6:16–17. The spiritual goal is clearly formulated: to glorify God in body and spirit. His emphasis in these verses is not merely on what a Christian should (not) do. It is primarily on power and authority exercised through sexuality—independent of the concrete kind of intercourse (good/lawful or bad/πορνεία):

> The language of power, already introduced in 6:12 and implicit in the references to the Lord in whose name the believers have been baptized [6:11], suggests that something more [than a simple prohibition] is intended. The mutuality, the body for the Lord and the Lord for the body, echoes the structure of mutuality assumed to be created in Gen 2:24 between a man and a woman.... The focus on power continues in 6:14 where Paul links Christ's resurrection to the believers. διὰ τῆς δυνάμεως αὐτοῦ ('by his power') is emphatically placed in the final position [... as] a statement about resurrected bodies. The issue is about bodies and the powers which govern them. 6:15 presses home the point by identifying the bodies of believers as members of Christ.... As sexual intercourse was widely understood to constitute a marriage, a permanent state of affairs, so sexual intercourse with a prostitute brings me into a relationship with a prostitute in which my body becomes a member of hers and hers a member of mine.[436]

---

435. Batey, *Nuptial Imagery*, 35.

436. Loader, *LXX, Sexuality, and NT*, 89–90. It is further interesting that the understanding of Gen 2:24 in *Gen. Rab.* 18 is that "when two men engage in sexual intercourse with a prostitute, only the second commits adultery because the first through sexual intercourse creates marriage. This understanding of the effects of sexual union and thus its key role in establishing marriage reflects a widespread assumption in the texts and informs Paul's argument here. The focus certainly includes

So the leading motif in the rest of chap. 6 is the topic mentioned in v. 12: "I will not *be mastered* by anything"—except Jesus Christ and the Spirit of God who "washed, . . . sanctified, [. . . and] justified" (v. 11; cf. vv. 17–20), and who are able to "benefit" (v. 12) the church.

What Christ did, according to the message of Eph 5:21–33, is what husbands should do: love, nourish, and cherish their wives.[437] Correspondingly, in 1 Cor 6 Paul speaks about what every individual church member should do, again appealing to the intimate union every Christian may enjoy with Christ through a "one spirit" union. The Edenic pattern thus functions as a mutual condition, applicable to both spheres (literal and spiritual) and to both covenant partners (God and man) in (almost) the same way. Both have their tasks and their own responsibility. The foundation is the same: (1) leaving; (2) cleaving; (3) becoming (one flesh/spirit). Especially the "cleaving" (κολλάω) is emphasized in 1 Cor 6:16–17 as the "instrument" of establishing the union between two persons; it functions as a summary of the two steps cleaving and becoming (one flesh) in Gen 2:24. This may allude to the fact that becoming "one flesh" is the inevitable result of a "cleaving" of this quality.[438] And this is even more than just a simple, temporary act; it further involves spiritual and psychological aspects. „Die Besonderheit der paulinischen Interpretation von Gen 2,24 liegt darin, daß sie von κολλᾶσθαι eine Regel ableitet, die für alle Beziehungen gilt, die so umschrieben werden müssen. Sie besagt, daß ein Mensch mit jeder Größe, der er anhängt, eins wird."[439] As the texts demonstrate, "Paul conceives the union with Christ to be as real as the physical union created by sexual intercourse."[440]

---

sexual intercourse, but the primary concern is not the act but what it produces." Ibid., 90/fn.21; (referring to Kirchhoff, *Sünde*, 163–64).

437. Similarly Beale and Carson, *NT Use*, 826, 828; Schnackenburg, *Epheser*, 262–63; Lincoln, *Ephesians*, 374, 389; Son, "Concept," 114; Beattie, *Women and Marriage*, 79; Lambrecht, *Collected Studies*, 303: "The husband is 'head,' man and bridegroom: he must behave as Christ." Cf. Farla, "The Two," 75: "They [the Christian husband and wife] must give form to their marriage with the ideal of Christ's love for the Church as an example. The Genesis quotation has, in this summons, the same function and meaning as in the synoptical texts: the ideal of mutual love between husband and wife in marriage is founded on God's plan of creation." Note also Theobald, "Heilige Hochzeit," 253: „Die Hingabe Jesu 'definiert' neu, nicht nur was Liebe bedeutet, sondern vor allem was sie tut. Deshalb steht sie im Eph im Zentrum einer umfassenden Vision sich realisierender Einheit, die in der Gemeinschaft von Juden–und Heidenchristen (2, 11 ff.), aber auch im pluralen Miteinander der einzelnen Glieder der Kirche (4, 1 ff.) ihre ekklesiologische Erdung besitzt. Daß sie daneben erfahrbar wird auch in der ehelichen Gemeinschaft, insoweit diese sich vom Urbild der Bundes-Liebe Christi leiten lässt, entspricht ganz dem präsentischen Zug der Eschatologie des Briefes . . . ." In Ephesians Paul obviously speaks solely about the ideal; he does not speak about the problems of mixed marriages and he also "offers little practical assistance to those whose marriages are, for whatever reason, less than splendid." Beattie, *Women and Marriage*, 81. This, however, will be balanced by his remarks in 1 Cor 7 (to be investigated below about "Paul's Practical Application").

438. Hence, in context of Gen 2:24 or its echoes, it seems as if κολλάω must mainly be understood as denoting a cleaving in a sexual sense; cf. Dautzenberg, "Φεύγετε τὴν πορνείαν," 280; Schmidt, "κολλάω," 822; Lohmeyer, *Markus*, 201; similarly Isaksson, *Marriage and Ministry*, 106; Son, "Concept," 108/fn.3, against Miller, "Fresh Look," 127 who suggests that Paul in 1 Cor 6:16–17 removes the sexual connotation by omitting the prefix (προσ-), although esp. 1 Cor 6:16 clearly deals with sexuality (harlotry).

439. Kirchhoff, *Sünde*, 195.

440. Son, "Concept," 109.

It is a spiritual fact to become "one spirit" and thus "one body/flesh" with Christ through "cleaving," just as a man becomes "one flesh" with his wife.

Although both passages deal with different contexts and therefore contain differing applications of the Edenic ideal, they evidently have quite a lot in common. Hence, to reemphasize the spiritual level of the Edenic ideal Paul is referring to as his theological basis, I will now present a synoptical overview of both passages (in 1 Cor 6 beginning even with v. 11), stressing the paralleling aspects concerning the spiritual sphere.

Eph 5:21–33	1 Cor 6:11–20
(vv. 23–24) Christ is: Head of the church Savior of the body [i.e., his church] The Church is: Subject to Christ	(v. 13) The Lord is: For the body The Body is: For the Lord
(v. 30) We are: Members of Chirst's body (out of his flesh and out of his bone)	(v. 15) You are: Members of Christ
(vv. 31–32) Gen 2:24 as referring to: Christ and the church Being "one flesh"	(v. 17) Gen 2:23–24 as referring to: The Lord and the church member(s) (=CM)[441] Being "one spirit"

(vv. 21, 25–29)
Christ did:
He   gave up   himself
        loved   the church
(to) sanctify,   "
(has) cleansed, "
        nourishes, "
        cherishes, "
 	
Christ will do:
        present, "
 	
Goal:
        holy,   "
        blameless, "
 	
Christ feared by, "
 	
Husb. love   their wives
Wives fear   their husbands
	(vv. 11, 14, 19–20)
	Christ (=C), Spirit (=S), and God did:
	C+S washed the CM
	        sanctified
	        justified
	
	God raised the Lord
	bought the CM
	
	God will do:
	Raise us up through his power
	
	Goal:
	CM being a temple of the
	                     Holy Spirit
	
	CM glorifying God in body
	                       and spirit
	
	CM choosing sound intimacy
	                       as explained in
	                       1 Cor 7

441. The individual church member, of course, represents the entire "body" of the church, which consists of its different members, as the many plural pronouns in 1 Cor 6:15–20 distinctively point out. Yet, the passage 1 Cor 6 seems to stress a bit more the individual responsibility than the one in Eph 5. (As to be seen even by the simple fact that in 1 Cor 6:11–20 nowhere the term "church" appears, while in Eph 5:21–33 ἐκκλησία occurs altogether six times!)

The various common features may be regarded as the pillars of the Pauline "one flesh" (or "one spirit") theology, being congruent in both specific applications. These would be the following "elements:"

1. Christ is head and savior of every Christian
2. The Christian is subject to him
3. The Christian is a member of Christ, being "one flesh" with him
4. Through the Holy Spirit the Christian further is "one spirit" with him
5. Christ fulfills his tasks faithfully (bought by self-sacrifice, loving, sanctifying, cleansing, nourishing, cherishing)⁴⁴²
6. The Christian should perform his tasks faithfully (fearing Christ, glorifying God in body and spirit)
7. Then the common goal will be reached (presenting the church holy and blameless, raising up the individual member as well as the entire church as Christ's "body" being a temple of the Holy Spirit)

These "pillars" surrounding the Pauline application of the Edenic ideal very clearly allude to what the apostle himself so significantly called a great μυστήριον: The consummation of the divine covenant by the blood of Christ according to a model of intimacy already established in Eden and entrusted to the first human couple. It is the εὐαγγέλιον ("good news/message") of God seeking reconciliation with man by the redeeming work of Jesus Christ, basing on the Old Testament covenant ideal as introduced by the Edenic marriage and continued throughout the Old Testament as an intimate covenant relationship between Yahweh and Israel for the purpose of restoring (re-creating) the godly image in man (cf. Col 3:10; 2 Cor 5:17)⁴⁴³ as a preparation of the final world-wide establishment of Edenic ideals (cf. Gen 1:28; Rev 21:1–4; then actually even excelling the glory and perfectness of the original Eden; "for the first heaven and the first earth passed away;" Rev 21:1)—including the intimacy and faithfulness exemplified in Gen 2:24, which was taken up in context of the בְּרִית שָׁלוֹם.

---

442. Please notice additionally the following thoughts on the redemptive works of Christ and their meaning in the marital context: "Christ has expressed his love concretely in the flesh, sacrificing himself on the cross (Eph 2:15, 16). As betrothal was effected by the giving and receiving of a valuable gift; so Christ has given himself—a gift the value of which reveals the magnitude of his love. The acceptance of this gift by the church is the response in faith which completes her betrothal (Eph 2:8, 9) . . . Those who accept in faith the redemptive work of God wrought in Jesus Christ are sanctified. Just as a betrothed girl, they are separated from their former manner of life, consecrated and dedicated to the honor and glory of another (Eph 1:11–14) . . . The love of Christ for the church, as for the individual, does not begin with a perfect church. Sanctification in this context does not designate perfection but rather consecration for a purpose. However, Christ has provided the means by which the church might be worthy of her status as Bride elect . . . Christ's initial preparation of the church is the cleansing bath of baptism. As a bride was bathed in preparation for the wedding, so the church has submitted to the purification of her Lord provided by baptism." Batey, *Nuptial Imagery*, 27–28.

443. Cf. e.g., Kirchschläger, *Ehe im NT*, 21, 49.

Paul consequently applies the Old Testament images to the New Testament church, thus also consequently amplifying Jesus' sayings which focus more on the everlastingness and general indissolubility of the "one flesh" union. Paul further explains that these heavenly principles are universal, and thus even apply to certain elements associated with pagan worship services. Hence, it is most important to "flee" from anything establishing such an influential union with idolatry (1 Cor 6:18; 1 Cor 10:14), thereby abusing what is meant to be an "instrument of righteousness" (Rom 6:13) by turning the "members of Christ" into "members of a prostitute" (1 Cor 6:15), injuring the Christian's high calling of being God's temple and even "one spirit" with him (1 Cor 6:17, 19).[444] The sound alternative to this threatening danger is consequently further dwelt upon in 1 Cor 7, which will be further investigated below.

To sum up, in Eph 5 as well as in 1 Cor 6, Paul's fundamental idea and priority seems to be the spiritual integrity and loyalty of the church. In this context, the "one flesh" metaphor is meant to set up a vision for this great spiritual union and intimacy with Christ. This possibly is Paul's most potent image for salvation as individual *participation*, rather than perceiving it in sole legal/juristic categories. As was developed in the foregoing investigations, it emphasizes (1) the redemptive quality of the one flesh union; (2) the possibility of experiencing the redemptive covenant relationship between God and his people on the personal one-to-one sphere of marriage; (3) a deeper evaluation and estimation of the gospel "mystery" by living a marriage through good and bad times (blessings and curses, forgiving and being forgiven); (4) the potential to create a spiritual union by physical unification; (5) the connection to the goal of rightly representing the image of God (Gen 1:26–27).

II.3 Further Allusions

In this last section on further New Testament notes basing on the Edenic ideal, there are two main streams that deserve attention for the purpose of rounding off the NT references pointing back to the Edenic covenant pattern of Gen 2:24: first, the practical Pauline application of the marriage ideal to the conditions and requirements of the Corinthian church as given in 1 Cor 7, and second, the echoes of the Old Testament marriage metaphor as reflecting the relationship between Christ and the New Testament church.

---

444. Similarly Dunstan, "The Marriage Covenant," 251: "If, too, the harlot of I Corinthians 6 was a temple prostitute, then union with her was to become 'one flesh' with the devilish or idolatrous company which she had her temple symbolized. For the Christian, already 'one flesh' with Christ, and a 'living stone' in that 'temple of his body' which is indwelt by the Holy Ghost, this was the ultimate apostasy. St Paul wrote as heir to the prophets, for whom apostasy from the covenant was 'whoredom.'"

II.3.1 Paul's Practical Application (1 Cor 7)

While the investigated text of 1 Cor 6:12–20 represents the depiction of the theological "problem," chap. 7 seems to further illuminate the author's understanding of the "solution" dealing with sound sexuality and marriage as contrary to what he previously called πορνεία (1 Cor 6:18) making the church members to become πόρνης μέλη instead of μέλη Χριστοῦ (v. 15). The passage focusing on the Edenic ideal and its spiritual application by pointing to the goal of being ἓν πνεῦμα with the Lord through κολλάω (1 Cor 6:17) ends, as a first stage, with the appeal to glorify God in body (and spirit). The following remarks, consequently, deal with practical instructions on how to reach that goal.

Since the investigated passage is placed in context of two prominent pagan practices, prostitution and the cultic meal (see v. 13), it is not surprising that both topics are consequently dealt with in the subsequent chapters. At first, in chap. 7, we find the practical elucidation of what to consider regarding πορνεία; and in chap. 8 we find Paul's admonitions concerning εἰδωλόθυτος, the "food sacrificed to idols." Thus, both elements of the initial problem statement in 1 Cor 6:12–14, and especially its core v. 13 (βρώματα/πορνεία), are comprehensively dealt with and both parts of the glorification mentioned in v. 20 (σῶμα/πνεῦμα) are correspondingly taken into consideration, still based on the solid foundation of Gen 2:24 as given in the central rationale of 1 Cor 6:16–17.

Furthermore, following the same pattern of the previous problem statement in 1 Cor 6:12,[445] it seems that Paul again quotes a Corinthian slogan to introduce his additional instructions (1 Cor 7:1): καλὸν ἀνθρώπῳ γυναικὸς μὴ ἅπτεσθαι ("it is good for a man not to touch a woman").[446] On the one hand, he again (partially) refutes this basically erroneous principle by a brief, tentative response: διὰ δὲ τὰς πορνείας ἕκαστος τὴν ἑαυτοῦ γυναῖκα ἐχέτω καὶ ἑκάστη τὸν ἴδιον ἄνδρα ἐχέτω ("but because

---

445. Please remember the pattern that came to light within the investigation of the literary context of 1 Cor 6:12–20 concerning 1 Cor 10:23 and Matt 19:3, 9 with its brief, refuting response followed by a larger dealing with the matter.

446. On reasons for interpreting this line (v. 1) as Corinthian slogan see e.g., Garland, *1 Corinthians*, 248–51; Merklein, "Paulus und die Sexualität," 230–32, 241; cf. Collins, *Sexual Ethics*, 18. The main arguments are the contradiction of v. 1 and vv. 2–5 if supposed that v. 1 is a Pauline doctrine, and the resemblance of structural parallels given in 6:12–13; 8:1–4; 10:23 also using a short catchphrase and providing immediate refutation. However, even if understanding v. 1b as Pauline statement, it would only correspond with his own opinion in v. 7 (thus Baltensweiler, *Ehe im NT*, 156), and therefore there should be no problems in interpreting vv. 2–6 in the same way as it is given above assuming a Corinthian slogan. Perhaps, as speculation, this might be the reason why Paul does not concretely mark it as a Corinthian statement by saying, for instance, "each one of you is saying" (1 Cor 1:12); "one says, . . . and another" (1 Cor 3:4); or "some among you say" (1 Cor 15:12). To assume a Pauline declaration in v. 1, therefore, is not unreasonable (Isaksson, *Marriage and Ministry*, 106–7; Farla, "The Two," 76, 78; Niederwimmer, *Askese und Mysterium*, 80–81/fn.3), albeit certain problems remain (see Isaksson, *Marriage and Ministry*, 107). However, the observation of Barth, *Ephesians 4–6*, 733 may easily solve the "problem:" "Paul leaves it to the Corinthians to call physical contact with a woman 'not good' (I Cor 7:1). But he does not call it 'good' either (I Cor 7:8, 26)." Both views (v. 1 and vv. 8, 26, 32–33) are apparently overlapping.

of sexual immoralities, each man is to have his own wife, and each woman is to have her own husband") (1 Cor 7:2). On the other hand, however, at least in the subsequent passages, he provides rationales as to why the principle of v. 1 could also be something good: because of the present or impending crisis and the distraction (from being "concerned about the things of the Lord, how to please the Lord;" v. 32) due to marital cares (cf. vv. 25–40).[447] It seems that Paul is not completely rejecting the idea uttered by the Corinthians, but he corrects their understanding by providing a Christian basis and proper aims of celibacy, clearly rejecting the idea of dissolving already existing partnerships (see e.g., v. 27) or eschewing sexuality even within marriage (vv. 3–5).[448]

What follows in vv. 3–9 is a larger dealing with the matter, again reflecting the pattern of 1 Cor 6:15–20. Also, in 7:4 Paul again speaks about ἐξουσιάζω ("to exercise power/master"), which occurs only thrice in the NT and, leaving out the instance of Luke 22:25 speaking about the "authority" of kings, clearly parallels the only further occurrence in 1 Cor 6:12. 1 Cor 7:4 knows a sound kind of "exercising power," thus contrasting the general rejection of "being mastered" in 1 Cor 6:12.[449] All these considerations further affirm that Paul contrasts the immoral sexuality of chap. 6 with the moral sexuality of chap. 7. The pattern is very similar, and the foundation is still the Edenic ideal. Therefore, we should assume that it must be possible to derive some further hints concerning Paul's "one flesh/one spirit" thinking by briefly dwelling on main aspects of 1 Cor 7 that may contribute to a better understanding of his perception.

II.3.1.1 Notes on Lawful Sexuality

First of all, Paul's previous argumentation concerning πορνεία in chap. 6 could have been misunderstood as a warning to possibly refrain from any kind of a "one flesh" union for the sake of the "one spirit" union with God. At least v. 1, which most probably was a Corinthian slogan so popular that they even stated this principle in a letter to Paul, could be used as a support of this erroneous idea. Paul apparently intends to prevent that and at the same time he uses the opportunity to explain what the real

---

447. Cf. Dunn, *Theology*, 697: "Those who marry may have 'trouble for the flesh' (7:28), but there is no attempt to promote ascetic views or practices as such. Nor can the ethical principle which emerges be defined solely as an 'interim ethic'. It is the primacy of the affairs of the Lord, rather than simply the immanence of his coming, which relativizes (not abolishes or diminishes) all other concerns."

448. Schrage, *1. Korinther*, 2:59–60 puts it thus: "Zwar kann Paulus das καλόν in gewisser Weise unterschreiben, aber während καλόν im Mund der Korinther ein 'moralisches Axiom' von hohem, wenn nicht abolutem Wert sein wird, möglicherweise im Sinne des Superlativs, versteht er es eher im Sinne von wünschenswert und vorteilhaft, aber nicht als Verherrlichung von Virginität und Askese." Cf. also Loader, *Jesus Tradition*, 151, 154; May, *Body*, 212, 216.

449. Baltensweiler, *Ehe im NT*, 158 adds concerning the "atmosphere" of this assertion: "Es fehlt aber im Griechischen an dieser Redensart jegliche Herabwürdigung des andern Geschlechtes. Es will eine sachliche Feststellung gemacht werden."

Christian principles concerning sexuality and celibacy are like. Beginning with verses 2–9, Paul elucidates:

1. It is wrong to assume that a complete rejection of sexuality is the best life style; in order to prevent πορνεία it is reasonable to marry (v. 2).

2. Everyone should "have"[450] his or her *own* spouse; stressing the principle of monogamy (v. 2).

3. Conjugal sexuality is nothing to be negotiated and particularly not to be rejected; in fact, it is the only instance where both partners may ἐξουσιάζω over their spouse's σῶμα; both bear the special "duty" (ὀφειλή)[451] not to "rob" (ἀποστερέω) their spouses of sexuality "except by agreement for a time" in order to pray (vv. 3–5).[452] But afterwards "come together again [to have sexual relations]" (v. 5).[453]

---

450. Please note: "'Haben' ist antithetische Substitution von 'nicht anfassen' (V. 1 b) und tendiert daher zur Bedeutung 'geschlechtlichen Umgang haben' (vgl. 1 Kor 5, 1 b). Dies wird durch V. 3 a bestätigt. V. 4 bringt die Begründung: In der Ehe wird das Verfügungsrecht über den eigenen Körper dem Partner übertragen." Merklein, "Paulus und die Sexualität," 233.

451. It is most interesting that the same term for "duty" (ὀφειλή) is used in Eph 5:28 in the verbal form (ὀφείλω—"owe/must/indebted/ought") explaining that the Ephesian husbands "*owe* to love their wives as their own bodies." The structural parallelism with the quotation from Gen 2:24 in Eph 5:31 was demonstrated in the corresponding paragraph of the exegesis on Eph 5:21–33 above (see "Paul's Spiritual Application: Textual Analysis"). The congruency regarding the "marital duty" as particularly referring to conjugal sexuality is striking. On the "sexual accessibility of husband and wife" as "mutual duty" see also Beattie, *Women and Marriage*, 23; Baltensweiler, *Ehe im NT*, 157; Domanyi, "Anthropologie und Ethik," 236–37; Schrage, *1. Korinther*, 2:63–64; Martin, *Corinthian Body*, 209; Strack and Billerbeck, *Talmud und Midrasch*, 3:368–72; Külling, *Ehe und Ehelosigkeit*, 45–47 (on the "power" over each other's body see pp. 48–49).

452. Beattie, *Women and Marriage*, 23 (referring to Poirier and Frankovich, "Celibacy and Charism," 4) points to a similar idea in the rabbinic material: "*T. Naph.* 8.8: 'There is a time for having intercourse with one's wife and a time to abstain for the purpose of prayer.' However, Paul does not *command* such periods of abstinence; he merely *permits* them. It is also by no means obvious that Paul sees it as necessary for people to abstain from sex in order to be pure." (Italics given; the same point is made by Epstein, *Soncino Babylonian Talmud*, 93/fn.54; cf. also Loader, *Jesus Tradition*, 158–59; Friedrich, *Sexualität und Ehe*, 83; Collins, *Sexual Ethics*, 120–21; and Fitzmyer, *First Corinthians*, 281, who further hints at Tob. 8:4–8 which in the Latin Vulgate translation speaks about abstaining from sexual intercourse for three nights in order to pray.) This observation concerning sex and ritual purity is completely in harmony with Heb 13:4 and the results found by investigating Lev 15:18 in the chapter "Ritual Purity." (The external [mostly Hellenistic] support from Paul's days perceiving sexuality as rendering a person ritually impure as provided by Poirier and Frankovich, "Celibacy and Charism," 5–10 is interesting, indeed. It lacks convincing biblical support, however, in OT and NT, especially in the other Pauline writings.)

453. The emphasis clearly is upon coming together for the purpose of sexual intercourse, as the rationale at the end of v. 5 and the underlying subject confirm. Similarly Merklein, "Paulus und die Sexualität," 233; Garland, *1 Corinthians*, 258; Beattie, *Women and Marriage*, 23. The Jewish tradition even formulated how often this intercourse should happen and it is interesting to notice that; see *m. Ketub.* 5:6; cf. also *'Ed.* 4:10: Depending on different cases, those who swore to abstain from sex may do according to their oath no longer than two weeks (the school of Shammai) or even no longer than one week (Hillel). For studying Torah and without consent of one's wife no longer than 30 days, a simple worker only one week. The interpretation of the frequency of the "conjugal duty" in Exod 21:10 is: every day for the unemployed, a worker twice a week, a driver of mules once a week, a driver of

It is not reasoned as legitimate only for the purpose of procreation, or as being adequate only as an expression of love and companionship, but as in itself inherently being part of the one-flesh union/marriage relation.⁴⁵⁴

4. The ultimate rationale for the previous instructions is ὁ ἀκρασία ὑμῶν ("your lack of self-control;" v. 5).

5. Paul is not supporting the contrary opinion that everyone has to marry. Marriage is "a concession, not [. . . a] command" (v. 6; cf. vv. 7–9).⁴⁵⁵

6. It is a special χάρισμα ἐκ θεοῦ to be able to live without sexuality (v. 7). Man's usual condition apparently is including the desire to have intimate relations with a עֵזֶר כְּנֶגְדּוֹ (Gen 2:18). However, it is καλόν (v. 8) to remain unmarried.⁴⁵⁶

---

camels once per month, a seaman once in six months, according to R. Eliezer.

454. Cf. Loader, *Jesus Tradition*, 157; Schrage, *1. Korinther*, 2:82. It further alludes to gender equality in matters of marital sexuality; cf. Fitzmyer, *First Corinthians*, 275.

455. Concerning the prominent τοῦτο at the beginning of v. 6, it seemingly refers to the instructions in vv. 2–5 altogether (i.e., marriage), not just to the immediately preceding agreement to be abstinent for a short period (against Baltensweiler, *Ehe im NT*, 161–63; Schrage, "Frontstellung," 232–33; Yarbrough, *Gentiles*, 99–100; Beattie, *Women and Marriage*, 24; Fitzmyer, *First Corinthians*, 281), or only referring to the sexual intercourse dealt with before (cf. e.g., Merklein, "Paulus und die Sexualität," 233–34). Considering Paul's own desire that all would have the gift to be unmarried like him (v. 7), this contrast seems to make more sense "wenn das in V. 6 auszuräumende Mißverständnis sich auf die Ehe als solche bezogen hat." Ibid., 234; cf. Loader, *Jesus Tradition*, 161–62. Yet, the actual reference of the τοῦτο remains ambiguous and even the interpretation of Isaksson, *Marriage and Ministry*, 107 is reasonable: "However, after saying that the husband and wife each have a right to sexual intercourse and that neither is entitled to refuse, Paul is careful to emphasize that this is a concession and not a command (7.6). He here employs a common rabbinical distinction between a command (κατ' ἐπιταγήν), which must be obeyed, and a concession (κατὰ Συγγνώμην). . . . The husband and wife have a right to sexual intercourse: this is not a right which they *must* exercise but one which they *may* exercise." Yet, the echo of Exod 21:10–11 in 1 Cor 7:3 using ὀφειλή ("duty") rather indicates an appeal to take care of this part of the relationship, although it may be the case that Paul himself declares that "it is good for a man not to touch a woman" (v. 1)—but that certainly only under the conditions of 1 Cor 7:25–40, and not within an already existing marital relationship. Especially v. 35 ("this [τοῦτο] I say for your own benefit; not to put a restraint upon you") points unambiguously to the understanding of τοῦτο as referring to marriage per se (not just sexuality) and could be understood as parallel to the foregoing exposition (vv. 2–5). In my opinion, the immediately following argument about the gift of celibacy (v. 7) is to function as a further elucidation of the τοῦτο in v. 6 and has to be read in common with v. 6. Then it is even more obvious that Paul at this place splits two topics: (1) marriage and sexuality in vv. 2–5 and (2) celibacy in vv. 1, 7–9 (in vv. 7–9 he evidently returns to his starting point of v. 1: the Corinthian's inquiry).

456. By using this καλόν Paul takes up the Corinthian slogan of v. 1, but significantly alters the statement by omitting any debasing of sexuality: "Allerdings weist bereits die Tatsache, daß er das sexuell fixierte ‚nicht anfassen' der Parole nicht übernimmt und durch 'wenn sie bleiben wie ich' ersetzt, darauf hin, daß der Standpunkt des Paulus, kaum durch eine Disqualifizierung der Sexualität motiviert sein kann. Dies unterstreicht im Übrigen V. 9. Paulus will seine Ausführungen in V. 8 nicht als Parole oder gar als Prinzip verstanden wissen. Ehelosigkeit erfordert das Charisma der Enthaltsamkeit (vgl. V. 7 b). Wo dies nicht gegeben ist, ist der Stand der Ehe die bessere christliche Möglichkeit." Merklein, "Paulus und die Sexualität," 235. Similarly Külling, *Ehe und Ehelosigkeit*, 71: "1Kor 7,7 ist somit kein Plädoyer zugunsten der Ehelosigkeit, die Paulus als die bessere Möglichkeit propagiert. Aber es dokumentiert seinen verbindlichen Willen, dass jeder Einzelne seine eigene

This constitutes the first passage of chap. 7 that deals with the general topic of correcting the (possibly) Corinthian slogan καλόν ἀνθρώπῳ γυναικὸς μὴ ἅπτεσθαι ("it is good for a man not to touch a woman")—at least the negative results like abstaining from sex within marriage that could be derived therefrom. Even when interpreting v. 1b as Pauline opinion—either in harmony with a group in Corinth that encouraged abstinence or with the group of chap. 6 that dealt carelessly with sexuality under the premise "anything is permitted"—the argumentation in vv. 2–5 clearly demonstrates that

> abstinence cannot and may not become an ideal for married persons; it would only be asking for trouble to demand that these people should deny themselves sexually. This is indeed how [vv.] 2–5 should be read and understood. These verses deal with the married man and the married woman. The surrounding arguments διὰ δὲ τὰς πορνείας and διὰ τὴν ἀκρασίαν ὑμῶν are in defence of marriage as a sexual relationship per definition, against the fanatical demands for abstinence.[457]

As outlined by Garland, there is a chiastic structure given in the introductory verses 1–5 which further stresses the sexual quality of marriage:[458]

(A) But because of fornications (7:2a)
  (B) Let each one have his own wife or her own husband (7:2bc)
    (C) Let the husband fulfill his sexual obligations to his wife (7:3a)
      (D) and likewise the wife to her husband (7:3b)
      (D') The wife does not have authority over her own body but her husband (7:4a)
    (C') and likewise the husband does not have authority over his own body but his wife (7:4b)
  (B') Do not deprive one another . . . (7:5ab)
(A') because of your lack of self-control (7:5c)

This structure points to the importance of sexuality for the marital life, while Paul is significantly silent on the purpose of procreation, thus rejecting the perceptions of Josephus (*C.Ap.* 2:199) and Philo (*Spec.* 3:36, 113).[459] Furthermore, Paul points out that sexuality may not be an instrument to demonstrate the husband's power over the wife, since just like the wife's body belongs to the husband, so the husband's body equally belongs to the wife (v. 4). Consequently, "was im entscheidenden Kern der Begabung ergreife, wie er selbst es tut."

---

457. Farla, "The Two," 78.

458. Garland, *1 Corinthians*, 246; also observed by Baltensweiler, *Ehe im NT*, 158.

459. Cf. Domanyi, "Anthropologie und Ethik," 237–38; Garland, *1 Corinthians*, 259: "By contrast, Paul apparently believes that sexual relations within marriage are justifiable as such. . . . He assumes that God ordained marriage to include sexual relations and that sexual relations in marriage were not solely intended for the procreation of the human species." See about the anthropological aspect of sexuality and its undissolvable relation to marriage also Domanyi, "Anthropologie und Ethik," 230–32.

Ehe, d. h. in der Pflege der Intimität als Prinzip etabliert ist, das kann nicht ohne Auswirkungen auf die Gesamtgestaltung der Partnerschaft bleiben."[460] The pattern given for the intimate core of marriage as delineated in vv. 2–5, thus, affects the entire partnership in its various facets.

There are two more passages following: precepts concerning separation and general apologia of marriage (vv. 10–24); and instructions for singles (vv. 25–40). The first two passages (vv. 1–24) make up the first part of 1 Cor 7, while the third passage (vv. 10–24) constitutes part two; this basic outline is supported by Paul's usage of the Greek περί at the beginning of the respective introductory sentences (vv. 1, 25).[461] The second passage of the first part (vv. 10–24) is again divided into three sections: (A) Married Christians (vv. 10–11); (B) mixed marriages (vv. 12–16); and (C) general considerations concerning different callings (vv. 17–24). The outline of the chapter's structure, therefore, looks as follows:[462]

General Topic: Refutation of καλὸν ἀνθρώπῳ γυναικὸς μὴ ἅπτεσθαι

Investigation: (I) (1) Defending sound Sexuality (vv. 2–9)

    (2) Precepts concerning Separation:

        (a) Both Christians (vv. 10–11)

        (b) Mixed Marriages (vv. 12–16)

        (c) General: Different Callings (vv. 17–24)

    (II) Instructions for Singles (vv. 25–40)

The issues I.2–II will now be dealt with in the subsequent sections.

II.3.1.2 Paul on Marital Separation/Celibacy

Most important are vv. 10–11, for they refer concretely to what "the Lord commands" (v. 10) as investigated above within the gospels. His "instructions in 1 Corinthians 7 regarding marriage presupposed the teaching of Jesus concerning the permanence of the matrimonial bond and Paul recognized no condition in which a Christian might initiate a divorce."[463] Paul repeats that Christians generally must not separate (v. 10). Yet, if it happens, the verbal modes Paul uses in vv. 10b and 11 are interesting (the verbs in italics are passive):

(A) General Principle (γυναῖκα ἀπὸ ἀνδρὸς μὴ χωρισθῆναι)

(B) Distortion (ἐὰν δὲ καὶ χωρισθῇ)

---

460. Domanyi, "Anthropologie und Ethik," 237.

461. Similarly Merklein, "Paulus und die Sexualität," 232.

462. See for a similar outline e.g., Garland, *1 Corinthians*, 245; more detailed and also slightly differing: Farla, "The Two," 76–77.

463. Batey, *Nuptial Imagery*, 34.

(C) Suboptimal Principle 1 (μενέτω ἄγαμος)
(C') Better Principle 2 (καταλλαγήτω)
(A') General Principle (καὶ ἄνδρα γυναῖκα μὴ ἀφιέναι)

The aorist passive forms "being separated" (χωρισθῆναι) and "she has been separated" (χωρισθῇ) again emphasize the wife as the passive subject being separated (perhaps better: "allowing herself to be separated") from her husband;[464] basically not necessarily departing herself actively, although the contrast between (A) and (A') points to the fact that in A the wife is the one who encouraged the separation.[465] The reconciliation is also described in the aorist passive form, even in its jussive sense (καταλλαγήτω): "let her be reconciled." Thus it is the husband who bears a responsible part of the reconciliation by generally offering the possibility to return. But it is the wife, however, who is called to favorably respond to this kind offer, as Paul points out by applying this imperative in regard to her (τῷ ἀνδρὶ καταλλαγήτω). Interestingly, a very similar usage of the same verb (καταλλάσσω), again in its passive imperative form, is to be witnessed in 2 Cor 5:20, bringing into line both invitations of reconciliation:

> God was in Christ reconciling the world to Himself, not counting their trespasses against them, and He has committed to us the word of reconciliation. Therefore, we are ambassadors for Christ, as though God were making an appeal through us; we beg you on behalf of Christ, be reconciled to God (καταλλάγητε τῷ θεῷ). (2 Cor 5:19–20.)

This καταλλάγητε τῷ θεῷ strongly echoes the τῷ ἀνδρὶ καταλλαγήτω of 1 Cor 7:11. Since the previous verse (2 Cor 5:19) clearly emphasizes God's resp. Christ's efforts to obtain reconciliation, finally again using the passive imperative form of καταλλάσσω in regard to the party that separated itself, it may be proper to assume that the husband in 1 Cor 6:11 thus again functions as representative of Christ, behaving towards his wife as Christ towards the church, just as Eph 5:21–33 pointed out very distinctively. Furthermore, 1 Cor 6:10–11 as well as 2 Cor 5:19–20 hint that most likely the departing party is the causer of the separation, although the husband seems to bear further responsibility even in this respect, as alluded to by the last finite verb form (ἀφιέναι; "let go/allow/send away") now using the active mode while referring

---

464. While some scholars interpret these forms as a deponent verb, actually connoting an active meaning (see e.g., Collins, *Divorce*, 15, 19), others (as, for instance, Fitzmyer, *First Corinthians*, 293; Murphy-O'Connor, "Divorced Woman," 602) understand it as a real passive, while it is sometimes used in Paul with the connotation "to allow oneself to be." Ibid. at both references; (cf. verses like 1 Cor 6:7 and Rom 12:2).

465. Beattie, *Women and Marriage*, 28–29 adds by reference to MacDonald, *Early Christian Women*, 189 and Plutarch's Coniugalia Praecepta (140D) that "the use of feminine pronouns here is not inappropriate... women were more likely than men to find themselves in this situation, for it was expected that a woman should adhere to her husband's religious tradition." And adhering to the husband's religious tradition could mean, especially in Corinth, to forsake Christ. The group of persons addressed in this instance, however, seems to be a Christian marriage, not a mixed marriage, as will further be argued.

to the husband. It seems Paul adds a slight reproach on the husband for letting her go—probably without greater efforts to keep her and to secure a high quality of their partnership. The husband should have taken up his responsibilities to win his wife back even before a separation could take place, again resembling the efforts and the serious struggles Christ took and takes upon himself to win and keep his church closely bound to himself (cf. again Eph 5:21–33).

Finally, the only active part of the separated woman to be adhered by her alone (i.e., without her husband's cooperation), is μενέτω ἄγαμος ("she should remain unmarried"). Concerning this task, the husband is without responsibility, for he cannot force his wife to keep the way open for reconciliation. Once she is married to someone else, he would not be able to take her back (due to Deut 24:1–4, and simply since that would mean striving for divorce, now from her new husband).

There is a most interesting philological hint that distances the Pauline exposition slightly from the main topic Jesus and the Pharisees were discussing. It even seems that Paul took it for granted that the Corinthians were already acquainted with the Lord's teaching on divorce (ἀπολύω).[466] Hence, while in the gospels the issue under debate was ἀπολύω ("releasing/divorcing"), Paul instead speaks about χωρίζω ("departing/dividing/separating"), which appeared only once in the gospels: in immediate context of the Edenic ideal referred to by Jesus in Mark 10:9 and Matt 19:6. The difference between the legal act of divorce indicated by the Greek verb ἀπολύω as a term of legal acquittal[467] in contrast to the more personal, individual χωρίζω seems noticeable and meaningful.[468]

---

466. This is widely held, cf. e.g., Isaksson, *Marriage and Ministry*, 105–6; Weiß, *Der erste Korintherbrief*, 178.

467. Cf. BDAG s.v. ἀπολύω. See on this also the investigations on the corresponding terms within the textual analysis of the gospel passages.

468. Interestingly, Josephus uses very similar terms in a similar context: "But some time afterward, when Salome happened to quarrel with Costobarus; she sent him a bill of divorce and dissolved her marriage with him (. . . γραμμάτιον ἀπολυομένη τὸν γάμον), though this was not according to the Jewish laws; for with us it is lawful for a husband to do so; but a wife, if she departs (διαχωρίζω) from her husband, cannot of herself be married to another, unless her former husband put her away (ἐφίημι)." (*A.J.* 15:259.) Josephus apparently uses the Greek διαχωρίζω in the same way as it is applied by Paul in 1 Cor 7:10: It is a severe separation from the own husband including the intention to dissolve the marital bond, yet without legal force—as further indicated by the use of the optative διαχωρισθείσῃ in reference to the wife. The seriousness of the wife's desire is further stressed by Josephus' usage of διά-χωρίζω ("pass through/abscond/part asunder/divide/depart/separate;" LSJ/BDAG s.v. διαχωρίζω; it further denotes a separation *for good*, as the usages in Gen 1:4, 6–7; 13:9; Luke 9:33; *A.J.* 1:28 indicate) instead of the more lenient χωρίζω ("I. in local sense, *separate, divide, exclude* [. . .]; II. *separate in thought, distinguish*; III. Pass. . . . *divorced*; IV. later in Pass. *depart, go away*" LSJ s.v. χωρίζω; italics given) in Paul's text. In addition, the ἐφίημι ("let go/give up/allow/permit/[. . .];" LSJ s.v. ἐφίημι) used by Josephus refers to the husband's consent regarding his wife's desire to divorce, not necessarily to his own active initiative. Thus it corresponds to the use in Paul's instruction (there: ἀφίημι, similarly meaning: "let go/give up/allow/tolerate/set free/put away/leave/dissolve/[. . .];" cf. BDAG/LSJ s.v. ἀφίημι), as passive consent, not active "divorce." This is further stressed by the position of the very brief, final remark concerning the husband's single part in the foregoing context of *the wife's* desire to separate (καὶ ἄνδρα γυναῖκα μὴ ἀφιέναι): The husband should not consent to the wife's

Paul apparently refers to the "Lord's command" (1 Cor 7:10) concerning χωρίζω (Mark 10:9; Matt 19:6), not necessarily regarding ἀπολύω. Taking into consideration the basic assumption behind καλὸν ἀνθρώπῳ γυναικὸς μὴ ἅπτεσθαι (v. 1) and Paul's preceding efforts to reject this perception at least concerning marriage (vv. 2–9), the meaning of vv. 10–11 using the exceptionally rare appearing of χωρίζω (only 13 times in the NT), which is used almost exclusively in context of a local distance[469] or a loss of emotional devotion,[470] must allow to draw an apparently close connection to vv. 3–5.[471] There, Paul already spoke about μὴ ἀποστερεῖτε ἀλλήλους ("do not rob/deprive each [from the] other"), for both have to fulfill their conjugal duties towards each other (v. 3), not having (exclusive) authority over their own bodies (v. 4) to separate from their spouses, thus neglecting conjugal sexuality. Thus his omission of Jesus' exception clause is not strange any more, and demanding to remain unmarried (i.e., not to seek official, legal divorce in order to remarry) until reconciliation might be possible is utterly reasonable.[472] It does not seem that Paul is addressing legally valid divorce, but rather temporary separation/leaving of a spouse, perhaps for the purpose

---

wish for separation (he should instead make efforts to win her back). The topic of both verses is the wife's intention, not the husband's, and legitimate divorce is not obtained, but a severe (local) separation occurs. While χωρίζω is indeed also used in extra-biblical literature to describe divorce (see e.g., Collins, *Divorce*, 21; Murphy-O'Connor, "Divorced Woman," 605; Fitzmyer, "Matthean Divorce Texts," 211; Meier, *Marginal Jew IV*, 101), it nevertheless seems reasonable to detect a slightly different level in the biblical texts given above (thus also Thatcher, *Marriage*, 266: ". . . a less final meaning [compared to ἀπολύω] is intended. Paul is not talking about divorce but about separation." Cf. further Luck, *Divorce and Remarriage*, 166; Elliott, "Paul's Teaching," 224–26).

469. Cf. Acts 1:4; 18:1–2; Rom 8:35, 39; Phl. 1:15; Heb 7:26. The LSJ lexicon makes the same point, indicating that χωρίζω denotes a local separation. Cf. also the discussion of this verb within the chapter about Jesus' saying. While he (Jesus) refers to the Edenic ideal of Gen 1:27 and 2:24, he uses χωρίζω as counterpart of what in Hebrew is expressed by דָּבַק ("cleave/cling/stick;" Gen 2:24), clearly pointing to "the idea of *physical* proximity." BDB s.v. דָּבַק; my italics.

470. See e.g., BDAG s.v. ἀφίημι; cf. LSJ: "let loose/let fall/give up . . . ." Consider also the usage in a corresponding context in 1 Esd 4:21: "A man (ἄνθρωπος) leaves (ἐγκαταλείπει) his own father that brought him up, and his own country, and cleaves (κολλᾶται) unto his wife. He stickes not to spend his life with his wife, and remembers neither (=forgets/gives up; ἀφίησι) father, nor mother, nor country" (KJV). The similarities to Gen 2:24 are obvious; cf. on that further Sampley, *One Flesh*, 58–59; Kirchhoff, *Sünde*, 162; Berger, *Gesetzesauslegung*, 530. The Greek κολλᾶται is the same verb as used in 1 Cor 6:16–17 to describe the "cleaving" as instrument to create a new union; and the ἀφίησι is the same verb Paul uses in the text investigated above. Again it indicates an inner position, an attitude, not a legal act (against Shaner, *Christian View*, 60–61). Just like the man in Gen 2:24 "left behind" his parents (cf. Matt 4:22; Mark 1:20) implying a change of the man's sympathy, so Paul is here now writing against "leaving behind/letting go/giving up" one's wife, thus "separating" the "one flesh" union God has "yoked together" (Matt 19:6; Mark 10:9). There is no legal act of ἀπολύω given (yet).

471. Similarly Schrage, *1. Korinther*, 2:100: "Von daher ist nicht auszuschließen, daß ganz normale Zerwürfnisse und profane Querelen vorliegen, zumal die Aufforderung zur Versöhnung sicher nicht Zufall ist."

472. Similarly Merklein, "Paulus und die Sexualität," 243. I am differing from Heinz, "Mischehen," 196 due to the understanding of the separation in this passage as being different from legal divorce. If understanding 1 Cor 7:10–11 as dealing with divorce, his conclusion concerning remaining "unmarried" is comprehensible. But I suppose that is not what Paul is actually dealing with in this instance.

of practicing the celibacy fostered within some groups in the Corinthian church as v. 1 indicates.[473] Thereby they are neglecting their conjugal duties (vv. 3–5) and are unfaithful regarding the "command of the Lord" (v. 10) which emphasizes the "one flesh" union as necessary requisite for the marital relationship that should, therefore, not be "separated" (using exactly the same verb as Paul: μὴ χωριζέτω; Mark 10:9; Matt 19:6).[474] Celibacy is no option for married Christians, "under no circumstances may people be allowed to bow to external pressure and exchange the married state for that of celibacy."[475] That fits the given context and particularly the previous train of thought concerning sexual abstinence in the best way, representing some final summary on the preceding instructions concerning each of the individual groups in the church.

It is further important to note that it is the wife who "has been separated" (χωρισθῆναι; vv. 10–11; see (A) and (B) above), but the husband who "lets go/allows" (ἀφιέναι; v. 11; (A') above). This usage of the verb regarding the husband again rather indicates a departure concerning locality and emotional devotion with the husband's *permission* or *neglect*; but not a complete "releasing" as a legal act of divorce, in which we would have to expect a more active, supportive involvement of the husband.[476]

Therefore, to sum up what we found regarding the application of unusual terminology ("unusual" at least if Paul indeed intended to speak about divorce!), we may assert that 1 Cor 7:10–11 actually deals with local "separation" due to some personal differences resulting in irreconcilability or simply because of mistaken efforts to reach the ideal of celibacy (cf. vv. 3–5). If Paul intended to deal with divorce, we would have

---

473. The same interpretation is presented e.g., by Farla, "The Two," 79; similarly Ryrie, "Biblical Teaching," 190; Schrage, *1. Korinther*, 2:100; and many others. On the mere temporary character of the separation (as contrary to divorce) see also Crispin, *Divorce*, 46. One has to keep in mind, however, that the command to "remain unmarried" (v. 11) would be odd if the only reason of the separation would be the aim of celibacy—the command would be superfluous!

474. Nevertheless, preventions against the legal act of divorce as a final consequence may also be implied, as the command to remain unmarried as well as some incidents of a synonymous (to the terminus technicus ἀπολύω) usage in classical texts may indicate (see Collins, *Divorce*, 21; Fitzmyer, "Matthean Divorce Texts," 211). Cf. e.g., Shaner, *Christian View*, 60–62; yet he hesitates on pp. 64–65 concerning the usage of χωρίζω in 1 Cor 7:15 suggesting that "certainly this provision allows separation *a mensa et thoro* [i.e., bed and board], and probably complete divorce" (italics given). Farla, "The Two," 80, explains in harmony with my interpretation concerning marital celibacy regarding the command to remain unmarried: "However, if celibacy should, after a period of time, turn out to be a disappointment, then the former relationship should be re-established; the ideal of celibacy should not be improperly used as an intermediary step towards another marriage."

475. Farla, "The Two," 79.

476. Thus, the remark of Beattie, *Women and Marriage*, 28, (stating that Paul is "making an exception to the rule [of the Lord in v. 10] in the very next verse! It would seem that his relationship to dominical commands was a creative one, to say the least.") is turned into its contrary, for the text is not at all referring to Jesus' instructions about divorce in general, but about the more personal "separating" (χωριζέτω; Mark 10:9; Matt 19:6) even within marriage. Yet, of course, this "separation" comes very close to "official" divorce, since marriage basically consisted of συνευδοκεῖ οἰκεῖν μετ' αὐτοῦ/ συνοικέω ("agreeing to live together;" 1 Cor 7:12–13/1 Pet 3:7) and therefore Paul even warns about remarriage while actually, from a Christian viewpoint, still being bound to a spouse—albeit being separated locally could indeed even be understood as being "divorced."

to expect at least once the terminus technicus ἀπολύω,⁴⁷⁷ but that is entirely absent.⁴⁷⁸ The complete omission thereof is—especially in the given context of vv. 1–7—more than just conspicuous.

However, given the case that Paul also wanted to deal with the legal act of divorce (which consequently would be the next step, following the tentative "separation"),⁴⁷⁹ we firstly have to assert that he omits the exception clause of Matt 5:32 and 19:9, apparently speaking merely about the Pharisees' reasons for divorce: κατὰ πᾶσαν αἰτίαν (Matt 19:3). But this divorce, of course, is invalid and both partners are still married before God, regardless of any formal certificate professedly affirming the releasing. Therefore, there are only two possibilities left in Paul's reasoning: (1) remain unmarried; or (2) reconcile. Any new sexual partnership would be tantamount to adultery, since there actually was no proper reason for the divorce. Hence, it should only be temporarily—and sexual abstinence until reconciliation is demanded. The way Paul thus would be dealing with "divorce" is reasonable and the omission of the exception clause is justified, too, for there actually is no "divorce" between Christians (except for a few reasons, which obviously are not given in the case Paul is dealing with above). Paul just speaks about temporary irreconcilability due to any reason.⁴⁸⁰

477. On ἀπολύω as terminus technicus for divorce consider the finding of a divorce document in Qumran as provided by Benoit et al., *Les Grottes*, 104–9, 243–54; cf. Isaksson, *Marriage and Ministry*, 95; Baltensweiler, *Ehe im NT*, 64; Shaner, *Christian View*, 39, 42–43; Blomberg, "Exegesis," 165. Josephus is likewise precise in his usage, omitting the term ἀπολύω completely in reference to the "separation" of Salome; cf. *A.J.* 15:260. For him the "withdrawal from her husband" (ἀποστῆναι τἀνδρός) is no legal divorce, because it is merely according to "the law of her (own) authority" (ἀπ' ἐξουσίας) and not to "the law of her country" (τὸν ἐγγενῆ νόμον). He also uses ἀπολύω as terminus technicus in context of the divorce certificate (see *A.J.* 15:259: γραμμάτιον ἀπολυομένη τὸν γάμον).

478. In v. 27, however, Paul uses λύω evidently meaning legal "divorce:" "Are you bound to a wife? Do not seek to be released [λύσιν]. Are you released [λέλυσαι] from a wife? Do not seek a wife." Obviously he is well aware of the correct term denoting the "official" dissolution of marriage ("divorce"). Yet, he does not employ it in his instruction about "separation" in the passage above. If not simply used synonymously, it indeed seems that Paul speaks about (slightly) differing cases. In this verse 27 it is likely to assume the case of the separation of a mixed marriage, which would easily result in divorce (considering vv. 15 and 21; similarly Beattie, *Women and Marriage*, 32; more on this will follow).

479. We further have to consider that "a legal act" of divorce in those times was unlike the judicial procedures in our modern times. In fact, a legal divorce could simply consist of a permanent separation, with both partners accepting the fact that reconciliation is unattainable. See on this e.g., Crispin, *Divorce*, 47. The difference, then, is primarily the tentative/temporal or permanent character of the separation.

480. The only exception he mentions follows in v. 15: mixed marriages with the unbelieving partner willing to "separate" may be "separated" (again χωρίζω). It is very interesting that even in this case of obvious "divorce" Paul does not use ἀπολύω—and he immediately supplies the reason for it: "the brother or the sister is not under bondage in such [cases]" (οὐ δεδούλωται ὁ ἀδελφὸς ἢ ἡ ἀδελφὴ ἐν τοῖς τοιούτοις; v. 15). As will be demonstrated below by considering the verbal forms of the verbs used in this passage (see "Mixed Marriages and Singleness"), the marital relationship between a believing and an unbelieving partner is not equal to the marriage of two Christians. It is not of the same quality and stability, not even of the same seriousness concerning divorce, as Paul makes clear in v. 15. Hence, (local) separation or the will to live abstinent on part of the unbelieving spouse is indeed reason enough to declare the believer as "not being bound," being free to (legally "divorce," if necessary, and to) remarry. See the mentioned passage below for more details.

The New Testament Echoes of the Edenic Ideal

Even the "divorce" Jesus is dealing with actually alludes to the fact that there is no licit "divorce" between Christians, but only a covenant breach and replacement of the first bond by "cleaving" and being "one flesh" with a new partner.[481] This replacement is not simply a common legal act; for if the unfaithful spouse does not repent and/or the betrayed spouse refuses to reconcile, the former marriage is actually replaced by the new partnership. In all cases, as explained above in context of Jesus' speeches, the actively dealing partner (in NT times primarily the husband) is responsible for the consequences. That also means he is responsible for the adultery committed if the wife he divorced due to κατὰ πᾶσαν αἰτίαν and strict, permanent irreconcilability on his part, is cleaving to a new partner having sexual relations with him.

A state of irreconcilability and separation should, if ever, only be temporary, as one might conclude from v. 5 with reference to the ἀκρασία ("lack of self-control") of those people who decide to marry. A doctrine of permanently remaining "unmarried" (v. 11), however, cannot firmly be derived from the two short words μενέτω ἄγαμος ("she should remain unmarried"). It may only be interpreted as prevention of quick separations without earnestly trying to reconcile, for Paul himself speaks of a conjugal right (v. 3) that would be "robbed" (v. 5), and he therewith most likely refers to Exod 21:10–11 which also speaks of letting the woman go out freely in case of not properly providing her with food, clothing, or "her sexual intercourse"[482] (τὴν ὁμιλίαν αὐτῆς/ עֹנָתָהּ: Paul obviously understood that difficult term in the same way as the Jewish tradition uniformly perceived it, namely, as meaning sexuality).

Although the first impression may support the prominent idea that Paul in 1 Cor 7:11 imposes a possibly lifelong celibacy on the passively divorced partner, by

---

481. In this instance, I am leaving out other possible legitimate reasons of divorce, as will be discussed in the corresponding chapter below (see "Further Legitimate Reasons for Divorce"). I am only dealing with Jesus' statement in the gospels, since Paul is referring to this "instruction of the Lord" (1 Cor 7:10).

482. Cf. HALOT s.v. עָנָה. The same connection between Exod 21:10 and the main line of 1 Cor 7 is recognized by Beale and Carson, *NT Use*, 714; Instone-Brewer, *In the Bible*, 193; cf. Instone-Brewer, "What God has Joined," 29; Garland, *1 Corinthians*, 258; Friedrich, *Sexualität und Ehe*, 79; Luck, *Divorce and Remarriage*, 34 (indirectly); and others. "The LXX [on Exod 21:10] translates that the husband is not 'to deprive' her of association (τὴν ὁμιλίαν αὐτῆς οὐκ ἀποστερήσει, . . .). The word ὁμιλία is also used for sexual intercourse (LSJ 1222), and Paul uses the same verb 'to deprive' (ἀποστερεῖν) in 7:5 to refer to withholding sexual contact." Garland, *1 Corinthians*, 258/fn.21. Although, as discussed above (see "Polygamy as Cultural Digression"), it is difficult to interpret the Hebrew עֹנָה in Exod 21:10, the ancient rabbis clearly understood it as referring to conjugal sexuality; cf. *m. Ketub.* 5:8–9; *b. Ketub.* 47b–48a; *t. Qidd.* 3:7; *Mekilta de Rabbi Ishmael: Nezikin* 3 on Exod 21:10; Instone-Brewer, *In the Bible*, 100; Rubenstein, "Jewish Tradition," 11. The justified comments of some researchers pointing out that the Hebrew ענתה originally meant "oil/ointment" (in harmony with ancient Babylonian marriage stipulations; cf. Instone-Brewer, *In the Bible*, 9, 38) or simply "habitation/quarters/dwelling" (see Du Preez, *Polygamy*, 68; cf. also Propp, *Exodus 19–40*, 201; Cassuto, *Exodus*, 269) are not really relevant for the understanding of the NT application of this text, since Paul used the Greek LXX version and the Jewish tradition (at least the ancient rabbinical) interpreted the term as sexuality (see the foregoing; cf. also *m. Ketub.* 5:6; *'Ed.* 4:10). In fact, it seems that Paul understood Exod 21:10 differently compared to modern exegetes, rather holding on to his ancient Jewish tradition. Consequently, he stresses the importance of conjugal sexuality.

taking into consideration his previous remarks on the importance of conjugal sexuality (vv. 1–9), admitting that it is a special gift of God to remain unmarried (vv. 7–8), further considering the different textual hints and the arguments presented within the exegesis on the gospel texts, it seems too far-fetched to argue in favor of a forced lifelong sexual abstinence on part of the unjustified released spouse;[483] albeit Paul actually knows good reasons for staying unmarried and clearly states that celibacy indeed has merit—but always on a voluntary basis (vv. 28, 38). Moreover it seems as if the interpretation of the middle and passive forms concerning the woman "being adultered" in the gospel texts are pointing to the former husband's responsibility when the wife he released due to unlawful reasons (κατὰ πᾶσαν αἰτίαν), and not for unlawful sexuality (πορνεία), remarries; she is not condemned or reproved. "What the victimized spouses of Matthew 19 and 1 Corinthians 7 have in common is that 'they find themselves in the situation not through choice,' the responsibility now falling entirely on the other partner (though obviously earlier actions by both parties may well have led to the current situation)."[484]

The irreconcilable husband is responsible for the sin of adultery if the divorced spouse remarries: "*he makes* her to be adultered" (ποιεῖ αὐτὴν μοιχευθῆναι; Matt 5:32). The woman is passive in this act of adultery which is on the one hand committed actively by her new spouse, according to Luke 16:18b ("the one marrying a [woman] released from her husband, commits adultery") and Matt 5:32b ("whoever would marry a released [woman], commits adultery [for himself]"). Yet, on the other hand, it actually is her former husband who is responsible for that adultery (*he makes her to be adultered [by the new partner]*) and it seems difficult to call it the sin of the new partner—as Luke and Matt 5:32b could be (mis-)understood when not considering the paralleling, more detailed elucidation of Matt 5:32a. But, according to Luke 16:18, he had (and has) nothing to do with the sins of the former spouses and therefore is in no way responsible for it.

As mentioned in the investigation of the gospel texts, the previous husband is the only one to be blamed, the only one responsible for the adultery, irrespective of the fact who of both former spouses will finally be the first to enter a new (sexual/marital) relation. That is, self evidently, also applicable to a wife releasing her husband due to unlawful reasons. The instance in 1 Cor 7:10–11 seems to lead in this direction, declaring the wife to be the one who separates (but the husband, however,

---

483. Hence, exegetes clinging to the interpretation of the text as speaking about a general prohibition of remarriage cannot avoid admitting: "Die Wiederheirat Geschiedener kommt für Paulus in diesen Fällen [1 Cor 7:10–11] offenbar nicht in Frage. Dies ist umso erstaunlicher, als der Apostel zu Beginn schreibt, daß im Hinblick auf die in Korinth vorgefallenen Unzuchtsfälle jeder Mann seine Frau und jede Frau ihren Mann haben soll (7,2)." Kremer, "Jesu Wort," 58–59. Similarly wrong in his conclusions is Shaner, *Christian View*, 63 claiming that "it is implicit in Paul's teaching that remarriage to a new partner [always/in any case] constitutes adultery . . ."

484. Blomberg, "Exegesis," 193; agreeing with the conclusions of Lövestam, "Divorce and Remarriage," 65.

to be the one who takes up no efforts to prevent that). The texts know just two elements: The one actively releasing and the other passively being released. Consequently, if both mutually encourage divorce, both are responsible and remarriage is sinful to both. Only the passively, innocently divorced partner is excepted and goes out free; if his or her efforts to reconcile were permanently without success, he or she is free to "go out for nothing" (ἐξελεύσεται δωρεάν/יָצְאָה חִנָּם; Exod 21:11), without any further duties, and without any further claims of the former spouse. The sin of the possibly following "adultery" of remarriage apparently is within the responsibility of the willfully divorcing partner. And, finally, due to the "lack of [sexual] self control" (1 Cor 7:5) even a temporary "separation" (χωρίζω) of the spouses, thus denying their intimacy, is distinctively disapproved of; whether this kind of separation is due to an exaggerated and erroneous religious ambition (vv. 3–5) or the result of irreconcilability (vv. 10–11), the only solution is to remain unmarried until the separation is finally abandoned through reconciliation—or through lawful divorce due to the few licit reasons given in the Bible.[485]

At this place another possible explanation of the μενέτω ἄγαμος of v. 11 must be mentioned. Külling understands this phrase as a "right" to remain unmarried (as contrary to public and particularly Jewish opinion), not as a "duty:"

> [Es] ist nun aber die Frage berechtigt, ob denn aufgrund von 1Kor 7,11 ein Verbot zur Wiederverheiratung abzuleiten sei. Die eigentliche Absicht dieser Aussage ist ja, der von ihrem Mann getrennten Frau das Recht zu gewähren, entgegen der allgemeinen Meinung und Sitte ehelos zu bleiben. Denn die Ehelosigkeit ist wie das Verheiratetsein eine von Gott verliehene Begabung. Die Trennung hat aber an den Tag gebracht, dass sich die betreffende Frau in ihrer Ehe nicht bewähren konnte und gezwungen war, ihren Mann zu verlassen, um fortan in ihrem nunmehrigen Stand verbleiben zu dürfen. Das ist der einzige Gesichtspunkt, den Paulus hervorhebt. Die geschiedene Frau kann mit gutem Gewissen ehelos bleiben und muss nicht ein Joch auf sich nehmen, für das sie nicht begabt ist. Jedoch die Konsequenz, dass jede geschiedene Frau nicht mehr heiraten soll, wird hier von Paulus nicht ins Auge gefasst. Seine Aussage ist somit nicht ein allgemeines Verbot der Ehe für Geschiedene. Wenn sie ihnen die Erlaubnis gewährt, entgegen der Meinung und Forderung ihrer jüdischen und heidnischen Umgebung ehelos zu bleiben, heisst dies nicht zugleich, dass ihnen der Eintritt in eine neue Ehe durchweg untersagt ist. Es ist nämlich damit zu rechnen, dass sie in der Ehelosigkeit nicht ihre wahrhaftige Begabung erkennen, sondern in einer neuen Verbindung mit einem anderen Partner in der Hoffnung, dass sie sich nun in ihrer Berufung bewähren werden.[486]

The possibility and legitimacy of interpreting the imperative form of v. 11 (μενέτω: "she should stay") as a priviledge rather than a duty is demonstrated just a

---

485. More on these few reasons see below: "Further Legitimate Reasons for Divorce."
486. Külling, *Ehe und Ehelosigkeit*, 85–86; see pp. 83–87 for his full argumentation.

few verses below, where Paul in v. 15 argues concerning the opposite direction: "If the unbelieving one leaves, let him leave" (εἰ δὲ ὁ ἄπιστος χωρίζεται, χωριζέσθω).—Of course, this is a concession, not a demand! To stay lifelong unmarried because of the illegal, unjustified divorce of one's spouse is demanded neither by Jesus nor by Paul.

II.3.1.3 Mixed Marriages and Singleness

Following the Pauline interpretation of Christ's instructions about separation between Christian partners (1 Cor 7:10–11), in vv. 12–24 Paul at first deals with "the rest" being somehow different from those partnerships spoken about before (apparently with both spouses being Christians),[487] until he finally turns to the unmarried members in vv. 25–40. In context of the foregoing statements, v. 15 is particularly significant. According to my previous investigations, even if Paul actually intended to say something about the legal act of divorce, the unguilty, passively released partner is not bound to lifelong celibacy. Yet, v. 15 is frequently understood as granting this "freedom" (from the previous marriage and therefore the right to remarry) to only those Christians who are married to unbelievers, and if the unbelieving spouse endeavors to divorce. However, there are at least two significant philological hints pointing to a slightly, but nevertheless decisively, different interpretation. At first, the topic is again (local/emotional) "separation" (εἰ δὲ ὁ ἄπιστος χωρίζεται, χωριζέσθω; v. 15), not necessarily the legal act of divorce (that would rather be ἀπολύω). This is even more affirmed by the interesting Pauline explanation about what virtually means to "have a wife/husband" (vv. 12–13), namely: συνευδοκεῖ οἰκεῖν μετ' αὐτοῦ/αὐτῆς ("she/he agrees to live with him/her;" vv. 12–13; cf. 1 Pet 3:7: συνοικέω!). Consequently, when this "agreement of cohabitation" is abandoned through χωρίζω ("separating locally"[488]/withdraw emotionally by neglecting sexuality), the partnership itself is impugned, and Paul consequently declares the Christian "not [to be] under bondage in such [cases]" (v. 15).[489] Χωρίζω has the potential to destroy the marital bond and divorce may be reasonable, although at least Christian spouses are strongly expected to reconcile (v. 11).[490]

---

487. Most likely, "'the rest' refers to marriages where one partner had been converted to Christianity and the other was then an 'unbeliever.'" Shaner, *Christian View*, 63.

488. Cf. LSJ s.v. χωρίζω.

489. Thus answering Shaner's open question on what the Christian should do "if an unbeliever deserts but does not divorce the Christian." Shaner, *Christian View*, 66. Instone-Brewer, "What God has Joined," 29 adds: "Anyone in first-century Palestine reading this phrase would think immediately of the wording at the end of all Jewish, and most Roman, divorce certificates: 'You are free to marry anyone you wish!'" There certainly was no doubt that a new partnership (or official "remarriage") was permitted.

490. Isaksson, *Marriage and Ministry*, 105 explains that "they should not try at any cost to maintain such a marriage in the hope of converting the unbeliever presuppose that there were men and women in the Corinth church who were married to non-Christians and who felt the prohibition of divorce to be so binding that they would not consent to a divorce when the non-Christian spouse wanted one." However, even with Christian spouses it is hardly possible to maintain the marriage

So what do sexual infidelity and desertion have in common? Once one recalls that the marriage covenant contained two main components—personal allegiance or loyalty and interpersonal intimacy culminating in sexual relations—the answer emerges with surprising ease. Both infidelity and desertion break one half of the marriage covenant. Unfaithfulness destroys sexual exclusivity; desertion reneges on the commitment to 'leave and cleave.'[491]

Second, the crucial text says: οὐ δεδούλωται ὁ ἀδελφὸς ἢ ἡ ἀδελφὴ ἐν τοῖς τοιούτοις, which is mostly translated as present tense. But actually it is in the perfect and correctly means: "the brother or the sister *has not been bound* in such [cases as] these." It apparently is meaningful that Paul does not use the present or future time, but the perfect of δουλόω (ind. pass. 3rd pers. sg.).[492] Corresponding to the English present perfect, he is thereby pointing to a present state that is a result from an action that took place in the past.[493] In other words, he is not just referring to the time at which the separation happens declaring the Christian to be "not bound in such cases;" he rather points to the time before, when the mixed marriage was consummated and the entire period it existed. The time in the past, as well as the time in the present, the believer is not "bound" as he would be with another Christian (vv. 10–11).[494] That is further affirmed by the fact that in vv. 10–11 he evidently speaks about "the married" (τοῖς γεγαμηκόσιν; again using the perfect!), while from v. 12 onwards he speaks

---

when one partner permanently and persistently seeks divorce. It rather seems that Paul's teaching bases on his other maxim concerning bonds/close relationships with unbelievers: "Were you called while a slave (δοῦλος)? Do not worry about it; *but if you are able also to become free, rather do that*" (1 Cor 7:21)—when all hope for the conversion of the unbelieving party is gone (1 Cor 7:16). Please note the similar wording in 1 Cor 7:15 (οὐ δεδούλωται) considering that the Greek lemmata δοῦλος and δουλόω only occur in 1 Cor 7:15, 21–23 (and 9:19; 12:13)! Cf. also 2 Cor 6:14–16.

491. Blomberg, "Exegesis," 192.

492. The Greek δουλόω is actually a very strong verb, rather meaning "to enslave" than only "to be bound." BDAG s.v. δουλόω; cf. Heinz, "Mischehen," 194, 198/fn.39. Furthermore, it is differing from what Paul uses in vv. 27, 39, where he employs δέω ("to bind/tie;" BDAG s.v. δέω), which is not as intensive and negative in its meaning. Besides, δουλόω is very rare in the NT (only in Acts 7:6; Rom 6:18, 22; 1 Cor 7:15; 9:19; Gal 4:3; Titus 2:3; 2 Pet 2:19), and is always used in context of salvation or its opposite, namely, eternal ruin (slave of sin or of righteousness; Paul enslaved himself to win the Corinthian church; slaves of the world; enslaved to much wine (endangering salvation: 1 Cor 5:11; 6:10); slaves of corruption)! Thus, supporting one's spouse to win salvation as an important aim of the marriage relation is again emphasized (as e.g., in Eph, see above: "Paul's Spiritual Application;" cf. vv. 14, 16) and marriages with unbelievers are declared to be useless regarding this important goal.

493. Cf. e.g., Schwyzer, *Griechische Grammatik*, 768; Mehrlein et al., *Ars Graeca*, 209–10; Bornemann and Risch, *Griechische Grammatik*, 222: „Gewöhnlich handelt es sich um einen *erreichten Zustand*: das Perfektsystem ist resultativ, weil in den betreffenden Zuständen eine verbale Handlung nachwirkt." (Italics given.)

494. Similarly Baltensweiler, *Ehe im NT*, 193, 195; Murphy-O'Connor, *1 Corinthians*, 66; Fee, *Corinthians*, 303; Shaner, *Christian View*, 65–66. Shane rightly concludes concerning the "bond" of mixed marriages by giving two summarizing statements: "1. If the unbeliever desires to separate, let him depart, for the Christian is not bound necessarily to seek his conversion. 2. If the unbeliever gets a divorce, let it be so, for the Christian is not bound to this old relationship but may remarry if the new partner is also a believer." Ibid., 66.

about "the rest" (τοῖς λοιποῖς)—obviously not entirely equating these relationships with Christian matrimony. It even seems as if the only "bond" uniting both is the fact that they live together (συνευδοκέω; vv. 12–13; cf. 1 Pet 3:7)![495]

However, this does not mean that those mixed marriages are not binding, as Paul clearly states in vv. 12–13! But the quality and the spiritual depth certainly are not the same. Paul is not granting the Christian to encourage separation or divorce himself, for "God has called us to peace" (v. 15), thus contrasting the events around Ezra (cf. Ezra 9–10) and certain Jewish prescription demanding divorce from heathens or the right for Jewish wives to divorce their husband if he became apostate.[496] But a "real" (Edenic) marriage bond is, consequently, only given when both partners are believers, thus sharing the same spiritual oneness (1 Cor 6:17), both being "members of Christ" (1 Cor 6:15), belonging to the same heavenly family (Gen 2:23), and being brought together by God (Gen 2:22; Mark 10:9; Matt 19:6). Therefore, "Paul did not suggest that marriage be a method for missionary endeavor (I Cor. 7:39; II Cor. 6:14);" although they "can have a missionary character,"[497] for "if only one party were a Christian, their mutual identification could lead to the consecration of the unbelieving spouse."[498] While even cleaving to a prostitute results in an (inferior) "one flesh"

---

495. That might be meaningful considering today's problems when encountering couples living together without officially being married. According to Paul's instructions above, συνευδοκέω οἰκεῖν apparently constitutes a legal partnership (cf. 1 Pet 3:7). Thereby he even exceeds Philo's understanding of concubinage as virtual marriage: "Some people think that a licensed concubinage is an offense, something between seduction and adultery, when the two parties come together, and agree to live as man and wife by a certain agreement, but before the marriage ceremony is completed, some other man meeting with the woman, or forcing her has connection with her; but in my opinion this also is a kind of adultery; for such an agreement as is here mentioned is equivalent to a marriage, for in it the names of the woman and of the man are both registered, and all other things which were to lead to their union." *Spec.* 3:72. Philo evidently does not regard wedding ceremonies as necessary prerequisite to constitute legal marriage, for he despises those glamorous rites and feasts anyway; cf. *Opif.* 103. Just the mutual "confession/agreement" (ὁμολογία) seems to be important in order to be lawfully "married." Philo uses the expression ὅταν ὁμολογίαι μὲν ὑπερεγγυήσωσι μήπω δὲ τῶν γάμων ἐπιτελεσθέντων to express this "licensed concubinage." *Spec.* 3:72. The phrase literally means: "When, on the one hand, confessions have been made, but the ceremonies are not yet completed." The important term which has been translated as "licensed concubinage" is ὁμολογία and rather means "confession/acknowledgement" (BDAG), "statement of allegiance" (FRI) and "agreement/compact" (LSJ). Hence, for him the mutual agreement creates what is called "marriage." Consequently, even seducing one of the (concubinage-) spouses is tantamount to committing adultery, and should be punished accordingly; cf. *Spec.* 3:73. Perhaps this was a widespread idea in ancient Judaism, since concrete procedures were not given in the scriptures.

496. Cf. on this e.g., Amram, *Divorce*, 75, 89–92. Similarly Kirchschläger, *Ehe im NT*, 77: "[Es] wird dem heidnischen Partner das Vorrecht der Entscheidung eingeräumt: Will er die Ehe weiterführen, so bleibt sie bestehen; die eventuelle Bereitschaft des christlichen Partners wird nicht angefragt, er hat sich hingegen nach dem Willen des Heiden zu richten." Cf. Heinz, "Mischehen," 194.

497. Farla, "The Two," 80; similarly Beattie, *Women and Marriage*, 30.

498. Batey, *Nuptial Imagery*, 34; cf. Batey, "The ΜΙΑ ΣΑΡΞ Union," 278. On the meaning of consecrating the unbeliever see also Heinz, "Mischehen," 196–97; Beattie, *Women and Marriage*, 29–30.

union (1 Cor 6:16), the real, original Edenic marriage ideal seems to be fulfilled only with two partners both "cleaving to the Lord" (1 Cor 6:17).

Paul clearly declares that

> wünscht der heidnische Gatte oder die heidnische Gattin die Scheidung, dann soll der christliche Partner die Ehe nicht um jeden Preis fortsetzen wollen. Er oder sie ist dann nicht mehr an die Ehe oder an das Wort des Herrn ‚gebunden'. Die Fortsetzung der Ehe erzwingen zu wollen, wäre ja Anlass zu beständigem Zwist, wo doch Gott will, dass Eheleute im Frieden miteinander leben sollen (V. 15b). Nicht einmal die gute Absicht, den anderen für Christus gewinnen zu wollen, rechtfertigt die Ehefortsetzung, denn niemand kann wissen, ob er je dieses Ziel auch erreichen wird (V. 16). Einen stellvertretenden Glauben gibt es im Neuen Testament nicht.[499]

The Corinthians might inquire, then, whether mixed marriages are lawful at all. Just upon this fictitious question Paul seems to dwell in the following verses (17–24), again arguing on basis of a general Christian principle saying: "In whatever situation someone was called, brothers and sisters, let him remain in it with God" (v. 24). Of course, he is still talking about the situation of τοῖς λοιποῖς (v. 12), before he subsequently deals with the last group of the underlying topic concerning lawful sexuality as positive contrast to πορνεία: the group of the unmarried. The fact that Paul obviously has to substantiate so extensively the instruction to remain in the individual calling and not to encourage divorce in mixed marriages (vv. 16–24), stresses the result of my previous hypothesis: He apparently declared mixed marriages to be no real marriages in its highest sense (i.e., Gen 2:24). Nevertheless, since "God has called us to peace" (v. 15) and "has assigned to each one, as God has called each" (v. 17), Paul sees it justified to accordingly "direct in all the church" (v. 17) to restrain from divorcing. But if the unbeliever desires to leave, and thus the Christian is able "to become free, [he should] rather do that" (v. 21).[500] Finally, once being free to remarry (due to the lawful divorce of v. 15 or the death of one's spouse in v. 39),[501] Paul reemphasizes the principle of marrying only a Christian: μόνον ἐν κυρίῳ (v. 40).[502]

The last part of chap. 7 concerns unmarried Christians (vv. 25–40). The main basis Paul is building his instructions on is the impending crisis which affects the

---

499. Heinz, "Mischehen," 198.

500. Similarly Beattie, *Women and Marriage*, 31, who adds the interesting observation: "The etymological connection between δοῦλος (7.21) and the perfect passive of δουλόω in 7.15 would suggest that it is the married person (the one who is 'bound') whom the slave represents. Any who find themselves in this situation are encouraged not to worry about it; but if they find themselves 'freed' (by divorce or widowhood), then they ought to make the best of this new situation."

501. On the freedom to remarry see Heinz, "Mischehen," 199 referring to Morris, *1 Corinthians*, 107 and F. F. Bruce in Thiselton, *1 Corinthians*, 535.

502. Cf. Shaner, *Christian View*, 66; Rodríguez, "Konfessionsverschiedene Ehen," 201; Hasel, "Eheverständnis," 32–33, 38; Domanyi, "Anthropologie und Ethik," 243; Rodríguez, "Konfessionsverschiedene Ehen," 219.

Christian in all fields of life. Again he has "no command of the Lord, but I give an opinion as one who by the mercy of the Lord is trustworthy" (v. 25). He reiterates the καλὸν ἀνθρώπῳ ("it is good for a man;" v. 26) of the (at least partly) erroneous Corinthian slogan (v. 1) and uses it for his own instructions. His introduction to this new block of "precautions" is meaningful. In v. 26 he again uses the (participle) perfect ἐνεστῶσαν ("has been present/coming"), not the aorist (pointing to a punctual time in the past), and not the future tense. He is not just dealing with some eschatological crisis, but with the "distress" (ἀνάγκη) that even existed in Paul's time (cf. 2 Thess 2:7).[503] Hence, the apostle's admonition was directed to his (New Testament) times, and it likewise applies all through the ages until the last days of this earth's history. It is no concrete future date he is envisioning, it were the hard conditions of his own time he was reasoning by, drawing general conclusions also for the future. Nevertheless, it seems he anticipated even more dangerous times to come. The Christian evidently always has to consider the threats and advantages of his moves and decisions. But it is clear from the Edenic ideal which Paul is emphasizing as a "preamble" of his treatise (1 Cor 6:16) that the creational conditions, including the divinely pronounced and thus immovable fact that "it is not good for the man to be alone" (Gen 2:18), are still applicable—and will be until the end of time. Paul's "trustworthy" instructions therefore are "not to put a restraint upon you, but to promote what is appropriate and [to secure] undistracted devotion to the Lord" (v. 35). And that may be better secured by not seeking a wife (v. 27); "so then both he who gives his own virgin in marriage does well, and he who does not give her in marriage will do better" (v. 38).[504] Finally, one still has to consider that Paul

> makes it clear that these are 'opinions' and do not have the force of 'commands.' He leans over backwards to indicate that other options are just as acceptable to the Lord. And when we look at the counsel he actually gives, it becomes clear that his primary concern is with priorities and the realism with which

---

503. See also John 4:23; 5:25; 16:32: "an hour is coming, and has already come"—"the time of the end" (Dan 8:17, 19; 11:35, 40) began already and the danger is constantly increasing towards the ultimate ending. On the usage of ἐνίστημι as referring to *present* conditions cf. Rom 8:38; 1 Cor 3:23; Gal 1:4; Heb 9:9; Baltensweiler, *Ehe im NT*, 169. Yet, it could also refer to (exclusively) future events (2 Thess 2:2; 2 Tim 3:1), which, nevertheless, may commence right away. However, it is certainly too far-fetched to assume that "Paul confidently believed that the End [sic.] was near.... Hence, the reproductive act ceased to have any relevance for him." Rubenstein, "Jewish Tradition," 6. Paul is nowhere even slightly addressing the subject of procreation, he is only dealing with undistracted devotion to the Lord in perilous times. Nevertheless, "a large part of the reason for Paul's preference for the unmarried state is his conviction that the time is short." Dunn, *Theology*, 693.

504. Baltensweiler, *Ehe im NT*, 172 summarizes: "Angesichts der Endzeit, angesichts dessen, dass diese Welt jetzt schon im Vergehen ist . . . kann die Ehe nicht das Vordringliche und Gebotene sein. Auf der andern Seite ist die Ehe aber keineswegs zu verdammen oder abzulehnen, schon gar nicht etwa aus einer Abwertung der Leiblichkeit heraus. Paulus sagt ja, dass der Leib ein Tempel Gottes sei (1. Kor 6, 19). Somit kann er den Leib und auch die Leiblichkeit der Ehe nicht verachten. Die Zurückhaltung gegenüber der Ehe resultiert bei Paulus allein aus der nahen Erwartung des Endes." Similarly Beattie, *Women and Marriage*, 32.

they should be pursued, not to promote a particular attitude to marriage or marriage relations, or to promote a policy of asceticism.[505]

II.3.1.4 Summary and Final Considerations

To sum up, the basic, underlying structure of the given passages, including the findings of the exegetical investigation on 1 Cor 6:12–20 above, looks as follows:

(A) General Problem Statement (1 Cor 6:12–20)
  (B) *Hypothesis* (v. 12): Universal Claim of a Corinthian Slogan (πάντα μοι ἔξεστιν)
    (C) *Investigation* (vv. 13–20): Concrete Application to Two Aspects:
      (1) βρώματα corresponding to σῶμα
      (2) πορνεία corresponding to πνεῦμα
(A') Closer Investigation of Aspect Two (1 Cor 7): πορνεία (1 Cor 6:13b)
  (B') *Hypothesis* (v. 1): Universal Claim of a Corinthian Slogan
    (καλὸν ἀνθρώπῳ[506] γυναικὸς μὴ ἅπτεσθαι)
    (C') *Investigation*: Concrete Application to Three Conditions:
      (1) Conjugal Sexuality (vv. 2–9)
      (2) Separation (vv. 10–24)
        (a) Both Christians (vv. 10–11)
        (b) Mixed Marriages (vv. 12–24)
      (3) Singles (vv. 25–40)
(A") Closer Investigation of Aspect One (1 Cor 8): βρώματα (1 Cor 6:13a)
  (B") *Hypothesis* (v. 1): Universal Claim of a Corinthian Slogan (πάντες γνῶσιν ἔχομεν)
    (C") *Investigation* (vv. 2–13): Concrete Application to Three Kinds of Eaters:
      (1) Free Men (vv. 4–6)
      (2) Former Idolaters (vv. 7–8)
      (3) Free Men responsible for Former Idolaters (vv. 9–13)

As this basic structure demonstrates, chaps. 7–8 reemphasize their theological foundation as given in the first part (1 Cor 6:12–20) and its central core basing on the Edenic ideal (vv. 16–17), which is the basis of the following elucidations concerning the two central levels of 1 Cor 6:13 and vv. 16–17 (σῶμα/πνεῦμα).

---

505. Dunn, *Theology*, 695.

506. Please note that ἄνθρωπος is used, not ἀνήρ as contrasted in v. 3! The claim is indeed universal, speaking about any human, not necessarily only a male. That also fits the second part of v. 1 which is a euphemism of sexual intercourse and does not necessarily point to a man touching "a woman" as referring to the female sex. Thus, the Corinthian slogan deals with any intimate heterosexual intercourse (similarly, Collins, *First Corinthians*, 258; Garland, *1 Corinthians*, 254; Fee, "1 Corinthians 7:1," 307–14; Baltensweiler, *Ehe im NT*, 156).

Consequently, in the following sections it is stressed what the author of Hebrews puts thus: "The marriage relation is honorable in all parts, and the [conjugal] bed is pure" (Heb 13:4). Yet, a "perfect" fulfillment of the Edenic marriage ideal is only given between two Christian spouses and those who consider marriage are instructed to marry μόνον ἐν κυρίῳ ("only in the Lord;" 1 Cor 7:39). Those who are already married to unbelievers when being called (by God to be Christians) may regard themselves as free to leave when the unbeliever desires to separate. If he does not, they are, of course, not allowed to seek separation, but to be faithful spouses trying to win their partner for Christ, thus assisting in their salvation.

The basic "doctrine" underlying Paul's practical application of the Edenic ideal is the maxim "to promote what is appropriate and [to secure] undistracted devotion to the Lord" (1 Cor 7:35)—and that may even result in celibacy (vv. 32–34). However, he makes clear that this "undistracted devotion" may not be gained by rejecting conjugal intercourse, for it is a sound and important "duty" (ὀφειλή) of both wife and husband; to neglect that part of marriage is equal to "robbery" (ἀποστερέω; vv. 3, 5).

II.3.2 Nuptial Imagery

In Matt 9:15; Mark 2:19–20; and Luke 5:34–35 Jesus calls himself the bridegroom (νυμφίος) and describes his disciples as wedding guests (lit. "the sons of the wedding chamber:" οἱ υἱοὶ τοῦ νυμφῶνος). The parable of the wedding banquet (Matt 22:1–14) and the one about the ten bridesmaids (Matt 25:1–13) similarly depicts Jesus' followers as mere guests passively attending the wedding of Jesus. Only John the Baptist is differently called φίλος τοῦ νυμφίου ("friend of the bridegroom"); Jesus' "bride" (νύμφη), however, is not described in the gospels but only once rather anonymously referred to without giving any details (John 3:29). Until John's eschatological vision of "the holy city, new Jerusalem" (Rev 21:2) in the book of Revelation the Greek term νύμφη disappears. There it is this holy, new Jerusalem which is "coming down out of heaven from God, made ready as a bride adorned for her husband" (ibid.) being "the bride, the wife of the lamb" (Rev 21:9). "His bride has made herself ready. It was given to her to clothe herself in fine linen, bright and clean; for the fine linen is the righteous acts of the saints" (Rev 19:7b-8). Again, resembling the statements and parables of the gospels regarding the saint's passive attendance, "blessed are those who are invited to the marriage supper of the Lamb" (v. 9). In 2 Cor 11:2–3, however, the church is described as the παρθένος "betrothed to one husband, Christ;" and in Eph 5:31–32 it is the central verse Gen 2:24 which is applied to Christ and his church. This is, in short, all the New Testament says about the bride-bridegroom metaphor.[507]

---

507. For further investigations of these texts containing the wedding metaphor of Jesus as bridegroom see Syreeni, "Bridegroom's Time," 343–69, whose emphasis is on the gospels and who oversees the parallels of Rev 21:1–4 with Gen 2:22–25 as given above. See also Schlier, *Epheser*, 265, who

In order to obtain further, deeper insights, it will be interesting to compare the nuptial imagery given in Rev 21:1–4 with the Edenic pattern of Gen 2:22–25. While Genesis represents the initial marriage covenant ideal, the passage in Revelation seemingly depicts the regained ideal, still following the same pattern as given at the world's foundation.[508]

The Initial Ideal (Gen 2:22–25)	The Regained Ideal (Rev 21:1–4)
(1:1) *In the beginning* God created the *heavens* and the *earth*. Extensive Description of the first, lost Paradise (1:1—2:25)	(v. 1) [*At the end*] I saw a *new heaven* and a *new earth*; for the first heaven and the first earth passed away. Extensive Description of the new, regained Paradise (21:1—22:4)
(2:22) And YHWH <u>God built</u> into a woman . . . and brought her/taken *out of* man (v. 23) to the man.	(v. 2) And I saw the holy city, new Jerusalem, coming down *out of* heaven <u>from God</u>, made ready as a bride adorned *for her husband*.
(2:23) [*Direct Speech:*] And *the man said*: [*Signs of Kinship:*] "This finally is bone of my bones, and flesh of my flesh . . . ."	(v. 3a) [*Direct Speech:*] And I heard *a loud voice from the throne, saying*: [*Signs of Kinship:*] "Behold, the tent of God *is* among men,
(2:24) [*Explanatory comment:*] "For this reason a man . . . *is joined to his woman*; *and they become one flesh*."	(v. 3b) [*Explanatory comment:*] and he *will spread the tent with them*, and *they will become his peoples*, and God himself will be among them (, their God).
(2:25) [*Clear eyesight:*] And the two of them were *naked*, the man and his woman, [*Innocence:*] and *were not ashamed* before one another.	(v. 4) [*Clear eyesight regained:*] And he will *wipe away every tear* from their eyes; [*Innocence regained:*] and there *will no longer be any death*; there *will no longer be any mourning, or crying, or pain*; for the first things have passed away."

Resembling the creation story of Gen 1–2, the vision of Rev 21:1—22:4 depicts the "restoration,"[509] respectively new creation of "a new heaven and a new earth" under pre-Fall conditions—without death, mourning, crying, and pain, with free access to the creator-God. Again this is created by God and again everything is perfect, without any hint to the results of sin. Again there is a clear focus on the "masterpiece" of this new creation; while in the Genesis creation report that has been the human pair (Gen 1:26–31), and particularly the creation of the woman (Gen 2:18–25), now it is the holy Jerusalem. Both the woman and the new Jerusalem are "built" by God, "brought before" the man or "coming down" to the lamb from God. Both "brides" (the woman and the new Jerusalem) are presented as a gift to their new "spouses" (the man and the

---

recognizes the connections mentioned above. More general on the character of the metaphor of Jesus as bridegroom and the church as his bride e.g., Zimmermann, *Geschlechtermetaphorik*, 276–324.

508. Agreements of the paralleling sequences are marked by italics and underlining.

509. Cf. Younker, *God's Creation*, 65–66 for the same understanding of the "new creation" in terms of a "restoration" of Edenic conditions.

lamb). While the woman is "taken out of" the man, the holy city is "out of heaven"—both reflecting the glory of their origin: Just like the first couple was made in the image and likeness of God (Gen 1:26–27), so the new bride of the lamb will reflect "the glory of the Lord" (Rev 21:11).

The beauty and significance of the scenes is further emphasized by the sudden change of the "speakers." In Gen 2:23 there is a change into the direct speech of the "bridegroom" exclaiming his pleasure about the newly "built" bride who corresponds to his own human nature. Similarly, in Rev 21:3a there is a change into the direct speech of "a loud voice from the throne" exclaiming the meaningful familiarity between God and man, finally living together as one family, with the *imago dei* (Gen 1:26–27) completely restored to redeemed humankind. The direct speech is continued in the following sentences which by their shortness and the way the conjunctions are used are again reflecting the Edenic pattern of Gen 2:23–25:

Subject	Gen 2:23–25 (MT/LXX)	Rev 21:3–4 (NA²⁷)
Direct Speaker:	And said (וַיֹּאמֶר/καὶ εἶπεν)	And . . . saying (καὶ λεγούσης)
Kinship:	This finally is (זֹאת הַפַּעַם/τοῦτο νῦν)	Behold (ἰδού)
[Insertion] Rationale:	For this reason (עַל־כֵּן/ἕνεκεν τούτου)	[see at the ending]
Cohabitation:	And is joined (וְדָבַק/καὶ προσκολληθήσεται)	And spread the tent (καὶ σκηνώσει)
Oneness:	And become [one] (וְהָיוּ/καὶ ἔσονται)	And will be [his] (καὶ ἔσονται)
Clear Sight:	And they were (וַיִּהְיוּ/καὶ ἦσαν)	And he will (καὶ [ἐξαλείψει])
Innocence/Sinlessness:	And [were] not (וְלֹא/καὶ οὐκ)	And will not be (καὶ οὐκ . . . ἔσται)
[Insertion] Rationale:	[see at the beginning]	Because (ὅτι)⁵¹⁰

The center regarding the intimate union and its innocent, sinless state is marked by the rationale of Gen 2:24a at the beginning of the direct speech. The counterpart is the rationale of Rev 21:4b at the ending of the direct speech. Thus it is like an inclusio of the inner core, although spread over the different books. That also fits the basic pattern as given by the use of the verbal times; the Genesis report uses mainly past and present tense, while the vision in Revelation is described in present and future tense. Thus even the narrative style alludes to the final, positive *ending* of what since its original, perfect *beginning* lost all its innocence. This is further affirmed by the position of both passages in relation to the rest of the account on the two creations:

510. Please note that the Greek ὅτι is slightly uncertain: "On the one hand it can be argued that the reading τὰ πρῶτα, which is strongly supported by A P 051 1006 1611 2053 al, is original and that copyists sought to avoid asyndeton by inserting ὅτι or γάρ. On the other hand, however, it is altogether possible that the shorter reading originated through an accident in transcription when, because of the preceding ἔτι, copyists overlooked ὅτι. In order to represent the balance of probabilities the Committee decided to include ὅτι enclosed within square brackets." Metzger, *Greek NT*, 689.

(A) First Creation (Gen 1–2)
  (B) First Covenant (Gen 2:22–25): Man-Woman
    (C) Fall of Man and God's Work for Redemption (Gen 3–Rev 20)
  (B') Final Covenant (Rev 21:1–4): Lamb-Jerusalem
(A') Final Creation (Rev 21–22)

Regarding the Greek LXX version of Gen 2:24, the change from passive ("[the man] will be joined with") to active ("[God] will spread the tent with") in the corresponding verse Rev 21:3 further points to God's active working for humankind concerning both covenants: (1) The marital covenant between man and woman; (2) The redemptive covenant between Israel and God. Their paralleling position in this chiasmus further demonstrates the congruence of both covenant spheres of the Edenic ideal. Both result in a clear sight of the spouse, intimate intercourse including "knowing" (יָדַע) each other,[511] and the perfect innocence once given and finally regained (Gen 2:25; Rev 21:4).

Both direct speeches stress the normative pattern of kinship, covenantship, closest intimacy, and loyalty as alluded to by the absence of the results of sin. In both scenes the almost "inherent" presence of the Lord is remarkably prominent, and in Rev 21:3b it is even emphasized by a small chiasmus:

(A) He [i.e., God] will spread the tent with them,
  (B) and they [i.e., the men] will become his peoples,
(A') and God himself will be among them (, their God).

In Gen 2:24 there are no procedures, no oaths, no forms given as necessary requirements of establishing (or legalizing) the intimate union. Only the "joining/cleaving" by cohabitation is the sign of what now became one unity ("one flesh") alluded to by introducing the personal pronouns "his" peoples (λαοὶ αὐτου) and "their" God (αὐτῶν θεός),[512] echoing the Hebrew and Greek "his" woman (אִשְׁתּוֹ/τὴν γυναῖκα αὐτοῦ) of Gen 2:24. Thus, the ultimate goal of the redemptive covenant between Israel (respectively man) and God is finally reached, still using the original covenant pattern of Gen 2:24. Again there are both spheres mingled; the literal (man and woman) and the spiritual (Israel/church/man and God/Christ/the lamb). The "happy ending" of God's plan of redemption and the fulfilling of his covenant purposes are further marked by an inclusio given by the same rationale enclosing vv. 1–4: *"for the first heaven and the first earth passed away"* (ὁ γὰρ πρῶτος οὐρανὸς καὶ ἡ πρώτη γῆ ἀπῆλθαν; v. 1) *"for the first [things] have passed away"* (ὅτι τὰ πρῶτα ἀπῆλθαν; v. 4).

---

511. As investigated earlier; see above ("Marriage as Model of the Divine Covenant") and the further exposition below in this section concerning the "covenant of peace."

512. It is uncertain whether the αὐτῶν θεός may be regarded as the original reading. There is important evidence in favor of and also against it. Hence, it is put into square brackets within the NA[27] version. On discussion of the textual evidence and reasons for the decision to insert it using brackets see the NET note on Rev 21:3 and Metzger, *Greek NT*, 688–89.

The spreading of God's tent (σκηνόω) in v. 3 strongly alludes to the first spreading of God's "tent of meeting" (אֹהֶל מוֹעֵד/σκηνὴ μαρτυρίου) in the wilderness.[513] Again the purpose is personal intercourse, a close union of God with "his" people. While that was not possible in the same way as it will finally be attained at the new earth, it is interesting that in the new Jerusalem there is "no temple in it, for the Lord God the Almighty and the Lamb are its temple" (v. 22) and "the glory of God lights it up" (v. 23). Similarly, men should reflect the image and likeness of God (Gen 1:26–27) by "glorifying God in body (and spirit)" being "a temple of the Holy Spirit" (1 Cor 6:19–20).

Furthermore, this intimate "tabernacle union" depicted in Rev 21:3 stands in close connection to the purposes of the meaningful "covenant of peace" (בְּרִית שָׁלוֹם) as investigated within the studies on the Old Testament foundation (see above). It will be worthwhile to thoroughly compare the main, representative passage of Ezek 37:26–27 with what we found in Rev 21:2–3.[514]

Intended Intimacy (Ezek 37:26-28)	Intimacy Coming True (Rev 21:2-3)
(v. 26) *The Covenant of Peace:* I will make a covenant of peace with them; it will be an everlasting covenant with them. And I will place them [i.e., taking home the bride] and multiply them [i.e., procreation],	(v. 2) *The Covenant of Marriage:* And I saw the holy city, new Jerusalem, coming down out of heaven from God, made ready as a bride adorned for her husband.
Cohabitation: and will set my sanctuary (מִקְדָּשׁ) in their midst forever. (v. 27) My home/dwelling place (מִשְׁכָּן) also will be with them;	*Cohabitation:* (v. 3) . . . Behold, the tent (σκηνή) of God is among men, and he will spread [his] tent (σκηνόω) among them,
Intimacy and Kinship: and I will be their God, and they will be my people. (Cf. Gen 2:23–24!)	*Intimacy and Kinship:* and they shall be his people(s), and God himself will be among them, their God.

---

513. On the implications of σκηνόω concerning the close divine presence and God's tabernacle see also Mounce, *Revelation*, 383; Stefanovic, *Revelation*, 577.

514. The similarity between Ezek 37:27 and Rev 21:3 is also recognized by Osborne, *Revelation*, 731, 734: "Probably the verse behind the wording here." He further perceives a link to another passage dealing with the "covenant of peace:" Isa 54:5–6. Cf. also ibid., 733; Stefanovic, *Revelation*, 577.

(v. 28) *Influencing the Nations:* And the nations will know that I am the Lord who sanctifies Israel,	(v. 3; cf. 24, 26) *Influencing the Nations:* "They will be his *peoples*."[515] The nations will walk by its light [i.e., the glory of the Lord; v. 23], and . . . bring their glory [i.e., sanctified people; v. 27] into it.
Reemphasizing, final Note: when my sanctuary (מִקְדָּשׁ) is in their midst forever.	*Reemphasizing, final Note:* (22:4–5) they will see His face . . . the Lord God will illumine them [that means: God himself is as their tabernacle among them; cf. 21:22–23]

Rev 21:2 as paralleling Ezek 37:26 interprets the "covenant of peace" as the marriage covenant between the new, holy Jerusalem and Christ, the lamb. As pointed out within the investigations on the בְּרִית שָׁלוֹם in the first part of this treatise, this significant covenant is founded on the following important "pillars:"

1. There is *one* divine leader (the Messiah/Christ)
2. God works mightily to redeem his people
3. There will finally be only *one* people
4. There is only *one* God
5. There is *one* covenant between them (the eternal בְּרִית שָׁלוֹם)
6. The covenant's blessing is peace, fertility, and spiritual welfare (deliverance, sanctification, righteousness)
7. God's presence is the major/basic feature
8. An intimate relationship ("Their God"/"My people") is reached
9. There is a deep experience/intercourse by "knowing" (יָדַע) each other

These basic principles are all fulfilled by the covenant described in Rev 21:1–4 and its context. Even the concrete structure of the covenant's final "consummation" agrees remarkably with the prediction in Ezek 37:26–28, as the table above further affirms. That alludes to the perfect union foreshadowed in Gen 2:24 as it will at last be

---

515. It is important to note that the Greek NA text supports the reading λαοί (plural: "peoples") instead of the singular λαός ("people"), although the decision was considerably difficult. Metzger, *Greek NT*, 688. Nevertheless, "apparently, John modified the traditional concept (Jer 7:23; 30:22; Hos 2:23) and substituted a reference to the many peoples of redeemed humanity. Jesus had spoken of 'other sheep that are not of this sheep pen' that must become part of the one flock (John 10:16). It is with the redeemed peoples of all races and nationalities that God will dwell in glory." Mounce, *Revelation*, 383. Similarly, Osborne, *Revelation*, 734 and Bauckham, *Climax of Prophecy*, 310–13. Bauckham further explains that the generic τῶν ἀνθρώπων in v. 3 corresponds to the plural αὐτοὶ λαοί in the same verse, both indicating that the redeemed of all nations are meant here. Ibid. Yet they are *one* people in God, thus reflecting the *one* people in Ezek 37:16–22.

restored through the בְּרִית שָׁלוֹם in the future world. The Edenic marriage covenant and the "covenant of peace" are, consequently, one and the same. While the first primarily refers to the literal (human) realm, the last one primarily refers to the spiritual (human-divine) level. Nevertheless both are following the same ideals and both result in the same blessings.

However, it still needs to be explained why the new Jerusalem is called the bride of the lamb (i.e., Christ), and not Christ's disciples. How can the church and Christ be "one flesh," or the individual church member "one spirit" with God, if the church members are only passive guests, as pointed out within the different gospel texts and even Rev 19:9? Again, there are different spheres to be considered: The new, holy Jerusalem is the symbol of the new-born, holy saints who dwell within the city. Therefore Rev 21:14 states that on the foundation stones are "the twelve names of the twelve apostles of the Lamb." Additionally, while those are "blessed" (μακάριος) "who are invited to the marriage supper of the lamb" (Rev 19:9), it is the city of Jerusalem that is clothed with "the righteous acts (τὰ δικαιώματα) of the saints" (v. 8). There evidently is a close identification of the holy city and its holy inhabitants, wearing their righteous deeds and the names of their apostles. The entire city must be a symbolic metaphor of the Christian church and its individual members being "living stones, . . . built up as a spiritual house for a holy priesthood" (1 Pet 2:5)—certainly the holy priesthood of 1 Pet 2:9 (the Christian church). The holy city as bride thus is a symbol of the holy church and its members who finally reach the heavenly wedding as "those who *spread their tent* in the heaven" (τοὺς ἐν τῷ οὐρανῷ σκηνοῦντας; Rev 13:6; cf. 12:12). "The saints and the city together are the bride of Christ. They are closely connected. Both are arrayed as the bride beautifully dressed. . . . The new Jerusalem belongs to Christ. It is populated by God's faithful people who are finally at home."[516]

With these holy Christians who make up the new, holy Jerusalem, the Edenic covenant pattern, the marriage bond, the "one flesh/one spirit" union, and the "covenant of peace," which all allude to the same Edenic "oneness," are finally coming true; "now, at the consummation, the new Jerusalem is where God tabernacles with his people in 'ultimate unity' . . . ."[517] These holy ones experience the final, ultimate, and real, extensive שָׁלוֹם transmitted by the holy human-divine covenant. This covenant is the plan of redemption, the gospel, the good news, foreshadowed even in Gen 2:24 as a promise of the final goal to be reached by God's intervention as firstly predicted in Gen 3:15 and henceforth throughout the Old Testament.

Corresponding to the "competition of covenants" as experienced in the Old Testament apostasy and judgment stories,[518] which all stress the changing of loyalties away from God, now clinging to a new "Lord/Husband" (cf. esp. Num 25:3), what in Christian interpretation is Belial (2 Cor 6:14–15)/Satan, in Revelation there also is a

---

516. Stefanovic, *Revelation*, 576–77.
517. Stefanovic, *Revelation*, 577.
518. See the first part of this study: Gen 3:1–7; Gen 6; Exod 32; Num 25.

"counter-bride" (Rev 17–19:5) standing for a counter-μυστήριον (Rev 17:5, 7; cf. 2 Thess 2:7) attacking the Edenic ideal referred to in Eph 5:31–32 as the great, true, genuine "one flesh" μυστήριον of unity with Christ. This false "bride" is thoroughly depicted and immediately precedes the wedding day of the lamb's bride, thus emphasizing even more the stark contrast between both elements. The harlot is called "Babylon," the virgin bride "holy Jerusalem," thereby creating a startling opposition.[519] While even in Paul's days "the mystery of lawlessness is already at work" (2 Thess 2:7), it grows until being ready for harvest by destruction, but that is not before the bride of the lamb is made ready, adorned with "righteous deeds"—thus again contrasting the "lawless" (ἀνομία) works of the counter-μυστήριον, namely: the counter-εὐαγγέλιον.[520] Considering the equation of the εὐαγγέλιον-μυστήριον with the σὰρξ μίαν union of Gen 2:24 in the theology of Eph 5:31–32, the larger context of Revelation 17–22 evidently deals with two opposing marital covenant relationships, both derived from the Edenic pattern. Consequently, it is again the Edenic ideal that inherently consist of the New Testament εὐαγγέλιον of restoring the divine image, presence, and union to the NT church and her individual "members" as finally coming true with the wedding of the lamb (Rev 19:7–9; 21:1–4), the ultimate establishment of the "covenant of peace," forever abandoning the counter-covenant of Gen 3:1–7. Then, at last, Christ "might present to Himself the church in all her glory, having no spot or wrinkle or any such thing; but that she would be holy and blameless" (Eph 5:27)—completely differing from the counter-covenant's bride, who is "fallen" and "has become a dwelling place of demons and a prison of every unclean spirit, and a prison of every unclean and hateful bird." (Rev 18:2).

Furthermore, just as the beginning of the בְּרִית שָׁלוֹם ("covenant of peace") is marked by a holy zeal, describing the affection and love for the own dear spouse (Num 25:11, 13), the same Greek verb as used in the Septuagint version of Num 25:11, 13 (ζηλόω) is later used by Paul in 2 Cor 11:2–3, again in a marital context, describing more closely his work of preparing Christ's bride, the NT church:

> For I am jealous (ζηλῶ) for you with a godly jealousy (θεοῦ ζήλῳ); for I betrothed you to one husband (ἀνδρί), so that to Christ I might present you as a pure virgin (παρθένον ἁγνήν). But I am afraid that, as the serpent deceived Eve by his craftiness, your minds will be led astray from the simplicity and purity of devotion to Christ.

Paul even returns to the events in Eden and thus again builds a connection to the covenant conditions and the marital patterns given there.[521] The language and the terminol-

---

519. See for a table of contrasting qualities both cities stand for Stefanovic, *Revelation*, 373–75.

520. As investigated above in context of Eph 5:32 (see "Paul's Spiritual Application: Textual Analysis"), the term μυστήριον evidently refers to the gospel (cf. Rom 11:25; 16:25; 1 Cor 2:1, 7; 4:1; (13:2; 14:2; 15:51;) Eph 1:9; 3:3–4, 9; 5:32; 6:19; Col 1:26–27; 2:2; 4:3; 1 Tim 3:9, 16; Rev 10:7.) The μυστήριον of the harlot, therefore, must be a counter-εὐαγγέλιον propagated by the harlot.

521. It is even possible to recognize a connection between Eph 5, Gen 2 and the text of 2 Cor 11:2, as depicted in Theobald, "Heilige Hochzeit," 241: "Beide Texte, Eph 5 wie 2 Kor 11,2–3, lassen

ogy used by him in this remarkable text obviously are marriage language. Although the church is nowhere in the New Testament called the "bride" of Christ, by the implication of the Revelation texts mentioned above and particularly the way Paul depicts the New Testament "people of God" in this passage, the links to the marital ideal of Eden and the "covenant of peace" become even more evident. Again it is the significant ζῆλος which leads to the consummation of the covenant, again only the serpent may be the one to endanger this "oneness" by his deceptive craftiness, and again the παρθένον ἁγνήν is presented to the bridegroom by a third person (cf. Gen 2:22).

It further seems relevant to notice that Paul only speaks about betrothal, not marriage. Thus matching the vision of Rev 21, he foresees the final, ultimate union consummated at the second advent of Christ and his marriage to the glorious bride, the church of the new, holy Jerusalem.[522] The "one spirit" union of 1 Cor 6:17 or the "mystery" of virtually being "one flesh" with (i.e., members of) Christ in Eph 5:30–32, therefore, indicate the seriousness of the betrothal and allude to the Holy Spirit as the betrothal gift, the "down payment/pledge... of redemption" (ἀρραβών... εἰς ἀπολύτρωσιν).[523] "Paul believes that the church lives *zwischen den Zeiten*, during which she experiences the presence of her Lord and yet hopes for a future consummation.... The betrothal day has passed when these Christians had accepted Jesus Christ as Lord; the wedding day will be celebrated at the parousia."[524]

In Revelation it is even permissible to speak of betrothal and marriage as (almost?) one and the same thing, saying: "I will show you *the bride, the wife* of the Lamb." (Rev 21:9.) Consequently, the quotation of Gen 2:24 in Eph 5:31 on the one hand alludes to the marriage between Christ and his church at the end of this world's history, when Christ's tasks of purification, glorification, and sanctification (Eph 5:26–27) are completed; on the other hand it simultaneously points to the close intimacy already to be experienced through the gift of his Holy Spirit.[525]

---

demnach einen Bezug auf die Urgeschichte erkennen, Eph 5,31–32 auf Gen 2,24 in einer allegorischen Deutung der Beziehung Adams und Evas auf Christus und die Gemeinde, 2 Kor 11,3 auf Gen 3,1–6 als Exempel, das zur Warnung der Gemeinde herangezogen wird." On the influence of the LXX version of Gen 3:13 ("the serpent 'seduced' [ἠπάτησέν] me") leading to sexualize the downfall of the woman see Loader, *LXX, Sexuality, and NT*, 105.

522. Cf. Schlier, *Epheser*, 265.

523. Quotation from Eph 1:14; cf. Eph 4:30; 2 Cor 1:22; 5:5. Similarly expressed by Batey, *Nuptial Imagery*, 14. "Paul's metaphor of the church as Bride implies that the End has begun. The church is the eschatological community whose betrothal is a past fact, effected by the acceptance in faith of Jesus as Christ and Lord. Betrothal in Israel, as among other nations, was a far more serious contract than are present-day engagements. During the approximate year between the betrothal and nuptial ceremonies, the betrothed girl was legally the man's wife even though she was still a virgin, since the marital relation did not begin until the nuptial ceremony. The betrothal could be abrogated only by a formal written divorce or death." Ibid., 13. Cf. on the corresponding ancient Jewish laws e.g., *m. Ketub.* 5:2 (twelve months for a betrothed virgin to prepare for marriage); *Song Rab.* 4:8; *m. Qidd.* 3:7 (certificate of divorce to dissolve the betrothal).

524. Batey, *Nuptial Imagery*, 14.

525. As mentioned above in context of 1 Cor 6:17 (see Paul's Spiritual Application—Textual

To sum up briefly, the most significant paralleling reflection of Gen 2:22–25 in Rev 21:1–4 is like an afterword about the ultimate victory of God's plan of redemption—basing on his holy, Edenic covenant ideal, and pursued with his divine, holy zeal. The bridge from the first creation to the new creation, and the perfectness and holiness both stages of man's history are marked by, is permanently oriented on the Edenic ideal, the first, perfect model. God's work for the sake of humankind all through the extensive accounts and times of human history is finally reaching the ultimate goal to reestablish the intimate relationship of Eden by God's presence and the overwhelming blessings of the בְּרִית שָׁלוֹם in the new world. Although once they have been God's "enemies" (Rom 5:10), the members of his holy covenant people are finally restored to be in "peace" (שָׁלוֹם) with him for eternity, newborn through God's Holy Spirit, now being of divine origin (זֶרַע אֱלֹהִים; Mal 2:15), reflecting God's image (Gen 1:26–27), ready to experience an intimacy of its relationship with God that is comparable only with marriage.

> Indeed, we have in the marriage-metaphor an excellent illustration of the meaning of the doctrine of the 'one body,' 'one flesh,' 'one spirit,' of the Pauline teaching. For the marriage-relationship is the deepest, richest, and most satisfying personal human relationship of which we have experience; it is an experience of surrender without absorption, of service without compulsion, of love without conditions.[526]

Analysis), it seems 1 Cor 8:3 is also hinting at this loving union with Christ: "But if anyone *loves* God, he is *known* by Him." (My italics; cf. 1 Cor 6:17.) This "known" (γινώσκω) is interesting, being the same as used e.g., in Gen 4:1 as translation of the Hebrew יָדַע, the euphemism for sexual intimacy. Cf. further on Paul's use of metaphors concerning "salvation history" and "apocalyptic" as denoting both "conversion and . . . the final consummation" at the same time: Dunn, *New Perspective*, 252; particularly about the "already—not yet" theology of Paul: Dunn, *Theology*, 466–72.

526. Richardson, *NT Theology*, 258.

III

Results: Permanent Commitment to the Edenic Ideal

THIS THIRD AND LAST part is meant to gather the important results obtained in the foregoing investigations. This will not be a repetition of the conclusions given at the end of the different sections of this study; therefore, only certain significant aspects contributing to a refinement of the previous results concerning the New Testament "one flesh" concept will be taken into account. This treatise focused on both levels of the Edenic ideal: the literal (husband—wife) and the "symbolical," "figurative," or "spiritual" sphere (Yahweh/Christ—Israel/church). Consequently, both spheres and corresponding features that deserve further consideration and emphasis will be dealt with in the two sections of this last chapter.

It seems important to notice beforehand that one of the first observations when investigating the evidence on biblical "marriage" as constituted in Gen 2:24 is the absence of any complete "marriage theology." There are certain hints on how to deal with different situations, but even the mainly discussed aspect in the New Testament, divorce, still leaves several questions open. Hence, it is advisable to heed the admonition to "learn not to exceed what is written" (1 Cor 4:6). It will further be wise and meaningful to consider the close, mutual connections between the two spheres (literal: human-human/spiritual: human-divine) which lead to a deeper understanding of the idea behind what is described so artfully as the Edenic marriage ideal in Gen 2:18–25.

III.1 The Spiritual Level (Christ–Church): Toward a Successful Representation

As pointed out throughout this study, the literal marriage is a representation of the relationship God intends to establish with his followers. Unfortunately, this representation is frequently deformed and gives only a distorted view of what God originally wanted (and of course still wants) the intimate relationship with his disciples to be like.¹ As conclusion of the investigations on the spiritual sphere of the Edenic pattern, a final comparison of the significant qualities of both levels will be presented, but beforehand, there are two more issues to be briefly dealt with. These are the significance of the Edenic basis of Jesus' and Paul's expositions concerning marriage, and the soteriological oneness introduced by Paul's marriage metaphor.

III.1.1 Edenic Basis and Soteriological Oneness

As became apparent especially during the investigations on the "one flesh" echo in Ephesians 5, Paul is consequently applying the Old Testament nuptial imagery of Yahweh and Israel to the New Testament church. This church is the continuation of the Old Testament bride, while Jesus is the bridegroom paying a very expensive price for his bride (1 Cor 6:20; Eph 5:25), preparing her for the wedding (Eph 5:26–27), looking forward finally to dwelling with her (Rev 21:2–3). Jesus himself refers to the OT Edenic ideal for the purpose of justifying his rejection of divorce "on any reason," thus even interpreting Deut 24:1–4 as instrument against (not because of) the Israelites' "hardness of heart" for diminishing divorce and thus leading at least partly back to Eden.

Apparently there is no break, no new marriage theology developing in the NT, not even a cultural adaption is to be witnessed. Hence, "in Bezug auf Stellung und Bewertung der Institution Ehe kann unmittelbar am alttestamentlichen Verständnis angeknüpft werden."² The right understanding of the OT marriage and "one flesh" concept is the foundation of a right understanding of the NT perceptions; much more important than literary and cultural backgrounds that evidently were not determining the expositions of Jesus and Paul concerning the original ideal. Additionally, Jesus points out that the perfect state of Eden is to be understood as hermeneutical foundation when trying to interpret later ordinances touching patterns given in the first two chapters of Genesis. That is also affirmed by Paul and his numerous references to Eden as the foundation for interpreting other topics.³

The theological basis particularly for marriage is, therefore, in every case the creational pattern of a perfect, mutual covenant—not to be changed, not to be dissolved,

---

1. Please note that I am only speaking about analogy and typology, not about any sacramental understanding of the marriage relation as inherently containing redemptive elements. "There is nothing in marriage itself as an institution that 'mystically' dispenses divine grace. It is not the case, as the Roman Catholic Church maintains, that when marriage is entered into under the auspices of the Church it is in itself an institution where Christ is 'personally present' in a mystical way. There is no intrinsic power in . . . marriage [itself . . .]." Köstenberger, "The Mystery," 87.

2. Kirchschläger, *Ehe im NT*, 25.

3. This is in addition to the investigated texts of 1 Cor 6:16–17 and Eph 5:30–32 cf. e.g., Rom 5:12–21; 1 Cor 11:7–9; 15:20–28, 42–49; 2 Cor 11:3, etc. Cf. on this also Son, *Corporate Elements* 45–91; Son, "Concept," 121. Beale and Carson, *NT Use*, 59 reminds us: "The more ancient the practice, the weightier it remains."

not to be broken. The original aim is perfect faith, completely trusting the covenant partner, living together in harmony, rejoicing about the blessings promised by the covenant of שָׁלוֹם. God is witnessed by Jesus and Paul as the active initiator, the one who "yokes together" and therefore prohibits separation as well as legal divorce. While the church (just as Israel before) dwells on this earth waiting for the final restoration or new creation of paradise, she is nevertheless betrothed to the redeemer, being prepared for the wedding according to the Edenic model. There is no deviation in between, no deformation of the ideal due to earthly circumstances. The original marriage pattern is not an ideal to be realized only under ideal conditions—it is a universal pattern presented to humankind as ideal fulfillment of its needs for closeness, intimacy, and help. It further is presented as metaphor of the partnership God offers to humankind *although* paradise is lost and God is generally invisible for man.

Although the final, visible consummation lies in the future, the spiritual consummation is already performed through the coming of his Holy Spirit, already dwelling in the believer, making him and the entire church as body of Christ a holy temple (1 Cor 6:17–20; 3:16), fulfilling the most intimate relationship ever possible by being of "one spirit" (1 Cor 6:17) sharing even "the mind of Christ" (1 Cor 2:16). "The Spirit is the medium of Christ's union with his own."[4] Considering these remarkable ideals and purposes, it is not surprising that the events of Eden always had a high estimation within Judaism, although these elaborate expositions frequently led to strange interpretations. Yet, Jesus and Paul meant to rediscover the original simplicity and beauty of the Edenic institution not only as ideal pattern for literal marriage, but also as spiritual norm providing the earliest pattern for the human-divine covenant and its redemptive purpose.

Given the equal pairs "Adam/Eve (sexual union) = husband/wife (sexual union) = Christ/church (spiritual union) = head/body," it becomes apparent that "Paul's 'one flesh (body)' concept is closely related to his Adam-Christ typology."[5] This typology is basically used as pattern for the plan of redemption; for instance, in Rom 5:12–21 (cf. 1 Cor 15:20–22, 45–49). Paul's usage of the "one flesh" concept in 1 Cor and Eph perfectly corresponds to this passage in the letter to the Romans which deals with Adam as the one who brought the curse of sin into the world and Christ as second Adam obtaining redemption from this curse, "that he might present to himself the church in all her glory, having no spot or wrinkle or any such thing; but that she would be holy and blameless" (Eph 5:27).

It is indeed adequate to use the Edenic marriage covenant ideal likewise as image for the plan of redemption, since both originally have saving purposes (encouragement to be loyal to the divine authority) and while through the first marriage Adam was led to sin and thus lost paradise (Gen 2:18—13:24), finally it is by the "second" marriage of the "second" Adam that a new paradise is created and inhabited by holy followers of the lamb (Rev 21:1–4). The striking parallels given between Gen 2:24 and Rev 21:2–3

4. Dunn, *Theology*, 264.
5. Son, "Concept," 117; cf. Schlier, *Epheser*, 262.

as pointed out in the investigations on the nuptial imagery, therefore, are all the more comprehensible and perfectly, precisely fitting the underlying, redemptive purpose of Gen 2:24. The curse of sin following the first marriage will be eradicated as soon as the second marriage is finally consummated. As elucidated in the exegesis of Gen 2:18–25, the first woman was meant to be man's עֵזֶר כְּנֶגְדּוֹ ("complemental helper") particularly in the task of preserving his faithfulness in allegiance to God. The conditions God created for this purpose were prefect. Yet she dared to stretch out her hand, grasp and eat of the forbidden fruit, thus seducing the man to break the only prohibition given immediately before the pericope about the woman's creation as man's "helper" (Gen 2:17–18). This close connection of both accounts, the forbidden tree and the creation of the woman, is certainly not given incidentally in exactly that way. The first marriage obviously missed the underlying goal of mutual strengthening faithfulness and allegiance to God. That is likewise true in reference to Adam, for he missed saving his wife by protecting her from approaching the forbidden tree. Instead he follows her (Gen 3:6) and shares in her transgression. Christ, the second Adam, overcame where Adam fell; he is the perfect, sinless bridegroom, always leading his betrothed wife on the perfect way of sanctification and holiness to the final salvation from the curse of sin.[6]

Interestingly, Paul recognizes the same goal in 1 Cor 7:16 within his exposition on the permanence of the marriage relation: "For how do you know, O wife, whether you will save your husband? Or how do you know, O husband, whether you will save your wife?" "The meaning is obviously that the husband/wife would be the human agent in leading his/her wife/husband to salvation."[7] Paul therefore explains that marriages with unbelievers may be dissolved if the unbelieving spouse desires to separate, since the purpose of saving him is apparently no more achievable (cf. 1 Cor 7:12–16).

The original purpose of the "one flesh" covenant, however, will finally be accomplished through Christ's redeeming work in preparing the church for the restored paradise—and for every individual believer the redemptive purpose of Gen 2:24 is already accomplished by the "one spirit" union through "cleaving" to the Lord (1 Cor 6:17). The close "one flesh," respectively "one spirit" unions referred to in 1 Cor 6:17 and Eph 5:31–32 thus allude to the "soteriological oneness" created by Christ's redemptive work for his people, shared by the believer and the entire church through covenantal "cleaving" to the Lord, thus being led the way back to the ideals of Eden and the newly created paradise at the final and ultimate wedding feast of Rev 21:1–4.

6. Cf. e.g., 1 Cor 1:30; 2 Cor 7:1; 1 Thess 3:12–13; 4:3, 7; 2 Thess 2:13; 1 Pet 1:2.

7. NET on 1 Cor 7:16. Son, "Concept," 110 further explains concerning 1 Cor 7:14 ("For the unbelieving husband is sanctified through his wife, and the unbelieving wife is sanctified through her believing husband; for otherwise your children are unclean, but now they are holy.") that "Paul seems to employ here . . . the OT principle of holiness by association: 'Whatever touches it [the altar] becomes holy' (for example, Exod 29:37; 30:29). In 1 Cor 7, the 'one flesh' marriage union sanctifies the unbelieving spouse. The familial corporate sphere is not limited to the union of husband and wife; it also extends to their children: 'they are holy' (1 Cor 7:14). The fundamental concept that underlies Paul's teachings on divorce is, therefore, the ontological corporate solidarity in marriage that includes not only the husband and wife but also their children."

III.1.2 Marriage as Image for the Plan of Redemption

Marriage as established in Gen 2:18–25 is per se a universal institution that belongs to all humankind. Nevertheless, its richest fulfillment is apparently found in Christian partnerships that acknowledge God's part in the marriage process and his leading authority in their lives. As already explained above, I am not speaking about modern ecclesiastical marriage procedures, but about recognizing God's divine working in creating a "complemental helper" (Gen 2:18), "bringing" the partners before one another (Gen 2:22), and "yoking" (συζεύγνυμι) them inseparably together (Matt 19:6; Mark 10:9). Yet, Jesus explains that God also cares for those who do not follow him (Matt 5:45). Hence, even those who do not know the God of Eden and his marriage ideal might nevertheless be led and "joined" by him, if not actively or passively opposing and refusing his efforts.

> The clause 'what God united' has led some to suppose that not all married couples have been united by God; perhaps other unions are merely human. By itself, v. 6b could sustain this interpretation, but in the context of a creation ordinance this is impossible. What Jesus is rather saying is that because all marriages are divinely made unions, they ought not be dissolved. Paul certainly viewed Gen 2:24 as equally applicable to believer and unbeliever, including even the pagan cult-prostitutes (1 Cor 6:16).[8]

Yet, further significant patterns connected with the marital bond in the New Testament are, of course, not equally applicable to unbelievers and not even to mixed marriages, as 1 Cor 7:12–16 and 2 Cor 6:14–16 indicate. Only a marriage of two believing spouses is a perfect representation of the human-divine relationship as intended by the holy covenant between Christ and his church, a perfect representation of the divine image as intended in Gen 1:26–27.

The text in Ephesians 5, for example, declares the church members to be bound to Christ as members to the body (cf. also 1 Cor 6:15; 12:27). 1 Cor 6:17 even states that a church member is "one spirit" with God through "joining" him, thus becoming "a temple" of the Holy Spirit (v. 19). Both use the image of Gen 2:24 to emphasize even more the remarkable intimacy created by choosing to follow the Lord. That obviously leads to a new level of the human-divine relationship that is comparable with the beginning of a marital bond. Turning to the spiritual sphere, we find that the consummation of the intimate relationship with God usually commences with baptism[9] by the "inauguration" of the "one spirit" union through the Holy Spirit (Acts 2:38), by whom "we were all baptized into one body" (1 Cor 12:13). However, there are cases alluding to the fact that even baptism in the name of Jesus is no

---

8. Blomberg, "Exegesis," 169.

9. Hasel, "Eheverständnis," 37 recognizes the same parallel (baptism—marriage). See also Eph 5:26 possibly hinting to a connection of marriage and baptism; cf. Schlier, *Epheser*, 256–58; Thatcher, *Marriage*, 77.

guarantee that the "one spirit" union is really established, since that only happens through the transmission of the Holy Spirit and it may be that these two aspects (baptism and receiving the Holy Spirit) do not occur together (cf. Acts 8:15–17). The reception of the divine spirit may even occur suddenly without any baptism planned (see Acts 10:44–46), but it usually leads to the official recognition through formal baptism with water (vv. 47–48).[10]

Becoming members of the "body of Christ" is obtained by the "one spirit union" through the baptism with the Holy Spirit (see also 1 Cor 12, esp. vv. 12–13),[11] while the church membership is officially initiated by baptism with water. Both may come together, but not necessarily. Acts 19:3 ("did you receive the Holy Spirit *when you believed?*") and Gal 3:2 ("This is the only thing I want to find out from you: did you receive the Spirit by the works of the Law, or *by hearing with faith?*"), for example, further elucidate that the Holy Spirit should be received by conversion (just as in Acts 10:44–46), not necessarily with water baptism (cf. Acts 2:38). Hence, there may be outward "signs" of the newly established covenant with God, but the only prerequisite actually demanded is the personal "joining/cleaving" unto the Lord (1 Cor 6:17).[12] Also, as the passive mode "[he] will be joined"[13] expresses, it is God's initiative and his efforts that succeed in winning a person to enter the "one flesh/spirit" relation with him;[14] we are joined and incorporated into his "one flesh" body (the church) through his efforts, his saving abilities, his perfect sacrifice that makes us instead of enemies to become his friends, even his children—he is the initiator of marriage as well as of redemption.

The newly converted believer thus is a "new creation" (καινὴ κτίσις; 2 Cor 5:17) through being "in Christ" (ἐν Χριστῷ; ibid.).[15] Henceforth he follows the Lord by the leading of his Holy Spirit through the new "one spirit" union (1 Cor 6:17) established in terms equal to those of literal marriage in Gen 2:24 (see also Eph 5:29–33), as was demonstrated throughout the several investigations within the New Testament

---

10. Perhaps, the following perception would be adequate: while the marriage itself is consummated through the intimate (sexual) contact (both becoming one flesh), an official recognition through a marriage procedure would be appropriate—however, not strictly biblically (re the Eden model) demanded.

11. Son, "Concept," 109 makes the same point: "Paul probably implies here [1 Cor 6:17] that the believer's union with Christ is effected by the Holy Spirit. Although Paul does not explain in this chapter how believers were united to Christ, he writes elsewhere that they were united to Christ in baptism, that is, baptism in the Spirit, and as a result they have become corporately the body of Christ and individually members of it (1 Cor 12:12–13, 27)." Cf. ibid., 120.

12. Dunn, *New Perspective*, 252 similarly interprets 1 Cor 6:17 as denoting conversion (through "cleaving;" κολλάω).

13. Gen 2:24; cf. Matt 19:5; (Mark 10:7;) 1 Cor 6:16–17; Eph 5:31.

14. Cf., for instance, Phil 1:6; Heb 2:10; 12:2; Rom 5:10; 2 Cor 5:18–19 and many more.

15. Cf. Batey, "The ΜΙΑ ΣΑΡΞ Union," 281: "There is no doubt, however, that the result is a new nature created in the 'likeness of God in true righteousness and holiness' (Eph iv. 24).'"

above.[16] The NT "one flesh" union in spiritual terms is substantially compatible with the Edenic pattern and the Old Testament realization thereof. The following table presents the similarities of the covenants in Gen 2, the OT, and the NT, based on the chart given at the end of the first part of this treatise.

	Literal Level (Gen 2)	Spiritual Level (OT)	Spiritual Level (NT: 1 Cor 6/Eph 5)
Initiator	God	God	God
Who	Man	Israel/Humankind	Church/Israel/Humankind
Familial Attributes	Human Pattern for Woman	God's Firstborn Son His Image and Likeness	God's Sons and Daughters/his newborn Children[17]
Pillar (1)	Forsake [parents] (עָזַב)	Forsake [false gods] (עָזַב)	Forsake [old life]/ Hate [old family]/Flee [idolatry] (καταλείπω/μισέω/φεύγω)[18]
Pillar (2)	Cleave (דָּבַק)	Cleave (דָּבַק)	Cleave/Follow ([προσ-] κολλάω/ἀκολουθέω)[19]
Pillar (3)	Be(come) One Flesh (הָיָה לְבָשָׂר אֶחָד)	Accept Divine Word (עַל כָּל־הַדְּבָרִים)	Be(come) One Spirit/One Body ("members of Christ") (ἓν πνεῦμα/μέλη Χριστοῦ)[20]
To Whom	Woman	God	Christ/God[21]

16. Thus "Christians are imitators of Christ (Eph v.1–2), but they are more than this. They are the historic continuation of his personality (σῶμα). Just as there is one God and Father, one Lord, one faith, one hope, one baptism, so there is one Spirit and 'personality.' As each individual encounters and surrenders himself to the power of Christ's personality, so all become conformed to a single 'Body' characterized by love. This personality transcends all barriers to genuine interpersonal relationships patterned on the love revealed in Christ. The personal unity sustained by Christ with his Body signifies that the Church is the visible locus of Christ's personal presence in history at the level of human experience and activity." Batey, "The ΜΙΑ ΣΑΡΞ Union," 281.

17. 2 Cor 6:17–18; John 3:5–7; 1 John 3:1; Rev 21:7.

18. Luke 5:28 (cf. LXX on Gen 2:24: καταλείπω); 14:26; 1 Cor 6:18/10:14.

19. 1 Cor 6:17; Eph 5:31; Acts 5:13; [17:34; Rom 12:9] (cf. LXX on Gen 2:24: προσκολλάω); Matt 4:20, 22, 25; 8:1, 10, 19, 22–23; 9:9, 19, 27; 10:38; 12:15; 14:13; 16:24; 19:2, 21, 27–28; 20:29, 34; 21:9; 26:58; 27:55; Mark 1:18; 2:14–15; 3:7; 5:24; 6:1; 8:34; 9:38; 10:21, 28, 32, 52; 11:9; 14:13, 54; 15:41; Luke 5:11, 27–28; 7:9; 9:11, 23, 49, 57, 59, 61; 18:22, 28, 43; 22:10, 39, 54; 23:27; John 1:37–38, 40, 43; 6:2; 8:12; 10:4–5, 27; 11:31; 12:26; 13:36–37; 18:15; 20:6; 21:19–20, 22; Acts 12:8–9; 13:43; 21:36; 1 Cor 10:4; Rev 6:8; 14:4, 8–9, 13; 19:14.

20. 1 Cor 6:15, 17, 19; Eph 5:30 (cf. LXX on Gen 2:24: εἰμί).

21. Even the other way around would be acceptable: Christ *left* his heavenly father and came into this world (Phil 2:5–8; cf. also for the future 1 Thess 4:16), he *cleaves* to his church all through the ages (Matt 28:20b), and will finally *become one flesh* at the ultimate wedding feast (Rev 21:1–4).

Results: Permanent Commitment to the Edenic Ideal

	Literal Level (Gen 2)	Spiritual Level (OT)	Spiritual Level (NT: 1 Cor 6/Eph 5)
Familial Attributes	"Bone of my bones, and flesh of my flesh"	Creator/Father/Divine Pattern for Man	Creator/Head/Divine Pattern for Man[22]
Establishing Act[23]	Sexuality	Sacrificing	Accepting Christ's Sacrifice/Conversion
Spiritual Result	Unveiled Seeing Knowing Blessing	Unveiled Seeing Communal Meal Blessing	Unveiled Seeing/ Knowing Communion Blessing[24]
Spiritual Sign	Lovingkindness/ Faithfulness	Lovingkindness/ Faithfulness	Baptism with the Holy Spirit: Love/Spiritual Fruit[25]
Formal Result	One Flesh (σάρκα μίαν)	Covenant	One Spirit/One Body ("members of Christ") (ἐν πνεῦμα/μέλη Χριστοῦ)
Formal Sign	Garment Marital Faithfulness	Circumcision Observing the Commandments, esp. the Sabbath	Baptism Observing the Commandments, esp. the Sabbath[26]
Long Term Outcome	Life Procreation Prosperity	Life Growth/Procreation Prosperity	Eternal Life Spiritual Growth Spiritual Prosperity

The compatibility of both spheres is striking. Paul's usage of the Edenic ideal concerning the divine-human relationship in 1 Cor 6:17 and Eph 5:30–32 is a consequent and appropriate application of comparable features. It is not surprising that

> the metaphorical use of sexual union to describe the divine human relationship occurs in many cultures and continues to do so. It is assumed in Jewish prophetic and wisdom literature. Later streams of Christian thought would elaborate the

22. Again, when accepting the hint I have mentioned within the section about the wider biblical context of Gen 2:24 and its "covenantal aspects," there is another accord given between these three levels, directly related to the "establishing act:" The "Blood of the Covenant" (דַּם־הַבְּרִית) as given by defloration (concerning literal level), the blood of sacrifices (concerning spiritual level OT), and the blood of Christ (concerning spiritual level NT; cf. Matt 26:28; Mark 14:24; 1 Cor 11:25).

23. Unveiled seeing/knowing: John 14:9, 17; 1 Cor 2:7–12, 16; 13:12; 1 John 3:2; Communion: Matt 26:26–28; Mark 14:22–24; 1 Cor 11:23–26; Blessings: John 12:24; 15:5, 8; Gal 5:22–23.

24. Importance of Holy Spirit: e.g., 1 Cor 6:17; Acts 19:3; Gal 3:2; Acts 10:44–46. Love and fruits of the Holy Spirit: John 13:35; Gal 5:22–25.

25. On the commandments and the role of the Sabbath consider these texts: Rev 12:17/14:9–10 (true followers have not the sign of the counter-God [i.e., the beast] on their hands or foreheads); Exod 13:9/Deut 6:8/11:18 (true followers have sign of God's commandments "between their eyes" and "on their hands"); Exod 20:8–11/31:13–18 (Sabbath is the special, eternal sign of true allegiance); Gen 1:26—2:23 (wedding night on Sabbath's eve).

26. Creator: John 1:3, 10; Col 1:16; 2:9; Heb 1:2; Head: Eph 5:23–27; Col 1:18; 2:19; Divine Pattern for Man: Matt 5:48; 1 John 2:6.

marital image so that conversion became a moment of sexual consummation in the spiritual bridal chamber (so *Gos. Phil.* 64; 70; 82; *Gos. Thom.* 22).[27]

Particularly impressive is the fact that the Christian's relationship with God is compared to the sexual union of spouses. While this on the one hand indicates that there is no biblical detraction of sound sexuality, it also points out how deep the intimacy is that God intends to establish between him and his church, with respect to the individual believer.

> We speak God's wisdom in a *mystery*, the hidden wisdom which God predestined before the ages to our glory; the wisdom which none of the rulers of this age has understood; for if they had understood it they would not have crucified the Lord of glory; but just as it is written, 'things which eye has not seen and ear has not heard, and which have not entered the heart of man, all that God has prepared for those who love him.' For to us God revealed them *through the Spirit*; for the Spirit searches all things, *even the depths of God*. For who among men knows the thoughts of a man except the spirit of the man which is in him? Even so *the thoughts of God no one knows except the Spirit of God. Now we have received*, not the spirit of the world, but *the Spirit who is from God, so that we may know the things freely given to us by God*, which things we also speak, not in words taught by human wisdom, but in those *taught by the Spirit, combining spiritual thoughts with spiritual words*. . . . For 'who has known the mind of the Lord, that he will instruct him?' But *we have the mind of Christ*. 1 Cor 2:7-16; (my italics).

III.2 The Literal Level (Husband-Wife): Toward a Sound Foundation

Throughout the few biblical incidents dealing with different aspects of "marriage," or rather the significance of the "one flesh" union, there is basically only one important train of thought continually reoccurring: the Edenic foundation—"to this creational reality is traced the institution of marriage as its sole appropriate expression ([Gen] 2:24)."[28] The largest text on what we nowadays call "marriage" is the description of Gen 2:18-25, while the few other texts dealing with instructions touching this pattern always point back to this instance. Jesus states this most clearly by referring to "the beginning," "the creation," and "he who created" (Matt 19:4; Mark 10:6) while additionally quoting the LXX on Gen 1:27 and 2:24; and Paul again refers to what Jesus said (1 Cor 7:10).

---

27. Loader, *LXX, Sexuality, and NT*, 109-10; on the "mystery" of marriage in the gospel of Philip see further Pagels, "Mystery of Marriage," 442-54. On a brief survey of Gnostic ideas about Gen 2:24 see Schnackenburg, *Epheser*, 260-61; Lincoln, *Ephesians*, 362, 382-83; Lincoln, "OT in Ephesians," 34-35; cf. Barth, *Ephesians 4-6*, 728-29, 740-41 (esp. concerning Eph 5:30-32).

28. Beale and Carson, *NT Use*, 197.

According to Gen 2:18 ("it is not good for the man to be alone"), the "one flesh" covenant ideal is a gift for all humankind, and compliance with its norms and purposes (vv. 19–25) is essential for every marital relationship. These norms are given "from the beginning" (Matt 19:4; Mark 10:6) by the creating God and, in New Testament times, reaffirmed by the one "in whom all things were created" (Col 1:16; cf. John 1:3, 10; Heb 1:2) and in whom "all the fullness of deity dwells in bodily form" (Col 2:9)—Jesus Christ, the Son of God. Since solely Gen 2:18–25 originally describes the divine ideal of marriage, it becomes evident that some modern Christian perceptions cherish cultural traditions and norms that are not given in the biblical text. This will now be addressed in the subsequent sections.

III.2.1 Significance and Responsibility of Sexuality

Sexuality means power (1 Cor 6:12; 7:4), it means becoming "yoked" to someone (Matt 19:6; Mark 10:9)—and this bond should ideally not be "unequal" (i.e., marriages of persons with different faiths) thus impairing the Christian's relationship with God (2 Cor 6:14–18). There is no careless or indifferent dealing with matters of sexuality, for it inherently contains the power to create a structure of dependency and mastery—be it for good or for evil. Marriage was originally meant to foster one's good ambitions in being loyal to the creator of man and marriage (cf. 1 Cor 7:16), for seeking salvation and being saved through the human-divine covenant that is even symbolized by that same institution of marriage. As was summarized at the end of the investigation on the Genesis creation account and its "Edenic ideal," there are altogether eight steps that represent the perfect marriage model: (1) Realizing the need of a partner (Gen 2:19–20); (2) the partner should be a real counterpart, complement, and helper (Gen 2:18, 23); (3) he/she should be created by God;[29] and (4) they should be brought together by divine intervention/providence (Gen 2:22).[30] If that is the case, further steps are: (5) leaving; (6) cleaving; and (7) becoming "one flesh" (Gen 2:24), not to be separated unless (8) God intervenes again (by the death of the spouse). Steps 5–7 are not to be made first; yet, they make up the final consummation on basis of the foregoing conditions (1–4). Hence, the following remarks about the responsibility of sex necessarily include at least the "preparatory steps" of "leaving" and "cleaving,"

---

29. Correspondingly, in the world after Eden, it would be anyone accepting God as his or her creator, being loyal to him. According to 2 Cor 5:17 this particularly applies to the "new creation" of Christian rebirth, as was argued in more detail above (see "Marriage as Image for the Plan of Redemption").

30. This "one flesh" union should be obtained by divine effort ("for love is as strong as death, passion is as severe as sheol; its flashes are flashes of fire, *the very flame of the Lord*;" Song 8:6); "so they are no longer two, but one flesh. What therefore God has joined together, let no man separate" (Matt 19:6). For a detailed story depicting the effort of "the angel of God" leading spouses together see Gen 24, especially vv. 7, 44, 50.

which are requisite for the relationship to grow and develop until its "finalization" through becoming "one flesh."[31]

III.2.1.1 Consummation of Marriage

Considering the aforementioned spiritual concepts, it is not surprising that marriage is one of the most personal and intimate affairs entrusted to humans. Just as conversion and becoming a newborn Christian are the most intimate and personal experiences resulting in a deep experience and knowledge of God, creating a soteriological "one spirit" (1 Cor 6:17) and even (spiritual) "one flesh" (Eph 5:30–32) union with Christ, so the creating and establishing act of Gen 2:18-25 is an equally personal experience.[32] It generally knows nothing about an institutionalization of marriage, of certain procedures or necessary rituals.[33]

---

31. This is just to explain clearly that I do not share the opinion that mere sexuality makes up an ideal "marriage." While it indeed represents the final consummation of the "one flesh" union, the other preceding steps are not to be omitted. Otherwise the biblical ideal is again marred.

32. Just as a short note on the contemporary understanding of how to consummate the one flesh-marriage union even in the times of the Gnostic gospel of Philip (late 3rd cent.): "No one will be able to know when a man joins with his wife except the two of them alone." (81:35) It is further described as "hidden . . . in darkness and night [. . . in] the bedchamber." *Gos. Phil.* 81:35—82:26; cf. Pagels, "Mystery of Marriage," 451.

33. This might be confirmed by a simple story about the wedding of Jacob in Gen 29:21-25: Jacob followed the cultural procedures to marry Rachel, but was deceived and thus had sexual intercourse with Leah. Although he followed the required procedures (the amount of work to fulfill in order to gain his wife and the final wedding meal) with Rachel in mind (and most likely even with her participation), in fact, he was wedded only to the woman he had (unintentionally and deceitfully!) had sexual contact with, and that was irreversible. The next wedding to Rachel is finally reduced to its simple, essential core: "Jacob went in to Rachel also" (וַיָּבֹא גַּם אֶל־רָחֵל; v. 30). There are no hints at all to recognize any "Hochzeitszeremonie" in Gen 2:24 as, e.g., Hasel, "Eheverständnis," 19, 23 presupposes. However, he admits that there is no "spezielle Form der Eheschließung in der Bibel," except the fact that the customs required an official character to guarantee legal security. Ibid., 30; cf. pp. 23, 36. Of course, Gen 2:24 contains covenantal language and represents a covenant; but there is definitely nowhere any (official) procedure required (against ibid., 26–27, 38; Domanyi, "Anthropologie und Ethik," 243–45, 252). So Rock, "Marriage and Family," 725 explains that "Scriptures nowhere prescribe or even describe a model marriage ceremony . . . ." The only "witnesses" mentioned as part of the marriage are (1) the parents who recognize the leaving; (2) husband and wife who are joined and become "one flesh;" (3) God who has joined them (cf. Mal 2:14). These are very intimate, personal processes, which will, of course, be recognized by their surrounding "social network"—yet this official recognition or any invented procedure is no prerequisite to regard them as married in the sense of Gen 2:24! Note also Fischer, "Primat," 352 about Luther's understanding of marriage as a basis for the perception of the Protestant church: "Soviel ist jedenfalls klar, daß das eheliche Leben nicht durch die Rechtsform der Ehe begründet wird und daß dasjenige, worin es für Luther begründet ist, nämlich die Erkenntnis des Glaubens, die Rechtsform der Ehe auch nicht voraussetzt. Denn das Wissen, daß dies der Mensch ist, den Gott mir an die Seite gestellt hat, wird nicht durch das Standesamt vermittelt. . . . Eheliches Leben, wie Luther es beschreibt, kann es daher grundsätzlich auch in einer nichtehelichen Lebensgemeinschaft geben." For Martin Luther the distinguishing quality of the marital life in contrast to harlotry is "daß ein Ehemann gewiß sei und sagen könne: das Weib hat mir Gott gegeben, bei der soll ich wohnen . . . ." Ibid.—thus supporting the marital "sign" of living together as mentioned in 1 Pet 3:7;

> Neither Gen 2 nor Eph 5 contains the materials for a legalistic casuistry which by definition would exclude a variety of marriage types as they have developed in the past and may still emerge in different cultural settings. Paul and the Gen 2 passage leave the door open for necessary changes, eventual progress, and the enactment of change and progress by reformations or courageous new experiments—if only the grace of God and the gift of freedom and responsibility remain fundamental—so that the solidity of marriage and the joy of those married shall not be exposed to neglect and contempt. God himself protects the freedom and steadfastness of love.[34]

Although certain cultural features are from time to time mentioned in the Scriptures (but altogether extremely seldom), it is conspicuous that we nowhere find the least hints concerning necessary rites making a marriage "real," "full," or "legal."[35] In fact, "[es] findet sich an keiner Stelle des Alten Testaments eine ausführliche Darstellung einer Eheschließung oder gar eine Lehre von der Ehe."[36] "Scriptures nowhere prescribe or even describe a model marriage ceremony . . . ."[37] Marriage is nowhere regulated, neither is divorce; both are just mentioned and dealt with concerning special cases and cultural conditions.

> In New Testament times and through most of recorded history, they [i.e., the three steps of Gen 2:24] were the only requirements for a valid marriage. Neither the Old nor the New Testament prescribes any kind of ceremony and the modern-day ceremonies required by law are a comparatively recent innovation. . . . When Isaac married Rebecca, he did so by the simple expedient of moving her into his tent and commencing married life . . . it may be instructive to remember that the Bible does not lay down any procedural requirements at all. It distinguishes between marriages and casual sexual encounters by virtue of the three characteristics referred to in Genesis, namely the creation of a separate household, the permanence of the relationship and the 'becoming one flesh.'[38]

---

1 Cor 7:12–13. Cf. also Joestel and Schorlemmer, *Luther und die Ehe*, 11, about Luther stating that "beide im Grunde ihres Herzens so gesinnt sind, daß sie gerne immer beieinander bleiben wollen in rechter ehelicher Treue, [. . .]; die zwei sind gewiß vor Gott verehelicht."

34. Barth, *Ephesians 4–6*, 749–50.

35. Fischer, "Primat," 354–55, further explains: "Um ein eheliches Leben führen zu können, bedarf es keiner rechtsgültigen Eheschließung. Zwei Menschen können—in Luthers Worten ausgedrückt—»ehelich sein«, ohne eine Ehe zu führen. . . . Läßt sich gleichwohl sagen, daß die rechtsgültig geschlossene Ehe einen Primat vor der nicht rechtsgültig geschlossenen ehelichen Gemeinschaft hat? Man wird dies nicht generell sagen können . . . . Konstitutiv für das eheliche Leben ist nicht das Standesamt, sondern der Glaube und die spezifische Erkenntnis, mit der dieser [i.e., Luther] das Wesen des ehelichen Lebens erkennt."

36. Niebergall, *Ehe und Eheschliessung*, 1; cf. ibid., 233: ". . . keine Zeremonie vorgesehen." On later Jewish ceremonies see pp. 24–30, 47–51.

37. Rock, "Marriage and Family," 725.

38. Crispin, *Divorce*, 13.

Although different cultures knew their own procedures, including the one Israel and the early Christians lived in,[39] according to the Scriptural evidence there remains solely one simple assertion that explains apparently everything that makes up the marital bond: "For this reason a man leaves his father and his mother, and is joined to his woman; and they become one flesh." Gen 2:24. This verse contains everything that needs to be said about marriage, and everything that constitutes the indissoluble, monogamous, lifelong bond that ecclesiologically even comprises so many soteriological aspects. Therefore it was just this verse that Jesus pointed to and emphasized as the true hallmark of marriage. There simply are no references or even commandments about necessary wedding procedures within the OT or NT that would perhaps be required in order to confirm a legal marital relationship. These are a product of the later church history.[40]

---

39. Similarly, Lehmann, "Kirchliche Feier," 271 about the marriage customs today: "Es stimmt, dass die Durchführung der Eheschließung stark von der Gesellschaft geprägt wird, in deren Umfeld sie stattfindet. Man heiratet nicht in allen Ländern auf die gleiche Art und Weise." And that further differed, of course, in the various times of the past. Hence, we must be careful not to make our own, temporary rules a normative, putatively "holy" standard.

40. Leslie and Korman, *Social Context*, 159–60 further explicate concerning the early Christian church and the introduction of procedures in church history: "The [early NT] church did not immediately take positions on marriage and divorce. It did not develop its own wedding ceremonies. It continued to accept the Roman ideas of marriage and divorce as private matters and sought to express its ideals within the framework of Roman law and customs. . . . Not until the ninth century was marriage within the church firmly established." Grubbs provides additional evidence concerning procedures that perhaps already existed at the end of the second and the beginning of the third century AD: "Occasionally we can get glimpses from stray remarks in apologetic or doctrinal literature. The arranged marriage preceded by betrothal seems to have been customary among Christians in the Empire, as it was among non-Christians. Tertullian implies that among Christians in Carthage (and probably elsewhere in the West), both nuptial and dotal contracts were drawn up, and betrothal rites (*sponsalia*) were marked by the exchange of a kiss and the clasping of hands. Interestingly, he also suggests more than once that men chose their own wives (rather than having their marriages arranged by their parents) and that sexual attraction, or at least approval of a prospective wife's physical appearance, was a determining factor. Tertullian also reproached Christian parents for marrying off their daughters at a later age than was customary among pagans. . . . Christian inscriptions from Rome (dating from the mid-third through the sixth century) indicate that in late antiquity Christian woman did tend to marry in their late teens, somewhat later than in pre-Christian Rome." Grubbs, "'Pagan' and 'Christian' Marriage," 388–89 (italics given). Since some Christians desired the special blessing of their church leaders, it became customary in some regions by the end of the fourth century, but initially there has not been such practice, and especially not as mandatory requirement. Generally Christians consented to the traditional procedures of their province, but rejected any customs of idolatry. "To judge from the prescriptions made by church leaders regarding the behavior of their flocks, it appears that many Christians were all to ready to accept traditional pagan wedding rites, including drunken carousing and serenading of newlyweds with obscene songs." Ibid., 389. The official procedures obviously depended solely on cultural customs (as was similarly the case within Judaism: Greenberg, "Jewish Tradition," 13–15) instead of (nonexistent) scriptural ordinances: "It needs to be remembered that within the world of the first century c.e. marriage was primarily a contractual relationship. Although usually accompanied by some form of feast, it was a contractual agreement, and not any further legal or religious ceremony, that constituted a marriage." Lincoln, *Ephesians*, 363. "Die Kirchengeschichte scheint diese Position zu bestätigen, da die religiöse Form der Eheschließung recht spät entstand und von der Reformation in Frage gestellt wurde." Lehmann, "Kirchliche Feier," 271; (see for a short

> In biblical terms one is married if one has a permanent relationship with a member of the opposite sex which involves living with him or her in the manner described in Genesis 2:24. One is divorced if that relationship terminates other than by death. There is simply no room for any kind of intermediate ground.[41]

Traditions usually grant a certain measure of secureness, of familiar patterns to categorize and judge social behaviour. These traditions, of course, also emerged in ancient Judaism, declaring what is right and wrong about marriage. Questions like what has to be done to consummate marriage, to rightly continue it, or to dissolve it have been settled in numerous ways by various ancient commentators on the Mosaic text. Shortly after the early Christian church's establishment and Jesus' appeal to go beyond man-made standards for the purpose of rediscovering the divine, Edenic norms, man has again introduced several traditions. Fisher rightly asserts that it is a "tiefsitzendes Missverständnis" ("deeply rooted misunderstanding/misapprehension") to think that "die Ehe im standesamtlichen Eheschluß begründet ist. Dieser Meinung ist vom evangelischen Eheverständnis her zu widersprechen."[42] Biblically, marriage is consummated when both partners become "one flesh"—independent of any human authority except the free will and decision of both man and woman who jointly take the steps of Gen. 2 as mentioned above.

If the state's government (cf. Rom 13:1–7; Titus 3:1; 1 Pet 2:13–14) does not require an official certificate as requisite for living together as a married couple, the Bible, basically, does not condemn those who faithfully dwell together—they are even precisely described as being under the marital bond: "If she consents to living together with him, he shall not send her away; . . . if he consents to living together with her, she shall not send away the man." 1 Cor 7:12–13.[43] It evidently is not according to Paul's instructions to recommend separation in cases of the nowadays so called "concubinage" (cohabiting without an official marriage document), which apparently pertains to the realm Paul is dealing with in 1 Cor 7:12–13.[44] To demand separation of con-

---

summary of the development and purpose of marriage rites in church history also ibid., 274–80). Since Jesus and Paul only trace marriage back to its introduction in paradise as the only standardizing biblical evidence, we must assume that ceremonies for them have been of less (actually even of no) importance and belonged only to the realm of "being in subjection to the governing authorities" (Rom 13:1; cf. Titus 3:1; 1 Pet 2:13–14).

41. Crispin, *Divorce*, 17.

42. Fischer, "Primat," 357.

43. Kovar, "Konkubinat," 151 only mentions the frequency of the Greek verb γαμίζω ("marry") in 1 Cor 7 without investigating the possibly differing understanding thereof (compared to today), as it is pointed out in vv. 12–13 (cf. 1 Pet 3:7). The only element mentioned in these texts that constitutes a marriage is the mutual, obliging agreement to live together and to have a sexual relationship (vv. 2–9).

44. At this place, the instance of Jesus speaking to the woman at Jacob's well should briefly be mentioned. John 4:16–18 is sometimes referred to as a text proving that Jesus rebukes her of having a "man" who is not her "husband" (v. 18). However, the Greek ἀνήρ can mean both, "man" and "husband;" therefore the text is at least unclear regarding this interpretation. But what makes Jesus' remark all the more interesting, and contradicts the previous idea, is the emphasis of the "*your* [husband]" (σου) in

cubinage is equal to demanding divorce, for "marriage" is constituted by becoming "one flesh"—at least when considering the scanty biblical evidence.[45] And this "one flesh" union is declared indissoluble by Jesus himself; only the unfaithful spouse is able to break it by committing πορνεία, thus concretely destroying the "one flesh" union through prohibited sexuality. The church, however, has no right to demand separation, estimating her own traditions higher than the simple verse of Gen 2:24 and the few instructions of Jesus and Paul concerning the concept of becoming "one flesh" to establish marriage.

These conclusions may not be used, of course, against governmental laws which indeed may require certain procedures and certificates to grant the marital status. Following Paul's argumentation in Rom 13:1–7 (cf. Titus 3:1; 1 Pet 2:13–14), Christians should always seek to live an exemplary live and therefore should heed the national laws. This study is focusing on the pure biblical view—and that does actually not require any procedure at all. But if the government does, Christians are to obey. If the state does not, pastors are not standing on biblical ground if they not only recommend

---

the Greek text; cf. Hasel, "Eheverständnis," 36/fn.82; Köstenberger, *John*, 153; apparently overlooked by Kovar, "Konkubinat," 145. That means: Jesus does not rebuke her of not being officially married, but of having a man who is not *hers*—but (most probably) married to someone *else*. It seems there is only one further reference that sometimes is put forward (see again ibid., 151–52; Hasel, "Eheverständnis," 36) to argue that sexuality without official procedures is per se sinful (even for a betrothed couple): The relationship of Mary and Joseph in Matt 1:18–25. It is explained that Joseph and Mary had no sexual relations, for she is called a virgin when becoming pregnant through the Holy Spirit. That is right, and it seems also clear that the Jewish culture of this time basically demanded virginity until the official marriage procedures were over (see *m. Ketub.* 5:2; *b. Ketub.* 7b; cf. Kovar, "Konkubinat," 152; Neusner, *Law of Women*, 266; Strack and Billerbeck, *Talmud und Midrasch*, 1:45–47; Ilan, "Premarital Cohabitation," 259). It is to be considered, however, that Judaism brought up many different customs, which are not divinely ordained simply because they emerged within Judaism! While Christians argue (as Jesus did) against many Jewish inventions that misrepresent God's original plans and ideals, it is inconsequent to accept this custom without clear biblical support, simply because it is mentioned. Especially since Jesus himself explains official divorce to be invalid, because it does not fit the Edenic ideal of Gen 2:24—although Deut 24:1 could have supported the contrary position! It is not proper to take a simple description of a couple (even when the man is called "righteous;" Matt 1:19) and make it prescription, a normative example. Furthermore, it is clear that the moral standards even in this respect in ancient Judaism were not unequivocal, as is to be seen in *y. Ketub.* 1:5, 25c (see about these texts and their interpretation esp. pp. 261–62, 264) and by the fact that cohabitation before marriage occurred even within the Jewish society. Ibid., 247–64; cf. also Lewis, *Greek Papyri*, 130. Jesus in his discussion about divorce makes clear that it is the becoming of "one flesh" that constitutes marriage, and therefore it can only be the breaking of this "one flesh" union through adultery/sexual immorality (Matt 5:32; 19:9), which dissolves it. Procedures evidently are worthless.

45. The brief and deficient argument of Ryrie, "Biblical Teaching," 179, pointing to the fact that the Old Testament sometimes distinguishes between "wives" and "concubines" (1) fails to explain the missing hint in the Genesis institution of marriage (Gen 2:18–25), (2) disregards the cultural requirements prevailing in the OT times allowing to have "wives" of different estimation (first and secondary wives or "Haupt- und Nebenfrauen" as German versions translate the Hebrew פִּלֶגֶשׁ "concubine") (cf. Gen 22:24; 25:6; 35:22; 36:12; Judg 8:31; 19:passim; 20:4–6; 2 Sam 3:7; 5:13; 15:16; 16:21–22; 19:6; 20:3; 21:11; 1 Kgs 11:3; 1 Chr 1:32; 2:46, 48; 3:9; 7:14; 2 Chr 11:21; Esth 2:14; Song 6:8–9 [; Ezek 23:20]) not at all void of legal recognition and "marital" care, and (3) overlooks completely the contrasting laws of Exod 22:16–17 and Deut 22:28–29 (more about these instances on the next pages).

but *demand* certain rites that are definitely only human invention—even though they may be reasonable and good (and I am personally convinced they are in most cases).

III.2.1.2 Social Security and Protection

There is, however, a concrete biblical precept demanding some kind of a preparatory "ceremony" or official recognition as basis of marriage which should be heeded before marrying by becoming "one flesh." This is the law of Exod 22:16-17 which demonstrates that social protection (in Mosaic times by paying a dowry) is divinely demanded. This function is nowadays usually fulfilled through an official, legal wedding. It grants legal protection and security in cases of divorce or premature death of the "breadwinner"—and this, in fact, is divinely commanded.[46] In order to understand these two different principles, (1) social security as basis of (2) marriage, which are mostly merged today through legal wedding, it is necessary to have a closer look at the most interesting and instructive texts dealing with cases of what is nowadays called "premarital" intercourse.

The most frequently cited text of Deut 22:13-21 (on blaming one's newly wedded wife of not being a virgin) is, actually, not speaking about a couple that did not wait until the official procedures were over and the wedding night came. This text in Deut 22 unambiguously speaks about indulging in "harlotry" (זָנָה; v. 21), since she previously had sex with some other man—and not with the one she married. That is, of course, harlotry. It is right that "the law here encourages premarital sexual purity and the value of sexual abstinence prior to marriage"[47]—but it actually does not speak about a virgin couple having sexual relations prior to any official procedures. It only speaks about the immoral case of a spouse who has had sexual contacts before with someone else than his or her current partner that he/she is about to wed. And that, indeed, is harlotry, for it injures the Edenic ideal of two spouses having no other partners before or after their first becoming "one flesh" (at least, of course, until one of the partners died—but, naturally, death was not part of sinless Eden).

But there is another situation described and regulated, which is really appropriate for what we today understand as "premartial" intercourse (a couple having sex before legal wedding). In Exod 22:16-17 we read: "And if a man seduces a virgin who is not engaged, and lies with her, he must pay a dowry for her to be his wife. If her father absolutely refuses to give her to him, he shall pay money equal to the dowry for virgins." It is interesting to realize that in this case the couple will not be punished—they

---

46. So what this chapter is aiming at should not be misunderstood as breaking down protective cultural elements like an official wedding. The object is just to give these cultural "instruments" the right meaning (as a social protection) and to point out that marriage, in its inner core and its pure biblical meaning, cannot be consummated through rites or by signing certificates—just as divorce cannot (at least not in any case) be sanctioned through simply signing a corresponding declaration by human authorities.

47. Christensen, *Deuteronomy 21:10—34:12*, 522.

are not called sinners, their act is not described as "harlotry," and they do not have to die.[48] Yet, the man was obliged to care for the social security of his "wife" by paying a dowry—a very important instrument in the sinful and unstable world outside of Eden to guarantee a livelihood for the wife if the spouses would divorce in the future or the husband as the "breadwinner" would die prematurely. Corresponding to the responsibility involved in sexual intercourse as creating a new "one flesh" union, the man is no more allowed simply to leave her behind. The biblical text of Exod 22 regards them as a newly established marital unit; it does not esteem them transgressors of God's moral principles or laws—but, however, as having disregarded a reasonable, protective precaution demanded to protect this fragile union in a dangerous, sinful world.[49]

The text says that "if her father absolutely refuses to give her to him" both are released from this partnership, but the man still has to pay the dowry—another witness to the fact that this single sexual encounter was indeed sufficient to be regarded as consuming a marriage between both partners.[50] Besides, there is no reference to widows, divorcées, or any other non-virgin women. It seems that these, being independent from their parental home, consequently could not claim a refusal through parental authority afterwards. In such cases, apparently, neither of the partners had the right to withdraw from the responsibilities incurred by sexual intercourse, since both partners were of age, and not under the patriarchal authority of a virgin's father.[51]

Interestingly, the father's behavior in Exod 22:17 is implicitly disapproved by stressing that he "*absolutely* refused" (מָאֵן יְמָאֵן) to give his consent—such behavior is apparently unreasonable and unadvisable in such cases.[52] Furthermore, the emphasis of the

---

48. Unfortunately, Hasel refers to Exod 22:16–17 (see Hasel, "Eheverständnis," 26, 32) without investigating it, and so concludes in the opposite direction (similarly Kovar, "Konkubinat," 143). Of course, Exod 22:16–17 deals with a non-ideal situation, but it does not interfere with the simple steps of Gen 2:24.

49. Stuart draws the reader's attention to the couple's responsibility in regard to property and compensation, for they obviously had made no provisions. He emphasizes that "almost any bypassing of arranged marriage betrothal requirements ... were designed not only to compensate the bride's family properly but to ensure a proper marriage and a proper start for a marriage." Stuart, *Exodus*, 509. Durham, *Exodus*, 327 also recognizes the law's "primary focus is financial."

50. As Propp, *Exodus 19–40*, 253 understands it, the dowry in this passage could alternatively (or as well) be understood as a recompensation for the woman's virginity. However, it must not be perceived as some kind of punishment.

51. As is also to be witnessed in the rabbinic traditions, they are clearly considered a married couple—and dissolving the partnership would therefore even require an official bill of divorce. Cf. *m. Qidd.* 1:1; Isaksson, *Marriage and Ministry*, 40–41; Ilan, "Premarital Cohabitation," 256; Kirchhoff, *Sünde*, 163–65. For an ancient document (dated August 131 AD) witnessing that a Jewish couple "officially" lived together even before their marriage contract was drawn up see Ilan, "Premarital Cohabitation," 247–64.

52. This construction of the verbal infinitive absolute with the finite verb form thereof, both even as piel (!), is a very strongly emphasis of the father's action and apparently denotes a divine disapproval of this behavior, for it seems to be unreasonable and inappropriate. Nevertheless, the father evidently still has the right to decide for his daughter, since she was still under his authority, and God respects this important patriarchal role. Apparently in this context we have to interpret the cases of

man's act of "seducing" (פִּתָּה) bears a negative connotation, for the Hebrew פִּתָה denotes an act of changing another one's will in favor of a certain thing or person by persuasion, enticement, or deception.⁵³ Thus it also becomes clear why this text is placed right at the end of a large passage dealing with compensations for negligent or deliberate loss of another one's property (Exod 21:33—22:17): the father of Exod 22:16-17 has been cheated out of his daughter's virginity by the seducer's deceptive efforts and thus might have lost the opportunity to find a better husband for his daughter. That the (possibly angry) father, therefore, may tend to refuse to give his consent to this partnership is thus better understandable, although the double piel construction all the more indicates that the father's behavior, nonetheless, is inappropriate; viz., the man actually "acquired" the virgin through sex,⁵⁴ as is further pointed out in the very similar case of Deut 22:28-29.⁵⁵ Another reason for the negative overtone of this case law concerning the term "seduction" may be derived from the fact that by this seemingly hasty and probably thoughtless

---

rape in Gen 34 and 2 Sam 13, which also required the parental approval although both partners have already had sex.

53. Cf. BDAG s.v. פָּתָה.

54. Please note the law on rape in Deut 22:25-26: "But if in the field the man finds the girl who is engaged, and the man forces her and lies with her, then only the man who lies with her shall die. But you shall do nothing to the girl; there is no sin in the girl worthy of death, for just as a man rises against his neighbor and murders him, so is this case." The rationale on the sentence elucidating that "just as a man rises against his neighbor and murders him, so is this case" is meaningful. The following law concerning an unbetrothed virgin indicates that a marital relationship was created between both by sex, but it will be annulled due to the violence involved (see below; Deut 22:28-29). Also, this law concerning a betrothed virgin indicates that sex created a marital bond, for the rationale points to the fact that the bond to her future "husband" is now broken since he is "as if murdered"—killed by the rapist. Therefore, the rapist has to die, and the illegitimate marital relationship created through violent sex is thus again dissolved, leaving the young woman free to "remarry" whom she wishes. It is also important to recognize that she is not prohibited from marrying the one she was betrothed to before (as could be argued from Deut 24:1-4), for she has not been divorced from him, but he figuratively "died"—she is not a figuratively "divorced" woman, but a "widow." Thus, the case law of Deut 24:1-4 does not apply and she really goes out free—without sin and without any restrictions concerning her future marriage.

55. There it reads, "If a man finds a girl who is a virgin, who is not engaged, and seizes her and lies with her and they are discovered, then the man who lay with her shall give to the girl's father fifty shekels of silver, and she shall become his wife because he has violated her; he cannot divorce her all his days." (Deut 22:28-29) It is unlikely and unreasonable, however, to assume that the father has the right of refusal in cases of seduction which, after all, resulted in mutual consent on the couple's part, but has no right to protect his daughter from being bound lifelong to a rapist. In fact both texts (Exod 22:16-17 and Deut 22:28-29) are almost identical, the only difference is that the force of seduction changed into violence. Both texts are clear on the man's responsibility, while Deut 22:29 emphasizes that the woman has the right never to be divorced; thus, the man's responsibility now is even greater— just as his "seductive force" was stronger, even violent. It is not stated, however, that the virgin's father is unable to refuse the partnership and the close similarity to the law on seduction may indicate that this right is presupposed (overlooked by e.g., Frymer-Kensky, "Law and Philosophy," 94)—hence, the law solely deals with the man's duty, not with the father's rights. Furthermore, it is not stated that the woman would have no right to divorce. It seems this law is, again, aiming at the protection of abused women, who now could choose between (1) being married to a man who (hopefully only once) used force, or (2) to divorce from this man while having "earned" a very generous livelihood through the considerable amount of silver he had to pay as a dowry.

act the couple may have skipped some of the first six steps (those required in preparation of seventh—becoming "one flesh") given in the Edenic model presented above.

So on the one hand it is generally right to agree with other commentators finding that it is only the element of sexual intercourse which is the "sign" of the marriage covenant and what therefore is able to represent the marriage's consummation or "ratification:"

> Sexual intercourse functions as the sign of the covenant of marriage whether or not other formal, legal undertakings have been completed. In other words, sexual intercourse makes a couple 'one flesh' or married *virtually* even if not legally and properly (as Paul contends in 1 Cor 6:16). Thus a couple who have engaged in sexual intercourse before marriage are 'as if' married, and the bride price is due the woman's family whether or not they are finally allowed to get married.[56]

On the other hand, however, we lear from Exod 22:16–17 that God demands to make provisions beforehand. Responsibilities must be considered seriously, social protection/security is divinely demanded. There definitely is no room for a careless dealing with sexuality. It involves large responsibilities actually influencing the whole person (1 Cor 6:16–17) and "yoking" (Matt 19:6; Mark 10:9) two persons indissolubly together as a couple under the Edenic covenant (Gen 2:24). Before daring to take this far-reaching step, the couple must follow the divine instruction to care for their social security, as given in ancient times through a dowry, nowadays in most countries through legal wedding.

III.2.1.3 Summary and Final Considerations

It is not true that "it is an ill-service not only to marriage but to humanity to play down this *consensus* in order to play up *concubitus*. Without the vow the covenant is not made; without this, other bonds are counterfeit."[57] The distinguishing quality of marriage is not a vow, there is not even a single vow at least mentioned in the entire Bible as an element to constitute marriage.[58] Vows occurred often in different affairs and the most common alliances were frequently affirmed by holy promises. Not so with marriage. Marriage is constituted by much more than a simple *declaration*. It is consummated by the only *act* involving the couple's whole personality (body and spirit)—through sexuality, adequately providing a "formal sign" (cf. Deut 22:17: the garment) and the most holy witness ever possible (see Mal 2:14: Yahweh himself).[59]

56. Stuart, *Exodus*, 509; italics given; cf. also pp. 483–84.

57. Dunstan, "The Marriage Covenant," 248; italics given.

58. The attempts of Brueggemann, "Flesh and Bone," 532–42 or Hugenberger, *Covenant*, 216–39 to find vows in Gen 2:23–24 are completely unconvincing.

59. Again, when accepting the hint I have mentioned within the section about the wider biblical context of Gen 2:24 and its "covenantal aspects," there is another significant sign given, the "blood of

Consequently, when declaring certain vows and/or traditional rites to be necessary requirements, the responsibility and far-reaching impact of sex as the only instrument creating a corporate body is lost sight of. Hence, it rather "is an ill-service not only to marriage but to humanity to play down" the responsibility of those engaging in sexual relations. Simply having sex with someone and then leaving him or her behind is impermissible divorce in its truest, Jewish-Christian sense; and afterwards "officially" marrying someone else is rightly called "harlotry/fornication" (זָנָה; Deut 22:21). Demanding separation of "concubinage" actually is, therefore, an invitation to divorce, and not just an invitation to "repent" and leave behind a "sinful" cohabitation. It is my personal conviction that the widespread problems with modern ("premarital") promiscuity are better dealt with when explaining the true biblical view of the far-reaching spiritual consequences of sex, not the inapropriate view of declaring any abstract procedures to be calling forth this significant influence,[60] thus explaining "premarital" intercourse as something to repent of and easily leave behind. In cases of unmarried concubinage, especially concerning incautiously consummated mixed marriages of a Christian with an unbeliever, the instructions of Paul apply ("Let him/her not send away [i.e., separate]" 1 Cor 7:12–15; and if both are Christians: "Do not separate" 1 Cor 7:10), and the command of Exod 22:16–17 has to be heeded.

It is good and reasonable to recommend the heeding of certain procedures for the purpose of demonstrating the official and obliging character of the marital union as well as guaranteeing important (and divinely demanded) social protection for the spouses. To care for social security by cultural means (as, for instance, the dowry mentioned above) must come first. Independent of this, however, it is important to inform about the far reaching spiritual consequences of sex honestly, and thus to help make responsible decisions at an early stage of the relationship—either to become "one flesh" (with all its consequences) or to refuse it in light of the high responsibilities and the everlasting character demonstrated in Gen 2:24 and its New Testament echoes.

This biblical view is necessary to gain the moral strength in withstanding the great amount of sexual temptations presented to humans today. Only when the person understands how far-reaching his or her responsibilities concerning sexuality really are, he/she will have enough strength to resist temptation and wait until the previous steps of Gen 2 (incl. social protection according to Exod 22:16–17) are dependably and faithfully taken. So, finally, the following table should demonstrate the different steps to a full, licit, biblical marriage, including a column with cultural procedures aiming at the protection of wives in a strongly patriarchal society:

---

the covenant" through defloration.

60. Therefore, it seems problematic to introduce terms like "sacrament" or "marriage liturgy" even in protestant churches and evangelical (free) churches in order to emphasize the ecclesiastical "power" concerning the establishing of the marriage covenant.

Edenic Ideal	Doer/Initiator	Cultural Means (Social Recognition/Security)
Realizing the need of a partner	God (man & woman are led and respond)	
Finding a real counterpart, helper, newborn Christian	God (man & woman are led and respond)	
	Man	Parental Agreement & Payment of Dowry
Leaving	Man & Woman	
Cleaving	Man & Woman	
Becoming "One Flesh"	Man & Woman	
	Man	Certificate of Divorce
Dissolution through Death	God	

In Mosaic times, the parental agreement and the payment of a dowry were means to secure the uprightness of the future husband's intentions. The father of the bride could reject the bridegroom's endeavor in case of dubious motives or negative prospects. The requirement of a dowry made it further difficult to thoughtlessly marry a wife—men would naturally be much more careful when a considerable sum must be paid. Furthermore it demonstrated the husband's ability to care for their livelihood. The certificate of divorce, finally, secured a stable, unambiguous social status and reputation for the divorcee, while the dowry would help her to make ends meet until a new husband would be found. Thus it becomes clearer that the function of these few cultural means was to protect women. It has no concrete moral function concerning the Edenic marriage ideal. When the marriage was successful throughout the partners' lives, the cultural procedures were virtually renounceable. Yet, since we live in an insecure, sinful world, no Christian will run the risk to marry without taking the precaution divinely demanded in Exod 22:16–17 and thus caring for a case of failure (divorce) or premature death of the family's provider.

III.2.2 Further Legitimate Reasons for Divorce

As was pointed out within the investigations on Jesus' speech about divorce, it was only the law of Deut 24:1–4 and the obscure עֶרְוַת דָּבָר ("matter of nakedness;" v. 1) that was the subject of the Pharisees' inquiry about divorcing one's wife κατὰ πᾶσαν αἰτίαν ("for any reason;" Matt 19:3). It was "neither . . . intended to cover all possible scenarios"[61] nor to have a discussion about any further aspect of marital life; Jesus consequently focused on the basic practice of the ancient Jews who in fact frequently allowed divorce "for any reason [whatsoever]." There is no comprehensive discussion about problematic conjugal situations. Blomberg rightly emphasized that there are nu-

---

61. Beale and Carson, *NT Use*, 61.

merous instances, particularly in Matthew, where seemingly exceptionless absolutes may certainly not be interpreted thus strictly;[62] these instances are actually mostly even perceived as stressing only a significant theological *principle*, which certainly is not the case with the topic of divorce in our texts. The literary style suggests that Jesus' pronouncement is not meant to represent a law covering everything related with divorce, but it rather represents a response to the prevailing Jewish practice concerning Deut 24:1.

> The climactic focus of the passage will be Jesus' main pronouncement in [Matt 19] v. 9 and it will take the form of proverbial or gnomic truth—a generalization which admits certain exceptions. Mark and Luke do not spell any of these out (Mark 10:11–12; Luke 16:18); Matthew makes clear there is at least one. Few try to make the pronouncements in various other controversy or pronouncement stories absolute (cf. e.g., Matt 19:21; 9:15, and esp. 13:57, a particularly interesting parallel because of its similar exception clause—yet prophets are sometimes without honor away from home or with honor at home), so one should be equally wary of elevating 19:9 (or Mark 10:11–12) into an exceptionless absolute. The casuistic legal form ('whoever...') does not undermine this claim; parallel 'sentences of law' (e.g., Matt 5:22, 27 [f.], 39, 41) also contain implicit qualifiers.[63]

Another example in Paul's writings is further instructive in this context: while Rom 7:1–3 and 1 Cor 7:39 know no divorce, Paul clearly refers to Jesus' instruction about divorce in 1 Cor 7:10 (without mentioning the exception clause), and in v. 15, he finally mentions an exception, even a supplement to the teaching of Christ! In Rom 7:1–3 he evidently concentrates on a theological principle to be employed in favor of his argumentation, he does not intend to develop a theology of marriage or divorce; and even in 1 Cor 7:10–11 he truncates his explanations by referring to the Lord's saying (which he most likely presupposed to be well known) and dwelling solely on the only aspect he wishes to develop in more detail (i.e., here: the ideal of living closely together, "one flesh" as contrary to separation; see the context 1 Cor 7:3–5, 12–14).[64] And in 1 Cor 7:39, even in immediate context of a clearly stated reason for divorce

---

62. Cf. Blomberg, "Exegesis," 162–63; quoted in the indented text below.

63. Blomberg, "Exegesis," 162–63; he refers for further support to Guelich, *Sermon*, 239–52. The texts mentioned by Blomberg deserve quotation: Matt 19:21; ("If you wish to be complete, go and sell your possessions and give to the poor, and you will have treasure in heaven; and come, follow me."); 9:15; 13:57 ("A prophet is not without honor except in his hometown and in his own household."); 5:22 ("But I say to you that everyone who is angry with his brother shall be guilty before the court; and whoever says to his brother, 'You good-for-nothing,' shall be guilty before the supreme court; and whoever says, 'You fool,' shall be guilty enough to go into the fiery hell."); 5:28, 39; 5:41 ("Whoever forces you to go one mile, go with him two"). I like to add the following statement: "If anyone comes to Me, and does not hate his own father and mother and wife and children and brothers and sisters, yes, and even his own life, he cannot be My disciple" (Luke 14:26).

64. On Paul's abbreviated style in these passages and the fact that he presupposed a considerable range of knowledge about marriage cf. also Dunn, *Theology*, 694.

(v. 15), Paul dares simply to utter that husband and wife are bound until death—most evidently truncating the whole story (as already eloquently elucidated in the previous verses) to its simplistic and idealistic core in order to prepare his audience for his final statement about widows. The same has to be assumed in Jesus' speech within the gospels, where Jesus apparently intends to explain the right understanding of the עֶרְוַת דָּבָר of Deut 24:1, focusing on the ideal pattern of marriage as given in Eden, not concentrating on all matters about divorce.[65] He is nowhere (at least not with the necessary clarity) abrogating the few other hints within the Pentateuch pointing to further legitimate reasons of divorce (e.g., Exod 21:10, see below). Besides, another problem would then occur: the problem of Jesus contradicting Moses' instructions, while at the same time claiming: "Do not think that I came to abolish the Law or the Prophets; I did not come to abolish but to fulfill. For truly I say to you, until heaven and earth pass away, not the smallest letter or stroke shall pass from the Law ... " (Matt 5:17–18).

As pointed out within the exegesis on Matt 19 and Mark 10, the situation in which the Pharisees' loaded question is posed further affirms the assumption of understanding Jesus' remark as focusing on Deut 24:1 and not as a complete theology of divorce in general, for

> whatever his [i.e., Jesus] reply, someone stood ready to condemn him. The argument that because Jesus did not here address other possible grounds of divorce such as desertion or wife-beating, he therefore categorically excluded them is thus flawed. He was asked specifically about a man who wished to divorce his wife. Women then as now seldom left their only source of sustenance or beat themselves; desertion and abuse were almost uniquely male offenses. But Jewish law afforded little provision for wives to divorce their husbands, so the Pharisees here do not even raise this issue. The setting makes the occasional nature of Jesus' teaching inescapable."[66]

Correspondingly, I dare to suggest that beside the strictly limited discussion of Jesus with the Pharisees there indeed are further legal, permissible reasons for divorce. By interpreting the עֶרְוַת דָּבָר of Deut 24:1 Jesus affirms the everlasting validity of the Mosaic commandments (cf. Matt 5:17–18; Luke 16:31). He does not abolish the case law of Deut 24:1–4, but he interprets it in light of the Edenic ideal and clearly explains that

---

65. Besides, one finds that the Gospel's viewpoint is (almost) strictly the husband's active dealing with the wife as passive subject. The possibility for a wife to initiate divorce from her husband is, if ever, only indirectly mentioned (cf. Mark 10:12, please remember the textual critique on this instance, which makes it less reliable). Nevertheless, it is hardly reasonable to argue that Jesus' saying is meant only for husbands, simply because of its male perspective, and that it would not be equally applicable to wives. This again demonstrates its abbreviated, occasional character. (See further on the topic of women's rights to divorce esp. Brooten, "Scheidung," 65–80; Schweizer, "Scheidungsrecht," 294–300; Brooten, "Debatte," 466–78; for Palestinian evidence of divorce by the wife: Frankemölle, "Wiederverheiratung," 31–33; similarly Ilan, "Divorce Bill," 195–202.)

66. Blomberg, "Exegesis," 164–65.

it is meant to restrict the Israelite's "hardness of hard" and that such a commandment would never have been necessary if the Edenic ideal had still been the prevailing pattern in Moses' times. Hence, it must be permitted to assume that the laws working for the same purpose (against the Israelite's emotional hardness), by regulating situations of improper hardships in different relationships, may equally apply to the marital bond, the integrity of which is to be protected above any other partnership.

While Deut 24:1–4 is a law concerning a serious misconduct of *wives*, there are, as already mentioned briefly above, also severe laws protecting different people from the misconduct of the *man* they are subjected to. The abuse of his authority would cost the master his slave, if he knocks out only his or her tooth (Exod 21:27). How much more must *free Hebrew wives* have been free to leave their marital "master" (cf. Gen 3:16; Eph 5:22; 1 Pet 3:6) in such cases of domestic violence, for they were meant to enjoy a much higher status and many more rights and privileges than simple (possibly *foreign*) *slaves*; the obligations of the husband are likewise greater (cf. Eph 5:28–29, 33; Lev 19:20).[67]

> Note that the abuse in question is not a simple slap or a raised voiced, but a serious attack. Hebrew scholars suggest that the eye-tooth reference may be a *merism*, that is, a term-set that goes from the greatest to the last. The implication of a *merism* at this location in the text would be that if the contract partner sustains any lasting physical damage, the covenant has been broken . . . we see that the rights of a wife will at least equal those of a slave woman. In fact, logic implies that if a slave may not be beaten seriously, a full wife may not be beaten at all.[68]

It cannot unambiguously be said from the text in Exod 21:26–27 that any "negative, aggressive touching" of a husband against his wife (or the other way around!) would be valid, tangible evidence for divorce. But, at least, it seems clear that any physical damage is sufficient lawful reason to regard the marriage bond as violently broken.

Paul further refers to indispensable obligations (as given in Exod 21:10) in 1 Cor 7:3 when speaking about the "duty" (ὀφειλή) not to refuse sexual intercourse in marriage. The text his teaching is basing on most likely was Exod 21:10–11 speaking about three minimum requirements that had to be guaranteed to a slave wife: (1) food, (2)

---

67. Cf. Instone-Brewer, *In the Bible*, 100–101; Luck, *Divorce and Remarriage*, 35–36, 38–39. As already mentioned, this way of reasoning corresponds to "the most commonly employed" ancient Jewish exegetical technique, the so called "Qal Vahomer" (from minor to major; Instone-Brewer, *Techniques and Assumptions*, 17). For a similar argumentation see Gane, "Old Testament Principles," 55–56; cf. Davidson, "Scheidung und Wiederheirat," 164–65. Note Lev 19:20: "Now if a man lies carnally with a woman who is a slave acquired for another man, but who has in no way been redeemed nor given her freedom, there shall be punishment; they shall not, however, be put to death, because she was not free." This verse demonstrates, even in concrete context of sexual intimacy, that free wives clearly enjoy a better position with more privileges than slave women/wives.

68. Luck, *Divorce and Remarriage*, 35–36.

clothing, and (3) cohabitation/marital intercourse.[69] Without these three basics "she shall go out for nothing" (v. 11). Of course, these three marital rights are not abolished by Jesus' specific answer to the specific question of the Pharisees.[70]

> Although the church forgot the other cause for divorce, every Jew in Jesus' day knew about Exodus 21:10–11, which allowed divorce for neglect. Before rabbis introduced the 'any cause' divorce, this was probably the most common type. Exodus says that everyone, even a slave wife, had three rights within marriage—the rights to food, clothing, and love. If these were neglected, the wronged spouse had the right to seek freedom from that marriage. Even women could, and did, get divorces for neglect—though the man still had to write out the divorce certificate. Rabbis said he had to do it voluntarily, so if he resisted, the courts had him beaten till he volunteered! [. . .]

> Paul taught the same thing. He said that married couples owed each other love (1 Cor 7:3–5) and, material support (1 Cor 7:33–34). He didn't say that neglect of these rights was the basis of divorce because he didn't need to—it was stated on the marriage certificate. Anyone who was neglected, in terms of emotional support or physical support, could legally claim a divorce.[71]

The passage in Exod 21:10–11 referring to a *slave* wife is placed in immediate context to the one mentioned above about releasing *slaves* (v. 27) and further instructions on certain hardships and violence of persons with authority. It is most unlikely

---

69. As investigated above (see "Polygamy as Cultural Digression"), the Hebrew word for "marital intercourse" (עֹנָה) is unclear. It could also mean "oil/ointment/dwelling/cohabitation" without any sexual connotation. The LXX as basis of Paul's reference in 1 Cor 7:3, however, renders the ambiguous Hebrew term as ὁμιλία, meaning a "state of close association of persons" (BDAG s.v. ὁμιλία) and, in the context of the unequivocal interpretation thereof in ancient Judaism as "sexuality" (cf. e.g., Strack and Billerbeck, *Talmud und Midrasch*, 368–72; Domanyi, "Anthropologie und Ethik," 236–37), it may be apparent that Paul speaks about sexuality as a marital duty on the basis of Exod 21:10–11 (thus also Instone-Brewer, "What God has Joined," 29; Luck, *Divorce and Remarriage*, 34). Even in case of rejecting the translation of the Hebrew term as "sexual intercourse," Paul's understanding in 1 Cor 7:3–5 nevertheless supports this perception and, consequently, sexuality as a marital "duty."

70. Similarly Beale and Carson, *NT Use*, 199: "The fact that Jesus says nothing about non-'no-fault' divorces is probably best understood as an acceptance of those grounds as outlined in Exod 21:10–11." The same point is strongly defended by Instone-Brewer, *In the Bible*, 166, 184–87; cf. Instone-Brewer, "What God has Joined," 28–29.

71. Instone-Brewer, "What God has Joined," 28–29. He further explains: "These three rights became the basis of Jewish marriage vows—we find them listed in marriage certificates discovered near the Dead Sea. In later Jewish and Christian marriages, the language became more formal, such as 'love, honor, and keep.' These vows, together with a vow of sexual faithfulness, have always been the basis for marriage. Thus, the vows we make when we marry correspond directly to the biblical grounds for divorce. . . . Jewish couples listed these biblical grounds for divorce in their marriage vows. . . . When these vows were broken, it threatened to break up the marriage. As in any broken contract, the wronged party had the right to say, 'I forgive you; let's carry on,' or, 'I can't go on, because this marriage is broken.'" Ibid., 29. He concludes that "theologians who have long felt that divorce should be allowed for abuse and abandonment may be vindicated. And, more importantly, victims of broken marriages can see that God's law is both practical and loving." Ibid.

that a violation of these stipulations would not have to be equally applied concerning *free wives*, thus covering these further scenarios in that context as well. Deuteronomy 21:14 additionally explains that even a female foreign captive who became a Hebrew man's wife is to be better treated than a slave even when he is not pleased with her anymore. He has to send her away as she desires (וְשִׁלַּחְתָּהּ לְנַפְשָׁהּ). Evidently this foreign captive wife is specially protected by divine instruction; how much more must this apply to a Hebrew wife in contrast to "simple" slaves. It seems reasonable that

> Divorce for neglect included divorce for abuse, because this was extreme neglect. There was no question about that end of the spectrum of neglect, but what about the other end? What about abandonment, which was merely a kind of passive neglect? This was an uncertain matter, so Paul deals with it. He says to all believers that they may not abandon their partners, and if they have done so, they should return (1 Cor 7:10–11). In the case of someone who is abandoned by an unbeliever—someone who won't obey the command to return—he says that the abandoned person is 'no longer bound.'[72]

According to ancient Jewish (rabbinic) law, a wife had the right to demand divorce in cases of domestic violence. Concerning ill-treating one's own wife Amram sums up:

> The opinion of Rabbi Isserles, as reported in Eben Haëzer, Cap. 154, Sec. 3, sums up the ancient Jewish law and its bearing on the question [i.e., wife beating]. He says, 'A man who beats his wife commits a sin, as though he had beaten his neighbor, and if he persists in his conduct the court may castigate him and excommunicate him and place him under oath to discontinue this conduct; if he refuses to obey the order of court, *they will compel him to divorce his wife at once* (though some are of the opinion that he should be warned once or twice) *because it is not customary or proper for Jews to beat their wives; it is a custom of the heathen.* This is the law where he is in fault; but if she curses him or insults his parents, some are of the opinion that he may beat her, and others say even if she is a bad woman he may not beat her; but I am of the first opinion. If it is not known who began the quarrel the husband is not permitted to testify that she was the aggressor; for all women are presumed to be innocent.' To this opinion is appended the opinion of the Rabbi Jacob Weil, that 'he who beats his wife is in greater fault than he who beats his neighbor, for he is not obliged to protect the honor of his neighbor, but he is obliged to protect the honor of his wife; he must honor her more than himself; she rises with him but does not descend with him [*b. Ketub.* 60a]; she was given him as a companion for life and not for misery [*b. Ketub.* 61a], and his punishment for ill-treating her is greater than for ill-treating his neighbor, for she trusts in him and confidingly rests under his roof.'[73]

---

72. Instone-Brewer, "What God has Joined," 29.
73. Amram, *Divorce*, 71–72; my italics. Crispin, *Divorce*, 33 adequately adds: "There is, however,

Domestic violence was a serious offence for the ancient rabbis and naturally resulted in releasing the ill-treated woman. The same could apply in cases of apostasy, when a Hebrew husband forsook his Jewish faith.[74] That is another important remark concerning the instructions of Paul in 1 Cor 7:12–16. If a former Christian spouse radically changed his mind and henceforth denies his former faith, turning into open apostasy and betraying "the heavenly gift" (Heb 6:4), the rules of 1 Cor 7:12–16 apparently apply to him as well. If he wishes to separate, "let him leave" (v. 15).[75]

> For in the case of those who have once been enlightened and have tasted of the heavenly gift and have been made partakers of the Holy Spirit, and have tasted the good word of God and the powers of the age to come, and then have fallen away, it is impossible to renew them again to repentance, since they again crucify to themselves the Son of God and put Him to open shame." (Heb 6:4–6; cf. the rationale in 1 Cor 7:16!)

However, in these further cases of probably permissible, legal divorce, may it be due to

1. πορνεία/עֶרְוַת דָּבָר (Deut 24:1; Matt 5:32; 19:9),

2. permanent, willful (physical) abuse/negligence by withholding "food, clothing, or conjugal rights [i.e., sexuality]" (Exod 21:10–11, 26–27; 1 Cor 7:3–5),[76] or

3. the unbelieving (resp. apostate) spouse's (irreversible) desire to separate (1 Cor 7:15),

the pattern of behavior presented by Yahweh himself should ever be thoroughly considered and preferred. Just as he did not "divorce" Israel at the next best opportunity, but even in case of spiritual πορνεία, of complete abuse of divine regulations, and of Israel's desire to separate itself from God, he did his best to fulfill the purpose of

---

some significance which can be gleaned from the fact that sexual sin is used as a metaphor for unfaithfulness to God. Clearly God was saying through the words recorded in Ezekiel 16 that other sins involved the same breach of faith as adultery. This is precisely what one would expect because sin is simply rebellion against God. It is the fact of that rebellion or lack of faithfulness which is of critical importance rather than the particular form it takes. Equally it is the fact of a serious and persistent violation of faithfulness to the other party which is important. That lack of faithfulness will undermine and ultimately destroy the marriage. It matters not one whit whether that unfaithfulness is reflected in adultery, desertion or violent and cruel behaviour."

74. On these and further reasons of divorce see Amram, *Divorce*, 63–77.

75. "Dabei wird dem heidnischen Partner das Vorrecht der Entscheidung eingeräumt: Will er die Ehe weiterführen, so bleibt sie bestehen; die eventuelle Bereitschaft des christlichen Partners wird nicht angefragt, er hat sich hingegen nach dem Willen des Heiden zu richten." Kirchschläger, *Ehe im NT*, 77.

76. It might be of special interest for those in a Protestant faith tradition that Martin Luther himself recognized sexual neglect as severe "robbery" and denial of one's marital "duty" (cf. 1 Cor 7:3–5), thus justifying legitimate divorce (see Joestel and Schorlemmer, *Luther und die Ehe*, 20–22). And if there has never been a sexual relationship between the spouses, in fact, "es ist vor Gott keine Ehe . . . ." (Ibid., 20.)

marriage by bringing them to salvation (1 Cor 7:16).[77] And even after finally divorcing Israel (Jer 3:8) in order to lead her to repentance, Yahweh still declares: "'Return, faithless Israel,' declares the Lord; 'I will not look upon you in anger. For I am gracious,' declares the Lord; 'I will not be angry forever. . . . Return, O faithless sons, I will heal your faithlessness'" (vv. 12, 22). There is no sin that "uniquely destroys a marriage; restoration always remains the ideal . . . divorce should never be considered unless all other approaches to healing a broken relationship have been exhausted."[78] Divorce is always a most sad defeat; Christians should always seek the victory about any crisis in their marital life, whatever it may be—since marriage is a display of the gospel of Christ's irrevocable faithfulness:

> Staying married, therefore, is not mainly about staying in love. It is about keeping covenant. . . . Therefore, what makes divorce and remarriage so horrific in God's eyes is not merely that it involves covenant-breaking to the spouse, but that it involves misrepresenting Christ and his covenant. Christ will never leave his wife. Ever. . . . There may be times of painful distance and tragic backsliding on our part. But Christ keeps his covenant forever. Marriage is a display of that! That is the ultimate thing we can say about it. It puts the glory of Christ's covenant-keeping love on display. . . . It's about portraying something true about Jesus Christ and the way he relates to his people. It is about showing in real life the glory of the gospel.[79]

At last, however, one must accept that it is a question of one's own conscience whether or not it is possible and reasonable to continue an evidently detrimental and destructive marriage, which may endanger one's physical and psychological (including spiritual) health.[80] God has nowhere commanded to perhaps slowly and steadily commit "suicide" by clinging to a partner who destroys one's own life. In fact, in some cases it may be more advisable to give up the aim of covenantal everlastingness in order to hold up the original covenant quality meant to be inherently present within

---

77. Corresponding to this godly endurance, another, more practical negative consequence of divorce must also be considered carefully, as Rubio, "Three-in-one Flesh," 66, concludes her survey of sociological studies concerning the long-term consequences of divorce for the concerned children: "Today, divorce is justified on the grounds that commitments can be broken, relationships can end, and ideals are not reality. Theologians claim that Christians ought to recognize human failure and allow people to move on with their lives. However, sociological research shows that often when relationships become unfulfilling for parents, they are nonetheless important to children. These same studies also show that remarriage does not mitigate (and may even increase) the negative effects of divorce on children. While divorce in high-conflict cases generally decreases children's suffering, divorce in low-conflict marriage most often increases their pain. Based on these findings, it can be argued that while some high conflict marriages should end, most low conflict marriages ought to endure." As Yahweh's behavior demonstrates, patience, endurance, and hopefully a final reconciliation must always be the first consideration and demand the highest priority and consequently the most diligent efforts.

78. Blomberg, "Exegesis," 196.

79. Piper, *Momentary Marriage*, 25–26.

80. Similarly Crispin, *Divorce*, 34.

the Edenic (i.e., biblical) marriage ideal.[81] Crispin explains appropriately: "Let us not encourage immorality or a watered-down commitment to marriage but, on the other hand, let us not emulate the Pharisees by putting great burdens on the shoulders of those least able to bear them."[82]

Finally, it is not biblical or Christ-like to ostracize persons who have to make such bitter decisions as to divorce. While the church is to decidedly emphasize the holiness and everlastingness of the marriage bond, she also has to respect strongly the individual responsibility of her members, even in cases of divorce—whenever those above mentioned biblical reasons exist. Regarding remarriage, it should be remembered that, according to 1 Cor 7:7–9 and the other hints discussed in the corresponding chapters above, there is no biblical reason to prevent someone from starting a new relationship. The sin committed was what led to divorce (or perhaps the divorce itself), it is not the remarriage—when all efforts of reconciliation were (and most likely will be) permanently unsuccessful. Therefore, I support Crispin's explanation:

> If a Christian has been guilty of such a sin in terminating his marriage then he should confess it and obtain forgiveness. Having done so he must treat it in the same manner as he would treat any other sin that he has had to confess; that is, he should accept God's forgiveness and put his sin behind him, secure in the knowledge of Christ's atonement. He must not, under any circumstance, permit it to cripple or restrict his future life. If he later contemplates remarriage there may be many factors which he needs to consider . . . but he need not ever feel that he may be held back from remarriage by some real or imagined sin either in his former marriage or in the act of divorce.[83]

III.3 Eternal Ideal or Final Abolishment?

Now, at the end of this thorough investigation of the biblical theology of marriage as constituted in Gen 2:24, there is a last, but very important, question left: there is a word of Jesus that is, on the one hand, apparently very clear, but on the other it yet stimulates wide-ranging speculations about its original meaning and, most interestingly, about its sense and a possible, reasonable rationale—if it would at all be possible to discover an explanation before the coming of the new world. This "apple of discord" in rather personal discussions, less in more objective scientific investigations, is the statement that "in the resurrection they neither marry nor are given in marriage, but are like angels in heaven" (Matt 22:30; Mark 12:25; cf. Luke 20:34–36).

---

81. See on a practical discussion of the urgent necessity of "other exceptions" Keener, . . . *and Marries Another*, 105–9; Instone-Brewer, *In the Church*, 93–106; Instone-Brewer, *In the Bible*, 189–212; Crispin, *Divorce*, 29–37.

82. Crispin, *Divorce*, 53.

83. Crispin, *Divorce*, 47–48.

We found that Scripture is very clear as to the high ideal of marriage, employing this very intimate and personal relationship even to compare a Christian's (or the church's) relation to God. This Edenic ideal of the most personal human relationship is strongly protected by other instructions of Jesus and his apostles. Jesus himself points back to paradise in order to confirm his strict view on divorce (cf. Matt 19:4–6; Mark 10:6–9), thus stressing the Edenic pattern as still being valid and demanded in this world; it is still God who cares about marriage and the faithfulness of both spouses; he still desires to see his blessed idea of an intimate human partnership come true. So why should it be abandoned in the future?

The idea expressed by Jesus was also shared by some of the ancient rabbis and was already present in ancient Jewish apocalyptical (post-canonical) literature; yet it seems that it was no widespread perception in Jesus' time, and important questions about the concrete meaning of these statements remain.[84] The remarks do not present even a speculative hint at possible reasons for God's decision to abandon marriage.

Modern scholarly research about these verses is quite homogenous and consists mainly of linguistic, stylistic, and synoptic investigations—rather seldom one finds a broader dealing with its concrete content. If so, it usually tends to emphasize the "newness" or "difference" of the conditions in the new world and its close connection to the remarks of Paul in 1 Cor 7:29–35 (on Christian marriage); 15:35–54 (on resurrection), and Gal 3:28 (on the abolition of gender differences). Once it is accepted that Jesus indeed speaks about conditions of the life in the world to come (i.e., after the resurrection of the righteous), it is usually also admitted that there will be a change concerning marriage, sexuality, and procreation—it will be abolished. It is conspicuous, however, that inquiries about the reason(s) for that great "modification" in the new life are missing.[85] The widest step is to recognize a connection between the final overcoming of death and the procreative (life-giving) aspects of marriage which might, then, not be needed anymore.[86]

The meaning of Jesus' saying in Matt 22:30 (the same in Mark 12:25) and Luke 20:34–36 seems unambiguous. So what we have is simply that there will not be marriage anymore in the new world. There are no hints what the conditions regarding personal relationships in the new earth will be like.

---

84. See Strack and Billerbeck, *Talmud und Midrasch*, 1:888–91 and the various common commentaries. It remains unclear about which time these texts speak. It is possible that the "future world" rather deals with the time of the Messiah, the Jews' return from the exile, or with the supposed conditions of the righteous souls right *before* the resurrection. Other rabbis taught that there will be sexuality even in the new world.

85. The attempt of Maier, *Matthäus-Evangelium*, 223–24 is not really helpful, since he overlooks the early hint at procreation even in Gen 1:28 by turning to Gen 4:1 as the first event of giving birth, thus claiming that Jesus held sexuality and procreation to be a part of the sinful post-Fall world, which will, consequently, be overcome in the resurrection.

86. See e.g., Pohl, *Markus*, 441.

Once this is accepted, a more interesting and significant question arises and at times results in various speculations: What might be the reason for the unexpected, rather sudden suspension of marriage in the world to come? Marriage was part of the sinless pre-Fall world (Gen 1:26–27; 2:24), the first paradise—why, then, should it no more be a part of "human" life in the newly established, sinless world that's soon to come, the second paradise? If the borders of sinless conditions (Eden) into sinful circumstances (this world) were once crossed with marriage untouched—then why not again from sinful (this world) into reestablished sinlessness (the new world)? When this world with its perilous seductions and negative results of sin (Satan's reign and its ultimate result: death) ends (1 Cor 15:26; Rev 20:10, 14), leading into the world's (and heaven's) greatest wedding feast (Rev 21:3–4)—what at all does this have to do with human marriage? Why could that lead to an abolishment of this great Edenic institution so closely linked to biblical anthropology and, by its comparative features, even to the plan of redemption (cf. esp. Eph 5:22–32)? Could it be that marriage has much more to do with redemption than usually acknowledged and would thus be linked to the finalization of this divine plan amid the final, ultimate wedding feast at the beginning of the new era under the reestablished reign of Christ?

These questions will now be discussed, starting with an investigation of the permanent, unalterable character of marriage in the New Testament that is at times doubted, leading to a fresh look at important "redemptive" features of marriage, concluding with a possible, Scripture-based rationale for Christ's statement against marriage in the new earth. While we cannot (or should not) conjecture about the conditions of this future world, there are at least some hints in Scripture that allow to illuminate the reasons for the future change.

III.3.1 Alterable or Permanent Pattern?

This first section of the investigation intends to answer two basic questions: (1) Is the statement of Jesus linked to other NT texts dealing with possible modifications of marriage in the Christian era, within the time of the end, or the world to come? (2) Are there any real, substantial hints at all pointing to modifications of the original, Edenic marriage ideal?

At first, it is important to note, as aforementioned, that Jesus himself reconfirms the Edenic marriage ideal by not disputing with the Pharisees about Moses' instructions (which were certainly foremost in meaning to check the spread of unholy divorce customs), but rather, pointing backwards to the original, Edenic pattern: one man, one woman, becoming one flesh, henceforth being one life long bound. While this ideal evidently still prevails, there are, nevertheless, some instances speaking about (suspected) changes.

"Those who have wives should be as though they had none." The main passage about a "new" attitude towards marriage is presented by Paul in 1 Cor 7: "But this I say, brethren, the time has been shortened, so that from now on those who have wives should be as though they had none; . . . and those who use the world, as though they did not make full use of it; for the form of this world is passing away" (1 Cor 7:29–31). The context of the whole chapter clarifies that Paul intends to present instructions on attitudes, not on concrete behavior. Those who are married should, of course, still behave as if married (vv. 1–16), everyone according to his own calling (vv. 17–24), one should not divorce or suspend marital intercourse. Yet it seems that Paul still tries to prove his maxim of vv. 1, 8, 40 (viz., that it is better to be unmarried) true even for those who are already married: While they should not give up marital life (especially concerning sexuality, vv. 2–5), he apparently recognizes the necessity to explain the actual core of his reservations against marriage—after all it is against the meaningful divine statement, "It is not good for the man to be alone; I will make him a helper suitable for him" (Gen 2:18). So Paul elaborates:

> But I want you to be free from concern. One who is unmarried is concerned about the things of the Lord, how he may please the Lord; but one who is married is concerned about the things of the world, how he may please his wife, and his interests are divided. And the woman who is unmarried, and the virgin, is concerned about the things of the Lord, that she may be holy both in body and spirit; but one who is married is concerned about the things of the world, how she may please her husband. And this I say for your own benefit; not to put a restraint upon you, but to promote what is seemly, and to secure undistracted devotion to the Lord. (1 Cor 7:32–35)

Being obvious from numerous other instances in the letters of Paul, he is a very practical theologian, always considering the practical results of his teachings, speaking "with the voice of the deeply caring pastor."[87] Especially in this most practical chapter on marriage and sexuality he is permanently concerned about the consequences the Corinthians may derive from his exposition (cf. vv. 6–9, 15–16, 26–28, 35–36). He is afraid of marriages being dissolved for the purpose of better serving the Lord. The result is the reduction of his practical counsels to remain unmarried by elucidating that his actual (single) concern is to secure "undistracted devotion to the Lord" (v. 35). Marriage is not per se minor to singleness—but it will be if this distraction is the result. Paul deals with priorities, not with general and absolute ideals.

Jesus seems to hint at the same general thrust by his "afterword" about marriage in Matt 19:12 ("there are eunuchs [i.e., presumably unmarried] who made themselves eunuchs for the sake of the kingdom of heaven"). But that has not to do with marriage itself, not even with some future modification to better fit the requirements of the perilous times immediately before Christ's return. We should consider that persecutions

---

87. Quotation from Dunn, *Theology*, 698.

harassing Christians were already present in Paul's own times and that the NT Christian church was convinced they lived within the last time of this world's history. So there was no need of pointing to some future changes concerning the basic marriage pattern; all preparations to meet the returning Jesus would have to be performed right away during the times of the apostles. Yet, marriage was not abolished or somehow altered—just the greater distress waiting for those who would be married is emphasized by Paul.

"Not Male and Female." There are no further instances within the entire New Testament that could be understood as altering the principles or basic theology of marriage. But could it be that at least some modification concerning the different genders is already observable, hinting at some present or future change(s) of marriage? There is one text that is at times used to support such claims: "There is neither Jew nor Greek, there is neither slave nor free man, there is not male and female; for you are all one in Christ Jesus" (Gal 3:28).

Although this verse is not dealing with a future, heavenly setting, but with the realities of the New Testament churches in Paul's days, and the liberation through faith in Christ, there might be a tiny hint pointing to the abrogation of gender and any other cause of discriminating between "social statuses" even in the world to come: "Once it is recognized that Galatians 3:28c is a citation of Genesis 1:27c the implication is that Paul . . . envisions that the creation ordinance which differentiates and separates humanity on the basis of sex has been negated in Christ."[88] Gal 3:28c ("there is not male and female:" οὐκ ἔνι ἄρσεν καὶ θῆλυ) indeed echoes Gen 1:27c and might even be a quotation of the LXX "male and female" (ἄρσεν καὶ θῆλυ).[89] To assume that Paul really intended to go beyond that creation ordinance, reasoned solely by the reoccurrence of this short phrase (ἄρσεν καὶ θῆλυ), however, is too vague to draw profound conclusions.

These three words further appear in context of another story: the Flood account (Gen 6:19–20; 7:2–3 (twice in each verse); 7:9, 16). Comparing the number of instances, the Flood story is clearly outnumbering the references to creation as given in Gen 1:27; 5:2; Matt 19:4; Mark 10:6 by eight to four. That makes the implied hint to Gen 1:27 even more unlikely. However, in either way the common feature of the texts is the implied power (even necessity) to procreate in order to fill an empty earth. It seems clear that Paul does not "transcend the Law itself and thereby even the order of creation"[90] by means of abrogating any social difference (see the complete verse of Gal 3:28), even between man and woman. This is no contradiction to any creation ordinance, for hierarchy was not introduced until sin entered the world in Gen 3. Thus, to

---

88. Litke, "Beyond Creation," 178.

89. LXX text according to the most current version in Rahlfs and Hanhart, *Septuaginta*, 2. Cf. for reasons supporting the assumption of a LXX-quotation: Stendahl, *Role of Women*, 32; Litke, "Beyond Creation," 174–76.

90. Stendahl, *Role of Women*, 34.

the contrary, it rather is a restoration of the creation ideal even in the case of equality, and it is by no means a "conflict"[91] with any divinely commanded status.

The Christian church on earth, as the instrument to reflect God's divine image (Gen 1:26–27; cf. Eph 5:22–33), consequently, is the first institution to return to this creation ideal of basic gender equality, thus even more widely recreating the original character of Gen 2:24 and the intents of God for marriage in its twofold significance (literal: husband/wife; spiritual: Christ/church). The practical instructions concerning hierarchy given, for example, in Eph 5:21–33, Col 3:18, and 1 Pet 3:1 do not interfere with this perception, since Paul evidently deals with given (secular) conditions, applying them in a Christian way, without calling them perfect or unalterable. This is supported, for instance, by the instructive statements about slavery (which is also mentioned in Gal 3:28 as being void!), which, of course, is no ideal institution for humanity (see 1 Cor 7:21–23). Considering hierarchy as a necessary instrument to guarantee order in a sinful world, Gal 3:28 may point to a time when this provisional and certainly imperfect "tool" will be extinct.[92]

These different aspects are an important background to explore the saying of Jesus: (1) marriage is basically not altered in the NT; (2) yet a new dimension about the perils for Christians is emphasized, and, at least, (3) an ambition to restore the Edenic hierarchy (gender equality) is witnessed—although (as particularly Eph 5:22, Col 3:18 or 1 Pet 3:1 indicate) evidently not yet implemented in this world, but most likely coming true in the future world of Edenic restoration.

III.3.2 Text, Translation, and First Hints

The Greek text in Matt 22:30 and Mark 12:25 is solid. Only the following variant readings are possible, but unlikely and without altering content and meaning:[93]

Matt 22:30: ἐν γὰρ τῇ ἀναστάσει οὔτε γαμοῦσιν οὔτε γαμίζονται (ἐκγαμίζονται/γαμίσκονται), ἀλλ' ὡς (οἱ) ἄγγελοι ((τοῦ) θεοῦ) ἐν τῷ οὐρανῷ (τοῖς οὐρανοῖς) εἰσιν.

Trans.: For in the resurrection they neither marry nor are given in marriage (. . .),[94] but are like (the) angels (of (the) God) in heaven (/the heavens).

---

91. Thus Stendahl, *Role of Women*, 34.

92. For a connection of Gal 3:28 even with the passage of 1 Cor 7 (esp. vv. 17–24) see further Beattie, *Women and Marriage*, 30–31.

93. The variants are so small and insignificant that there is only one short note in Metzger, *Greek NT*, 48, concerning Matt 22:30: "While the evidence for ἄγγελοι is limited in extent, it nevertheless includes the leading representatives of the Alexandrian and the Western types of text. The addition of τοῦ θεοῦ is a natural expansion, which, if present in the text originally, would not have been likely to be omitted." As there are no real textual challenges, the alternate readings above are only mentioned within round brackets, without any further discussion about the different traditions and probabilities. The common reading according to NA^{27} is certainly to be preferred, the variants do not change the meaning.

94. The variants express the same meaning as the usual reading of γαμίζονται: "They are given

Mark 12:25: ὅταν γὰρ ἐκ νεκρῶν ἀναστῶσιν οὔτε γαμοῦσιν οὔτε γαμίζονται, ἀλλ' εἰσὶν ὡς ἄγγελοι ((οἱ)) ἄγγελοι οἱ/ἄγγελοι θεοῦ οἱ) ἐν τοῖς οὐρανοῖς.

Trans.: For when they rise from the dead, they neither marry nor are given in marriage, but are like (the) angels (of God)[95] in the heavens.

The more interesting text is presented in Luke 20:34-36, offering more information about Jesus' remark:

Luke 20:34-36: καὶ (ἀποκριθεὶς) εἶπεν αὐτοῖς ὁ Ἰησοῦς· οἱ υἱοὶ τοῦ αἰῶνος τούτου (γεννῶνται καὶ γεννῶσιν) γαμοῦσιν καὶ γαμίσκονται (ἐκγαμίσκονται), οἱ δὲ καταξιωθέντες τοῦ αἰῶνος ἐκείνου τυχεῖν καὶ τῆς ἀναστάσεως τῆς ἐκ νεκρῶν οὔτε γαμοῦσιν οὔτε γαμίζονται (γαμίσκονται)· οὐδὲ (οὔτε/(οὐ)) γὰρ ἀποθανεῖν ἔτι (μέλλουσιν) δύνανται, ἰσάγγελοι γάρ εἰσιν καὶ υἱοί εἰσιν (τοῦ) θεοῦ (τῷ θεῷ) τῆς ἀναστάσεως υἱοὶ ὄντες.

Trans.: And (answering) Jesus said to them: The sons of this age (are begotten and beget,) marry and are given in marriage (...)[96], but those who are considered worthy to attain to that age and the resurrection from the dead, neither marry nor are given in marriage (...)[97]; for they cannot even (...)[98] die anymore (/ they will not die anymore), because they are like angels, and are sons of (the) God (/for God), being sons of the resurrection.

While there are no variants that would alter the meaning of Jesus' saying, the insertion γεννῶνται καὶ γεννῶσιν is interesting, since it emphasizes not only the cessation of marriage, but also the end of procreation. However, it seems natural and should certainly be expected that procreation will cease once the institution of marriage is abolished. Further, "instead of saying flatly, 'they cannot die anymore,' several witnesses (chiefly Western) soften the statement by using μέλλουσιν ('they will not die anymore')."[99]

The central expression in Jesus' saying is the Greek comparative adjective ἰσάγγελοι in respect to the expression ὡς ἄγγελοι—"like angels." Unfortunately Jesus does not clarify in detail what he means by this comparison, and the Bible is rather silent about the angels' nature. What we know from Scripture as rather general characteristics is their ability to change appearance, not being bound to materia, being able to appear and disappear suddenly, being superhumanly strong, fast, and

---

in marriage" (indicative present passive 3rd person plural from γαμίζω, ἐκγαμίζω, or γαμίσκω).

95. The οἱ before ἐν τοῖς οὐρανοῖς emphasizes their connection with "the heavens" and is almost untranslatable, to be read perhaps as: "... like *those* angels in the heavens [as different from others]."

96. Just as in Matt 22:30 above, there is no difference between γαμίσκονται and ἐκγαμίσκονται.

97. Again, just like the variants in Matt 22:30 above, there is no difference between γαμίζονται and γαμίσκονται.

98. Again, the variant readings (οὔτε or οὐ instead of οὐ δὲ) are just synonyms.

99. Metzger, *Greek NT*, 146.

intelligent. The only hints we further get about our bodies as "sons of the resurrection" (τῆς ἀναστάσεως υἱοί; Luke 20:36) point to a "powerful" (ἐν δυνάμει), "imperishable" (ἐν ἀφθαρσίᾳ), "spiritual" (πνευματικόν) body, being a "human from/(out) of heaven" (ἄνθρωπος ἐξ οὐρανοῦ; see all 1 Cor 15:42–49). These indisputably "angelic" characteristics seem to be what Jesus focuses on; particularly the new state of imperishability, for he solely emphasizes the fact that "they cannot even (/will not) die anymore."[100] Significantly, this inability to die is the rationale of his entire argument, and thus necessarily represents the key to discovering the theological connection between the cessation of marriage in heaven and its relation to the new earth.

It should be clear that the death spoken of by Jesus and Paul, which the resurrected will not be able to suffer anymore, is the so-called "second death" (δεύτερος θάνατος; cf. Rev 20:6, 14; 21:8), the death of the unrighteous; the first death actually was part of the experience of most of the redeemed and does, of course, not exist anymore now that the decisions for or against eternal life are past. While death in general is a result of sin (Rom 6:23), it is confined to the age of this earth's sinful history. The first, temporary death can be overcome through faith in Jesus; the second death is irreversible, everlasting. The difference between the two "stages" of death is important to perceive more deeply their theological connection to marriage: Only as long as the possibility to die the *second* death exists, marriage exists. The second death, on the other hand, is closely connected to Satan and his rebellion, which will finally and completely be eliminated in the "lake of fire"—the second death.[101] The point that now becomes clearer is: Marriage seems to be closely linked to the rebellion of Satan; when this is over, marriage is dispensable.

III.3.3 Marriage Between Sin and Redemption

Once the foregoing conceptual basis is recognized, we find an instance in Scripture that again deals very concretely with this idea and which is able to illuminate further Jesus' rationale of abolishing marriage due to the fact that "they cannot even (/will not) die anymore." This instance is found in Gen 2:16–18:

> The LORD God commanded the man, saying, "From any tree of the garden you may eat freely; but from the tree of the knowledge of good and evil you shall not eat, for in the day that you eat from it you will surely die." Then the LORD God said, "It is not good for the man to be alone; I will make him a helper suitable for him."

---

100. Another aspect, although not stressed that much in Jesus' saying above, certainly is the human quality to consist of male and female genders according to Gen 1:27 ("God created man in His own image, in the image of God He created him; male and female He created them."). If that (gender difference) ceases, we are no more "human" in its original (Edenic) sense, but rather angelic.

101. Cf. Rev 20:10, 14–15; 21:4; 1 Cor 15:26; Isa 25:8.

This passage is usually not read as a unit, containing a problem statement (vv. 16–17) followed by a possible solution (v. 18). Mostly it is divided into two independent parts: Gen 2:4b–17 and vv. 18–25, the first dealing with man alone in paradise (the rather general "setting"), the second with the introduction of marriage. It is important, however, to remember that the report about Eden in Gen 2:4b–25 is already shaded by the results of Satan's rebellion. One recognizes several allusions to problems connected with Satan's agenda, or to the imperfect circumstances the humans will experience once they become disloyal to God. The entire introduction of marriage, although presented in paradise, seems to be a threshold to the human's transgression, as has already been demonstrated above on the several "post-Fall elements" and various terminological connections in Gen 2 to the world outside of Eden after the Fall of Man.[102] We found the following hints associated with the change of life's conditions after the transgression, particularly concerning the central passage about the constitution of marriage in Gen 2:18–25:

1. In Gen 2:5, the chapter's "introduction," we already read about (A) the "shrubs/plants of the field" (שִׂיחַ/עֵשֶׂב הַשָּׂדֶה), the (B) divinely caused "raining" (הִמְטִיר יְהוָה אֱלֹהִים), and the man in future (C) "cultivating the ground" (לַעֲבֹד אֶת־הָאֲדָמָה). A word and phrase study revealed that this particular terminology points to (A) the curse of man's working field and God's working for his slavish people; (B) the human's unholy descendants and God's divine working in judgment and deliverance, and (C) the expulsion of man from paradise.

2. The most obvious connection to the Fall was given, of course, by the depiction of the tree of knowledge in the centre of the garden and God's warning about the death punishment resulting from eating it's fruit (Gen 2:9, 16–17).

3. Concerning the phrase וַיֹּאמֶר יְהוָה אֱלֹהִים ("and YHWH God said") we saw that there are no occurrences of this seemingly common expression in the entire Hebrew Bible, except in Gen 2:18 and 3:13–14, 22. This led to the conclusion that, instead of linking Gen 2:18 (and thereby the entire passage about marriage which is introduced here) with the "very good" working of God in Gen 1:26–27, 31, the author discreetly forged links to the final results of the woman's creation as reported in Gen 3, namely: transgression and expulsion from Eden. We also recognized that this phrase is always connected with the tree of knowledge, thus further stressing the mentioned conclusion.

4. The most important observation was the woman's description in Gen 2:18 as a "helper" (עֵזֶר). Regarding the foregoing narration focusing on the tree of knowledge (Gen 2:8–17), the last part of chap. 2, beginning with this crucial v. 18, seemed to be God's special dealing for the sake of man. He created the woman not only as a "helper" in the everyday "business" of Adam cultivating the garden

---

102. See the section on "The Edenic Constitution of Marriage."

(v. 15), or for the purpose of procreation and ruling (Gen 1:28), but particularly as a helper in heeding the only prohibition God gave to man: keeping away from the tree of knowledge (vv. 16–17). The close connection between the "problem statement" in vv. 16–17 and the "solution" immediately following in v. 18 was further supported by the fact that the only time God spoke about something not being good (in Eden) are exactly these verses 16–18. Additionally, we noted that Hebrew צָוָה ("to command/order") occurs for the first time in Gen 2:16, and the other instances in Edenic context (Gen 3:11, 17) again refer to this single command. There apparently was no other "command" of that urgency in Eden, no other order worthy to be referred to by this strong expression. The divine remark of man's conditions being "not good" (Gen 2:18) was understood in the same respect, namely: "not [yet] good" regarding man's obedience and faithfulness; he still needed someone at his side for assistance, to strengthen him in securing his loyalty amid the danger emerging from the tree of knowledge.

5. Finally, we noticed that the depiction of the transgression in Gen 3:1–7 was thoroughly reversing the course presented in Gen 2:18–25. Contrasting both passages it turned out that by means of narrative style the very creation of woman was already linked to the sad event of the Fall.

While Eden itself was pure and perfect, we have to acknowledge that the narration in Gen 2:4b–25 is not free from traces of (later, future) sin. Consequently, it seems rather natural that the main content of this chapter, namely, marriage, also has something to do with it.—But then it becomes more obvious how the blotting out of sin and death might be connected with the future abolishment of the originally pure, sinless institution of marriage.

We already saw at different places that all through the Scriptures there is a close propinquity between the representation of the marriage ideal and the intimate relationship God desires to obtain with his people respectively with each individual believer. Marriage is a pattern for the relationship God offers every human—and the final result is redemption. This fact was emphasized within the investigations of texts like 1 Cor 6:16–19, 1 Cor 7:13–16, 2 Cor 11:2–3, Eph 5:21–33, 1 Pet 3:1–2, Isa 54, Ezek 16, Hos 1–2. They all led to a more profound recognition of the marriage's aim to deepen the spouses' understanding of the intimacy God intends to share with humans, the purpose of assisting in being faithful to God, and thus to finally attain salvation.

In fact, it seems that the major purpose of marriage, right from its beginning in paradise and reaching down until the end of this world, up to the completion of the plan of redemption, is to strengthen one's faithfulness to God, and thus, one's personal way to salvation.[103] So the most significant fulfillment of the Edenic purpose of mar-

---

103. Thus it is even better comprehensible why the death of one's spouse so suddenly enables to marry someone else: The primary purpose of (the former) marriage is over, the dead spouse's fate is settled. A new partnership is permissible, for there is no possibility any more to endanger the former relationship and its redemptive goal.

riage will come true at the end of this world's history, with the great wedding feast between God and his people, thus finally accomplishing this relationship's ultimate goal: salvation (Rev 21:1–4). Then it is time for a new era to begin—an era without the necessity of redemption, thus making the spiritual purpose of marriage void and therefore, possibly, the entire institution dispensable.

III.3.4 Summary and Final Considerations

We saw that marriage, although introduced in paradise while in a state of sinlessness, is nevertheless embedded in a context foreshadowing the Fall of man. It seems that Scripture even links this institution with the danger of Satan's rebellion: it was meant to encourage and support faithfulness towards God, particularly regarding the only express command that was given in Eden: "From the tree of the knowledge of good and evil you shall not eat, for in the day that you eat from it you will surely die" (Gen 2:17). The woman should be a "complemental helper" (עֵזֶר כְּנֶגְדּוֹ; v. 18), not just for the purpose of procreation (Gen 1:28), but primarily to help man reach the goal of fully representing the image of God (Gen 1:26–27) by remaining faithful and obedient towards God.[104]

While the entire context of marriage in Gen 2 already connotes the Fall of the first couple and is thus connected to Satan's rebellion, the main link to Jesus' statement about the abolishment of marriage in the new paradise is given by his rationale: "They cannot even (/will not) die anymore." Just as Jesus' remark thus links the end of marriage with the end of Satan's rebellion by the second death, so the first biblical statement about death as a result of partaking in Satan's rebellion in Gen 2:16–17 is closely linked to the beginning or introduction of marriage in the immediately following verses (Gen 2:18–25).

The other evidence particularly from the New Testament epistles further strengthened the idea that the most profound fundament, the deepest principle, and the highest aim of marriage is both spouses' mutual assistance in reaching this life's most important goal: salvation. Marriage was apparently meant to be an instrument to secure one's faithfulness towards God. Unfortunately it has been misused ever since and influenced many (formerly) devout men to transgress God's commandments.[105]

---

104. Please note that the command to shun the tree of knowledge was the first instruction given; only then—after building the woman and thus providing the necessary requirements to multiply—the blessing on procreation could have been given. And previous to that blessing, there was the idea to have man as God's representative(s) as they rule over God's creation on earth. Gen 1–2 present the following priorities: (1) Primary goal: representing the image of God (Gen 1:26–27a); (2) Provision: not being alone, helping each other to remain faithful towards God (Gen 1:27b; 2:16–25); (3) Blessing: procreation (Gen 1:28).

105. Consider the "sons of God" in Gen 6:1–7; Samson & Delilah, David & Bathsheba, Solomon & his foreign wives, Ahab & Jezebel etc. (Of course, in most cases it rather was mere sexual desire than sincere love and true, personal intimacy/marriage.) The danger of unwise (mixed) marriages leading believers astray instead of strengthening their faithfulness toward God is well known in many biblical texts, as e.g.: Gen 24:3; 28:6; Exod 34:16; Deut 17:17; Judg 14:3; 1 Kgs 11:3–4; Ezra 9:11–14; Neh 13:25–26.

Instead of vividly representing and deeply intensifying the human's relationship to God, it frequently became an instrument of temptation, transferring one's life's priorities and loyalty away from the Almighty to one's perishable spouse.[106]

In response to the question formulated in the heading of this last chapter, we may generally assert that marriage is both: an eternal ideal *although* it is temporary, restricted to this sinful earth's history, and will be abolished at the end. Yet, its underlying principle of reflecting the divine plan of redemption will remain throughout eternity, although the human institution of marriage as we know it today will finally be abolished. The statement of Jesus is unambiguous. While there will be no marriage between humans in the world to come, we are nevertheless married—to Christ (Rev 21:2–3). The former, earthly principle (support in redemption) is suspended; but the spiritual ideal still continues to exist: intimate spiritual relationship with our redeemer, unmarred by sin, pain, or death (Rev 21:4).

We saw that what we as humans experience during marital life is a representation of our way with Christ—albeit there is, of course, a huge difference: God as Jesus is perfect, we are not. Once this gospel is fully exemplified by bringing the sad history of rebellion and sin to its ultimate end through the second, final death and the subsequent wedding between God and his people (Rev 20–21), the ultimate purpose of marriage will be reached. The divine covenant ideal it represents and the plan of redemption it symbolizes are, then, completely fulfilled and finished.[107] At this final, happy day, these redemptive goals will belong to the past—and consequently marriage itself, too. The status of paradise formerly evaluated as being imperfect ("not good;" Gen 2:18), will then be appraised as perfect: "there will no longer be any death; there will no longer be any mourning, or crying, or pain; the first things have passed away" (Rev 21:4). The era of human mortality is over; the danger once emanating from the tree of knowledge (Gen 2:17) is gone. Now they know their God by a deep spiritual intimacy that is comparable only to the marital relation of becoming "one flesh" (Gen 2:24; cf. 1 Cor 13:12). Thus they will not be tempted anymore to doubt God's character and motives as Eve did (Gen 3:6) and, therefore, "they cannot even (/will not) die anymore . . ."

Now the variant reading "will not" yields an interesting idea: in case this was the original reading, it alludes to the fact that, of course, immortal "man" is still able to sin by transgressing God's commandments; he still possesses a free will just as Adam and Eve in the first paradise did. But now things have changed dramatically—"they will not die anymore," because they will not sin anymore. There will not be the least doubt about God's infinite love. The redeemed will know by experience that what God

---

106. Please remember again Paul's reservations in 1 Cor 7:32–35.

107. Piper, *Momentary Marriage*, 52, puts it thus: "Marriage is a pointer toward the glory of Christ and the church. But in the resurrection the pointer vanishes into the perfection of that glory." Similarly Greeven, "Aussagen," 125, who speaks about the marriage's "Christusbezogenheit" in the present (i.e., this world's) era.

commands is the best way to eternal happiness; thus there will be no more death, mourning, crying, or pain; thus "the first things have passed away" (Rev 21:4).

Hence, at the end of this world, after the resurrection, the extermination of Satan's rebellion, sin, and death, having completed the marriage ideal's highest goal through the wedding between God and his people, human (earthly) marriage, with its connection to Satan's rebellion and the danger of death and mortality, indeed seems dispensable. This represents at least a possible Scripture-based explanation of Jesus' baffling statement in Matt 22:30, Mark 12:25, or Luke 20:34–36 and it perfectly fits into the general theology of marriage as constituted in Gen 2.

Epilogue

THERE IS NO COMPLETE, comprehensive marriage theology (as a dogmatic description) in the entire Bible, but there is an Edenic ideal of a mutual, intimate partnership that is the basis of the different remarks about marriage and divorce: Gen 2:24. "Dieser erste Bericht ist das Urmuster, das für alle späteren biblischen Aussagen über die Ehe die Grundlage bildet."[1] This ideal of Gen 2:24 apparently contains everything that is necessary to understand the essence of marriage from the first day it was introduced in paradise until the last day it will be consummated on this earth. This intimate union consists of one man and one woman, and lasts as long as both shall live; it represents holiness, everlastingness, exclusiveness, and purity. Its covenant pattern is significant far above the literal sphere of a relationship between human spouses. The spiritual application demonstrates that Gen 2:24 is applicable even to the bond between Yahweh and Israel, respectively Christ and the church. It is a representation of God's intentions and purposes with its highest aim to save the spouse (may it be the human partner or the covenant people Israel/NT church).

The biblical theology of marriage basing on Gen 2:24 as developed in this study, finds that marriage is actually consummated by becoming "one flesh," presupposing the foregoing (rather psychological) steps of "leaving" and "cleaving." The responsibilities evolving from sexual contact, therefore, are enormous. Sex develops power and figuratively creates a corporate body of the ones engaging in it. This new "one flesh" union is not to be separated, and leaving the partner for having relations with someone else is equal to adultery. However, in order to hold up the original ideal, for certain reasons it is permissible, in some cases perhaps even necessary (e.g., in cases of mortal danger), to suspend the principle of "everlastingness" due to the marriage's miserable quality. If one spouse decides to imperil severely this intimate "one flesh" union and its grand aims through sexual immorality, permanent (willful) abuse, or by dissolving the partnership in terms of neglecting to continue "to live together," the other, ill-treated spouse is free to let go and marry someone else. Without these

---

1. Hasel, "Eheverständnis," 18; cf. Von Rad, *Erstes Buch Mose*, 59–60; Schlier, *Epheser*, 263. As derived from the biblical evidence investigated in the previous chapters, this consequently is also my own conviction.

reasons, however, the biblical texts indicate that remarriage is not allowed and divorce should not be pursued. Finally, as a general rule, reconciliation always remains the ideal, encouraged by the divine pattern of forbearance, patience, and forgiveness.

Considering the literal as well as spiritual responsibilities and powerful, far-reaching results of violating these most profound principles of Gen 2:24, it is not surprising that the prohibition of πορνεία

> im frühjüdischen und urchristlichen Kontext keiner Begründung im eigentlichen Sinne [bedarf]; das zeigt sich an ihrer herausgehobenen Stellung in den Lasterkatalogen Mk 7,21; Röm 1,29; 2 Kor 12,21; Gal 5,19; Eph 5,3; Kol 3,5, in der Paränese 1 Thess 4,3 und an ähnlichen Stellen. Das Urchristentum steht hier in der Tradition des frühjüdischen Gesetzesverständnisses.[2]

Texts like those mentioned in this citation and additionally Eph 5:5; 1 Cor 5:9–11; 6:9; Heb 13:4; or Rev 21:8; 22:15 clearly point to the serious fact that no one scorning, despising, and transgressing the principles of Gen 2:24 will enter the kingdom of the heavens, for he is called a πόρνος ("sexually immoral person"). The sin of πορνεία and those committing these sins (οἱ πόρνοι) are frequently even the first ones to be mentioned in considerable detail within the prominent "sin catalogues" (cf. esp. 1 Cor 5:11; 6:9; Eph 5:5). Furthermore, of all things it is depraved sexuality which is depicted in such detail in Rom 1:26–28 as a result which God has allowed to capture persons who deny him (see vv. 18–28). This fits exactly the pattern of apostasy given in the OT stories investigated in this study, which frequently combine prohibited sexuality with idolatry.[3]

Jesus' remark about the repentant πόρναι ("sexually immoral women/prostitutes") entering the kingdom of God (cf. Matt 21:31–32) and his grace against the adulteress in John 8:2–11 are, therefore, even more significant and meaningful. God's grace still prevails; there is sufficient forgiveness for everyone, even for those who committed one of the most prominent and most serious sins, thereby distorting the image of God and his divine covenant they should represent among humankind.

Living in harmony with the literal marriage ideal as well as the divine covenant ideal hidden in Gen 2:24 and its NT echoes results in the sanctification Paul described in his letter to Timothy in words applying most properly to the topic of this study:

> For this is the will of God, your sanctification; that is, that you abstain from sexual immorality; that each of you know how to possess his own vessel in sanctification and honor, not in lustful passion, like the Gentiles who do not

---

2. Dautzenberg, "Φεύγετε τὴν πορνείαν," 284; cf. Niederwimmer, *Askese und Mysterium*, 67; Collins, *Sexual Ethics*, 76, 80.

3. See above ("Interaction Between the Two Levels") about the accounts of Gen 6; Num 25; Exod 32. Consider further, for instance, 1 Kgs 11:1–4; 16:31; 21:25; and the references to prostitutes and temple whores throughout the OT (e.g., 1 Kgs 14:24; 15:12; 2 Kgs 23:7; Hos 4:14).

know God; . . . because the Lord is the avenger in all these things, just as we also told you before and solemnly warned you. (1 Thess 4:3–6.)

A commentator expressed concerning the ideal of Gen 2:24: "The holier a person is, the closer his life must conform to the Genesis 2 ideal for marriage."[4]—And at the end of this treatise I would like to add: As one's life conforms more closely to the Gen 2:24 ideal for the covenant of redemption by "cleaving" (κολλάω) to the Lord and becoming "one spirit" with him (1 Cor 6:17), the more it is incorporated into one spiritual body with Christ (Eph 5:30–32)—just as spouses "cleave" together and become "one flesh." It is right to the point that "the description of human marriage in Genesis finds its true fulfillment in the relationship between Christ and the church; yet its significance for human marriage is not thereby set aside, but on the contrary, deepened and transformed."[5]

Finally, the lost intimate intercourse with God is restored and deepens until the final consummation of the ultimate wedding feast at Jesus' return. Then God will again be cohabitating with his redeemed people at the re-created, Edenic earth as beautifully depicted in Rev 21:1–4. Then, having all purposes of marriage fulfilled unto its glorious ending, marriage itself is apparently dispensable and will be abolished.

---

4. Gane, "Old Testament Principles," 54.
5. Beattie, *Women and Marriage*, 82.

Appendix

THE FOLLOWING TABLES CONTAIN the main passages dealing with sexuality in the Pentateuch, the New Testament, Josephus, Philo, and the main tractates of the Mishnah.

Pentateuch

Reference	Content
Gen 2:18	"It is not good for the man to be alone. I will make a helper suitable for him."
Gen 2:22–24	Adam and Eve as one flesh, building a new family (leaving father and mother).
Gen 3:16	New arrangements after the first sin; the husband "will rule" over the wife.
Gen 4:1	The first son (Cain) fathered by sexual intercourse ("Adam knew his wife").
Gen 4:19	Lamech was the first man who took two wives. First instance of polygamy.
Gen 6:1–4	"Sons of God" and "daughters of men" marry, God is offended.
Gen 9:20–27	Noah became drunk, his son (Ham) sees him naked, he is cursed.
Gen 16:1–4	The handmaid of Sarai becomes Abrams wife to give birth to a child. (Besides there seems to be not necessarily a connection between infertility and a sinful live (despite Exod 23:16 and Deut 7:14), but certainly a sinful life may be cursed by the captivity of children: Deut 28:41.)
Gen 18:9–15	God deals with infertility and impossibilities regarding pregnancy. (Cf. for a similar story in the NT: Luke 1:11–20.)
Gen 19:1–11	Sodom and Gomorrah are destroyed because of their obvious wickedness in sexual behavior. (Cf. 13:10, 13 and Ezek 16:49: the cities were situated with best geographical conditions and had peace, wealth and prosperity all around; that became a snare to them.)
Gen 19:30–38	Lot fathers two sons (later the people of Moab and Ammon) with his two daughters.
Gen 20:3	Taking a married wife is adultery and brings in death.
Gen 24:67	Rebekah gets married to Isaac by "bringing her into Sarah's tent and taking her."
Gen 25:1	Abraham weds a second wife not before his first spouse has died.
Gen 26:34–35	The "gentile" wives of Esau brought a lot of grief to his parents. (See also 28:9.)

Appendix

Gen 29:20–27	Jacob gains his wife through hard working; he touches her not before the scheduled time. He has to marry two women. The wedding procedure lasts a whole week.
Gen 30:1, 14–16	Competition between both wives of Jacob about bearing children. "Buying" sexual intercourse with the husband from one another.
Gen 34	Jacob's daughter Dinah is raped by Shechem. The sons of Jacob retaliate by slaughtering all men of the city and spoiling everything.
Gen 38:8–10	Onan takes the levirate, but selfishly refuses to father his brother descendants while engaging in sexual intercourse.
Gen 38:14–18, 24	Judah goes to a prostitute (Tamar) and gives her a special payment. As he finds out that his daughter-in-law (Tamar) has become pregnant without being married, he wants to burn her. Then he gets aware that she was the "prostitute" who now is pregnant by him.
Gen 39:7–10	Joseph rejects the attempts of his master's wife to have sex with him, because otherwise he would sin against God. God blesses him mightily as a result (vv. 21–23).
Exod 1:7	Israel multiplies and increases very fast. (Cf. Jer 25:6—procreation is important)
Exod 1:16–17	The midwives fear God and therefore do not kill the newborn.
Exod 6:20	The father of Moses and Aaron married his aunt. (Contrary to the laws given later by Moses; cf. e.g., Lev 18:12.)
Exod 19:15	The people are instructed not to take their wives in order to be prepared to meet God.
Exod 20:14, 17	The Decalogue forbids to commit adultery or to covet the neighbor's wife or servants. And by prohibiting to murder (v. 13), the killing of newborns in order to limit the family's growth, is strictly forbidden. (Cf. Exod 1:16–17)
Exod 21:3–11	Slaves are not allowed to take their wives and children with them when they are released if they married while being a slave already. Incl. laws on polygamy (v. 10).
Exod 22:16–17	Sexual intercourse before wedding results in paying the dowry and, if allowed by the father, in official marriage.
Exod 22:19	"Anyone who has sexual relations with an animal must be put to death."
Exod 23:16	Not being infertile is a blessing of the Lord. (Cf. Deut 7:14.)
Exod 34:15–16	Relationships, especially marriages, between Israel and the pagan nations are not allowed.
Lev 15	About bodily discharges. No sexual intercourse allowed when "unclean."
Lev 17:7	Introduction of the *prostitution symbolism*: ". . . sacrifices to the demons to which they *prostitute* themselves."
Lev 18:6–23	Several prohibited sexual relations.
Lev 19:20–22	Special instructions on punishment of a man who intercourses with "a slave acquired for another man."
Lev 19:29	"Do not degrade your daughter by making her a prostitute, or the land will turn to prostitution and be filled with wickedness."
Lev 19:34	All these instructions are valid for aliens as well as for natives.

Lev 20:5–6	Apostasy from Yahweh and serving other Gods or demons is like prostituting oneself. *Prostitution symbolism.*
Lev 20:10–21	Additional laws regarding sexual sins punishable by death.
Lev 21:3–4	Sexual intercourse means belonging to/being affiliated with the person (possible implication). But a priest is not allowed to defile himself by a dead person who is a relative only by marrying.
Lev 21:7	Priests "must not marry women defiled by prostitution or divorced from their husbands."
Lev 21:9	"If a priest's daughter defiles herself by becoming a prostitute, she disgraces her father; she must be burned in the fire."
Lev 21:13–15	A priest is not allowed to marry any woman that is not a virgin from his own people.
Num 5:11–31	Procedure to test a woman suspected of adultery.
Num 12:1	"Then Miriam and Aaron spoke against Moses because of the Cushite woman whom he had married."—Even though Moses had a pagan wife, the marriage is lawful because she is believing in Jahweh (cf. e.g., Lev 16:29; Isa 56:3–5).
Num 15:39	"Going after the lusts of the own hearts and eyes" against the laws of God is prostituting oneself. More detailed defining of the peculiar *prostitution symbolism.*
Num 25:1–13	Israel "began to indulge in sexual immorality with Moabite women, who invited them to the sacrifices to their gods." Phinehas took vengeance on a (sexual) sinning man inside the camp of Israel; God therefore blessed him and his descendants.
Num 36:5–9	Special directions concerning women who inherit land to marry only men of their own tribe.
Deut 5:18	Repetition of the Decalogue; prohibition of adultery.
Deut 7:3–4, 14	Repetition of the prohibition of marrying pagan men and women. Keeping God's commandments brings fertility (v. 14).
Deut 17:17	The king "must not take many wives, or his heart will be led astray."
Deut 21:10–14	About marriages with captive women.
Deut 22:13–30	Special laws concerning the calumniation of not being a virgin when marrying. Instructions about dealing with rape and rapists.
Deut 23:2	"A bastard shall not enter into the congregation of the LORD." (KJV)
Deut 23:17–18	There must not be temple prostitution among Israel. No payment of prostitution must be given to the house of God.
Deut 24:1–4	When a man gets divorced from his wife and she weds and gets divorced again, he may not take her anew.
Deut 24:5	"When a man is newly married, he shall not go out with the army or be liable for any other public duty. He shall be free at home one year to be happy with his wife whom he has taken." (ESV)
Deut 25:5–10	The levirate marriage.
Deut 27:20–23	Special curses on sexual transgressions.
Deut 31:16	"This people will rise up, and go a whoring after the gods of the strangers of the land." *Prostitution symbolism.*

Appendix

New Testament[1]

Reference	Content
Matt 1:5–6	Rahab, the harlot (cf. Josh 2), is one of the ancestors of the Messiah (Jesus). Bathsheba, the wife of Uriah, has been the mother of King Salomon (son of King David and ancestor of Jesus) who has been borne by this (formerly) illegal relationship.
Matt 1:18–19, 23	Mary "was found to be with child through the Holy Spirit"—not by sexual intercourse. Her future husband, already betrothed to her, "was a righteous man and did not want to expose her to public disgrace, he had in mind to divorce her quietly." Even prophesy is fulfilled by the young virgin becoming pregnant (v. 23). (Cf. Luke 1:26–31, 35)
Matt 5:17–18	Jesus does not abolish the law (the OT, the Torah; cf. Luke 16:17–18). (See also Matt 8:4: Jesus observes even the ceremonial laws.)
Matt 5:27–32	Jesus talks about adultery: "Anyone who looks at a woman lustfully has already committed adultery with her in his heart. . . . If your right eye causes you to sin, gouge it out and throw it away. . . . But I tell you that anyone who divorces his wife, except for marital unfaithfulness, causes her to become an adulteress, and anyone who marries the divorced woman commits adultery."
Matt 9:20–22	"A woman who had been subject to bleeding for twelve years came up behind him and touched the edge of his cloak" in order to be healed. She did not regard the restrictions concerning uncleanness. Jesus is not defiled by this act, but he purifies her. (Cf. Mark 5:25–34; Luke 8:43–48.)
Matt 10:35–37	Jesus came "to turn a man" against his own household. The spouse is not directly mentioned, but perhaps he/she may be implied as well. (Cf. Luke 12:51–53.)
Matt 11:23–24	Sodom would have remained to Jesus' day, if his miracles would have been performed there. So it will be "more bearable for Sodom on the day of judgment." (Cf. Matt 10:15; Luke 10:12.)
Matt 12:39	Jesus calls the Scribes and Pharisees a "wicked and adulterous generation." (Cf. Matt 16:4.)
Matt 12:46–50	Jesus' disciples are his relatives, like one household. (Concerning marriage/family. Cf. Mark 3:31–35; Luke 8:19–21; 9:59–62.)
Matt 14:3–4	John the Baptist was imprisoned (and finally executed) by Herod Antipas, because he rebuked him for taking his brother's wife. (Cf. Mark 6:17–18; Luke 3:19–20)
Matt 15:1–9, 18–20	Some of the Pharisee's traditions are against God's laws and therefore sinful (cf. Luke 11:46). True uncleanness comes from sinful thoughts (like "adulteries, fornications, lasciviousness") and not from outward "uncleanness." (Cf. Mark 7:1–23; see also: Titus 1:13–14!)
Matt 18:6–9	"But if anyone causes one of these little ones who believe in me to sin, it would be better for him to have a large millstone hung around his neck and to be drowned in the depths of the sea." So "if your hand or your foot causes you to sin cut it off and throw it away." (Cf. Mark 9:42–47; Luke 17:1–2)

---

1. The New Testament is of special importance. Therefore, every text that is in any way associated with sexuality or sexual morals/ethics will be mentioned.

Matt 18:15–17	How to deal with a church member sinning against the laws of God; he will finally be expelled from the church.
Matt 19:1–12	Jesus teaches about marriage, divorce and singleness. (Cf. Mark 10:2–12.)
Matt 19:18	The law against adultery (within the Decalogue) is valid and important for Jesus, when pointing out the way to eternal life. (Cf. Mark 10:19)
Matt 19:29	Jesus talks again about giving up the family bonds in order to follow him. Again, he does not talk about leaving one's own spouse!—That seems to be only possible when the infidel partner wants to divorce: cf. 1 Cor 7:15. (Cf. Mark 10:29–30) But it is interesting that Luke adds the wife who may be left behind (cf. Luke 18:29).
Matt 21:31–32	The prostitutes will more likely enter the kingdom of God than the priests and elders, because they (the harlots) believed John the Baptist.
Matt 22:1–14	*Marriage symbolism.* A great feast, many (humble) guests. The right garment is important.
Matt 22:23–30	About the levirate marriage. One woman had seven brothers but no children; whose wife will she be in the resurrection? There is no marriage in heaven. (Cf. Mark 12:18–25; Luke 20:27–36.)
Matt 24:19	Pregnant women and nursing mothers are in peril when the time of tribulation comes. (Cf. Mark 13:17; see also: Luke 23:27–31 and especially 1 Cor 7:26.)
Matt 24:38–39	Eating, drinking and marriage will so occupy the mind of the people that they do not regard the signs before Jesus' second coming. (Cf. Luke 17:26–30; here even the time of Lot and the destruction of Sodom and Gomorrah are mentioned.)
Matt 25:1–13	*Marriage symbolism.* Ten virgins waiting for the arrival of the bridegroom, but only five are prepared.
Luke 1:5–7	Zacharias and Elisabeth are childless even though they were "observing all the Lord's commandments and regulations blamelessly." There is no connection between sin and infertility.
Luke 1:15	Even the fetus may be filled with the Holy Spirit; there seems to be no clue that sexuality in itself and its "fruit" is inherently sinful.
Luke 1:25	Being infertile brings disgrace before the people. (They may perceive a divine curse, perhaps deriving from Exod 23:16 and Deut 7:14.)
Luke 15:13, 30	The prodigal son went to the harlots, but his father (God) forgives him when coming back.
Luke 16:17–18	Not one of God's laws is or will be abolished (cf. Matt 5:17–18). Adultery and divorce (!) is and will ever be sinful.
Luke 18:11	The Pharisees look down disparagingly upon adulterers and other sinners.
John 2:1–11	Jesus attends a wedding and performs his first miracle.
John 3:29	*Marriage symbolism.* Jesus is called a bridegroom by John the Baptist.
John 4:16–19	Jesus and the Samaritan woman. He knows her (illegal) relationships.
John 8:1–11	Jesus and the woman caught in adultery.
Acts 15:20, 29	The council at Jerusalem passes some doctrines, so e.g., to abstain from "sexual immorality." (Cf. 21:25.)
Rom 1:24–32	Sexual impurities are forbidden by God's law and deserve death-penalty.

Appendix

Rom 2:22–23	Adultery is breaking the law and therefore dishonoring God.
Rom 6:12	Evil desires shall not reign in the body of the new life. (Cf. 7:5.)
Rom 7:2–3	A married couple is bound to one another as long as both live.
Rom 7:7, 12	The law is holy, righteous and good and it tells us what sin is.
Rom 13:9	Adultery is against the holy law of loving ones neighbor as oneself.
Rom 13:13–14	"Walking honestly" means to life "not in sexual promiscuity and sensuality."
1 Cor 5:1–13	A man having his father's wife shall be expelled. "I have written you in my letter not to associate with sexually immoral people [within the church]." (Cf. 2 Cor 7:11; 12:21; see also: Titus 3:10–11; Jude 23c.)
1 Cor 6:9–20	"Neither fornicators, nor idolaters, nor adulterers, nor effeminate, nor homosexuals . . . shall inherit the kingdom of God." So have been some of the Corinthians, but now they are cleansed and called "holy" (cf. 1:2). "The body is not meant for sexual immorality, but for the Lord." (v. 13) Whoredom is a very special sin against the Lord, his spirit and the temple of his spirit (the human body).
1 Cor 7	About marriage, divorce, singleness and widows.
1 Cor 9:5	Peter (Cephas) and other apostles were married and took their wives with them. There is nothing bad associated with it.
1 Cor 10:8	Israel's harlotry killed them—Christians shall shun that.
1 Cor 11:3, 11	Christ as head of the man and man as head of the woman; but "in the Lord, however, woman is not independent of man, nor is man independent of woman." (Cf. Gal 3:28!)
1 Cor 13:1–8	The nature of true love.
2 Cor 6:14—7:1	"Do not be bound together with unbelievers . . . let us cleanse ourselves from all defilement of flesh"—could also easily be interpreted concerning marriage.
2 Cor 10:3–5	Obedience begins with thoughts and thinking. (Cf. Phil 4:8.)
2 Cor 11:2	*Marriage symbolism.* Jesus is the bridegroom, the church is the virgin.
2 Cor 12:21	Some of the fornicators have not repented. (Cf. 7:11; the church dealt just with them.)
Gal 5:16–24	The fruits of the flesh (fornication etc.) are sinful and contrary to the fruits of the spirit. There are certain results coming from the works of flesh or spirit (cf. 6:8).
Eph 2:1–6	The church members once were "dead" by obeying the lusts of the flesh, but now they have changed and are "saved."
Eph 4:19–22	They have to keep themselves undefiled from "sensuality" and "every kind of impurity" in order to be righteous.
Eph 5:3, 5–7	"But do not let immorality or any impurity . . . even be named among you, as is proper among saints." No immoral will enter God's kingdom (v. 5), "for because of such things God's wrath comes on those who are disobedient." (v. 6; cf. Col 3:5–6)
Eph 5:22–33	The right order of husband and wife; the basic principle of Christ-like love. (Cf. Col 3:18–19; 1 Tim 2:11–12; 1 Pet 3:1, 5–7.)
Col 3:5–6	"Put to death . . . whatever belongs to your earthly nature: sexual immorality, impurity, lust, evil desires . . . Because of these, the wrath of God is coming." (Cf. Eph 5:5–7.)

1 Thess 4:3–5, 7	"For this is the will of God, your sanctification; that is, that you abstain from sexual immorality."
1 Tim 1:10	The law is against "immoral men and homosexuals."
1 Tim 3:2, 11–12	"Now the overseer must be . . . the husband of but one wife, temperate, self-controlled." The same is valid for deacons and the women shall be faithful. (Cf. Titus 1:6.)
1 Tim 4:3	False teachers tell that marriage is forbidden.
1 Tim 5:2–16	Timothy has to rebuke young sister (church members) in all purity. Several instruction how to deal with widows.
2 Tim 2:22	"Flee the evil desires of youth!" (Certainly, fornication is included here.)
2 Tim 3:3–4	In the last times there will be "lovers of pleasure rather than lovers of God."
Titus 2:11–12	The grace of God teaches to live self-controlled, without worldly lusts. (Cf. 3:3.)
1 Pet 1:14–15	Do not obey the lusts, but be holy like God. (Cf. 2:11; 4:2–3; 2 Pet 1:4; 2:2.)
1 Pet 2:11	Christians have to abstain from "fleshly lusts, which wage war against the soul."
1 Pet 4:2–3	Sensuality and the lusts of men are against the will of God and have to be shunned.
2 Pet 1:4	The world is corrupted through (evil) lust.
2 Pet 2:5–8, 14, 18	The great flood and Sodom and Gomorrah are examples for the succeeding generations of God's dealing with the impure. (Cf. Jude 7–8) The just man suffers when he witnesses those sins. There are people "with eyes full of adultery . . . —accursed brood." (v. 14) They seduce others to live according to the carnal lusts. (v. 18; cf. 3:3)
1 John 2:16	"For all that is in the world, the lust of the flesh and the lust of the eyes . . . is not from the Father, but is from the world."
1 John 3:3–4	"Everyone who sins breaks the law; in fact, sin is lawlessness." Holy people do not break the laws (of the OT/Torah), but cleanse themselves.
Heb 11:31–32	The harlot Rahab is called a hero of faith and as is Jephtah (the illegitimate son of a harlot; cf. Judg 11:1) is named among that list. (Cf. Jas 2:25: Rahab became righteous by helping the Israelite spies.)
Heb 12:16	There should be no "immoral . . . person like Esau" among the churches.
Heb 13:4	"Marriage should be honored by all, and the marriage bed kept pure, for God will judge the adulterer and all the sexually immoral."
Jas 1:14–15, 25	The lusts of the flesh are tempting the man. Obeying them is sin and results in death. The commandment keeper will be saved.
Jas 2:10–12	Breaking one commandment (e.g., adultery) is breaking the whole law; Christians shall live according to the commandments.
Jas 4:4	Friendship with the world is adultery (against God).
Rev 2:14, 20–22	Some people in the church of Pergamos and Isebel of Thyatira go on to teach harlotry and are rebuked and finally punished by the Lord.
Rev 9:21	Mankind does not repent of immorality (whatever it may be exactly).
Rev 11:8	The Lord was crucified in a city mystically called "Sodom."

Appendix

Rev 14:4, 8, 12	The redeemed people will be virgins, undefiled by women (v. 4). Babylon, the great harlot, is introduced (v. 8; cf. chaps. 16–18: finally she will be destroyed. Cf. 19:2; she corrupted the earth with her immorality). Those who are not with her, but who are undefiled, are the followers of the lamb of God (v. 4), the keepers of God's law (cf. v. 12).
Rev 16:15	Nakedness is a shame/disgrace. (Cf. 3:17.)
Rev 19:7–9	*Marriage symbolism.* Jesus is the bridegroom and the bride is the congregation of the holy people.
Rev 21:1–3, 9–10	*Marriage symbolism.* Jesus is the bridegroom, the bride is the new (heavenly) Jerusalem.
Rev 21:8, 27	Fornicators will not enter the new world. (Cf. 22:12, 15.)

Mishnah

Reference	Content
Yebam.	The Levirate.
Ketub.	Marriage contracts.
Soṭah 1:1—9:8	Adultery suspicion and how to settle the matter.
Giṭ.	The Bill of divorce.
Qidd.	About engagements.
Nid. 1–10	Uncleanness during menstruation. (Times when sexual intercourse is prohibited.)

Flavius Josephus[2]

Reference	Content
A.J. 1:194, 200–203	The Sodomites "abused themselves with sodomy." Finally they were cursed.
A.J. 3:92	The commandment against adultery within the Decalogue.
A.J. 3:261–277	Summary of several instructions given by Moses concerning sexuality. (On the wedlock, the dealing with the suspicion that a wife committed adultery, special laws for the priests etc.).
A.J. 4:206	No money from prostitution shall be brought to the temple.
A.J. 4:244–259	Further precepts on sexual behavior (marriage, divorce, rape, levirate).
A.J. 8:251–252	The people follow the examples of their kings, even in wickedness/licentiousness.

2. Only those passages will be presented here that deal with Jews and their sexuality, or general Roman and Greek attitudes towards sexual ethics; simple remarks on some practices without any reference concerning sexual morals will be passed over. The remarks within the first eleven books of the *Antiquities*, as a kind of commentary on the Mosaic Laws, will also be included, but only as far as they are directly connected with sexuality. I will not give any reference on marriages in general or events of the OT paraphrased by Josephus; that will only occur in special cases, where a good benefit for a deeper study of the main subject is to be expected (e.g., the commentary on the Mosaic Laws).

A.J. 15:259–260	Salome sends her husband a bill of divorce, but that is contrary to the Jewish laws.
A.J. 15:319–322	Herod takes another wife, due to his lusts.
A.J. 16:185	Licentiousness is a popular accuse for executing unpopular, disturbing persons.
A.J. 17:51	Antipater is suspected to have forbidden sexual intercourse with Pherora's wife.
A.J. 17:121	Antipater had done lasciviously with Pherora's women.
A.J. 17:350–353	Glaphyra caused the divorce of her new husband and is now married for the third time. She has dream in which she is accused of acting immorally and dies a few days later. (B.J. 2:115–116)
A.J. 16:339–340	Sylleus is accused of adultery with Arabian and Roman women.
A.J. 19:356–357	After King Agrippa's death his daughters were brought to the brothel and then were severely abused.
A.J. 20:106–112	One Roman soldier "exposes his privy members" at the Passover feast and the multitude becomes furious because of that "impious action." Thus "the impudent obscenity of a single soldier" meant death to twenty thousand men.
A.J. 20:145	Bernice had her uncle for husband. She is also suspected to have immoral intercourse with her brother.
B.J. 1:438–439	Herod's wife Mariamne is accused of adultery and that her lust is very "extravagant."
B.J. 1:486	Salome's former husband has been put to death because of adultery.
B.J. 2:120–121, 160–161	The Jewish sect of the Essenes thinks disparagingly about marriage, because of the sexual pleasures and the general lasciviousness of women. On the other side they see a necessity in giving birth to children. They have special rules to prove the faithfulness of their future wives.
B.J. 4: 558–563	Some crazy Jews (Zealots) behave during the war "as in a brothel house."
B.J. 5:402	Adultery is one of the sins that are responsible for the destruction of Jerusalem.
Vita 415, 426–427	Josephus himself has been divorced three times and married four times.[3] He got divorced from his second wife without mentioning any reason. The third wife he got divorced from because he was "not pleased with her behavior."
C.Ap. 2:199–203	Marriage and sexual regulations according to the laws of Moses.
C.Ap. 2:215	Moses imposed the death penalty on adultery, raping, homosexuality.
C.Ap. 2:234	There are "inviolable rules in lying with wives."
C.Ap. 2:244–246	Pagan Gods love all sexual immorality; men are following their pattern.
C.Ap. 2:270–277	The gentile punishments on adultery etc. are too small.

---

3. His first wife he lost in Jerusalem during the siege (cf. *B.J.* 5:419), so it is no divorce in a juridical sense. The second wife he took on command of Vespasianus (*Vita* 415), but she soon left him. His third and fourth wives are now described in *Vita* 426–425.

Appendix

Philo of Alexandria[4]

Reference	Content
Opif. 103–104	Philo agrees with the Athenian Solon that a man should wed between 28 and 35 years.
Leg. 3:148	Adultery pollutes the soul and belongs to the "passions of the belly."
Leg. 3:197	Abraham sent back the horses of the king of Sodom, because it was "wages of harlots."
Cher. 91–92	The wedding feast (at day) is among Philo's list of absurd festivals among the nations.
Sacr. 21–25	Description of the prostitute woman living "with each individual among us," as opposite of the modest woman described in the following verses. (Cf. *Spec.* 2:1; repetition of that text.)
Sacr. 100–103	Every sex has its own purposes. There should not be any mingling between them. The evil passions are female; the good virtues of the soul are male.
Det. 102	Not just because the sexes are given we have to use them in anyway. "Impure connections" are to be avoided.
Agr. 37	"Gluttony is followed by its usual natural attendant, an eagerness for the connections of the sexes."
Conf. 144	Children of harlots are expelled from the assembly of the Lord.
Migr. 69	Worshipping many Gods is harlotry.
Congr. 23–63	Concubine symbolism referring to Gentiles and bad passion.
Fug. 114	About the marriage regulations for priests.
Fug. 144	The Sodomites had "unnatural and impious desires" when intending to rape the male guests of Lot.
Mut. 205	Polytheism is harlotry. The Lord God would be the only husband and father of all men. (Cf. *Decal.* 8; *Spec.* 1:332)
Abr. 133–135	The cause of the wickedness of Sodom is in its "overmuch prosperity." They became accustomed to every kind of sexual immorality and "intolerable evil . . . corrupting in this way the whole race of man." Therefore God had to destroy them.
Abr. 149	The beasts which are "the most strongly inclined to sexual connections are the most vehemently excited." Implications on similar expectations regarding men?
Ios. 42–56	The Hebrews have special laws on sexuality. Comparison with the morals of gentiles.
Mos. 295–304	The story of Balaam and the Moabite women seducing Israel to prostitution and apostasy. (Cf. Num 25:1–13)

4. Here, just like the table on Josephus, only those passages will be mentioned, which refer directly to a sexual context, respectively which deal with obvious judgments on morals concerning that subject. The mere parallel-texts on OT stories will be avoided to assure a straighter overview and a better access to really illuminating sequences about their personal convictions. In the same way the various lists of sins in his works will not be mentioned. That would go too far without providing significant new insights. Yet, all references to the corresponding laws of Moses are regarded as valuable hints for a broader interpretation thereof.

Decal. 8	More than one God is like having more than one man, i.e., harlotry. (Cf. *Mut.* 205; *Spec.* 1:332.)
Decal. 121–131	Philo's interpretation of the Decalogue: Adultery is the greatest of all violations of the law. He explains its bad results on body and soul.
Decal. 168–169	The law against adultery comprises many other commands (incl. pederasty).
Spec. 1:101–112	Commands on marriages of priests. Harlots who repent, may be forgiven and are allowed to marry again. No harlot's wages are allowed in the temple (cf. 1:280).
Spec. 1:138	Qualities of a blessed marriage.
Spec. 1:324–326	There are people who will be driven away from the assembly of the Lord, e.g., harlots and their children.
Spec. 1:332	Polytheism is spiritual whoredom. (Cf. 1:344 and *Decal.* 8; *Mut.* 205)
Spec. 2:1	Cf. *Sacr.* 21–25 (repetition of that text). A defiled soul is like a concubine.
Spec. 2:12–13	Making oaths on sins like adultery or rape is bad. One should not ratify them.
Spec. 2:50	An adulterer is not eligible to join any feast of the Lord.
Spec. 3:8–82	On the Mosaic Laws of sexual limits.
Spec. 4:89	Pederasts are sinners.
Spec. 4:203–204	Adultery is like "copulation between irrational animals of different species."
Virt. 28–30	On the direction that a newly married husband shall not go to war/military service.
Virt. 34–42	The Arabians tried to seduce the Israelites to adultery: "Man may be caught by pleasure, and especially by such pleasure as proceeds from connections with women."
Virt. 110–115	On the laws about marriage with captive women.
Virt. 199	Adam and Eve "came together for the propagation of offspring."
Praem. 139	". . . married in holy wedlock for the purpose of propagating legitimate children."
Contempl. 48–63	About "the luxury and extravagance of the Italians which both Greeks and barbarians emulate:" Pederasty injures soul and body. It is nothing but violence on young men.
Gai. 72	Marriage is the bond which can unite very different families as long as it exists.
QG 2:49	While living in the ark, Noah and his sons had no sexual intercourse with their wives. That would have been impious; the wrath of God would first have to cease.
QG 3:21	Abraham is a good pattern, for he has not left his wife for the sake of another.
QG 3:57	Abraham's first son Ishmael is illegitimate (from the "concubine" Hagar), not like Isaac, the son of his wife Sarah.

Bibliography[1]

Abrahams, Israel. *Studies in Pharisaism and the Gospels.* 2 vols. Cambridge: Cambridge University Press, 1917.

Adams, Jay E. *Marriage, Divorce, and Remarriage in the Bible.* Phillipsburg, NJ: Presbyterian and Reformed, 1980.

Albright, William Foxwell, and C. S. Mann. *Matthew.* The Anchor Bible 26. Garden City, NJ: Doubleday, 1971.

Allen, Leslie C. *Ezekiel 20–48.* Word Biblical Commentary. Dallas: Word, 1990.

Allen, Ronald B. "Numbers." In *Expositor's Bible Commentary*, edited by Frank E. Gaebelein. 655–1008. Grand Rapids: Zondervan, 1990.

Alter, Robert. *The Art of Biblical Narrative.* New York: Basic, 1981.

Amram, David W. *The Jewish Law of Divorce, According to Bible and Talmud with Some Reference to its Development in Post-Talmudic Times.* New York: Hermon, 1968.

Andersen, Francis I., and David N. Freedman. *Hosea. A New Translation with Introduction and Commentary.* The Anchor Bible. Garden City, NJ: Doubleday, 1980.

Anderson, Gary. "Celibacy or Consummation in the Garden? Reflections on Early Jewish and Christian Interpretations of the Garden of Eden." *Harvard Theological Review* 82 (1989) 121–48.

Archer, Gleason Leonard. *A Survey of Old Testament Introduction.* Chicago: Moody, 1994.

Armstrong, Gregory T. *Die Genesis in der Alten Kirche.* Tübingen: Mohr, 1962.

Arzt-Grabner, Peter et al. *1. Korinther. Papyrologische Kommentare zum Neuen Testament.* Göttingen: Vandenhoeck & Ruprecht, 2006.

Ashley, Timothy R. *The Book of Numbers.* The New International Commentary on the Old Testament. Grand Rapids, MI: Eerdmans, 1993.

Atkinson, David J. *To Have and to Hold. The Marriage Covenant and the Discipline of Divorce.* London: Collins, 1979.

Bachmann, Philipp. *Der erste Brief des Paulus an die Korinther.* Kommentar zum Neuen Testament. Leipzig: Werner Scholl, 1921.

Bailey, Kenneth E. "Paul's Theological Foundation for Human Sexuality: 1 Cor. 6:9–20 in the Light of Rhetorical Criticism." *Near Eastern School of Theology Theological Review* 3 (1980) 27–41.

Balorda, Aron, "The Jealousy of Phinehas in Numbers 25 as the Embodiment of the Essence of Nominal Marriage." MA Thesis, Andrews University, 2002.

---

1. The following list of titles is a reference list containing the bibliographic information of the works concretely referred to at some place within this book. It is not an exhaustive list of all books and articles consulted during the process of research and writing.

Bibliography

Baltensweiler, Heinrich. *Die Ehe im Neuen Testament. Exegetische Untersuchungen über Ehe, Ehelosigkeit und Ehescheidung*. Zürich: Zwingli, 1967.

———. "Die Ehebruchsklauseln bei Matthäus." *Theologische Zeitschrift* 15 (1959) 340–56.

Balz, Horst R. *Christus in Korinth. Eine Auslegung des 1. Korintherbriefes*. Kleine Kasseler Bibelhilfe. Kassel: Oncken, 1970.

Barrett, Charles K. *A Commentary on the First Epistle to the Corinthians*. Harper's New Testament Commentaries. London: Harper & Row, 1968.

Barth, Markus. *Ephesians. Introduction, Translation, and Commentary on Chapters 1–3*. The Anchor Bible. Garden City, NJ: Doubleday, 1974.

———. *Ephesians. Translation and Commentary on Chapters 4–6*. The Anchor Bible. Garden City, NJ: Doubleday, 1960.

Batey, Richard A. "Jewish Gnosticism and the 'Hieros Gamos' of Eph. V:21–33." *New Testament Studies* 10 (1963/64) 121–27.

———. "The ΜΙΑ ΣΑΡΞ Union of Christ and the Church." *New Testament Studies* 13 (1966/67) 270–81.

———. *New Testament Nuptial Imagery*. Leiden: Brill, 1971.

Batto, Bernard F. "The Covenant of Peace: A Neglected Ancient Near Eastern Motif." *Catholic Biblical Quarterly* 49 (1987) 187–211.

———. "The Institution of Marriage in Genesis 2 and in Atrahasis." *The Catholic Biblical Quarterly* 62 (2000) 621–31.

Bauckham, Richard. *The Climax of Prophecy: Studies on the Book of Revelation*. Edinburgh: T&T Clark, 1993.

Beale, G. K., and D. A. Carson, eds. *Commentary on the New Testament Use of the Old Testament*. Grand Rapids, MI/Nottingham, UK: Baker Academic/Apollos, 2007.

Beattie, Gillian. *Women and Marriage in Paul and His Early Interpreters*. London: T & T Clark, 2005.

Beeston, A.F.L. "One Flesh." *Vetus Testamentum* 36 (1986) 115–17.

Benjamins, H. S. "Keeping Marriage out of Paradise: The Creation of Man and Woman in Patristic Literature." In *The Creation of Man and Woman: Interpretations of the Biblical Narratives in Jewish and Christian Traditions*. Edited by Gerard P. Luttikhuizen. Themes in Biblical Narrative: Jewish and Christian Traditions, 93–106. Leiden: Brill, 2000.

Benoit, Pierre et al., eds. *Les Grottes de Murabba'ât*. 2 vols, Discoveries in the Judaean Desert 2. Oxford: Clarendon, 1961.

Bergen, Robert D. *1, 2 Samuel*. The New American Commentary. Nashville, TN: Broadman & Holman, 1996.

Berger, Klaus. *Die Gesetzesauslegung Jesu. Ihr historischer Hintergrund im Judentum und im Alten Testament*. Wissenschaftliche Monographien zum Alten und Neuen Testament. Neukirchen-Vluyn: Neukirchener, 1972.

———. "Hartherzigkeit und Gottes Gesetz. Die Vorgeschichte des antijüdischen Vorwurfs in Mk 10,5." *Zeitschrift für die neutestamentliche Wissenschaft* 61 (1970) 1–47.

Berkouwer, G. C. *Man: The Image of God*. Grand Rapids, MI: Eerdmans, 1962.

Best, Ernest. *A Critical and Exegetical Commentary on Ephesians*. The International Critical Commentary on the Holy Scriptures of the Old and New Testaments. London: Continuum, 2004.

———. *One Body in Christ. A Study in the Relationship of the Church to Christ in the Epistle of the Apostle Paul*. London: S.P.C.K., 1955.

Bird, Phyllis. "'To Play the Harlot:' An Inquiry into an Old Testament Metaphor." In *Gender and Difference in Ancient Israel*, edited by Peggy L. Day. Minneapolis: Fortress, 1989.

Blenkinsopp, Joseph. *Isaiah 40–55. A New Translation with Introduction and Commentary*. The Anchor Bible. New York: Doubleday, 2002.

Bloch, René S. *Antike Vorstellungen vom Judentum. Der Judenexkurs des Tacitus im Rahmen der griechisch-römischen Ethnographie*. Historia Einzelschriften. Stuttgart: Steiner, 2002.

Block, Daniel I. *The Book of Ezekiel: Chapters 25–48*. The New International Commentary on the Old Testament. Grand Rapids, MI: Eerdmans, 1998.

Blomberg, Craig L. "Marriage, Divorce, Remarriage, and Celibacy. An Exegesis of Matthew 19:3–12." *Trinity Journal* 11 (1990) 161–96.

Bornemann, Eduard, and Ernst Risch. *Griechische Grammatik*. Frankfurt am Main: Diesterweg, 1978.

Botterweck, G. Johannes et al., eds. *Theologisches Wörterbuch zum Alten Testament (=TWAT)*. 10 vols. Stuttgart: Kohlhammer, 1973–2000.

Brayford, Susan. *Genesis*. Septuagint Commentary Series. Leiden/Boston: Brill, 2007.

Bromiley, Geoffrey W. *God and Marriage*. Grand Rapids, MI: Eerdmans, 1980.

Brooten, Bernadette J. "Konnten Frauen im alten Judentum die Scheidung betreiben?" *Evangelische Theologie* 42 (1982) 65–80.

———. "Zur Debatte über das Scheidungsrecht der jüdischen Frau." *Evangelische Theologie* 43 (1983) 466–78.

Brown, William P. "The Moral Cosmologies of Creation." In *Character Ethics and the Old Testament: Moral Dimensions of Scripture*, edited by M. Daniel Carroll R. et al., 11–26. Louisville: Westminster John Knox, 2007.

———. *The Structure, Role, and Ideology in the Hebrew and Greek Texts of Genesis 1:1—2:3*. Society of Biblical Literature Dissertations. Atlanta: Scholars, 1993.

Brueggemann, Walter. *Genesis:* Interpretation. A Bible Commentary for Teaching and Preaching. Atlanta: John Knox, 1982.

———. "Of the Same Flesh and Bone (Gn 2:23a)." *The Catholic Biblical Quarterly* 32 (1970) 532–42.

Bruner, Frederick D. *Matthew. Vol. 2: The Churchbook*. Dallas: Word, 1990.

Budd, Philip J. *Numbers*. Word Biblical Commentary. Waco, TX: Thomas Nelson, 1984.

Budin, Stephanie. *The Myth of Sacred Prostitution in Antiquity*. Cambridge: Cambridge University Press, 2008.

Cassuto, Umberto. *A Commentary on the Book of Exodus*. Jerusalem: Magnes/Hebrew University of Jerusalem, 1967.

———. *A Commentary on the Book of Genesis. Vol. 1. From Adam to Noah*. Translated by Israel Abrahams. Jerusalem: Magnes/Hebrew University of Jerusalem, 1961.

Charles, R. H. *The Apocrypha and Pseudepigrapha of the Old Testament in English. Volume Two: Pseudepigrapha*. Oxford: Oxford University Press, 1913.

———. *The Teaching of the New Testament on Divorce*. London: Williams & Norgate, 1921.

Christensen, Duane L. *Deuteronomy 1:1—21:9*. Word Biblical Commentary. 2 vols. Dallas: Word, 1991.

———. *Deuteronomy 21:10—34:12*. Word Biblical Commentary. 2 vols. Waco, TX: Thomas Nelson, 2002.

Clark, Elizabeth A., and Herbert W. Richardson. *Women and Religion: A Feminist Sourcebook of Christian Thought*. New York: Harper & Row, 1977.

Bibliography

Clines, David J. A., ed. *The Dictionary of Classical Hebrew.* 6 vols. Sheffield: Sheffield Academic, 1993–2007.

———. "The Etymology of Hebrew *selem.*" *Journal of Northwest Semitic Languages* 3 (1974) 19–25.

———. "The Image of God in Man." *Tyndale Bulletin* 19 (1968) 53–103.

———. "The Significance of the 'Sons of God' Episode (Genesis 6:1–4) in the Context of the 'Primeval History' (Genesis 1–11)." *Journal for the Study of the Old Testament* 13 (1979) 33–46.

Cole, R. Dennis. *Numbers.* The New American Commentary. Nashville, TN: Broadman & Holman, 2000.

Collins, C. John. *Genesis 1–4: A Linguistic, Literary, and Theological Commentary.* Phillipsburg, NJ: P&R, 2006.

———. "The (intelligible) Masoretic Text of Malachi 2:16." *Presbyterion* 20 (1994) 36–40.

Collins, Gary R. *The Secrets of Our Sexuality: Role Liberation for the Christian.* Waco, TX: Word, 1976.

Collins, John J. "The Sons of God and the Daughters of Men." In *Sacred Marriages: The Divine-Human Sexual Metaphor from Sumer to Early Christianity,* edited by Martti Nissinen et al., 259–74. Winona Lake: Eisenbrauns, 2008.

Collins, Raymond F. "The Bible and Sexuality." *Biblical Theology Bulletin* 7 (1977) 149–67.

———. *Divorce in the New Testament.* Good News Studies 38. Collegeville, MN: Liturgical, 1992.

———. *First Corinthians.* Sacra Pagina. Collegeville, MN: Liturgical, 1999.

———. *Sexual Ethics and the New Testament: Behavior and Belief.* Companions to the New Testament. New York: Crossroad, 2000.

Colson, F. H. et al., eds. *Philo.* 10 vols, The Loeb Classical Library. Greek Authors. London/Cambridge: Heinemann/Harvard University Press, 1929–1953.

Comfort, Philip W., and David P. Barrett, eds. *The Text of the Earliest New Testament Greek Manuscripts: A Corrected, Enlarged Edition of the Complete Text of the Earliest New Testament Manuscripts.* Wheaton: Tyndale, 2001.

Conzelmann, Hans. *Der erste Brief and die Korinther.* Kritisch-exegetischer Kommentar über das Neue Testament. Göttingen: Vandenhoeck & Ruprecht, 1969.

———. "Korinth und die Mädchen der Aphrodite." In *Theologie als Schriftauslegung. Aufsätze zum Neuen Testament,* edited by Hans Conzelmann, 152–66. München: Kaiser, 1974.

Cook, James I. "The Old Testament Concept of the Image of God." In *Grace upon Grace: Essays in Honor of L. J. Kuyper,* edited by James I. Cook et al., 85–94. Grand Rapids, MI: Eerdmans, 1975.

Cooper, Lamar E. *Ezekiel.* The New American Commentary. Nashville, TN: Broadman & Holman, 1994.

Cornes, Andrew. *Divorce and Remarriage. Biblical Principles and Pastoral Practice.* Tain, UK: Christian Focus, 2002.

Cosby, Michael R. *Sex in the Bible: An Introduction to What the Scriptures Teach Us About Sexuality.'* Englewood Cliffs, NJ: Prentice-Hall, 1984.

Countryman, William L. *Dirt, Greed and Sex: Sexual Ethics in the New Testament and Their Implications for Today.* Philadelphia: Fortress, 1988.

Craigie, Peter C. *The Book of Deuteronomy.* The New International Commentary on the Old Testament. Grand Rapids, MI: Eerdmans, 1976.

Craigie, Peter C. et al. *Jeremiah 1–25.* Word Biblical Commentary. Dallas: Word, 1991.

Crispin, Ken. *Divorce: The Forgivable Sin?* London: Hodder and Stoughton, 1989.

Dana, H. E., and Julius R. Mantey. *A Manual Grammar of the Greek New Testament.* New York: MacMillan, 1957.

Danker, Frederick W. et al. *A Greek-English Lexicon of the New Testament and other Early Christian Literature (=BDAG).* Chicago: University of Chicago Press, 2000.

Daube, David. *The New Testament and Rabbinic Judaism.* Jordan Lectures in Comparative Religion. London: University of London, Athlone, 1956.

Dautzenberg, Gerhard. "Φεύγετε τὴν πορνείαν (1 Kor 6,18): Eine Fallstudie zur paulinischen Sexualethik in ihrem Verhältnis zur Sexualethik des Frühjudentums." In *Neues Testament und Ethik*, edited by Helmut Merklein. 271–98. Freiburg, 1989.

Davidson, Richard M. "Divorce and Remarriage in Deuteronomy 24:1–4." *Journal of the Adventist Theological Society* 10 (1999) 2–22.

———. *Flame of Yahweh. Sexuality in the Old Testament.* Peabody: Hendrickson, 2007.

———. "Scheidung und Wiederheirat im Alten Testament." In *Die Ehe. Biblische, theologische und pastorale Aspekte*, edited by Roberto Badenas et al., 157–79. Lüneburg: Saatkorn, 2010.

———. "The Theology of Sexuality in the Beginning: Genesis 1–2." *Andrews University Seminary Studies* 26 (1988) 5–24.

Davies, W. D., and Dale C. Allison. *A Critical and Exegetical Commentary on the Gospel According to Saint Matthew.* The International Critical Commentary on the Holy Scriptures of the Old and New Testaments. 3 vols. Edinburgh: T&T Clark, 1997.

Davis, John J. *Moses and the Gods of Egypt: Studies in the Book of Exodus.* Grand Rapids: Baker, 1971.

Deines, Roland. *Die Pharisäer. Ihr Verständnis im Spiegel der christlichen und jüdischen Forschung seit Wellhausen und Graetz.* Wissenschaftliche Untersuchungen zum Neuen Testament. Tübingen: Mohr, 1997.

Dibelius, Martin. *An die Kolosser, Epheser, an Philemon.* Tübingen: Mohr, 1953.

Domanyi, Thomas. "Sexualität und Ehe aus theologischer Sicht: Ein Beitrag zur biblischen Anthropologie und Ethik." In *Die Ehe. Biblische, theologische und pastorale Aspekte*, edited by Roberto Badenas et al., 229–52. Lüneburg: Saatkorn, 2010.

Doukhan, Jacque B., "The Literary Structure of the Genesis Creation Story." Doctoral Dissertation, Andrews University, 1978.

Driver, Samuel R. *A Critical and Exegetical Commentary on Deuteronomy.* The International Critical Commentary on the Holy Scriptures of the Old and New Testaments. Edinburgh: T. & T. Clark, 1902.

———. *A Treatise on the Use of the Tenses in Hebrew.* Oxford: Clarendon, 1892.

Du Preez, Ronald A. G. *Polygamy in the Bible.* Adventist Theological Society Dissertation Series. Berrien Springs, MI: Andrews University Press, 1993.

Dunn, James D. G. *The New Perspective on Paul: Collected Essays.* Wissenschaftliche Untersuchungen zum Neuen Testament. Tübingen: Mohr Siebeck, 2005.

———. *The Theology of Paul the Apostle.* Grand Rapids, MI: Eerdmans, 1998.

Dunstan, Gordon R. "The Marriage Covenant." *Theology* 78 (1975) 244–52.

Durham, John I. *Exodus.* Word Biblical Commentary. Waco, TX: Thomas Nelson, 1987.

Egger, Wilhelm. *Methodenlehre zum Neuen Testament. Einführung in linguistische und historisch-kritische Methoden.* Freiburg: Herder, 1987.

Ellens, Deborah L. *Women in the Sex Texts of Leviticus and Deuteronomy: A Comparative Conceptual Analysis.* Library of Hebrew Bible/Old Testament Studies. New York: T & T Clark, 2008.

Elliott, J. K. "Paul's Teaching on Marriage in 1 Corinthians: Some Problems Considered." *New Testament Studies* 19 (1972/73) 219–25.

Ellis, E. Earle. *Christ and the Future in New Testament History.* Leiden: Brill, 2000.

———. *Making of the New Testament Documents.* Leiden: Brill, 1999.

———. *Paul's Use of the Old Testament.* Edinburgh/London: Oliver and Boyd, 1957.

Epstein, I. *Soncino Babylonian Talmud.* London: Soncino, 1935–1948.

Erickson, Millard J. *God in Three Persons: A Contemporary Interpretation of the Trinity.* Grand Rapids, MI: Baker, 1995.

Farla, Piet. "'The Two Shall Become One Flesh.' Gen 1.27 and 2.24 in the New Testament Marriage Texts." In *Intertextuality in Biblical Writings. Festschrift in Honor of Bas van Iersel,* edited by Sipke Draisma. Kampen: Kok, 1989.

Fee, Gordon D. "1 Corinthians 7:1 in the NIV." *Journal of the Evangelical Theological Society* 23 (1980) 307–14.

———. *The First Epistle to the Corinthians.* New Testament International Commentary on the New Testament. Grand Rapids, MI: Eerdmans, 1987.

Feldman, David M. *Marital Relations, Birth Control and Abortion in Jewish Law.* New York: New York University Press, 1968.

Field, Fridericus. *Origenis Hexaplorum Quae Supersunt: Veterum Testamentum Graecorum in totum Vetus Testamentum fragmenta.* Oxford: Clarendon, 1875.

Fischer, Johannes. "Hat die Ehe einen Primat gegenüber der nicht ehelichen Lebensgemeinschaft?" *Zeitschrift für Theologie und Kirche* 101 (2004) 346–57.

Fischer, Karl-Martin. *Tendenz und Absicht des Epheserbriefes.* Göttingen: Vandenhoeck & Ruprecht, 1973.

Fitzmyer, Joseph A. *First Corinthians: A New Translation with Introduction and Commentary.* New Haven: Yale University Press, 2008.

———. "The Matthean Divorce Texts and Some New Palestinian Evidence." *Theological Studies* 37 (1976) 197–226.

———. *To Advance the Gospel: New Testament Studies.* Grand Rapids, MI: Eerdmans, 1998.

Fockner, Sven. "Reopening the Discussion: Another Contextual Look at the Sons of God." *Journal for the Study of the Old Testament* 32 (2008) 435–56.

Fossum, Jarl. "Gen 1:26 and 2:7 in Judaism, Samaritanism and Gnosticism." *Journal for the Study of Judaism* 16 (1985) 202–39.

France, Richard T. *The Gospel of Mark: A Commentary on the Greek Text.* Grand Rapids, MI: Eerdmans/Paternoster, 2002.

———. *The Gospel of Matthew.* The New International Commentary on the New Testament. Grand Rapids, MI: Eerdmans, 2007.

Frankemölle, Hubert. "Ehescheidung und Wiederverheiratung von Geschiedenen im Neuen Testament." In *Geschieden, Wiederverheiratet, Abgewiesen? Antworten der Theologie,* edited by Theodor Schneider, 28–50. Freiburg im Breisgau: Herder, 1995.

Freedman, David R. "Woman, A Power Equal to Man." *Biblical Archaeology Review* 9 (1983) 56–58.

Freedman, H., and M. Simon. *Midrash Rabbah.* 10 vols. London: Soncino, 1951.

Friedrich, Gerhard. *Sexualität und Ehe. Rückfragen an das Neue Testament.* Biblisches Forum 11. Stuttgart: Katholisches Bibelwerk, 1977.

Frymer-Kensky, Tikva S. "Law and Philosophy. The Case of Sex in the Bible." *Semeia* 45 (1989) 89–102.

Gane, Roy. *Leviticus/Numbers*. The NIV Application Commentary. Grand Rapids, MI: Zondervan, 2004.

———. "Old Testament Principles Relating to Divorce and Remarriage." *Journal of the Adventist Theological Society* 12 (2001) 35–61.

Garland, David E. *1 Corinthians*. Baker Exegetical Commentary on the New Testament. Grand Rapids, MI: Baker Academic, 2003.

Garrett, Duane A. *Genesis 1 and the Primeval History*. Grand Rapids, MI: Baker, 1991.

———. *Hosea, Joel*. The New American Commentary. Nashville, TN: Broadman & Holman, 1997.

Gaster, Theodor H. *Myth, Legend and Custom in the Old Testament*. New York: Harper & Row, 1969.

Gehring, René. *Die antiken jüdischen Religionsparteien. Essener, Pharisäer, Sadduzäer, Zeloten und Therapeuten*. Schriften der Forschung. St. Peter am Hart: Seminar Schloss Bogenhofen, 2012.

Gellman, Jerome. "Gender and Sexuality in the Garden of Eden." *Theology & Sexuality* 12 (2006) 319–35.

Gilmour, S. MacLean. *The Gospel According to St. Luke*. The Interpreter's Bible. New York: Abingdon, 1952.

Ginzberg, Louis. *The Legends of the Jews*. 7 vols. Philadelphia: Jewish Publication Society, 1909–1938.

Gnilka, Joachim. *Das Evangelium nach Markus*. Evangelisch-Katholischer Kommentar zum Neuen Testament. 2 vols. Zürich/Einsiedeln/Köln/Neukirchen-Vluyn: Benziger/Neukirchener, 1978–1979.

———. *Das Evangelium nach Markus*. Bd. 2. Leipzig: St. Benno, 2001.

Green, William Scott. "What Do We Really Know About the Pharisees, and How Do We Know It?" In *In Quest of the Historical Pharisees*, edited by Jacob Neusner et al., 409–23. Waco, TX: Baylor University Press, 2007.

Greenberg, Blu. "Marriage in the Jewish Tradition." *Journal of Ecumenical Studies* 22 (1985) 3–20.

Greeven, Heinrich. "Ehe nach dem Neuen Testament." *New Testament Studies* 15 (1968/69) 365–88.

———. "Zu den Aussagen des Neuen Testaments über die Ehe." *Zeitschrift für evangelische Ethik* 1 (1957) 109–25.

Grelot, Pierre. "The Institution of Marriage. Its Evolution in the Old Testament." In *The Future of Marriage as Institution*, edited by Franz Böckle. 39–50. London: Herder and Herder, 1970.

Grossfeld, Bernard, trans. *The Targum Onqelos to Genesis. Translated, with a Critical Introduction, Apparatus, and Notes*. The Aramaic Bible. Edinburgh: T&T Clark Ltd., 1988.

Grubbs, Judith E. "'Pagan' and 'Christian' Marriage: The State of the Question." *Journal of Early Christian Studies* 2 (1994) 361–412.

Guelich, Robert A. *The Sermon on the Mount*. Waco, TX: Word, 1982.

Gulley, Norman R. "Trinity in the Old Testament." *Journal of the Adventist Theological Society* 17 (2006) 80–97.

Gunkel, Hermann. *Die Urgeschichte und die Patriarchen. Das erste Buch Mosis*. Schriften des Alten Testaments 1. Göttingen: Vandenhoeck & Ruprecht, 1911.

———. *Genesis*. Handkommentar zum Alten Testament. Göttingen: Vandenhoeck & Ruprecht, 1910 (= 1966/1977).

Haag, Herbert, and Katharina Elliger. *Zur Liebe befreit. Sexualität in der Bibel und heute*. Zürich: Benziger, 1998.

Habel, Norman C. *Literary Criticism of the Old Testament*. Philadelphia: Fortress, 1971.

Hagner, Donald A. *Matthew 1–13*. Word Biblical Commentary. Dallas: Paternoster, 1993.

———. *Matthew 14–28*. Word Biblical Commentary. Dallas: Paternoster, 1995.

Hamilton, Victor P. *The Book of Genesis: Chapters 1–17*. The New International Commentary on the Old Testament. Grand Rapids, MI: Eerdmans, 1990.

———. "Marriage." In *The Anchor Bible Dictionary*, edited by David N. Freedman. 559–69. New York: Doubleday, 1992.

Harrelson, Walter J. *The Ten Commandments for Today*. Louisville, KY: Westminster John Knox, 2006.

Harris, R. Laird. "Leviticus." In *The Expositor's Bible Commentary*, edited by Frank E. Gaebelein. 499–654. Grand Rapids, MI: Zondervan, 1990.

Harrison, R. K. *Numbers*. The Wycliffe Exegetical Commentary. Chicago: Moody, 1990.

Hartley, John E. *Leviticus*. Word Biblical Commentary. Waco, TX: Thomas Nelson, 1992.

Hasel, Frank. "Das biblische Eheverständnis." In *Die Ehe. Biblische, theologische und pastorale Aspekte*, edited by Roberto Badenas et al., 17–40. Lüneburg: Saatkorn, 2010.

Hasel, Gerhard F. "Equality from the Start: Woman in the Creation Story." *Spectrum* 7 (1975) 21–28.

———. "The Meaning of 'Let Us' in Gen 1:26." *Andrews University Seminary Studies* 13 (1975) 58–66.

Hauck, Friedrich, and Siegfried Schulz. "πορνεία." In *Theologisches Wörterbuch zum Neuen Testament 6*, edited by Gerhard Friedrich. 579–95. Stuttgart: Kohlhammer, 1959.

Hauser, Alan J. "Genesis 2–3: The Theme of Intimacy and Alienation." In *Art and Meaning. Rhetoric in Biblical Literature*, edited by David J. A. Clines. Sheffield: JSOT, 1982.

———. "Linguistic and Thematic Links between Genesis 4:1-6 and Genesis 2-3." *Journal of the Evangelical Theological Society* 23 (1980) 297–305.

Hays, Richard B. *First Corinthians*. Interpretation. Louisville, KY: John Knox, 1997.

———. *The Moral Vision of the New Testament: Community, Cross, New Creation. A Contemporary Introduction to New Testament Ethics*. Edinburgh: T&T Clark, 1996.

Heinemann, Isaak. *Philos griechische und jüdische Bildung. Kulturvergleichende Untersuchung zu Philos Darstellung der jüdischen Gesetze*. Reprint (Breslau 1932). Hildesheim: Olms, 1962.

Heinisch, Paul. *Die Heilige Schrift des Alten Testaments. I.1. Das Buch Genesis*. Bonn: Peter Hanstein, 1930.

Heinz, Hans. "Das Problem der Mischehen in 1. Korinther 7,12–16." In *Die Ehe. Biblische, theologische und pastorale Aspekte*, edited by Roberto Badenas et al., 193–200. Lüneburg: Saatkorn, 2010.

Hering, James P. *The Colossian and Ephesian Haustafeln in Theological Context: An Analysis of their Origins, Relationships, and Message*. American University Studies: Theology and Religion. New York: Peter Lang, 2007.

Heth, William A. "The Meaning of Divorce in Matthew 19:3–9." *Churchman* 98 (1984) 136–52.

Heth, William A., and Gordon J. Wenham. *Jesus and Divorce*. Nashville, TN: Thomas Nelson, 1985.

Hill, Andrew E. *Malachi. A New Translation with Introduction and Commentary*. The Anchor Bible. A New Translation with Introduction and Commentary. New York: Doubleday, 1998.

Hoek, Annewies van den. "Endowed with Reason or Glued to the Senses: Philo's Thoughts on Adam and Eve." In *The Creation of Man and Woman: Interpretations of the Biblical Narratives in Jewish and Christian Traditions*, edited by Gerard P. Luttikhuizen. Themes in Biblical Narrative. Jewish and Christian Traditions, 63–75. Leiden: Brill, 2000.

Hoekema, Anthony A. *Created in God's Image*. Grand Rapids, MI: Eerdmans, 1986.

Hoffmann, Pad. "Jesus' Sayings about Divorce and Its Interpretation." In *The Future of Marriage as Institution*, edited by Franz Böckle, 51–66. London: Herder and Herder, 1970.

Höhner, Harold W. *Ephesians. An Exegetical Commentary*. Grand Rapids, MI: Baker Academic, 2002.

Holwerda, David E. "Jesus on Divorce. An Assessment of a New Proposal." *Calvin Theological Journal* 22 (1987) 114–20.

Hugenberger, Gordon P. *Marriage as a Covenant: Biblical Law and Ethics as Developed from Malachi*. Supplements to Vetus Testamentum. Leiden: Brill, 1994.

Ilan, Tal. "Notes and Observations On a Newly Published Divorce Bill from the Judean Desert." *Harvard Theological Review* 89 (1996) 195–202.

———. "Premarital Cohabitation in Ancient Judea: The Evidence of the Babatha Archive and the Mishnah (Ketubbot 1.4)." *Harvard Theological Review* 86 (1993) 247–64.

Instone-Brewer, David. "Deuteronomy 24:1–4 and the Origin of the Jewish Divorce Certificate." *Journal for the Study of Judaism* 49 (1998) 230–43.

———. *Divorce and Remarriage in the Bible: The Social and Literary Context*. Grand Rapids: Eerdmans, 2002.

———. *Divorce and Remarriage in the Church. Biblical Solutions for Pastoral Realities*. Downers Grove, IL: InterVarsity, 2003.

———. *Techniques and Assumptions in Jewish Exegesis before 70 CE*. Texte und Studien zum antiken Judentum 30. Tübingen: Mohr, 1992.

———. "What God Has Joined. What Does the Bible Really Teach About Divorce?" *Christianity Today* 51 (2007) 26–29.

Isaksson, Abel. *Marriage and Ministry in the New Temple: A Study with Special Reference to Mt. 19.13–12 and 1. Cor. 11.3–16*. Lund/Copenhagen: Gleerup/Munksgaard, 1965.

Jewett, Paul K. *Man as Male and Female: A Study in Sexual Relationships from a Theological Point of View*. Grand Rapids, MI: Eerdmans, 1975.

Joestel, Volkmar, and Friedrich Schorlemmer, eds. *Und sie werden sein ein Fleisch. Martin Luther und die Ehe*. Wittenberg: Drei Kastanien, 1999/2007.

Jones, David C. "A Note on the LXX of Malachi 2:16." *Journal of Biblical Literature* 109 (1990) 683–85.

Josephus, Flavius. *Against Apion*. Translated by John M. G. Barclay. Flavius Josephus. Translation and Commentary. Leiden: Brill, 2007.

———. *The Works of Flavius Josephus*. Translated by William Whiston. New York: W. Borradaile, 1828.

Joüon, Paul, and Takamitsu Muraoka. *A Grammar of Biblical Hebrew*. Subsidia Biblica. Rome: Editrice Pontificio Intituto Biblico, 2006.

Kaiser, Walter C. "Divorce in Malachi 2:10–16." *Chriswell Theological Review* 2 (1987) 73–84.

———. "Exodus." In *The Expositor's Bible Commentary*, edited by Frank E. Gaebelein, 285–498. Grand Rapids, MI: Zondervan, 1990.

———. *Toward Old Testament Ethics*. Grand Rapids, MI: Zondervan, 1983.

Kalland, Earl S. "Deuteronomy." In *The Expositor's Bible Commentary.*, edited by Frank E. Gaebelein, 3–238. Grand Rapids, MI: Zondervan, 1990.

Kaye, Bruce. "'One Flesh' and Marriage." *Colloquium* 22 (1990) 46–57.

Kearney, Peter J. "Creation and Liturgy: The P Redaction of Exod 25–40." *Zeitschrift für die Alttestamentliche Wissenschaft* 89 (1977) 375–87.

Keener, Craig S. *. . . and Marries Another: Divorce and Remarriage in the Teaching of the New Testament*. Peabody: Hendrickson, 1991/1996.

Keil, Carl Friedrich. *The Book of Numbers*. Biblical Commentary. Edinburgh: T. & T. Clark, 1869.

———. *The First Book of Moses*. Grand Rapids, MI: Eerdmans, 1949.

———, and Franz Delitzsch. *The Pentateuch: Three Volumes in One*. Biblical Commentary on the Old Testament in Ten Volumes. 10 vols. Grand Rapids, MI: Eerdmans, 1976.

Kidner, Derek. *Genesis. An Introduction and Commentary*. London: Tyndale, 1967.

Kinlaw, Dennis F. "A Biblical View of Homosexuality." In *The Secrets of Our Sexuality: Role Liberation for the Christian*, edited by Gary R. Collins. Waco, TX: Word, 1976.

Kirchhoff, Renate. *Die Sünde gegen den eigenen Leib. Studien zu πόρνη und πορνεία in 1 Kor 6,12–20 und dem sozio-kulturellen Kontext der paulinischen Adressaten*. Studien zur Umwelt des Neuen Testaments. Göttingen: Vandenhoeck & Ruprecht, 1994.

Kirchschläger, Walter. *Ehe und Ehescheidung im Neuen Testament. Überlegungen und Anfragen zur Praxis der Kirche*. Wien: Herold, 1987.

Klauck, Hans-Josef. *1. Korintherbrief*. Neue Echter Bibel. Würzburg: Echter, 1984.

Klawans, Jonathan. *Impurity and Sin in Ancient Judaism*. New York: Oxford University Press, 2000.

Klein, Ralph W. *1 Samuel*. Word Biblical Commentary. Waco, TX: Thomas Nelson, 1983.

Kleinschmidt, Frank. *Ehefragen im Neuen Testament. Ehe, Ehelosigkeit, Ehescheidung, Verheiratung Verwitweter und Geschiedener im Neuen Testament*. Arbeiten zur Religion und Geschichte des Urchristentums 7. Frankfurt am Main: Peter Lang, 1997.

Kline, Meredith G. "Creation in the Image of the Glory-Spirit." *Westminster Theological Journal* 39 (1977) 250–72.

Koch, Klaus. *Imago Dei*. Göttingen: Vandenhoeck & Ruprecht, 2000.

Koltun-Fromm, Naomi. "Sexuality and Holiness: Semitic Christian and Jewish Conceptualizations of Sexual Behavior." *Vigiliae Christianae* 54 (2000) 375–95.

Köstenberger, Andreas J. *John*. Baker Exegetical Commentary on the New Testament. Grand Rapids, MI: Baker, 2004.

———. "The Mystery of Christ and the Church. Head and Body, 'One Flesh.'" *Trinity Journal* 12 (1991) 79–94.

Kovar, Johannes. "Eheähnliche Lebensgemeinschaft (Konkubinat)." In *Die Ehe. Biblische, theologische und pastorale Aspekte*, edited by Roberto Badenas et al., 131–56. Lüneburg: Saatkorn, 2010.

Kraetzschmar, Richard. *Die Bundesvorstellung im Alten Testament in ihrer geschichtlichen Entwicklung untersucht und dargestellt*. Marburg: Elwert, 1896.

Kramer, Samuel N. *The Sumerians, their History, Culture and Character*. Chicago: University of Chicago, 1963.

Kremer, Jacob. "Jesu Wort zur Ehescheidung." In *Geschieden, Wiederverheiratet, Abgewiesen? Antworten der Theologie*, edited by Theodor Schneider, 51–67. Freiburg im Breisgau: Herder, 1995.

Külling, Heinz. *Ehe und Ehelosigkeit bei Paulus. Eine Auslegung zu 1. Korinther 6,12–17,40*. Zürich: Theologischer Verlag Zürich, 2008.

Kuntz, Paul G., and Thomas D'Evelyn. *The Ten Commandments in History. Mosaic Paradigms for a Well-Ordered Society*. Emory University Studies in Law and Religion. Grand Rapids, MI: Eerdmans, 2004.

Kvam, Kristen E. et al. *Eve and Adam. Jewish, Christian, and Muslim Readings on Genesis and Gender*. Bloomington, IN: Indiana University Press, 1999.

Lambrecht, Jan, ed. *Collected Studies on Pauline Literature and on the Book of Revelation*, Analecta Biblica, vol. 147. Rome: Editrice Pontificio Istituto Biblico, 2001.

Laney, J. Carl. "Deuteronomy 24:1–4 and the Issue of Divorce." *Bibliotheca Sacra* 149 (1992) 3–15.

Lawton, Robert B. "Genesis 2:24: Trite or Tragic?" *Journal of Biblical Literature* 105 (1986) 97–112.

Lehmann, Manfred R. "Gen 2:24 as the Basis for Divorce in Halakhah and New Testament." *Zeitschrift für die Alttestamentliche Wissenschaft* 72 (1960) 263–67.

Lehmann, Richard. "Die kirchliche Feier der Eheschließung." In *Die Ehe. Biblische, theologische und pastorale Aspekte*, edited by Roberto Badenas et al., 271–89. Lüneburg: Saatkorn, 2010.

Leslie, Gerald R., and Sheila K. Korman. *The Family in Social Context*. New York: Oxford University Press, 1985.

Levine, Baruch A. *The JPS Torah Commentary: Leviticus: The Traditional Hebrew Text with the New JPS Translation*. Philadelphia: Jewish Publication Society, 1989.

———. *Numbers 21–36: A New Translation with Introduction and Commentary*. The Anchor Bible. New York: Doubleday, 2000.

Lewis, Naphtali. *The Documents from the Bar Kokhba Period in the Cave of the Letters. Vol. 2: Greek Papyri*. Jerusalem: Israel Exploration Society, 1989.

Lietzmann, Hans, and Werner G. Kümmel. *An die Korinther I-II*. Handbuch zum Neuen Testament 9. Tübingen: Mohr, 1949.

Lincoln, Andrew T. *Ephesians*. Word Biblical Commentary. Dallas: Paternoster, 1990.

———. "The Use of the OT in Ephesians." *Journal for the Study of the New Testament* 14 (1982) 16–57.

Litke, Wayne. "Beyond Creation: Galatians 3:28, Genesis and the Hermaphrodite Myth." *Studies in Religion* 24 (1995) 173–78.

Loader, William. *The Dead Sea Scrolls on Sexuality: Attitudes towards Sexuality in Sectarian and Related Literature at Qumran*. Grand Rapids, MI: Eerdmans, 2009.

———. *Enoch, Levi, and Jubilees on Sexuality: Attitudes towards Sexuality in the Early Enoch Literature, the Aramaic Levi Document, and the Book of Jubilees*. Grand Rapids, MI: Eerdmans, 2007.

———. *The Septuagint, Sexuality, and the New Testament: Case Studies on the Impact of the LXX in Philo and the New Testament*. Grand Rapids, MI: Eerdmans, 2004.

———. *Sexuality and the Jesus Tradition*. Grand Rapids, MI: Eerdmans, 2005.

Lohfink, Norbert. *Das Hauptgebot. Eine Untersuchung literarischer Einleitungsfragen zu Dtn 5–11*. Analecta Biblica 20. Rome: Pontifical Biblical Institute, 1963.

Lohmeyer, Ernst. *Das Evangelium des Markus.* Meyer's Kommentar I/2. Göttingen: Vandenhoeck & Ruprecht, 1957.

Loretz, Oswald. *Die Gottesebenbildlichkeit des Menschen.* München: Kösel, 1967.

Lövestam, Evald. "Divorce and Remarriage in the New Testament." *The Jewish Law Annual* 4 (1981) 47–65.

Luck, William F. *Divorce and Remarriage. Recovering the Biblical View.* San Francisco: Harper & Row, 1987.

Luz, Ulrich. *Das Evangelium nach Matthäus.* Evangelisch-Katholischer Kommentar zum Neuen Testament. 4 vols. Düsseldorf/Zürich/Neukirchen-Vluyn: Benziger/Neukirchener, 1989–2002.

Maccoby, Hyam. *Ritual and Morality: The Ritual Purity System and Its Place in Judaism.* New York: Cambridge University Press, 1999.

MacDonald, Margaret Y. *Early Christian Women and Pagan Opinion: The Power of Hysterical Woman.* Cambridge: Cambridge University Press, 1996.

Maher, Michael, trans. *Targum Pseudo-Jonathan: Genesis. Translated with Introduction and Notes.* The Aramaic Bible. Edinburgh: T&T Clark Ltd., 1992.

Mahoney, Aidan. "A New Look at the Divorce Clauses in Mt 5,32 and 19,9." *Catholic Biblical Quarterly* 30 (1968) 29–38.

Maier, Gerhard. *Matthäus-Evangelium.* Edition C-Bibelkommentar. Neuhausen-Stuttgart: Hänssler, 1995.

Marks, Herbert. "Biblical Naming and Poetic Etymology." *Journal of Biblical Literature* 114 (1995) 29–50.

Marrs, Rick. "The Sons of God (Genesis 6:1–4)." *Restoration Quarterly* 23 (1980) 218–24.

Martin, Dale B. *The Corinthian Body.* New Haven: Yale University Press, 1995.

Martin, Ralph P. *2 Corinthians.* Word Biblical Commentary. Waco, TX: Word, 1986.

Martínez, F. García. "Man and Woman. Halakha Based upon Eden in the Dead Sea Scrolls." In *Paradise Interpreted. Representations in Biblical Paradise in Judaism and Christianity.*, edited by Gerard P. Luttikhuizen. 95–115. Leiden: Brill, 1999.

Mathews, Kenneth A. *Genesis 1—11:26.* The New American Commentary. 2 vols. Nashville, TN: Broadman & Holman, 1996.

May, Alistair Scott. *The Body for the Lord. Sex and Identity in 1 Corinthians 5–7.* Journal for the Study of the New Testament Supplement Series 278. London: T&T Clark, 2004.

McCarter, P. Kyle. *1 Samuel. A new Translation.* Garden City, NJ: Doubleday, 1980.

McNamara, Martin, trans. *Targum Neofiti 1: Genesis. Translated with Apparatus and Notes.* The Aramaic Bible. Collegeville, MN: Liturgical, 1992.

Mehrlein, Rolf et al. *Ars Graeca. Griechische Sprachlehre.* Paderborn: Ferdinand Schöningh, 1981.

Meier, John P. *A Marginal Jew: Rethinking the Historical Jesus. Vol. 4: Law and Love.* The Anchor Bible Reference Library. New Haven: Yale University Press, 2009.

Meier, Samuel A. "Linguistic Clues on the Date and Canaanite Origin of Genesis 2:23–24." *The Catholic Biblical Quarterly* 53 (1991) 18–24.

Merklein, Helmut. "'Es ist gut für den Menschen, eine Frau nicht anzufassen.' Paulus und die Sexualität nach 1 Kor 7." In *Die Frau im Urchristentum*, edited by Gerhard Dautzenberg et al., 225–53. Freiburg: Herder, 1983.

Merrill, Eugene H. *Deuteronomy.* The New American Commentary. Nashville, TN: Broadman & Holman, 1994.

Mettinger, Tryggve N. D. "Abbild oder Urbild? 'Imago Dei' in traditionsgeschichtlicher Sicht." *Zeitschrift für die Alttestamentliche Wissenschaft* 86 (1974) 403–24.

Metzger, Bruce M. *A Textual Commentary on the Greek New Testament. A Companion Volume to the United Bible Societies' Greek New Testament.* Stuttgart: Deutsche Bibelgesellschaft/ United Bible Societies, 1994.

Meyers, Carol. *Discovering Eve: Ancient Israelite Women in Context.* New York: Oxford University Press, 1988.

Miles, Herbert J., and Fern H. Miles. *Husband-Wife Equality.* Old Tappan, N.J.: F. H. Revell Co., 1978.

Miletic, Stephen F. *"One Flesh:" Eph. 5.22–24, 5.31. Marriage and the New Creation.* Analecta Biblica. Rome: Editrice Pontificio Istituto Biblico, 1988.

Milgrom, Jacob. *The JPS Torah Commentary: Numbers. The Traditional Hebrew Text with the New JPS Translation.* Philadelphia: Jewish Publication Society, 1990.

———. *Leviticus 1–16. A New Translation with Introduction and Commentary.* New York: Doubleday, 1991.

Miller, J. I. "A Fresh Look at 1 Corinthians 6:16f." *New Testament Studies* 27 (1980) 125–27.

Miller, J. Maxwell. "In the 'Image' and 'Likeness' of God." *Journal of Biblical Literature* 91 (1972) 289–304.

Moberly, R. W. L. "Did the Serpent get it right?" *Journal of Theological Studies* 39 (1988) 1–27.

Moore, George Foot. *Judaism.* Vol. 2. Cambridge: Harvard University Press, 1972.

Morris, Leon. *1 Corinthians.* Tyndale NT Commentaries. Leicester: Eerdmans, 1985.

Mounce, Robert H. *The Book of Revelation: Revised.* The New International Commentary on the New Testament. Grand Rapids, MI: Eerdmans, 1998.

Muilenburg, James. "Form Criticism and Beyond." *Journal of Biblical Literature* 88 (1969) 1–18.

Müller, Karlheinz. "Die Haustafel des Kolosserbriefs und das antike Frauenthema." In *Die Frau im Urchristentum*, edited by Gerhard Dautzenberg et al., 263–319. Freiburg: Herder, 1983.

———. "Zur Datierung rabbinischer Aussagen." In *Neues Testament und Ethik*, edited by Helmut Merklein, 551–87. Freiburg: Herder, 1989.

Murphy-O'Connor, Jerome. *1 Corinthians.* New Testament Message. Wilmington, DE: Glazier, 1979.

———. "Corinthian Slogans in 1 Cor 6:12–20." *The Catholic Biblical Quarterly* 40 (1978) 391–96.

———. "The Divorced Woman in 1 Cor 7:10–11." *Journal of Biblical Literature* 100 (1981) 601–6.

———. *St. Paul's Corinth. Texts and Archaeology.* Wilmington, DE: Glazier, 1983.

Murray, John. "Divorce." *Westminster Theological Journal* 9 (1946) 31–46.181–97.

———. *Principles of Conduct.* Grand Rapids, MI: Eerdmans, 1957.

Nembach, Ulrich. "Ehescheidung nach alttestamentlichem und jüdischem Recht." *Theologische Zeitschrift* 26 (1970) 161–71.

Neudecker, Reinhard. "Das Ehescheidungsgesetz von Dtn 24,1–4 nach altjüdischer Auslegung. Ein Beitrag zum Verständnis der neutestamentlichen Aussagen zur Ehescheidung." *Biblica* 75 (1994) 350–87.

Neufeld, Ephraim. *Ancient Hebrew Marriage Laws, with Special References to General Semitic Laws and Customs.* London: Longmans, 1944.

Bibliography

Neusner, Jacob. *From Politics to Piety: The Emergence of Pharisaic Judaism.* Englewood Cliffs, N.J.: Prentice-Hall, 1972.

———. *A History of the Mishnaic Law of Women.* Leiden: Brill, 1980.

———. "The Rabbinic Traditions about the Pharisees before 70 CE: An Overview." In *In Quest of the Historical Pharisees*, edited by Jacob Neusner et al., 297–311. Waco, TX: Baylor University Press, 2007.

———. *Uniting the Dual Torah: Sifra and Problem of the Mishnah.* Cambridge: Cambridge University Press, 1990.

Nichol, Francis D., and M. L. Andreasen. *The Seventh-Day Adventist Bible Commentary. The Holy Bible with Exegetical and Expository Comment (=ABC).* 7 vols. rev. ed. Washington, DC: Review and Herald, 1976/2002.

Niebergall, Alfred. *Ehe und Eheschliessung in der Bibel und in der Geschichte der alten Kirche.* Marburger Theologische Studien 18. Marburg: Elwert, 1985.

Niederwimmer, Kurt. *Askese und Mysterium. Über Ehe, Ehescheidung und Eheverzicht in den Anfängen des christlichen Glaubens.* Göttingen: Vandenhoeck & Ruprecht, 1975.

Nies, Richard D., "Divorce and Remarriage." Transcript from Taped Presentations, Avondale College Library, 1979.

NN. *Das Buch Henoch. Das sogenannte Slawische Henochbuch in der längeren Redaktion.* Kassel: Rosenkreuz, 1974.

Nolland, John. *The Gospel of Matthew: A Commentary on the Greek Text.* Grand Rapids, MI/Bletchley: Eerdmans/Paternoster, 2005.

Noort, Ed. "The Creation of Man and Woman in Biblical and Ancient near Eastern Traditions." In *The Creation of Man and Woman: Interpretations of the Biblical Narratives in Jewish and Christian Traditions*, edited by Gerard P. Luttikhuizen. Themes in Biblical Narrative. Jewish and Christian Traditions, 1–18. Leiden: Brill, 2000.

Noth, Martin. *Das vierte Buch Mose. Numeri.* Das Alte Testament Deutsch. Göttingen: Vandenhoeck & Ruprecht, 1982/1995.

Ortlund, Raymond C. *Whoredom. God's Unfaithful Wife in Biblical Theology.* New Studies in Biblical Theology. Leicester: Apollos, 1996.

Osborne, Grant R. *Revelation.* Baker Exegetical Commentary on the New Testament. Grand Rapids, MI: Baker Academic, 2002.

Osiek, Carolyn. "The Bride of Christ (Ephesians 5:22–33): A Problematic Wedding." In *Sacred Marriages: The Divine-Human Sexual Metaphor from Sumer to Early Christianity*, edited by Martti Nissinen et al., 371–92. Winona Lake, IN: Eisenbrauns, 2008.

Oster, Richard E. "Use, Misuse, and Neglect of Archaeological Evidence in some Modern Works on 1 Corinthians (1 Cor 7:1–5; 8:10; 11:2–16; 12:14–26)." *Zeitschrift für die neutestamentliche Wissenschaft* 83 (1992) 52–73.

Pagels, Elaine H. "The 'Mystery of Marriage' in the Gospel of Philip Revisited." In *The Future of Early Christianity: Essays in Honor of Helmut Koester*, edited by Helmut Koester et al., 442–54. Minneapolis: Fortress, 1991.

Paul, Shalom M. "Exod. 21:10: A Threefold Maintenance Clause." *Journal of Near Eastern Studies* 28 (1969) 48–53.

Pedersen, Johannes, and Fru Aslaug Møller. *Israel, Its Life and Culture I-II.* London: Oxford University Press, 1926.

Pesch, Rudolf. *Freie Treue. Die Christen und die Ehescheidung.* Freiburg: Herder, 1971.

Phillips, Anthony. *Deuteronomy.* The Cambridge Bible Commentary: New English Bible. Cambridge: Cambridge University Press, 1973.

Pickup, Martin. "Matthew's and Mark's Pharisees." In *In Quest of the Historical Pharisees*, edited by Jacob Neusner et al., 67–112. Waco, TX: Baylor University Press, 2007.

Piper, John. *This Momentary Marriage: A Parable of Permanence*. Wheaton, IL: Crossway, 2009.

Piper, Otto A. *The Biblical View of Sex and Marriage*. New York: Scribner, 1960.

Pohl, Adolf. *Das Evangelium des Markus*. Wuppertaler Studienbibel. Ergänzungsband. Wuppertal: R. Brockhaus, 1986.

Pöhler, Rolf J. ""Dies Geheimnis ist groß": Ist die Ehe eine Sakrament?" In *Die Ehe. Biblische, theologische und pastorale Aspekte*, edited by Roberto Badenas et al., 253–70. Lüneburg: Saatkorn, 2010.

Poirier, John C., and Joseph Frankovich. "Celibacy and Charism in 1 Corinthians 7:5–7." *Harvard Theological Review* 89 (1996) 1–18.

Pröbstle, Martin. "Söhne Gottes auf Abwegen." *Salvation & Service* 19 (2009) 48–51.

Proksch, Otto. *Die Genesis*. Kommentar zum Alten Testament. Leipzig: Deichert, 1913.

Propp, William H. *Exodus 19–40: A New Translation with Introduction and Commentary*. New York: Doubleday, 2006.

Rahlfs, Alfred, and Robert Hanhart. *Septuaginta*. Stuttgart: Deutsche Bibelgesellschaft, 2006.

Reiser, Werner. "Die Verwandtschaftsformel in Gn 2, 23." *Theologische Zeitschrift* 16 (1960) 1–4.

Richardson, Alan. *Introduction to the Theology of the N.T.* New York: Harper, 1958.

Richter, Hans-Friedemann. *Geschlechtlichkeit, Ehe und Familie im Alten Testament und seiner Umwelt*. Beiträge zur biblischen Exegese und Theologie. 2 vols. Frankfurt am Main: Peter Lang, 1978.

Rivkin, Ellis. *A Hidden Revolution*. Nashville, TN: Abingdon, 1978.

Robertson, A. T. *A Grammar of Greek New Testament in the Light of Historical Research*. Nashville, TN: Broadman & Holman Academic, 1947.

Rock, Calvin B. "Marriage and Family." In *Handbook of Seventh-Day Adventist Theology*, edited by Raoul Dederen et. al., 724–50. Hagerstown: Review & Herald, 2000.

Rodkinson, Michael L., ed. *New Edition of the Babylonian Talmud*. Boston: The Talmud Society, 1918.

Rodríguez, Ángel Manuel. "Konfessionsverschiedene Ehen: Eine Studie über 2. Korinther 6,14." In *Die Ehe. Biblische, theologische und pastorale Aspekte*, edited by Roberto Badenas et al., 201–26. Lüneburg: Saatkorn, 2010.

Roig, Miguel Ángel. "Jesus und die Frage der Scheidung. Eine exegetische Studie über Matthäus 19,1–12." In *Die Ehe. Biblische, theologische und pastorale Aspekte*, edited by Roberto Badenas et al., 181–92. Lüneburg: Saatkorn, 2010.

Rooker, Mark F. *Leviticus*. The New American Commentary. Nashville, TN: Broadman & Holman, 2000.

Rösel, Martin. *Übersetzung als Vollendung der Auslegung*. Berlin: de Gruyter, 1994.

Rosenzweig, Michael L. "A Helper Equal to Him." *Judaism* 139 (1986) 277–80.

Rosner, Brian S. *Paul, Scripture and Ethics. A Study of 1 Corinthians 5–7*. Arbeiten zur Geschichte des antiken Judentums und des Urchristentums. Leiden: E.J. Brill, 1994.

———. "Temple Prostitution in 1 Corinthians 6:12–20." *Novum Testamentum* 40 (1998) 336–51.

Rubenstein, Richard L. "Marriage and the Family in Jewish Tradition." *Dialogue & Alliance* 9 (1995) 5–19.

Rubio, Julie H. "Three-in-one Flesh: A Christian Reappraisal of Divorce in Light of Recent Studies." *Journal of the Society of Christian Ethics* 23 (2003) 47–70.

Rudolph, Wilhelm. "Zu Mal 2,10–16." *Zeitschrift für die Alttestamentliche Wissenschaft* 93 (1981) 85–90.

Rudolph, Wilhelm, and Karl Elliger, eds. *Biblia Hebraica Stuttgartensia*. 5th ed. Stuttgart: Deutsche Bibelgesellschaft, 1997.

Rylaarsdam, J. Coert. "The Book of Exodus: Exegesis." In *The Interpreter's Bible: The Holy Scriptures in the King James and Revised Standard Versions with General Articles and Introduction, Exegesis, Exposition for each Book of the Bible*, edited by George A. Buttrick. 851–1099. New York: Abingdon-Cokesbury, 1952.

Ryrie, Charles C. "Biblical Teaching on Divorce and Remarriage." *Grace Theological Journal* 3 (1982) 177–92.

Sailhamer, John H. "Genesis." In *The Expositor's Bible Commentary*, edited by Frank E. Gaebelein. 1–284. Grand Rapids, MI: Zondervan, 1990.

Sampley, J. Paul. *"And the Two Shall Become One Flesh": A Study of Traditions in Ephesians 5:21–33*. Society for New Testament Studies Monograph Series. Cambridge, U.K.: University Press, 1971.

Sanders, E. P. *Jesus and Judaism*. Philadelphia: Fortress, 1985.

———. *Paul and Palestinian Judaism: A Comparison of Patterns of Religion*. Philadelphia: Fortress, 1977.

Sapp, Stephen. *Sexuality, the Bible, and Science*. Philadelphia: Fortress, 1977.

Sarna, Nahum M. *The JPS Torah Commentary: Exodus. The Traditional Hebrew Text with the New JPS Translation*. Philadelphia: Jewish Publication Society, 1991.

———. *The JPS Torah Commentary: Genesis. The Traditional Hebrew Text with the New JPS Translation*. Philadelphia: Jewish Publication Society, 1989.

Satlow, Michael L. *Jewish Marriage in Antiquity*. Princeton, NJ: Princeton University Press, 2001.

———. "Rabbinic Views on Marriage, Sexuality, and the Family." In *The Cambridge History of Judaism*, edited by Steven T. Katz. 612–26. Cambridge, 1989.

Scharbert, Josef. *Genesis 1–11*. Würzburg: Echer, 1983.

Schlatter, Adolf. *Der Evangelist Matthäus. Seine Sprache, sein Ziel, seine Selbständigkeit. Ein Kommentar zum ersten Evangelium*. Stuttgart: Calwer, 1929.

Schlier, Heinrich. *Christus und die Kirche im Epheserbrief*. Tübingen: Mohr, 1930.

———. *Der Brief an die Epheser. Ein Kommentar*. Düsseldorf: Patmos, 1962.

Schmidt, Karl L. "κολλάω." In *Theologisches Wörterbuch zum Neuen Testament*, edited by Gerhard Kittel et al. Stuttgart: Kohlhammer, 1938.

Schnackenburg, Rudolf. *Der Brief an die Epheser*. Evangelisch-Katholischer Kommentar zum Neuen Testament. Zürich: Benzinger, 1982/2003.

Schneider, Norbert. *Die rhetorische Eigenart der paulinischen Antithese*. Tübingen: Mohr, 1970.

Schrage, Wolfgang. *Der erste Brief an die Korinther*. Evangelisch-Katholischer Kommentar zum Neuen Testament. 4 vols. Zürich/Düsseldorf/Neukirchen-Vluyn: Benziger/Neukirchener, 1991–2001.

———. "Zur Frontstellung der paulinischen Ehebewertung in 1 Kor 7,1–7." *Zeitschrift für die neutestamentliche Wissenschaft* 67 (1976) 214–34.

Schreiner, Stefan. "Mischehen-Ehebruch-Ehescheidung. Betrachtungen zu Mal 2,10–16." *Zeitschrift für die Alttestamentliche Wissenschaft* 91 (1979) 207–28.

Schüle, Andreas. *Die Urgeschichte (Genesis 1–11)*. Zürcher Bibelkommentare AT 1.1. Zürich: Theologischer Verlag Zürich, 2009.

Schwartz, Matthew B., and Kalman J. Kaplan. *The Fruit of Her Hands. A Psychology of Biblical Woman*. Grand Rapids: Eerdmans, 2007.

Schweizer, Eduard. "Scheidungsrecht der jüdischen Frau?" *Evangelische Theologie* 42 (1982) 294–300.

Schwyzer, Eduard. *Griechische Grammatik. Auf der Grundlage von Karl Brugmanns Griechischer Grammatik. Band 1: Allgemeiner Teil. Lautlehre. Wortbildung. Flexion*. Handbuch der Altertumswissenschaft. München: Beck, 1953.

———. *Griechische Grammatik. Auf der Grundlage von Karl Brugmanns Griechischer Grammatik. Band 2: Syntax und Syntaktische Stilistik*. München: Beck, 1988.

Scotchmer, Paul F. "Lessons from Paradise on Work, Marriage, and Freedom: A Study of Genesis 2:4—3:24." *Evangelical Review of Theology* 28 (2004) 80–85.

Seeligmann, Leo I. "Aetiological Elements in Biblical Historiography." *Zion* 26 (1961) 141–69.

Sellin, Gerhard. *Der Brief an die Epheser*. Meyers kritischer Kommentar über das Neue Testament. Göttingen: Vandenhoeck & Ruprecht, 2008.

Shaner, Donald W. *A Christian View of Divorce. According to the Teachings of the New Testament*. Leiden: Brill, 1969.

Shields, Martin A. "Syncretism and Divorce in Malachi 2, 10–16." *Zeitschrift für die Alttestamentliche Wissenschaft* 111 (1999) 81–85.

Sigal, Phillip. *The Halakhah of Jesus of Nazareth According to the Gospel of Matthew*. SBL Studies in Biblical Literature 18. Leiden: Brill, 2008.

Simpson, Cuthbert A. "The Book of Genesis: Exegesis." In *The Interpreter's Bible. The Holy Scriptures in the King James and Revised Standard Versions with General Articles and Introduction, Exegesis, Exposition for each Book of the Bible*, edited by George A. Buttrick, 465–829. New York: Abingdon-Cokesbury, 1952.

Skinner, John. *A Critical and Exegetical Commentary on Genesis*. The International Critical Commentary. Edinburgh: T. & T. Clark, 1956 (=1930).

Sly, Dorothy. *Philo's Perception of Women*. Brown Judaic studies. Atlanta, GA: Scholars, 1990.

Smedes, Lewis B. *Sex for Christians: The Limits and Liberties of Sexual Living*. Grand Rapids, MI: Eerdmans, 1976.

Smith, Morton. *Tannaitic Parallels to the Gospels*. The Society of Biblical Literature Monograph Series. Philadelphia: Society of Biblical Literature, 1951.

Smith, Ralph L. *Micah-Malachi*. Word Biblical Commentary. Waco, TX: Thomas Nelson, 1984.

Soden, Hans von. "ΜΥΣΤΗΡΙΟΝ und sacramentum in den ersten zwei Jahrhunderten der Kirche." *Zeitschrift für die neutestamentliche Wissenschaft* 12 (1911) 188–227.

Soggin, Jan Alberto. *Das Buch Genesis*. Darmstadt: Wissenschaftliche Buchgesellschaft, 1997.

Sohn, Seock-Tae. *The Divine Election of Israel*. Grand Rapids, MI: Eerdmans, 1991.

Son, S. Aaron. "Implications of Paul's 'One Flesh' Concept for his Understanding of the Nature of Man." *Bulletin for Biblical Research* 11 (2001) 107–22.

Son, Sang-Won. *Corporate Elements in Pauline Anthropology: A Study of the Selected Terms, Idioms, and Concepts in the Light of Paul's Usage and Background*. Analecta Biblica. Rome: Editrice Pontificio Istituto Biblico, 2001.

Speiser, E. A. *Genesis: A New Translation with Introduction and Commentary*. The Anchor Bible. Garden City: Doubleday, 1964.

Spero, Shubert. "Sons of God, Daughters of Men?" *Jewish Bible Quarterly* 40 (2012) 15–18.

Stefanovic, Ranko. *Revelation of Jesus Christ. Commentary on the Book of Revelation*. Berrien Springs, MI: Andrews University Press, 2002.

Stein, Robert H. *Mark*. Baker Exegetical Commentary on the New Testament. Grand Rapids: Baker Academic, 2008.

Stendahl, Krister. *The Bible and the Role of Women. A Case Study in Hermeneutics*. Translated by Emilie T. Sander. Biblical Series. Philadelphia: Fortress, 1966.

Sternberg, Meir. *The Poetics of Biblical Narrative: Ideological Literature and the Drama of Reading*. Bloomington, IN: Indiana University Press, 1987.

Steudel, Annette. "Ehelosigkeit bei den Essenern." In *Qumran kontrovers. Beiträge zu den Textfunden vom Toten Meer*, edited by Jörg Frey et al., 115–24. Paderborn: Bonifatius, 2003.

Stienstra, Nelly. *YHWH is the Husband of His People: Analysis of a Biblical Metaphor with Special Reference to Translation*. Kampen: Kok Pharos, 1993.

Stordalen, Terje. *Echoes of Eden: Genesis 2–3 and Symbolism of the Eden Garden*. Contributions to Biblical Exegesis and Theology. Leuven: Peeters, 2000.

Strack, Hermann L., and Paul Billerbeck. *Kommentar zum Neuen Testament aus Talmud und Midrasch*. 6 vols. 4th ed. München: Beck, 1965.

Stuart, Douglas K. *Exodus*. The New American Commentary. Nashville, TN: Broadman & Holman, 2006.

———. *Hosea-Jonah*. Word Biblical Commentary. Waco, TX: Word, 1987.

Stuhlmiller, Wayne J. H. "'One Flesh' in the Old and New Testaments." *Consensus* 5 (1979) 3–9.

Sturdy, John. *Numbers*. Cambridge Bible (NEB). New York: Cambridge University Press, 1976.

Sun, Henry T. C., "An Investigation into the Compositional Integrity of the So-called Holiness Code (Leviticus 17–26)." PhD diss., Claremont Graduate School, 1990.

Syreeni, Kari. "From the Bridegroom's Time to the Wedding of the Lamb." In *Sacred Marriages. The Divine-Human Sexual Metaphor from Sumer to Early Christianity*, edited by Martti Nissinen et al., 343–69. Winona Lake, IN: Eisenbrauns, 2008.

Tarwater, John K. *Marriage as Covenant: Considering God's Design at Creation and the Contemporary Moral Consequences*. Lanham: University Press of America, 2006.

Taylor, Joan E. "Virgin Mothers: Philo on the Women Therapeutae." *Journal for the Study of the Pseudepigrapha* 12 (2001) 37–63.

Taylor, Richard A., and E. Ray Clendenen. *Haggai–Malachi*. The New American Commentary. Nashville, TN: Broadman & Holman, 2004.

Taylor, Vincent. *The Gospel According to St. Mark*. London: MacMillan & Co, 1959.

Terrien, Samuel. "Toward a Biblical Theology of Womanhood." In *Male and Female: Christian Approaches to Sexuality*, edited by Ruth T. Barnhouse et al., 17–23. New York: Seabury, 1976.

Terry, Milton S. *The Sibylline Oracles*. New York/Cincinnati: Eaton & Mains/Curts & Jennings, 1899.

Thatcher, Adrian. *Marriage after Modernity: Christian Marriage in Postmodern Times*. New York: New York University Press/Sheffield Academic, 1999.

Theobald, Michael. "Heilige Hochzeit. Motive des Mythos im Horizont von Eph 5.21–33." In *Metaphorik und Mythos im Neuen Testament*, edited by Karl Kertelge, 220–54. Freiburg im Breisgau: Herder, 1990.

Thiel, Josef Franz. "The Institution of Marriage. An Anthropological Perspective." In *The Future of Marriage as Institution*, edited by Franz Böckle, 13-24. London: Herder and Herder, 1970.

Thiselton, Anthony C. *The First Epistle to the Corinthians: A Commentary on the Greek Text*. The New International Greek Testament Commentary. Grand Rapids, MI: Eerdmans, 2000.

Thompson, John A. *The Book of Jeremiah*. The New International Commentary on the Old Testament. Grand Rapids, MI: Eerdmans, 1980.

Thrall, Margaret E. *The Second Epistle to the Corinthians*. A Critical and Exegetical Commentary. 2 vols. Edinburgh: T&T Clark, 1994.

Tigay, Jeffrey H. *Deuteronomy: The Traditional Hebrew Text with the New JPS Translation*. The JPS Torah commentary. Philadelphia: Jewish Publication Society, 1996.

Tobin, Thomas H. *The Creation of Man. Philo and the History of Interpretation*. The Catholic Biblical Quarterly Monograph Series. Washington, DC: Catholic Biblical Association of America, 1983.

Torrey, Charles C. "The Prophecy of Malachi." *Journal of Biblical Literature* 17 (1898) 1-15.

Tosato, Angelo. "The Law of Leviticus 18:18: A Reexamination." *The Catholic Biblical Quarterly* 46 (1984) 199-214.

———. "On Genesis 2:24." *The Catholic Biblical Quarterly* 52 (1990) 389-409.

Trible, Phyllis. "Depatriarchalizing in Biblical Interpretation." *Journal of the American Academy of Religion* 41 (1973) 30-48.

———. "Eve and Adam: Genesis 2-3 Reread." *Andover Newton Quarterly* 13 (1972-1973) 251-58.

———. *God and the Rhetoric of Sexuality*. Overtures to Biblical Theology. Philadelphia: Fortress, 1978.

Trobisch, Walter. *I Married You*. New York: Harper & Row, 1971.

Turner, David L. *Matthew*. Grand Rapids, MI: Baker Academic, 2008.

Van Gemeren, Willem A. "The Sons of God in Genesis 6:1-4: An Example of Evangelical Demythologization?" *Westminster Theological Journal* 43 (1981) 320-48.

Van Ruiten, J.T.A.G.M. "The Creation of Man and Woman in Early Jewish Literature." In *The Creation of Man and Woman: Interpretations of the Biblical Narratives in Jewish and Christian Traditions*, edited by Gerard P. Luttikhuizen. Themes in Biblical Narrative. Jewish and Christian Traditions, 34-62. Leiden: Brill, 2000.

Vawter, Bruce. "Divorce and the New Testament." *Catholic Biblical Quarterly* 39 (1977) 528-42.

Veith, Walter J. *The Genesis Conflic:. Putting the Pieces Together*. Delta, BC: Amazing Discoveries Foundation, 2002.

Verhoef, Pieter A. *The Books of Haggai, Malachi*. The New International Commentary on the Old Testament. Grand Rapids, MI: Eerdmans, 1987.

Von Rad, Gerhard. *Das erste Buch Mose: Genesis*. Das Alte Testament Deutsch. Göttingen: Vandenhoeck & Ruprecht, 1976.

———. *Genesis: A Commentary*. Translated by John H. Marks. The Old Testament Library. Philadelphia: Westminster, 1956/1972.

———. *Old Testament Theology*. New York: Harper, 1962.

Wallace, Daniel B. *Greek Grammar Beyond the Basics. An Exegetical Syntax of the New Testament*. Grand Rapids, MI: Zondervan, 1996.

Ware, Bruce A. "Male and Female Complementarity and the Image of God." In *Biblical Foundations for Manhood and Womanhood*, edited by Wayne A. Grudem. Foundations for the Familiy Series. Wheaton, IL: Crossway, 2002.

Warren, Andrew. "Did Moses Permit Divorce? Modal *wĕqāṭal* as Key to New Testament Readings of Deuteronomy 24:1–4." *Tyndale Bulletin* 49 (1998) 39–56.

Weisengoff, John P. "The Impious of Wisdom 2." *Catholic Biblical Quarterly* 11 (1949) 40–65.

Weiß, Johannes. *Der erste Korintherbrief*. Kritisch Exegetischer Kommentar 5. Göttingen: Vandenhoeck & Ruprecht, 1910.

Wenham, Gordon J. *Genesis 1–15*. Word Biblical Commentary. Waco, TX: Thomas Nelson, 1987.

———. *Numbers: An Introduction and Commentary*. The Tyndale Old Testament commentaries. Leicester, UK: Inter-Varsity, 1981.

———. "The Restoration of Marriage Reconsidered." *Journal of Jewish Studies* 30 (1979) 36–40.

———. "The Syntax of Matthew 19:9." *Journal for the Study of the New Testament* 28 (1986) 17–23.

———. "Why does Sexual Intercourse Defile (Lev 15:18)?" *Zeitschrift für die Alttestamentliche Wissenschaft* 95 (1983) 432–34.

Westermann, Claus. *Creation*. Philadelphia: Fortress, 1971.

———. *Das Buch Jesaja. Kapitel 40–66*. Das Alte Testament Deutsch. Göttingen: Vandenhoeck & Ruprecht, 1970.

———. *Genesis 1–11. A Commentary*. Minneapolis: Augsburg, 1984.

———. *Genesis. 1. Teilband. Genesis 1–11*. Biblischer Kommentar. Altes Testament. Neukirchen-Vluyn: Neukirchener, 1974.

Wevers, John William. *Notes on the Greek Text of Deuteronomy*. Septuagint and Cognate Studies Series 39. Atlanta, GA: Scholars, 1995.

Whidden, Woodrow et al. *The Trinity: Understanding God's Love, His Plan of Salvation, and Christian Relationships*. Hagerstown, MD: Review and Herald, 2002.

Whitekettle, Richard. "Leviticus 15:18 Reconsidered: Chiasm, Spatial Structure, and the Body." *Journal for the Study of the Old Testament* 49 (1991) 31–45.

Williams, William C. "שכב." In *New International Dictionary of Old Testament Theology and Exegesis*, edited by Willem A. Van Gemeren. Grand Rapids, MI: Zondervan, 1997.

Williamson, Ronald. *Jews in the Hellenistic World: Philo*. Cambridge Commentaries on Writings of the Jewish and Christian World, 200 BC to AD 200. Cambridge: Cambridge University Press, 1989.

Winter, Paul. "Sadoquite Fragments IV 20, 21 and the Exegesis of Genesis 1:27 in late Judaism." *Zeitschrift für die Alttestamentliche Wissenschaft* 68 (1956) 71–84.

Witherington, Ben. *Conflict and Community in Corinth: Socio-Rhetorical Commentary on 1 and 2 Corinthians*. Grand Rapids, MI: Eerdmans/Paternoster, 1995.

Wolff, Hans J. *Written and Unwritten Marriage in Hellenistic and Post-Classical Roman Law*. Haverford, PA: American Philological Association, 1939.

Wolff, Hans W. *Anthropology of the Old Testament*. Philadelphia: Fortress, 1974.

Woudstra, Marten H. "The Toledot of the Book of Genesis and Their Redemptive-Historical Significance." *Calvin Theological Journal* 5 (1970) 184–89.

Yarbrough, O. Larry. *Not Like the Gentiles. Marriage Rules in the Letters of Paul*. Society of Biblical Literature. Dissertation Series 80. Atlanta: Scholars, 1985.

Yonge, Charles D. *The Works of Philo Judaeus, the Contemporary of Josephus*. 4 vols. London: Henry G. Bohn, 1854–1855.

Young, Richard A. *Intermediate New Testament Greek. A Linguistic and Exegetical Approach*. Nashville, TN: Broadman & Holman, 1994.

Younker, Randall W. *God's Creation. Exploring the Genesis Story*. Nampa, ID: Pacific, 1999.

Zeller, Dieter. *Der erste Brief an die Korinther*. Kritisch-exegetischer Kommentar über das Neue Testament. Göttingen: Vandenhoeck & Ruprecht, 2010.

Zimmerli, Walther. *1 Mose 1–11. Die Urgeschichte*. Zürich: Zwingli, 1943.

Zimmermann, Ruben. *Geschlechtermetaphorik und Gottesverhältnis. Traditionsgeschichte und Theologie eines Bildfelds in Urchristentum und antiker Umwelt*. Wissenschaftliche Untersuchungen zum Neuen Testament. 2. Reihe, Bd. 122. Tübingen: Mohr Siebeck, 2001.

www.ingramcontent.com/pod-product-compliance
Lightning Source LLC
Chambersburg PA
CBHW081148290426
44108CB00018B/2474